Tolstoy and the Religious Culture of His Time

Tolstoy and the Religious Culture of His Time

A Biography of a Long Conversion, 1845–1887

Inessa Medzhibovskaya

LEXINGTON BOOKS

A division of
ROWMAN & LITTLEFIELD PUBLISHERS, INC.
Lanham • Boulder • New York • Toronto • Plymouth, UK

LEXINGTON BOOKS

A division of Rowman & Littlefield Publishers, Inc.
A wholly owned subsidary of The Rowman & Littlefield Publishing Group, Inc.
4501 Forbes Boulevard, Suite 200
Lanham, MD 20706

Estover Road
Plymouth PL6 7PY
United Kingdom

British Library Cataloguing in Publication Information Available

Library of Congress Cataloging-in-Publication Data

Medzhibovskaya, Inessa, 1964–
    Tolstoy and the religious culture of his time : a biography of a long conversation,
    1845–1887 / Inessa Medzhibovskaya.
      p. cm.
    Includes bibliographical references and index.
    ISBN-13: 978-0-7391-2533-5 (cloth : alk. paper)
    ISBN-10: 0-7391-2533-8 (cloth : alk. paper)
    eISBN-13: 978-0-7391-3265-4
    eISBN-10: 0-7391-3265-2
    1. Tolstoy, Leo, graf, 1828–1910—Religion. 2. Tolstoy, Leo, graf, 1828–1910—
Philosophy. 3. Conversion. 4. Europe—Religion—19th century. 5. Russia—
Religion 19th century. I. Title.
PG3415.R4M43 2008
891.73'3—dc22   2008000011

Printed in the United States of America

∞™ The paper used in this publication meets the minimum requirements of American
National Standard for Information Sciences—Permanence of Paper for Printed Library
Materials, ANSI/NISO Z39.48-1992.

For my parents and grandparents

"In order to live honestly, one must fret, become confused, struggle, make mistakes, resume all over again and give up, and then resume again and again give up, and struggle and fail eternally. As regards serenity—it is sordidness of the soul."

—Leo Tolstoy to his second aunt, A. A. Tolstaya, October 18–20, 1857

"To live is to change, and to be perfect is to change often."

—John Henry Newman, "Essay on the Development of the Christian Doctrine," 1845

Contents

Preface and Acknowledgments

My concern in this study is to explore the origin, progress, and result of a seemingly sudden change that took place in Tolstoy the novelist's psyche in the mid-1870s, namely, his conversion. Religious conversion in the age of modernity is not an especially well understood phenomenon. Is it a process or a transport, divine illumination or conscious effort? A change for the better once and for all, or a meandering narrow path, a long road to Damascus? The pattern of St. Paul's conversion will hardly help to explain that of Tolstoy. He had no revelatory experiences similar to St. Paul's or Luther's "tower experience" [*Turmerlebnis*] or Augustine's encounter with the divine presence in the Roman garden or Aquinas's experience on the Feast of St. Nicholas in 1273. He did not enjoy a life-altering acquaintance like Pascal's with Jansenius.

In Tolstoy studies there is no agreement on whether there is one or two Tolstoys, that is, no agreement on whether he was ever "born again." In the past thirty years, Mikhail Bakhtin's verdict on Tolstoy, namely that he or his hero is not a threshold, a crises-ridden type; that he thrives or suffers exclusively in biographical or chronological time—has adversely influenced thinking about Tolstoy's spirituality. In 1987, Gary Saul Morson offered an important correction of Bakhtin by suggesting that one view Tolstoy's fictional or fictionalized autobiographical subjects as time-enriched human "aggregates" of life experience, an extension of Lydia Ginzburg's earlier theory of psychological conditionedness of every ideological and spiritual change.[1] The views of these critics, extremely valuable in their own right, share the same ideational intent, as well as a Marxist belief in socially evolving individuals and in the importance of the external, temporal event that shapes the psyche. These views stem from Nikolai Chernyshevsky's proposition, made at the dawn of Tolstoy's writing career, concerning his "dialectics of the soul," whose evolution is conditioned by material reality: "Count Tolstoy is most of all interested in the psychological process itself, its stages, forms, its laws, the dialectics of the soul."[2] In short, Tolstoy does change, albeit not spiritually, not cataclysmically, not as converts do, but with some doctrinaire absolute vision in mind if any ideology is at work there. It is symptomatic that the few recent studies of Tolstoy's spirituality concentrated on its pathological aspect.[3]

While insisting on the special autonomy in Tolstoy's spiritual development, I do not neglect culture, which is mentioned in the title. However, I do not limit my purview with considerations of cultural perceptions, including those of mental health, or theories of narrative. In presenting a history of Tolstoy's effort in relation to the religious culture of his time, I necessarily cross academic genres and fields. Conversion today is as much a topic for literary scholars and intellectual historians as it is for psychoanalysts, sociologists, anthropologists, cultural historians, theologians, and philosophers of religion. I attempt to demonstrate that Tolstoy's particular change was both subjective and a product of his time, that it was a conversion initially predisposed toward engaging in a dialogue with his culture.

Combining the genres of intellectual biography and history of religious ideas, while also including literary discussion and analysis, this study analyzes several things in complex. First, it applies the contemporary theory of conversion to Tolstoy. Second, it critically examines received notions of Tolstoy scholarship. Third and most important, it considers the realities of religious culture in Tolstoy's time and how they affected his evolving spiritual personality.

Culturally, conversion is not a forum for free discussion in Russia. In 1845–1847 Nikolai Gogol announced his birth as a religious writer and failed miserably. Religious zealots and atheistic radicals hounded him mercilessly, with the result that he experienced the slow agony of spiritual self-immolation, no longer able to write. Such a violent reaction to a self-guided conversion has its deep roots in the history of the ritual. Foreigners traveling through modern Russia who left eyewitness accounts of baptism were always amazed at the elaborate order and rigorous seriousness of its participants, parents and godparents alike. In the name of the Holy Trinity, godparents rejected Satan on behalf of the baptized and the priest put a cross on their necks that was not to be removed for the rest of their lives. Afterward the priest kissed the baby and lightly touched it with the altar crucifix to complete its transition to Christian life. Godparents were instructed to remember the event and explain its meaning to the growing godchildren.[4] Conversions of the heart and conversions of consciousness that are not part of the Orthodox sacrament are suspect, and if they do take place, they usually occur in abeyance. The Russian language contains several terms that describe spiritual changes other than literal baptism. The one that is closest in meaning to conversion proper is *obrashchenie* (turnaround or revolution). Formally the word contains within itself all the meanings that the young Martin Luther also assigned to conversion, including form of address, turn toward, revolution, and conversion. However, for the true Orthodox believer the only true conversion occurs at baptism, the first of the New Testament's seven sacraments and the most important sacrament of Orthodox Christianity, involving the "drowning" of the old self in triple immersion.[5] All other so-called conversions—and Gogol's was one in the way it was received—signify anguished crises of belief. Relying on Saint Paul's permission to "put away from yourselves the evil person" (1 Cor. 5.9–11) as a guideline for excommunication, Orthodoxy judges only those who are within its pale to determine whether they can remain. By excommunicating them, thereby placing them outside, it leaves them to be judged solely by God's court (*sudy gospodni*).

Although Tolstoy publicly acknowledged his conversion from atheism to a personal version of Christianity around 1880, whether it ever occurred is still a moot point. Tolstoy scholars often enclose the word "conversion" within quotation marks—whether or not they are comparing his act to Gogol's—and even oftener preface it with "so-called." The chagrin of Tolstoy scholars is clear. Unlike Gogol, who expired within five years of his attempt to convert, Tolstoy lived thirty years of robust, feisty, and productive life. We scholars do not begrudge Tolstoy his long life, but feel that it is regrettable that in his last thirty years he ceased writing "regular," secular novels. We treat *Resurrection* (1899) as grounds for Tolstoy's excommunication from the arts, in the same way that the Holy Synod of Russia treated it as grounds for his excommunication from the Church in 1901. However, the fact remains. Whatever happened to Tolstoy while he was working on *Anna Karenina* (1873–1877) gradually led to the emergence of a transformed, extraordinarily active religious writer whose worldwide influence in this area would prove to be enormous.

Walter Kaufmann's classic anthology *Religion from Tolstoy to Camus* opens with a complaint about our scarce knowledge of Tolstoy's religion. Today the problem is still imperfectly understood and conversion remains one of the least understood and most suspect periods in Tolstoy's life, home and abroad. The Russian Orthodox Church excommunicated Tolstoy after about fifteen years of a militant crusade of the establishment against Tolstoy. Vicious attacks on Tolstoy and his alleged spirit of hatred toward God (*dukh vrazhdy na Boga*) begin from the early 1880s when his new religious ideas started circulating in lithograph copies. A typical example comes from one of Russia's most revered prelates, Theophanous the Recluse, who labels Tolstoy the servant of Satan: "Our Lord Jesus Christ is to him a regular man. [. . .]

He is a destroyer of the Kingdom of Truth, the enemy of God. He is the worst counterfeiter without shame, liar and a deceiver. If any of his ravings reaches you, reject it with disgust. . . ."[6]

Even those who were sympathetic to Tolstoy's conversion, such as Russian religious philosophers, found fault with him—and Gogol. Witness the opinion of Simon Frank (1877–1950), a Jew who converted in 1912 to Russian Orthodoxy, but professed a very conflicted form of faith suspended between philosophy and theology. According to Frank, Gogol's scandalous book, *Selected Passages From Correspondence With Friends* (1844–1847; publ. 1847) that confessed his religious change of heart publicly was artificial and yet a "shattering document of a deep and truly Russian tragic religious striving." Tolstoy's need of spiritual cure forced him to live through "the same shattering tragedy." From this crisis emerged someone who rejected art and beauty even more indubitably and preached his "limited moral didacticism" more confidently than Gogol.[7] Russian intellectual culture has been more forgiving to born-again revolutionaries than to its born-again writers. It is in this very sense, that Sergey Bulgakov described his return to faith after his Marxist years. In 1908, he made his way to a solitary hermitage, but when the prayers for those preparing for confession began, he almost bolted. Distressed, Bulgakov suddenly arrived at the elder's cell. Here the miracle finally occurred. Bulgakov returned to the chapel and was greeted by bells calling him to prayer: "The next morning at the Eucharist I knew that I was a participant in the Covenant, that our Lord hung on the cross and shed his blood for me and because of me. [. . .] It was on that day that I partook of the blessed body and blood of my Lord." [8]

Surveying his own spiritual development at the end of his life, Nikolai Berdiaev, another former Marxist, offers an alternative view in his essay "Self-Knowledge" (*Samopoznanie*): "My turn was not a conversion into a confession, such as Russian Orthodoxy or simply Christianity. This was a turn toward spirit and conversion to spirituality, . . . a turn toward Truth-searching."[9] Despite the egocentric title of his work, Berdiaev's self-knowledge is tied to the historical process and its success is judged by how well Berdiaev's spiritual rebel responds to the demands of history in the struggle against commonality and meaningless reality.

The dominant and state-sponsored view on Tolstoy's conversion in the Soviet era may be best illustrated by the authoritative voice of Boris Eikhenbaum, Tolstoy's renowned critical biographer, the great literary scholar of the last century. In his influential essay "On Tolstoy's Contradictions," along with creative parameters for the study of Tolstoy's evolution, Eikhenbaum offered a confining and confounding methodology for the interpretation of conversion. Tolstoy's contradictions, including the "crisis of 1880," "as Lenin convincingly showed," writes Eikhenbaum, "were created by a special position of Tolstoy between the warring classes and ideologies, and not by his individual qualities." According to Eikhenbaum, Tolstoy soon realized that he was letting himself be involved in decadent games with spirituality and made an ideological turnaround; by targeting the decomposition of human character and personality in his new genres—parables, satiric mysteries and so on, Tolstoy made his historical choice.[10]

Ninety years later, freedom of the press in Russia made possible the reissue of Tolstoy's iconoclastic writings. However, the ongoing religious revival in Tolstoy's homeland has changed pitifully little in terms of the reception of Tolstoy's religious persona. Although no longer a shibboleth of Bolshevik and Communist propaganda (a "peasant Count," "a mirror of the Russian Revolution," the most anticlerical voice in the history of Russian letters), Tolstoy is still cursed by official Orthodoxy, and by ultra-Orthodox nationalistic and democratic critics alike. Ultranationalists hold him responsible for the events of 1917, the ensuing reign of atheism, and the persecution of the clergy. To pro-Western democrats, Tolstoy's resistance to politics, state institutions, and his anarchic condemnation of large-scale property ownership make him an unappealing ally. Given the fact that current conditions in Russia are not conducive to an unbiased study of Tolstoy's conversion, the cultural meaning of his religious experience has not been addressed. Russians still call Tolstoy's change a *krizis* (crisis), which in Russian is strongly suggestive of some internal malfunction or temporary pathology.

In the West—which proclaims its tolerance, inclusiveness, and respect for religious heroism—Tolstoy the religious seeker is understood primarily as an exile from his native context. He continues to be viewed as a curious quasi-Protestant anomaly within that same context. Inspired by the recent Bakhtinian fascination with open-endedness and novelistic "unfinalizability," existentialist and then postmodern literary theory in the West have come to distrust cohesive truth-seeking parables, excepting those in the dystopian or absurdist category (e.g., Kafka, Borges). Such distrustful approaches, which have been dominant in the past thirty years, routinely dismiss Tolstoy's work after *Anna Karenina* as a didactic diversion from the novelistic genres in which he had achieved world acclaim. The great liberal philosopher Isaiah Berlin provided an intellectual underpinning for negative assessments of Tolstoy's religion. It bemused Berlin to even think that Tolstoy, with his naive empiricist ideology, might have experienced something close to religious conversion. In relation to religion, Tolstoy was Voltaire's twin brother where Berlin was concerned: "There are descriptions in Voltaire of religious processions as if written by somebody who had no idea what their purpose was, just men in funny garments carrying one stick crossed with another plus an effigy of a small man, etc, etc.—you can imagine the elaborate mockery of this kind of distanced view, as if it were by some Chinaman or visitor from Mars." The same happened with Tolstoy's description of the Eucharist in *Resurrection*, and his excommunication was well deserved, intoned Berlin.[11]

Beginning with Wittgenstein and Heidegger, Tolstoy has been received with almost unalloyed enthusiasm by major Western philosophers of the twentieth century. These philosophical raptures are biased, however, in that they interpret Tolstoy's influence on twentieth-century thought as a cursory artistic prompt to grand theories. (One typical example is the now common reading of *The Death of Ivan Il'ich* as an illustration of Heidegger's *Being and Time*.[12]) Tolstoy scholarship is vast and rich, yet the writer's religious evolution has not been studied in terms of its own intrinsic worth. The current study attempts to bridge this gap by tracing the roots of conversion since Tolstoy's formative years. In addition, it demonstrates that the conversion was itself a novelistic event and that it enabled Tolstoy, the great realist, to perform an act of spiritual heroism. He created a unique religious worldview and language that, in its flexibility and sophistication, served him well as both artist and religious thinker during the final third of his life.

The two studies that motivated my work are Richard Gustafson's *Tolstoy: Resident and Stranger: A Study in Fiction and Theology* (Princeton: Princeton University Press, 1986) and Donna Orwin's *Tolstoy's Art and Thought, 1847–1880* (Princeton: Princeton University Press, 1993). Gustafson's comprehensive study of Tolstoy's moral universe argues that Tolstoy needed to be—in his fiction as well as in his theology—both a "resident" (a member of the brotherhood of man) and a "stranger" (a proud loner who seeks truth far from home). Synchronic and encyclopedic in its scope, this work treats Tolstoy's mature theology with utmost respect, but does not specifically address Tolstoy's conversion or his transitional states. Donna Orwin's work, philosophical and chronological in its approach, embraces the period before the conversion. The current study addresses Tolstoy's maturation more directly, explaining, among other things, his religious roots, his discipleship in the genres of intellectual biography and confession, and offering an alternative reading of *War and Peace* and *Anna Karenina* and their consequences for Tolstoy's religious evolution. The second part of my study expands the chronological scope of Tolstoy's growth as a thinker and artist beyond *Anna Karenina* and provides a systematic study of his conversion-related documents, with their incipient allegorical orientation and a symptomatic change in his artistic outlook and language, culminating in a discussion of *On Life* (1887), the summit of Tolstoy's conversion prose.

My primary task is to analyze sources of distrust toward Tolstoy's conversion and to locate them as the starting point of Tolstoy's change. His thoughts on death and immortality ("a fear of dying," the oldest fear of existentialism), although legitimate reasons according to most influential theorists of conversional experience (e.g., Lewis Rambo), are considered inauthentic sources of conversion in Russian contexts—in Tolstoy studies, Orthodox theology, and Russian religious thought. The second problematic point concerns the course and result of Tolstoy's spiritual shift. When studied day by day, it offers a glimpse into a process that is overly long, laden with suffering, and punctuated by painful setbacks, with none of those sanctioned illuminations or moments of serenity that we expect in a conversion, especially one so private and so public as Tolstoy's. The pattern of conversion that Tolstoy displays to the postrealist age as the only authentic conversion is far too demanding. For this reason, the third point of distrust concerns the way Tolstoy relates his conversional experience. For all his openness about his struggle for faith, many of his powerful critics refuse to grant Tolstoy the benefit of the doubt.

The source of these and other dissatisfactions, as I argue, should be sought in the following striking characteristic normally overlooked in studies of Tolstoy's conversion: this experience was a gigantic philosophical and religious project, the search for a new outlook rather than a crisis-begotten tragic moment. This study undertakes a critical formulation of Tolstoy's conversion process as he experimented with forms of knowledge gleaned from widely differing fields and disciplines: the natural sciences; pragmatist religious solutions; theories of social progress and evolution; the historical school of Christianity; and other influential intellectual currents present during this time. Furthermore, the study shows how Tolstoy steadily reworks the fundamental concepts of neoidealism concerning space, time, and the role of a metaphysical subject in the acquisition of immaterial, eternal knowledge. As I demonstrate, Tolstoy's progress of faith or, better, his progress *into* faith is unsuccessful until he elaborates an individual form of communication with God—in which he explains how and why he chooses to bypass the benefit of revelation and the havens of secret knowledge pursued by Russian religious mystics.

Finally, I show how Tolstoy's newfound principles of philosophy, harmonized with religion, are joined in a new, reborn Christian art, with all the consistency of inspired faith. By offering a strict intellectual and spiritual chronology of the decades during which Tolstoy's faith was shaped this study thus provides a significantly modified view of Tolstoy's conversion, beginning with its unusually protracted chronology and continuing with Tolstoy's reworking of major terms generally included in accounts of conversional experience. I analyze how Tolstoy redefines terms and conditions of self-analysis, repentance, and how he works out creative resources of a new belief, starting with a will to change. Consequently, this study critically reexamines some longstanding contentions about the conversion, including: it was a midlife crisis caused by a fear of dying; it was a family crisis; it was not a crisis but rather a bout of clinical depression; he had written himself out in all the accepted forms and despaired of ever finding a new language.

There is also a "professional corrective" that I would like to introduce into the theory of novelistic discourse. Tolstoy's reputation over the past thirty years has been that of a "monologic despot," one who eclipsed every inch of narrative space on which his characters might have grown and experienced life on their own. Such a view, begun with Merezhkovsky and Berdiaev, became especially influential with the arrival of Mikhail Bakhtin's ideas of dialogue and carnival in studies of Tolstoy. Bakhtin's views on conversion, communication, artistic responsibility, and communion were grounded in Dostoevsky's novelistic cosmos, which, in select but highly visible points of Bakhtin's analysis, is in every way antagonistic to Tolstoy's. Tolstoy's word emerged in Bakhtinian interpretations as impoverished, noncreative, unfree. In the process of working through my dissatisfaction with Bakhtin's hypotheses on Tolstoy, I developed an alternative reading that would not only overcome the predictable juxtaposition of Dostoevsky and Tolstoy but would also help us to see Tolstoy's special use of religious language as a unique tool for survival. This is all the more difficult and imperative because Tolstoy—unlike Dostoevsky—avoids exultation and mysticism. In fact, Tolstoy seeks to dissolve narrative authority and authorship as such if, as he believes, religious experience is indeed true and life is indeed as it should be. One means of countering the myth of the incommunicable and authoritarian Tolstoy is by practicing what I call inductive and amplified readings of his closed forms, namely, the syllogisms, metaphors, and parables. Concentrating on *The Death of Ivan Il'ich*, I offer several examples of inductive readings: Tolstoy's artistic reformulation of the philosophical metaphor of agency (man as flying stone); the categorical syllogism (Ivan Il'ich defies his mortality: Caius may be mortal, but Ivan Il'ich is not necessarily so); mottoes of antiquity and Christian allegory ("respice finem" ["looke forward to the endynge," a phrase from *Everyman*]). The art of reading allegorical language after the age of realism is an exercise in true communion: all but humorless, highly ironic, intensely empathetic, and productive of fruitful (and surprising) results.

The book is structured as follows. In part 1, the introduction discusses the chief conversional tropes and shows that Tolstoy falls firmly within the tradition of other notable converts. It also explains the reasons why Tolstoy's conversion was not taken as seriously as those of his predecessors. Chapter 1, "Challenges of Modernity: The Russian Vertigo in Personal Experience and Literature to 1847" introduces thinkers and seminal concepts related to conversion (Western and Russian) important for Tolstoy. The chapter also presents a critical survey of the culture and theology of conversion in Russia through the age of Tolstoy and discusses the special challenges that Tolstoy's predecessors and contemporaries faced in their individual search for faith. In its last section, the chapter focuses on the development of religious experience in Russian secular literary genres of the nineteenth century that played a role in Tolstoy's religious growth. Chapter 2, "Portrait of the Artist as a Young Nonbeliever," traces Tolstoy's religious growth from his earliest philosophical efforts to 1851–1852. Chapter 3, "Superfluity and the Religion of Writing," follows the development of Tolstoy's creative effort to 1863, the year he began writing *War and Peace*. Chapter 4, "Belief System of *War and Peace*," argues that Tolstoy's indecisiveness and his inability to tie up the loose ends of his masterpiece led him to experience a crisis in the 1870s. Chapter 5, "The Unfinished Battle: The Case With the Epilogues" examines the philosophical repercussions of the epilogues to *War and Peace* and their role in the change in Tolstoy's spiritual orientation. Chapter 6, "Tolstoy's Path toward Conversion: 1869–1875," summarizes the writer's religious experience before 1875, the year the first signs of his crisis of faith become apparent.

In part 2, chapter 7, "The Course of Tolstoy's Conversion, evaluates the development of Tolstoy's religious thought from the mid-1870s through 1881. The chapter studies Tolstoy's conversion by examining personal documents, eyewitness accounts, the writer's dialogues with God and with his spiritual predecessors. The chapter also addresses intercessions and appeals by other writers urging Tolstoy to return to literature, and it looks as well at Tolstoy's communications with advocates and adversaries. Chapter 8, "Turning with Christ," provides a careful analysis of key moments in Tolstoy's rewriting of the Gospels and his appropriation of the religious experience of Christ. Chapter 9, "Religious Experience and Forms of Accounting," studies the various forms of Tolstoy's spiritual biography composed before and after the completion of his conversion, including diaries, autobiographical writings, memoirs, and the recorded moments of the process of thinking itself, with special emphasis on the narrative strategies in *A Confession* (1878–1881) and *What I Believe*? (1883–1884). The chapter specifically examines forms of dialogue at different moments of his conversion that Tolstoy employs to lend a sense of agony and tension to his descriptions. The polyphony of discrete spiritual moments that Tolstoy creates is arguably his greatest artistic contribution to spiritual autobiography. Going back to the introduction, and to chapter 1, chapter 9 compares and contrasts key narratives in the genre of the spiritual memoir (e.g., Saint Augustine, Rousseau, Gogol, Newman) as they challenge the now dominant claims concerning Tolstoy's absolute language and his alleged inability to process moments of threshold consciousness. Chapter 10,

"Logos and Its Life in the World," discusses how Tolstoy accommodates his religious discoveries in everyday situations and develops new terms for artistic creation. The chapter investigates Tolstoy's conversion narratives in diverse but thematically related genres, such as the historical parable, kenotic drama, picaresque adventure, religious parable, and allegorical tale. This chapter also shows how Tolstoy's post-conversion art assimilates the new parameters of spiritual and artistic behavior summarized in his rewriting of the Gospels and several artistic manifestos, forerunners of *What Is Art?*—all featuring a paradoxical spiritual chronology that operates outside space, time, history, and society life.

Chapter 11, *The Death of Ivan Il'ich*, provides a comprehensive reading of the tale as a conversion narrative. Among the various aspects of the story discussed is the choice of the tale's structure (from the moment after death through the story of life, death, and salvation), including the writer's important decision *not* to publish the tale in its original form of a diary assembled from the records of the late Ivan Il'ich. Another important focus of this chapter is Tolstoy's artistic refashioning of "closed forms": syllogistic statements, mottoes, and other metaphors of conversion based on his own experiences as a polemic with philosophical and religious imagism of the thinkers important to Tolstoy (Kant, Schopenhauer, Kierkegaard), and with picaresque medieval tales (such as the *Gesta Romanorum* and *Everyman*). Chapter 12, "*On Life* and Conclusion," focuses on Tolstoy's magisterial treatise *On Life* (1887) to interpret his moral position in relation to self-justification for what he described as a lonely and difficult road toward the light. The chapter summarizes the results of Tolstoy's own journey and evaluates the form and message of his religious counsel shared with *urbi et orbi*. Appendixes I and II provide readers with previously unavailable translations of Tolstoy's thoughts on prayer, which illustrate the enormous progress of Tolstoy's faith from his youth in 1852 to 1909.

Like all books, mine has a history of its own, and it owes many debts of gratitude. The sources of the book may be traced to my lifelong fascination with Tolstoy's genius. But I would also like to acknowledge the more immediate professional influences. After taking Caryl Emerson's graduate seminar on Tolstoy at Princeton, in the summer of 1998, I was reading Schopenhauer's essays on logic and rhetoric and came across the syllogism "All men are mortal; Caius is a man; Therefore, Caius is mortal." This decidedly monologic trope of thinking was compared by Schopenhauer—in a more than lively metaphor—to a voltaic pile on which communication of both thinking and ontological processes takes place. This lively Schopenhauer metaphor reminded me of the same syllogistic trope used by Tolstoy in *The Death of Ivan Il'ich*. Residence as a doctoral fellow at the Center for Human Values presided over by Amy Gutmann resulted in a dissertation, *Tolstoy's Projects of Transcendence (Reading the Conversion)* (PhD Dissertation. Princeton University, 2001), taking the year 1880 as a starting point. Caryl Emerson and Ellen Chances supervised the writing of my dissertation and gave me a blessing to continue my work on the topic. Over the past few years, the project has been radically rethought—in terms of genealogy, chronology, methodology, and execution. In trying to contextualize Tolstoy's conversion, I researched other cases of conversion and I studied religious theory and history intensively. Gradually, I arrived at a conclusion that only a complete history of Tolstoy's religious growth starting from his early days considered within the context of the religious culture of his time—broadly investigated—would bring me to the desired destination. I would like to thank Justin Weir and Julie Buckler, the organizers of the conference "Tolstoy: the Over-Examined Life," that took place at Harvard University (April 19–20, 2002) for inviting me to present my paper and later write the expanded version for the conference volume, "Tolstoy's Conversion: Reexamination and Definitions," that became the cornerstone of the future book. A generous grant from the Mellon Foundation allowed me to spend the year 2002–2003 in residence at the Society for the Humanities at Cornell University. I am grateful to Dominick LaCapra, Society Fellows, and postdoctoral fellows of that year who shared their knowledge and gave me salient advice about avoiding pitfalls in the preparation of my first scholarly book. Colleagues in the Russian Department: Pat Carden, Slava Paperno, Nancy Pollack, Gavriel Shapiro, and Peter Holquist—then part of the Cornell History department—were wonderfully supportive in every sense of academic and intellectual life. Doreen Silva made many difficulties of adjustment seem small.

In the process of writing and finishing my work on the book, I have been fortunate to communicate with the following colleagues in the fields of Tolstoy studies, literature, intellectual history, philosophy, and religion who either offered their astute advice on various aspects of research and writing or served as discussants or fellow presenters at conference panels where parts of this project were read: Galina Alexeeva, Jeffrey Brooks, Ellen Chances, Michael Denner, Caryl Emerson, Richard Gustafson, Robert Louis Jackson, Gary Jahn, Dominick LaCapra, Jeff Love, Marge McShane, Donna Orwin, Gabriella Safran, Michael Wachtel, and Theodore Ziolkowski. I would not have dared to delve this far into Tolstoy without the encouragement of Lydia Dmitrievna Opulskaya during our only meeting in the summer of 2000 and ensuing correspondence in the spring of 2001.

During my research sojourns at Yasnaya Polyana and subsequent communications, the following colleagues offered their generosity and expertise in making vital Tolstoy materials available. I would like to thank

Vladimir Tolstoy for granting me permission to study books from Tolstoy's library, Galina Alexeeva, Liudmila Miliakova, Tatiana Nikiforova, Alla Polosina, and Tatiana Shchitsova for their guidance and generous assistance with precious documents and the archives.

Many thanks to my wonderful colleagues in Literature and other departments at Eugene Lang College and at the New School who offered their good humor, spiritual support, and sound advice. Ferentz LaFargue, Laura Liu, and Ann Murphy, members of the New Research reading group at Eugene Lang in 2004–2005, read early versions of my introduction and offered sound advice. A research fund from the Dean's office allowed me to do the necessary travel and complete the final stages of research and writing. Special thanks go to my students at Lang, for their indefatigable curiosity, sparkling intelligence, and razor sharp metaphysical challenges. They are the best in the whole world.

Michael Denner generously shared an image from his collection and permitted me to reproduce it on the front cover of my book. In the preparation of this manuscript, I owe special thanks to my patient proofreaders Adele Brinkley, Mary Gilpatrick, and Henry Krawitz, whose stylistic discipline and linguistic expertise proved invaluable.

I would finally like to extend my gratitude to Joseph C. Parry of Lexington Books/Rowman and Littlefield. His enthusiasm concerning the project and his wise guidance during and after the review helped me to improve the manuscript in its final stage. Donna Orwin, Richard Gustafson, and Caryl Emerson read the entire manuscript for the press and made valuable comments and suggestions. Lynda Phung and Melissa Wilks steered the manuscript through the production stage and made this process enjoyable. Sunday Oliver assisted me in preparing an extensive index.

Earlier versions of several segments in the book have been presented as conference talks and appeared as essays. I would like to acknowledge the following publications with thanks for the permission to reproduce some of the sections of these earlier versions with emendations: "On Moral Movement and Moral Vision: *The Last Supper* in Russian Debates." *Comparative Literature* 56, no. 1 (winter 2004): 23–53; "Aporias Of Immortality: Tolstoy Against Time." Pp. 370–74 in *Word, Music, History. A Festschrift for Caryl Emerson.* Edited by Lazar Fleishman, Gabriella Safran, and Michael Wachtel. *Stanford Slavic Studies*, volumes 29–30 (2005): 29: 370–84; "Tolstoy, evkharisitiia i Tainaia vecheria." *Leo Tolstoy and World Literature. Papers Delivered at the 3rd International Tolstoy Conference. Yasnaya Poliana 28–30 August 2003. In Memory of Lydia Dmitrievna Opulskaya.* Edited by Galina Alexeeva. Moscow/Tula/Yasnaya Polyana: Yasnaya Polyana Publishing House 2005 (155–70); "Kritika teleologicheskoi sposobnosti suzhdeniia v *Smerti Ivana Il'icha*." Pp. 246–55 in *Tolstoy i o Tolstom: Materialy i issle-*

dovaniia. 2nd vol. Moscow: IMLI (Institute of World Literature, Russian Academy of Science), 2002; "Teleological Striving and Redemption in *The Death of Ivan Il'ich.*" *Tolstoy Studies Journal* 12 (2000): 35–49.

Finally, it is to my parents and grandparents, to their love, devotion, and unflagging faith that I owe not only the completion of this book, but all of my accomplishments. It is to them that I dedicate my book.

NOTES

1. See Gary Saul Morson, *Hidden in Plain View. Narrative and Creative Potentials in War and Peace* (Stanford, Calif.: Stanford University Press, 1987), 193–227. See also Ginzburg's insistence on the connection between conditionedness and responsibility (obuslovlennost' i otvetstvennost') and on the responsible choice that should necessarily take place within causes, conditions, and situations of any psychological change. Lydia Ginzburg, *O psikhologicheskoi proze* (Moscow: Intrada, 1999), 399, and Lydia Ginzburg, *On Psychological Prose*, trans. Judson Rosengrandt (Princeton, N.J.: Princeton University Press, 1981), 365.

2. Nikolai Gavrilovich Chernyshevsky, *Polnoe sobranie sochinenii v piatnadtsati tomakh* (Moscow: Gikhl, 1949), 3:422. See Chernyshevsky's reviews of Tolstoy's *Childhood,* and *Boyhood* (*Detstvo i Otrochestvo*) and Military Sketches (*Voennye rasskazy*) published in *Sovremennik* (1856).

3. See chapter "Tolstoy and the Beginning of Psychotherapy in Russia." Irina Sirotkina, *Diagnosing Literary Genius. A Cultural History of Psychiatry in Russia. 1880–1930* (Baltimore: Johns Hopkins University Press, 2002), 74–116 and Daniel Rancour-Laferriere's "Does God Exist? A Clinical Study of the Religious Attitudes Expressed in Tolstoy's *Confession.*" *Slavic and East European Journal* 49, no. 3 (Fall 2005): 445–73.

4. See Aleksandr Ivanovich Almazov, *Soobshcheniia zapadnykh inostranstev XVI–XVII vv o sovershenii tainstv v russkoi tserkvi* (Kazan': Tipografiia Imperatorskogo universiteta, 1900), esp. 8, 17. See also the same author's *Istoriia chinoposledovaniia, kreshcheniia i miropomazaniia* (Kazan': Tipografiia Imperatorskogo universiteta, 1884).

5. The seven sacraments include baptism, confirmation, Eucharist, penance, extreme unction, holy orders, and matrimony. The oft-practiced annual immersion in cold water during Epiphany reinforces the sacramental tie to the original baptism.

6. *Rossiia pered vtorym prishestviem v dvukh tomakh.* 2 vols (Moscow: Rodnik, edition of Sviato-Troitskii Monastery, Moscow, 1994), 2:108. Another example of Tolstoy's harassment by religious authorities may be witnessed in a fragment of a fresco formerly found in the church at the village of Tazovo in the Kursk Province. In the lower tier at the far right in this fresco, Tolstoy was shown embraced by Satan who received him in hell while the holy prelates and apostles of Orthodoxy gave blessing to the act. The fresco was removed at Lenin's special order during the Bolshevik crusade against religion in the early years of the Soviet regime. The fresco was later

transferred to the Museum for the History of Religion and Atheism of the Soviet Union. The photograph of this fresco is reproduced in *Istoriia pravoslaviia i russkogo ateizma* (Moscow: USSR Academy of Sciences, 1960), 95.

7. See Frank's "Religioznoe soznanie Gogolia" [Gogol's Religious Consciousness] in S. L. Frank, *Russkoe mirovozzrenie* (St. Petersburg: Nauka, 1996); quoted passage, 306–7. The essay originally appeared in German, "Nikolaj Gogol als religioser Geist," *Hochland* 1934/1935, vol. 1, 251–59.

8. Sergius Bulgakov, *A Bulgakov Anthology*, ed. James Pain and Nicholas Zernov. (Philadelphia: Westminster Press, 1976), 10–11.

9. Nikolai Berdiaev, "Samopoznanie (1940–1947)," in Nikolai Berdiaev, *Izbrannye proizvedeniia* (Rostov-on-Don: Feniks, 1997), 378–79.

10. See Boris Eikhenbaum, "O protivorechiiakh L'va Tolstogo," in Boris Eikhenbaum, *Lev Tolstoy. Semidesiatye gody*. (Leningrad: Sovetskii pisatel', 1960), 229–68. Quoted text, 229, 252.

11. I have in mind Isaiah Berlin's correspondence with Robert Grant in relation to Grant's negative review in *The Times Educational Supplement* July 8, 1988 of A. N. Wilson's biography of Tolstoy and a more benevolent review of Berlin's *The Hedgehog and the Fox*, a famous exposition on Tolstoy's dogmatism. See Robert Grant, *The Politics of Sex and Other Essays*. Foreword by Raymond Tallis (Hampshire and London: Macmillan Press Ltd, 2000), 201–11. Quotation occurs on page 210.

12. "L. N. Tolstoy in his story 'The Death of Ivan Il'ich' has portrayed the phenomenon of the disruption and collapse of this 'one dies'." Martin Heidegger, *Being and Time*, trans. Joan Stambaugh (Albany: State University of New York Press, 1996), 409.

Introduction

In 1869, Tolstoy published the last installment of *War and Peace*. Although he could not have known it then, he had written what was to become one of the greatest novels of the modern period. He had plenty of other reasons to celebrate life. He was only forty-one years of age, and in excellent health, enthusiastic and thirsty for life and love, with a growing family. Tolstoy was being acknowledged, both home and abroad, as the most famous Russian writer of his time, and was living the good life on his ancestral estate, Yasnaya Polyana, in Tula province. With serfdom abolished in 1861, Russia was in the grip of Great Reforms implemented only a few years earlier. Radical social activism vis-à-vis the government's eccentric pan-Slavism and internal political reaction—whose very forces would eventually tear the empire apart in 1917—were growing rapidly. On the eve of the Paris Commune and the Franco-Prussian War, Europe was experiencing a period of political upheaval. The United States was convalescing from the ravages of its own civil war. With war breaking out all over the world, Tolstoy's Yasnaya Polyana (which in English means the bright or ash-tree clearing) remained an island of peace. Simply stated, Tolstoy and his kin prospered.

Tolstoy was happy in the precise manner he had desired and dreamt back in 1852 as a ne'er-do-well twenty-three-year-old artillery cadet posted to the Caucasus. Tolstoy joined the military to expiate financial losses due to gambling and what seemed like an impending loss of his moral constitution. In a letter to his aunt, Tatiana Ergolsky, who had raised him, Tolstoy nonetheless confessed his dream of a perfect and quiet domestic life with wife and children at his beloved Yasnaya. The simple happiness of this life is so complete that Tolstoy adds: "If they made me Emperor of Russia, if they gave me Peru, in a word if a fairy came with her wand to ask me what I desired; my hand on

my heart, I would reply that my only desire is for this to become a reality.
... Dear Aunt, tell me: would you be happy?"[1] In 1869, all these dreams were
now a reality.

On September 2, 1869, Tolstoy and his manservant ordered a room for the
night in a shabby hotel at Arzamas, a small provincial Russian town on the
way to the eastern province of Samara, which was their destination. At his
most vigorous, Tolstoy was the living embodiment of Aristotle's prosperous
household, destined to eternal renewal thanks to a masterful and successful
ordering of "the things that nature supplies"—as master to his servants, husband to his wife, and father to his children and charges.[2] He undertook the trip
with an almost epic goal in mind: to expand the familial space beyond the visible horizon of his estate, stake out the success of his bloodline, and buy more
land. Samara lands were good and cheap and they had the best horses and
horse herds. That night, while staying at the Arzamas inn, Tolstoy suddenly
experienced an inexplicable panic attack, which he related to his wife in a letter written two days later: "The day before yesterday I spent the night at Arzamas, and something extraordinary happened to me. It was 2 o'clock in the
morning. I was terribly tired, I wanted to go to sleep and I felt perfectly well.
But suddenly I was overcome by despair, fear and terror, the like of which I
have never experienced before. I'll tell you the details of this feeling later: but
I've never experienced such an agonizing feeling before and may God preserve anyone else from experiencing it."[3]

Fifteen years after this episode and at the pinnacle of his conversion, Tolstoy wrote "The Memoirs of a Madman" (1883–1886), which describes the
experience in an expanded but unfinished fictionalized memoir.[4] The hero relates in autobiographical fashion his escalating madness by tracing those aspects of his character that might explain why madness set in. What sorts of
episodes does his memory retrieve? They are mostly those where he recognizes, from the earliest days of his childhood, the injustices and pain that others failed to notice. He became hysterical and inconsolable after hearing from
his nanny the tale of Christ's Passion and receiving no answer as to why
Christ was tortured. The second blow to his sanity occurred when the same
nanny was reprimanded unjustly, and a third when a serf boy was thrashed
mercilessly by a seemingly kind man named Foka. Adopting the morally abnormal but universally accepted behavior of his environment, the hero learns
the means and ways of neglectful and expedient normality—an attitude that
rewards him with a blissful marriage and wealth. Suddenly he encounters
death at midlife and everything changes.

Immediately connecting his childhood insights about evil with this vision
of death, the hero sees the life around him and within him in its true light: the
lies, the injustice, the cruelty, and the misery. As was the case earlier, no one

else in his family or immediate circle sees things nearly as clearly and thus he admits to his "madness" or, rather, to the solitude of his clairvoyance. To gain some private, silent space and continue thinking or doing his "mad work," as he puts it, he permits his family to have him investigated by medics. The extraordinary nature of his discovery displays itself in his low spirits, lack of interest in leisurely activities, and a few minor acts of charity to which he is able to commit himself. There is every reason to believe that he is in the grips of a grand folly: "But what folly is this? I told myself. 'Why am I depressed? What am I frightened of?' 'Of me,' answered the voice of Death. 'I am here!' . . . My whole being was conscious of the necessity and the right to live, and yet I felt that Death was being accomplished."[5] The unfinished memoir ends on the Madman's repudiation of official religion and a secret pledge to seek a life-affirming accomplishment that could counter death (26: 474).

Despite its transience and brevity, this episode from "The Memoirs of a Madman" is popularly cited by professional psychoanalysts studying midlife crises. Denigrating psychoanalytic explorations of Tolstoy's crises before and after 1869 are often used for comic relief to exemplify the commonalities of mad spells that intensify in midlife and undermine the uniqueness of the event even as it occurs in the life of a genius. Genius, after all, is a disease that can itself be diagnosed.[6] Irrespective of whether they entertain the likelihood that Tolstoy's crisis was actual, or that it had anything but clinical explanations, nearly every serious biographer of Tolstoy agrees that the 1869 episode signified the beginning of the end for Tolstoy the novelist and that it prepared the way for that strange collapse less than ten years later, which Tolstoy described equally as graphically in another autobiographical document entitled *A Confession* (*Ispoved'*, 1878–1882): "'Well, fine, so you will have six thousand desyatins (acres) in the Samara province and three hundred horses, and then what? Well fine, so you will be more famous than Gogol, Pushkin, Shakespeare, Molière, more famous than all the writers in the world—and so what?' And I had absolutely no answer. My life came to a standstill. I could breathe, eat, drink and sleep and I could not help breathing, eating, drinking and sleeping; but there was no life in me because I had no desires whose gratification I would have deemed it reasonable to fulfill. . . . If a magician had come and offered to grant my wishes I would not have known what to say."[7]

Everything is curious in the above-quoted paragraph about the awful, debilitating soberness that overtook the phase of literal intoxication with life. Curiosity increases once we compare Tolstoy's *Confession* with another masterpiece of crisis lore, namely, John Stuart Mill's *Autobiography*: "'Suppose that all your objects in life were realized; that all the changes in institutions and opinions which you are looking forward to, could be completely effected at this very instant: would this be a great joy and happiness to you?' And an irrepressible self-consciousness distinctly answered: 'No!' At this my heart sank within me: the whole foundation on which my life was constructed fell down. All my happiness was to have been found in the continual pursuit of this end. The end had seemed to charm, and how could there ever again be any interest in the means? I seemed to have nothing left to live for."[8]

Only hardcore skeptics would deny the arresting similarity between the two passages. Per his instructions, Mill's *Autobiography* was published posthumously in the year of his death (1873). Tolstoy must have come across it when rereading the earlier Mill while writing *Anna Karenina* (1873–1878). One cannot help but be startled and excited by this unsettling discovery. While obviously endorsing Mill's crisis memoir, Tolstoy was simultaneously criticizing Bentham's, Spencer's, and Mill's "spider web" of accommodations that these utilitarian critics had woven between an individual and society, bearing in mind their view that reliance on God's laws alone failed to make everyone happy. How can one reconcile Tolstoy's deliberate borrowing with the criticisms he had advanced against Mill?[9]

Some years later Tolstoy received from Charles Wright, his distant foreign in-law, the *Autobiography* of Herbert Spencer (1904), for whose ideas he did not care. Nevertheless Tolstoy thanked Wright profusely, confessing: "In autobiographies, quite independent of the will of their authors, psychological data of supreme importance become revealed. The same staggered me, as I now recall, in the autobiography of Mill."[10] Mill's periodic breakdowns indicated to Tolstoy that Mill was wrong about God, that the inborn yearning for God dwelt even in utilitarians, these masters of hedonic calculus, who first deny the existence of nonempirical spiritual responses in man but then find themselves in bewilderment when they, to borrow Mill's own words, awake from this delusion "as from a dream," just like the as-yet faithless subject in Tolstoy's memoir *A Confession*. Mill's autobiography provided Tolstoy with an archetype for a memoir of doubt "in an age of transition in opinions . . . in noting the successive phases of any mind," so much so that he decided to borrow it in such an obvious manner from Mill.[11]

Mill divided his life into chapters of relatively equal length, corresponding to the phases of his intellectual growth. Young as he was at the time, the crisis chapter is the center of the book, which ends on the longest and tranquil general view of the remainder of his life. Here the similarities end. According to Mill, he knew of no better means to cure himself from the defects of Bentham's teaching than to read. Gradually books did help, all of them relentlessly clear about the impossibility of perfect happiness on earth or complete, all-absorbing faith in life eternal: Coleridge's "Dejection," Wordsworth's meditative "Excursion" and "Ode: Intimations of Immortality," and especially Marmontel's "Mémoires d'un père" (1804), about the decision of a young boy, who has just lost a father, to take care of his family, which proved decisive for Mill in casting off the illusion of egotistical profit due one for being "moral" in a society that was, according to utilitarian doctrine, built on picking up one's rewards.

Tolstoy's *A Confession* marks the beginning of a flight from literature that bears little resemblance to the passing cloud of Mill's youthful dejection, which heralded the appearance of a confident born-again utilitarian. Unlike Mill's *Autobiography*, Tolstoy's memoir does not end with the discovery of a belief system but rather a will to believe. Moreover, it is enigmatically subtitled: "A Preface to the Unpublished Work." Although William James had strong doubts about the positive outcome of Tolstoy's religious transformation and assigned his case to chronic *anhedonia*, or inability to be happy, he never doubted the transformation itself and named Tolstoy—who all but abandoned literature—a mystic capable of belief.[12] While Mill's "crisis of apathetic melancholy" produced a healthy, extroverted intellectual keen on maintaining his hale-and-hearty social functioning, James doubted whether any transformation of spiritual energy had ever occurred in Mill's case. ("Heaven save the mark!" James exclaimed in a derisive footnote while referencing Marmontel among Mill's reading choices.)

Of what precise variety was Tolstoy's religious experience? Why did he forgo the easy route to saintliness owed to the best poet of his age? Why did he instead pursue a route of what can be termed "anhedonic calculus," of calculated unhappiness amid total success: "well fine, and then what?" He was like the famed Paulinus in the fifth Christian century, who renounced his art and took vows, following which he engaged in a beautiful polemic with Ausonius, who reprimanded him, and which itself became a poetic genre of laments about the voluntary descent from Parnassus. Tolstoy also constructed his conversion narratives with the deliberate goal of harmonizing the main facets of modern man's spiritual quest within one's life experience.

"Want to convert? Join me if you dare, but read this warning first," cautions Leon Shestov (1866–1938), one of the keenest existentialists of the twentieth century. "Nur für Schwindelfreie" (Only for those who are not subject to vertigo) announces the epigraph to the second part of his controversial *Apotheosis of Groundlessness* (1903).[13] Shestov's epigraph is simultaneously expressing two thoughts: Follow me if you (think you) do not have problems with vertigo *and* follow me if you are not afraid of being in a state of vertigo. For Shestov vertigo is a precursor to conversion. So-called normal men—not madmen—assert that they have solid ground under their feet. The vertigo effect is meaningful only to those who are not afraid of losing their balance. Shestov knows that those who submitted to vertigo are few in number, and Leo Tolstoy, Shestov's namesake, was among those few—Shestov also names Jesus, Saint Paul, Martin Luther, and Blaise Pascal—who "suddenly" saw through the law in whose name criminal deeds were done, tilted the scales of that law violating the balance of normalcy, and became "mad." After their moment of vertigo, they could not see the world through their old eyes. The old world still stood firm as before, but they now had a new center of gravity and a new focus of vision.[14] In his exploration of Tolstoy's vertigo, Shestov was the first to appreciate its heroism and the importance of the abyss metaphor, that "beauty of terror over the abyss" that Tolstoy would not have been able to experience had he not been destined to write *War and Peace* (the peak he has ascended) first.[15] Shestov also understood Tolstoy's journey as an upward climb that resulted in a standstill—vertigo—an image that will remain central throughout this study. We shall see that the imagery of the staircase or ascent is common to those who experience conversion as vertigo and how peculiar Tolstoy's interpretation of the metaphor is.

Shestov's discussion of Tolstoy's conversion is unusual for the Russian tradition, which will be explored in subsequent chapters. Yet it also goes against the grain of the Jamesian paradigm of "normal" or good conversions that prevailed among its earliest serious students and subsequent generations of their disciples. In his book *The Varieties of Religious Experience* (1902), which predates Shestov's book by only a year, William James provided a celebrated and influential definition of conversion as "*the process, gradual or sudden, by which a self, hitherto divided, and consciously wrong, inferior and unhappy, becomes unified and consciously right, superior and happy, in consequence of his firmer hold upon religious realities.*"[16] This soothing definition immediately follows a discussion of the conversional pathologies of John Bunyan and Tolstoy under the rubrics of "the sick soul" and "the divided self."[17] According to the morbid Jamesian diagnosis—as if he truly was one of those medics on the investigative board—Tolstoy suffered "accidental vitiations of his humors," complicated by chronic *anhedonia*, or inability to experience joy.[18] No wonder he failed to sustain himself in a superior, happy state requisite for correct conversions and hence failed to become healthy-minded. In the eyes of the scientific community at the dawn of professional psychology, Tolstoy experienced no real conversion.[19]

The only case study of Tolstoy's conversion used by James at the time of the delivery of his Gifford Lectures, which was reworked into a book a year later, was *A Confession*. Fairly soon James would start paying attention to Tolstoy's salvation thanks to the latter's invocation of delusional mysticism in *War and Peace* and *Anna Karenina*. But *A Confession*—with its protracted period of suspense before the final vertigo ending in a nightmare, and which, in turn, immediately follows the conclusion of Tolstoy's testimony of the sick soul—sets itself this final task at the very end of the text, which is already in proofs: "I have no doubt that there is truth in the teachings (of the Holy Fathers), but I also have no doubt that there is falsehood in them too, and that I must discover what is true and what is false and separate one from the other. This is what I have set out to do. That which I found false in the teachings, and that which I found true, and the conclusions I came to comprise the following section of this essay, which, if someone should consider it worthwhile and useful to people, will probably be published someday, somewhere."[20]

To James the document was indeed precious enough. The nightmare description that followed right after the just-quoted conclusion must have suited him especially well. The nightmare in question described Tolstoy lying on a bed suspended by ropes. He feels uncomfortable and moves his legs too briskly, realizing the supports are pushed too far away, and he is no longer lying but hanging, dangling by a thread, suspended from an unimaginable height over the "bottomless abyss":

> The infinity below repels and frightens me; the infinity above attracts and reassures me. . . . I was saved from my terror by looking upwards. . . . I grope about, look around and see that beneath me, under the middle of my body, there is a single support and when I look up I am lying on it in a position of secure balance, and that alone gave me support before. . . . It appears that there is a pillar at my head and the solidity of this slender pillar is beyond doubt, although there is nothing for it to stand on. A rope is hanging very ingeniously, yet simply, from the pillar, and if one lies with the middle of one's body on the rope and looks up there can be no question of falling. This was all clear to me and I was glad and tranquil. It was as if someone were saying to me "See that you remember." And I woke up.[21]

In the figurative jargon of the nightmare replete with epithets such as "dreadful," "terrifying," "terror," "terrified," while optimistically misquoting Pascal's anthological fright at the sight of the silent expanses above him, ingeniously hanging ropes must have looked not only too threadbare but too grossly comical a tool for counterpoising the vertigo. Ropes in such states are used to decide the matter by different methods, except that even a good hook above his head was not available to this miserable convert. James disbelieved that Tolstoy could save himself and regain a firmer hold other than by indulging in intoxication with the joys available in life (the mysticism of his choice).

Who is right about Tolstoy, James or Shestov, a pragmatist or an existentialist? Shestov agreed that a "second look" after the first experience of vertigo during the night at Arzamas (terror and nothing more thereafter, dismissed as "groundless fears") allowed Tolstoy to reconsider his position vis-à-vis the reality or illusion of what is good or evil by employing the technique of continually turning back to face his past (*ogliadyvaias' na svoe proshloe*).[22] Looking back is essential in order not to turn back, to keep one-self turned away from the old delusions and skewed visions of life. However, not everyone agrees with such an interpretation. The act of "looking back" is discussed by James as a faulty Tolstoyan technique.

Nonetheless, I would like to propose that it is not James but Mikhail Bakhtin who helped to secure the negative reputation of Tolstoy's conversion in the lit-erary sense. Arguably the most influential advocate of co-experiencing the world in an ongoing dialogic relationship that negates death because human beings individually are mortal but humanity as a whole is immortal, Bakhtin has influenced serious scholars of literature and religious experience in the past thirty years. Bakhtin and his followers interpret human personality from a novelistic point of view that, at first glance, looks to be ideally suited for con-version or change. It is therefore all the more intriguing to determine why an opportunity to experience this change is denied Tolstoy by them. Bakhtinists believe in what James would think was too bad and Tolstoy would think was only too normal, namely, that a human being is never whole, never coincident with himself, and is thus a divided soul seeking to repair the disease of divi-siveness in a constant drive toward "finalizing" himself. Recall Tolstoy's let-ter to A. A. Tolstaya involving erring often and tirelessly.

Herein lies the difference. To Bakhtin the striving to become whole can never be achieved until death. The whole human being is only in evidence and available as a body and a complete life story not to himself but to an-other following death. One's own death, and therefore one's own life that precedes death, are of no use to oneself. Ideally, to become whole in the process of life, one should become involved in an act of co-experiencing, the creation of life events together (*so-bytie*). Only novels allow that to happen. In other genres, Bakhtin claims, heroes are either smaller than their fate or bigger than their humanity. Only in modes that possess novelistic con-sciousness can the author and hero enter into a dialogic relationship in which, to be of use to one another, they never coincide, presuming only one absolute authority over either (their absolute other or God/Christ). A person-ally led conversion or a conversion one on one with God may not be such a mode. According to Bakhtin and his dialogic scheme of personal "unfinaliz-ability," genuine change and salvation occur when one submits one's inferior capacity and need for self-discovery to the rescuing powers of another party. This is required not only because any quest is unsolvable through one's own resources but because revelation, goodness, and grace—those powers that do enact and sustain conversion—are available only through a gift of coexist-ing and co-creating with God through another. However, one cannot talk or listen to God directly since that would be a lapse into so-called monologic consciousness and the selfishness of a life that closes in on itself, completing the vicious "I-for-myself" existence that the "non-dialogic" Tolstoy allegedly suffered all his life.

Bakhtin began his academic career by accusing Tolstoy of the spiritual crime of always *turning back upon himself* (*samoogliadka*). That crime, which the dialogic, outward-looking Dostoevsky—Bakhtin's preferred type of controversial novelistic consciousness—completely lacked, has still not been lifted off Tolstoy.[23] According to Bakhtin's interpretation, the denial of others to Tolstoy devolved into the denial of any ability to change oneself religiously. Tolstoy, that deaf, monologic, self-ogling despot, eventually descended into dank preaching of uninspired, dogmatic Protestant fables. It is interesting to note that Dostoevsky, Bakhtin's preferred conversional model, accused Tolstoy of committing quite the opposite flaw: Tolstoy, who changes often, turns away from his old self forever. Commenting on Tolstoy's ability to experience change or demand it of his characters, in his *Diary of a Writer* (1877) Dostoevsky complained that Tolstoy "needs to perform a complete turn" (*Tolstomu nado povernut'sia vsem korpusom*) *away from himself.* It follows that it is wrong, in Dostoevsky's view, to change radically and irreversibly since such a change is too self-willed and too principled, sincere yet one-sided (*iskrennost' odnostoronnosti*).[24] Dostoevsky's evaluation achieves only a partial correction of Bakhtin. After all, Dostoevsky does believe that complete conversions also imply a complete break with one's intimate others and social environment and with sinful humanity as a whole.

Not only Dostoevsky but more recent theorists of conversion also reject Bakhtin—and more radically. Martin Heidegger forcefully asserts that "the conversion must lie in . . . having-seen," that our pain in the world is a result of our lost connection with the dizzying Open. Without "having-seen"—turning back upon ourselves, our memory of ourselves in the world, our sense of guarded security—it is impossible to turn back completely and carry out "that daring venture, which is at times more daring than even life itself." Heidegger's conversion is always a conversion of the "inside sphere of consciousness."[25] Recent theorists concede that real conversions are painful, long, and largely solitary engagements that shift back and forth and do involve and affect society. But society at large (or individual significant others)—here the difference with Dostoevsky is evident—can at best fulfill a conducive or compassionate role. Gauri Viswanathan, an eminent scholar of conversion, writes the following in the preface to her study *Outside the Fold: Conversion, Modernity, and Belief*: "In its most transparent meaning as a change of religion, conversion is arguably one of the most unsettling political events in the life of a society. This is irrespective of whether conversion involves a single individual or a community, whether it is forced or voluntary, or whether it is the result of proselytization or inner spiritual illumination."[26]

After more than thirty years of observation and theoretical study of conversion in thousands of people and numerous historical cases, Lewis Rambo, a social psychiatrist who concentrates on the *fragility context* of human change, became convinced that a conversion is most likely a process, and that it is more accurate to refer to it as conver*ting* rather than a conver*sion*. Rambo writes, "My choice of the word *process* over *event* is a deliberate distinction resulting from my personal interpretation that, contrary to popular mythology, conversion is very rarely an overnight, all-in-an-instant, wholesale transformation that is now and forever. I do not, however, exclude the possibility of sudden conversions."[27] Rambo is deeply sympathetic to the pain that people experience when changing themselves spiritually and he finds no wrong motives in the desire to find faith. According to Rambo, people convert or decide to convert in order to "gain . . . a sense of ultimate worth." He has observed intellectual converts (people who actively seek and explore alternatives), prototypical mystics (that is, followers of Saint Paul), experimentation converts (those who shop around: show me what you've got to offer), and revivalists and returnees to faith after periods of collective and personal apostasy. He has also observed apostates who leave their original faith system and community and for whom the end result may or may not be an institutional or tradition transition. A negative reflection of the latter, there are "backward converts" who revitalize their commitment to the faith of their previous affiliation.

With the sole exception of a coercive conversion that contradicts one's inner callings or desires of one's soul at every stage of a person's religious journey, every conversion is a salvation phenomenon, the causes and motives behind which are not to be considered shameful. Instead of denying our fragility, according to Rambo conversion allows us to experience both our inner resources and our helplessness to the fullest extent. There are simply no wrong conversions, and each is an improvement over the previous one. Converts need time and space to fulfill their new spiritual task; otherwise, painful regressions are not excluded. Rambo's approach is very liberal and original. He has repeatedly criticized all forms of reductionism in going about the conversion—pragmatic, phenomenological, behaviorist, or sociological reductionism—beginning with James, continuing with Freud, and ending with his contemporaries and colleagues, who treat the human predicament solely in terms of clinical methods. He is also against the so-called normative method, which monitors conversions in order to subsume them under the existing structure and ensure their obedience to its laws or, conversely, violates and invalidates the improper structure. Given his keen attention to conversional needs at every step in the process—involving quest stages, encounters with true or false advocates, interaction with the community of believers or other seekers and, last but not least, the elaboration of the new language of transformation and then of testimony—Rambo is a friend that Tolstoy would have greatly appreciated but sadly didn't encounter in his own day.[28]

Contemporary theorists thus follow Shestov and Heidegger and not Bakhtin in acknowledging that conversion is always about the loss of orientation that accompanies radical turn—disastrous, painful, with its lonely rituals, and sometimes, in fact, offering salvation. Terms such as "turning," "turn," and the like provide a crucial clue to describing and understanding a conversion. In a splendid and fairly recent semiotic study of conversional stances from the "vertiginous point of view," Massimo Leone has persuasively shown that case after case involving converted saints (Saint Isabella and Saint Ignatius of Loyola are his foci) reveal the same pattern: an attack of vertigo halts a person's ability to continue living in the old manner and interferes with his or her daily functioning and decision-making ability in such a way that everything is changed irrevocably. Leone is specifically interested in the poses and stances of vertigo victims and how they discover various means of countering the effects of vertigo by finding props, convenient turns, and turnarounds.[29] They have to do this because they are being attacked or resisted from within and from without. Feeling threatened, the community demands explanations from the vertiginous person, which is its dialogic engagement with the convert: like a good totalitarian dictator, society first demands a story and then amends the original story "in order to stabilize the role of the converted people."[30] Here one should recall Tolstoy's tale "The Memoirs of a Madman," where the hero agrees to see the medics. He shows great wisdom by pretending to be mad and placating his listeners with the story of madness they expect to hear in order to carry on with the vertigo project.

Leone offers a serious reinterpretation of what appears to him as simplistic on the part of James. The latter, for example, conflates the meaning of being converted and conversion, the workings of grace and unconscious mechanisms within the mind of a person visited by vertigo. Unity of any sort (what I earlier called balance) is available to someone only *after* the conversion but *not during* it, and even then one *can* find unity of belief, although rarely will there be a unity of one's religious experience as it is represented in the accounting of conversion unless unity is specifically imposed.[31] One finding by Leone is especially intriguing. He insists on the importance of the same body undergoing conversion, a body with a changing consciousness. Leone believes that "conversion . . . is neither the time of disbelief nor the time of belief. It is the passage between them." In conversion, Leone writes, "different beliefs must belong to a single body at different times, while in controversy different beliefs belong to different bodies at the same time. . . . In a controversy, different narrative roles, . . . including different beliefs, are supposed to be embodied by different actors. . . . In religious conversion, on the contrary, a single actor embodies different beliefs."[32] Upon reading this paragraph, I immediately recalled what continued to be the sticking point of Tolstoy studies in the deliberations between Bakhtin's camp and Dostoevsky adherents versus Tolstoy, namely, whether or not Tolstoy and his central characters genuinely change, and how narratives of Tolstoy's religious experience interact with the world.

In 1985 Caryl Emerson, the most authoritative exponent and critic of Bakhtin's views on Tolstoy, published a groundbreaking essay in which she succinctly explained, in a style similar to Leone's, what differentiates Dostoevsky from Tolstoy and why Bakhtin—who prefers crises situations ("the most of what happens") to the so-called biological, evolutionary chronotope of life ("what happens the most")—misreads Tolstoy.[33] According to Emerson, Dostoevsky's heroes (or various bodies) process one idea at the same time. Thus there is dialogue, controversial and scandalous as it might be, in the Dostoevsky that we know at his best. Compared to Dostoevsky's craftily impassible theodic dilemmas (the happiness of humanity at the expense of a child's tear or the necessity to choose between the beauty of Christ and the possibility of truth), in Tolstoy we find the monotony of an exhausting monologue of one body that processes different ideas at different times, in the order of their pressing appearance. When Tolstoy's bodies do convene at the same time in the same place, they are awkward around one another and need to find moments of sympathy and dialogue, which, when found, are the most memorable instances in Tolstoy's fiction. Then bodies are sundered apart from each other again. As it appears to us at this point, the theater of Dostoevsky, with its many actor-contrarians, is deliberate in its rhetorical controversy. Tolstoy's one-man show, with ropes and visits to the psychoanalytic examiner, is on a path through the conversion process. Thanks to its pioneering study of conversional semiotics or the pictorial theater of conversion, Leone's book provides insight into what at first appeared incomprehensible, ridiculous, and feigned in Tolstoy's descriptions of the various conditions and situations of his vertigo. According to Leone, "Conversion is the moment when one ceases to disbelieve and starts to believe. There can be oscillations between belief and disbelief, but there cannot be any coexistence of both. It is a consequence of the principle of non-contradiction: one may believe in God and not believe in the Holy Trinity, but one cannot both believe in God and not believe in him at the same time. . . . Conversion therefore is a punctual event, and not a durative one."[34]

Leone implies that although we do need time in duration to convert, following the propositions of Rambo, we should distinguish between conver*ting* and conver*sion*. Conversion, strictly speaking, is indeed that moment within the process of converting when one stops disbelieving and starts believing once and for all. Tolstoy's character, as he appears to us from the passages in which he represents his searches, wishes to overcome the moments of controversy inherent in the conversional process even if that means performing the stunts of conversion theater, namely, hanging over the precipice or dangling from the ropes.

The doubts that Tolstoy's religious character experiences figuratively are the antinomies of faith inherent in the age of pragmatism and the denigration of idealistic reason. In sharp contrast to Tolstoy, Dostoevsky's most famous seekers of faith celebrate controversy. Dostoevsky's portrayal of controversial characters clashing with the holy believers, of hell and heaven, are the most unforgettable moments of his novelistic and ideological universe. Tolstoy's dynamic of describing searches of faith is more concentrated in the body of *one* individual. This, I will argue, is his greatest contribution to our modern understanding of religious experience. Tolstoy's seeking subject obeys only his conscience, the silent voice of God that he learns how to hear, moment by moment, and then addresses this word in a new type of literary-religious dialogue to the community of readers. This makes Tolstoy the true protean modern man and Russia's first truly modern man.

Especially intriguing will be the task of making Tolstoy face the highest standard established by Bakhtin for Russian and contemporary art, namely, that of co-experiencing sympathy. I am implying the application to Tolstoy of Bakhtin's planes of responsibility for the artist toward the reader and God. According to Bakhtin, in *everyday life* the other corrects and completes me in cognitive-ethical activity. In *creative life*, the author and hero are two persons, and the author transcends the hero. While the hero exists in the event of being, on his own ethical-cognitive plane, the author embraces the hero's "event of being" (*sobytie-bytiia*) and endows it with aesthetic meaning. In the triadic *absolute aesthetic* life, God is the Absolute Other, the highest instance providing all meaning for everyday and aesthetic creation. In the absolute aesthetic life one achieves the pure self-consciousness of life that is faith (that is, the awareness of need and of hope, of one's lack of self-sufficiency, and of possibility), which creates the necessity of forgiveness and lifts norms of justice to achieve the possibility of a true event or conversion.[35]

As the subsequent discussion will show, in his religious choices Tolstoy was less anarchic and more disciplined than is commonly thought. If he was so selfish and satanic as Bakhtin and Theophanous the Recluse have implied, then it is strange to discover that Tolstoy was not swayed by the demonic patterns of the Romantic conversions or by rather unsubtle conversions of the members of "les poètes maudits" group of Paul Verlaine's generation—Tristan Corbière, Stéphane Mallarmé, Paul Claudel. He was untouched by the experimentation with religious faith of Joris-Karl Huysmans that occurred in the 1880s. Nor did Nietzsche's counterexample, with his proclamation of the death of God and the new Anti-Christ impress him. Nevertheless, Nietzsche and Tolstoy were the two most important psychological cases examined at the International Congress of Psychology, where the positivist William James met with Tolstoy's friend, the neo-Kantian and anti-positivist philosopher Nikolai Grot, who was at work on an essay comparing Tolstoy's faith and Nietzsche's nihilism. The two, he thought, were not completely "un-alike."[36] Like Nietzsche, Tolstoy was a quintessentially modern phenomenon. His genealogy begins with the Christians who are made, or self-made, not born, to paraphrase Saint Jerome.

Various dictionaries of theology usually include the following stages and categories by way of explanation of conversion: turning from sin to God; repentance; regeneration; a change of man's status in the sight of God; and, finally, opting for Christ.[37] In his influential study of conversion, A. D. Nock introduced the pioneering term "peripety," or conversion, as the turning point after which there is no going back.[38] In the Gospels conversion literally means "turning around" (*epistrophē*).[39] Some factions within Eastern Christianity trace the institution of the rite to the words uttered by Christ to his disciples on the Galilean mountain before his Ascension: "Go therefore and make disciples of all nations, baptizing them in the name of the Father and of the Son and of the Holy Spirit" (Matt. 28.20).

Rather than focusing on the examples that describe the act of converting others, by means of persuasion or coercion, we should consider active, crisis-ridden conversions of individuals who seek the help of others (advocates or fortuitous encounters) and then tell the story of their findings (employing witnesses and gathering a community of their followers). As an impetus to such changes, recall Jesus' words to Nicodemus: "Unless born anew, you can't enter the Kingdom" (Matt. 5.20).

One finds such a convert in Tolstoy, who, in the fitting words of Saint Augustine, is involved in a struggle for his faith "in which I was my own contestant," engages in communication with God, asking for help so that His faith may prevail: "Give me what you command and command me what you will."[40] A successful turn requires a radical change. An integral part of God's redemptive plan of restoring and renewing life, conversion requires repentance (*metanoia*) and inner change for the turn to take place. Numerous verses in the Gospels speak of baptism as repentance in the original Greek translations from the Aramaic and ancient Hebrew. In Byzantine icons John the Baptist is often portrayed making a sign of the cross with an inscription on the tablet from Matt. 3.11 or Mark 1.14–15 that he holds: *metanoete* (bethink yourselves or change yourselves) and *metamelomai* (change your minds, repent).[41] This understanding of conversion as the reception of the fundamental gift (*metanoia*), which, if lost through sin after baptism, is restored and rein-vigorated in those who avail themselves of the sacrament of mercy has been firmly embedded in the Catholic catechism.[42]

The first example reflecting a conscious change against one's will in the acceptance of grace should, of course, be that of Saint Paul and his agonizing illumination on the road to Damascus (Acts 9.1–19) and in the retelling of Paul during his trial by Agrippa (Acts 28.18). Paul's conversion is aided by Jesus's revealing his identity and explaining to Paul the reason why his jour-ney was blighted and the new journey should commence. He also tells Paul what to do: "And immediately there fell from his eyes as it had been scales: and he received sight forthwith, and arose, and was baptized." Paul's conver-sion is the best possible example of so-called unidirectional, irrevocable con-version, or peripety. Through Paul we have a connection that the New Testa-ment establishes between repentance, instantaneous change lasting forever, and the hand baptizing/converting others. Already in Justin the Martyr, the miracle of the encounter is problematic. Justin saw the presence of logos, and consequently the presence of Christ, in every person. This conviction allowed him to advance a belief in the sowing and renewing *logos spermatikos*. In a long succession of sowing of the whole logos, Moses was a forerunner of Socrates and Plato, of John the Baptist, of Jesus, and then of Saint Paul.[43] The truth was revealed to Justin after a now legendary encounter he had at sea with an old sage, who drew a line between philosophers and the blessed men, the prophets who predict truths that are miracles invisible to the mind's eye. After his meeting with the old man, Justin "expected immediately to gaze upon God, for this is the goal of Plato's philosophy."[44] Since he did not, he referred to what had happened to him as a special illumination in the mind through the "open gates of light," which is how he interpreted conversion to his friends, a found philosophy, the gospel of his heart (divorced from the old mythology of demonological wonder-working) in the dialogues he set him-self to write next. Although his audience in the dialogues laughed in mocking disbelief, Justin held his own records to be part of a long tradition of prophetic memoirs.[45] Justin's problem with miracles forecasts doubts arising around Augustine's path of interpreting conversion. The birth of the will to turn and the turn itself are described by Augustine in supernatural terms. Like Saint Paul, Augustine believed that his turn to God was a supernatural process. God's agency was by far more important to Augustine than his own ability to conform or resist. During the famous scene in the garden, like Paul he realized that his mind cannot command itself and its will should obey a higher will.[46] "Conversion" was useful to Augustine as a bifocal term of turn-ing: it suggests both turning toward God (conversion) and turning away from one's own sin in disgust.

Nock, Morrison, Leone, and other scholars of early Christianity and conversion in the Middle Ages argue that conversion after Augustine became a metaphor, a semantic link of the soul to God, with a specific paradigm of representation that relied on the techniques of religious art to portray the change.[47] Conversion was meant to finish the artistic work commenced by God. Augustine set the example of a follower of Saint Paul, a convert released by God's redemptive grace from his deliberate wrongs and cataclysmic doubts. He also set the record for the imitative nature of medieval conversions, most of which, since based on other ready paradigms, became empathetic conversions by extension. Thomas Aquinas' criticism of Augustine's imperfect understanding of sin and evil opened the discussion of conversion as an act of free will.[48]

Aquinas's arguments against the Catholic tenet of all-embracing grace, operating on man without justification, remain central for Martin Luther's belief in continuous regeneration. It is necessary to recall our baptism at birth and trust in the Lord's forgiveness for our salvation.[49]

Luther's personal breakthrough happened one night in 1518 while he was in a study tower reading the Gospels and the Psalms (the so-called *Turmerlebnis* or "experience in the tower"). He entrusted himself to God and His ability to convert man, without his aid, through justification by faith alone. After the conversion, Luther considered himself to be no more than an "instrument of the Word" and made a mental distinction between his *true* conversion (his forgiveness by means of God's grace thanks to his faith in Christ) and a false one, that which Rambo has called the "final straw" effect (Luther achieving his faith in Christ through his own effort, culminating in the tower episode).[50] Particularly important for the present discussion is Luther's conception of man in the process of change, his loss of "the old man" of his body and his "putting on the new man" of his converted spirit.[51] Tolstoy was interested in many of Luther's works, beginning with his rewriting of the psalms and religious hymns in the vernacular, which Tolstoy used as a guide in drafting the literary curriculum for his peasant school in the early 1860s.[52] Luther's *De servo arbitrio* (On the Bondage of the Will, 1525) was discussed in the philosophical passages of *War and Peace* (15:189, 225, 243, 279). Most profitable for Tolstoy's own rewriting of the Gospels and his critiques of dogmatic theology were Luther's translations of the Bible and his anticlerical works. Luther was consulted often and his imprecise translations were criticized quite frequently. During his years of transition (mid-to-late 1870s) from nonbeliever to believer, Tolstoy used Luther's *Catechism*, which survived in his library and was quoted in his most famous work on religion, *The Kingdom of God Is Within You* (1894).[53] Tolstoy especially appreciated in Luther a decisive turn to modern freedom of conscience, initiated by Protestantism, which generally considers human life to be a recurring regeneration from the old man into the new, and conversion to be a slow process and a *task*, a unique duty of those who are "born again."[54] It remains to examine the roots of Tolstoy's disquiet in the context of the Russian vertigo, specifically in the areas of religious tradition, philosophy, and literary art. The next chapter will study the tradition of vertigo that Tolstoy inherited in 1847, the year when he retired from Kazan University to commit to the tasks of self-improvement.

NOTES

1. Mozdok to Yasnaya Polyana, January 12, 1852, in Tolstoy, Lev Nikolaevich. *Polnoe sobranie sochinenii*. Ed. V. G. Chertkov. 90 vols. (Moscow: Khudozhestvennaia literatura, 1928–1958), 59: 159–60. Unless otherwise specified, all future references are to this edition of *Tolstoy's Complete Works*. Further references (volume: page) are thereafter cited parenthetically in the text. Certain diary entries or letters requiring further elaboration will be referenced in the text and explained in footnotes. Unless otherwise specified, all translations from Tolstoy's letters and diaries from *Tolstoy's Complete Works* are mine. Selected translations of Tolstoy's letters in English are from *Tolstoy's Letters* (volume 1: 1828–1879; volume 2: 1880–1910), trans and ed. R. F. Christian (New York: Charles Scribner's Sons, 1978), hereafter cited *Tolstoy's Letters*, volume: page. This translation is from *Tolstoy's Letters*, 1: 23–24.

2. Aristotle, "Politics," Book One, 1252–60, in Aristotle, *The Complete Works of Aristotle*, 2 vols. Revised Oxford translation, ed. Jonathan Barnes (Princeton: Princeton University Press, 1984), 2: 1988–96.

3. Letter to S. A. Tolstaya from Saransk, 4 September 1869 (83: 167–68). *Tolstoy's Letters*, 1: 222.

4. "The Memoirs of a Madman," trans. Louise Maude and Aylmer Maude, in *The Portable Tolstoy*, ed. John Bayley (London: Penguin, 1978), 653–65. Hereafter cited as "Memoirs."

5. "Memoirs," *The Portable Tolstoy*, 658.

6. See Sirotkina, *Diagnosing Literary Genius*, 74–116. Sirotkina does not discuss the connection between Tolstoy and Mill.

7. Translation quoted from Leo Tolstoy, *A Confession and Other Religious Writings*. Trans. Jane Kentish (London: Penguin Books, 1987), 30–31.

8. John Stuart Mill, "A Crisis in My Mental History," in John Stuart Mill, *Autobiography and Other Writings*, ed. Jack Stillinger (Boston: Houghton Mifflin, 1969), 81.

9. In *Anna Karenina*, references to Mill are ironic. In part 1, chapter 3, the philanderer and near bankrupt social servant Stiva Oblonsky read a financial review on Bentham and Mill (18: 10) and Konstantin Levin remained dissatisfied with Mill's social theories in part 3, chapter 39 (18: 361). In a letter to his new friend the Russian philosopher Nikolai Strakhov, Tolstoy criticized Mill's ideas about emancipation of women (unsent version dated March 19, 1870 [61: 232–34]). Further encounters of Tolstoy with Mill will be addressed in subsequent chapters.

10. Letter to Charles Wright, April 22-May 7, 1904 (75: 82).

11. See the preface that Mill wrote to his work explaining its purpose, in Mill, *Autobiography*, 3.

12. William James, *The Varieties of Religious Experience* (London: Penguin, 1982), 204. On Tolstoy the mystic who experienced states of faith, see page 424.

13. Lev Shestov, *Apofeoz bespochvennosti: Opyt adogmaticheskogo myshleniia* (Leningrad: Izdatel'stvo Leningradskogo universiteta, 1991), 110.

14. Lev Shestov, "Gefsimanskaya noch': Filosofiia Paskalia," in Lev Shestov, *Sobranie sochinenii*, 2 vols. (Moscow: Nauka, 1993), 2: 278–324, esp. 306.

15. See Lev Shestov, "Na strashnom sude (Poslednie proizvedeniia L'va Nikolaevicha Tolstogo)" in *Sobranie sochinenii*, 2: 98–150; see also Shestov's letter to his daughters concerning Tolstoy, 519.

16. James, *The Varieties of Religious Experience*, 189.

17. See lecture-chapters "The Sick Soul," and "The Divided Self," in James, *The Varieties of Religious Experience*, 127–65 and 166–88.

18. Ibid, 185.

19. Ibid, 187. Tolstoy read James's book in the original in 1904. At the end of 1909 the Russian translation came out. Tolstoy was visited by Varvara Grigorievna Malakhieva-Mirovich, its translator. Tolstoy would not dispute James's diagnosis, mentioning with his characteristically sly meekness that it was "good for his health." See his diary entry for December 13, 1909 (57: 187–88). To Mirovich he mentioned pseudoscientific terms in James's book and a day later, running a very high fever, he was pleased to notice, no doubt in response to James, how good he felt in his soul. In the evening, he took to reading James again—and pitied James's own scientific malaise: "Read James's book. A wrong attitude to the subject, a scientific one. Oh, this science!" (57: 188). James' book in the Russian translation is catalogued under No. 1013 in Tolstoy's library at Yasnaya Polyana. See *Biblioteka L.N.Tolstogo v Iasnoi Poliane: Bibliograficheskoe opisanie* (Moscow: Kniga, 1972), vol. 1, part 1, 256.

20. Tolstoy, *A Confession and Other Religious Writings*, 78.

21. Ibid, 79.

22. Lev Shestov, "Derznoveniia i pokornosti," fragment no. 9 (IX), in Shestov, *Sobranie sochinenii*, 2:151–250, esp. 155.

23. See Bakhtin's excerpts "Man at the Mirror" (*Chelovek u zerkala*) and "Regarding self-consciousness and self-evaluation" (*K voprosam samooznaniia i samoot-senki*) (both 1943?) in Bakhtin, M. M. *Sobranie sochinenii*. 5 vols. (Moscow: Russkie slovari, 1996), 5: 71–72. See also the "Mirkina Notes," the notes from Bakhtin's lectures on Russian literature delivered in Vitebsk and Leningrad (1922–1927) taken by one of his students, Rakhil' Moiseevna Mirkina, where Tolstoy's *samoogliadka* is identified as his definitive and lifelong artistic flaw. Bakhtin, M. M., "Zapisi kursa lektsii po istorii rus.lit., 1922–1927. Lev Tolstoy" in Bakhtin, *Sobranie sochinenii*, 2: 255.

24. See chapter "My Conversation With a Moscow Acquaintance. A Note on One New Book Release" of Dostoevsky's *Diary of a Writer* (*Razgovor moi s odnim moskovskim znakomym. Zametka po povodu novoi knizhki*) (July–August, 1877). See Dostoevsky, *Polnoe sobranie sochinenii v tridtsati tomakh*. (Leningrad: Nauka,

1972–1988), 25: 175. Unless otherwise indicated all future references to Dosto-evsky's works (hereafter, Dostoevsky, volume: page) are to this complete edition.

25. See Martin Heidegger, *Poetry, Language, Thought*. Trans. Albert Hofstadter (New York: Perennial Classics, 2001), 119, 124–25.

26. Gauri Viswanathan, *Outside the Fold: Conversion, Modernity, and Belief* (Princeton, N.J.: Princeton University Press, 1998), vi.

27. Lewis Rambo, *Understanding Religious Conversion* (New Haven and London: Yale University Press, 1993), 1; on the fragility element, see p. 31.

28. For types of conversion and an explanation of motives, see Rambo, *Understanding Religious Conversion*, 12–14; for normative regulation of conversion, see 6, 18–19. For the psychology of conversion, see Lewis R. Rambo, "The Psychology of Conversion," in H. Newton Malony and Samuel Southhard, eds., *Handbook of Religious Conversion* (Birmingham, Ala.: Religious Education Press, 1992), 159–77; see esp. 164–66 on the fragility of the self in conversion.

29. Massimo Leone, *Religious Conversion and Identity: A Semiotic Analysis of Texts* (London: Routledge, 2004), ix.

30. Ibid, xii.

31. Ibid, 70–72.

32. Ibid, 64–67.

33. Caryl Emerson. "The Tolstoy Connection in Bakhtin," in *Rethinking Bakhtin: Extensions and Challenges*, eds., G. S. Morson and Caryl Emerson (Evanston, Ill.: Northwestern University Press, 1989), 149–70. The essay first appeared in *PMLA*, volume 100, No. 1 (January 1985), 68–80. Bakhtin associates modes with "chrono-topes," spatio-temporal organizations of narrative that reflect the author's attitude. Thus, we have crises or the threshold consciousness of Dostoevsky that encourages the battle of ideas and discourages taking the evolutionary course in the biological time. We also have Bakhtin's narcissistic Tolstoy, to whose gradual self-realizations the reader is bound in the biology of life's transitions. Emerson used the terms "the most of what happens" in relation to Dostoevsky and "what happens the most" in relation to Tolstoy in her opening lecture for the course "Tolstoy, Dostoevsky, and the Tasks of the Russian Novel" (spring semester, 2001; Course packet, p. 21). On Tolstoy's habits of "always" and "for the most part," see George R. Clay's elaboration of the phrase, "what happens the most" in his *Tolstoy's Phoenix. From Method to Meaning in* War and Peace (Evanston, Ill.: Northwestern University Press, 1998), 7–40.

34. Leone, 64.

35. See M. M. Bakhtin, "Author and Hero in Aesthetic Activity," in *Art and Answerability: Early Philosophical Essays by M. M. Bakhtin*, ed. Michael Holquist and Vadim Liapunov, trans. Kenneth Brostrom (Austin: University of Texas Press, 1990), 4–256; esp. 129.

36. See Joan Delaney Grossman, "'Philosophers, Decadents, and Mystics': James's Russian Readers in the 1890s," *William James in Russian Culture*, eds. Joan Delaney Grossman and Ruth Rischin (Lanham, Md.: Lexington Books, 2003), 93–112.

37. See T. H. L. Parker, "Conversion," in *A Dictionary of Christian Theology*, ed. Alan Richardson (Philadelphia: Westminster Press, 1969), 73–75.

38. A. D. Nock. *Conversion: The Old and the New in Religion from Alexander the Great to Augustine of Hippo* (1933; reprint, Oxford: Oxford University Press, 1969).

39. See the reports of turning the gentiles "from darkness" as they are sanctified by "faith in Me" (Acts 15.3 and 28.13). Romans, 1 Corinthians, 2 Thessalonians, and 2 Timothy describe new converts to Christianity as "first fruits" and those "newly planted." If not indicated otherwise, all references to the Bible are to *New Oxford Annotated Bible*, eds. Bruce Metzger and Ronald Murphy (New York and Oxford: Oxford University Press, 1994).

40. Saint Augustine, *Confessions*, trans. R. S. Pine-Coffin (London: Penguin, 1961), bk IX, 171.

41. On this point see Malony and Southhard, *Handbook of Religious Conversion*, 1–8, 41–77, 93–107.

42. Quoted in John A. Hardon, S.J., *The Catholic Catechism: A Contemporary Catechism of the Teachings of the Catholic Church* (New York: Doubleday, Image Books, 1981), 556–57.

43. See Saint Justin Martyr, *The First and Second Apologies*, trans. Leslie William Barnard (New York: Paulist Press, 1966), 5–10, 54–67 and Saint Justin Martyr, *Dialogues With Trypho*, trans. Thomas B. Fallsand, ed. Michael Shlusser (Washington, D.C.: Catholic University of America Press, 2003), 55, 60, 65, 80. My readings of Justin were aided by the interpretations of Craig D. Allert, *Revelation, Truth, Canon and Interpretation: Studies in Justin the Martyr's Dialogue With Trypho* (Leiden: Brill, 2002), and L. W. Barnard, *Justin Martyr: His Life and Thought* (Cambridge: Cambridge University Press, 1967).

44. Saint Justin Martyr, *Dialogues With Trypho*, 7.

45. Allert, *Revelation*, 23.

46. Saint Augustine, *Confessions*, 170.

47. On the paradigmatic conversions, see Morrison, *Understanding Conversion* (Charlottesville: University Press of Virginia, 1992), xxv, 7, 41, 133.

48. See Saint Thomas Aquinas, *The Pocket Aquinas*, ed. Vernon J. Bourke (New York: Washington Square Press, 1960), 206–11, 340–41. For Aquinas' criticism of Augustine and Augustinians, see Jan A. Aertsen, "Aquinas Philosophy in Its Historical Setting," in *The Cambridge Companion to Aquinas*, eds. Norman Kretzmann and Eleanore Stump (Cambridge: Cambridge University Press, 1993), 12–37, esp. 28. For Aquinas's revival of moral obligation in the reception of the teaching of Saint Paul, see, in the same collection, Joseph Owens, "Aristotle and Aquinas," 38–59, esp. 42.

49. Marilyn Harran, *Luther on Conversion: The Early Years* (Ithaca, N.Y.: Cornell University Press, 1983), 21.

50. For a basic explanation of Luther's attitudes toward conversion, see John Baillie, *Baptism and Conversion* (London: Oxford University Press, 1964), 22–25. Harran describes Luther's night in the tower in terms of the "last straw," the final moment resulting from long and tortuous searches for this truth. See Harran, *Luther on Conversion*, 177, 191.

51. See Martin Luther, *Christian Liberty*, ed. Harold J. Grimm (Philadelphia: Fortress Press, 1957), 7, 29.

52. See the following references to Luther in Tolstoy's volume on pedagogy (8: 4, 6, 10, 106, 225, 329–31, 383, 408).

53. See *The Kingdom of God is Within You* (*Tsarstvo bozhie vnutri vas*), 28: 1–293, esp. 46, 48. The copy of Luther's *Catechism* in Tolstoy's library, entitled *Dr. Martin Luthers Kleiner Katechismus: Mit Erklärung und biblischen Beweisstellen*, was published in Moscow in 1875 by a German press owned by a certain A. Lang. See *Biblioteka L. N. Tolstogo v Iasnoi Poliane*, vol. 3, pt. 1, 699.

54. See Eric W. Gritsch, *Born Againism: Perspectives On a Movement* (Philadelphia: Fortress Press, 1982).

Part One

Chapter One

Challenges of Modernity: The Russian Vertigo in Personal Experience and Literature to 1847

DOCTRINE AND GOVERNMENT POLICIES

In the modern era, conversion was increasingly becoming a matter of individual conscience and personal choice. In the West, confessions of faith and public declarations of one's religious change became an all-important open forum. Most Enlightenment thinkers believed that through the gift of reason noticeable in Spinoza's *amor intellectualis Dei* or Descartes's "mind's eye," God has already accomplished the conversion of man to Himself. John Locke favored separating reason and faith into two distinct provinces of human activity and placing each in its own respective room. New scientific discoveries further questioned the possibility of miracles and, with them, the possibility and nature of revelation, of which reason, this *ultimo ratio*, served the verifier. According to Locke, reason should "declare for it [revelation] as for any other truth."[1] In the literary-religious field, the last bloody Protestant revolutions left in their wake Milton's great iconoclastic epics affirming religion for the new age, as well as a spate of heavy-handed yet entertaining allegorical conversion stories by John Bunyan, Thomas Hobbes, and Izaak Walton, along with revelatory re-creations of the debaucheries celebrating freedom (Casanova, Sade, Voltaire). Rousseau's principle of self-love influenced uncountable millions of youths encouraging their drive toward self-perfection.[2] Literal conversion changes little in such a self-loving man. Rousseau himself converted twice in his life, to Catholicism and then back to Protestantism, making a literal belonging to a confession a form of sport and his *Confessions* bears a very conflicted witness to this new religious liberalism.

The growth of religious consciousness in the Russian secular tradition has been much slower. Its stirrings toward independence are evident in how the

3

baroque times catered to the yearnings of the mind and the flesh in their handling of temptations. Penetrating through the westernmost provinces of Poland and Ukraine, Western didactic genres intermingled with local apocryphal legends. The genre of graphic temptation tales flourished in the sixteenth and seventeenth centuries. The first printed books in Russia were of a traditional religious nature; the development of printing culture contributed to creating an intimate link between the act of reading and the life of faith. Mikhail Lomonosov (1711–1765), Russia's first significant poet and a scientific genius, developed a taste for bookish wisdom after learning the Psalter by rote, the first and only book available to him, a son of a fisherman near Arkhangelsk. In the final reckoning, Russia may well owe the formation of its Academy of Science to psalmody. The German-trained Lomonosov and such contemporary neoclassical men of letters as Antioch Kantemir, Vassily Trediakovsky, and Alexander Sumarokov (whose tastes were informed by the French) sharpened their poetic craft and learned how to write in the same mode as they learned how to read, namely, by translating psalms from the Old Church Slavonic into the Russian poetic vernacular and sponsoring a contest for the best spiritual ode, in which Trediakovsky proved superlatively clumsy. Yet it was not articles of faith that caused discord among the authors and ridicule rather than awe in the readers but what articles of poetic grammar, meter, and rhyme scheme were better suited for the Russian idiom. For the sake of the latter, Trediakovsky and Sumarokov soon switched to more accessible genres (for example, love songs, madrigals, animal fables, and tragedies in their more solemn moods). Poetic rhyme and religious reason survived the longest in the metaphysical poetry of Lomonosov, who composed dazzling meditations on the splendor of the universe and the secrets of intelligent design.[3]

Dissent and heterodoxy that is of interest to this study, the dissent of the spirit, had a complex reflection in the literature, intellectual, and spiritual life of the Russians. From Lomonosov onward, Enlightenment thinkers preferred inflexible neoclassical high genres—mostly odes—to discuss faith. On the eve of the nineteenth century, Ivan Pnin resigned himself to honoring God in silence: "to say *what* he is—one should himself be a god" (1798).[4] The nature of poetic conversations with God was finally altered by Gavrila Derzhavin (1743–1816), who proclaimed himself the original feature of divinity: "I am tsar—I am slave—I am worm—I am God!"[5] In nervous convolutions and transmutations of the Baroque verse, Derzhavin composed his epitaphs that were forms of metaphysical revolt against death, heart-breaking farewells to his dead friends ("Where hast thou gone, Meshchersky?") and wives ("Half of my heart and soul, farewell") in forbidding tones that should have made death go about its grim business uneasy. Derzhavin's poems on death opened more intimate channels of communication between the poet and God, as well as with the reader. His final poem, "The River of Time," an epitaph to himself, was a metaphysical reconciliation with eternity that will swallow everything, even that what remains in the sounds of the lyre.[6]

Profoundly spiritual and engaged in a relentless quest for justice, Russian literature rightfully enjoys the renown of a holy literary tradition. Only in the 1840s, however, Russian literature became what it is now famous for, and what Berdiaev described as one of the forms of Russian truth-searching. Literature provided an outlet for religious experience that had a limited and unremittingly guarded space for independent self-exploration. No wonder that prodigal sons and daughters lost to truth-searching, who also wished to be Christian, were left with no choice but to return in the most conventional way and revert in the mode of Bulgakov. Although Berdiaev remained outside the church and Bulgakov returned to become a rather controversial priest, when placed side by side their tales exemplify two facets of a uniquely Russian personal conversion: a sense of participation in the common act of brotherhood (the cause of existential-social justice of Berdiaev; the Sophianic unity of Bulgakov). Both men resented the role of breakaway "little Russian Luthers."[7] How was the birth of Bulgakovs and Berdiaevs possible and where may we find the Russian roots of Tolstoy's iconoclasm?

The seriousness of the baptismal rite to the Orthodox majority, who do not expect acts of grace to occur outside the church, may be explained in terms of how Orthodox theology interprets man's place in the world according to its three aspects: his natural and uncorrupted state before the Fall; his state after the Fall and banishment from Paradise; and his state after his inclusion in the sphere of divine grace following his joining the body of the Orthodox Church.[8] Russian Orthodoxy translates the Greek word *ortodoksia* as *pravoslavie*, or "correct glorification [of God]," and has as its antonym *inoslavie*, or "other [types of Christian] glorification," which is considered to be heretical.

Orthodoxy rejects the *filioque* ("and through the son"), the amendment to the teaching of the Holy Trinity introduced by the Catholic Church in the fifteenth century, on the grounds that the Holy Spirit may issue only from the Father to the Son. Objections to the *filioque* had far-reaching consequences, disqualifying individual imitations of Christ and all identification with his human and divine person. Russian Orthodoxy does not acknowledge purgatory, an additional obstacle to self-engendered regeneration outside the church, based on the freedom to repent, which further curtails the independent struggle for faith.[9] More doctrinal barriers to personally guided conversions relate to the rights of biblical interpretation. Although it permits a believer to read the Bible on his own, the Russian Orthodox faith does not presume his right to interpret the Bible according to his own understanding (*lichnoe razume-nie*), a concept crucial to the life and fate of independent seekers and a form of heresy for the Orthodox.

In establishing these restrictions, Orthodoxy relies on its unique means to make man's communion with God complete. To its faithful laity, who accept the Holy Eucharist and the gifts of the Lord's redemption, it reveals the mystery of divine providence. Orthodoxy interprets the end of the world and the resurrection of the dead as the beginning of the new life. According to the *Paterik* (A Collection of Saints' Lives) compiled in the thirteenth century by Bishop Simeon and Monk Polycarp, the practice of humility and other Christian virtues is impossible without *internal conversion*, which ideally leads to a life of silent prayer. Internal conversion—turning to God with one's entire being so that the whole life becomes an *uninterrupted inner prayer*—is a state of the soul achieved through consistent repetition of the Lord's Prayer and attained through much spiritual labor. Dmitry of Rostov and Father Makarius—the compilers of the *Menology*, or *Saints' Lives* (*Chet'i Minei*; 1702–9), both of whom Tolstoy studied seriously in the late 1860s and 1870s as part of his editorial involvement in the publication of educational books for peasant children and the common people—also devised a special spiritual technique for the discovery of one's "inner man" (*vnutrennii chelovek*) involving silent prayer before the icons or without them. The inner man who knows himself knows God and uses his reason for mental deeds (*umnoe delainie*).[10]

Equally dog-eared among Tolstoy's books, as well as in the libraries of his countrymen, was a Russian translation of an anthology of late-eighteenth-century mystical Greek Orthodox texts entitled *Philokalia* (love of the fine), by Nikodemus of the Holy Mount (Hagiorite) and Makarios of Corinth. The translation was corrected in the middle of the nineteenth century by Theophanous the Recluse (the same Theophanous who later referred to Tolstoy as Satan), an important Russian elder, who completed the serial publication of *Dobrotonravie* (good behavior) in 1878. In this work, Theophanous reinterpreted the ascent toward uninterrupted, complete prayer *with feeling*: "To pray is to stand spiritually before God in one heart in glorification, thanksgiving, supplication, and contrite penitence. The root of all prayer is devout fear of God; from this comes belief about God and faith in Him."[11]

The Orthodox preamble on conversion and religious change has remained unaltered down through the centuries. Maximus the Greek (Maxim the Confessor, or Maksim Ispovednik, A.D. 580–662), one of the most revered Greek fathers—from whom Russian Orthodoxy has adopted its tenets of deification of human nature in Christ—stated that he did not wish for heretics to suffer and did not delight in their misfortune but grieved for them.[12] In the same vein, Nilus Sorsky (1433–1555), the leader of the ascetic faction of non-possessors in the sixteenth century, allowed for greater freedom of religious conscience by arguing that those who disagreed with Orthodox principles should not be persecuted but rather excommunicated. In order to be allowed to return to Orthodoxy, they must repent, recant, and formally re-convert. Truth be told, those cases of second baptism are rare indeed.[13] One of the more liberal-minded Orthodox hierarchs of Tolstoy's time, the Metropolitan of Moscow Filaret (Vasilii Drozdov, d. 1867) wrote that tolerance does not mean consent to all conversions or acceptance of heresies, but only lack of persecution. Regarding conversion, he used an eloquent metaphor of the believer's progress with his eyes fixed forward on the shepherd in whose service he was baptized at birth. Desire of self-appraisal and temptation to look back (*zret' vspiat'*), the Tolstoyan symptom criticized by Dostoevsky and Bakhtin, is a form of self-persecution requiring no further punishment, for it is already a guarantee of not getting into the Kingdom of God.[14]

Difficulties of self-directed conversion in the age of Tolstoy had doctrinal as well as socio-political reasons that date back to the dawn of modernity in Russia. Mass heresies spread throughout Russia during the reign of Peter the Great's father, Tsar Aleksis, during the schism between the supporters of Patriarch Nikon, who attempted to modernize the doctrine and liturgy by bringing it into conformity with the Greek standard, and opponents of any collaboration with either the Greeks or the papacy, the so-called Old Believers, heroic retrogrades who preferred to live "priest-less," stateless, and church-less. Peter the Great instituted the Holy Synod, a ministry in his government in place of the Patriarchate (1721), put in charge of regulating the spiritual behavior of Peter's subjects. The metropolitans of the greater eparchies became ministers responsible to the *Ober prokuror* (Chief Procurator). On the one hand, the state assumed the role of guardian of the religious conscience of its subjects. On the other hand, it became an enforcer of religious conscience. Nevertheless, the spread of secularism and religious creativity continued unabated, ensured by the progressive personal qualities of the first procurators. In 1763 Chief Procurator Melissino submitted his Points (*Punkty*) to the young wife of Emperor Peter III, the soon-to-be Catherine the Great, which advocated ridding Orthodox liturgy of repetitions and cumbersome elements, calling off prayers for the dead, and expunging everything that smacked of "feigned miracles" (*pritvornye chudesa*) and superstitions.[15] These developments caused Alexander Pushkin's indignation years later, condemning modern Russian monarchs and their governments for being more revolutionary in terms of religious creativity than their subjects. He argued that only Old Believers and a handful of Russian Protestants enjoyed a real life of the spirit unendorsed from above.[16]

The government changed religion on their political whim. Catherine sent
mixed signals about the extent of personal religious freedoms. She did not allow Melissino's project to go forward and preferred to heed the petitioning
clerics and the Holy Synod, who, at her request, submitted "Instructions" for
the new legislature, points 5 and 6 of which drastically restricted the extent of
personal freedom in matters of religious interpretation and banned public debates on religion.[17] Even though Catherine soon blotted out the remnants of
her Enlightenment and cracked down on Russian Masons, Nikolai Novikov
(1744–1818) and Alexander Radishchev (1749–1802), important notions relating to freedom of conscience developed. Freethinking (*svobodomyslie*), a
synonym of Voltairianism (*vol'terianstvo*) and a near-relative of Freemasonry
(*frankmasonstvo*), became awful charges. They were preambles to an ideological and intellectual crime deemed much worse, namely, *inakomyslie*
(thinking differently from us), which joined *inoslavie* (glorifying God otherwise than us) as its secular counterpart. With their innocent belief that it was
possible to extirpate evil in the hearts and minds of men and prepare for the
descent of heavenly grace on earth, Russian Masons and Radishchev were the
first secular intellectuals who fell victim to charges of *inakomyslie*.

From that point on, Russian dissidents of conscience had greater trouble
with the government than with the Church doctrine and had trouble with the
latter because the government controlled the doctrine. Catherine's son, Paul
I, and her grandson, the future Alexander I, responsible for his father's murder, were mystics whose Orthodoxy represented a curious mix of belief in
Protestant election and Catholic good deeds. Paul's favorite prelate Platon
Levshin (1737–1812), the author of a progressive "Orthodox Doctrine"
(1765), insisted in his work *Slovo* (Logos) that it was religious holy men or
churchmen, not lay pranksters, who could interpret the Lord's Word. Levshin
blessed the opening in 1792 of Optina Pustyn' Cloister, which soon became a
pilgrimage site for those seeking advice from the holy elders concerning the
righteous way of life, a place visited by Dostoevsky and Tolstoy.[18] In Alexander's cabinet Masons rubbed shoulders with liberal Russian Catholics and
with Orthodox clerics—from the morbidly ultraconservative Photius Spassky
to the more enlightened Filaret Drozdov. In his effort to blend Enlightenment
thinking with Christian piety, Chief Procurator Prince Alexander N. Golitsyn
who had strong Catholic leanings urged a chapter of the Bible Society to open
a branch in Saint Petersburg, which in 1814 was renamed the Russian Bible
Society. The latter concentrated on translating the Old Church Slavonic Bible
into Russian and publishing the Scriptures in the major languages of the empire. During these years pro-Catholic aristocratic salons flourished in Saint
Petersburg, where the Bible was read and mystical rites were performed by
specially invited mediums.

After the defeat of Napoleon, Alexander became noticeably less liberal and took advantage of his victory to bolster Orthodoxy against his allies in the conservative Holy Alliance, making it the leading ideology in the new ecumenical church movement. Toward the end of his life, Alexander I was again in the grips of a pious panic, dying mysteriously and suddenly in December 1825.[19] During Alexander's reign educated religious intellectuals of the 1820s were strongly influenced by German idealism—mostly Kantian in the universities— as well as by the younger correctors of Kant from the Jena and Berlin schools of philosophy.[20] German idealism flourished in select Muscovite intellectual circles, especially one that came to be known as *liubomudry* (Lovers of Wisdom). The works of Luther, Leibniz, Wolff, Herder, Kant, Fichte, Schelling, Schleiermacher, the brothers Schlegel, and Hegel became staples in the academic curricula. Differences among these early Russian idealists soon gave rise to intellectual schisms more fateful than the religious fallouts of the previous century.

In December 1825, just days after the passing of Alexander I, the simmering resentment among both military and civilian aristocrats regarding the establishment of justice in deed—as it had been established in principle for them by decades of Enlightenment thought—finally erupted. The aristocratic coup of December 14 on Senate Square in Saint Petersburg, as well as the armed revolt in the Ukraine and other southwestern regions, brought to a bloody conclusion the debates on how one redeems oneself through what is just. Tolstoy was born less than three years after the revolt and his youth was spent in the atmosphere of religious reaction. Nicholas I began by executing and exiling the Decembrists and shutting down the Bible Society in 1826. He ordered Prince Sergey Uvarov—a brilliant intellectual and connoisseur of Schelling who was the new minister of education and president of the Russian Academy of Sciences and had ties to the Decembrists—to draw up a religious state doctrine that would keep the country in check. The triadic guidance for life in the Russian empire that Uvarov devised called for "Orthodoxy, Autocracy, National Spirit." Applied as universal state policy, this formula, reflecting an infatuation with the ideas of the German Enlightenment and Romanticism, became odious. On the day of his coronation in August 1826, Nicholas appointed Filaret Drozdov the metropolitan of Moscow. Filaret was known for his *Prostrannyi khrsitianskii katekhizis* (Extended Christian Catechism), composed in the Russian vernacular with the encouragement of Alexander I, which earned him the reputation of a reformed theologian thanks to its stress on *knowing* Christ through creative mental coexistence in the events of his mystery. Under Nicholas and in response to Decembrist catechisms, the more cautious Filaret wrote a pro-monarchist work entitled "Christian Teaching on the Tsar's Power and the Duties of His Faithful Subjects."

THE BIRTH OF MADMEN OUT OF
THE SPIRIT OF ORTHODOXY

The Tsar's doctrinal response to the Decembrists was hardly overstated. In terms of their religious affiliations in 1825, the Decembrists—who differed politically regarding the degree of violence permissible in promoting either republicanism or constitutional monarchy—were a motley crew (Orthodox, Lutheran, Catholic, deists, and agnostics). Their fathers, Enlighteners and masons raised them with respect for the Master of the Universe and instilled in them a sense of civic duty.[21] However, the majority of enlightened children grew up to believe that faith contradicts reason and refused to pray or confess before tried. They were inspired by Pushkin's four-line rhyme written in imitation of Pierre-Jean Béranger and the French Revolution: "We shall amuse good citizens / And on the pillar of shame / We shall strangle the last tsar / With the intestine of the last cleric."[22] Others believed in the possibility of employing religion in the new version of the earthly paradise. Sergey Murav'ev-Apostol, one of the five Decembrists hanged by the new emperor, Nicholas I, wrote *Pravoslavnyi Katekhizis* (The Orthodox Catechism) in the name of the Father and the Son and the Holy Spirit, from which all the earthly tsars were expunged and where man could believe in God, and be free. Whence the misfortune of the Russians? The tsars and their subservient church have usurped their freedom. And where is salvation to be found? In repenting their long-drawn-out servility, taking arms against the tyrants, and struggling for the Truth of Christ, the one tsar in earth and heaven.[23] Seeing in it the nearest relative of universalizing Christian socialism, many Decembrists, including radicals like Mikhail Lunin, ultimately embraced Catholicism. They considered themselves opposition leaders within the general religious movement for liberation rather than rebels and apostates.

In 1829, Peter Chaadaev (1794–1856), Tolstoy's second cousin once removed, a friend of the Decembrists and of Pushkin, a former officer of the guards, an independent scholar of French mysticism and German Romanticism who knew Schelling, and a famous dandy began a correspondence with a social acquaintance, Ekaterina Panova (1804–1858). Panova was contemplating conversion to Catholicism. While composing the epistles Chaadaev decided to publish his part of the correspondence as *Lettres Philosophiques addressée à une dame* (Philosophical Letters Addressed to a Lady) concealing the identity of his addressee while serving as the lady's pastor in response to her hypothetical laments and uncertainties. In 1836, Chaadaev dared to publish "Letter One" out of eight, translated into Russian, in the Moscow journal *Telescope*. The letter essentially claimed that Russians lacked a religious conscience and, with no religious home of their own, were "illegitimate children of civilization" excluded from the history of Christendom and living in "Necropolis," the city of the dead. The journal was immediately closed, its editor exiled, Chaadaev proclaimed mad and put under house arrest by imperial decree, and required to undergo regular checkups by a medic competent in treating mental diseases.[24]

Although extreme and radical in terms of his historical prognosis for Russia, on the level of personal religiosity Chaadaev's path toward inner conversion is modest, involving the reentry into the European religious home, preferably with a Catholic or Anglican pass. To accomplish this, Chaadaev recommended the establishment of a personalized "regimen for the soul," and implies that "putting on the garments of humility" and strict fulfillment of all church rites is not only aesthetically proper to his friend's sex, but also helps to realize personal "fascinating plans." Here Chaadaev craftily rephrased the prayers of Ephrem (Ephraim) the Syrian, who was familiar to everyone baptized in the Russian faith: the image of a robe of divine grace redeemed by the Incarnation, which was thrown on everyone at baptism. Ephrem's robe was obviously combined in Chaadaev's imagination with the putting on of the new man, as suggested by Kant.

The leitmotif of Chaadaev's appeal is modest indeed: "Apprenons à vivre raisonnablement dans notre réalité donnée" ("let us learn how to live reasonably in the reality given to us").[25] The Chaadaev of *The Letters* believes in the power of providence to guide men toward good deeds and implies dissolving reason in the life of the soul in order to apprehend the voice of the spirit and thus reach the end point of life's pilgrimage. *The Letters* concludes with a call to continue writing the book of Christian history that commenced with the Word of Jesus. For all its imitative inconclusiveness, Chaadaev's *Letters* started circulating immediately and alerted Russia's intellectual conscience to the fact that personal religion is a dangerous, "mad" force. In 1837, Chaadaev took advantage of the popularity of the madman theme after the appearance of Gogol's *Notes of a Madman* (Zapiski sumasshedshego; 1835) and published his *Apologie d'un fou* (Apology of a Madman). Its Russian title, *Apologiia sumasshedshego*, echoed the title of Gogol's *Notes*. In the *Apology* Chaadaev expressed bitter disappointment at the reversal of the scales of reasonableness in his country: his penetrating thoughts about the state of Christianity in Russia were considered insane, whereas Gogol's religious farce hurled at God and decency in the style of a Scaramouch was applauded. Perhaps too mean-spirited, a few years later Chaadaev's barb succeeded in swaying the already wavering Gogol toward a seminal change in his attitude toward religious laughter and the role of a Christian writer. The *Apology* drew a decisive line between the untouchable Holy Fool of Orthodoxy, who wore his prophetic garb in all his erratic earnestness, and the new Holy Fool, who only pretended to be mad to continue on the sly in his well-reasoned foolish business. Chaadaev's *Apology* anticipates Tolstoy's *The Memoirs of a Madman* while distancing itself from Gogol's work, which intentionally blurs the difference between the high vocation of a writer and the writing of doggerel.

Tolstoy's earliest years in the literary sphere in the 1850s were spent among the writers belonging to the Westernizer persuasion, one of the two intellectual camps, the Westernizers and the Slavophiles, which Chaadaev had unwittingly consolidated in 1836. The older Westernizer group—which included such luminaries as the writer Ivan Turgenev, the "frenetic" critic Vissarion Belinsky, the anarchist revolutionary Mikhail Bakunin, and the Christian socialist, writer, revolutionary, critic, and publisher Alexander Herzen—carried Chaadaev's banner high. However, most of the Westernizers of the 1840s were atheists wherein Bakunin's dicta on religion represented the summa of Russian atheism. Baptized by a comet, according to Herzen, Bakunin reportedly modified and adapted Voltaire's statement—"If God did not exist, he had to be invented"—to serve as an epigraph to his posthumously discovered work *God and the State*: "If God really existed, it would be necessary to abolish him."[26] The early Westernizers were ardent Hegelians for whom reconciliation with reality was a pretext for a critical investigation of the truth and the ideas of the age with an eye to change. Belinsky was fixedly and blindly atheistic. "According to you," wrote this son of a priest to Gogol, in his open address to Gogol's *Selected Passages from Correspondence with Friends* in 1847, "the Russian people are the most religious in the world: this is a lie! The foundation of religiosity is pietism, goodwill, fear of divine judgment. But the Russian man utters the name of God while scratching his behind. He speaks thus about the holy image: if it suits me I pray, if it doesn't I use it to cover chamber pots."[27] Alexander Herzen, Tolstoy's valued personal acquaintance since 1860, and a defining voice of the group since Belinsky's death in 1848, doubted that Christianity could balance the unbounded freedom of the individual in a neat Western package of moral civility and sociability and gave preference to Saint-Simon's version of the new Christianity, which he hoped to realize in the Russian peasant commune.

The Slavophile group lived in Moscow and on their estates not far from Optina Pustyn', their unofficial headquarters, which they also financed. In Ivan Kireevsky's periodical *Moskvitianin* (The Muscovite) they intoned their belief that Orthodoxy was providentially inspired to rescue a narcissistic Europe from its spiritual morass. The Slavophiles relied on the so-called Orthodox *conciliarity (sobornost')*, their version of Schelling's All-Unity (*vseedinstvo*), to combine the church, society, and man into one organic spiritual unity, providing society with an organizational and legal structure that would obviate the need for a Western-style bureaucratic state, which was foisted on his nation by Peter the Great.[28] The strictest restraints on religious freedom, within the allegedly limitless freedom granted by *conciliarity*, were espoused by Aleksei Khomiakov (1804–1860), whose "Christ is the Law. Church is the Judge" became an informal Slavophile motto. Khomiakov's essays claimed that Western congregations had lost the sense of the living logos and the sacraments, and were about to slump into their final heresy, moving against the source of their possible salvation present in the unity of individuals in the Orthodox church, which embodied the life of the living logos.[29] These views, however, were fully expressed only in the 1850s to respond to the so-called Catholic threat posed by the sermons of the two converts, Father Ivan Gagarin and Vladimir Pecherin, and by the growing threat of a military conflict with the West.[30]

From the point of view of iconoclasm, Pecherin's example is especially illuminating.[31] This man made his name legendary by abandoning a very promising academic and literary career in Moscow and defecting in 1836 from the autocratic hell of Nicholas I Russia. After four years of destitute wanderings and rubbing shoulders with mostly harmless revolutionary fanatics in Switzerland and Belgium, he stunned his compatriots and European radicals by shaving his beard of hobo extremism and taking Redemptorist vows in one of the strictest Catholic orders of Europe. At the height of his fame as a multilingual preacher in 1845, Pater Petcherine earned the admiration and respect of John Henry Newman, a new Catholic convert and future cardinal.[32]

Let us take a look at the more typical youth of the 1830s described in the chapter "The World of Superstition" from a memoir by Apollon Grigoriev (1822–1864), a brilliant critic and rather questing ally of Dostoevsky in the years following his exile. Grigoriev adumbrates items on his childhood reading list approved of by his commoner grandfather, an amateur theologian so well read in the Scriptures that he debated archpriests: Russian romantic historical novels by Mikhail Zagoskin and Ivan Lazhechnikov varying in nationalistic prejudice, *Dobrotoliubie*, John Bunyan's *Pilgrim's Progress* in translation, and journalism of the Russian Enlightenment from the Novikov era.[33] As a result of these readings, Grigoriev characterizes his religious mind-set as sensible (*zdravyi*) and his faith in the just God of Israel and His Truth prevailing over the New Testament.

Through the effort of radical critics, the image of a religious ignoramus priest and his young ignoramus student became ingrained in the popular imagination. Herzen's first novel, *Kto vinovat?* (Who Is to Blame?, 1845–1847), presented a typical despot landowner Negrov who has just mistakenly hired a mathematician, to teach his thirteen-year-old son Mitenka the skills needed to run a successful capitalist enterprise, this science for the new age. To demonstrate the brightness of his son, Negrov demands a report on

Mitenka's progress with the priest, his former teacher. Mitenka famously replies: "We covered the Russian grammar to adverbial participles, dear daddy, and read Catechism up to the mysteries section."[34] From this account, it appears that the nation has made little progress since pre-Lomonosov times to 1847.

Church authorities themselves pointed to the all-consuming collapse of faith in the religious habits of nineteenth-century Russians. Modern studies dispute this opinion and support the Slavophiles' insistence that a Russian was a believer and that "faith activated his whole being."[35] Parishes maintained strong and cohesive communities (*soobshchestva*) and played a decisive role in the renewal of religious and ethical norms among lay believers.[36] In their lived religion, parishioners shared the conciliatory notion of the Slavophiles and adhered to what Vera Shevzov calls "Churchness," or ecclesia of the temple.[37] Personal testimonies of faith-seeking individuals are rare since they went against the grain of the religious habit rather than against the habit of spiritual life.[38]

Icons continued to hold their sacred appeal and their reputation of sacred presence. At least once in a lifetime every Russian would visit the site of a miracle-inducing or venerated icon.[39] Pilgrimages to Palestine were undertaken by pious Russian commoners. Eighteenth-century scrap pictures, depicting dancing and carousing priests and showing scenes of the Last Judgment and tales of the prodigal son were complemented by the new posters, "Stages on Life's Journey" or "The Return of Prodigal Son." After the decline of the Sarov Cloister since St. Seraphim's death in 1833, Optina pustyn' became a virtual pilgrimage site in the nineteenth century. The majority of educated Russians knew the *Catechism* of Filaret Drozdov, the Staircase (*Lestvitsa*) of John Lestvichnik, could recite the prayer of Saint Vladimir, chant verses from the liturgy of John Chrysostom, say the Lord's prayer, and know at least the main points of *Dobrotloliubie*. The nobility continued to seek the tsar's blessing for marriages or promotions or the archbishop's blessing in the provinces and on the estates. Lockets containing name saints continued to be given and worn as protection during war. Artisanal icon painting prospered. Personal Bibles were in great demand.[40] Early on religious communities clustered around the manorial patrimony of the noble family, which organized life around religious holidays, gave to charity, became godparents to peasants, and often acted in concert with parish priests and higher-level clergy from the district centers in guiding the life of the laity. Holy Fools and pilgrims were housed for weeks and even months in the servants' quarters, telling tales from and about the capitals and of unknown distant lands. It was through household serfs, especially wet nurses and male under-tutors, that the aristocratic child retained a link with popular Christianity. From their serfs, and less often from grandparents, the noble child learned how to read and speak Russian, say prayers, empathize with Passion stories and saints' vitae, and imbibe the legends and lore of folk religiosity. However, it was from their foreign tutors that they often adopted Protestant, Catholic, Anglican, and Methodist habits.

THE EPARCHY OF LITERATURE

Russian literature itself was developing its identity of a very special ecclesia. Some of the ties of the eparchy of literature with the Church were anecdotal, others were serious. For years Filaret had supervised Pushkin unofficially as a solicitous supporter of his genius, first mistakenly giving Pushkin a passing grade on the subject of divine law at his graduation from the Imperial Lyceum in 1818, then complaining to the censors that jackdaws alight on church crosses of his Moscow eparchy in the seventh chapter of *Eugene Onegin*, and scolding Pushkin for spells of dejection in his poem "Vain gift, casual gift" (May 26, 1828) by writing him his own poem to the effect that life is never given in vain because there is faith and the soul is immortal. Pushkin wrote back a luminous poem saying that his vain diversions were interrupted by Filaret's voice, and that his "fragrant speeches" healed the wounds of Pushkin's conscience like unction. Shedding penitent tears, Pushkin accepted Filaret's warnings against swaying off his prophetic path: "By thy fire my soul is scorched / It rejects the gloom of earthly vanity / And (the poet) harks to the harp of the seraph / In sacred horror." In January 1830, Pushkin wrote to his society friend, Elizaveta Khitrovo, "The poetry by a Christian, the Russian Bishop, in response to skeptical couplets! Isn't this a real godsend?"[41]

Such sincere penitence was not the dominant mood of a rapidly secularizing young literature. Before the complete edition of Rousseau's *Confessions* appeared in 1790, educated Russians had already read most of the memoirs and confessional classics from the West (Seneca, Marcus Aurelius, Vauvenargues, Montaigne, Pascal), as well as the fictional novelties of the age, such as the erotic novels of Richardson and the works of Laurence Sterne, the connoisseur of the capricious whims of mind and spirit. For writers seeking emotional bonds in the age of sentimentalism, new genres permitted the flexibility of escape from ruthless satire and picaresque merrymaking in favor of the more serious. This was the case with Denis Ivanovich Fonvizin (1745–1792), Russia's best satiric playwright who routinely targeted clerics and sycophants. At the age of forty-five Fonvizin suffered a debilitating stroke and set about composing his cry of the heart entitled "Chistoserdechnoe priznanie v delakh moikh i pomyshleniiakh" (An Open-Hearted Confession about My

Deeds and Thoughts, 1790–1792). Fonvizin appropriated the conventional divisions of a secular life, common in the literature of his time, in which human existence was thought to consist of four ages: childhood, youth, maturity, and old age. However, the work remained unfinished. The youth and young adult whom we see in the early chapters is a rake who regrets his delusions (zabluzhdeniia), the result of a sharp wit that is not complemented by common sense. But his progress is not a conventional rake's story. Fonvizin relies on Saint Augustine to explain how his encounters with friends or superiors at his government post affect him and how he learns to distinguish the brilliant from the blasphemous. He also describes the three meetings with good counselors in preparation for the decisive turn: with Lomonosov, who compels him to undertake serious study; with the Enlightenment statesman and Mason Nikita Panin, who shields him from exposure to the atheistic sophisms of his friends; and a fortuitous encounter with the old philosopher Teplitsky. The latter informs the young Fonvizin that Hobbes and Spinoza were proven wrong by Samuel Clarke's work *The Unchangeable Obligation of Natural Religion and Truth* and Alexander Pope's *Essay on Man*. Fonvizin's confession ends with a promise to supply the reader with quotations from the wondrous books that rescued his mind and soul—once he corrects the translations.[42]

The moralizing and repenting voice did not suit Fonvizin the satirist. Patterning his life according to Old Testament sayings, he was forced to switch from the chatty, humorous colloquial Russian that made him famous to the unwieldy Church Slavonic of the holy books, in which his most pedantic characters previously spoke. If the dying satirists were converting to a faith-based existence and retreating from service just when the motherland needed educated cadres, younger and more robust sentimentalists recycled themselves into castigators of religious sloth. In Nikolai Karamzin's best-seller *Poor Liza* (1792), a sentimental lover of humanity narrates the story of a repentant seducer, Erast, who, after having wronged Liza, the bucolic maiden, confessed his wrongdoing and dissolute life to the author. Languid monks of the Simeon Monastery add to the tale's enchanting poetry as they gaze at the darkened icons of the Last Judgment and preserve the tale of Liza's wronged love. However, in 1802 Karamzin wrote and sent to *The Messenger of Europe* (*Vestnik Evropy*) "My Confession: A Letter to the Editor," a vicious satire on repenting gentlemen past their prime. Taking advantage of the commonplace shamelessness with which private lives are made public in his age, Count NN, who is about to turn forty, decides to add grist to his confessional mill: "just recall your pranks and the book is ready."[43] In his zeal to ridicule Rousseau and Fonvizin, Karamzin tells the story of an unrepentant swindler who sells his wife to an old and ugly prince on condition that the prince rescues him from debtor's prison. NN seduces his wife anew and deceives her again after their elopement. No bad dreams lead the rake to repent and fling himself into the lap of God. After his wife dies, he seduces old heiresses and takes on usury and is proud of his accomplishments: "I have fulfilled my predestination, and, like a pilgrim standing on the top watching the places he has traversed, I recall with joy what has happened to me and I do tell myself: thus I have lived!—Count NN."[44]

Karamzin did not preach debauchery in lieu of religion. His point was otherwise: to be appealing to the reader, morality could not afford to speak in a register higher or lower than the sphere of the reader's daily experience. Thus, oddly, the story of an "honest" rake told in a completely transparent voice provided the immediacy necessary for a confessional relationship, which was lacking in the soul-baring and morally correct Fonvizin. Known as the creator of precisely this *middle language* suitable for men, women, and "their younger daughter" (his specific provision), Karamzin was the first Russian writer who mastered the portrayal of minute changes in often ironic emotional experiences. Karamzin soon left literature to accept the post of court historiographer, in which capacity he authored the magisterial *History of the Russian State*, and transformed the Slavonicisms, Byzantine-style oratories to the tsars, and biblical quotations of his archival sources into genuine poetry in prose. Before his death in 1826, Karamzin remained at the head of a flamboyant and libertine school of writers, poets, and intellectuals who clustered around the societies The Green Lamp and Arzamas—the latter named after that same town where Tolstoy's nightmare of 1869 would occur. Karamzin and those who frequented his home—Vasily Zhukovsky, Dmitry Bludov, Sergey Uvarov, Petr Chaadaev, Petr Viazemsky, Vasily L'vovich (Pushkin's uncle), and the teenage Pushkin among them—supported aesthetic reforms against Admiral Shishkov and other so-called archaists, who congregated around his Society for the Lovers of Russian Letters (Beseda), and who insisted that archaisms and the Church Slavonic Bible should supply literature with inspiration and themes.[45]

The first Arzamas nightmare of Russian literature was not Tolstoy's. Recorded in the fuzzily otherworldly tones of a literary spoof it represents a milestone in the exploration of religious experience. In his inaugural speech, Dmitry Bludov, one of the founding members of Arzamas and a close acquaintance of Tolstoy's in the late 1850s, announced the beginning of the new Arzamas calendar starting in 1815, the historic year the liberated Russian logos was born. The pseudo-biblical story involved a nightmarish vision that a certain guest at the Arzamas inn had experienced there one night, which another future Arzamasian had the good fortune to witness and record on paper. The sleepwalking guest, in the throes of his nightmare, discoursed like a Shishkovite, mumbling apocalyptic prognostications to himself. But salvation was near. Suddenly he heard a harsh voice telling him not to fear. An old sage—suffused in a halo of light and encircled by icicles, from the Arzamasian Zhukovsky's Romantic ballad "Thunder Clapper" (*Gromoboi*)—appeared to him in a vision. Like a seraph from Isaiah 6, the elder unfurled before the bedazzled Shishkovite a scroll with commandments of a zany Arzamasian nature, pressing him to convert to the new literature. The reborn Shishkovite, now turned Arzamasian, recalled: "And the elder finished his prophesy, and inserted a head of a small serpent in my heart, and I was suffused with that elder's spirit and the vision vanished, and so it will be fulfilled."[46]

With the birth of Russia's new literary scripture, its antediluvian times were past. The Golden Age that had saved and baptized itself in the waters of Arzamasian Shakhovskoy's spa comedy *The Lipetsk Waters* (*Lipetskie vody*, 1815), had commenced.[47] The brilliant Karamzin school had won, enjoying the support of sermonizer Filaret, a rising star, as well as the good-humored deserters from Shishkov (the fable writer Ivan Krylov, among others). The real nightmarish effects of the Arzamasian victory took time to show. At first, the tastes of the new Romantic age transformed death, life, and God into an anthology of aesthetic facts and categories. In its perfectly executed aesthetic shape, death was now as graceful as the muse—and it could be flirted with. Elegant blasphemy sported one striking pose after another in the poetry of the young Pushkin and his circle. Prophets were cuckolds, arch-angels seducers, and God was invoked in a bevy of chummy soubriquets. Pushkin's uncle Vasily made famous a madrigal on the occasion of a rumor that he had died (1815).[48] Pushkin's juvenile "Elegy" written a year later, confirmed that the heart already had its stable poetic genres to express joy and sorrow: elegies, sonnets, dedications that *became* lyrical and religious confessions. "And traces of my grievous life / Nobody will ever notice."[49] The poet was permitted to hint at his sorrow, even evoke melancholic thoughts and wear a melancholic mien, but piercing through the horrific vision to reach for the final meaning was *not* the goal of poetry.[50]

The developing attitudes of the Golden Age toward death, confession, and faith may best be summed up in the example of Dmitry Venevitinov (1805–1827), member of a Lover of Wisdom circle and a Schellingian, who died of consumption at twenty-two. Already on his deathbed, in the sonnet "Consolation" Venevitinov announced that he defeated death and that his suffering was not in vain.[51] Venevitinov's last Platonic dialogue, "Anaxagoras," which imitates Schelling's *Bruno*, gives his poetic age its proper name, the Golden Age of innocence. In order to become true logos of resurrection, gold needs to be tarnished by experience and learn how to become genuinely, not merely aesthetically, unhappy. Venevitinov bequeathed to Russian literature the science of self-knowledge (*nauka samopoznaniia*), which, if mastered, and even if destined to be consumed by a more powerful cosmic force, will have uttered its logos and fulfilled its task (*naznachenie*).[52]

Venevitinov's insight was greeted with a disquieting indifference by the early Russian Romantics to the genre of genuine confession. The science of self-knowledge had to be learned firstly by mastering the Russian romantics' oddly *least* common subject: themselves. The famous world weariness (*la maladie du siècle*), with its vagueness of passions (*le vague des passions*), instantaneous conversions and apostasies was no more than formulaic in the Russian Romantic reception. The Western despondent seeker and challenger of God was born out of "the lowest abyss of human calamity," out of a Faustian "presentient holy dread" that impels him to stop his daily "restless action" and scrutinize, out of love "of our fellow man," the worth of "what's celestial," daring to rewrite its beginning from the point of view of "mind," "power," and "action" rather than divine word.[53] As for his passive counterpart, the fatal introspection of Chateaubriand's *Atala* and *René* (1802) doomed "victims of imagination" to "total solitude and the spectacle of nature," the latter reminding them of man's true destination: "Man, thou art but a fleeting vision, a sorrowful dream. Misery is thy essence, and thou art nothing save in the sadness of thy soul and the eternal melancholy of thy thought!"[54] In lieu of earthly unhappiness, the poetic malady intimated narrative immortality enjoyed by the poet, most famously but cautiously in Wordsworth's "Ode: Intimations of Immortality" (1804–7) and most emphatically verbalized in Shelley's *Prometheus Unbound*: "But from these create he can / Forms more real than living man, / Nurslings of immortality!"[55]

Pushkin was the only writer in Russia who truly mastered all these registers through contemplation and conversations with other literatures. Pushkin's progress toward his belief in Christian diffidence began with a charming, gallantly obscene youth who made his precocious debut at fourteen in narrative poetry that hailed Voltaire, the catechism, and the Psalter and sent John of Novgorod to gallop astride the devil to Jerusalem ("The Monk," 1813). Pushkin's transition to a lucid personal religion of bright sorrow was gradual. One of its many expressions comes from Pushkin's letter while in exile to Viazemsky's lament that without political liberty life is lost: "Don't take the hope of paradise and the fear of hell away from the hermit."[56] The "heeding with indifference to goodness and evil," the virtue of a historical chronicler, the old monk in his *Boris Godunov* (1825) was not suited for the mature life philosophy of the poet who made up his mind "to live and suffer" in his "Elegiia" ("Elegy") and related poetry of the late 1820s and 1830s.

Documented by almost four hundred quotations and references, Tolstoy's interest in Pushkin's works and his religion, like that of many other writers, was accorded to Pushkin's humble stoicism in the face of misfortune and death, to his ability to repent in his work, and to his prophetic use of the word. Pushkin's "The Prophet" (1826) folded in his breast pocket during his interview with the tsar who just amnestied him from exile is not only an ingenious reenactment of Isaiah 6, it describes the transformation of the poet—a degenerate wanderer in the desert, with a tongue idle yet cunning, parched by his desiccated spirit—into a prophet who is the first in Russian literature to hear the voice of God and survive: "Rise, o prophet, behold and listen, Suffuse thyself in my will / And walking the seas and lands / Burn the hearts of men with the Word" (Pushkin, 3: 30–31). Pushkin's rendition alters Isaiah so significantly that it combines the paradigm of this transformation with the conversion of Saint Paul. Pushkin leaves the command unresolved; it is not known whether the poet will obey it. However, it is abundantly clear that the replacement of the snake tongue (*iazyk*) signifies his retreat from the Arzamasian ridicule of piety in the same reenactment of Isaiah and a return to the divine roots of logos (in Russian, also *iazyk*).

Pushkin's lonely strife is even more telling in the poem entitled "A Memory" (*Vospominanie*, 1828), written in the year of Tolstoy's birth and on which Tolstoy would spend several decades rethinking its pattern of accounting. Here the tongue of the snake is a metaphor of the poet's nocturnal repent spent in torturous wakefulness, as his memory begins to unfold its long scroll before him. He reads his life in disgust, trembling, cursing, and shedding bitter tears. Yet he does not erase the sad lines (3: 102). This is not how the poem ends but rather where Pushkin drew the line in order to publish it in 1828. What he revealed to the reader is a sad yet not shameful acceptance of his past. Pushkin's rendition of the beginning of Bunyan's *Pilgrim's Progress* in his "The Wanderer" (Strannik, 1835) afforded Tolstoy a pattern of spiritual labor, to which one is condemned for an unspecified crime. The "spiritual laborer" (*dukhovnyi truzhenik*) has an encounter with the advocate of conversion, his spiritual doctor, at the seashore. The youth reading *the* Book, points out to him the source of light, which is a means of entering "the narrow gates to salvation." The wanderer starts on his course immediately, fleeing from his family and townsfolk, who are in hot pursuit to stop him. The significant changes that Pushkin made to Bunyan's tale—especially involving the search for meaning and how his family's reaction affects the conduct of the search— influenced Tolstoy in terms of the structure of the eighth part of *Anna Karenina* and "The Memoir of a Madman," which conform to the scheme of conversion outlined by Pushkin.

Pushkin's interest in the confessional genre was based on his conviction that poetic repentance had to take place in and through poetry. Repentance looms large in an unfinished youthful fragment entitled *A Confession* (*Ispoved'*) written sometime before 1820. An unidentified sinner wishes to confess his unheard-of sacrilege to a monk. The latter allows him to begin speaking, which is where the fragment breaks off (Pushkin, 1: 252). One could say that the theme of the fragment continued in everything Pushkin wrote subsequently. Perhaps the most open confession of submission to religion that Pushkin ever made is his rewriting of the prayer by Ephrem the Syrian, "that one that the priest repeats during the sad Days of the Holy Lent." Pushkin starts by quoting the prayer: "Lord of my days, / The spirit of despondent idleness, lustfulness, that hidden snake, / And idle talk forswear to my soul / But give me o Lord the knowledge of my sins / And let me not pass reproach on my neighbor / And the spirit of humility, patience and love / And chastity revive in my heart."[57] In the margins of the manuscript Pushkin drew a figure kneeling by the latticed window of a cell and covered by Ephrem's cloak.

In his and Delvig's *Literaturnaia gazeta* (The Literary Gazette) and his journal *Sovremennik* (the Contemporary) Pushkin resurrected or published reviews of confessional writings, among them Fonvizin's, Radishchev's, and Silvio Pellico's. Honoring Fonvizin's *Confessions* in 1830, Pushkin advanced his defense of honest self-accounting in a seminal review of Silvio Pellico's *Dei Doveri Degli Uomini* (On the Duties of Men, 1836), equating it with faith: "Reading these notes in which there does not fall one word of impatience, reproach or hatred from the unfortunate prisoner's pen, we involuntarily assumed there to be a hidden intention beneath this unruffled benevolence towards everyone and towards all things; this moderation struck us as artificial. And filled with admiration for the author, we reproached the man for insincerity. The book, *Dei doveri*, put us to shame, and solved for us the secret of a beautiful soul, the secret of a man and a Christian."[58]

In addition to handing down a legacy about how to believe, pray, and repent, and respect the religion of his fathers by examples of his poetry, correspondence with friends, and his own stoic death Pushkin left lessons of how to pass through stages of life's way and die with grace and honor. In the decade following Pushkin's death (in 1837) when Tolstoy made his decision in 1847 to begin writing, the road to spirituality in Russian literature diverged in several directions.[59] By dint of literary demographics, for the first time in its history Russian literature had produced a whole generation of secular writers old enough to die yet totally overwhelmed and unready to deal with the pessimism of dying as such. In the chorus of voices on the topic one hears notes of disillusion, the meaninglessness of art, the irreparable wrongs of creation, or delirious deathbed propaganda, such as in Wilhelm Küchelbecker's "In me, my soul outlives the body" that implies only the uselessness of physical survival. On the eve of his death in 1845, Küchelbecker, Pushkin's friend from the Lyceum and an exiled Decembrist, wrote a heartbreaking confession reflecting a disillusioned lack of faith.[60] In the 1840s the

aesthetic attitude toward death is similar among poets of Pushkin's generation (Viazemsky, Baratynsky, and Iazykov): tired, frightened, subdued, and
prosaic in tone; cautious in spirit as to how far they can push the intimations
of immortality.

Religious tastes among the very diverse group of young writers in the
1840s were informed by several factors: by their attitude toward outgoing Romanticism and by incoming Hegelian aesthetics, which demanded objectivity
of historical types. Literary norms of the "natural" or physiological school
within critical realism punctuated the growing ideological polarity between
the Westernizers and the Slavophiles, official religion and the need for a private, creative space. The gradual retreat of poetry, which used to be the main
repository of religious ideas and a home for religious experience, created a
vacuum that existed for quite some time. The new generation's memoirs were
still to be written, psychological prose was only gradually emerging, metaphysical poetry was ceding its position to new democratic voices, while
tragedy and old hagiographic masterpieces were hijacked by the Slavophiles
and nationalistic writers, whose focus was not on individual faith but rather
on history as part of their attempt to repaint Russia's past, present, and future
in monarchist-Orthodox hues. The school based on officialdom's religiosity
did not yield any masterpieces.[61]

In the opposite direction, the heirs of the Decembrist writers, the new democratic, physiological, critical realist school represented by Belinsky, Botkin,
Druzhinin, Kavelin, Grigorovich, Nekrasov, Herzen, and Ogarev—the majority of them militant Hegelians—restored the archaic religious pathos to the
description of revolutionary struggle. Nikolai Ogarev continued the tradition
of religiously colored revolutionary poetry, offering in his early poem "Jesus"
(Iisus, 1830s), the first Russian image of Jesus as a revolutionary figure rising up amid torture and doubt to change history: "And he alone is sent forth
to announce / The word of love to the mercenary people, / Joy to the unhappy
and freedom to the slaves."[62] A dreamier version on the cusp of the aesthetics
of Fichte, Schelling, and Hegel may be found in the poetry and essays of
Nikolai Stankevich (1813–1840), the precursor of the group and their beloved
martyr, the first serious Russian literary Hegelian, who died of consumption
at twenty-seven. The confessions of the Byronic heroes were only rhetorically
connected with democratic agendas, while the unhappiness of Stankevich and
his fictional heroes was associated with noble ideals of progress and reconstruction. The Stankevich legend was mostly oral since practically nothing of
his legacy—except the short tale "Several Moments from the Life of Count
T***" (1834)—appeared in his lifetime. The tale presents the typical stages
in a life of these Russian superfluous heroes, which begins with ideas and
ends on a note of picturesque bankruptcy. The various stages include: truth-

searching, skepticism, heroic dreams, failed practical activity, and love at the very end of life.[63] Ideas from Stankevich's short essay "My Metaphysics" (*Moia metafizika*) developed the Schellingian and Fichtean belief that man is not lost in the infinity of creation, and that his destiny is to attain the summit of nature.

Nature is Force, Life, and Creativity, writes Stankevich. The whole of nature consists of indivisible particles of life in which life continues independently of their consciousness or volition. Only life distributed among the innumerable multitude of its particles is conscious of itself, because it acts purposefully. Therefore, it is called *razumenie* (understanding): "Life within the whole is called Razumenie. . . . All (das All) is life, and life acts reasonably, therefore it is harnessed with Razumenie." Life as a whole is revealed in human life; "Here life, conscious of itself as part of the whole, reasonable and free, becomes a life that knows itself separately—as reasonable and free . . . man, this crown of creation, is the repetition of nature and the repetition of reasonable life." By constant work and thanks to his *will to love* man transforms his soul, his nation, the whole of humanity, and history.[64] Stankevich's terms "razumenie" and harnessing (*sopriazhenie*) and his conception of wholeness and separateness of human life will play an enormous role in Tolstoy's intellectual development.

Stankevich's death was the breaking point for Belinsky, Ogarev, and other Hegelians, weighing the benefits of reflection for the dialectics and of spiritual immortality (*Unsterblichkeit*).[65] They felt the awkwardness of confession best expressed by Ogarev: "I feel ashamed of complaining; / And whatever miraculously lives / In the depths of my soul / I feel difficulty in expressing."[66] In 1840, Belinsky prepared a programmatic statement on death and strategies to cope with it on a literary scene. In a letter to Botkin he wrote his thoughts on Stankevich: "Yes, to each of us it seemed impossible that death would dare to approach prematurely such a divine personality and turn it into nothingness. Into nothingness, Botkin! Nothing remains of it except bones and flesh, by now infested with worms. He lives, you will say, in the memory of his friends, in the hearts he inflamed and where he kept alive the sparks of divine love. Yes, but how long will these friends last? For how long will these hearts beat? Alas! Neither faith, not knowledge, neither life nor talent, not even genius is immortal! Death alone is immortal."[67]

Belinsky paused to compare Derzhavin's ode to Meshchersky—with its famous line "Where is he?—he is *there*! Where is '*there*'?—We don't know!"—with feelings about death of his own time and gravely acknowledged the nonexistence—even hypothetically—of any *there* and *thereto*, "never resorted to even for fun." Belinsky further paused to consider whether this *aporia* could promise a productive, tragic resolution in literature and decided it could not.

The authentically tragic required a collision of passion and duty for the instantiation of the moral law, for which a hero was selected to be sacrificed. But how can a literary hero clash with the god of annihilation? Rejecting this possibility as a vulgar sentimental comedy, Belinsky would eventually launch a campaign against pseudo sufferers and their woeful genres.[68] In a single breath he condemned Zhukovsky's late-career collected volumes of religious prose (1844), as well as another religious dinosaur, Fonvizin, who, although deceased for over fifty years, was still enjoying the second edition of his complete works in a single decade (1830 and 1838). Belinsky also called into question the merits of translating Pascal's *Pensées*. Sizing up Pascal's legacy, Belinsky felt that only the *Provincial Letters*, which combated retrograde Jesuits, mattered historically.[69] Belinsky actively endorsed new translations of Shakespeare plays that paraded the cerebral fraying of mighty natures alongside the ideas of the age, but not old epics.[70] Belinsky concurred with Hegel, considering lyrical digressions, complaints, and solicitations a sign of self-pity and religious hypocrisy. Belinsky's other target was Apollon Grigoriev. In a literary review of his poems (1845), Belinsky called him a sufferer by trade. By contrast, Lermontov brought Byronic sufferers back in vogue. What, then, makes Lermontov's sufferers more deserving than Grigoriev's? Lermontov's sufferers are ready to "destroy themselves and the world [rather] than adjust to what their proud thought rejects. But Mr. Grigoriev makes an effort to turn his poetry into an apotheosis of suffering. . . . This is hardly a proud mind. . . . There is in his hymns a sign of a rather cheap reconciliation, aided by mysticism."[71]

Belinsky's irritation with Grigoriev was also due to his invention of types to represent national and religious life. Although his major characters of the 1840s all supported ideas of Christian socialism, they were divided along the lines of scientific versus artistic perceptions of existence. In such works as "Leaves from the Manuscript of an Itinerant Sophist"(1843–1844), "Man of the Future" (1845), and "My Acquaintance with Vitalin" (1845), the truth was partially Hegelian, reminiscent of Stankevich, and partially Hamletian—and, according to Grigoriev, characteristic of his generation of nugatory dreamers (Botkin; Kavelin [to whom he lost his bride], Stankevich, Chicherin, Buslaev), all of whom studied Hegelian philosophy at Moscow University in the 1830s. Grigoriev invented a representative literary prototype for a Russian-Hegelian-Hamlet named Vitalin (from *vitalis*, an immaterial living energy), who, together with a talent for life, lacks this energy, wallowing for days in a disabling comedy of ratiocination, "in a state of permanent negation and tedious, tortuous apathy. . . . He believed neither in sin nor in goodness; he did not believe to such an extent that it seemed ridiculous to him to convince anyone in his disbelief, but he maintained a fiery belief in one thing: that in every nature there rests an anticipation of its vocation, its right to happiness, and the right to life."[72] Vitalin's pragmatic character had much in common with Kavelin, and Grigoriev made sure to point out the difference in their outlook: "The whole evening we—Kavelin and I—sat down together—and all in vain as before. We shall never understand each other: social suffering will forever remain a phrase for me, as will searches for God for him. His calm and reasonable view of love is more than unclear to me."[73] However, Grigoriev, that self-appointed "itinerant sophist," who raves about "mystic immortality," is afraid to die a slow death and is ready to die "now," provided a walking illustration of Hegelian unhappy consciousness and unfulfilled dreams, of beauty defiled, and a prototype of the superfluous hero of the 1840s.[74]

In addition to Lermontov, Belinsky found several more exceptions to the rule against despondent complaining.[75] He singled out the following three works by younger writers: Turgenev's "Conversation" (*Razgovor*, 1844), Herzen's novel *Who Is to Blame?* (*Kto vinovat?*, 1845–1847), and Goncharov's *Same Old Story* (*Obyknovennaia istoriia*, 1847). All three featured the disease of the age, best described by Turgenev as "the apathy of feeling and will," coupled with "[all-] devouring mental activity."[76] Herzen's novel, a "criminal case, masterfully related," on the fates of destroyed lives, especially its protagonist, Vladimir Beltov, this "clever uselessness," perennially and without reason "out of sorts," solicited attention to endangered human dignity.[77] Goncharov's novel, strictly speaking, is a story of the subjugation of an unsteady young idealist, Aleksandr Aduev—praying to some indefinite "divine spirit"—to his tightfisted and pragmatic bourgeois-minded uncle, Petr Ivanovich. At the end of the story Aleksandr succumbs to "aduevshchina": married into money, he sports a pleased face, well-rounded belly, and an order of merit.[78] Whereas in Beltov Belinsky observed traces of Pushkin's Onegin and Lermontov's Pechorin, in Goncharov's hero he found a follower of Lensky, whose susceptibility, mistaken for a yearning for "loftier reality," is more common among Russian Romantics, and is really only a charming replacement of life's comforts with dreams about these comforts, without any ability to procure them.[79] Both Belinsky and Herzen were more interested in assigning blame for Beltov's departure from the battlefield of history.[80] In Beltov, one finds the tragic hero courting death without Aduev's mockery of human character. Beltov's withdrawn attitude transpires in a decisive conversation he has with the materialistic Doctor Krupov, who says: "—Your pulse is no good. You live twice as fast, sparing neither the wheel nor the grease—you can't go far this way.—Why, do I need to live long?—Strange question! I don't know why; it is better to live than to die; every animal has love of life. . . . Byron said quite rightly that a decent man can't live longer than thirty-five. And why do you need a long life? This must be very boring."[81]

Unlike Belinsky, in his last years Gogol found the line of Lermontov, Turgenev, Belinsky, and Herzen to be questionable. Gogol met Lermontov in Moscow during those surreal Slavophile dinners hosted by Konstantin Aksakov, where Chaadaev, Lermontov, on leave from the Caucasus, and Gogol, a visitor from Rome, could peacefully convene in one room. He was less taken aback by Lermontov's strange condescension than by his disdain for himself and his talent. Gogol responded to Lermontov's path in poetry several years later in the chapter entitled "What Is, Then, the Essence of Russian Poesy and What Is Its Peculiarity?" in his *Selected Passages from Correspondence with Friends*. According to Gogol, Lermontov's epoch championed a spirit of "charm-lessness" or "un-enchantment" (*bezocharovanie*) in Russian literature, replacing Byron's simpler and more humane disenchantment (*razocharovanie*), which, in turn, had replaced the "charm-fullness" (enchantment) of Schiller.[82] Lermontov's path would be perilous for Russian literature. What is "charm-lessness"? It is "meetings without joy, separations without sadness" and an absolute lack of love. Deluded by the demon of ridicule, Lermontov fell by the wayside. There was Pushkin's prophet, with the bearing of a high priest, not a speck of dirt on his chasuble and no sign of untidiness. And there was Lermontov's useless and spiteful prophet, mocking the crowd, which mocked him back. In 1847, Gogol sees the future of incorruptible art in the new policy of the golden mean: "No, it is not Pushkin or anybody else who should become our pattern: other times have come."[83]

Significantly, Gogol separated chapters on the coming of the Christian Believer from his discussions of art, subjugating the role of the poet to the role of a modest Christian and subordinating art to the festival of Divine Resurrection that concludes the book. The word that knows no mitigating circumstances if it strives toward the divine deed is described in "On the Nature of the Word" (1844), the celebrated fourth chapter of *Selected Passages*.[84] Never mind that there are no signs of repentance or conversion to true spirituality in Gogol's own heroes, who never approach the degree of spiritual readiness for figuratively entering into their catechumen status. The death of the Prosecutor at the conclusion of the first volume of *Dead Souls* written after Lermontov's death rivals the best parts of Gogol's theater of the grotesque, both the fact of death and the suddenly discovered lost soul being no more than rhetorical figures: "Go figure the man . . . he does not believe in God, yet believes that if the bridge of his nose itches, he'll die. . . . And can one possibly resist the devil? This is none of the author's business," comments the narrator in the tenth chapter, which precipitates the death of the Prosecutor.[85] Most significantly, Gogol denied his Chichikov the right to experience repentance after driving him cruelly and masterfully to the point of near-confession not only at the end of this first volume but also in the surviving drafts of the second.

How different is this new policy of Gogol's from Lermontov's treatment of a theme of a prophet who would do his best by staying devotedly incommunicado? "How everyone despises him!" is the last line of Lermontov's poem on the topic.[86] Lermontov's masterpiece, *A Hero of Our Time* (1838–1840), was patterned on Karamzin's mocking parody of sincere confessions, *The Knight of Our Time* (*Rytsar' nashego vremeni*, 1803) and Musset's *Confession of the Child of the Century* (*Confession d'un enfant du siècle*, 1836). In the preface to his novel Lermontov advises the reader to exercise irony and seek no ethical advice: "The malady has been pointed to; how it is supposed to be treated—God alone knows!"[87] In the preface to Pechorin's journal, Lermontov adds that even the story of a trivial soul resulting in social inaction can be "more interesting and instructive than the story of a whole nation."[88]

His first literary and philosophical sketches in 1845–1847, written while still a student of oriental languages (and then of law) at Kazan University, as well as everything he wrote up to and including *War and Peace*, put Tolstoy in closer contact with the ideas emanating from the atheistic literary responses to the Belinsky-Stankevich-Lermontov and Belinsky-Gogol-Lermontov affairs. The latter unfolded in February 1847, when Gogol's book began appearing in bookstores across the country, in society rags and journal reviews, and was unquestionably the event of the year. Already in 1846, Zhukovsky published several cameo pieces called "On Melancholy in Life and Poesy" that were written in response to Viazemsky's skeptical rejection of the religious meaning of death in Gogol: "If we are, it is not, if it is, we are not." Why do Christians believe that death is the beginning of all? Living in Germany with his Lutheran young wife, Zhukovsky predicted that acceptance of death is the prerogative of the new Christian melancholy initiated with Gogol and that it would replace the Romantic grimacing of Lermontov's tradition. Paraphrasing Lermontov, Zhukovsky put it strongly that the turning experienced by one man, finding faith individually and living in God's permanent presence, is more instructive than the life of one nation or of all historic humanity.[89]

Zhukovsky continued his conversation with Gogol, while reading *Selected Passages*, in the three letters of 1847–1848. In the letter entitled "On Prayer" (*O molitve*) he discussed problems relating to the reception of Gogol's book. He claimed that these problems were the result of Gogol's lack of confidence in his handling of the word and lack of true collaboration with God in the act of writing. In his personal letter to Gogol, Zhukovsky asked his friend not to indulge in indiscriminate play with words that begets the "disheveled word" (*neopriatnoe slovo*) of the Romantics.[90] Reacting with shock to Gogol's death in his letter to Pletnev, Zhukovsky expressed no surprise about Gogol's behavior prior to his death. He ought to have become a monk, but the unfortunate duality in his spirit—of a mystic piety competing with intellectual sarcasm and irony—ultimately brought his writing career to a halt.[91] Following these dialogues with Zhukovsky, in April 1847, Viazemsky rushed to Gogol's defense and published an essay claiming that Gogol's conversion meant a turning point (*krutoi povorot*) for art in general. He witnessed in Gogol the rebirth of religious art generated by "terrible consciousness" (*strashnoe soznanie*). As a phenomenon of precisely such terrible consciousness, Gogol's *Selected Passages* was a book of both literary and psychological importance that the uneducated Russian religious mentality did not know how to view as a single entity. Gogol's example should have become a seminal episode in the religious education of his countrymen. Instead, their pathos for religious explorations only lasted several weeks and Gogol's book was soon forgotten as a clumsy joke.[92]

In May 1847, a month later, Tolstoy decided to withdraw from the university and become a young landowner-intellectual. To suggest that Gogol's book—especially its points about the religious importance of the land-owning class—might have influenced Tolstoy's decision would be an exaggeration. Tolstoy had more pressing and immediate reasons. However, in view of Tolstoy's disillusion with the profession of civil law, and the prominence of what was becoming a scandal over Gogol, it is equally wrong to disregard the fact that amid this scandal, in his first conscious retreat, Tolstoy had joined the ranks of these socially ineffectual young men, who wore quilted gowns and dabbled in writing, and who had yet to decide how to accommodate their despondency in the form of a literary statement. Tolstoy was settling in on his estate when in his mailed response to Belinsky Gogol admitted that their generation was not prepared for the fulfillment of spiritual toils, predicting that "the coming age will be *the age of reasonable consciousness*" (*vek razumnogo soznaniia*), possessed of the required *spiritual calm* (*spokoistviia dushevnogo*), that first principle of goodness without which one is unable to perform in any vocation. The term was altogether new in the Russian vocabulary. It replaced the failing "personal understanding" (*lichnoe razumenie*) of the eighteenth century, the motto of Radishchev and Fonvizin.[93] Forty years later, in his work *On Life* (1887), the crown of his conversion, Tolstoy will define the principles of reasonable consciousness and act as its mouthpiece.

NOTES

1. John Locke, "Of Faith and Reason and Their Distinct Provinces," in *Essay Concerning Human Understanding* (Amherst: Prometheus Books, 1995), 583–89.

2. For a succinct definition of self-love, see Richard Velkley, *Being After Rousseau: Philosophy and Culture in Question* (Chicago: University of Chicago Press, 2002), 18.

3. See Lomonosov's morning and evening meditations on the Lord's magnificence. See *Russkaia poeziia XVIII veka*, ed. G. P. Makogonenko (Moscow: Khudozhestvennaia literatura, 1972), 142–43, 144–45.

4. Quoted in *Russkie prosvetiteli (ot Radishcheva do dekabristov): Sobranie proizvedenii v dvukh tomakh* (Moscow: Izdatel'stvo sotsial'no-ekonomicheskoi literatury Mysl',' 1966), 1:168.

5. Quoted from the ode "God" (1780–84) in Gavrila Derzhavin, *Sochineniia* (Moscow: Pravda, 1985), 54.

6. My translations refer to the following poems by Derzhavin: "On the Death of Meshchesrky," "On the Death of Katerina Yakovlevna That Occurred July 15, 1794," and "The River of Time," in *Sochineniia*, 29–31, 149–50, and 255, respectively.

7. See Sergey Bulgakov, "My Life in Orthodoxy and as a Priest" (*"Moia zhizn' v pravoslavii i sviashchenstve"*) in *Pravoslavie*, 456–57 and 462.

8. See V. V. Zenkovskii, *Osnovy khristianskoi filosofii* (Moscow: Kanon, 1996), 261.

9. The Orthodox Church permits repentance as rarely as once a year, usually during Lent.

10. See George Florovsky, *Puti russkogo bogosloviia* (Paris: YMCA-Press, 1983), 27.

11. Quoted in *The Art of Prayer: An Orthodox Anthology*, comp. Igumen Chariton of Valamo; trans. E. Kadloubovsky and Elizabeth Palmer (London: Faber and Faber, 1997), 93.

12. See Lars Thunberg, *Man and the Cosmos: The Vision of St. Maximus the Confessor* (Crestwood, N.Y.: St. Vladimir's Seminary Press, 1985).

13. See George A. Maloney, *Russian Hesychasm: The Spirituality of Nil Sorskij* (The Hague: Mouton, 1973), 73–77.

14. Vasilii Drozdov, *Sochinenie Filareta, mitropolita Moskovskogo i Kolomenskogo. Slova i rechi 1803–1867*. 5 vols. (Moscow: Tipografiia Mamontova, 1873–1885), 5:419–423.

15. *Russkoe pravoslavie: vekhi istorii*, 295.

16. See Pushkin's letter to Petr Chaadaev (October 19, 1836). Pushkin, *Polnoe sobranie sochinenii*, 19 vols. (Moscow: Vozrozhdenie, 1994–1997). (Reprint of *Polnoe sobranie sochinenii*, 17 vols. [Moscow: Izdatel'stvo Akademii Nauk, 1937–59]), 16:171–73.

17. See Gregory L. Freeze, *From Supplication to Revolution: A Documentary Social History of Imperial Russia* (New York: Oxford University Press, 1988), 39.

18. See Florovsky, *Puti russkogo bogosloviia*, 109–13. See also I. M. Kontsevich, *Optina pustyn' i ee vremia* (New York: Jordanville, 1970).

19. For a history of religious views in Alexander I's time, see Yury E. Kondakov, *Gosudarstvo i pravoslavnaia tserkov' v Rossii: evoliutsiia otnoshenii v pervoi polovine XIX veka* (St. Petersburg: Izdatel'stvo Rossiiskaia natsiolanl'snaia biblioteka, 2003). See also: Elena Vishlenkova, *Zabotias' o dushakh poddannykh: religioznaia politika v Rossii pervoi chetverti XIX veka* (Saratov: Izdatel'stvo Saratovskogo universiteta, 2002); Valerie Kivelson and Robert H. Green, *Orthodox Russia: Belief and Practice Under the Tsars* (University Park, Pa.: Penn State University Press, 2003).

20. See Vladimir Pustarnikov, "Russko-nemetskie filosofskie sviazi v sotsio-kul'turnom kontekste," in his *Filosofskaia mysl' v Drevnei Rusi* (Moscow: Krug, 2005), 169–82; esp. 176–81.

21. See *Russkie prosvetiteli (ot Radishcheva do dekabristov)*, 1: 83–165; esp. 160–62.

22. Pushkin, *Polnoe sobranie sochinenii*, 2: 488.

23. See *I dum vysokoe stremlen'e*, ed. N. A. Arzumanova (Moscow: Sovetskaia Rossiia, 1980), 61–65; 69–71.

24. Panova's fate was equally disastrous. At the insistence of her husband, Vasilii Panov, an agrarian and a spy for the secret service, she was confined to a psychiatric clinic, where she shared a room with a deranged tramp. Panova's letters have not survived except for several guarded responses in 1836. Chaadaev most likely destroyed most of them so as not to compromise her.

25. Quoted in Petr Iakovlevich Chaadaev, *Polnoe sobranie sochinenii i izbrannye pis'ma*, 2 vols., ed. Z. A. Kamenskii (Moscow: Nauka, 1991), 1:90.

26. Michael Bakunin, *God and the State* (New York: Dover, 1970), 1.

27. "Letter to N. N. Gogol <15 July New style 1847 Salzbrünn> ("Pis'mo k N. N. Gogoliu <15 iiulia n. s. 1847 Zaltsbriunn), in V. G. Belinsky, *Sobranie sochinenii v deviati tomakh*, 9 vols. (Moscow: Khudozhestvennaia literatura, 1982), 8: 284. All future references are to this edition (volume: page) unless otherwise noted.

28. On the Slavophile movement and its ideology of Romantic nationalism, see the following: Edward C. Thaden, *Conservative Nationalism in Nineteenth-Century Russia* (Seattle: University of Washington Press, 1964), 32–56; Nicholas Riasanovsky, *Russia and the West in the Teaching of the Slavophiles* (Cambridge, Mass.: Harvard University Press, 1952), 90–153; Andrzej Walicki, *A History of Russian Thought*, trans. Hilda Andrews-Rusiecka (Stanford, Calif.: Stanford University Press, 1979), 92–114; idem, *The Slavophile Controversy: History of a Conservative Utopia in Nineteenth-Century Russian Thought*, trans. Hilda Andrews-Rusiecka (Notre Dame, Ind.: Notre Dame University Press, 1989), 121–283; and James Billington, *An Icon and the Axe: An Interpretive History of Russian Culture* (New York: Vintage, 1970), 307–28; 329–51.

29. See Khomiakov's "Letter to the Editor of *L'Union Chrétienne*, on the Occasion of a Discourse by Father [Ivan] Gagarin, Jesuit," in *On Spiritual Unity: A Slavophile Reader. Aleksei Khomiakov. Ivan Kireevsky. With Essays by Yury Samarin, Nikolai Berdiaev, and Pavel Florensky*, trans. and eds., Boris Jakim and Robert Bird (Hudson, N.Y.: Lindisfarne Books, 1998), 135–39.

30. The conflict had been brewing since the Straits Convention in 1841. Russian worries intensified after a Suez concession was signed over to the French in 1854. The Crimean War became inevitable.

31. Tolstoy purchased Pecherin's work as soon as it was finally published in Mikhail Gershenzon's rendition of his life, which contained lengthy quotations from Pecherin's diary and poetry. See an off-print of M. O. Gershenzon's, *V. S. Pecherin*, 1904. *Nauchnoe slovo* 1904, book 4, pp. 65–88; book 10, pp. 63–111. See the description of this item in *Biblioteka L. N. Tolstogo v Iasnoi Poliane*, vol. 1, part 1, p. 182.

32. In reality, Pecherin refused to deliver Papal addresses to Russian pilgrims that could hurt Russia. Pecherin's life is now available in an informative biography by Natalia M. Pervukhina-Kamyshnikova. *V. S. Pecherin. Emigrant na vse vremena.* (Moscow: Iazyki slavianskoi kul'tury, 2006).

33. See Apollon Grigoriev, *Vospominaniia*, ed. B. F. Fedorov (Moscow: Nauka, 1988), 13–14.

34. Alexander Herzen, *Sobranie sochinenii v vos'mi tomakh.* 8 vols. (Moscow: Pravda, 1975), 1:129.

35. See Riasanovsky, *Russia and the West in the Teaching of the Slavophiles*, 157–86; esp. 157.

36. See the following: S. V. Kuznetsov, "Pravoslavnyi prikhod v Rossii v 19 v," in *Pravoslavnaia vera i traditsii blagochestiia u russkikh v XVIII-XX vekakh. Etnograicheskie issledivaniia i materially*, eds., O. V. Kirichenko and Kh. V. Poplavskaya (Moscow: Nauka, 2002), 156–78, esp. 176; G. N. Melekhova, "Dukhovenstvo i ego rol' v zhizni naseleniia Kargopol'ia, 19—pervaia tret' 20-go vekov," *Pravoslavnaia vera i traditsii blagochestiia u russkikh*, 179–208, esp. 184; and Vera Shevzov, *Russian Orthodoxy on the Eve of Revolution* (New York: Oxford University Press, 2004).

37. Vera Shevzov, "Letting People into Church: Reflection on Orthodoxy and Community in Late Imperial Russia," in Kivelson and Green, *Orthodox Russia*, 66–67. See also the chapter on "temple Dialectics" in Shevzov's study *Russian Orthodoxy on the Eve of Revolution*, 54–94; esp. 68.

38. See Daniel H. Kaiser, "Quotidian Orthodoxy: Domestic Life in Early Modern Russia," in *Orthodox Russia*, 179–92; and L. A. Tul'tseva, "Tainaia milostynia," in *Pravoslavnaia vera i traditsii blagochestiia u russkikh*, 90–100.

39. See Shevzov, *Russian Orthodoxy on the Eve of Revolution*, 171–213.

40. See O. V. Kirichenko, "Pochitaniia sviatykh russkim dvorianstvom (18 stoletiia)," in *Pravoslavnaia vera i traditsii blagochestiia u russkikh*, 6–65, esp. 23, 26, 53.

41. Pushkin, *Polnoe sobranie sochinenii*, 3: 104; 14: 57. Further references to Pushkin's poems will be referenced parenthetically in text, volume: page.

42. Denis Ivanovich Fonvizin, *Sobranie sochinenii*, 2 vols. (Moscow and Leningrad: Gosudarstvennoe izdatel'stvo khudozhestvennoi literatury, 1959), 2:81–105.

43. Nikolai Karamzin, "Moia ispoved': Pis'mo k redaktoru zhurnala," in Karamzin, *Sochineniia v dvukh tomakh*, 2 vols. (Leningrad: Khudozhestvennaia literatura, 1984), 1: 534–35.

44. Ibid., 543.

45. In "Discourse on the Old and New Style in the Russian Language" (*Rassuzhdenie o starom i novom sloge rossiiskogo iazyka*); 1802, publ. 1803) Shishkov insisted on the Church Slavonic roots of the Russian language and its folk poetry and, moreover, that the ecclesial high style of the Church Slavonic Bible should be used for elevated topics as occurred in Lomonosov's odes, while colloquial Russian was proper for popular epics and lifelike scenes.

46. Dmitry Nikolaevich Bludov, "Videnie v kakoi-to ograde izdannoe obshchestvom uchenykh liudei" (1815), in *"Arzamas" sbornik v dvukh knigakh*, eds., Vadim

E. Vatsuro and Aleksandr L. Ospovat (Moscow: Khudozhestvennaia literatura, 1994), 1: 261–65.

47. At their meetings the Arzamasians often referred to Shakhovskoy's comedy in the postdiluvian sense.

48. The madrigal confirmed that the poet Vasily had died to the world, but that he was alive to poetry and friends. See Vasily Pushkin, *Stikhi, proza, pis'ma* (Moscow: Sovetskii pisatel,' 1989), esp. 106–7.

49. A. S. Pushkin, *Polnoe sobranie sochinenii*, 1:439.

50. See Anton Del'vig's "Death, the consolation of my soul!" (*"Smert,' dushi us-pokoen'e!"*; 1830–31) written months before his fatal illness. Anton Del'vig, *Stikhotvoreniia* (Moscow: Sovetskaia Rossiia, 1983), 228.

51. See Dmitry Vladimirovich Venevitinov, *Stikhotvoreniia. Proza*, ed. E. A. Maimin and M. A. Chernyshev (Moscow: Nauka, 1980), 59–60.

52. Venevitinov, *Stikhotvoreniia. Proza*, 122–27.

53. The quotation is taken from volume 1, chapter 3, of Charles Maturin's *Melmoth the Wanderer* (London: Oxford University Press, 1989), 45. Johann Wolfgang von Goethe, *Faust I & II*, ed. and trans. Stuart Atkins (Princeton: Princeton University Press, 1984), pt. I, 33. The quote is taken from the scene in Faust's study.

54. François-Auguste-René de Chateaubriand, *Atala/René*, trans. with an introduction by Irving Putter (Berkeley: University of California Press, 1980), 96 and 82, resp.

55. See Percy B. Shelley, *The Major Works, Including Poetry, Prose, and Drama*, eds. Zachary Leader and Michael O'Neill (Oxford: Oxford University Press, 2003), 256.

56. Pushkin to Viazemsky, September 13 and 15, 1825. Pushkin, 13: 225–27.

57. Pushkin, "Ottsy pustynniki i zheny neporochny" (3: 421).

58. Quoted in *Pushkin on Literature*, rev. ed., ed. and trans. Tatiana Wolff (Evanston, Ill.: Northwestern University Press, 1998), 449. Pushkin's review, "On the Duties of Men, by Silvio Pellico," appeared anonymously in his journal *The Contemporary*.

59. See Pushkin's letter to Chaadaev of October 19, 1836, defending the sanctity of Old Russian Orthodoxy uncorrupted by modern politics and also defending the creative spirit of Protestantism against Papacy. Pushkin, 16:171–73.

60. Vil'gelm Karlovich Kiukhelbecker, *Izbrannye proizvedeniia v dvukh tomakh*. 2 vols. (Moscow and Leningrad: Sovetskii pisatel,' 1967), 1:286–89, 316–17, resp.

61. The following works fall within this tendency: Nestor Kukolnik's "Ruka vsevyshnego otechestvo spasla" (1834), Nikolai Polevoy's "Istoriia russkogo naroda" (vol. 6 was published in 1833); Fedor Bulgarin's "Dmitry Samozvanets" (1830) and "Mazepa" (1834); Mikhail Pogodin's "Marfa Posadnitsa"; Alexei Khomiakov's poems "Ermak" and "Dmitry Samozvanets" (1833), Mikhail Zagoskin's "Yuri Miloslavskii ili russkie v 1612 godu" (1832) and "Roslavlev ili ruskie v 1812 godu."

62. Nikolai Ogarev, "Jesus" (Iisus, date unknown), in Nikolai Platonovich Ogarev, *Stikhotvoreniia i poemy*, 2 vols., eds. S. A. Reyser and N. P. Surina (Moscow: Sovetskii pisatel,' 1937), 1:16.

63. Nikolai Vladimirovich Stankevich, *Izbrannoe*, ed. G. G. Elizavetina (Moscow: Sovetskaia Rossiia, 1982), 68–82. See also Stankevich's letter to Diakova

of November 3, 1837, in Stankevich, *Izbrannoe*, 180. The meaning of Stankevich's correspondence with friends for Tolstoy is discussed in the next chapters of the present study.

64. See "My Metaphysics" (*Moya metafizika*) in Nikolai Vladimirovich Stankevich, *Perepiska ego i biografiia*, ed. P. V. Annenkov (Moscow: Tipografiia Katkova, 1857), 17–22, esp. 18.

65. See especially the letters to Botkin dated December 16, 1839; February 10, 1840; February 3–10, 1840; and February 22, 1840. Belinsky, 9: 291–97, 301–10, 325–26.

66. Ogarev's poem, "Confession" (Ispoved,' 1840–41), addressed to Herzen, in *Stikhotvoreniia i poemy*, 1: 115–16.

67. Belinsky, letter dated August 12, 1840, in *Sobranie sochinenii*, 9: 389–91. See other letters on the same topic to A. P. Efremov (August 1840) and Botkin (September 5, 1840), 9: 394–96, 398–402, resp.

68. Belinsky, 9: 390.

69. See Belinsky, 5: 314–21, 456–58.

70. In the 1840s, Belinsky closely monitored and reviewed Russian translations of Shakespeare.

71. Belinsky, "Stikhotvoreniia Apollona Grigorieva," in *Sobranie sochinenii*, 8:494.

72. Apollon Grigoriev, "Arseny Vitalin" [a chapter in the novella Man of the Future (Chelovek budushchego)], in *Vospominaniia* (Moscow: Nauka, 1988), 110–13.

73. Grigoriev, "Leaves from the Manuscript of an itinerant Sophist" (*Listki is rukopisi skitaiushchegosia sofista*), *Vospominaniia*, 90.

74. Ibid., 91.

75. See Belinsky, "Hero of our Time: Composed by Mikhail Lermontov, 3rd edition (1843)" ("*Geroi n. vr. Soch. M. Lermontova* 3-e izd, [1843]") and "Stikhotvoreniia M. Lermontova. Chast' 4, 1844," in Belinsky 7: 435–36 and 493–96, resp.

76. Belinsky, "Razgovor: Stikhotvorenie Iv. Turgeneva," 7: 528.

77. Belinsky, "Russkaia literatura v 1845 godu" and "Vgliad na russkuiu literaturu 1847 goda," 8: 23–24 and 8: 378–81, resp.

78. Ivan Aleksandrovich Goncharov, *Sobranie sochinenii v shesti tomakh*. 6 vols. (Moscow: Gosudarstvennoe izdatel'stvo khudozhestvennoi. literatury, 1959–60), 1: 255; 259–60.

79. Belinsky, "Vzgliad na russkuiu literaturu 1847 goda," 8: 382–89.

80. The reference is to Beltov's famous self-comparison to "a hero of our folk tales" who has not found a soul alive on this field of active life, "and one person is no warrior. . . . So I left the battlefield." Herzen, *Sobranie sochinenii*, 1: 280.

81. Herzen, *Sobranie sochinenii*, 1: 268–70.

82. Gogol, "XXXI. V chem. Zhe, nakonets, sushchestvo russkoi poezii i v chem. ee osobesnnost.'" *Vybrannye mesta iz perepiski s druz'iami* in N. V. Gogol, *Sobranie sochinenii v vos'mi tomakh* (Collected Works in 8 vols.) (Moscow: Terra, 2001), 7: 238–39. For an excellent translation of Gogol's essay and the whole of *Selected Passages*, see Nikolai Gogol: *Selected Passages from Correspondence with Friends*, trans. Jesse Zeldin (Nashville, Tenn.: Vanderbilt University Press, 1969), 240–42.

83. Gogol, *Sobranie sochinenii*, 7: 238–39.

84. In the only earlier example, Gogol let the amateur painter Vakula daub the devil in the church of his *Dikanka Cycle* to make the devil too repellent to be dangerous, yet he also let the philosopher Khoma Brut be seduced in church by fearing evil's charms.

85. Gogol, *Sobranie sochinenii*, 5: 211, 214.

86. In Lermontov's poem, "Prorok" (The Prophet, 1841), his delusion that he is God's mouthpiece and, most of all, his gloominess, pale looks, poverty, and unhappiness, attract ubiquitous contempt. M. Iu. Lermontov, *Izbrannye proizvedeniia v dvukh tomakh*, ed. Irakly Andronikov (Moscow: Khudozhestvennaia literatura, 1973), 1: 332.

87. Lermontov, 2: 384. See Lermontov's preface to *A Hero of Our Time*, 2: 290–91. See also Karamzin, *Rytsar' nashego vremeni*, in *Sochineniia*, 1: 584–607 and his related half-page "Autobiography," ibid.

88. Mikhail Lermontov, *A Hero of Our Time*, trans. Paul Foote (London: Penguin, 1966), 75.

89. The essays were published in *Russkaia Beseda* (1845). See V. A. Zhukovsky, *Sochineniia v stikhakh i proze*, 10th ed., ed. P. A. Efremov (St. Petersburg: Izdanie knigoprodavtsa I. Glazunova, 1901), 922–26, 926–30, and 930–38.

90. Zhukovsky, "Pis'ma k N. V. Gogoliu" (*I. O smerti; II. O Molitve; III. Slova poeta—dela poeta*) in *Sochineniia v stikhakh i proze*, 945–53.

91. Letter to Pletnev dated March 5 (17), 1852, in V. A. Zhukovsky, *Izbrannoe*, ed. I. M. Semenko (Moscow: Pravda, 1986), 528–29.

92. See Viazemsky, "Iazykov i Gogol'" and "Iz avtobiografii." P. A. Viazemsky, *Sochineniia v dvukh tomakh*. 2 vols. (Moscow: Khudozhestvennaia literatura, 1982) 2: 162–84, 239–81, esp. 170–73.

93. See Gogol's response to Belinsky, August 10, 1847. Gogol, *Sobranie sochinenii*, 8: 229–30.

Chapter Two

Portrait of the Artist as a Young Nonbeliever

A MERRYMAKING "PART OF THE GREAT ALL"

In 1847, Tolstoy departed Kazan University with Rousseau medallion in place of the baptismal cross. The opening passages of *Émile* taught him to adhere to the precept that a free life is something more than the freedom to breathe and eat: "To live is not [merely] to breathe; it is to act, to make use of our organs, our senses, our faculties, of all parts of ourselves which give us the sentiment of our existence."[1] In the 1840s, Tolstoy's goal is earthly happiness (*zemnoe schasti'e*).[2] While pursuing a legal path as a student of law at Kazan University, Tolstoy hoped that through law he would grasp the "system of his being" and discover nothing less than the goal of human life and the organizing principle of the life of humanity (46: 272).

The syllabus for a course on the encyclopedia of law that Tolstoy was given by a young professor named Anton G. Stanislavsky was broadly philosophical and historical, devoted to "the defining qualities of human nature, from which human law," in its relation to jurisprudence, ethics, and religion, can be deduced.[3] The second part of the course dealt with the French philosophy of law of Montesquieu and Rousseau, as well as the German idealist teachings of Kant, Fichte, Schelling, and Hegel. All of these high-minded approaches, whose humanistic focus would loosen starting with Hegel, differed profoundly from the pragmatic, case-oriented norms of real legal practice.[4] In his legal studies, Tolstoy placed the greatest value on moral will, on "thought that influences itself," and on "force of the soul," this chief instrument of human striving for absolute perfection that "produces goodness" (46: 8, 30, 269). Out of a conviction that necessity ought to be respected and arbitrary will made obedient, from his earliest days Tolstoy designed the types of pragmatic rules to coincide with what he understood to be the demands of necessity (46: 242).[5] After all, Montesquieu taught him that laws, in general, are the *necessary relations* derived from the nature of things. According to Rousseau's Savoyard Vicar, divine laws fulfill themselves without our participation, and we should pursue activities that quench mental and spiritual instability. One of the articles in Diderot's and d'Alembert's *Encyclopédie* defined religious melancholy as a kind of theological sadness, born of the false idea that religion proscribes people all innocent pleasures and ordains instead tears and contrition of the heart. Said melancholy is a disease of the body and the soul, a tragic error in need of extirpation when it cannot be controlled.[6]

German idealism taught Tolstoy different lessons about "the necessary practical employment of . . . reason—of *God, freedom, and immortality.*" If Tolstoy appealed to this famous phrase from Kant's *Critique of Pure Reason* like those obscure seekers of spiritual advice some eighty years earlier, he would find the answer that it is necessary to deny *knowledge*, in order to make room for *faith* (Glaube).[7] This "room for faith" is a hope and a binding moral duty and is very different from Locke's separate compartments.[8] The earliest traces of Tolstoy's preoccupation with Kant's most important questions date back to his younger days. A dog-eared French translation of *The Critique of Pure Reason* (1835) from his library must have accompanied Tolstoy everywhere in his youth. Patterns of Tolstoy's underlining in agreement or disagreement with Kant bear out his searching in every corner of Kant's text to find that precious little room of salvation. Underlining, worn paper, and bent corners furnish telltale evidence that Tolstoy spent a lot of time pondering over Kant's undying and unanswerable three questions—from the section on the "Ideal of the Highest Good" (A 805/B833), which he read in French— concerning how we can "fulfill our vocation in this present world . . . to adapt ourselves to the system of all ends": (1) Que puis-je savoir? (What can I know?); (2) Que dois-je faire? (What ought I to do?); (3) Que m'est-il permis d'espérer? (What may I hope for?).[9]

Kant advised effecting a change of heart through "a revolution in the cast of mind," and insisted on human task in the cause of salvation, on "what we are to do to become worthy of God's assistance."[10] Kant defined radical goodness as a "putting on of a new man," the supreme maxim of moral will under whose guidance something like a covenant for converts in the ethical commonwealth, "a union of men under merely moral laws, . . . an ethico-civil (in contrast to a juridico-civil) society" would gradually transform itself "to the exclusive sovereignty of pure religious faith."[11] Kant's followers refined with their emotionalism their mentor's much drier injunctions against the selfishness of a self-satisfied moral subject. Friedrich Schleiermacher admitted to two opposing yet complementary impulses in the human soul, of individualism, and of "the dread fear to stand alone over against the Whole, the longing to surrender" that worked toward establishing a fellowship of free believers.[12] However, there was a conflict of interest in the teachings of the German philosophy about personal religious change.

Fichte produced a scheme replicating the conversion that man repeatedly underwent in his lifetime. Through its activity the "I" separates itself from the objective world of the "non-I," ultimately arriving at the "pure I."[13] In this way a sphere was created in which the human will fights against the inertia and abstractness of Kant's scheme of salvation wherein "man persists and continues to *act*."[14] Fichte also fundamentally changed the romantic perception of brotherhood involved in the process of communal perfection, in which the church was transformed into a historical community of seekers united by the spirit of the All. Friedrich Schelling's philosophy of identity, expressed in his *System of Transcendental Idealism* (1800), posited a belief in the pure, absolute Ego as the endless object of faith. Schelling insisted that God must be present to man as an object if we are not to do away with the believing subject as such. The subject and object of faith exist in an eternal equilibrium in the act of self-consciousness: "The eternal, timeless act of self-consciousness which we call *self* is that which gives all things existence."[15] Schelling moved on to postulate the primordial ground, or abyss, in God, which does not annihilate human freedom but rather necessitates it, following from the intelligible nature of man: "Inner necessity is itself freedom; man's being is essentially *his own deed*. Necessity and freedom interpenetrate as one being which appears as the one or the other only as regarded from various aspects; in itself it is freedom, but formally regarded, necessity."[16]

Tolstoy's hesitation between the French and the German routes of spiritual self-improvement finds its eloquent reflection in his first bestseller, his strongly autobiographical trilogy *Childhood, Boyhood, Youth* (1852–1857). In an earlier version of chapter 19 of *Boyhood*, Nikolen'ka Irteniev, the narrator-protagonist, does not know what to make of Pascal's "order of the heart" (*l'ordre du Coeur*) and his calculating wager. (If God exists, the one believing in Him is saved; if God does not exist, one has nothing to lose since everything is already lost in that case).[17] Nikolen'ka gives Pascal's wager a try after his fiascos with the epicurean style for which he was too young and lacked funds. He also mocks Pascal's theory of a hidden God, demanding proof of God's existence in the form of making Nikolen'ka a better person.

I was also an atheist. With the arrogance strikingly characteristic of that age, which, once allowing religious doubt, [made me] ask myself why God would not prove it to me that all what I have been taught is true. And I prayed to Him sincerely, so that He would prove to me His existence either in myself by some miracle or somehow else. Brushing aside all beliefs inculcated in me since childhood I was drawing up my own, new beliefs. It was hard for me to part with a comforting idea about the future, immortal life; while considering that nothing vanishes but only changes shape in reality, I have arrived at the pantheist idea, the one about an infinite and forever changing ladder of beings. I was so gripped by this idea that I became seriously preoccupied by the question what I had been before I became a man—a horse, a dog or a cow. This thought, in its turn, was replaced by another idea, Pascal's idea more precisely, that even if all that religion teaches us were untrue, we would lose nothing by following it; by not following it, on the other hand, we risk receiving eternal damnation instead of eternal bliss (2: 287).

Taking Anselm's famous term *deus absconditus* (the hidden God), or "Dieu caché" in French, Pascal arrived at the next formulation: What *can* be seen proves neither the absence nor the presence of divinity, but the presence of a hidden God (fragment 449). With the same awe present in his most famous fragment (201), which speaks of the fright of the eternal silence of infinite spaces above him, Pascal posited the possibility of a dialogue with God from His hiddenness and His silence.[18] God's silence invites the seeker into a special dialogic relationship. In order to receive grace, one learns to listen to God's inaudible voice. Eternal bliss in a tangible form of gingerbreads supplies stronger proofs for Nikolen'ka. What Pascal could not supply Tolstoy and the skeptical European and Russian youths of his generation, was more than compensated by Schelling. In the final version of Tolstoy's *Boyhood*, Nikolen'ka Irteniev struggles to choose a better faith system relying on "inalienable attributes of the mind" that he senses in himself before he can "know of the existence of the philosophical theories." The Schelling whom Nikolen'ka invokes in this connection reinforces his philosophizing on the fatally attractive subjectivity of all inwardness. Schelling wins over Pascal and his wager and takes his place in the final version: "I fancied that besides myself nobody and nothing existed in the universe, that objects were not real at all but images which appeared when I directed my attention to them, and that so soon as I stopped thinking of them these images immediately vanished. In short, I came to the same conclusion as Schelling that objects do not exist but only my relation to them exists. There were moments when I became so deranged by this *idée fixe* that I would glance sharply in some opposite direction, hoping to catch unawares *the néant* where I was not. What a pitiful trivial spring of moral activity is the mind of man! My feeble intellect could not penetrate the impenetrable."[19]

Tolstoy's philosophical youth was also spent under the spell of Hegel, who put the aspiring and suffering divided soul in the untenable position. At the time of Tolstoy's youth, Kazan University was one of the intellectual hotbeds of practical Hegelianism in Russia. He switched to the faculty of law, where Dmitry Meier, one of the brightest Hegelians and most promising intellectuals in the field, had just accepted appointment.[20] The Hegelian ethos of service to what is real and necessary, vetoing the right to unhappy consciousness, must have only compounded for Tolstoy the meaning of Rousseau's precepts for active happiness without immediately contradicting them, as it soon would.

Hegel posited that for a separate being or organism there can be no legitimate end outside universal existences; thus, individual teleology was a contradiction in terms.[21] When law students read Hegel's *Rechtsphilosophie*, they discovered that positive ends for individuality outside of social collectives were a "hypocrisy."[22] The young Tolstoy's endlessly guilty dealings with his personal idleness and ineffectualness, which, in his opinion, separated him from active life within the universal whole, were the result of his exposure to the rhetoric of social utility.[23] Disputing La Bruyère's maxims, the Hegelian-minded Tolstoy jokingly disagrees in 1845–1847 with La Bruyère that at the time of leaving this world one should feel useless.[24] Tolstoy argues that anyone is assured of usefulness if he consciously tries to contribute to the common good. Of course, at the time of his death man should feel how insufficient— even trifling—the good done by him is, compared to the sum total, the *summum bonum* of good (*obshchei summoi blaga*) (1: 218). A genius (Tolstoy surely has himself in mind) will greatly outperform the median requirement for usefulness (1: 219). As regards the utility of law, in Tolstoy's view its political underpinnings in the modern period consisted of demonstrating "how state politics and the needs of justice may be combined in the positive law [*Strafgesetz Kunde*] of a given state" (1: 237).

Tolstoy's almost demonstrative negligence could not fool Meier, who discerned a gleam of dormant genius in the young man. Meier assigned to Tolstoy the writing of a comparative study of Catherine the Great's legal *Instructions* to her nation and Montesquieu's *Esprit des Lois*.[25] Working on his assignment, Tolstoy arrived at the conclusion contradicting the spirit of Hegelian Right. He discovered that society (*obshchestvo*) is not All (*tseloe*), or the source of all (*istochnik vsego*), but rather is the same sordid part (*chast'*) as is a flawed individual, and thus to serve justice best one must first work on self-improvement and elaborate one's *own laws* in order to merge with the All. Tolstoy thought it outrageous for Catherine, a Christian monarch and a woman, to demand capital punishment for minor public offense.[26] He started working on the assignment in the infamous quarters of an infirmary, where he had to serve time due to his debauched behavior. While taking notes on despotism and *jura reservata*, and checking every now and then to see whether his nose started sinking due to syphilis yet, Tolstoy evaluated the options left to the self in a society, coerced by the normative restrictions of "universal good." He contemplated the benefits of forced solitude for the study of iniquities in one's own character.[27] Because of his discovery, Tolstoy decided to withdraw from legal service without taking the degree and retire into his personhood. Quite inadvertently, Hegelianism pushed Tolstoy—the Rousseauian "part of the great all" that wanted to act and was straddled by conventions, eating and breathing in vain—out of society.[28]

"Man is born for solitude," Tolstoy wrote in his diary when he was already a landed manager of his estate, specifying that it needs to be *moral* seclusion and not the mere fact of isolation. There are feelings that ought not to be shared. The urge to share (or verbalize feelings) is the urge to "reveal one's strivings" (June 12, 1851; 47: 63). Just as it would for Nikolen'ka Irteniev— the hero of *Youth* (*Iunost'*, 1857), the third and last tale of Tolstoy's debut trilogy, who commences the journal of his life's mistakes at the end of the final part—"an enormous and dazzling field of moral perfection was opening for him" (2: 343).

However, both before and after making this decision, Tolstoy was spending his time in Kazan, and then Saint Petersburg and Moscow, most pleasantly: serious work was followed by "comme-il-faut" (*komil'fotnye*) distractions, and the motto "wild oats should be sowed" ("il faut que jeunesse se passe") was the only religion he strictly followed. The old Tolstoy reminisced: "I felt no protest against anything. . . . I am very grateful to fate that my first youth I spent . . . without touching upon punishing questions and living a life that may well have been leisurely and luxurious, but far from wicked."[29] Raised by devout Orthodox aunts, Yushkova and Ergolskaya, a Protestant German tutor whose favorite book was the Bible, and a French tutor who was at least a token Catholic, in a household friendly to holy beggars, itinerant miracle makers, and various and sundry pilgrims, Tolstoy was not completely barred from the rather contradictory practices of godly life, and he even earned a respectable good grade on his entrance exam for the Lord's Law (*Zakon Bozhii*). Nevertheless, he must have taken them for fashions of yesteryear inapplicable to the generation of the 1840s.[30]

Many pages of *Childhood*, and drafts of the first part of its incompletely realized forerunner, *Four Epochs of Development* (1851–1852), describe faith and innocence in the year 1833 as forever gone: "Where are those brave prayers and that sensation of closeness to God?"[31] *Childhood* reveals Tolstoy's envy of the itinerant Holy Fool Grisha, who has the ability to pray incoherently albeit sincerely and unselfconsciously (chapter 12, "Grisha"). Nikolen'ka Irteniev and his siblings watch him pray, in shirt and chains, from a dark hideout: "Though incoherent, his words were touching. He prayed for all his benefactors . . . , he prayed for himself, asking God to forgive his grievous sins, and he kept repeating: 'Oh, God, forgive my enemies!' Then he prayed 'Forgive me, O Lord, teach me how to live . . . teach me how to live, O Lord. . . .' O truly Christian Grisha! Your faith was so strong that you felt the nearness of God. . . . And what lofty praise you brought to glorify His majesty when, finding no words, you fell weeping to the floor!"[32]

Such keen sensitivity could not be part of Rousseau's influence. As he presents him in his *Confessions*, Rousseau's man of nature and truth always had near-fickle and opportunistic reasons for changing faith, but he enjoyed doing so—and often. His abjuring of the Protestant faith on the prompting of one M. de Pontverre, the dull curé without firm opinions, and his senseless and uninspiring stay at the hospice for catechumens in Turin invite the reader's ironic misgivings. Nothing compares with the "dying will" and deathbed reversal of Mme Vercellis, his dear friend, who proudly relieves herself of a bout of flatulence as she departs into the better world without a tint of melancholy. Her last defiant words, as she congratulates herself on her physical liberties in order to partake of spiritual ones, leave an indelible impression on Rousseau. Following Rousseau, the eighteenth and nineteenth centuries practically entitled one to change religions as part of life's adventure.

Even at the height of his youthful atheism, Tolstoy never played this loosely with baptismal issues. In fact there is no record of Tolstoy's baptism other than his own description, which appears in the very first line of *A Confession*, where it is stated that it took place under the most normal circumstances: "I was baptized and brought up in the Orthodox Christian faith" (23: 4). There is no reason to doubt Tolstoy's word. One of the earliest surviving fragments (1840) written by the twelve-year-old Léon is his ultra-Orthodox note on patriotism ("Amour de la patrie" 1: 215–16). Although written in French, the note's perfervid spirit of official religiosity could easily have earned its author the laurels also worn by minor Slavophiles and nationalistic writers of the 1830s and 1840s who portrayed Russia's past, present, and future in monarchist-Orthodox hues.

Tolstoy's father, Count Nikolai Il'ich, was interested in philosophy, science, and the arts, albeit not overly religious. Tolstoy remembered that his godfather, Semyon Ivanovich Iazykov, his father's close friend and neighbor, used to visit and stay with them often, mainly to hunt with the other adults and to hear the children recite Pushkin—especially little Leo—or watch them draw.[33] Tolstoy's extremely religious mother, Maria, née Princess Volkonsky, whom he lost at age two and about whom he retained no distinct memory, chose a patron saint for each of her four sons and her daughter, also named Maria. She ordered an icon of the four male saints (Nicholas the Mirleckean, Sergiy of Radonezh, Demetrios of Solun, and Leo the Great) each of whom was portrayed giving a sign of blessing, while Mary Magdalene, in the center, was shown kneeling to the Archangel and displaying the Mandylion (the face of the Lord on the handkerchief). Leo was named after Pope Leo I (Leo the Great), a Christian saint who wrote what is popularly remembered as the "Tome of Leo," which was accepted at the Council of Chalcedon in the fifth century A.D. establishing the doctrine of the divinity of Christ ("truly God and truly man"), the foundations of the Nicene Creed of Christendom.[34] Little did Maria Tolstoy realize that her youngest son would also write his "Tome of Leo," reinterpreting Christ's divinity according to himself and would opt to follow in the footsteps of another Leo, Leo III the Isaurian, the iconoclastic Byzantine emperor of the eighth century, who protested the creation and worship of holy images.[35]

In the first chapter of *A Confession*, Tolstoy described his precipitous falling away from faith (*otpadenie ot very*) once he attained the age of adolescence, especially after entering the University of Kazan (23: 5–5). Once again, biographical evidence supports this admission suggesting that Tolstoy was more of a selfish son of the century than a Rousseauvian, a sentimental deist. Comparing his reckless behavior with the unusually devout life of his older brother Mitin'ka, the old Tolstoy reminisced that he and his other two brothers ridiculed Mitin'ka's religious moods (34: 381). Mitin'ka stunned his family by spending long hours talking with a sickly, ugly, foul-smelling, and generally despised hanger-on relative, Liubov' Sergeevna. He often went to pray with convicts at a neighboring prison chapel, attending night vigils by their side, running their errands, and fulfilling their commissions. The prison priest referred Mitin'ka to Gogol's *Selected Passages*, the book Tolstoy remembered seeing on Mitin'ka's table next to the Bible, whose precepts of humbling and useful social service in public office or on his estate, he vainly attempted to realize after graduating. The frustration this caused Mitin'ka was so devastating that, without reneging on his faith, he nonetheless plunged into violent debauchery, which ended with his premature death due to consumption.[36] Nonetheless, Tolstoy also retired to honest landowning. Then in 1852, while in the army, the twenty-four-year-old Tolstoy wrote a confident note about prayer, coldly adumbrating the reasons why it is wrong to pray for people of his generation, and the false gains those who do pray vainly hope to procure (1: 247–48).[37]

The note breaks off abruptly. Tolstoy was writing the note after long hours of carousing, intending to use it for one of the chapters of *Boyhood*, then thought better of it, burned half of it, and preserved the remainder as a "memorial" (*pamiatnik*), certainly intending to preserve the piece in the form of his anti-Pascalian memorial of doubt. Given the circumstances surrounding the writing, the logical "seams" of the note, which are quite visible, retain the argument surprisingly well. The young Tolstoy is toying with his own expectations, trying on the three categories of "old men" and "new Men," and the category in between all at once. He is an implacable and destructive intellectual who tears down his only foundation and support, and who would return to faith in old age (category one). He is a weak young man, shamed by his godless peers, who suppresses his timid will to believe (category three). He is a practical connoisseur of intellectual and social trends who creates a religion of convenience (category two). Because the second category buttresses the analysis and supports the scheme of reasonable faith found in novels accessible to everyone, the Tolstoy of 1852 seems to be willing to lean toward this category.

In tandem with Tolstoy's sketch on writing, "Why People Write" (*Dlia chego pishut liudi*; 1: 246), his note "On Prayer" represents his polemic with Zhukovsky's letters to Gogol relating to *Selected Passages*, namely, "On Prayer" and "The Poet's Words, the Poet's Deeds."[38] Tolstoy's explanations regarding the reasons why people write feign the same cynicism regarding why people pray: some do so in order to earn money, others to attain fame, and the rest for money and fame. Yet a few say that they do so to teach people virtue. In the last category Gogol's reasonable consciousness seems to be implied. It is reasonable, says Tolstoy (emphasizing this word), to read only those books that teach virtue and offer their authors fame and money. What are these books? They are dogmatic, based on the foundations of reason, and speculative—because sound reason would not admit any others. Instead of inducing people to pursue reasonable actions by developing their reason, poets and novelists, as well as historians and natural scientists, incite people's passions and induce them to pursue unreasonable actions. That Tolstoy is joking becomes apparent only when, in his implied refutation of Zhukovsky's dogmatic attack on Gogol's "disheveled word" (*neopriatnoe slovo*), he completes his send-up with a Gogolian conclusion, imitating Gogol's *Diary of a Madman*: "Certainly, everything has its utility. It has been proven that the existence of a flea benefits man, whom it, moreover, bites, but the utility thereof is objective and is best called the necessary influence, and there is a subjective benefit, too. It is to the latter that I have been referring" (1: 246).

The visionary power and foresight into the very marrow of religious experience of both casually written notes is astonishing. It is not hard to believe that the young author must have been describing his various leaps and alternations between the few religious choices available, as well as his fears at not finding faith at all. One of the inspirations for these notes was Gogol's *Selected Passages*. In the summer of 1851 Tolstoy fell upon "Gogol's last book . . . which resonated like a song in my soul" (46: 71), and that made him think about the boundary separating life and art.

MAN AND FAITH AS SUCH

Yet even at this faithless stage, Tolstoy prayed to God and thanked Him unreservedly for His many services and saving graces. God was thanked most often for preventing Tolstoy's gambling disasters, and for waiting patiently until Tolstoy listed his debts: "I lost another 75 rubles. God spare me for the time being. [. . .] My sole hope is in Him!" (January 28, 1855; 47: 35). A real miracle was related to Auntie Ergolskaya (January 6, 1852, from Tiflis), a proof of God's existence and personal beneficence: Tolstoy lost hopelessly upon arrival in the army and prayed ardently through the night to God to help him find a way out. In the morning a note from brother Nikolai arrived, with a voucher reflecting his winning back of Leo's debt. Tolstoy was overjoyed: "Isn't it marvelous that the following day my wish was granted?" (59: 148). On May 31, 1852, God was thanked twice—for helping Tolstoy finish *Childhood* and for granting him diffidence, which was saving him from debauchery (46: 119). When Tolstoy felt reluctant to write, God's help was again solicited: "Dear Lord, thank you. Don't abandon me" (December 6, 1852; 46: 151). These prayers strongly remind of Alfred de Musset's bitterly ironic condemnation of the children of his faithless age in *Confession d'un enfant du siècle* (1836). The children either spit on the communion of Christ, or take a few minutes to give vent to their paroxysms of despair and appeal to celestial powers for small personal favors or for bread to benefit all humanity: "Who knows? In the eyes of Him who sees all things, it was perhaps a prayer."[39]

Little can be gained in trying to understand Tolstoy's religious evolution if we remain convinced that nothing of import happened between these evocations of feeble religiosity and the proverbial "crisis of 1880." Tolstoy's youthful attempts to rewrite official prayers of Orthodoxy (The Lord's Prayer and Saint Vladimir's Prayer recited by the troops) in order to adapt them to his spiritual needs (minimal as they might appear) anticipated his future struggle to achieve a sense of faith. Even if he lacked the convictions of Mitin'ka, Tolstoy's inner life remained intense. "Grant me to create what is good and avoid evil; but whether it be good or evil, Thy holy will be done! Grant me the good that is right! Forgive me, Lord! Forgive me, Lord! Forgive me, Lord!" (47: 12). Such prayers did not emerge from the skeptical spirit of Savoyard Vicar's sermons, which Tolstoy had placed, along with Hume's *Dialogues on Religion*, next to the notebook containing drafts of *Childhood* and *Boyhood*.

The surviving philosophical fragments of the 1840s and the early 1850s testify to the seriousness and complexity of Tolstoy's quest for religious truth. He is concerned with such high points of Romantic theosophy as the presence of the eternal in man's immediate experience (1: 217). He is keen on discovering the unifying principle and complete continuity of human existence (1: 227). He also sharply criticizes Rousseau for his moral indifference to goodness and evil (1: 221–23). Aside from serving as a sounding board for his gambling troubles and selfish requests, Tolstoy's youthful God was also synonymous with everything most beautiful, poetic, and inexpressible. In one act of prayer, as Tolstoy writes, he "connected everything, both entreaty and gratitude. . . . I was spirit solely and nothing else" (46: 62–63). In a telltale scene from *Boyhood*, Tolstoy's Nikolen'ka Irteniev struggles to find a better faith system relying on inalienable attributes of the mind that he senses in himself before he can know of the existence of any philosophical theories. The Schelling whom Nikolen'ka invokes in this connection reinforces his philosophizing over the fatally attractive subjectivity of all inwardness, redesigning, like Coleridge, Kant's room for faith most radically, calling in his dreams for the "willing suspension of disbelief for the moment which constitutes poetic faith."[40] Tolstoy's respect for the ineffable was the result of terrifying yet exciting insights into the figural visions of the supernatural, experienced during endless night vigils or induced by and remembered from dreams (46: 150). In such moments, he is not far from Blake's "fury of Spiritual Existence" treating God as an artist and not a moral "mathematical diagram."[41] Tolstoy of the diaries in the late 1840s and the early 1850s, and his heroes of those years celebrate man's return to God via the spiritually-sensitive language that only those whom He "anointed as his favorites" can speak, of Nature and Art.[42] Tolstoy recalls such spiritually intense moments in the scenes of Grisha's prayer and in chapter 15 of *Boyhood*, in which the punished Nikolen'ka falls asleep and has a vision of his late mother, who descends from heaven to caress him. At the words "and we soar higher and higher" he awakes and disdains his return to mundane consciousness. Well before the epilogues to *War and Peace*, Tolstoy reached important conclusions: "Freedom is comparative; man is free in his relation to matter, but he is not free in his relation to God" (46: 240).

Tolstoy never doubted that his striving was also part of God's beneficent design: "Don't leave me, O God! Instruct me, and not for the satisfaction of paltry desires, but for the attainment of the eternal and great, incomprehensible goal of being, of which I am nonetheless conscious" (April 14, 1855; 47: 42). In the surviving fragments of his philosophical exercises of 1847, Tolstoy stumbled upon the reason behind man's unstoppable striving to discover the truth: "I have found within myself the kind of activity of which I was not the cause" (1: 226).[43] In order to pinpoint the immediate nature of this cause, the alias of the divine, he decided to study himself in four continuous states: limited activity, unlimited activity, limited inactivity, and limitless inactivity (1: 228). Impossible for humans to apprehend on initial perusal, the second and fourth states were the closest link to the divine cause in human behavior. While man could not observe his activity in its limitless continuity—which could well transform itself into "limitless inactivity" or immortality—he could well imagine that his striving had as its impetus an infinite, outgoing, and active desire: "Desire has no cause and, moreover, possesses within itself that toward which it strives, namely, independence. And because that desire is dependent neither on the body nor on time, it follows that this desire is independent, infinite, self-defining, self-satisfying, and immortal" (1: 234).[44] Man's activity, meanwhile, is all unsatisfied striving and struggle, or "strife" (1: 236). "Man strives, hence man is active. But where is his activity directed?" Tolstoy's answer was Fichtean: man strives where his "consciousness of I," understanding of oneself, leads him: "*What is consciousness?* It is the understanding of *I* to be existing at different stages of activity or motion" (1: 230).[45]

If, following Fichte, striving is possible because the self posits itself both as infinite and unbounded and as finite and bounded,[46] then two outcomes are possible. If "the drive determines the action, it also determines the object; the latter is adapted to the drive" and a temporary contentment of inclination ensues. But in case the action is not determined by the drive, "the object is contrary thereto, and there results a feeling of *disinclination*, of discontent."[47] The entire German idealist tradition—beginning with Kant, continuing in Fichte's *Vocation of Man* and *Speeches to the German Nation*, and Hegel—defined the direction of man's activity as mediate, aimed toward the highest spiritual goal.

"EMPTY FELLOW" STRIVING AFTER THE GOAL

Before his departure from Kazan, Tolstoy jotted down this very characteristic note in a diary entry for 1847: "What is the final goal of human life? I would be the most unhappy among human beings were I not to find the goal of my life—the goal common to all and useful; useful because the immortal soul, having developed, would be naturally transported into the Supreme Being, commensurate with it. For now, my life in its entirety will be an active and perpetual striving toward this one, single goal. What is my life in the country in the next two years going to be like?" (April 17, 1847; 46: 30–31).

His letters written from Saint Petersburg in 1849, where he had gone with the intention of reenrolling in the law faculty at the best university in the country, are infatuated with the idea of service and the social ranks of a practical man. They are not unlike Gogol's dispatches to his mother and rich uncle, his patron, twenty years earlier; both are in a similarly modest social situation, reporting on progress made thus far toward future conquest of the world.[48] On February 13, 1849, Leo wrote to Serge Tolstoy in tones unmistakably Gogolian, simultaneously mocking and self-important: "I know you will never believe that I could have changed; you'll say: 'This is the umpteenth time, and still no good, the same empty fellow'; but, no, this time I have changed quite differently from before: earlier I'd say: 'Let me change,' but now I see that I have changed and I am saying: 'I have changed'" (59: 29). Tolstoy's searches for change were becoming the stuff of family folklore, and the only way to justify himself was to turn them into a profession—either that of a thinker or a writer.

His daily accounts heap one burst of self-flagellation upon another for slacking either in gymnastics, at the wake-up hour, or in terms of the number of hours dedicated to reading and writing. Although at times he calls himself superfluous and at other times "empty," Tolstoy rejects despair and thoughts of suicide (46: 74). Tolstoy consoles himself, like Lermontov's Pechorin, that life has no worse tricks up her sleeve except for death. Reading Lermontov incessantly throughout 1853 and 1854, he tried on the mask of a disenchanted son of the century, a victim of excessive mental toil.[49] Two resultant quatrains in the erroneous meter of a bland, ballad-style amphibrach, in imitation of Lermontov's war ballads about sun-scorched vales littered with corpses, were completed in Sebastopol on November 20, 1854. They shook off Tolstoy's melancholy with such energy that his self-epitaph resounded with the hale and hearty tones of a drunken cossack's lament:

When, when exactly shall I stop
Spending my age without goal or passion
Feeling this deep wound in my heart
And knowing no means how to heal it.
Who made this wound, Lord alone knows,
But I am tortured from birth
By a bitter pledge of future insignificance,
By gnawing sadness and doubts (47: 30).

Lermontov's representative man, a "malicious irony" of his generation— who goes to Persia in order to die of malaria—did reflect Lermontov's faith, a belief that a thirst for death marked his faithless contemporaries, who were doomed to disappear without a trace. In his programmatic poem "A Thought" (*Duma*; 1838) Lermontov concluded: "Sadly I look on our generation: it will get old in inaction." The leitmotif of the poem is lack of faith: "And our ashes, with the exactitude of a judge and a citizen, / Our descendant will insult with a contemptuous verse, / With a bitter mockery of a deceived son / Over his bankrupt father."[50] In this as well Lermontov was prophetic, but Tolstoy's was a different kind of gloom.

On June 4, 1851, gazing the whole night at the star-bedecked sky, he experiences the "two highest feelings, religion and love," and fantasizes about a divisional female companion Zinaida (46: 78–79). "God? Visions? Nonsense." As he eyes the stars, his imagination wanders across areas not quite so nebulous (46: 81). On the occasion of his twenty-fourth birthday (1852), Tolstoy would still be castigating himself for not having found that perfect single goal: "I am twenty-four years old; and I have not done anything yet.— I feel that it has not been in vain that for eight years now I have been combating doubts and passions. But what is my purpose? The future will show. Today I killed three snipe" (46: 140). Three days earlier, he had killed only one snipe but settled on a more decisive compromise about finding the goal for sure (46: 139–40). It is easy to observe that the young Tolstoy's desire for change is articulated in terms of snipe terminology. However amusing this association with the goal of very highbrow philosophical teleology might appear, sniping, too, is about discovering and hitting a hidden and elusive target.

Several months later Tolstoy was receiving laudatory reviews from liberal-minded and progressive readers of his early suicide tale "Notes of a Billiards Marker" (1853). Before blowing his brains out after an especially unlucky day, its hero, an army officer and pathetic loser in games of chance, pens a resentful litany against the life that wronged him. His suicide note—framed by the comical hysterics of his illiterate orderly, who can't quite make it all out— comprises the text of the story. Although he quickly came to despise this story, the practical Tolstoy received positive reviews gladly and without his customary self-questioning, acknowledging the "joyous pleasure" of such an attitude: "By sparking ambition, they induce activity" (47: 40). Ultimatums to either change "in three days" or die were lackadaisically announced and jovially ignored (March 14, 1854; 47: 4).

The shifting, almost clueless direction of Tolstoy's striving is especially evident once its external trajectory, after leaving Kazan, is traced. In May 1847 Tolstoy was engaged in agricultural improvements on his estate. However, in 1848 he abandoned solitude for the social whirl of Saint Petersburg, where he made friends with Ivan Turgenev. In 1849 Tolstoy decided to take up law studies again. He applied to the faculty of law at Saint Petersburg University, passed all exams, yet ultimately decided to return to Yasnaya Polyana to practice music and open the first school for peasant children. A year later Tolstoy was formally employed as a petty clerk in Tula province. The next year he went to Moscow to gamble, pursue women, and, incidentally, write his first psychological sketch, "A History of Yesterday" (*Istoriia vcherashnego dnia*) (1851; 1: 279–95). Neither the first drafts of 1851, nor assurances to his aunt, nor the near-death experience of a shell exploding virtually at his feet, nor the success of *Childhood* (published in 1852 by Nekrasov) put an end to the infelicities of Tolstoy's profligate behavior. After the Romanian campaign and the siege of Silistria, the gambling and womanizing of the second lieutenant who had been decorated for bravery intensified.

When compared to truth searching of another successful young author, Dostoevsky, Tolstoy's real-time searches look innocuous. The author of "Mr. Prokharchin" and *Poor Folk*, was a member of Mikhail Butashevich-Petrashevsky's political circle (1845–1849). Its leaders, Petrashevsky and Nikolai Speshnev, were known for reviling icons in public, deriding piety in a few of their God-fearing comrades, and making sport of shaking the foundation of faith from under their feet. Driven by their belief that Jesus the man and the first Christians, if resurrected, would join their circle as present-day communists and atheists, they were nurturing the idea of driving religion from the socialist temple. Whereas Tolstoy in 1847–1851 was on the side of Gogol, Dostoevsky participated in circulating Belinsky's denunciation of Gogol. In December 1848 Dostoevsky complained to his doctor of the fatal presence of a Mephistopheles in his life.[51] In a revealing gesture, Dostoevsky lent his copy of the French Bible to Petrashevsky, in which both made notations in the margins. This copy of the Bible served the prosecution as a weighty piece of evidence favoring the death sentence for Petrashevsky, while Dostoevsky, together with Speshnev, were among the second round of convicts to be executed. Those notations must have elaborated on the ideas of violent Christian socialism that Belinsky's letter to Gogol contained against "priests, archpriests, metropolitans and patriarchs, the Eastern and Western ones."[52] The Petrashevsky circle was disbanded in 1849, its members incarcerated for six months in the cells previously occupied by the Decembrists awaiting trial, whose death sentences were commuted at the site of the intended execution. Dostoevsky was sent by convoy to Siberia to undergo conversion in prison and hard labor and return in 1859 a new man.

Choosing politics or a path of martyrdom in his early days to seek faith never crossed Tolstoy's mind. Tolstoy was becoming a new man strictly in his art. Apart from sequels to *Childhood*, his extraordinary military tales appeared in a steady stream: "The Raid," "Wood Felling," and—following Tolstoy's voluntary transfer to the Crimean campaign in September 1854—such masterpieces of the short-story genre from the Sebastopol cycle as "Sebastopol in December" and "Sebastopol in May" (1854–1855), whose hero is "truth." It has practically become axiomatic among scholars that Tolstoy's stories of maturation—especially his military tales—are an example of didactic autobiography and reportage.[53] Indeed, in his passionate desire to reveal the whole truth in both its wide and narrow sense, the narrator never loosens his hold on the reader. He achieves an unbelievable continuity in his descriptions of fighting along the ramparts, an improvised armistice, drinking binges following the battle, amputation of limbs in hospitals ("if your nerves are strong, walk into the room to your left"), or the sight of a child who curiously touches corpses and flees in horror. The same continuity taunted and eluded Tolstoy in his philosophical fragments.

Keeping the reader captive in the "dirty space of war" by constantly addressing him with an imperious "look," or "as you go," or "the way people always do," Tolstoy is conducting him—as if on a leash and with equal ease—inside a character's mind, revealing his dying thoughts, disputing his "made-up and precocious expression of suffering," forgiving him his instinctive egoism or unconscious decency, his curious explorations of the metaphysical, and his withdrawal into the routines of life. The final effect of unrelenting presence is not so much the result of a didactic voice or eye as it is an extension of Tolstoy's preoccupation with capturing the act of striving in its mediate and immediate manifestations, thought, consciousness, and reason, the "I" that is and is not its own author. If we turn back to Tolstoy's philosophical fragments on striving—with their obsession with "thought related to future life"—or to his fragments on music of the late 1840s and early 1850s—with their hidden interest in capturing, through the continuity of sounds and perception, the "uninterrupted flow of being" considered subjectively and objectively—Tolstoy's narrative exercise involving truth as seen through the "soldier's story of how he was killed" (47: 42) in "Sebastopol in May" will not look much different.[54] Both deal with measuring the "capacity . . . of 'I' as it exists at different stages of motion," of self-consciousness explained in the fragments, or "memory of the body": "memory depends completely on the body, and so a deformity of one part of the body destroys this capacity, and so death should destroy it completely" (1: 230).

In the story, two officers are anxiously expecting the enemy's shell to explode. The death of the mortally wounded Praskukhin, who thinks he is only slightly wounded, and the survival of Captain Mikhailov, who, although hit by a stone rather than a shell, imagines himself to have been killed, are both portrayed from a necessarily misguided subjective perspective, reflecting the mind's inability to gauge the extent of physical damage done to the body and the brain. The narrator does not withhold for long his voiceover of truth from without the body, which is twitching in its final agony. Responding to Praskukhin's hope that he is only slightly wounded, he curtly announces that Praskukhin is actually already dead (4: 47–49). Inviting the reader to join him on the tour of the battlefields and hospitals and become a witness, Tolstoy seeks to supplement the subjective perspective, absorbing the facts from an indiscriminate sensory perception of self-awareness and sharing this perception spontaneously from an objective viewpoint. In other words, Tolstoy is looking for ways to represent an unbroken sequence of "truth," life, or God through expressive means. Aside from a few fleeting comments, Tolstoy does not expound on patriotism or the glory of Orthodox military might. His bird's-eye perspective is that of a participant in the slaughter who does not want to forget about the law necessarily connecting everything that exists. In his diary he lauds "the great moral force of the Russian people" (47: 27) and informs his aunt that he wept at the sight of enemy flags waving over the ceded bastions. At the same time, using his direct access to God, on November 2, 1854, Tolstoy entered the following comment in his diary: "A terrible manslaughter. It will oppress the souls of many! Lord, forgive *them!*" (47: 27).

NOTES

1. Jean-Jacques Rousseau, *Émile, or On Education*, trans. Allan Bloom (New York: Basic Books, 1979), 42.

2. See diary entry for April 7, 1847 (46: 31). See also Boris Eikhenbaum, "Iz stat'i 90 tomnoe Sobranie sochinenii L. N. Tolstogo (Kriticheskie zametki)," in B. Eikhenbaum *O proze* (Leningrad: Khudozhestvennaia literatura, 1969), 117.

3. See Boris Eikhenbaum, "Iz studencheskikh let L. N. Tolstogo," in *O proze*, 110.

4. I agree with Harry Walsh's opinion that even before his closer acquaintance with the work of Schopenhauer, Tolstoy "was not innocent of German idealist philosophy, contrary to the general opinion." Harry Walsh, "The Place of Schopenhauer in the Philosophical Education of Leo Tolstoi," in *Schopenhauer: New Essays in Honor of His 200th Birthday*, ed. Eric von der Luft, Studies in German Thought and History, vol. 10 (Lewiston, USA: Edwin Mellen Press, 1988), 301.

5. Inspired in particular by his study in 1847 of Benjamin Franklin's *Autobiography*, Tolstoy wrote and revised endless sets of rules for training and regulating his wanton behavior in accordance with the three divisions of will, namely, physical, mental, and moral.

6. See entry "Mélancholie religieuse" signed "de Jacourt" in *Encyclopédie ou dictionnaire raisonné des sciences, des arts et des métiers*, 2 vols. (Paris: Flammarion, 1986), 2: 228–29.

7. Immanuel Kant, *Critique of Pure Reason*, trans. Norman Kemp Smith (New York: St. Martin's Press, 1929), (fragment B xxx), 29. Among the most eloquent appeals to Kant is the letter, dated August 1791, from a Maria von Herbert, a resident of Carinthia: "My reason abandons me just where I need it most. Answer me, I implore you, or you yourself will not be acting according to your own imperative." See Immanuel Kant, *Philosophical Correspondence, 1759–1799*, ed. Arnulf Zweig (Chicago: University of Chicago Press, Midway, 1967), 174–75.

8. On Tolstoy and Kant's "room for faith," see Inessa Medzhibovskaya, "Tolstoy's Conversion: A Modified View" in *The Over-Examined Life: New Perspectives on Tolstoy*. Edited by Justin Weir and Julie Buckler. Essay accepted by the editors December

31, 2002. Forthcoming and "Tolstoy's Conversion: Reexamination and Definitions." (Paper presented at the conference "Tolstoy: The Over-Examined Life" at Barker Center, Harvard University on April 19–20, 2002.)

9. Kant, *Critique of Pure Reason*, 635, 644. As regards Tolstoy's reading habits, I refer to the following volume from Tolstoy's library at Yasnaya Polyana, which I examined in August 2005: No. 1720, Kant, Immanuel. *Critique de la raison pure*. Traduite de l'allemand par C.-J. Tissot, 2 vols. (Paris: Ladrange, 1835–1836). Tolstoy's notations to Kant's three questions can be found on page 414. See the description of this book in *Biblioteka L. N. Tolstogo v Iasnoi Poliane*, vol. 3, part 1, 554–55.

10. Immanuel Kant, *Religion Within the Limits of Reason Alone*, trans. Theodore M. Greene and Hoyt H. Hudson (New York: Harper Torchbooks, 1960), 109.

11. Kant, *Religion Within the Limits of Reason Alone*, 42–43, 86, 105, 181.

12. Friedrich Schleiermacher, *On Religion: Speeches to Its Cultured Despisers*, trans. John Oman and ed. E. Graham Waring (New York: Ungar, 1955), 4. On Schleiermacher's poetic emotiveness, see Bernard Reardon, *Religion in the Age of Romanticism* (Cambridge: Cambridge University Press, 1985), 30. On Schleiermacher's concept of the "divided self," see Gerald N. Izenberg, *Impossible Individuality: Romanticism, Revolution, and the Origins of Modern Selfhood, 1787–1802* (Princeton: Princeton University Press, 1992), 18–27.

13. Johann Gottlieb Fichte, *Science of Knowledge: With the First and Second Introductions*, trans. and ed. Peter Heath and John Lachs (Cambridge: Cambridge University Press, 1982), 97.

14. Johann Gottlieb Fichte, "Concerning Human Dignity," in Fichte: *Early Philosophical Writings*, trans. and ed. Daniel Breazeale (Ithaca, N.Y.: Cornell University Press, 1988), 84–85.

15. Friedrich Schelling, *System of Transcendental Idealism*, trans. Peter Heath (Charlottesville: University Press of Virginia, 1997), 32.

16. Friedrich Schelling, *Philosophical Inquiries into the Nature of Human Freedom*, trans. James Gutmann (La Salle, Ill.: Open Court, 1992), 63.

17. Unless otherwise noted, all references are to Blaise Pascal, *Oeuvres complètes* (Paris: L'Integrale/Seuil, 1963), which harmonizes Lafuma and Brunschvicg numbering of Pascal's fragments. In identifying fragments by their number, I will be adhering to Louis Lafuma's numbering system. See fragment 418 in Pascal, 550–51.

18. See fragments 68, 198, 199, 228, 242, 394, 427, 781, 793, and 921 in Lafuma's numbering system.

19. Quoted from Leo Tolstoy, *Childhood. Boyhood. Youth*, trans. Rosemary Edmonds (London: Penguin, 1964), 159.

20. See Eikhenbaum, *O proze*, 110. See also: Victor Shklovsky, *Lev Tolstoy*, trans. Olga Shartse (Moscow: Progress Publishers, 1978), 80. On Meier's reputation see Richard S. Wortman, *The Development of Russian Legal Consciousness* (Chicago: University of Chicago Press, 1976), 230.

21. G. W. F. Hegel, *Phenomenology of Spirit*, trans. A. V. Miller, intro. J. N. Findlay (Oxford: Oxford University Press, 1977), C. (AA.) 256: 156.

22. G. W. F. Hegel, *Elements of the Philosophy of Right*, trans. H. B. Nisbet, ed. Allen W. Wood (Cambridge: Cambridge University Press, 1991), 170.

23. Echoes of these Hegelian ideas may be found in Tolstoy's lecture notes on criminal law, published as "Fragment on Criminal Law" (*Otryvok ob ugolovnom prave*) (1: 237–40).

24. "Notes sur le second chapitre des 'Caractères' de La Bruyère" (1: 219–20).

25. Victor Shklovsky cites Meier's opinion of Tolstoy from P. Pekarsky's recollections of Meier published four years after the professor's death. Meier's prediction is astounding, especially since in 1859, when it went into print, Tolstoy was already known and yet far from famous. See Shklovsky, *Lev Tolstoy*, 81.

26. See the diary entry for March 18, 1847 (46: 6–7).

27. See diary entries for March 17–26, 1847 (46: 3–28). Tolstoy records his impressions of Meier and of his own work on the civil code in his diary entry for March 27–29, 1847, and then drafts a page on this in his 1904 memoirs (*Vospominaniia* 1903–6) dictated to biographer Pavel Biriukov (34: 398). Tolstoy's assiduous study of Latin and Roman law is also recorded in the pages of his daily planner for 1848 (46: 249, 251, 255, 256). Eikhenbaum makes several apt remarks about Tolstoy's work on Meier's assignment: Tolstoy strives for the application of the science of law (*justitia*) to private life ("à notre vie privée"). See Eikhenbaum, *O proze*, 106–7. In this same vein Tolstoy compares Montesquieu and Catherine's *Instruction*. According to Tolstoy, she was mistaken in concentrating solely on public law instead of dealing with private law. While reading Biriukov's biography, Tolstoy stressed that in addition to civil law he was also interested in the encyclopedia (theory of law) (34: 109).

28. Tolstoy reminisced that his work on Catherine's *Instruction* and *L'Esprit des lois* by Montesquieu, opened for him "the new vista for independent intellectual labor. With its demands, the university did not facilitate such work, but only prevented it." See Tolstoy's corrections to Biriukov's records of his *Biography* (Record no. 21; 34: 398). In a conversation with Alexander B. Goldenweiser (June 26, 1904) Tolstoy added that Montesquieu led him to Rousseau and he "left the university because he wanted to study" (Shklovsky, 81). Meier was a progressive-minded idealist, a truthfighting fanatic who collaborated with Antonin Kraevsky's *Notes of the Fatherland* (*Otechestvennye zapiski*), admired Belinsky, and was himself admired by Chernyshevsky as "one of our top professors of law" (Eikhenbaum, *O proze*, 101).

29. This notation was made by Tolstoy to contradict Biriukov's misrepresentation of his young life as too serious in the forthcoming biography (34: 397).

30. See Tolstoy's grade chart in his memoir (34: 397). The only grade higher than this was a superlative assessment of his French.

31. See the drafts of *Chetyre epokhi razvitiia*, 1: 103–66, esp. the fictional entry on the calendar for August 12, 1833 (1: 110). Tolstoy never completed the fourth part of his original plan, covering adulthood, publishing what became his trilogy: *Childhood, Boyhood, Youth*.

32. Tolstoy, *Childhood. Boyhood. Youth*, 43, 44. According to Tolstoy's late memoir, which he dictated between 1902 and 1906 to his biographer, Pavel Biriukov, Grisha was only partly invented. The boys used to spy on their dullard gardener, Akim, who spoke with God as if He were a living character, and called Him pet names: "My doctor, my pharmacist." Grisha was a calqued image of all Holy Fools

and humble heroes, "enduring contempt for their good life," whom the little Tolstoy was taught to venerate (34: 395).

33. This detail is disclosed by Tolstoy in the same "Vospominaniia" (34: 357).

34. See Hardon, *The Catholic Catechism*, 138–41.

35. The illustration of the icon is reproduced in L. N. Tolstoy, *Dokumenty, fotografii, rukopisi*, comp. M. Loginova and N. Podsvirova, ed. L. Opulskakya (Moscow: Planeta, 1995), 31.

36. For Tolstoy's reminiscences of Mitin'ka, see chapter 9 of "Vospominaniia" (34: 345–93, esp. 379–85).

37. See Appendix I.

38. Editors date the sketch to the year 1851 (1: 340). For Zhukovsky's "Pis'ma k N. V. Gogoliu" (*I. O smerti; II. O Molitve. III. Slova poeta—dela poeta*) see *Sochineniia v stikhakh i proze*, 945–53.

39. Alfred de Musset, *Confession of a Child of the Century*, trans. Robert Arnot (New York: Current Literature, 1910), 1, 10–11.

40. Samuel Taylor Coleridge, *Biographia Literaria*, 2 vols. ed. James Engel and W. Jackson Bate (Princeton, N.J.: Princeton University Press, 1983), 2:5–6.

41. William Blake *The Complete Poetry and Prose of William Blake*, rev., ed. David V. Erdman (New York: Doubleday, Anchor Books, 1988), 41, 663–64.

42. See Wilhelm Heinrich Wackenroder and Ludwig Tieck, *Herzensergießungen eines kunstliebenden Klosterbruders* (Stuttgart: Reclam, 1994), 61.

43. See untitled fragment (dated no earlier than 1847) (1: 226–28).

44. See untitled fragment no. IX (1: 233–36).

45. See fragment no. VIII, "On the Goals of Philosophy" (*O tseli filosofii*) (1: 229–32).

46. See Fichte's "Foundation of the Knowledge of the Practical," in *The Science of Knowledge*, 225–26.

47. See Fichte's explication of the ideal action in "Foundations of the Entire System of Knowledge," in *The Science of Knowledge*, 286.

48. See especially Gogol's letter to Maria Ivanovna Gogol, February 2, 1830, Gogol, *Sobranie sochinenii*, 8: 27–28.

49. Tolstoy's diary mentions reading Lermontov in December 1852 (46: 154), on July 6, 1854 (47: 7), and a few days later (47: 10). Such reading inspired Tolstoy to write poetry involving a solitary death on the battlefield ("The Dying Gladiator"). The reading of *A Hero of Our Time* encouraged his laziness and vanity. While reading Pechorin's journal, Tolstoy gazed in the mirror, examining his moustache and unhealed venereal fistulas. See diary entry for July 11, 1854 (47: 11).

50. Lermontov, *Sobranie sochinenii*, 1: 248–49.

51. On Speshnev's influence on Dostoevsky, see Liudmila Saraskina, *Nikolai Speshnev: Nesbyvshaiasia sud'ba* (Moscow: Nash dom/L'Age d'Homme, 2000), esp. 163, 167–71, 181.

52. Belinsky, 8: 283–84. The episode is known from the memoir of I. Ar-ev, who used to lodge in the house where Petrashevsky's members were also tenants. Ar-ev relates that during one of Dostoevsky's visits to his home, the latter noticed a French edition of the Gospels, and borrowed the book from Ar-ev for several days. Ar-ev was

arrested and interrogated since the book was covered in the latter's and Dostoevsky's notations. See "Iz vospominanii o Fedore Mikhailoviche Dostoevskom," in *F. M. Dostoevsky v zabytykh i neizvestnykh voispominaniakh sovremennikov*, ed. S. V. Belov (St. Petersburg: Andreev i synov'ia, 1993), 42–44. In his commentary, Belov brushes away the possible sacrilege on Dostoevsky's part (295–96).

53. See Gary Saul Morson, "The Reader as Voyeur: Tolstoi and the Poetics of Didactic Fiction," *Canadian-American Slavic Studies*, 12, no. 4 (winter 1978): 465–80; for Morson's theory of Tolstoy's "absolute language," see his book *Hidden in Plain View*, 9–36. See also Andrew Baruch Wachtel, *The Battle for Childhood: Creation of a Russian Myth* (Stanford, Calif.: Stanford University Press, 1990), 7–57. Wachtel further develops his ideas in "History and Autobiography in Tolstoy," in *The Cambridge Companion to Tolstoy*, ed. Donna Tussing Orwin (Cambridge: Cambridge University Press, 2002), 176–90.

54. See the diary entry for April 14, 1854 (47: 42). See also "Three Fragments on Music" (*Tri otryvka o muzyke*) (1: 241–45).

Chapter Three

Superfluity and the Religion of Writing (1851–1863)

THE DANGEROUS POETRY OF SELF-ACCOUNTING

"A History of Yesterday," Tolstoy's fragmentary and unfinished first literary sketch (1851), encapsulates the great artistic merit of that permanent "looking back" on the endlessly converting self that so irked Mikhail Bakhtin.[1] The story's narrative focus and voice belong to a young idler who rides in a hired carriage and pays social visits on a predetermined day, one to a married woman whom he vaguely fancies, and who goes about other routine errands. The autobiographical narrator realizes that in him, as in others, the body remains oblivious of the will of the soul. When the narrative voice articulates its inner desire, the earnest intention to speak one's mind passes through so many distorting lenses and filters that it is doomed as well. Thus, every human being remains incomplete: from the society flirt to the cabbie, each states what others want to hear, distorting the shaky meanings forming in his brain. Like sounds in music, words disrupt wholeness, and yet they are constitutive of it, connecting as much as they disunite. In a double reality of soul and body, spoken word and hidden meaning, whose artistic aspect Tolstoy finally captured, constituted the discovery of the divided self as a source of poetic accounting rather than a cause for alarm of the future James patient suffering from "a divided soul." Tolstoy found it both a challenge and an invitation to become a writer. In April 1851, he translated passages from Sterne's *Sentimental Journey*, the scene at Calais with the solicitous Monk, in which Sterne's traveler provides one of his most famous ruminations about the ebb and flow of humors in someone who is vainly protecting his virtue from becoming "the sport of contingencies" (1: 251). Instead of frustration, the dependence on the body and the *peripety* of its humors suddenly reveals to Tolstoy a splendid possibility for artistic representation (46: 34). The imperfect self with his mild sinning and lapses into indolence becomes a poetic prize, "entertaining [. . .], poetic, and useful" (46: 185; 47: 6–7).[2]

One solution for stepping over the "the insurmountable barrier" of mental and verbal representation, Tolstoy discovered, was to artificially interrupt the fluidity of the self (46: 102).[3] A little distance from the act of writing, and a brief separation from the moment of self-consciousness, permit the stepping out from one's body to take place, such that rereading the experiences of that body would be delightful because memories are "pleasant only because they are memories" (46: 92). Memory negotiates the gaping void between antagonistic and incommunicable reason and consciousness.[4] It finds its moment of departure, or "serious point" (ser'eznaia tochka) (46: 93), retraces the steps (46: 82), and retains meaningful "moments of self-consciousness" (46: 214) in order to appreciate one's experience and forecast expectations for future actions that render the sea-changing self less chaotic and volatile. In the same chapter that Nikolen'ka Irteniev recalls Schelling in Boyhood, he discovers that "abstract thoughts are born thanks to man's capacity to grasp with his consciousness at a certain moment the states of his soul and to commit them to memory."[5] The conclusion of Youth recommends self-accounting as a tool for "pulling oneself together" so as never to "go back on resolutions" (2: 224–25).[6]

The finished parts of Four Epochs of Development (Childhood, Boyhood, Youth) supply ample evidence that self-accounting and its rituals—daydreaming; arguments with siblings, adults, and friends; journal keeping or repentance in church—may be not just charmingly self-deluding but also poisonous. Moments of self-consciousness may be dangerous because their mnemonic recognition arouses anticipation of a certain expedient type of behavior (46: 214). Daydreaming inflates expectations and leads to the question of unhappy consciousness: "And then what?" Repentant self-accounting smells strongly of Hegelian attacks on hypocrisy: When the confessor is involved, complete sincerity is impossible. As soon as Nikolen'ka repairs his oversight and goes to the second confession in order to be completely sincere, he still needs the third party (the coachman) to brag about his spiritual accomplishment. Imagining that one can be intimate with God is another dangerous delusion.

The struggle between sincerity and self-deception is ongoing in Masha, the title character and narrating voice of a slightly later Family Happiness (1859). Although she sees the fake facade of the religious ritual in which she comes to participate for self-validation, she nevertheless persists in proving to herself that she is not selfish and capable of sacrifice.[7] In its fervent social advocacy for abused art, the story Lucerne (1857) portrays the most complex case of pernicious self-validation. Prince Nekhliudov's defense of the poor street musician, who has been spurned by the rich crowd and its lackeys, is of no use to the musician. Nekhliudov interferes on the musician's behalf solely to denigrate the crowd and earn moral edge over it. The metaphorical collision of bondsman and master psychology in Nekhliudov's condescending act resulted in a rhetorical renunciation by the "unhappy and pitiful creature, man, [. . .] with his need of positive decisions" about all eternal questions addressed to the Supreme Being. Consequently, the story resulted in the ceding of the privileged second-person narrative perspective of the Sebastopol stories. In *Lucerne*, Tolstoy uses his favorite second-person address to denigrate moral arrogance: "Only to you, insignificant worm, who arrogantly tries to penetrate into His laws, His intentions, only you see contradictions. He humbly looks down from His immeasurable height and feels joy at infinite harmony, in which you all move in infinite contradiction. [. . .] And you too, with your tiny and vulgar indignation at the bondsmen, and you too responded to the harmonic requirement of the eternal and the infinite" (5: 24–25).

In 1857, Tolstoy settled on a very Hegelian definition of personal striving, subdividing all humanity into arrogant masters, who achieve the least, and humble bondsmen, "the snub-nosed," who are dialectically driven and useful.[8] In his attempts at recovering wholeness of socially-useful personality, Tolstoy involved himself in the struggle between subjectivity and objectivity that raged in Russian culture and society on the eve and in the first years of the Great Reforms. Under Hegelian influence in his letter to Pavel Annenkov in 1857, and convinced by his progressive editor Nekrasov that personal unhappiness is cured after the discovery of a proper social niche, Tolstoy swore to abandon subjective art for the "positive objective sphere" (60: 182). In this period of his career, Tolstoy's dialogues with the culture of his time on religion and faith do center on themes of death, usefulness and superfluity, pure and objective art, and participation in historical events.

TOLSTOY'S UNHAPPY CONSCIOUSNESS AND THE RUSSIAN SUPERFLUOUS MAN

In the entries of his army diary of 1854 that discuss various categories of human utility, Tolstoy assigns himself to the category of the ratiocinating and the irresolute, whose desire to be better equals a desire to be what they are not: "My wish to correct myself, isn't it also the desire to be what I am not?" (47: 13). In his detached and lengthy self-evaluation of July 7, 1854, entitled "What Am I?" Tolstoy mapped his objective self-appraisal against the matrix of a typical superfluous man, who is "mostly without rule," irate, immodest, hardly literate, "ugly, awkward, smutty and socially inept": "I am smart, but my mind has not been tested by anything fundamental. I am so ambitious and this feeling has been satisfied so little that I often fear that between glory and virtue I would choose the former—if I were to opt for this choice" (47: 8–9).

It remains to be determined how far this character—who failed to imitate the disenchantment of Lermontov's lyrics or Pechorin, his "hero of our time"—might be from the despairing, superfluous man of the 1840s and 1850s. In the wake of Belinsky's death, all active literary factions were expounding on the new wave of social melancholy. In "Letters of the Country Dweller" (1847), Ogarev retraced the origin of "ornate melancholy about something, high-strung tearfulness, searching for lofty feelings (as if they could be sought after when you lack them?)—all this diseased mental muddiness" and dated spiritual anxiety in his generation of reformers back to Voltaire's gall and Byron's cynicism.[9] Pushkin first depicted the type in Russian literature in his narrative poem "Prisoner of the Caucasus" (1821), "this indifference to life and its pleasures, this premature decrepitude of the soul that became the mark of the young in the nineteenth century."[10] Pushkin also added a fatal Russian blemish to the dignity of this sufferer, who "behaved like a sentient man" and did not kill himself following the drowning of a Circassian maiden, his lover and liberator, and why should he have?[11] In 1864, Dostoevsky may have driven the last nail in the coffin of Russian dejection when he allowed his underground man to vituperate against the very possibility that Russia might have real lily-livered transcendent types rather than spite-filled or vulgar practical types like Gogol's do-gooder Kostanzhoglo in *Dead Souls*. "We Russians, generally speaking, have never had any of those stupid, transcendent German Romantics, or, even worse, French Romantics. . . . We here on the Russian soil have no fools," only sublimely "honest scoundrels."[12]

Sentient sufferers minding their own business were not the specialty of Turgenev. His landmark superfluous man suffered the clash between Goethe's beautiful soul and banal reality, yet he was goaded on toward a disastrous action despite the odds of his own trivial dreaming. In Turgenev's tale "Hamlet of the Shchigrov District" (1849), the unnamed main character got to gain knowledge of Hegel, knew Goethe by heart, and was in love with a daughter of his German professor. On top of that, at home he married a consumptive maiden, who "was bald, but a remarkable personality."[13] When pressed to start living for real, Turgenev's Hamlet from a Russian province rebukes reality: "I'd love to take lessons from her, our dear Russian life,—but she is silent, my pet. I have become aware of poisonous exultations of cold despair."[14]

The hero of "Diary of a Superfluous Man" (1850)—unprepossessing, wearing an "incessant, forced smile" and assuming a sense of "agonized vigilance," trying to bewitch others by means of his "idiotic silence"—gave the superfluous type its name and established its questionable gold standard: a curser of life who undertakes the writing of deathbed confessions in the act of final self-immolation. "My little comedy has been played out. Having been destroyed, I cease to be superfluous. Live you, who are living!"[15] A foreign hand by a Mr. Zudoteshin (Mr. Itching to Scoff) inscribes gibberish over the dead man's notes to the effect that the content of his confessions has not been approved. Turgenev's whole career was a rehearsal of the type. The clownish Rudin died uselessly but picturesquely on the defeated Paris barricade of 1848 (*Rudin*, 1855–57); the Bulgarian insurgent Insarov died of consumption before actually going into battle (*On the Eve*, 1960); and the scientist-doctor Bazarov exposed himself to a poisonous infection before he embarked on his project to vanquish nature (*Fathers and Sons*, 1862). Before they succumbed to preposterous deaths, all of these heroes had lost their main battle, namely, the struggle for authenticity and the capacity to love. Of great importance was Turgenev's theory concerning the difference between the superfluous man of introspection and inaction (Hamlet) and the superfluous man of clownish self-oblivion and action (Don Quixote), expressed in a celebrated speech entitled "Hamlet and Don Quixote" (1860). Its main point was to demonstrate that "Don Quixotes explore—Hamlets exploit,"[16] that Hamlets are disliked by the masses, while Don Quixotes are beloved by them, but that the two, achieving their last epiphany before death, are in the end inseparable in the mind of modern man.

The speech fed the already raging storm of deathbed confessions about the progressive species losing its battle with life. The democratic critics Nikolai Dobroliubov and Dmitry Pisarev seized on the opportunity to channel this anger of the dying in the right direction. In his review of the deathbed poems of poet Alexander Polezhaev, a resentful radical imprisoned for a minor crime, who died in a prison hospital, Dobroliubov suggested that instead of his complaining in "this glum and sultry atmosphere," which killed the "mighty powers of the soul," Polezhaev should have learned from Stankevich's knowledge about how to suffer productively.[17] Chaadaev's death in 1856 also reminded the democrats about the connection between utility and dissident foolishness. In his review of Chaadaev's "Apology of a Fool" written in 1860, Chernyshevsky criticized Chaadaev's aristocratic habit of filling journal space with religious fluff instead of discussing the precise role of the masses in advancing progress.[18] *What Is to Be Done?*, his great fictional declaration of the religion of the "new men"—their philosophy of reasonable egoism in support of progress supplanting their futuristic dreams of the socialist paradise—was written in prison and published in 1863.[19]

In the 1850s, the democratic critics used confessions as a medium that bridged the gap between the concrete historical tasks of the sufferer and his individual defects. Herzen started his unique confessional work *My Past and Thoughts* (begun in 1852) as an intellectual chronicle of political struggle. He took for an example of productive suffering the memoir (*Zapiski, 1743–1810*) of Ekaterina Dashkova, the founder and first president of the Russian Academy of Science, an outstanding statesperson, and victim of political intrigue. Herzen wrote a note about her in 1859 that popularized her work and paraphrased the concluding lines of her memoir: "Without fear and anxiety, without tremor and with calm I look the approaching death in the eye," adding as an aside to himself: "What a woman! What a powerful and rich life!"[20] Dashkova's and Stankevich's examples supplied the radicals with the hardest and most personal connection of life and writing caught between the time of resigning from active involvement in politics and the transition into the waning phase of life.

During and following the revolution of 1847–1848, European radicals accused Herzen of panic-mongering and a shameless betrayal of the revolution. He took the occasion to write *S togo berega* (From The Other Shore, 1847–1850), in which he explained his religion of the "cruel court of reason" and demonstrated why it was more foolish to believe in heaven and God and not as foolish to believe in man and his faulty reason. Herzen's dedication to his son Alexander that he added to the second edition of this work in 1855, summarizes his faith: "The religion of the future social reconstruction is the one religion that I bequeath to you. It has no paradise, no retribution except for your own consciousness and conscience."[21] Alexander Herzen maintained his belief that it is clowns and holy madmen, injudiciously confined to institutions by so-called civilized society, who make things happen in history. Herzen first mounted his defense of madmen in his satiric tale of 1847 entitled "Doctor Krupov," and reinterpreted Krupov's historical theses on productive violence for the 1850s in a sequel, *Aphorismata*. The thesis of creative destruction reappeared in another tale entitled "The Damaged One" (*Povrezhdennyi*), which was beloved by Tolstoy and was at first more relevant to him than the former tales.[22] The hero of the tale suffers from an incurable melancholia and is sure that the sinful planet must "explode or break off its orbit to float in the void. . . . It is not right to live this way, this is obvious; something ought to happen in order for things to start improving; it is better for the planet to start over."[23] Years ago an injustice done to his beloved serf girl, a talented musician, was the cause of his mental disturbance. Tolstoy took the plot so much to heart that he rewrote it in his own version of blessed insanity in the story "Albert" (1857–1858), of which "The Damaged One" was an earlier title.[24]

However, Tolstoy's firsthand reaction to superfluous types was equivocal. In 1856, he applauded Ivan Goncharov's *Same Old Story* and also approved of the first public readings of his novel *Oblomov*, but his evaluation of Turgenev's *Diary of a Superfluous Man* was negative: "Have been reading 'The Diary of a Superfluous Man.' Terribly maudlin [*pritorno*], coy [*koketlivo*], clever [*umno*], and playful [*igrivo*]."[25] He was also vaguely negative about *Rudin*, *On the Eve*, and *Fathers and Sons*, calling Turgenev "cold," and "loving nobody."[26] However, he complimented Ogarev's tale "The Spa in the Caucasus" (*Kavkazskie vody*) and what must be the related drafts of "Confession of a Superfluous Man" (*Ispoved' lishnego cheloveka*) (1858–1859).[27] Both works describe the inglorious passing generation of Hegelian-minded idealists. Ogarev's "Confession" communicates the hero's helplessness against the torpid force of his environment. He feels so badly about his complete uselessness that he volunteers his body for research purposes to a doctor, another progressive thinker, who treats him gratis for the benefit of abstract humanity.[28]

Tolstoy again endorsed this type—"the idealist is good" (48: 9)—in Mikhail Saltykov-Shchedrin's tale "Two Fragments from the Book of the Dying" (1857), in which the dying idealist Petr Zhivnovsky strongly declaims against reality: "We are being accused of misunderstanding reality, but why, pray tell, did we need it if we stood above it?"[29] Tolstoy's endorsements of works of inferior artistic quality have only one explanation: The Russian superfluous man was the closest literary link to the literature of religious despair, and his deathbed confession the closest link to spiritual autobiography. Although even at the high point of reconciliation he never achieved a semblance of conversion, the Russian superfluous man paved the way for genres that would discuss psychological changes more minutely than was possible before.

Tolstoy's interest in superfluous men had another impetus. The democratic critics viewed the psychological flow and minutia of his early fictional exercises as examples of Hegelian dialectics, wherein useful deeds must "follow after meditations and conversations."[30] Despite their compliments, Tolstoy's earlier interpretations of superfluity in "Notes of a Billiards Marker" (1853), especially the suicide's curiosity about what they might think about his death at Rtishcheva's Salon the day after, are parodies of the type.[31] In the drafts of "Distant Hunting Grounds" (*Ot'ezzhee pole*), from the rejected eleven versions of the story "Albert," Tolstoy attempts a more serious return to the "terrible question 'what for?'"(*strashnyi vopros 'k chemu'*) (5: 216–17) from the perspective of an adult who fears the approach of life's final act. His ageing character Prince Vasily Ilarionovich looks ahead at what life can offer, and his outlook is grim: "Poor digestion—here comes death—foul smell and nothing more" (5: 217). Tolstoy makes the prince promptly remember several lines from Pushkin's *Eugene Onegin* about the contempt for the "chill of life" (*zhizni kholod*) in anyone "who has lived and thought": "Prince Vasily Ilarionych struggled with this chill and was weaker than it" (5: 216–17).[32] Pushkin's solution for regrets and pain involves a healthy reorientation of desires and wholesome, blissful sorrow: "I've learned the voice of new desires / And come to know a new regret; / The first within me light no fires, / And I lament old sorrows yet."[33] Tolstoy fails to choose between a poetic solution to immortality and plain, rationalized despair.[34]

After reading the just released edition of Stankevich's correspondence on the eve of his thirtieth birthday, Tolstoy wrote his most heartfelt letter to Boris Chicherin, identifying completely with life's dread: "What for? And with some sickly pleasure to know that otherwise than with sadness and horror you can't answer this question: *What for?* The same *What for?* echoes in my own soul to all of what is best in it; and this better part I wouldn't say is dearer to me, but more painful" (60: 272–73).[35] Despite its visible resemblance to Belinsky's response to Stankevich's death in the letter to Botkin in 1840, the letter also articulates Tolstoy's rejection of Belinsky's and Herzen's path of overcoming death via historical vehemence. Although he complains of wearing himself ragged and hanging over the abyss, Tolstoy unexpectedly summons the moral determinacy of Pushkin's *Boris Godunov* as well as that of Stankevich. The knowledge of death provided the attitude of heroic and stoic gloom: "this is something! And I did it" (60: 272).

ISLANDS OF ACTIVITY AND PURE ART

The obviously religious linking of activity and the purpose of being goes back to Tolstoy's last days in the army, namely, his tempered religion of life, reflecting an attempt to become useful. The death of Nicholas I in 1855 briefly filled Tolstoy's imagination with thoughts of religious reform and the need to be "courageous to participate in these important moments in the life of Russia" (47: 37). In several paragraphs recorded in the diary of March 1855, he sketched the Christian religion of the future "purified of faith and mysteriousness, a religion that is practical and does not promise future bliss, but one that creates bliss on earth" (47: 37–38). In the midst of unending debates among the elite officer corps of the defeated army, and witnessing displays of careerism and patriotic zeal everywhere about which we hear echoes in his diary and letters, Tolstoy surveys the ruins of his military career. His new desire to accommodate the "material basis" may be explained less by his exposure to liberal dreams of reform, or even naive Marxism, than by what earlier Russian reformers—the "madmen"—and Gogol's reasonable consciousness had taught him, namely, that spiritual goals should be pursued gradually, without neglecting the practical considerations of life. Using the pretext of poor health, in October 1856 Tolstoy forwarded through his artillery commander a rather dispassionate letter of resignation addressed to Tsar Alexander II, "the-all-dazzling-Majesty, most Sovereign, the Autocrat of Russia, tsar most charitable" (60: 468).

He finally discovered a complicated law of spiritual action, "a situational model where the satisfaction of bodily yearnings does not contradict spiritual striving" (47: 39–40). Instead of neglecting precarious situations, base cravings, and acting on impulse against high odds, Tolstoy decides to utilize all material means available to do the kind of good that *does not* contradict causality or chance. The new Tolstoy was acknowledging that an ordinary day in the life of a man happens when he commits neither good nor evil. In this critical year Tolstoy finally accepted the fact that his literary career was not a mere tool in procuring "the well-being of my neighbor" (*dobro blizhnego*) (47: 61), but rather that writing *was* that well-being.

Tolstoy started constructing his island of activity, his beehive, by dividing his time between writing, running the estate and a school for peasant children, and learning how to fulfill his literary duties and serve progress in an active correspondence with other writers, which preoccupied him during trips to Moscow, Saint Petersburg, and two trips abroad in 1857 and 1860. In a startling departure from the stereotypical image of a superfluous wearer of the quilted gown, Tolstoy also steered clear of the opposite extreme of the steely-willed successful landowner, and devised a new, dogmatic type of genre and character of the land-owning novel.[36] His twenty-chapter-long fragment entitled *The Morning of a Landowner*, which was published by Nekrasov in *Notes of the Fatherland* (1856), was mistaken for a condemnation of slavery by the editorial board and Turgenev.[37] Tolstoy's landowner, the nineteen-year-old Prince Nekhliudov, sees that peasants are cheating and yet realizes just as clearly that their bond is deeper than the religious decorum: it is a form of primordial unity. At the conclusion of the final chapter, Nekhliudov envies the peasant Ilyushka's ability to pray devotedly after hard day's work and fall asleep without regrets, and he dreams about the majestic airborne pilgrimage to Orthodox shrines in Constantinople (4: 17–71). The landowner daydreaming his peasant's dreams is a special kind of religious envy indeed.

In the army, Tolstoy did not combat serfdom accepting that it is evil, "but evil . . . rather charming" (47: 4). However, in an unsent letter to Count Dmitry Bludov, a former Arzamas president, and in its more elaborate fictional variant, "Diary of a Landowner," addressed to the same Bludov, a close social acquaintance, Tolstoy presents the peasant as a conniving, dogmatic despot in the making. He shared with Bludov his anxiety that proletarian wars, revolutions, and Napoleons are not the "finished historical phenomena" and that new wars might lead to the purification of the world and its second birth (5: 256). He called for reform, "the suffering are waiting," to avoid violent retribution (60: 67; 5: 257).

Tolstoy's revolutionary rhetoric about history's second birth and his religiously colored representation of a difficult bond between peasant and landowner may suggest Tolstoy's affinity with the outgoing Slavophile doctrine. After 1856, the doctrine was revised by the "men of the soil" doctrine of the post-Siberian Dostoevsky and his circle, "the soil in which to root yourself" and the faith that "stays between us and civilization."[38] Apollon Grigoriev and Nikolai Strakhov, the other members of the group, engendered an interesting polemic about the faith of the native soil and personal beliefs; both were critical of Dostoevsky's religious ambiguity. Grigoriev implied that Dostoevsky's slogan of universal unification in the name of Christ prevented Dostoevsky from climbing his own Mount Patmos and kept him captive "within his habitual consciousness."[39] Before he died of alcoholism in 1864, Grigoriev had made an important discovery concerning the future of Russian literature, and that he did not espy in Dostoevsky, but based his opinion solely on Tolstoy's published work. In 1862 he published two articles on the creative activity of Tolstoy. According to Grigoriev, Tolstoy dug far enough but not deep enough, stopping shy of faith and ending in his *Cossacks* (1852–1853) on a pantheistic note, seeking everywhere the "ideal of simplicity in spiritual matters." His main contribution was his sundering the connection between the meek, with a potential for faith, and the arrogant, with a potential for revolt. Grigoriev correctly predicted that it would be the ingenuous meek rather than the self-centered arrogant types who would establish the golden treasury of the Russian religious literary canon.[40]

Grigoriev was wrong in thinking that in his negativity Tolstoy was too far removed from the roots of life. In fact, the opposite was true. Tolstoy's fierce criticism of the Slavophiles and Khomiakov was recorded on numerous occasions in his diary entries for 1856 (47: 69–71) and was based on firsthand knowledge of peasant life and its elemental laws. In a letter to Botkin dated January 10, 1857, he called the Slavophile platform not only obsolete but indecent (60: 156–57). Tolstoy's transition to a peculiar religious view aimed against the late Slavophile doctrine coincided with his simultaneous distancing of himself from the supporters of progress within the Belinsky circle, notably Nekrasov and Botkin. In July 1856 in his letter to Nekrasov, Tolstoy disputed the legitimacy of Belinsky's "indignant tone" for literature (60: 74–76). In "Segments of the Swiss Diary, 1857" he took a vow to be content with the harmonious vacillation (*garmonicheskoe kolebanie*) of life (5: 199).

However, harmony proved unattainable. In addition to the episode of utter injustice at one of the Swiss inns that formed the basic plot of *Lucerne*, during the same European tour, Tolstoy accidentally witnessed a public execution in Paris. Voicing his disbelief in the commensurability of the acts of Gospel kissing and severing the head of the accused, a healthy young man, by means of a "skilled and elegant machine," in a letter to Botkin dated April 5, 1857, Tolstoy related his growing doubt about the place of organized religion in the life of modern man. Between its "arrogant, brazen desire to execute justice and God's law" (60: 167–68) and the rhetoric of social utility of Westernizers and men of the soil there was the last best choice, the religion of pure art. In a programmatic letter to Botkin and Turgenev on Russian literature in November 1857, Tolstoy voiced his disgust with its critical bent, calling it an abomination, perhaps even a lawless realm.[41] During Tolstoy's first public appearance on February 4, 1859, he delivered a speech at the Society of Lovers of Russian Literature. The speech acknowledged that every literary epoch contains two strands: accusatory literature and eternal literature. The former is one-sided, topical, and seeks to expose "pictures of evil." Nobody seems to care about the latter type.[42] The rumor soon spread—supported by Tolstoy's hints that he was "both only and not only a man of letters"—that he was abandoning literature for good.[43] As Botkin put it, unless one is a religious fanatic like Savonarola to find poetry in faith, the world of art should be the only religion for Tolstoy if he ever hopes in the Goethean manner to reach beyond (*dahin*) the cruelty of this life.[44] Tolstoy was no Savanarola indeed, stumbling again at his own failure to accept the poetry of Christ in the religious rite: "It is not strange that the Lord commands that a piece of bread is the body of His son. What is stranger, 1,000,000 times over, is that . . . we love what is good, while there are no captions saying anywhere that this is good, and that is evil" (October 21, 1857; 47: 160).

Tolstoy's letter to Chicherin about Stankevich had misled the Nekrasov circle. In April 1858 Turgenev sent Tolstoy a pleading letter, volunteering himself and his superfluous men as a negative example of the feeling that "life is over."[45] Tolstoy's disgust with literature of social utility and morbid pessimism, and his disgust with religion had a much simpler explanation. Despite the fact that it had become a virtual graveyard of enthusiasm and a crypt for the dying idealism, Russian literature had not yet succeeded in describing the art of dying. Neither did the church succeed in making its rites meaningful.

In the poetry of the era, Fedor Tiutchev, the Slavophile and career diplomat who lived outside Russia, was the only surviving metaphysical poet. He was the heir to Nikolai Iazykov who since the 1830s until his death in 1847 nursed himself back to health by way of nationalism, after having lived enough "among those *Schmerzen*" at the European spas. As Iazykov's health and poetic gifts

visibly declined, his animosity and hatred of the West grew, and so did his pa-
tronage of the religiously vacillating Gogol.[46] In his deep and doubting poetry,
like Iazykov, Tiutchev chose to invest all personal belief in Russia. Poets of a
non-ideological bent—Vladimir Benediktov, the future Schopenhauer enthusiast Afanasy Fet, and Polonsky—added little to create the new death canon. An-
ticipating his mortal hour, the vastly popular Benediktov (1807–1873) composed an ironic existential jest entitled "Bewilderment" (*Nedoumenie*) (1859),
the final word on conversional lore denoting the beginning of vertigo: "What if
death cheats on me?"[47] The reigning poetic tsar of the era, Kozma Petrovich
Prutkov, a fictitious philosopher-poet-dramatist and director of an assays office
created by the democratic pranksters, was laid to rest in 1863 "for reasons of
organic decay." Prutkov described his own death and his final gasp "Ah" in his
posthumously discovered masterpiece, "On the Eve of My Dying," which had
divined the exact moment of its author's giving up the ghost.[48]

It was against this lighthearted and nationalistic background that Tolstoy
conceived of his first remarkable enigma on death, the story "The Three
Deaths" (1857–1858). The story is a triptych describing the deaths of two human beings and a tree. Of the three the tree dies most usefully and most beautifully. A society lady who dies of consumption does so grotesquely—with
much fuss, complaints, and inconvenience to her family. A monotonous dea-
con reads the Psalter over the richly decorated corpse, which no one else
mourns: "The dead woman's face looked stern and majestic. She seemed all
attention. But had she understood those solemn words even now?" (5: 63).
The second person to die is a peasant, who expires without a single complaint
and hands over his boots to a young, healthy friend. In exchange, he asks that
a wooden cross be placed on his grave. In the springtime, the young peasant
fulfills his friend's last wish. To provide the cross, a tree must be cut down.
"The sap-filled leaves whispered gladly and peacefully on the treetops, and
the branches of those that were living began to rustle slowly and majestically
over the dead and prostate tree" (5: 64–66). This third death raised more eye-
brows than the dead landlady's incomprehension and lack of attention to the
words of the psalm. Turgenev complained to Tolstoy that the public would not
understand the meaning of the third death no matter how hard they tried.[49] In
his review of "The Three Deaths," Pisarev applauded Tolstoy's seriousness
"in recording man's rude collisions with reality" and his satire of the
landowning class.[50] Tolstoy's advocacy of pure art in 1858 took his audience
by surprise and called forth Khomiakov's derision. Pretending there was
nothing immortal about "The Three Deaths," he responded to Tolstoy's earlier criticism of his outdated views by claiming that he saw pure forms of social indictment in the "consumptive post boy dying on a stove" and that Tolstoy had been—and would continue to be—an "involuntary accuser!"[51] To

add to the confusion, in a letter to his aunt A. A. Tolstaya dated May 1, 1858, his closest spiritual confidante, Tolstoy denied that the story contained a Christian viewpoint (60: 265–66).

A possible explanation for this alleged unification with life through dying may be found in the fact that Tolstoy read Saltykov's fragments about dying while working on "The Three Deaths," which he finished on January 24, 1858.[52] Saltykov's influence can be found in the various angles from which Tolstoy depicted death. But Saltykov's bipartite tale in which the unhappy dying idealist hands over his diary to a sympathetic youth who discloses its dismal content in the second part, was a parody of Hegelian negation of negation without synthesis, whereas the structure of Tolstoy's tale indicated that a synthesis was achieved. Another possible source of influence that could explain the nature of this artistic trinity was Turgenev's story "Death," from his collection entitled *Sportsman's Sketches*. Opening with the death of a peasant who is killed by a falling tree, Turgenev considers more than three cases of how Russian people die, concluding that they all die with a wondrous religious resolve and without complaint. Turgenev's last positive example of a good death is really that of an old female landowner who refuses to pay the priest for his service of giving her the cross: "What are you in a hurry for, dear sir—she said with her tongue already stiffening. There was a ruble coin under the pillow: she was going to pay the priest for her own death prayer. . . . Yes, the Russian people die miraculously!"[53] Had Tolstoy intended to write a social polemic against Turgenev, he would limit his effort by making his own landlady far more repellent, as he did with the first death in his story, and Turgenev would have understood.

Tolstoy's reluctance to disclose the real identity of the tree had to do with poetic reticence, much like in Pushkin's penitent lyrics. *He* was the tree. It was his sap that was supposed to spill onto the ground and fuse with nature had he sacrificed his life to religious poetry. This was the voice of the repenting Job begging the Lord for forgiveness: "For there is hope for a tree, if it is cut down, that it will sprout again, and that its shoots will not cease. . . . But mortals die" (Job 14: 7–12). The poet was also likened to a tree by Tolstoy's beloved Hugo in his audacious defense of Christian poetry in the "Preface to *Cromwell*": "The poet . . . must take counsel of naught but nature, truth, and inspiration, . . . We must draw our inspiration from the primitive sources that must be tapped into. . . . *The true poet is a tree.*"[54]

Tolstoy's autobiographical fragment of the same year, "The Day of Lord Jesus Christ's Resurrection" (*Svetloe Khristivo voskresen'e*, 1858), describes the same reticent shame of a young nonbeliever who spends the whole day drinking with his friend. As he heads home to go to sleep "without participating in this common joy," he encounters jubilant crowds of every class, the majority of whom are commoners, going to church to pray. Something—perhaps a joyous memory from childhood—forces him to join the believers. He feels awkward but stays. Here the fragment breaks off.[55] Diaries in the spring of 1858 relate awkward arguments with Chicherin and Fet about Christ, while drinking at the veteran Slavophile Samarin's: "Christ has not ordered but revealed moral law, which will forever remain the yardstick of what is good or bad" (48: 11–12). Tolstoy's poetic religiosity retained his old contempt for Orthodoxy. In his 1858 and 1859 conversations with his devout Orthodox aunt, he kept referring to her "fake" ritualistic religion of fasting, listening to priests, Gospel reading, and gazing at the motley parish of a Sunday morning (48: 14; 60: 287–89). In his letter to Tolstaya dated at the beginning of May 1859, Tolstoy expressed his newly formulated *profession de foi* in Luther's terms "ich kann nicht anders" (*ia ne mogu inache*): "I can't otherwise," "every soul has its own path" (60: 293–94). His faith in immortality, and the necessity to live for another had some similarities with Christianity, but it was a "conviction. . . . I have found neither God, nor the Redeemer, nor the mysteries, nothing; but I have been searching with every string of my soul, crying, suffering, and wishing for nothing but the truth" (60: 293).

Inch by inch, Tolstoy was fashioning his religion of literature, scaring bigotry out of it with the help of the same scorn that he bestowed on the Orthodox "playacting of the sacristy" (47: 73). It remained for him to purify his muse of its prophetic playacting. In 1857, Tolstoy wrote one of the most impressionistic pieces of his early career, an unfinished fragment entitled "A Dream" (Son):

> I stood high, higher than all people. I was standing alone. Around me, level with my knees, heads flushed with attention, faces pressed together. An ancient toga was on me, which flew open with my passionate and beautiful gestures. The crowd understood me joyously. I was surprised and admired everything I was saying. The sound of my voice was strong, firm and (unusually) beautiful. I was delighted at this sound. The crowd responded to my words with frenzied applause and slavish compliance. I was the Tsar, and my power had no limit. Mad jubilation, which burned in me, gave me power, and I swam in this intoxication by power. My madness and the crowd's madness made me happy. But temporal ecstasy of my situation bothered me (7: 118–19).

His jubilation ends when he spots a modest woman in plain clothes, his Muse, who glides away in contempt:

> I called after her, I beseeched her to look at me yet another time, mocking me. . . . She was gliding away. She disappeared. I started crying about the impossible happiness, but these tears were sweeter than my former ecstasies (7: 119).

The mantle of the prophet bothered him. His "dizzy moral progress" (47: 109) intoxicated him with the desire to conquer the world through art, by effortlessly exposing its vice and imperfection. The fragment might have been part of the simultaneously written *Albert*. Comparing his prototype, the debauched violinist Kiesewetter, the "Holy Fool of a genius," with the poet Zhemchuzhnikov, the author of the immortal prophet Prutkov, Tolstoy noted Kiesewetter's "fire without strength" and Zhemchuzhnikov's "strength without a spark" (47: 110). In order not to be wasted by this prophetic fire, the artist should avoid the temptation of artificially combining the two roles without believing in either. This was the flaw of Turgenev's superfluous clowns and Herzen's historical madmen. Tolstoy's impatience with them grew.

DEATH, MORAL ART, AND HISTORY

Tolstoy's personal life was still unsettled. In the grips of these diverse religious moods, he was studying philosophy in the morning and writing at night. He went on his second trip abroad in the company of his divorced sister Masha, and Nikolen'ka, who was in the final phase of consumption. Before joining his siblings, he began reading Goethe: "March 16–28, 1860: To know—is to know by all—to merge all classes in the knowledge of science. One needs to feel a Mephistopheles in oneself, but give him no power. To be a Mephistopheles is to doubt this truth" (48: 82). In Switzerland, he saw another prophetic dream, proving the greatness of Luther and the importance of the Bible for teaching, but revealing the deceptive side of the religion of progress: "I saw an unusual dream/thoughts: This is a strange religion of mine and of our time, the religion of progress. Who was it who said that progress is a good thing? This is only the absence of beliefs and a need of practical activity draped in belief" (May 26, 1860; 48: 25). Tolstoy's world collapsed following Nikolen'ka's death in Hyères, early in October 1860. Nikolen'ka was privy to his most cherished dreams about immortality and a partner in metaphysical disputes during their time in the army and in July 1860.[56] In a letter to Fet Tolstoy confessed his shocked witnessing of *"this absorption of self into nothingness . . . you can't influence the stone to fall up instead of down, where it is being drawn. . . .* this state into which we have been placed by someone is the most terrible lie and evildoing, for which we (we the liberals) would find no words if it were a man who placed another man in such a situation. . . . I do take life as is, as the most vulgar, repellent, and false condition" (60: 357).

At the funeral, the thought crossed his mind to write the materialist Gospel, "the life of Christ the materialist" (48: 29–30). For the first time in his life

Tolstoy rebelled against God the "benefactor" and his law, which he also expressed for the first time as something as calamitously certain as the law of gravity, which reduces man's life to the destiny of a dropped stone. Nikolen'ka's death dried up and scorched Tolstoy's poetic tree. Yet his infatuation with materialist teleology quickly faded and already in early 1861 Tolstoy managed to suppress his Mephistopheles and reinstated hopes in immortality by invoking the "purposiveness of future life": "Nature has overstepped its goal by having granted man the need for poetry and love, if its only goal were teleology" (48: 31–32).

The announcement of the Tsar's Manifesto of March 1861 ending serfdom found Tolstoy in Brussels, corresponding with Herzen on the meaning of religious sacrifice in history. The manifesto's false tone, pretending to be a grand historic gesture of charity, rubbed Tolstoy's sensibility the wrong way. He brushed the news off, concentrating on the main thought that the reading of Herzen's chapter on Robert Owen's role as the "apostle among the factory owners" inspired in him.[57] Herzen's chapter revisited the meaning of doubting and *Grübelei* (soul-searching) in the life of a revolutionary, who serves revolution as if it were a form of religion. In its final section, Herzen's chapter celebrates Owen's heroic obstinacy as an example of free will in history. If the ancients were right and history is a carpet, then "we can change the carpet's ornament" (7: 235). Herzen is certain that the general human striving toward the harmonious organization of life will be sufficient to embrace Owen's liberating philosophy, and that the success of this common goal will depend "on you and me" (7: 235–36, 239). In his response to Herzen, Tolstoy communicated his unease that Herzen was placing the substitute religion of progress on the pedestal of human aspiration in place of the "enormous hopes for immortality, eternal self-perfection, and historical laws" (60: 373–74). Tolstoy also objected to the comparison of the historical process to a soap bubble. Whatever happens, history never stops or ends: "This proves that we are puffing to inflate the new bubble," which is just as legitimate as the bubble of the Decembrist Ryleev hanged in 1826 (60: 374).

In this polite rebuttal to his older friend, Tolstoy linked Ryleev to religious rather than historical progress. He also informed Herzen that he had started working on a novel about a Decembrist—an enthusiast, a mystic, and a Christian—who returns from Siberia to Russia in 1856 with his wife, son, and daughter, and who is applying his strict, slightly idealistic view to the reality of the new Russia (60: 374). In the next and last surviving letter to Herzen, dated April 9, 1861, Tolstoy issued another polite rebuttal by informing Herzen that his project about the Decembrists had been inspired by Ogarev's and not Herzen's work. Ogarev's tale "The Spa in the Caucasus," his rumination about the meaning of self-oblivion in the lives of the Decembrists, who were "Christian philosophers" with their conscience completely free and "did not look for ecclesial unity in Christianity" or Orthodoxy had just appeared in Herzen's and Ogarev's periodical *The Polar Star* (Poliarnaya Zvezda) in 1861.[58] The religion described by Ogarev was the closest to Tolstoy's in 1861. As he explained it to Herzen, in reading Ogarev and without knowing a single Decembrist personally, he was proud to have guessed "the kind of Christian mysticism characteristic of those people" (60: 376–77). Tolstoy's unrealized novel about the Decembrists was begun in 1856, continued from 1860 to 1861, and was lightly revised at the end of the 1870s. The surviving chapters portray sincere religiosity in the person of the old Decembrist Petr Labazov, who recognizes his Christian neighbor in anyone on first encounter, and in his wife, alternately identified as Maria and Natalia. They attend matins the day after their arrival and set up icons above their bed before they go to sleep. However, their son, Sergey, is not a believer and prefers doing family chores rather than standing at Mass.[59] It is not clear how and when Labazov's impeccable Orthodoxy was born, that is, whether he had departed for the Siberian mines with the same convictions or whether it was his suffering in Siberia that forced him to seek religious consolation.

Instead of engaging in speculative games, it is more profitable to trace in this character the immediate results of Tolstoy's polemic against Herzen. The first result was the appreciation of freedom of conscience in England and its liberated spirituality, which was a bit too disciplined for Tolstoy's taste (47: 205). The second result was Tolstoy's launching of an all-out war against progress as it contradicted the religious attitude toward history. This was a contradictory campaign, for progress and democracy alone could ensure religious and personal freedom. In a note entitled "On Violence" (late 1850s continued in early 1860–1862), Tolstoy equated civilization with wars and mass murder arguing that violence in society is the same pernicious law of destruction witnessed in the falling down of the dropped stone, and what makes people resign themselves to lives contrary to their wishes and needs. "What is this incomprehensible force to which people submit the way they submit to gravitational force, without asking themselves about its origin, its beginning, or whether this strange force has an end?" (7: 121). Violence—or subjugation and restraint in the name of justice—is only possible because the majority affected by the force so as to become its implementers should agree that the cause for their action is just. The same cause should strike the remaining part of population as unjust. In the dialectical movement reminiscent of Hegel's descriptions and early Marxist writings on class struggle, historical events are produced. There can be no evil or right cause in history according to such a view, only modulations of violence depending on the degree of unanimity or

lack thereof during power transfer (7: 124). Herzen's theory of social reconstruction did not satisfy Tolstoy because of its artificial scheme of catapulting
a torpid and unwilling force into violent historical action. In an illuminating
note written near Clarens, Tolstoy considered Napoleon to be a fruitful hand
at reworking a ready-made formula to produce action (47: 207).

These embryonic formulas for *War and Peace* could not be put into practice in 1861–1862. It took Tolstoy another year of looking into additional
sources of free action and spirituality in several redemptive dreams: "Today
the moon lifted me—but how? Nobody knows. It is not in vain that I thought
today that the same law as the law of material gravity exists for the sake of
what we call 'spirit,' gravity toward the spiritual sun. . . . It is terrible, horrifying, and senseless to bind up one's happiness with material conditions—the
wife, children, health, or wealth" (48: 54–55). Nevertheless the conviction
that "whoever is happy is right" (48: 53) won; marriage proposal to Sofiya
Andreevna Bers was proffered and accepted in 1862. Soon after the marriage,
on December 27, 1862, Tolstoy had another prophetic dream: "Schiller told
me in my dream: happiness is the greatest engulfing of divinity (*zakhvaty-
vanie bozhestva*) breadth-wise and depth-wise" (48: 83). Whether this was indeed Schiller or Goethe's Walpurgis Night concert, Tolstoy came up with the
beautiful metaphor of the bubbles of life engulfing life and God. The reversal
between this engulfing and death swallowing man becomes clear in letters
written after Nikolen'ka's death.

Tolstoy celebrated his return to Russia and into literature by breaking up
with Turgenev and by adopting religious undertones to guide his life.[60] During Tolstoy's courtship of the Bers sisters in Moscow in the summer of 1862,
a search was conducted on his estate, and his private diaries read by a Colonel
Durnovo. Secret police acted on a tip that revolutionaries taught at Tolstoy's
peasant school at Yasnaya Polyana. Tolstoy's fury expressed in an indignant
letter to Tsar Alexander II knew no limit (60: 440–41), but it is more illuminating to notice that in 1862 Tolstoy seeks no confrontation. In his letters to
Aunt Alexandrine, who was lady-in-waiting and his direct link with the court,
he claimed that the twelve young teachers under suspicion (there were actually only eleven in number), like the veritable apostles of the new word, abandoned Herzen's despicable broadsheets upon arrival and picked up parables
and Gospels from which to teach peasant children (60: 428–29, 437). Under
the banner of his new religious striving, his writing agendas needed revision,
and the recurrent theme of an almost monastic purity and tranquility of the
writer raised in 1862 by Tolstoy recalls Pushkin's mood of lucid sorrow and
timid joy (48: 43).

Tolstoy's growing seriousness about faith may be witnessed in how
quickly—within the short span from 1856 to 1861—his tone has changed

from mild blasphemy to sincere expositions of his creed and its defense. In November 1856 he wrote from Saint Petersburg to his love interest and country neighbor Valeria Arsenieva: "Ah, si je pouvais croire!" (Ah, if only I could believe!), using the occasion to accentuate his teasing double entendre with seven exclamation marks. Marriage gave him calm because he was "getting tired of squaring accounts" with himself, and "starting new lives" (60: 452). Instead of making peace with his former "filthiness," he decided not to "delete the sad lines," a precept from Pushkin's *Vospominanie* (60: 452).[61] In October 1863, Tolstoy sent Alexandrine another letter announcing the end of all symptoms of superfluity ("*grübeln* is left behind"). He even inquired whether he would be permitted to enter the sanctuary of her Orthodox spirituality if he wears his new, spotless moral waistcoat: "I am now a writer— with every fiber of my being" (61: 23–24).

The only type of "grave digging" that Tolstoy was performing in 1863—he confessed as much to Fet in May 1863—was foraging in his literary recycling bin (61: 16). Fished out of it were plots of the "Distant Riding Field," "A History of a Horse," and *The Decembrists* project. In his unwitting journey toward becoming a poet-historian, Tolstoy started *War and Peace*. In his 1863 rewriting of "A Dream," Tolstoy changed its tone. The elevation from which he spoke was unsteady. Although the crowd still listened to him, and his words and movements were measured, he felt loneliness and despair: "They were moving me as I was moving them. I could feel my power over them and my power had no limit. Only the voice within me was saying: dreadful!" The Muse departed the gathering, smiling to him with a look of pity and compassion: "Tremulous dusk concealed her from me. I shook off shame and was crying about the irretrievable happiness of the past, the impossibility of future happiness, about the happiness that wasn't mine. . . . But in these words there was real happiness too" (Signed "N. O.") (7: 118).[62]

In his essay "History" (1828), written the year of Tolstoy's birth, Thomas Macauley predicted that a new Shakespeare and Homer embodied in one person, a poet-historian, would soon arrive.[63] When Tolstoy read Macauley in 1858, he made a note in his diary: "No—history is too cold for my taste" (*Net, istoriia kholodna dlia menia*) (48: 14–15). His early notes on Rousseau named history a science of "by-products," the study of foliage rather than roots and tree-saps (1: 221–25). His bitter arguments with Herzen, relinquishing his role as a weaver of the historical carpet, and a monastic conception of writing signified the matching of Tolstoy's novelistic maturity with Pushkin's peak at the time of *Boris Godunov*. He now stood at the threshold of a major redefinition of the religion of writing.

In his fictional work before *War and Peace*, Tolstoy attempted to join the incompatible, namely, progress and moral art. The contradiction plays itself out most fully in the three works that precede *War and Peace*: the novellas *Family Happiness* (1859–1860), *Polikushka* (1861–1863), and *The Cossacks* (1862). *Family Happiness* restored the broken idyll of family life in Masha's voluntary abandonment of modernity and its lures, her return to the estate of her husband, and submission to the law of Christian loyalty and its sanctified patrimonial lineage, her love for the father of her son, Ivan Sergeyevich. This reparation of love was most awkward. Tolstoy expressed his dissatisfaction with the novella, calling it "shit."

Far more interesting was the solution he found for *Polikushka*, a work considerably less popular. Its hero, a village drunkard named Polikei, loses his landowner's money loan that he was supposed to deliver from town. The money falls through a tear in the lining of his cap. Polikei hangs himself in despair, his youngest child drowns in the washtub amid all the ensuing chaos, and his wife loses her mind (7: 31–34). All this nightmare happens during recruit selection in the village. Diatlov, the richest peasant, bails out his sons, but his married nephew, Ilya, hard up for cash, can't dodge the draft. Diatlov finds the money dropped by Polikei and rehabilitates Polikushka's honor. The discovery of the money is not enough for Tolstoy to end the story, since he is not interested in rehabilitating the innocent who are already innocent in his satisfied mind; he wants to see his Diatlov repent his wrong against Ilya. This is achieved in a circuitous way. The landlady refuses to take back the devilish money. Diatlov takes the sum to his prosperous home, where Ilya's wife wails for her husband. At night he hears Polikushka calling after him, falling on him in order to strangle him. Diatlov wakes up, burps, prays, and asks his forgiveness. Before the morning breaks, he buys Ilya's freedom back (7: 48). The strange naturalism and unusual economy of expression of this redemption story and its unclear end prevented its early recognition as a masterpiece. Turgenev alone was generous enough to send Tolstoy his appreciation via Fet.[64] Why this frugal moral art was art Tolstoy could not tell either. It was inspired by his reading of a similar plot in Pushkin's rendition of a southern Slavic ballad entitled "Ianko Marnavich," which concerns the wronging of an innocent man and the death of a repentant perpetrator when he sees the corpse of the dead man walking over to his window. On July 8, 1854, Tolstoy commented: "This is enchanting—But why? Go figure what a poetic feeling is or might be" (47: 10).

The Cossacks explores a diametrically different possibility of life that is free in the absolute sense and not bounded by moral duty (47: 205). The hero of the tale, Olenin, represents the last semblance of the superfluous man that Tolstoy would place on his fictional stage.[65] Olenin's absolute freedom, a Satanic challenge to God, is unrealized because he "could do *everything*, and *nothing* was necessary to him." He could, on an impulse, "plunge headfirst into a bottomless abyss, not knowing why or how" (6: 6–12). Olenin is blindly happy about this bracketing out of necessity, and covers the path of unrestricted striving already trodden and left by his creator. On his lonely snipe-shooting sprees as an army officer in the Caucasus, Olenin sets out on lone pheasant hunts during breaks from military duty to think about the purpose of his life.[66] After the sharp-eyed Olenin kills twelve pheasants plus a myriad of mosquitoes, which have bitten him on this sultry day, he is tempted by their blissfully purposeless end: "Just as they . . . I shall live a while and die. Still I must live and be happy, because happiness is all I desire! How then must I live to be happy, and why was I not happy before?"[67] The only way to show this mosquito envier that he has limits was to clash him with the human force naturally not subject to any law, the Cossacks. While trying to cope with Maryanka's and Eroshka's indifference to his presence or absence, Olenin represents envy of pure desire, of unrestricted existence in sync with the harmonic fluctuation of nature and unmediated connection with its atoms, sensations, and laws (48: 51). As a consequence of these explorations, Tolstoy's emerging program of topics for *War and Peace* includes death, necessity, history, and absolute freedom, a thoroughly Romantic combination that sets itself the goal of "the perfect spiritualization of all the laws of nature into laws of intuition and intellect."[68]

NOTES

1. Bakhtin, *Sobranie Sochinenii*, 2: 238–65. See Introduction to the present study.

2. See also diary entry for June 14, 1850 (46: 35).

3. Diary entry for March 29, 1852 (46: 102).

4. On the war between reason and consciousness, see the diary entry for November 16, 1853 (46: 198). On memory's negotiating force, see the previously discussed fragment entitled "On the Goals of Philosophy" (1: 230).

5. See chapter 19 of *Boyhood* (2: 58).

6. Tolstoy, *Childhood, Boyhood, Youth*, 319.

7. See part 1, chapter 4, of *Family Happiness*.

8. See the diary entry for April 19, 1857 (47: 205).

9. Nikolai Platonovich Ogarev, *Izbrannye proizvedeniia v dvukh tomakh* (Moscow: Gosudarstvennoe izdatel'stvo khudozhestvennoi literatury, 1956), 2: 525. Only published in 1953, the manuscript of "Letters of the Country Dweller" (*Pis'ma derevenskogo zhitelia*; 1847) was widely circulated.

10. Pushkin, letter to Vladimir Gorchakov from Kishinev to Gura-Galben, October–November 1822. Pushkin, 13: 52–53.

11. Ibid., see also Pushkin's letters to Viazemsky (January 23, 1825) and A. A. Bestuzhev (end of January 1825), in criticism of the insentient behavior of Alexander Griboedov's character Chatsky. Pushkin, 13: 135, 137–38.

12. Fyodor Dostoevsky, *Notes From Underground*, 2nd ed., trans. and ed. Michael R. Katz (New York: Norton, 2001), 32–33.

13. Ivan Sergeevich Turgenev, "Hamlet of the Shchigrov District" (*Gamlet Shchigrovskogo uezda*) in *Sobranie sochinenii v piati tomakh* (Moscow: Russkaia Pravda, 1994), 1: 232; subsequent quotes are identified parenthetically in the text. The story was included in Turgenev's first successful prose collection, *Sportsman's Sketches* (1852).

14. Turgenev, *Sobranie sochinenii v piati tomakh*, 1: 235, 245.

15. Turgenev, "The Diary of a Superfluous Man," in *The Essential Turgenev*, ed. Elizabeth Cheresh Allen (Evanston, Ill.: Northwestern University Press, 1994), 104, 150, resp.

16. Turgenev, "Hamlet and Don Quixote," in *The Essential Turgenev*, 562.

17. See Doborliubov's review of Stankevich's correspondence, "Nikolai Vladimirovich Stankevich (Perepiska ego i biografiia, napisannaia P. V. Annenkovym) Moscow 1858" in *Izbrannoe*, 241–60.

18. Nikolai Gavrilovich Chernyshevsky, "Apologiia sumasshedshego," in *Sochineniia v dvukh tomakh, Filosofskoe nasledie, 101* (Moscow: Akademiia Nauk, USSR. Institut filosofii. Izdatel'stvo Mysl', 1987), 2: 278–307; esp. 279, 306–7.

19. For distributing leaflets calling for peasant revolution Chernyshevsky was sentenced to the pillory (1862) and sent to prison, followed by exile. *The Contemporary* was reopened after 1862 and then shut down for good in 1866. Nekrasov purchased a franchise for *Notes from the Fatherland* and took the remainder of his crew to this new pro-democratic forum.

20. Aleksandr Herzen, "Kniaginia Ekaterina Romanovna Dashkova," in Ekaterina Dashkova, *Zapiski 1743–1810*, ed. G. N. Moiseeva, Yu.V. Stepniak (Leningrad: Nauka, 1985), 258.

21. Herzen, *Sobranie sochinenii*, 3: 225–26, 227, 259.

22. Herzen, "The Damaged One" (*Povrezhdennyi*), in *Sobranie sochinenii*, 1: 437–59. The story was written at Saint Helene, near Nice, in 1851. Tolstoy reprinted the tale in his late collection of useful readings, *The Circle of Reading* (*Krug chteniia*, 1904–8), 42: 366–74; 668.

23. Herzen, "The Damaged One," 1: 445.

24. In addition to "The Damaged One," other titles Tolstoy considered included "The Lost One" (*Propashchii*) and "The Destroyed One" (*Pogibshii*). In Tolstoy's version, a contemptible violinist is found freezing to death in the street at the beginning and end of the story. The drunk is deemed deranged and hopeless, but he revives and ultimately turns into "the best and the happiest man" in a free realm of inspiration and creative daring (5: 52). While not Tolstoy's most successful piece of fiction of the period, it champions sacred uselessness, which only art and the ineffable can consecrate. Coupled with Tolstoy's renunciation of civilization and personal understanding of justice and injustice to the world spirit in *Lucerne* of the same year, "Albert" represents Tolstoy's partial response to the insanity and agony of the superfluous being.

25. Diary entry for December 5, 1856 (47: 103). See also Tolstoy's letter to Arsenieva dated December 7, 1856 (60: 140). In a letter to Botkin and Turgenev on the future of Russian literature, Tolstoy praised the parts of the as-yet-unpublished *Oblomov*. See the letter to Botkin and Turgenev dated October 21-November 1, 1857 (60:

234–36). For Tolstoy's remarks concerning Turgenev's *Diary of a Superfluous Man*, see diary entry for May 20, 1856 (47: 73).

26. For additional acrimonious comments about Turgenev, see the diary entry for late February-early March 1857 (47: 117–18).

27. See Tolstoy's letter to Herzen dated April 9, 1861 (60: 376–77).

28. Ogarev, "Ispoved' lishnego cheloveka," in *Stikhotvoreniia i poemy*, 2: 267–84.

29. N. Shchedrin (M. E. Saltykov), "Dva otryvka iz knigi Ob umiraiushchikh," in *Polnoe sobranie sochinenii*, ed. Valery Kirpotin et al. 20 vols. (Moscow: GiKhl, 1933–1937), 4: 169–81. The future satirist was a recent exile to Viatka. Quoted passage, 4: 178. Tolstoy was so impressed with Saltykov's description of dying that he volunteered to bring the manuscript to the editor Mikhail Katkov and negotiate its publication in the *Russian Messenger (Russkii vestnik)*. See Tolstoy's letter to Katkov, March 18, 1858 (60: 256).

30. Dobroliubov, *Izbrannoe*, 295. See Dobroliubov's review of Turgenev's *On the Eve*, which is typical of such an approach. Dobroliubov's "When Will the True Day Come? On The Eve, The Novel by I. S. Turgenev" (Kogda zhe pridet nastoiashchii den'? nakanune, povest' I. S.Turgeneva") was published in the *Russian Messenger* in 1860. A similar view is expressed in Pisarev's review of Turgenev's *Fathers and Sons*, who is critical of Bazarov's suicide. Dmitry Ivanovich Pisarev, *Literaturnaia kritika v trekh tomakh*, 3 vols. ed. Yu. Sorokin (Leningrad: Khudozhestvennaia literatura, 1981), 1: 280–81.

31. Nekrasov, to whom Tolstoy sent the story, felt that the choice of the marker as a first-person narrator failed in terms of both authority and structure. The concept of social duty, despite all the faults of the idle class, had to be elevated.

32. The prince is here referring to stanza 10 of chapter 8 of *Eugene Onegin*.

33. Alexander Pushkin, *Eugene Onegin*, trans. James F. Falen (Oxford: Oxford University Press, 1995), 143. The passage is taken from chap. 6, stanza 44.

34. Although Tolstoy returned to "Distant Hunting Ground" in 1865, the story was never finished.

35. Pavel Annenkov, ed., *N. V. Stankevich: Perepiska i ego biografiia* (Moscow: Tipografiia Katkova, 1857). The publication of the correspondence and biography was a major public event. Tolstoy must be referring to these questions that Stankevich addresses to his friends about his condition: "what should I do in my present condition?" and the same questions addressed to himself in his diary of the last year of his life. The same temperament may be noticed in Stankevich's fictional account, "A Few Moments from the Life of Count Z." See *Stankevich: Perepiska i ego biografiia*, 121–22, 277, 380, 394.

36. This type of character is exemplified in Gogol's Kostanzhoglo (the counterpart of Tentetnikov in the second part of *Dead Souls*) and in Turgenev's Lezhnev (*Rudin*).

37. See Turgenev's letter to Druzhinin dated January 13, 1857; it is quoted by commentators of Tolstoy's novel in the edition of his complete works (3: 85).

38. Dostoevsky, "Notebook, 1860–1862" (Dostoevsky, 20: 170 and 27: 19).

39. Apollon Grigoriev, *Iz russkoi mysli o Rossii*, ed. Igor Trofimivich Ianin (Kaliningrad: Iantarnyi skaz, 1998), 77. See also Grigoriev's letters to Strakhov dated June 18, 1861, and September 23, 1861 (ibid. 78–79).

40. Apollon Grigoriev, "Literaturnaia deiatel'nost' grafa L'va Tolstogo: Stat'ia vtoraia," in *Biblioteka russkoi kritiki: Kritika 60-kh gg. XIX veka* (Moscow: Astrel', 2003), 276–306.

41. Letter from Moscow dated October 21-November 1, 1857 (60: 231–35).

42. Cf. Tolstoy's diary entry for March 21, 1858: "The political excludes the artistic, because the former, in order to be true, ought to be one-sided" (48: 10).

43. On Tolstoy's hints that he might be abandoning literature, see his letter to Druzhinin on October 9, 1859 (60: 308–9) and to Chicherin end of October-beginning of November 1859 (60: 315–16).

44. Lev Nikolaevich Tolstoy, *Perepiska s russkimi pisateliami*. 2 vols. (Moscow: Khudozhestvennaia literatura, 1978), 1: 218. "Dahin" (over there) was a term that the Russian Romantics and "men of the 1840s" borrowed from a famous refrain "Dahin! Dahin!" of Goethe's poem "Kennst du das Land" and that they used to refer to the transcendent. See Johann Wolfgang von Goethe, *Selected Poetry*. Bilingual edition. trans. with intro and notes by David Luke (London: Penguin Books, 2005), 56–57.

45. Tolstoy, *Perepiska s russkimi pisateliami*, 1: 164–66.

46. Iazykov returned to Russia in 1843. Cf. Iazykov's letter to Gogol dated May 10, 1845, which links Gogol's depressive moods and bad health to his life abroad. See quoted passage in N. M. Iazykov, *Sochineniia* (Leningrad: Khudozhestvennaia literatura, 1982), 384.

47. V. G. Benediktov, *Stikhotvoreniia*, ed. V. I. Sakharov (Moscow: Sovetskaia Rossiia, 1991), 230–31.

48. The easygoing "pure artists," the brothers Zhemchuzhnikov and Tolstoy's relative Aleksei Konstantinovich Tolstoy, joined forces in 1854 to create Kozma Petrovich Prutkov. See "Predsmertnoe: Naideno nedavno, pri revizii Probirnoi palatki, v delakh sei poslednei" (At the Moment of Dying: Discovered During the Inventory of the Assays Office). My translation from Prutkov's poem is based on *Koz'ma Prutkov* (Rostov-on-Don: Feniks, 1996), 60–61.

49. See Turgenev's letter to Tolstoy dated February 11, 1859, reprinted in Tolstoy, *Perepiska s russkimi pisateliami*, 1: 168.

50. Pisarev's review is reprinted in *Tolstoy: The Critical Heritage*, ed. A. V. Knowles (London: Routledge & Kegan Paul, 1978), 67–68.

51. *Tolstoy: The Critical Heritage*, 67.

52. "Three Deaths" appeared in the first issue of *Biblioteka dlia chteniia* the following year (1859), but it circulated widely and was read by Tolstoy's friends in manuscript.

53. Turgenev, *Sobranie sochinenii v piati tomakh*, 1: 188. See Irina Reyfman, "Turgenev's 'Death' and Tolstoy's 'Three Deaths'" on Tolstoy's "tight authorial control over the reader" that creates a feeling of claustrophobia, while Turgenev offers the reader a "loose, open-ended plot" (316) by exploring the same phenomenon of calm death that the Russian people of all social stations invariably display (317). Irina Reyfman, "Turgenev's 'Death' and Tolstoy's 'Three Deaths'." *Word, Music, History. A Festschrift for Caryl Emerson*, eds. Lazar Fleishman, Gabriella Safran, Michael Wachtel. *Stanford Slavic Studies*, volumes 29–30 (2005): 29: 312–26.

54. Victor Hugo, *La Préface de Cromwell*, ed. Maurice Souriau (Geneva: Slatkine Reprints, 1973), 256–57. Amended English translation is quoted from Victor Hugo,

Dramas. Oliver Cromwell. trans. I. G. Burnham (Philadelphia: George Barrie & Son, 1896), 69–70.

55. Tolstoy, "Svetloe khristovo voskresen'e" (5: 224–25). Tolstoy actually visited a church on March 22, 1858. He felt so awkward that he imagined that the crowd was gazing at him: "Good! Christ is risen!" (48: 10).

56. Tolstoy spoke with his brother about the Bible on July 28/August 9 (European calendar): "Nikolen'ka is dying, terribly smart, clear, and wants to live" (48: 27).

57. See the chapter "Robert Owen," in part 6 of Herzen's *My Past and Thoughts (Byloe i Dumy)*; Herzen, 7: 197.

58. Ogarev's Caucasus memoir "Kavkazskie vody (Otryvok iz moei ispovedi)" was finished toward the end of 1860 and the very beginning of 1861. See Ogarev, *Izbrannye proizvedeniia v dvukh tomakh*, 2: 386.

59. See fragments and various redactions of the novel (17: 256–300).

60. The fallout was ugly. Tolstoy accused Turgenev of falsely raising his illegitimate daughter, a half-peasant, who was mending torn and dirty peasant clothes. The writers would not speak or write each other for the next seventeen years. See Tolstoy's account of the event in his diary entry for October 8, 1861 (48: 38).

61. See chapter 1 in the present study.

62. The fragment was sent to Ivan Sergeevich Aksakov's newspaper *Day (Den')* as the debut piece of a young provincial girl aspiring to become a writer. Sophia Andreevna wrote it in her hand, signed it N. O., and sent it to Aksakov pretending it was authored by a Natalia Petrovna Okhotnitskaya (a relative who lived at Yasnaya Polyana). Aksakov turned the fragment down.

63. See chapter 5, "History and Literature: Thomas Babbington Macaulay," in *The Varieties of History. From Voltaire to the Present*, ed., selected and introduced, Fritz Stern (New York: Meridian Books, 1960), 89.

64. Although he considered the story too dark, its heroes too uncouth, and the drowning of Polikushka's son excessive, Turgenev confessed that "there are some truly wonderful pages" and that the story "even induces shivers up my spine." See Turgenev's letter to Fet dated January 25, 1864, reprinted in *Tolstoy: The Critical Heritage*, 66.

65. In a letter to Fet dated April 7, 1863, Turgenev wondered why Tolstoy's new type of poetry needed Olenin at all, "that tedious, unhealthy figure, always preoccupied with himself. Why does Tolstoy not rid himself of that nightmare?" See *Tolstoy: The Critical Heritage*, 65–66.

66. See Tolstoy's diary entries made in August 1852 while in the Caucasus (46: 140).

67. Tolstoy, *The Cossacks* (6: 76–77). Translation quoted from *Great Short Works of Tolstoy*, ed. John Bayley, trans. Louise and Aylmer Maude (New York: Harper and Row, 1967), 165.

68. Coleridge, "Requests and Premonitions," chapter 12 of *Biographia Literaria*, 256.

Chapter Four

Belief System in *War and Peace* (1863–1869)

Reason expresses the laws of necessity. Consciousness expresses the essence of freedom. (E2/10; 7: 350)[1]

The war is not a niceties game; it is the foulest thing in life, and one ought to understand this and not play at war. One ought to accept this terrible necessity with grave seriousness. (III/III/25; 6: 219)

The joyous sensation of freedom—of that complete, inalienable freedom common to man—filled Pierre's soul during his recovery. (IV/IV/12; 7: 217)

TOLSTOY IN 1863

The quotations above neatly sum up the nature of Tolstoy's philosophical and literary orientation, suspended between necessity and freedom, at a time when he finally substituted fragments of "1805" for the novel *The Decembrists*, opting to concentrate on the study of the rich historical period that shaped the Decembrists' mystical beliefs. Following a series of untimely deaths and incomprehensible misfortunes among the families of friends and intimates since 1858, he suggested to his aunt Alexandrine—whose niece had just died—that she accepts Stankevich's response to unendurable suffering in fulfillment of God's will because "God wills people to live with this wicked, refined grief" (60: 311–13).[2]

From the perspective of choosing history as a topic, Tolstoy was continuing on a quest undertaken to investigate the extended effect of radical evil on masses and individuals, while simultaneously answering old questions about the law of necessity, and the reasonableness of being that ends in death. This is how he theorized the equilibrium of the above forces in April 1857: "There are two wisdoms. According to one, logical and small, civilization moves ahead, and this is good. According to another, 'bird's-eye view,' there is an equal compensation if civilization were lacking. According to the third, still higher view—where I can gain insight for only a minute—both views are just.—Buy the Gospels" (47: 203–4). However, several aspects of Tolstoy's search for the Gospel synthesis were purely literary. Many examples were adduced demonstrating Tolstoy's indifference to literary types or predictable characters, and his great interest in situations to which people should respond.[3] This is certainly a literary precondition for examining the interplay of necessity and chance in human behavior. Whenever he discusses divisions into human types, such as the "snub-nosed" and the arrogant, Tolstoy's division is based on their attitude toward action. In the early stages of his work on *War and Peace*, Tolstoy rebuffed an inquisitive question from Alexandrine about the identity of Andrey Bolkonsky, simply saying he was a "nobody."[4] Focusing on attitudes rather than character traits was a step beyond his early "dialectics," in which dynamic personality was achieved thanks mainly to wide-angle reporting combined with microscopic sensory reactions, dreams, and inner dissatisfactions of the superfluous seeker. In the funeral overtures to Russian literature that Tolstoy sang to Fet and other friends at the end of the 1850s, he yearns for the kind of revolution that he feared in terms of the imminent historical future. Exactly what was Tolstoy trying to bury and rebuild? Among the possibilities were: the maudlin language of the Karamzinian literary salons (46: 198); the crude tones and the negative tricks of the accusatory school (Gogol, Ostrovsky); the lack of moral responsibility in catering to the ideal reader, of which he himself was guilty (46: 242); and Turgenev's and his own cute "short novels."[5] By 1863 necessity and freedom were most closely being probed in *Lucerne* and *Family Happiness* (submission), *Polikushka* ("wicked, refined grief" and moral retribution), and *The Cossacks* (pure desire).

The best studies of *War and Peace* traditionally questioned the validity of customary novelistic assessments of the novel, thereby pointing to the possibility of its special form of trust and faith.[6] This novel is simultaneously "not a novel" but rather a process "that enters from Tolstoy's mind into our own, constantly restructuring the entire edifice of our own norms, assumptions, prejudices, and perception"[7] in the ever-unfolding polyphonies of the present, sifting through the consciousness of author, characters, and readers, this center where finitude and infinity, necessity and freedom collide. According to Donna Orwin's masterful explanation, Tolstoy corrects Herzen's conception of individuality as both "woof and weaver" in relation to history by insisting that man's illusion of complete freedom outside of history is repaired by "natural equivalent[s] for history," by man's "unconscious life" ruled by harmonious reason of Tolstoy the poet, who sees the interconnectedness of all things. To reinforce such interconnectedness, Tolstoy introduces the figure of the Master of Ceremonies, who, like the God of the Old Testament, makes his appearances to orchestrate history and unmask the Napoleons.[8] Duration, immediacy, and time are key themes in Jeff Love's study *The Overcoming of History in War and Peace*. Love argues in favor of the "dynamic interplay between two radically different types of cognition, one rational and mediate, the other non-rational and immediate" and in favor of Tolstoy's affirmation of rationality and necessity in history (Love, 2, 17). This narrator also believes—and Love proves—that events are not chaotic but rather necessitated by infinite causes which allows Tolstoy the novelist practices of revelatory dogmatism for the inspired, or what Love calls "aggressive passivity," during which "reason is subordinate to desire [and] does not command but obeys" (Love, 40).

This chapter will provide a hermetic reading of the novel's text, treating it as the ultimate and self-sufficient expression of Tolstoy's belief system between 1863 and 1869. Given its emphasis on Tolstoy's narrative theology, this chapter examines Tolstoy's belief system in terms of faith and humanity as such, interprets Tolstoy's representation of God's universe and His aliases, and considers the problem of writing as a form of religion.

FAITH AS SUCH

That the narrator's voice in the novel tends to acquire ironic overtones whenever religious piety enters the picture is a fact impossible to deny. After one of their many revelatory debates, the two main male heroes of the novel, Pierre Bezukhov and Prince Andrey Bolkonsky, relieve metaphysical tension by impugning the tall tale about the healing power of icons told by the enchanted wanderer Pelageiushka, guest of Andrey's religious sister, Princess Maria. Pelageiushka is left shamed and confused, but Princess Maria's despair following the debate, in which she and her God's people are unable to dispel accusations of "sham" (*obman*), is deeper by far. Tolstoy does not rush to her rescue (II/II/13). Tolstoy's impatience with the ceremonial side of faith truly justifies the dismissive description as a rationalist assassin of religious hokum that he received from Sir Isaiah Berlin. The novel virtually opens with a hilarious underhanded assault on religious bigots, headed by Prince Vasily Kuragin, who compete for the inheritance of the dying Count Bezukhov, Pierre's father. All are possessed of a literal, businesslike faith in an inexhaustible divine providence ("La bonté divine est inépuisable") (I/I/19–20; 4: 104–6). Depending on the unfolding of the inheritance scheme, the most propitious timing for the administering of extreme unction is disputed over the insensitive body, which has committed a sacrilege in its own right by surviving the sixth stroke, given that the limit of human life was set by the medics of the day at three strokes at most.[9] We would do better to address more complex issues than the rustle of clothes and the shuffling of feet in the room where "all were silent and crossing themselves" while the atheist Pierre felt shamed and scared; the ceremony finally interrupted by the voice of the priest congratulating the unconscious man on the acceptance of the mystery.[10]

However, Tolstoy's irony rarely stoops to a heavy-handed satire of a sworn atheist or disillusioned skeptic. A good example is provided by the heaps of icons and coffers (*obraza i sunduki*) that Pierre notices in the deserted streets of Moscow upon his return from the battle of Borodino (III/III/33; 6: 404). The jumble of holy objects and private effects of evacuating burghers, who refuse to abandon the icons to the enemy, expresses Tolstoy's attitude of a dialectical ironist who constantly shifts perspectives regarding what is sacred and profane in human experience. Princess Maria is one such complex case. Maria's spiritual complexity is revealed at her first appearance, receiving from her father, Prince Bolkonsky, permission to read a letter from Julie Karagina, her friend in the capital. The enlightened and loving tyrant Prince Bolkonsky does not "get involved with anyone's faith" and permits Maria to read the accompanying volume that Julie has forwarded, Karl Ekkartshausen's *Gefühle und Tempel der Natur* (Emotions and the Temple of Nature) (I/I/22; 4: 114). When she pores over Julie's letter, what catches Maria's eye and puts her into a state of reverie is the fact that the mystic book in question "calms and elevates the soul" (I/I/22; 4: 116). However, upon reflection Maria refuses to read Julie's mystical book because mysticism arouses doubt.

Tolstoy reveals that he has a special agenda for Maria, who thinks that she already knows all the answers from the Gospels. He endows her with two identities that he lets her observe in the mirror during her very first appearance: one of unconscious, spontaneous inner beauty when she looks away; and the other of self-conscious control that makes her a living embodiment of Gospel truths. In the latter case, the mirror reveals her homeliness, narrow-mindedness, and cruelty. This is evident in her pity for Pierre, who, despite his good heart, is deemed cast further down from heaven after inheriting his father's vast fortune. Her refusal to read Julie's mystical book signals her potential bigotry and desire to shield herself against the probing questions of life. Tolstoy reveals Maria's special role in an eloquent scene in the icon room. Maria is praying, expecting God to answer her question regarding whether it is a sin to feel physical love for Anatol, the empty-headed love object of her affection. And God "already responded to her in her own heart": "'Will nothing for yourself; don't seek, don't agitate, don't envy. The future of people and your destiny must be unknown to you; but *live so that you are ready for anything*. If it is pleasing to God to test you in the duties of marriage, be ready to fulfill his will.' With this calming thought (but also with the hope that her forbidden earthly dream be fulfilled), Princess Maria sighed, crossed herself, and went downstairs, without thinking about her dress, or hairstyle, or how she will make her entry and what she will say. What meaning could all of this have, compared to God's providence, without whose will not a hair of man's head will perish" (I/III/3; 4: 279).

It is impossible to determine who thinks the last thought in this carefully blended narrative voice, but it is clear that upon setting Maria free to go downstairs and rejoin the world, the authority that commanded her to wait will not permit that a single strand of her hair be destroyed on the conjugal bed of the immoral Anatol.[11] In the novel, Maria will be punished by experiencing deep emotional wounds and setbacks every time she uses her ready-made religious principles to mimic her understanding of God's will. After her subjection to a humiliating discourse on religion with Pierre and Andrey, her vagabond outfit of God's servant at the ready, Maria retreats to her room, hoping that He will save her and command her to set out on the pilgrimage route. This time Tolstoy frames God's voice differently, making it inaudible and forcing Maria's inner monologue to assume that her vicious, subdued rancor is in compliance with God's will: "Prince Andrey loved his wife, she died, he is not sated, and he wants to join his destiny to another woman. My father does not want this because he wishes a more prominent and wealthy match for Andrey. And they all struggle, suffer, torture, and spoil their soul, their eternal soul, to achieve the good whose expiry term is a moment. We all know that. Christ, Son of God, came down to earth to tell us that this life is momentary and a test, and we still hold on to this notion and deem it possible to find happiness here. How come nobody understood this? Nobody but these contemptible God's people" (II/II/13; 5: 127–28). Tolstoy's irony implies that Princess Maria is *not* yet ready for everything with her complete abstinence from any involvement with life. Testing it instead of being tested by it is a desecration of God's will rather than a readiness to fulfill it.

Tolstoy's irony is not disputing the power of the holy effects on the Russian heart. On the contrary, he shows that the opposite is true. In the case of the penitent Natasha Rostova's desire to "change forever and for good" (*ispravit'sia navsegda, navsegda*) (III/I/17; 6: 77) following her failed elopement with Anatol Kuragin while a guest at the house of the thoroughly Orthodox Maria Dmitrievna Abrosimova, Tolstoy observes the same feeling of entitlement to God's favors as he did in Maria's case.[12] Natasha's daily church visits following her redemptive, near-fatal illness, consisting of long vigils in front of the "darkened face of the Mother of God," are also a form of beastly hunger to be the chosen one. She finds solace in thinking that she is worse than everybody and thus of special interest to God. Like Princess Maria or Masha of *Family Happiness* before, Natasha never loses herself completely and prays, imagining that He "rules her soul" (*upravlial ee dushoi*) (III/I/18; 6: 82–83). The reader quickly overcomes the initial impulse to read the scene merely as an exposé of religious sham. In her youthful refusal to give in to despair Natasha soon recovers her thirst to live, and she immediately contradicts the general mood in the church, refusing to pray for the destruction of Russia's enemies and noticing tasteless outfits and other improprieties near the central gates of the iconostasis. When she identifies spiritual falsehood and establishes her own priorities while praying, we know that Natasha is again alive and well. The recovery and mellowing of Princess Maria occurs almost simultaneously. After the loss of the old Prince Bolkonsky, she loses her capacity to pray and speak to God. When the demands of existence call her back to life with a new and heretofore undiscovered force (*s novoiu eshche neizvestnoiu siloiu*) that remains unconscious (*bessoznatel'no*), Maria recovers her ability to address God again: "She could now remember, could weep, and could pray" (III/II/10, 12; 6: 157, 162).

The above examples demonstrate that in his interpretation of faith Tolstoy adopts two clear tacks: personal faith works positively when it becomes the expression—even in spontaneous outbursts—of human adjustment to necessity; it works negatively when God's will is presumed to be understood in any preordained sense. Tolstoy demonstrates that although such a meaning cannot be grasped by religious means, it can be expressed through them. Platon Karataev (Plato Black Lake), who is usually interpreted as the embodiment of lived religion or folk wisdom in the novel, may well not qualify.[13] Platon's static, unthinking, "round" condition of readiness, without any will or desire to contradict, is not synonymous with Maria's or Natasha's unconscious thirst for life.[14] He relates his meaningless parables unlike Tolstoy's beloved Grisha prays, in the same mindless manner in which Maria's holy vagrants blather about the apocalypses while sipping tea, or when the priest offers his impassive consolations. Platon's unreflecting readiness for submission is naturally coupled with his little acts of indulgent kindness. He weeps in the middle of a tale told to fellow prisoners about a wrongly accused man who dies in prison, but his tears do not underscore the moment of catharsis in him or in his audience. His tales puzzle his listeners due to their all-encompassing, virtually nonsensical meaning. Pierre asks Karataev why prisoners had been shot, whereupon Karataev superstitiously silences his inquisitive impiety ("hush, hush . . . 'tis a sin"). His prayers are similarly nonsensical: "Lord Jesus Christ, Saint Nicholas, Frola and Lavra, Lord Jesus Christ, Saint Nicholas, Frola and Lavra, Lord Jesus Christ, forgive and save us,—he concluded, bowed down to earth, got up, sighed and sat down on his heap of hay." When Pierre attempts to inquire about the meaning of this strange prayer, Karataev is already half asleep (IV/I/12; 7: 53). The moment when Karataev himself is shot by the French is the first instance in his captive state that Pierre glosses and absorbs without questioning the necessity and inevitability of injustice and evil. He, too, succumbs to necessity. Is such a truce satisfactory? If Platon's name and his parables are symbolic of anything, they symbolize the unreflecting black abyss separating God's designs from human experience.

How much faith, then, does Tolstoy place in ritual when, in attending to the rhythms of life's eclipse and renewal, it points toward the affirmation of God's law? Tolstoy examines several different situations. The noblest of occasions to explore what is holy in human behavior would be a scene with public prayer before a decisive battle against the invader. Tolstoy's tactic in presenting the scene of Russian troops praying before the battle of Borodino consists of a restrained form of parody. An external, withdrawn view is given to Pierre, who watches the reflection of the effect of the prayer to the icons of Mother of God the Protectress of Iversky and Smolensky Regiments on those who are preparing to die. Pierre notices that soldiers and volunteers gaze at the icon with identically "hungry eyes" and listen with attention to the monotone chanting of the priests. As the solemnity of the scene reaches its climax, religious exultation mixes with the impetuosity of the crowd, which is eager to be saved individually. The crowd engulfs Pierre and he finds himself caught and near trampled in a stampede of roaring beasts trying to reach out to touch the icon (III/II/21; 6: 203).[15]

Portraying organized faith as the channel of the beastly unconscious, Tolstoy violates his earlier military canon, in which protective personal icons and collective prayer were shown to be inviting healthy and ennobling human reactions.[16] However, it is Masonic ritual and doctrine, more than Orthodoxy, that exerts claims of entitlement to divine law and supreme mastery in the same inventory of symbolic falsehoods: skull and bones, faint light, and the universe wound up like clockwork. Intercepted by the Mason Bazdeev at his most vulnerable hour, Pierre is convinced of the need to change by Bazdeev's identification of him with a child who plays with parts of the clock, ignorant of the mastery of the Architect of the Universe, who alone knows the secret of the mechanism and sets it in motion. The demands to renew his innermost man ritualistically attract Pierre as much as the prospect of being a part of the flawlessly wound mechanism. Getting used to the "weak light" that penetrates the cover over his eyes during the initiation ceremony enough to make out the skull, the casket, and the Bible, Pierre begs for assistance: "I . . . I wish a renewal. I hope for guidance and assistance in renewal" (II/II/ 3; 5: 81). This need is so great that Pierre prefers to overlook the ridicule that Bunyan's journey of labor suffers at the hands of Masonic pranksters from the Saint Petersburg lodge. When the "scales," or scarf, covering his eyes falls, Pierre sees a few people in aprons to whom he had already given away his money, his watch, and other valuables, and who had cheated him out of his money in social situations before. Pierre's Masonic period marks a new stage in his romance with elaborate self-delusion. His ambiguous Masonic oath for his "readiness for everything" (*Ia gotov na vse*) (II/II/3; 5: 83) mistakes financial charity, legal duties, bookkeeping and funneling millions into the pockets of Masonic confidence men for the birth of his new man. Pierre's readiness for change will not be born in his stylized diary of an exemplary Mason, laced with orchestrated dreams and illuminated visions, in pursuit of sensual satisfaction. In his diary of a Mason Pierre attempts to describe his flight from passions to a life of holiness (bright palace in the distance), but he is stuck on the fence pursued by the vicious dogs. In this scene deserving to be part of the Arzamas anthology of humor, Pierre resides neither in the province of Adonai (the creator) nor that of Elohim (the ruler of all). Rather, he dangles in between, legs and trunk straddling either side of the imaginary fence separating him from the beautiful palace in the near distance, while the dogs of his passion are leaping up to take a bite out of his meaty shanks (II/III/10; 5: 191). Pierre's diary is the endearing indulgence of an idle soul, fabricating stories of its lost integrity until this future deliverer of humanity from Napoleon sees life's real horror during the war and feels that "to return to faith in life was not in his power" (IV/I/12; 7: 49).

Religious needs in the novel have no individual value of an overweening truth of the law in the name of which necessity rules the universe. Prayer and conformity to ritual no less than patriotic glee or gambling are to Tolstoy only a means by which he explores human impulses involving spiritual freedom or dependence. Be it organized Orthodoxy, elemental forms of religious life in the human hive, or personal prayer, Tolstoy does not place his trust in man's ability to divine the moment of truth through involvement in standard religious practices or traditional forms of shared religious opinion. The collective faith of a human hive depends on the volatility level of its members; it lives united only for brief stretches of time when it subjugates self-consciousnesses and self-interest to a blind extenuating force. Nowhere in the novel do people pray joyously together or undergo conversional experiences simultaneously. It remains to be determined what role Tolstoy accords to faith as a vital spiritual force that can counter moral decay and death, especially in the presence of the physical vestiges of death, the most certain proof of the inevitable.

DEATH AND NECESSITY

Beginning with the early scenes set in the parlors of the dying Count Bezukhov, Tolstoy introduces the theme of the "border of death" (*cherta smerti*), the invisible line that separates the phenomenal from the metaphysical world. Situated at the foot of old Bezukhov's deathbed, Pierre is given his first chance to gaze into the metaphysical void—and he fails the test. The fault, however, is not his: "The Count was looking straight at Pierre, but his look was of the type whose sense and meaning man may not understand" (I/I/21; 4: 104–95). Tolstoy writes "may not" (*nel'zia*), a word that in Russian connotes both the physical inability to understand and a warning against attempting to understand; the way the phrase is constructed, it implies that no living man can understand the gaze of death. Transfixed, Pierre and the narrator wonder whether Bezukhov stares out because one can't avoid using one's eyes while one physically has eyes to look somewhere. Perhaps this gaze was saying *too much* (*govoril slishkom mnogo*) (I/I/21; 4: 104–5)?

The same gaze of death continues to paralyze Princess Maria when she bids farewell to the old Prince Bolkonsky, in whose place she finds "something alien and hostile, some terrifying, horrifying and repellent mystery" (III/II/8; 6: 146). The selfsame gaze of transcendent knowledge prevents Natasha and Princess Maria from looking the dying Prince Andrey in the eyes. A similar turning away is practiced in the presence of the old Countess Rostova, the household's memento mori: "She is not wholly in what can be seen of her now. Memento mori—these glances were saying" (E1/12; 7: 290). There is nothing to add to it to explain or do away with the absolute alienation of the two opposites of human life: the phenomenal and the transcendent.

The motif of a reproach and the haunting presence of a corpse in the life of the living changes in *War and Peace* compared with Tolstoy's earlier works. Lize Bolkonsky's charming, pitiful non-acceptance of death in her dead face will continue to torture Andrey, who felt that "something had torn loose in his soul, that he was guilty of a guilt that can't be undone or forgotten" (II/I/9; 5: 45–46). Even the old Bolkonsky turned away in his vulnerable and guilty anger when he saw Lize's face. Compare to this the reproachful expression in the face of the dead landlady in "Three Deaths," which quickly fades from the memory of the living. In *War and Peace*, death inspires fear and respect. Nothing more can be said for or against the awful death of sixteen-year-old Petya Rostov—except that at the moment of his death he is "ready" (*gotov*), as his commander Denisov avers (IV/III/11; 7: 161). With a grim economy that well illustrates the double meaning of death in the novel, Tolstoy employs the Russian word's double meaning, namely, being "ready for" and being "killed." The menacing sense of this ambiguous readiness is intensified when one recalls that years earlier the dozing little Petya had been placed in wagonette/hearse to ride home "like a dead body" after a merry late-night stay at his uncle's place (II/IV/7; 5: 278). The scene of Petya's killing is drawn in more plaintive, gentle tones in the earlier drafts, where the hussar Denisov sobs and the cold-hearted Dolokhov, who is never sorry, says: "What a pity!" (15: 134).

Human behavior is different on the battlefield where death is both massive and random. The glory of war intoxicates the bloodthirsty humor of the troops when they gleefully repeat the beautiful word "direct hit" (*krasivoe slovo napoval*) (I/II/8; 4: 188) to refer to a death just witnessed. The "beautiful death" of Prince Andrey—just one of the many whose death is mistakenly diagnosed by Napoleon (voilà une belle morte) while inspecting the field of Austerlitz after the battle—is indeed beautiful within the semiotics of impersonal warfare that allows to kill or die in a frenzy of self-oblivion. Such a death, moreover, does not elicit the same need for understanding in the viewer as does the "peaceful" deaths in the examples described above. In the war sections, Tolstoy's characters are curious about the boundary that separates life from death. Before the battle, when death looms as a hypothesis that is borne out in the future, the boundary is merely a line that separates today from tomorrow. It is a curiosity of life, agitated and excited, that loses part of itself every day by approaching death and by enriching itself with new experience: "It is terrifying to step over the boundary and yet one wants to step over it. . . . [S]ooner or later one will have to step over it and find out what there is on the other side of the line, as inevitably as one will find out what there is on the other side of death" (I/II/7; 4: 181).

During those rare moments when death literally stares at a human subject in a one-on-one confrontation, Tolstoy presents two reactions: instinctive flights of a frightened animal or a conscious, if futile, challenge to fear. Nikolai Rostov experiences the former reaction during his early days as a hussar. He prays to God or "that which is up there in the sky" to spare him, and he runs away imagining that every French barrel about to discharge is taking aim at him, "whom everybody loves so much" (I/II/8; 4: 188). A world-weary Prince Andrey experiences the latter reaction as heavy enemy fire decimates his reserve regiment waiting in vain to be called into action at Borodino. In a sickening duel with a spinning cannon ball that threatens to explode any second at his feet, Andrey resents losing a life that he loves, yet he simultaneously realizes that to attempt to control the outcome is futile. At the last moment, in full view of his charges, he simulates defiance in an attempt to shame a frightened aide-de-camp who is playing possum and shielding himself. Diffident survivors of the blast voice an awestruck repulsion at the fateful indiscretion that mortally wounded Andrey and spared them: "Ah, dear Lord! Dear

Lord! How come? In the belly! This is the end! Ah, dear Lord!—one could hear voices among the officers.—It whizzed a hair's distance at my ear, the aide-de-camp was saying" (III/II/36; 6: 263). The repulsion is unredeemed by the fact of survival itself, for everyone near Andrey's stretchers knows by now that their forethought and precaution did nothing to save them: destiny would have been delivered from the hands of "dear Lord."

The only character in the novel designated to challenge death and danger time and again is Dolokhov, the cool-headed seducer, calculating gambler, and immoral demolisher of all forms of peace whose beautiful, arrogant, immoral eyes stare at the fearful symmetry of necessity and freedom. In a duel that he incites against Pierre, never bothering to conceal his affair with Pierre's wife, Helene, Dolokhov's unblinking gaze hypnotizes Pierre into a complete stupor. But can Dolokhov hypnotize fate? With his enormous chest exposed, Pierre, this short-sighted conscientious objector to dueling and killing, this awful shot, deals a near-mortal wound to the arrogant despoiler. Dolokhov's wound, like Andrey's, are just two of the many proofs supplied by Tolstoy that no form of behavior excepting readiness for accepting everything may beat the odds of contingency.

Of the many deaths in the novel, only that of Prince Andrey proves to be a true illumination. Andrey's death is the first in Tolstoy's oeuvre to be revealed, at least partially, from within the dying man's consciousness and thus from within his sphere of freedom. The only comparable act of dying, that of Praskukhin in the Sebastopol cycle, cannot compare due to the purely sensual perspective of that death. Andrey's pageant is altogether different, a stunning power play between freedom and entitlement to life that is not physical but rather involves love, and the need to lose it. Tolstoy presents this death as a slow *process* of coming to terms—a new approach that is unique not only for Tolstoy but also for the modern literary tradition. In a series of exits through the portal of death in his sleep, Andrey rehearses his semiconscious dying and a temporary retreat back into life upon awakening. In his sleep, he misses the conscious attachment to physical life, which he calls love, the medium of freedom by means of which he comprehends his place in the world: "'Love? What is love?,' he thought. Love stands in the way of death. Love is life. Everything, everything that I understand, I do only because I love. All is connected through love alone. Love is God and to die means—to me, this *particle of love*—to return to the common and the eternal source" (IV/I/16; 7: 69). Although these thoughts spell seeming consolation, Andrey knows that something is missing. His mental re-creation associates love and God with everything that attaches one to physical existence. If such existence is ended, the object of love cannot be identical with the sensual object; it will have to become an Idea of God, the transcendence of the physical. Apparently Tolstoy and Prince Andrey find the

Platonic leap wanting. Concepts of immortal ideas appear to Andrey "one-sided and personal, mental, lacking in evidence. And there was the same anxiety and lack of clarity. He fell asleep" (7: 70).

In his sleep Andrey encounters "that thing" (*ono*), the force without a name, gender, or shape: "Yes, this was death. I died—I woke up. Yes, death is reawakening. *His soul suddenly brightened,* and the veil that had been obstructing the unknowable was lifted before his soul's eye."[17] Because the illumination is portrayed as the embrace of the unknowable in a state of readiness, Tolstoy necessarily merges the two realms—reason and consciousness, necessity and freedom—in a condition that makes one complete to the point of the ethereal. Tolstoy felt it proper not to let Andrey die in his sleep but rather to force him to come back to the world of the living and exercise, in his final moments, his knowledge of the secret of existence in the presence of other "particles of love," those whom he used to love the most. When his sister Maria arrives, Andrey begins to speak about the Gospels but suddenly cuts himself short: "With a great effort to control himself, he attempted to return to life and adopted their point of view. 'Yes, it should seem pitiful to *them,*' he thought. And this is so easy. 'Look at the birds of the air; they neither sow nor reap but flock into barns, and yet your heavenly Father feeds them.'" Andrey initially wanted to tell these words to Maria but thought otherwise. Tolstoy's disclosure of the reason is startling: "*They* won't understand; those words so important to '*us*' are not important to '*them*'" (IV/I/15; 7: 65).[18]

In his secret prayer for Marie, Natasha, and his son, Andrey quotes a verse from the Lord's Prayer, which ends: "And can any of you by worrying add a single hour to your span of life? . . . So do not worry about tomorrow, for tomorrow will bring worries of its own. Today's trouble is enough for today" (Matt. 6: 26). Andrey's prayer is thus a continuation of Maria's prayer in the icon room early in the book and an embodiment of the true and fulfilled acceptance of the Lord's will, "the simple and great mystery of death." There can be no doubt that in 1868–1869 Tolstoy understands this death as true conversion to the mystery of the eternal. The word "mystery" in Russian (*tainstvo*) is neutral in gender and is linked to the finally accepted "that thing" (*ono*). It is for this reason that instead of the more appropriate and expected "Has he passed?" (*Konchilsia?*) Princess Maria asks: "Is it over?" (*Konchilos'?*) referring with respect to the great mystery of being (IV/I/16; 7: 72). The dead body of Andrey is the only corpse in the novel that does not induce horror. Andrey's godlike status as a sacred memory prefigures the discussion of the "reason of reasons" in the final part of the novel and the two epilogues, undercutting the validity of frequent claims that Andrey's cold rejection of earthly love prior to dying completes his logical progress toward the final demise.

"THAT THING" AND MAN'S FREEDOM

One of the difficulties in correctly identifying the belief system of *War and Peace* is the elusive status of God. He is infinity and the reason of reasons (IV/II/1; 7: 73), the copula harnessing all arbitrary wills, the miller, the clock-maker, the Architect of the Universe, the globe and the globe holder, the master of ceremonies, and the hive overseer who sets up new hives or caulks the dying ones. God's many oblique images reflecting the active life—chaotic bubbles, the mysterious force, "something," "that thing"—firmly impresses on the reader the novel's special monotheism: one law in many guises. God is most closely associated with everything that happens out of necessity: faith is a state of readiness to fulfill God's will; death is a terrifying mystery and a silent pact dividing and uniting man and God.

When Tolstoy was himself a soldier, he asked the Lord to forgive "them" for the Sebastopol manslaughter (47: 27). He wondered where he himself was in all this, and listed an excuse of an "insignificant worm" thrown into the "dirty space of war" (4: 10, 13) elaborating in several versions of his military tales and notes on the negative aspects of contemporary warriors who are alien to self-sacrifice, selflessness, or hard work (4: 285). His explorations allowed him to calibrate them by their degree of susceptibility to violence: the oppressed (those at peace with the idea that they must suffer), the oppressors (those who force on others the evil they have earlier endured), and the desperados (those convinced that all is permissible) (4: 287–88, 92). From his explanation of violence in the early 1860s, it appeared to be an unavoidable part of life. Modernity and progress, its counterpart, have developed the most effective tools for *simulating* unanimity and public peace rather than truly providing them.[19]

In *War and Peace*, Tolstoy put to test tools of thought and power, the institutions that by default are supposed to appease violent outbursts (nationalism, wars, religion, trade, cultural life), and found them wanting. His findings were despairing for he could not overcome his conviction that violence indeed is no more than a safety valve opening during cataclysms to let out the zoological rage and fury, and institutions of progress are themselves blind tools that assist in opening this valve. In discussing what affects crowds Tolstoy invariably employs the impersonal epithet "that thing," "something" (*chto-to*) that sets masses of people in motion (I/II/19; 4: 237)—nullifying the effort of individual will. If God acts on human crowds, he does not act on them morally. The astonishing and horrifying readiness for crime of a human speck in the crowd (*peschinka v tolpe*) that is ready to commit any crime or die when the order to act is issued is all too evident in Rostov's readiness to kill at Emperor Alexander's first hushed order (I/II/19; 4: 237). Or consider the needless drowning of the regiment of Polish *uhlans*, who are impatient to demonstrate their fervor to please Napoleon. Tolstoy calls these moods an eclipse of reason by ending the scene with the *uhlan* drowning with a Latin maxim: "Quos [Jupiter] vult perdere, dementat" (He whom Jupiter wills should perish, he shall deprive of reason) (III/I/2; 6: 15). The conclusion is terrifying: when necessity requires more blood and sacrifice, the Master deprives those who must die of reason, shutting out their instinct of self-preservation. In this sense Jupiter (the master of necessity), God, Napoleon (who watches the scene), and the narrator (who assumes responsibility for allowing ambiguity to exist) are all mass murderers.

Such scenes do not pacify the reader, who is told elsewhere—as in the example with Rostov in battle—that conscious life seeks its own self-protection; faced with losing life, victims alone "knew what life was to them" (IV/I/10; 7: 100). Executions of the commoner Vereshchagin by the patriotic crowd of his compatriots and of arrested Muscovite townsfolk by the French firing squad in which Pierre nearly died repeat the same scenario. Neither Mayor Rostopchin's billboards nor martial court rulings that permit outlawed victims to be dispatched summarily would be sufficient to force people to commit organized murder. Another force motivates those intent on killing. It is the elemental realization of power, of implementers of necessity, vested with them against their potential victims. Vereshchagin's admonition to Rostopchin and his murderers—"There is one God above us" (*odin Bog nad nami*)—falls on deaf ears. However, his whimper of pity toward himself after the first hesitant blow unleashes the fury of the crowd, which is now reassured of its fatal power. When the crowd that has just murdered Vereshchagin looks at its deed, it regards with horror that which was again done impersonally, without the conscious participation of a moral will: "Everybody would come up, glance at *that which has been done* and jostle his way back with horror, reproach, and astonishment" (III/III/25; 6: 360).

Following his explanation to Pierre, before the slaughter at Borodino, that war is not a game of chess but a grave necessity, Prince Andrey shrieks in a "thin and squeaky voice": "They will clash, as they will do tomorrow, to murder each other. How can God bear to look down and see and hear them?!" (III/II/25; 6: 219). Andrey's shriek is a protest against human and divine cruelty. If man is so conditioned by necessity, and God tolerates good things and evil things with equal indifference, man's discretion, his freedom, appears to be the only alternative. "How can he permit this?" Andrey wonders, without going one step further to doubt whether God exists at all if such evil is permissible, or whether He suffers with humanity the sins of His own imperfection.

War and Peace establishes that although war, death, and atrocities happen in spite of human will, they are nonetheless committed by a human hand, the "blind carrier of necessity" (15: 120), as the drafts bluntly explain. A fair copy finds a more acceptable formulation and calls human agency the particle swept up by the "inevitable course of events" (III/II/16; 6: 182). "That force" almost never overtakes man completely unawares, but in his futile effort to avoid its fatal arrival man looks away. Pierre outfits a regiment to pretend that his fatal personal mistakes have no meaning. At the critical moment when he needs to survive, he pretends not to recognize the preparations for Karataev's murder. The famous scene in which, unable to tear his eyes from Dolokhov's hands that mechanically deal the cards, Nikolai Rostov punts against his will and loses what he cannot afford to lose is emblematic of the mutual instrumental dependence of the manipulated and manipulators in scenes that take place in peaceful times.

Nature in the novel is hardly antagonistic to "that force." Its "beautiful, rotten organic life" (15: 58, 61) traps and ensnares human freedom just as much, resulting in some of the novel's most mesmerizing poetic passages.[20] One could say that Petya Rostov falls prey to his unforgettable communion with the stars on the eve of the shootout at daybreak, which filled his soul with a sense of inviolability and cost him his life. The old oak, which unexpectedly sprouts new foliage in the spring, prompts Prince Andrey to comment that "life is not finished at 31." It also causes him to fall in love with Natasha, who will betray him, and engage in law reforms under the liberal Speransky, who will disillusion him (II/III/1, 3; 5: 161, 165). Natasha's simultaneous "narrowness and physicality" and "that infinitely great and indefinite" quality that finds it easy to imagine infinity (II/III19; 5: 220) makes it impossible for Andrey to forgive the "female Magdalene" (II/V/11, 21; 5: 347, 384). The rewriting of Montesquieu's "necessary relations derived from the nature of things" from the point of view of the Code Napoleon under Speransky (II/III/7; 5: 178) represents the temporary infatuation of a human lawgiver who wishes that his life be "reflected on all," the appointment ending in disappointment.

The numerous instances of gazing at the sky practiced by Maria, Andrey, and Pierre are perilous to the same degree that they are awe-inspiring. Andrey's thoughts about the possibility of death on the eve of the Austerlitz battle whet his expansionist appetites: "I treasure this secret power and glory that flies right here above me, in this mist" (I/III/12; 4: 334). Lying supine under the empty, unreachable, majestic skies and enfeebled by a grave wound the following day, Andrey achieves a rather questionable epiphany reflecting the "emptiness of everything," the realization that there is nothing but infinity, quiescence, and stillness (I/III/16; 4: 354) of the "high, just and kind sky" (I/III/19; 4: 366–70). This does more than diminish Napoleon; it also diminishes the presence of a personal God, whose icon, a gift of Mary, Andrey is still wearing. "Wither this force—indefinite, incomprehensible, to which I can't address myself, and which, moreover, I can't express verbally—this great *all or nothing*, he was saying to himself, or this is that very God that was sewn in right here into this amulet by Princess Marie? There is nothing, nothing true except for the worthlessness of everything that is comprehensible to me, and greatness of something incomprehensible but more important!" (I/III/19; 4: 370).

Staring at the sky following old Bolkonsky's death inflicts dreadful pain on Princess Maria: "She wanted to think about something different; she wanted to pray and could do nothing. With her big, wide-open eyes she gazed at the moonlit darkness, and at every second she expected to see his dead face and felt that the stillness that hung over the house and in the house fettered her.—Dunyasha, she whispered.—Dunyasha!, she shrieked in a wild voice, and, having broken free of stillness, she ran towards the maids' quarters" (III/II12; 6: 164).[21] The starry sky that taught Pierre the art of remonstrance had impelled him to do some Kabalistic number crunching and imagine the connection between the comet of 1812 and his predestination for the world-saving mission to kill Napoleon (III/III/29; 6: 389).

If nature is conspiring with necessity, so is the fatalistic moral voice. "This happiness is not for you," a protective inner voice informed Pierre in the middle of his infatuation with Helene. But Pierre would not hear of it: "She was terribly close to him. She had power over him; between him and her there were no other obstacles except his own will" (I/III/1; 4: 260). "This must be and could not be otherwise—thought Pierre. And therefore it is no good asking whether this is good or evil" (I/III/2; 4: 268–69). Before his inner voice can interfere, after he had been deceived by his wife and Dolokhov "something frightening and repugnant" has already been growing inside him to cancel out his reason, and the terrifying Pierre challenges Dolokhov to a duel (II/I/3; 5: 25–28). Like faith and excessive questioning, morality seduces people into assuming false duties. Curiosity, however, is rarely a vice according to Tolstoy's brand of providence.

The same curiosity that made Pierre feel excited in the early stages of the Borodino affair pushes Natasha toward the horrible body of the wounded Andrey. Her heart freezing from "fear, horror and love," Natasha is drawn to Andrey's deathbed: "She imagined to herself some *horrible* body and stopped in *horror*, but *some insuperable force* drew her forward" (III/III/31; 6: 395). Natasha's reunion with Andrey was hardly inspired by Pierre's forgiveness of her on Andrey's behalf. The positive force that returned her to Andrey had repaired a similarly strong and unaccountable dark impulse, which threw her into Anatol's embrace ("I have no will—I love him"; II/V/14; 5: 359). The same type of force helped her convince the Rostovs to donate their horse carriages to transport the wounded and to jettison all of their possessions. Good deeds appear as another form of collective drunkenness and intoxication rather than a conscious choice. Those who a second earlier were crowding their "icons and coffers" on horse carts while neglecting the helpless and the wounded, now thoughtlessly dump icons and coffers to make room for the wounded—as if this was their original instinct.

The force that accomplishes everything in *War and Peace* acts without regard for moral exigency, sufficiency, and even apparent reasonableness. In both outer and inner expression, a human being can be "perfectly good" only on the upper rung of happiness, after engulfing too much life, when "man becomes perfectly kind and good, does not believe in the possibility of evil, unhappiness, and grief" (II/III/14; 5: 214). Even then, possessed of selfish ecstasy, he feels capable of crime and murder or is insensitive to the misfortune of someone close.[22] In a well-functioning, peaceful human hive, whose existence is threatened only by the greed of individual particles of life eager to swallow as much of it as possible, forgiveness and unselfish, unconscious acts are celebrated as God's victories. Tolstoy tends to reward trust in "that force" more lavishly than goodness.

In 1812 the Rostovs are bankrupt and Nikolai Rostov, who falls in love with Princess Maria, an heiress, has a chance to settle down happily in a marriage that is made in heaven and not out of convenience and simultaneously repair his family's finances. However, he is bound by his word to Sonya, whom he no longer loves, and can't break the engagement partly out of honesty and partly out of pride as the impoverished groom. In need of a miracle, Nikolai wishes that he could pray to God so that the prayer "could move mountains" and, clasping his hands, kneels under the icon of the Savior. "Moved by tender remembrance of Princess Marie, he began to pray the way he had not prayed in a long time. Tears welled in his eyes and in his throat." At this instant, a letter from Sonya arrives, dissolving their engagement and granting him his freedom. "He ran his eyes over the letter, reread it, standing in the middle of the room, his jaw dropped and his eyes fixed." But the reader already knows Tolstoy's explanation of Sonya's letter. She was forced into writing by the old Countess Rostova, who exploited Sonya's belief that her sole worth in life is giving up her share of earthly fortune to benefit others. Tolstoy does not think that this umpteenth ambiguity belies the wonder. Without a hint of irony he adds this eloquent coda. "The same thing he had just been praying for, certain that God will fulfill his prayer, was fulfilled. But Nikolai was astonished by this to such a degree, *as if this were something unusual*, as if he never expected this, and as if the fact that this was fulfilled so fast proved that *this was not coming from God, whom he was begging, but because of a sheer contingency*" (IV/I/6; 7: 33–34).

PIERRE AND HARNESSING

As the formerly friendly French officer drives the prisoners out, Pierre shudders when he recognizes in his suddenly impassive face the same neutral and genderless force that possessed everybody—"that thing, that thing again" (*ono*) during his narrowly escaped execution. It declares itself to be fateful (*rokovaia*) rather than merely "strange" (*strannaia*) (IV/II/13; 7: 109). In what follows, Pierre devises a means of resistance and of physical self-protection by "unharnessing himself" from the yoke of necessity as if it did not concern him personally. He does not return to the campfire to be near his comrades but walks straight into the French guard, who pushes him back into the doomed circle. Again Pierre refuses to join others. He sits by the *unharnessed* cart and thinks for an hour. Then he breaks out into gruff and complacent laughter (*tolstym, dobrodushnym smekhom*): "Ha-ha-ha! Pierre laughed. And he spoke aloud to himself: The soldier would not let me pass. They caught me, locked me up. They keep me in captivity. And who am I? Me? Me—my immortal soul! Ha-ha-ha! . . . ha-ha-ha! . .—he laughed with tears in his eyes" (IV/III/12; 7: 164). The new moon allows Pierre a glimpse of the expanses beyond the camp, "the bright, blurry infinity that enticed into its distance. Pierre looked at the sky, into the depth of departing, playful stars. 'And all of this is mine, and all of this is within me, and all of this is me!'—Pierre thought. And all of this they caught, imprisoned me in the barracks, barred by planks! He smiled and walked over to join his comrades and go to sleep" (7: 164).

This scene, which displays Tolstoy's artistic genius at its best, is usually misread as proof of immortality. However, as in every reading of Tolstoy's most significant episodes, attention to detail is all. First, what Tolstoy proves here is not immortality but inebriation with life so extreme that the desire to expand the boundary of personal existence transports the self outside itself into the outside world. Second, the scene is mildly self-ironic. Pierre does not laugh hysterically like a madman but laughs softly. In his trick with the stars he recognizes the literary tales from his Swiss youth, Xavier de Maistre's "Voyage Around My Room" and "Nocturnal Expedition Around My Room" being the first to come to mind. In those tales the star-gazing dreamer neglected the perils lying in wait for his body. He imagined his existence to be transfused exclusively into his cosmos-dwelling soul, only to burn his fingers and bump into a parapet. Third, Pierre's challenge to the captors is not defiant. "They keep me in captivity. And who is me? (*Kogo menia?*)," he asks rather than threatens ("who—me?").

By mentally unharnessing himself from participation in the fulfillment of necessity, Pierre calmly eats horsemeat and goes to sleep. Inspired by witnessing too much evil and calling forth unbearable questing about how one "must harness" (*sopriagat' nado*) necessity and a sense of justice after the Borodino debacle, his previous dream at Mozhaisk after the battle sent him in the wrong direction. Neglecting the fact that the words uttered by the riding master the morning he was waking up merely meant "harness the horses" (*zapriagat' nado*), he connected the dream with predictions of the Apocalypse promised by the comet of 1812. The Masonic calculus that deciphered the name of the devil in the numbers associated with Napoleon reinforced Pierre's delusion about being called to act on behalf of providence, that in him necessity and freedom crossed, "harnessed" themselves, summoning him to stab or shoot Napoleon. Pierre's earlier harnessing dream was prompted by his unfinished dispute with Prince Andrey on the eve of Borodino, in which Pierre had been warned against playing chess with necessity and giving in to the precise temptation "to harness everything," for it is difficult to unite in one's soul the meaning of all (III/III/9; 6: 304). Andrey warns Pierre of the danger accompanying unimpeded understanding of one's role in the "coincidence of all arbitrary wills" (III/III/1; 6: 275–77) and recommends stopping short of the final "why" (III/II/24–25; 6: 211, 219).

Pierre, however, refuses to listen. His carefully replayed solitaire and manipulation of the French alphabet send him on his mission of "l'Russe Besuhof": "On behalf of all, I must accomplish this or die. Not me . . . but the hand of Providence puts you to death . . . I will say" (III/III/27; 6: 370–73).What he learned at the unharnessed cart is the same discovery of his "salvation valve" (*spasitel'nyi klapan*), which lets one continue to participate in the immortal movement of life (IV/III/12; 7: 164), or what the draft calls "life transference" (15: 137). The story at the campfire about the wrongly accused merchant who died an old man in prison before his proof of innocence and pardon arrived—the last tale by Karataev that warrants the acceptance of the transcendent evil to expiate human injustice through God's love—fills Pierre's heart with a mysterious awe (IV/III/13; 7: 166). However, it does not harness Pierre into a sense of responsibility for helping Karataev, who futilely looks at him the following day, too weak to walk and about to be shot by the French. Tolstoy requires this paradoxical discovery of the moment of truth through a conscious move toward softening submission (*smiagchenie*).When the gulf separating questioning and incomprehension widens beyond endurance, it should close and questioning should stop.[23]

Pierre's character is constructed in such a way that he moves endlessly forward and in reverse between the temptation to harness and the desire for submission. Let us revisit some earlier scenes from the times of peace. To prove himself right by forgiving Helene in order to move back in with her on Bazdeev's orders, Pierre assumes a comfortable principle that "nobody is right, nobody is guilty, and so she isn't guilty either"(II/III/8; 5: 183). In order not to think whether it is right to follow Bazdeev's invitation to join the Masonic order a few years earlier, Pierre thinks: "I am guilty and must bear . . . but what? . . . Ah, all is nonsense; all is relative and independent of me." Asking oneself about guilt is tantamount to asking who is responsible for Robespierre's Reign of Terror: "Who is guilty? Nobody. Live while you are alive. . . . The moment he soothed himself, the same round of questions returned" (II/I/2; 5: 34). When Pierre forgives Anatol and Natasha, without thinking whether his decision may serve the goals of the Grand Architect, he instinctively arrives at the right idea that as long as there is life nothing can be lost forever and he confesses his love to Natasha: "All is lost?—he repeated. If I were not myself but the handsomest, smartest, and best man in the world, and if I were free I would this minute fall on my knees to ask for your hand and your love" (II/V/22; 5: 387).[24] Immediately the terrible question about the vanity of everything earthly stopped bothering him.

"If I were not myself" is a motto of Tolstoy's disconsolate and dissatisfied, converting seeker practiced as well in Pierre's unending self-accounting.[25] Several chapters excerpted from his diary, running from mid-November to the end of December in fictional time, and which begins with Bazdeev's advice, offer a rare glimpse into this uninterruptible act, which Tolstoy almost never permits his favorite characters. The advice of a dying master with a cancerous bladder is, in effect, a rejection of the Masonic doctrine. To help Pierre out of his misery, Bazdeev replaces the artificial Masonic triad with an ontological task: a self-accounting that engenders change; perfection following the survival of life's real turmoil; and achievement of the love of death, or complete readiness, which Bazdeev is experiencing in his last days (II/III/8; 5: 184). By depriving Pierre of the comforts and conventions of civilized life, its difficult excesses, and its freedom to choose, his unconscious slip from the unrealized assassin into captivity helped him discover "a new . . . experience of joy and strength of life." Captivity filled him with a feeling of "*readiness for everything* and moral tidiness," while imposing a new responsibility on him, namely, that of respect for his friends in captivity, which "bound him" (*obiazyval ego*) (IV/II/12; 7: 107). However, in the ensuing retreat of the convoy at the urging of "that force," Pierre unharnesses himself from the bond and breaks away in order to survive, and his moral tidiness disappears in the process.

Pierre's last visionary dream in the novel, his dream about the globe, recaptures the theme of readiness, and is associated meaningfully with substitute God figures: the Masonic globe; Bazdeev's bladder; Karataev's dark lake (dew) and the living moisture; the poetic, life-affirming sap of Schiller, Goethe, and Tolstoy's earlier works. Pierre observes, "Life is everything. Life is God. All transposes and moves, and this movement is God. And while there is life, there is a delight of *divine self-consciousness*. To love life is to love God. It is more difficult and saintly to love this life in your suffering, and in the guiltlessness of [all] suffering" (IV/III/15; 7: 169). The dream, which occurs right after Karataev's shooting, balances two opposing movements: the maximum engulfing of life by man (his freedom) and the gradual engulfing of man's life by death (necessity). When Pierre thinks that he recognizes Karataev, the voice begins a dictation of a geography lesson through the person of his Swiss tutor, who speaks French.[26] Pierre is shown a globe that is a living, revolving orb without depth. The surface of the globe is covered in tightly compressed droplets or bubbles (*kapli*) that are moving, changing place, merging into one another, or splitting into many droplets. Every droplet attempts to spill its contents, thereby occupying more space, but other droplets, attempting to do the same, compress it, at times annihilate it, and sometimes merge with it. "'This is life,' said the old teacher. 'How simple and clear this is—thought Pierre.—How could I have not known this before?' God is in the middle and every droplet attempts to widen and reflect him in the greatest dimension. And it grows, merges, compresses, and is annihilated on the surface, retreats underneath, and comes to surface again. Here is Karataev, he spilled over and disappeared.—Vous avez compris, mon enfant—said the teacher." Pierre wakes up to hear the real address from the French soldier: "Vous avez compris, sacré nom" (IV/III/15; 7: 170).

The dream about engulfing and being engulfed ends on a disjunction of unity. In the dream "Mon enfant" would be an address from Father God and "Sacré nom" (sacred name) would not be a profanity, a desecrated name. Pierre wakes up into the desecrated reality: "Sacré nom" is a curse of the retreating French soldier, running around is the dog of the murdered Karataev, and he soon sees the dead body of Petya Rostov, whose squadron liberates him. This dream gives way to Pierre's temporary acceptance of the tense, ever-changing disjunction between freedom and necessity as the new norm of life. "The joyous feeling of freedom" after he wakes up from his illness is possible only because he stops thinking about necessity and the reason of reasons: "this very *absence of a goal* afforded him this *complete, joyous consciousness of freedom.* . . . He could not have a goal because he now had faith—not in some rules, or words, or thoughts, but a faith in the living, always palpable God . . . and the eternal and the infinite in everything. . . . Now to this question—what for? There was a ready answer in his soul: because there is god, *that God without whose willingness not a hair will perish off man's head*" (IV/IV/12; 7: 217).

By inserting this last phrase, Tolstoy achieves the desired circularity: we witness the state of readiness achieved in fulfillment of the promise God gave to Maria at the beginning of the novel. The necessary conclusion is achieved in the two human matches made in moments of coincident free desire: Pierre and Natasha, who both meet when they rediscover their revived power of life, and Nikolai Rostov and Maria, who are drawn together like magnets through their contrasting poles of submission and domination. Tolstoy, however, does not conclude the novel with their reunion. He frees Pierre from the untenable role of a moral purist who wears his "misfortunes, suffering . . . captivity and horse meat" with a new pride and misses no opportunity to verify his newly achieved correctness. The first question that he asks Maria and Natasha, following a long separation and a brief sermon to preface his visit, is whether Prince Andrey submitted and softened before he died: "Yes, yes, yes, this is so—Pierre was saying, bending forward over Princess Marie and *greedily listening* to her story.—Yes, yes: so he quieted down? Softened? . . . His shortcomings—if any—did not stem from him. So he softened?" (IV/IV/16; 7: 230). Tolstoy only concludes the last chapter of the narrative part of the novel when he makes Pierre drop his guard altogether without recourse to his little inner god and give in to his love for Natasha. Only when he is fully human and his happy madness, selfishness, and his new, faulty judgments are revived is he truly God's. "This is untrue, untrue"—Pierre cried out in response to Natasha's wish for a recurrent traumatic repetition of her elevating moment of suffering—"I am not guilty because I am alive and want to live, and neither are you" (IV/IV/17; 7: 236).

By liberating his human character's unpredictable reactions, Tolstoy saves him from becoming an automaton in the clutches of necessity, wound up by the Masonic watchmaker that the fictional Napoleon imagines him to be in the novel: "Our body is a living machine. It is constructed for this" (III/II/29; 6: 233). Napoleon places the bodies of his soldiers as well as his own on his chessboard of a battlefield: "The chess figures have been positioned; the play will begin tomorrow" (6: 231). Tolstoy invariably juxtaposes such mechanistic and theatrical treatments with the view he supports, in this case Andrey's comment to Pierre that the war is not a game of chess, but a serious form of necessity.

By rescuing man's freedom, Tolstoy simultaneously rescues the creative force of necessity. With the novel practically finished, in 1868 Tolstoy sent a remarkable letter to the literary veteran Mikhail Pogodin, a friend of Pushkin and Gogol, stressing that he had achieved what he had hoped for: "My thoughts about the boundary between freedom and necessity and my view of history is not an accidental paradox that has briefly preoccupied me. These thoughts are the result of mental toil spanning my entire life and comprise an inalienable part of that worldview, which the Lord alone knows what labors and sufferings have worked out in me to produce perfect tranquility and happiness" (61: 195). The disrobing of Napoleon and Pierre's new illumination do not complete Tolstoy's system of belief in 1868. He added the Epilogues to the narrative corpus of the novel around the time the letter to Pogodin was composed. The role of the Epilogues in the edifice of *War and Peace* is the subject of the next chapter.

NOTES

1. L. N. Tolstoy, second epilogue to *War and Peace*, in *Sobranie sochinenii v dvadtsati dvukh tomakh*, ed. M. B. Khrapchenko et al. (Moscow: Khudozhestvennaia literatura, 1978–1985): 7: 350. Based on accepted practice in Tolstoy scholarship, all references to the final, definitive text of the novel are to this edition. Subsequent parenthetical references appear as follows: the first roman numeral refers to the book; the second roman numeral refers to the part of that book; the Arabic numeral refers to the chapter; the arabic numeral following the semicolon refers to the volume; lastly, the arabic numeral following the colon refers to the page. The two epilogues are identified as follows: E1 refers to the first epilogue; E2 refers to the second epilogue. Both are followed by chapter, volume, and page. Drafts, prefaces, notes, explanations, and letters by Tolstoy concerning the novel that are not identified by standard references to the text (book/part/chapter, etc.) refer to volumes in Tolstoy's Jubilee edition (1928–58). References to Tolstoy's explanatory note concerning the novel, "A Few Words about the Book *War and Peace*" (Neskol'ko slov po povodu knigi "Voina i mir"), are to *Sobranie sochinenii v dvadtsati dvukh tomakh*. The note was first published in *Russian Archive* in March 1868.

2. Tolstoy is here relating to Aunt Alexandrine a misfortune that befell Ivan Borisov, his hunting friend and Fet's brother-in-law, on the night of October 11, 1859. A religious man, for thirteen years prior to their marriage Borisov had hopelessly courted Fet's sister. He proposed twice and was rejected, barely surviving a suicide attempt thanks to a misfire. Only after Fet's sister showed signs of a mental disease and doctors recommended marriage was Borisov's new proposal reluctantly accepted. The young wife soon recovered and fell in love with the good-hearted Ivan, delivering him a healthy son. One night in 1859, when Turgenev, Tolstoy, and Borisov were sharing a bungalow during a hunting excursion, Fet's letter arrived informing Turgenev about the irreversibility of his sister's worsened condition. It was Tolstoy's mission to inform his friend of the tragedy and thus ruin his short-lived happiness.

3. See, for example, his impatience with the literary routine of character creation, recorded in the diary in November 1856 (47: 199).

4. See the letter to A. A. Tolstaya dated January 18, 1865 (61: 71).

5. See especially Tolstoy's letter to Fet dated February 23, 1860 (6: 234–36).

6. For in-depth discussions of the novel's genesis, structure, chronology, causality, genre, design, dynamic, theology, psychology, and narrative voices see, in addition to the previously mentioned studies by Clay, Gustafson, Morson, Orwin: John Bayley, *Tolstoy and the Novel* (Chicago: University of Chicago Press, 1966); Isaiah Berlin,

"The Hedgehog and the Fox," in *Russian Thinkers*, ed. Aileen Kelly (London: Penguin, 1979), 22–81; Sergey Bocharov, *Roman Tolstogo Voina i Mir* (Moscow: Khudozhestvennaia literatura, 1978); R. F. Christian, *Tolstoy's War and Peace* (Oxford: Oxford University Press, 1962); Kathryn B. Feuer, *Tolstoy and the Genesis of War and Peace*, eds. Robin Feuer Miller and Donna Tussing Orwin (Ithaca, N.Y. and London: Cornell University Press, 1996); Jeff Love, *The Overcoming of History in War and Peace* (Amsterdam: Rodopi, 2004); Natasha Sankovitch, *Creating and Recovering Experience: Repetition in Tolstoy* (Stanford, Calif.: Stanford University Press, 1998); Rimvydas Silbajoris, *War and Peace: Tolstoy's Mirror of the World* (London: Prentice-Hall International, 1995); and Andrew Baruch Wachtel, *An Obsession with History: Russian Writers Confront the Past* (Stanford, Calif.: Stanford University Press, 1994).

7. Silbajoris, *War and Peace: Tolstoy's Mirror of the World*, 35. See also Morson's essay "War and Peace" in Orwin, *The Cambridge Companion to Tolstoy*, 65–79, in which he revised his bias against Tolstoy's "absolute language," this didactic voiceover hovering above the reader and characters. Morson celebrates infinite contingency, ordinariness, presentness, and the wisdom of practical knowledge, Tolstoy's guide for life's journey. Morson also finds that the novel works precisely in its "non-narrative" sphere, concluding: "Development itself: contingent events, unburdened by a predetermined futurity or overall structure. The shape of *War and Peace* derives precisely from its central ideas about time. Might not its unsurpassed realism be taken as demonstration that those ideas really do describe life as we experience it?" (78). The most theological reading of the novel thus far is Richard Gustafson's *Leo Tolstoy: Resident and Stranger*, specifically chapter 5, "The Ways to Know" (218–55). Although Gustafson is mostly interested in how characters overcome the dilemma of finitude and infinity, he often adduces extratextual proofs from Orthodox theology and Tolstoy's later diaries.

8. See Orwin, *Tolstoy's Art and Thought*, 102, 110. On Tolstoy and Herzen's weaving the carpet, see also Patricia Carden, "The Expressive Self in War and Peace" in *Canadian-American Slavic Studies*, vol. 12 (1978): 519–34, especially page 525. Donna Orwin beautifully sums up the discussion in her *Tolstoy's Art and Thought*, 233–38.

9. "But you can't wait, Prince, in these minutes. Pensez, il y va du salut de son âme. . . . Ah, c'est terrible, les devoirs d'un Chrétien" (Think of it. It is about the salvation of his soul. Ah! This is terrible, the duty of a Christian) (I/I/12; 4: 67). Note also the hesitation over the lateness of the holy father hired to perform the mystery (I/I/18; 4: 90).

10. Free movement is forbidden to the Orthodox even during regular services and especially during the performance of one of the seven greatest mysteries. See T. A. Bernshtam, "Russkoe tserkovnoe obshchestvo v kontse XV-pervoi polovine XIX veka," in *Prikhodskaia zhizn' russkoi derevni* (St. Petersburg: Russian Academy of Sciences/Peterburgskoe vostokovedenie, 2005), 147–69, esp. 151.

11. Cf. Luke 21.18: "But not a hair of your head will perish. By your endurance you will gain your souls."

12. For Abrosimova's expostulations of Orthodox piety, see Tolstoy's ironic but sympathetic description of her (II/V/12; 5: 349).

13. "Platon" is the Russian version of "Plato." "Kara-" is Turkic for "black" and "tal" / "tai" is Turkic for "lake" and Hebrew for "dew."

14. The rotund nature of Platon's physical body, plus his roundabout, ingratiating ways, although stressed in the final version, are especially emphasized in the drafts, which state unequivocally that "his figure approached the circle" (15: 27).

15. A similar stampede almost claimed the life of Petya Rostov during the service for the victory of Russian troops at the Cathedral of Dormition (III/I/21; 6: 96–97).

16. The protective icon given by Maria Ivanovna Khlopova to her son, Captain Khlopov, in "The Raid" (*Nabeg*, 1852), which does not prevent him from being wounded but keeps him alive, is played off harmoniously against Plato's maxim that courage is knowledge of what must be feared. A collective prayer of soldiers in "Wood-felling" (*Rubka lesa*, 1855) and "Sebastopol in December," "a slender choir of virile voices," is certainly unlike the above scene in *War and Peace* (3: 72, 4: 6–9 resp.). Cf. also Prince Andrey's contemptible reference to the Russian army, quoted from the cynical diplomat Bilibin: "And here is your dear Warrior Orthodoxy" (Voilà le cher pravoslavnoe voinstvo) (I/II/13; 4: 209).

17. In substituting "soul's eye" for the more idiomatic "mind's eye" I am remaining faithful to Tolstoy's original. It is important to Tolstoy that linguistic signs of eternal ideas coincide with the fulfillment of these ideas in Andrey's spiritual experience.

18. If it were not for its clearly religious overtones, Tolstoy's terminology, specifically his division into "us" (those who have made themselves privy to the form-shaping meaning of death) and into "they" (das Man, those who don't) could very well fit into Heidegger's discussion of the same in *Being in Time*, 107–22, 233–41.

19. For Tolstoy's developing views on progress, see chapter 3 of this book.

20. The only character in the novel who is immune to the perils of star-gazing is Natasha, who easily imagines immortality while looking at the sky the night Prince Andrey is a guest at Otradnoe. He falls in love with her vitality while overhearing her conversation with Sonya. See Orwin's different interpretation of the role of the sky and nature in *Tolstoy's Art and Thought*, 136–37.

21. There can be no doubt that Tolstoy derives a secret pleasure in forcing a conventional Orthodox believer to disbelieve in immortality.

22. Take, for example, Nikolai Rostov's thinking about the possibility of killing or stealing after he hears Natasha's singing or Prince Andrey's not noticing Pierre's sour expression when he comes to confess his love for Natasha. Consider also "the highest joy" enveloping Princess Maria's false sense of duty when she receives the erroneous dispatch about Prince Andrey's death at Austerlitz.

23. Morson feels that wise characters in the novel believe that everything that happens occurs for some unclear reason (*Hidden in Plain View*, 90). Orwin interprets Tolstoy's submission to necessity as a kind of protective epistemological modesty (*Tolstoy's Art and Thought*, 104).

24. In first castigating and then begging forgiveness of Anatol, Pierre apologizes for his own sins and selfishness. His speech to Anatol is also addressed to himself: "You can't fail to understand, lastly, that besides your own pleasure there is the happiness and peace of other people, that you destroy a whole life only because you are willing to have some fun" (II/V/20; 5: 380). We next see Anatol mortally wounded on

the operating table at Borodino, near Prince Andrey, who also mentally forgives his enemy.

25. It turns out that the triple goal of the Masonic order—preservation and cognition of the mystery; self-purification for the receipt of the mystery; correction of humanity via self-perfection—applies to Pierre only where the importance of self-scrutiny is concerned (II/III/8; 5: 184–85). The following passage is typical: "All this time there continued in Pierre's soul a complex and difficult work of inner development that was disclosing much to him and that led him to many spiritual doubts and joys" (II/III/9; 5: 188).

26. See Orwin's elaboration of the Rousseau link in *Tolstoy's Art and Thought*, 139.

Chapter Five

The Unfinished Battle:
The Case With the Epilogues

> I am free when I am conscious of myself. I am subject to laws when I mentally project myself (15: 255).

WRITING AS A FORM OF RELIGION

History would have remained an indifferent topic for Tolstoy had he not used the space and time of *War and Peace* to explore the simultaneous mutability and entrapment of human life in the constant ebb and flow of the historical sea. His desire to examine the nature of individual quests both in isolation and within massive social movements reflects his continued interest in German Romantic philosophy, which aimed at restoring the "lost image of God" in the "internal consciousness" and "the outward conduct and experiences of life."[1] At the start of his writing enterprise, Tolstoy held a similar view, first formulated in Friedrich Schlegel's philosophy of history, which combines bird's-eye view of the historical life of humanity with the limited scope of the everyday (47: 203–4).[2] Schlegel's lectures on the philosophy of history explained that as soon as you think about the present moment "now," it already belongs to the past. The historian divines the future by looking at the fragment in order to achieve "the progressive restoration in humanity of the effaced image of God."[3] Tolstoy agrees that only fragments are available for human perception. In the third volume of the book he practically repeats and supports Schlegel's points, namely, that in order to deal with fragments of historical time, the best methodology is that of creative and dynamic fatalism, or progressive restoration of the divine, for the explication of those phenomena whose significance we do not understand. Tolstoy echoes Schlegel that "to the all-seeing eye of providence every human life presents a point of interest" as a "species of history, cognizable and visible to that eye only."[4] Nevertheless, despite the predetermined nature and inevitability of his every action—more obvious in the fates of so-called outstanding men of history, "in which man inevitably fulfills the laws prescribed to him"—there is freedom in man (III/I/1; 6: 10).

Tolstoy's first premise for his philosophical postlude appears early in the first epilogue: "If one admits that human life may be governed by reason, the very possibility of life will be destroyed" (E1/I; 7: 249). Human questioning itself is as much an instrument of free will as it is of necessity. While claiming that there is reason for everything, Tolstoy simultaneously insists that "nothing is the reason" because any event is only "a coincidence of those conditions under which any vital, organic, elemental event" should take place (III/I/1; 6: 11). Before embarking on his epilogues, Tolstoy nowhere provides as strong a counterargument in favor of "inorganic" decisions, in which human will to do good or be spiritual has its own vital ground other than freedom of pursuing personal happiness. Consequently, it is hard to make the case for a reality of informed spiritual growth among his protagonists, who in their best moments decide that to be happy, they must accept that their goals are empty and meaningless. For Schlegel's philosophical enterprise, which overlooks personal destinies and concentrates on heroes and prophets, it is enough to penetrate "into the hidden decrees of divine wisdom" or at least "uplift a corner of the mysterious veil which covers them."[5] What, then is enough for literature?

In addition to the rather transparent presence of Schlegel's theories, Tolstoy's ideas about historical necessity and freedom were most likely—perhaps through Stankevich—also influenced by Hegel. Stankevich used Hegel's renowned metaphor involving the coupling (or harnessing) of world history and freedom in the catastrophic emptying of experience into time; in his discussion of the danger resulting from the narrowing of these concepts into a system of "beliefs" as applied to imaginative literature, Stankevich, Tolstoy's idol at the end of the 1850s, saw in Gogol the example of a good "coupling" or harnessing (*sopriazhenie*) of life and art to which Tolstoy aspired.[6] In the same vein as by admitting that human life may be governed by reason, the very possibility of life will be destroyed; by admitting that a work of writing may be governed by reason, the very possibility of writing will be destroyed.

Tolstoy was adamant in insisting that the novel partook of a typical novelistic setting rather than a typical novelistic denouement. He was unperturbed in denying the obvious because, where the story line is concerned, the novel ends on the theme of marriage and peaceful family life, with necessity only waiting to intervene and strike in the hazy future of the Decembrist debacle, whereas it begins at a salon where the idle chatter on the French terror concerns who makes history. Tolstoy claimed that each of the four books, as well as each part within those books, has its own "independent interest" (*nezavisimyi interes*).[7] Because he refused to rewrite the historical denouement of 1805, 1807, 1812, or 1820, all changes of attitude toward life must constitute that very independent interest that holds the novel together and propels its movement toward the appointed end. A careful analysis of what forces characters in *War and Peace* to change and how these changes occur reveals a startling picture of inconsistency and arbitrariness of their spiritual needs, on the one hand, and the seesaw motion of their choices and decisions, on the other. If these random choices accommodate necessity and the laws of life, as Tolstoy understands and upholds them in the novel, they should represent paradigms of positive conversion. If they do not, they celebrate the triumph of the casual, of blind chance and arbitrary whim, or the "nonsense of detail."[8]

"Can the freedom of the human will be demonstrated from self-consciousness?" Following Schopenhauer, we may well wonder how much Schopenhauer's prize-winning response to the question influenced Tolstoy in terms of the extent of freedom necessary to satisfy the "independent interest" of personal quest.[9] After all, the study of self-consciousness in history should be important for the author whose career now spans a decade and a half of relentless self-examining. Schopenhauer reckons as manifestations of willing all manner of desiring, striving, and detestation, in short, "all affects and passions."[10] Simultaneous with this picture of rather moody and fickle willing, Schopenhauer is strict about the absolute constancy of human character, which remains the same throughout life; man already *is* what he wills. Therefore, "all that he ever does follows of necessity."[11] Tolstoy's heroes of *War and Peace* do not react to situations as a result of their unchangeable character and often react out of character should necessity outside their will require it. This is Tolstoy's first correction of Schopenhauer.

The *fabula* of the fourth book that concludes the "narrative" part of the novel ends with Natasha accepting the necessity of Pierre's departure for Saint Petersburg: "This must needs be" (*Tak nado*). The first epilogue, in which we see a final glimpse of the surviving heroes, also ends with the acknowledgment of the unavoidable that serves the interest of a higher necessity. Unless circumstances beyond their control or unexpected personal decisions intervene, according to their face-off at the end of the first epilogue, five years later, during the Decembrist affair of 1825, Nikolai Rostov and Pierre Bezukhov will become political enemies. Because he is so willing to oblige, and because the conditions of the affair will override his will, Nikolen'ka Bolkonsky will perish in the fray. Nikolen'ka's sole preoccupation is with whether "He," his late father Prince Andrey, would support Pierre, and he imagines that Andrey would. Pierre replies unwillingly and equivocally to

Nikolen'ka's question about Prince Andrey's possible support of violent action—"maybe, I don't know."

Pierre now contemplates the removal of Napoleon's victor, Tsar Alexander I because "Sire only indulges in mysticism" and wants to know none of the dismal political situation at home and in Europe (E1/14; 7: 295). Because Alexander's mysticism and renunciation of his will to God is praised by the historical narrator a little earlier in reflection of the book's growing conviction that history needs indeed be left alone to necessity, Pierre's new regicide plans look in this context no better than another dangerous yet unavoidable folly. This interpretation by association would be misleading in its simplicity. Pierre engages in the secret society lest "tomorrow's Pugachev arrives to slaughter my kids and yours" (E1/14; 7: 297). Pierre's folly is his lack of foresight about historical agency. The Decembrist formations of the Union of Welfare of Saint Petersburg, which he joins in order to act preventively, were indeed notorious for their lack of agreement on the course and severity of action that could stop autocratic and popular violence. By leaving the results of the debate in chapter 14 of the first epilogue inconclusive, Tolstoy implies that neither Pierre nor anyone else could enjoy the gift of such foresight.

What is the meaning of these multiple reactions to the as yet unrealized decision? It is Tolstoy's fitting postlude to the novel on freedom and necessity and a prelude to the philosophical expostulation thereof in the second epilogue. If the new Pugachev arrives, it will not happen because of exemplary masters such as Count Nikolai. For Pierre the Russian peasant, the *moujik*, remains the unknown factor, which he accepted as the ultimate response to life's wisdom after captivity. Unlike Pierre, Nikolai knows the peasant firsthand. Moreover, Nikolai Rostov's political views might change in favor of evolutionary development of society once he has read Sismondi, Rousseau, and Montesquieu, the books on public peace and safety that represent his latest acquisitions.[12] Nikolai's up-to-date choice of books is anything but arbitrary. Tolstoy inverts Pierre's irony against his "unthinking" and plodding brother-in-law by turning it against Pierre. Nikolai and Countess Maria think that Pierre reads too fast and too voraciously and is indiscriminately swayed by certain novel opinions. Pierre's Kantian project to form an alliance of the virtuous is not necessarily a greater folly against higher reason than his earlier projects involving a duped Masonic tycoon, an epic *bogatyr'* arming a Russian military host, or a stymied political assassin. At least the way Pierre sees it, he has again "united all," harnessed all anew in his new plan of salvation. If neither Pierre nor anyone else could enjoy the gift of such foresight, the novel's conclusion on Nikolen'ka's obstinate "prophetic dream," which disregards Uncle Pierre's hesitant "maybe," should be given more attention than it commonly receives.

In his dream that Nikolen'ka Bolkonsky experiences that night and that concludes the first epilogue and the narrative sections of the novel, Pierre, with Nikolen'ka by his side, is seen leading an army of "fils de la Vierge." These celestial and surreal soldiers lightly hover in the autumn air like white tufts of slanting filament—perhaps threads of mite nets seen through the mist, perhaps remnants of blotting paper and down from the quills on Nikolai Rostov's table that Nikolen'ka had obliviously crumpled and destroyed during the debate on the Union of Welfare. The army, wearing helmets from the illustrated book by Plutarch, is marching toward glory. Suddenly the threads entangle the army and muddle their movements. With the abrupt disappearance of Pierre, the army is opposed by the menacing figure of Count Nikolai. An impending collision of progressive and regressive impulses notwithstanding, Nikolen'ka senses approval through a weak signal that he receives in what must be a sign of transcendent love sent by Prince Andrey to his son. The signal is too faint and Nikolen'ka wakes up in horror. Nightmare and terror only confirm his decision to "burn his hand" in the fire of history. He implores God to let him succeed in repeating the feats of Plutarch's heroes and do even more—so that even He, his Father, were glad.

In a slanting and oblique manner, the conclusion of the first epilogue informs the reader that in literary terms, Tolstoy prefers an arch-Romantic progressive-regressive doing and undoing through fancy of the edifice of historical experience. Nikolen'ka's dream is Tolstoy's tribute to free but reasonably ordered poetic imagination, which implants in the poet's mind the fantasy preordained by the highest laws of creation. At first Tolstoy was stymied in his enterprise: "The necessity to bind through fancy those images, pictures, and thoughts that were borne in me by themselves, became so repellent to me that I would give up what was already begun and would despair about the possibility of expressing all that I was willing and needed to say."[13] "Willing and needed" is an eloquent confirmation of the fact that writing itself is an embodiment of the struggle between freedom and necessity. The next phrase confirms Tolstoy's deliberate choice of words: "*War and Peace* is something that the author *willed* and *was able to* express in that form in which *it happened to be expressed.*"[14]

The creative dissonance of reason and consciousness (*raznoglasie*) thus occasioned two dynamic voices, themselves a necessity: "This dissonance is also not something that is erratic, but that is inevitable. While describing a historical epoch, a historian and an artist have two completely different subjects. Just as the historian would not be right in attempting to represent a historical personage in his entirety, in the vast complexity of his relationship to all aspects of life . . . so the artist would fail to fulfill his task if he interpreted the personage as a historian would, by presenting him always in his historical meaning."[15] Tolstoy adds that if the two professional tasks split, the two provinces of cognition—reasonable forms of perception (laws of necessity) and essential knowledge of life (consciousness and freedom)—will be sundered. Only by joining them together can "a clear representation of life result." Tolstoy's "clear representation of life," a polemical reference to Schopenhauer's *World as Will and Representation*, contains links to alternative conceptions of freedom and necessity that he left in a state of conditional truce in the copies of the novel he published. What he left unresolved continues to appear in his notebooks, in his engagement with the Gospels, Hobbes, Hume, Priestley, Augustine, Luther, Kant, Schelling, Schopenhauer, and Hegel. These confrontations that led him to the point of conversion are the subject of the next sections.

VITAL FORCE AND DEITY IN DEBATES ON CONSCIOUSNESS AND THE LAW

In one of his work notebooks Tolstoy outlined the idea for a second, "philosophical" epilogue to conclude *War and Peace*: "To show that people, in obedience to zoological laws, never understand these laws, and, in pursuing their personal goals, involuntarily carry out universal laws. And to show how this comes about. It is especially obvious during cataclysms. (There is lust, which halts the proliferation where there is overpopulation.) There is a safety valve everywhere."[16] This is an intriguing and adversely layered proposition. The novel just established for Pierre and others that the safety valve consists in distracting one's attention from the unanswerable probing of divine law and its brand of justice, and leaving open the possibility for freedom. It also established that freedom is not reducible to the pursuit of personal interest. In their best and freest, always intimate moments, characters in the novel are grateful for the divine richness of life, while even at their worst moments the collective scenes do not stoop to zoology, or mere animal life, but rise up to reflect the mystery of what triggers collective reactions. Yet the plan for the epilogue suggests that people should unwittingly obey zoological laws to serve the purposes of the universal, higher laws. The unthinkable denigration of the human role in history laid bare in Tolstoy's draft is only half as damaging as his equation of life solely with nature.

Tolstoy's teachers Montesquieu and Rousseau had suggested that laws are derived from the nature of things, but not exclusively from nature as such. Their explanation of the web of "necessary relations" that weigh down upon life put forward a more sophisticated, deistic legal network, in which all beings have their laws, the deity has its laws, the material world has its laws, and the intelligences superior to man have theirs, while man has his own laws too. "What a legalistic universe!" Tolstoy must have thought to himself. Precisely because there are so many different subsets of laws not governed by one universal, divine law, litigation between the legal systems is endless and meaningless. Kant suggested that the litigation should be conducted individually from the point of view of the autonomous moral law, fulfilling the *summum bonum* of history.[17] Hegel begged to differ, suggesting that the litigation of universal history reveals and fulfills the universal law socially, treating man as its tool.[18] Thus, society and the state are the two forms in which freedom in conformity with the absolute law is objectively realized: "Only that will which obeys law is free; for it obeys itself—it is independent and so free."[19] In between these points of view, first Schelling and then Schopenhauer interposed their theories of religious and atheistic freedom, respectively. These philosophies and their Russian refractions are the undercurrents behind the painstaking rewriting of the epilogue, a witness to Tolstoy's metaphysical quandary.

In the drafts Tolstoy relies heavily on the philosophical solutions of "the great thinkers of modern philosophy," including Aristotle, Cicero, Augustine, Aquinas, Hobbes, Descartes, Spinoza, Locke, Kant, Fichte, Schelling, Hegel, and ending with Schopenhauer. According to Tolstoy, starting from the observations of the will in nature (*der Wille in der Natur*), by a circuitous route Schopenhauer arrives at what appears to be the summit of his philosophy, the immediate consciousness of will (*neposredstvennoe soznanie voli*), which Tolstoy equates with Kant's consciousness of intelligible will (*Intelligible Wille*) or *immediate consciousness*.[20] In the drafts Tolstoy is partial to thinkers who praise the vitality of being and manifest their primary interest in the uninhibited, philosophically raw man (*der unbefangene, philosophisch rohe Mensch*) who can say whatever he wishes: "I can do all that I wish" (*Ia mogu vse, chto khochu*) (15: 246–47).[21] Note that Tolstoy omits from the above list his former idol Rousseau and his natural man as a numerical integer entirely of his own: the immediate consciousness of will is not the religion of the heart of the noble savage. Tolstoy similarly overlooks Schopenhauer's pessimism in favor of treating his philosophy as an affirmation rather than a denial of life: it is a will to live that we perceive in ourselves immediately (*volia k zhizni, kotoruiu my chuvstvuem v samikh sebe*) (15: 247).

Another remarkable substitution in Tolstoy's prefatory drafts occurs in his interpretation of Kant's vision of freedom. Kant posits that in his intelligible character man is free because he is not only and not always determined by the laws of nature but also by the autonomous moral law that guarantees the freedom of his moral acts. Although the immortality of the soul, God, and freedom remain closed to intelligible will and practical reason, Kant insists that it is our duty to obey them as postulates of moral conduct. Tolstoy appears absolutely indifferent to this side of Kant's teaching. To him freedom is good because it is *freedom*, as opposed to necessity, and not because freedom is *good*. (Tolstoy everywhere stresses that lack of freedom, pure necessity, is evil.)[22] Driven to elevate immediate consciousness to the status of self-sufficiency, the divine principle of life, Tolstoy transforms it into a *transcendent* rather than a transcendental category of Kant's Copernican revolution of philosophy, his own version of a thing-in-itself, open only to God's own contemplation. "The immediate consciousness that he [Kant] accepts to be the subject of transcendent thinking, pure reason or Ding-an-sich" (15: 246). The likeliest explanation for such a bizarre interpretation of Kant's account of the pure employment of reason in "Transcendental Dialectic" lies in Tolstoy's secret desire, undisclosed in the published epilogue, to accept the law of reason merely as a token and to leave the seemingly meaningless freedom untouched and untouchable for the present. Tolstoy writes, "The consciousness of freedom as freedom is immune to reasonable proofs or refutations" (15: 292).[23]

In his attempt to liberate consciousness, Tolstoy ascribes absolute value to what Kant understands only to be mediate volition of understanding. For Kant, "the feeling of our incapacity to attain to an idea that is a law for us, is respect," the same sublime respect and awe that strikes one at the sight of the starry skies above and the realization of the inner law within.[24] Pierre's hitching his wagon to Kant's starry skies is Tolstoy's exercise in freeing him from his moral bondage. In Kant's view, "this play of the speculative reason would, like a dream, at once cease," and the likes of Pierre would choose their principles "exclusively in accordance with practical interests" that are not dictated by ought.[25]

Tolstoy does not proceed to investigate the correlation between freedom and moral law. The final version of the second epilogue lays bare only to a limited degree what Tolstoy intended to share about the correlation and alignment of freedom and necessity that he hopes to achieve by means of writing. The first point that Tolstoy makes in the published epilogue is paradoxical and provocative. Unlike Schlegel's insistence on vivid descriptions, Tolstoy suggests that history should *not* study the visible or recoverable, always sketchy vestiges of power but rather its *causes*—all the more so because modern history rejects the view of the ancients that power has *divine* causes (E2/1; 7; 309). The same divine cause inspired Kant and Schlegel to stoop in respect. Tolstoy would not be stopped. Previous to our ability to determine the reason of reasons behind the movement of humanity through the ages, says Tolstoy, one can't accept the reasons for the execution of historical power that *seem real* to the human mind. This idea is a radical correction of Hegel meaning that no discernible historical episode or period, no geographical part of "revealed" phenomenal history, and no historical character should ever be privileged in assuming that history fulfilled itself better or worse, more fully or less fully. Tolstoy is canceling out the possibility that the radiant Hegelian spirit will ever recognize itself completely accomplished and self-identical in any version of its concrete and final incarnation. Tolstoy is less interested in establishing a point of synthesis or decisive points of negation. Rather, he is here insisting that unless history recruits the deity anew, or clearly explains an alternative reason of reasons expressing a *collective will* embodied in power, a dialectical fake would render any discursive explanation meaning-less. Whereas Hegel could and did furnish explanations concerning the role of Luther, Voltaire, Rousseau, and Napoleon in making the vital historical phenomena actual, Tolstoy is picking on his favorite thinkers to simulate skepticism. The fact that Luther had an irascible temper and delivered viru-lent speeches or that Rousseau was suspicious and wrote libertarian books could hardly explain why thousands or even millions of the populace—if this were accepted to be the aftermath of Luther's and Rousseau's activities—fell under the knife of Protestant wars or under the blade of the guillotine during the Reign of Terror following the French Revolution.[26]

If neither Luther nor Rousseau are to blame, then the real question posed by Tolstoy is whether the power that commands the masses to commit hor-rific atrocities and that which permits these atrocities to occur is the same. His skepticism concerning the ability of Luther's sermons or Rousseau's philos-ophy to sway the masses into action is telling, and not merely because their ideas had a powerful influence on Tolstoy personally. He does not question the individual connection with ideas. Rather, he questions how divine will, which is *not* connected with space and time, may be connected with histori-cal movement and permit immoral acts. That this is true is evident in Tol-stoy's choice of words to convey the idea of God's power. Instead of "God," "godly," and the "divine," from the outset of the epilogue Tolstoy continues to use the word "deity" (*bozhestvò*), which is of neutral gender in Russian and signifies an eclectic medley of contradictory traits: indifferent supernatural force; godly essence at its most abstract; and, lastly, a mere idol, that is, a sub-stitute for true divinity.

This deity, Tolstoy implies, can define, of its own volition, the direction of movement from beyond time, from the realm of the invisible and unknowable Law. By dint of his immediate participation in the events of history, man—this part of the Great All, primarily a part of the human mass—does not think him-self accountable to God but rather to the transferred power of the historical character put in charge, "the hero," the leader, or the prophet. This is how Kant's moral law is elided. Despite their individually conflicting goals, people always aggregate in specific associations to fulfill common goals, so that the majority takes part in immediate massive action while the minority participates passively in the same action. Being drafted into action by the majority (the base of the conic structure, as Tolstoy calls it), the minority assumes the reins of illusory power at the top of the conic structure and runs the beehive (E2/6; 7: 330). Mostly repeating the points about the dynamic of violence from his earlier essay entitled "On Violence," Tolstoy's description of this conic beehive, with base and superstructure, presents a strikingly Marxist, utilitarian, or neo-Hegelian picture of human organization.[27]

However, at precisely this critical point Tolstoy chooses to part ways with modern political philosophy and theory of social evolution. In his view, modern historical science effectively removed the necessity to consider primary, first causes of all historical movement. In addition to eliminating the issue of the "first push," it also removed existential and ontological content from modern historical accounts. This explains why, without losing sight of the still evasive reason of reasons, Tolstoy abruptly raises the question of moral responsibility, but not in the Kantian sense. At the top of the structure, only the minority (so-called heroes) appears to bear moral or any sort of responsibility to stand court and be judged. The irresponsible mass that carries out the brunt of the real historical action remains no more than a physical actor subject to Copernican and Newtonian laws, and to the orders passed on to it by the appointed Master of Ceremonies.

The secret behind Tolstoy's term "zoology" in its application to human movement finally becomes clear. Are there other laws than those supplied by Montesquieu, Mill, Darwin, and the new branches of natural science (such as cell pathology)? Tolstoy feels that a composite historical event should consist of a combination of true, not illusory, moral power and physical movement: "In the final analysis, we have come to the circle of eternity, to that final boundary at which the human mind arrives as long as it does not play with its inquiry" (E2/7; 7: 335). Tolstoy is looking for the kinds of laws that, in any explanation of the historical life of humanity, could equal the absolute certainty of Copernican and Newtonian laws—which might not be explicable or even "visible" but remain true nonetheless, without altering articles of faith in divinity. Tolstoy's oversight in failing to acknowledge Kant's Copernican revolution of modernity should not lead us to assume that he was oddly negligent. Tolstoy implies that eternal historical laws will be validated as axiomatic, like Newtonian laws, *if and only if* human freedom, or the free moral will, is acknowledged as the absolute corollary of historical necessity and not merely because historical science should be considered as much a science as the natural sciences.

Tolstoy demands that we bypass the preceding Copernican revolution realized by Kant's transcendental return from the empirical reality to our subjectivity and affect a higher leap from the "moral law within" to the not immediately apparent law. Like Schlegel in relation to sciences, he proposes to keep the attention fixed on the main thing and discarding "the European predilection for particular branches of history" so that the construction of "the great edifice of universal history," which is subject to laws, can be studied.[28] At this point Tolstoy switches to a discussion of freedom because he has not finalized his consideration of divinity in relation to historical evil. He attends to the perennial contradiction identified by philosophy, which posits the belief that if there is at least one free act down through the millennia, then the laws of necessity may not obtain absolutely and consequently free will exists. Tolstoy is interested in both when and how man acts and what man strives for when he acts. He dissociates himself from the possibility of relativism and refuses to cater to the casuistic cavils of the new immoralists and their exaggerated claims: "The soul and freedom are not there because human life is expressed in muscular movements, while the muscular movements are conditioned by nervous activity," and so on. Again like Schlegel, Tolstoy prefers the creationist rhetoric of the Bible to the discussions in man of the same muscular-neurological activity as in the monkey: "in man we can observe muscular-nervous activity *and* consciousness" (E2/8; 7: 340).

Although Tolstoy's objection to manipulators is generally expressed crudely as "muscular-skeletal" ("you tell me that there is no freedom, while I raise my hand," etc.), he is actually proving that when he is in his conscious, free, *willing* mode, man's relation to the laws—such as the laws of gravity— is not the same as it is for a stone or any other unconscious and nonfree body. "No matter how many times experience and speculation demonstrate to man that under the same conditions and with the same character [of his] he would do the same as before, he, setting about to act toward the same result for the thousandth time, under the same conditions and with the same character, undoubtedly feels as certain that he may act as he will, as he had felt before" (E2/8; 7: 338). However, were man to switch his focus and observe himself from without, he would notice that his life is bound by the same laws that force the stone to fall, and that his life is thus predetermined.

There can be no doubt as to the origin of this rhetoric. Tolstoy's first bemoaning the impossibility of influencing the stone to "fall up instead of down," away from death, occurs in his philosophical meditation on the death of Nikolen'ka contained in an October 1860 letter to Fet, the Schopenhauer adept and jovial pessimist (60: 357). Additional causes behind this unexpected remark about freedom become apparent once one realizes that it is only in the ninth of the twelve chapters included in the published second epilogue that Tolstoy finally discloses the reason why history may be in such a special position to deal with necessity and freedom. For history the issue of freedom *does not refer* to the very essence of human freedom but to the conception about *the expression of this will in the past* and under known circumstances. "History does not have as its topic human will per se but our conception of it. Therefore there does not exist for history, the way it would for theology, ethics, or philosophy, the [same] *unsolvable mystery* about the union of the two contradictions, of freedom and necessity" (E2/9; 7: 341).

TOLSTOY'S COPERNICAN REVOLUTION

It may seem that Tolstoy's Copernican revolution is just a compromise to deal with the epistemological stalemate. Only thanks to his securing this truce, Tolstoy returns to the point at which he had started, namely, whether any element of "deity" is really present in the life of humanity. Tolstoy adamantly argues that to think, watch, and understand, man—any man, from Rousseau, the sophisticated intellectual, down to his noble and ignoble savages—should conceive of himself as a living being that knows himself primarily in the willing mode. In response to the voice of reason, which claims that there are laws of gravity, man, who wills from within, defies these laws by raising his arm and then lowering it of his own accord (E2/8; 7: 338). Such a truly savage, muscle-flexing response to Rousseau and Hegel—philosophers who insisted on man's freedom essentially revealing itself in his social being—is not intended to claim that the reflexive rise of the hand equals the capacity to "fly upward" and be immortal. Tolstoy is certainly reacting to Rousseau's conflation of freedom and liberty and to Hegel's disdain for the formal freedom of the "natural man," whose inner content is free from objective universality.[29]

By bringing in history, Tolstoy is attempting to minimize damage to the volatility of freedom, the same "subjective particularity"—which is Hegel's concern—that evaporates with the rise of the hand, vanishes in discrete moments of self-reflection, or deceives with the blurring phantoms and false knots of equally discontinuous memory. When Tolstoy was trying to establish complete continuity in his youthful philosophizing or early fiction, the elusive split moment of the conscious "now" was never available to him except in short-lived poetic reveries. The closest precedent of the epilogue's discussion of the freedom of consciousness is the discussion of unstoppable striving in the 1847 fragment on consciousness as the mental representation of "I" existing at different stages of its activity or motion. Since the younger Tolstoy could not associate memory with immaterial causes, all hypotheses about future life in relation to consciousness ended up "hanging about as hot air" (1: 230).[30] In one discouraged early fragment, "Le Présent, le passé et le futur" (The Present, the Past, and the Future), consciousness is given no space of its own since the present is claimed *not* to exist: "The past is what has been, the future is what will be, and the present is what does not exist.—The life of man therefore consists only of the future and the past, and it is for the same reason that the happiness we desire to possess is only a chimera, just like the present" (1: 217).

In the 1840s Tolstoy halted his philosophical inquiries when he felt he had arrived at a coveted destination, which philosophically turned out to be a vicious circle: "But observing the reasons for desiring further, I find that its cause is the same reason; hence, desire has no cause and, moreover, it possesses within itself that toward which it strives, namely, independence. And because this desire is dependent neither on the body nor on time, it follows that this desire is independent, infinite, self-defining, self-satisfying, and immortal" (1: 234).[31] Neither personal nor fictional diaries created by Tolstoy succeeded in capturing complete and immortal continuity from a subjective viewpoint. Whether it be the eloquent failure of Nekhliudov in *Lucerne*, the idle musing of Nekhliudov in the landowner fragments, Olenin's bragging of a freedom to plunge headfirst at whim in *The Cossacks*, or the more persistent probing of Andrey and Pierre, the continuous dialogue of the observing reason and the self-conscious subject—the observed deeming itself free—proved impossible. Simultaneously, the relative failure also proved Hegel's theory and Tolstoy's own earlier philosophical positions, now reinforced in the second epilogue, namely, that from the perspective of the universal spirit or the Great All, moments of self-consciousness are but two "fixed moments in the form of the immediate being" taken out of historical context.[32]

Just because Tolstoy exposes his hidden or direct dialogues with dominant philosophies of freedom and historical necessity does not mean that he is writing the most philosophically inspired sections of his book under the aegis or direction of a single philosophical system—Schopenhauer's in particular, whose *Prize Essay on the Freedom of the Will*, as well as *World as Will and Representation* and *On the Basis of Morality*, he read most attentively between 1868 and 1869 at the prompting of Fet. Of all the philosophical minds involved, Schopenhauer is the only one who celebrates the fact that "now" is but a phantom.[33] For Tolstoy, the author in search of a link between the infinite historical motion and the essence of freedom, only Schopenhauer's theory of unstoppable will could serve the desired corollary of the unstoppable vital motion, but certainly not that will's indiscriminate blindness. On Schopenhauer's dreaming and waking orb of the conscious mind, the distinctly conscious idea-bubbles "are merely the surface," while the "mass of the water is indistinct."[34] Nowhere did Schopenhauer claim that self-consciousness is morally autonomous or, except in the mind of a genius, directly connected to the primal cause of being. For Schopenhauer, if he were the primary cause, God would be responsible for all the cruelty and chaos of existence. Schopenhauer even jokingly solved the enigma of gravity by recommending the removal of the earth from the equation so that the stone would never fall. Everywhere in *War and Peace* death is that lofty, majestic, terrifying mystery pertaining to the divine law of life and not a mere cessation of a phenomenon.[35]

Most importantly, Schopenhauer considered both the science and idea of history to be the greatest hoax and a deplorable waste of vital energy, a ludicrous desire to replace philosophy. After all, he argued, history only describes wars, but these merely replicate zoological laws and Clio, the muse of history, is "as thoroughly infected with lies and falsehood as is a common prostitute with syphilis."[36] Tolstoy's creative violation of the Schopenhauer canon started right here, in the midst of his infatuation with the controversies of the Frankfurt sage. Sharing Schopenhauer's Neoplatonic zest for endlessly renewing life, or "historical zoology," and his sarcasm about the prevalent flaws of history writing, by following the example of the *Prize Essay* and its sequel, *On the Basis of Morality*, Tolstoy attempted to situate the individual and make him more responsible. For this, he had to exclude history from the realm of moral choices. Essentially, Tolstoy rephrases Schopenhauer's pun about gravity and recommends the removal of moral laws so that history could continue.[37]

Being an experiential science, history is not required to deal with the same "unsolvable mysteries" that have for centuries plagued ethics, philosophy, theology, and Tolstoy's own superfluous seekers (E2/9; 7: 344–45). Tolstoy bargains a significant excuse from resolving the "mysterious" reasons for murder, cannibalism, and thievery that he described in the narrative corpus of *War and Peace*—or planned to describe in the drafts. With cold reserve Tolstoy lists terrible transgressions and explains that these crimes would implicate their perpetrators less if we knew the circumstances that impelled these criminals to commit such crimes, reasoning that they would appear more subject to necessity than to their free will while committing the crimes: "If any of these reasons is known to us, we already admit a certain degree of necessity and *do not require retribution* for the crime; we are less appreciative of the merits of a good deed and we are less free in an act we deemed original" (7: 345).[38]

This morally questionable prelude is needed to pit Schopenhauer's unprincipled but compassionate justice against Kant's theory of absolute moral will, *a final end* of history dedicated to the Author of the world.[39] Schopenhauer's criticism of Kant was based on his theory of permanent character, which Tolstoy did not share.[40] This contradiction would prove decisive in Tolstoy's creative refashioning of his own philosophical and artistic choices. Critiquing Kant, Schopenhauer noted that if all people are programmed to always behave correctly according to some internal moral law, they will become indistinguishable from one another. Only through our character do we have access to the freedom of being (or consciousness), but not to the freedom of acting as one should, according to Kant. Whence does the action spring? Schopenhauer achieved his breakthrough and received the prize by suggesting that it is in consciousness that we experience our being directly and feel responsible for our actions: "Responsibility for what we do, accountability for our actions—a feeling that rests in the unshakeable certainty that we ourselves are the doers of our deeds separate from necessity."[41] Schopenhauer's correction of Kant occurs in connection with his gloomy appraisals of human nature. Apart from the expected ill will, malice, petulance, hatred, and so on, compassion also motivates human behavior. By witnessing another's weal and woe, we fear the same privation and experience spontaneous sympathy for those less fortunate: "Compassion, not reason, stops men from being sheer monsters."[42] If, according to Schopenhauer, conscience exists, it is not a deterrent of evil but a reaction to a witnessed and experienced evil that "speaks only afterward" (197). Freedom of will creates an "unremovable gulf between the Creator and the sins of his creature."[43]

Like Schopenhauer, Tolstoy tries hard to imagine a situation in which man is totally free and thus completely responsible for himself (that is, minimally dependent on space, time, and causality) yet—and here is a crucial difference between him and Schopenhauer—thoroughly dependent on God (E2/10; 7: 348). Like Schopenhauer's adversaries, especially Schelling, Tolstoy finds that excepting time, space, and causality from human experience negates such experience as human. According to Schelling, all limitation through the act of self-consciousness is necessarily determinate in nature, yet infinitely so, and thus "determinacy must reach into the infinite."[44] Similarly nonexistent would be a person dependent only on the law of necessity and completely devoid of freedom. Consciousness perceives life by experiencing it directly from within, providing life with its content. Despite his retention of Schopenhauer's distinctions that freedom is what is being considered, while reason is what considers, and that freedom is content, while necessity is form, Tolstoy arrives at a desired epistemological crisis:

> Thus, in order to imagine human action subject only to the law of necessity, without freedom, we must admit to the knowledge of an *infinite* number of spatial conditions, an *infinitely* great period of time, and an *infinite* series of reasons. In order to imagine a person completely free and not subject to the law of necessity, we must imagine him alone, beyond space, time, and causes. . . . Beyond these two concepts, which are mutually defining in their union—like form with content—any idea of life is impossible. . . . From the perspective of reason the force of human freedom differs from other natural forces only according to the definition that reason gives it. Freedom without necessity, without, in other

words, the laws of reason that would define it, does not differ substantially from gravity, warmth, or vegetative force—it is for reason only a momentary, indefinable feeling of life (7: 349–51).

This is the crucial point of Tolstoy's inquiry. Schopenhauer claims that omnipresent and omnivorous will treats consciousness without regard to its uniqueness and does not endow man with a sufficient motive "any more than a stone can move without a sufficient push or pull."[45] Hegel claims that supreme historical will treats man as its tool and realizes itself without regard to man's interest or self-evaluation. Kant and Schelling offer a better solution for Tolstoy: despite man's inability to penetrate into the hidden plan of nature, one must still presume such a plan for humanity, its historical task. It is in history, which respects and recognizes man's contribution, *as well as* in its narratives, where everything is truly connected, the documents of his achievement, in these "innumerable linkages" that he overcomes his "shortness of life" and realizes his capacity for reason.[46] In order to understand why Tolstoy so swiftly tailgates from a Schopenhauer-inspired division into the discussion of the narrative that unifies "linked consciousness" and indifferent forces of nature, one should note a significant lapse in Tolstoy's argument. Tolstoy begins to distance himself from the inner life of man, freedom per se, and leaves this unknowable thing-in-itself to the futile purview of metaphysics, thus retaining the mysterious privacy for freedom, consciousness, and history. Through the medium of history, he moves toward judgments about the retrospective meaning of human acts, which make more obvious the fulfillment or violation of laws: "Freedom for history is *only* the expression of the *unknown remainder* of what we know about the laws of human life. . . . To espy and define these laws is the task of history" (E2/10/11; 7: 351–52).

In the remaining two chapters of the published epilogue, Tolstoy abandons the theme of human freedom and personal responsibility to concentrate solely on the tasks of history. In order to overcome the flaw of the old history, prone to splitting up the unknowable infinity of time and causal relations into the vile multitude of discreet particles, he relies on Schelling's imaginative scheme of integers linking consciousness and its *unknowable remainder* to infinity. Having arrived at a colossal number of infinitely small integers, each of which held an undisclosed link to the reason of reasons and causality, such reformers of science as Newton and Copernicus solved the problem by imposing a newly discovered, universal law of nature to explain life without questioning God's authority yet opposing the grave resistance of old theology. The new history should do the same, instantiating "the law of necessity in history" for the maintenance of the whole edifice and paying no heed to theological resistance fearing the collapse of its foundations (E2/12; 7: 354–55).[47]

Unlike the new compartmentalized sciences, his new historical law will not do any damage to the original edifice. At the end of the eighth chapter of the published second epilogue, Tolstoy likens "natural scientists and their fans" to plasterers who are asked to plaster one wall and, in their zeal and taking advantage of the absence of the Master of Ceremonies (*glavnogo rasporiaditelia rabot*), have also plastered windows, icons, and the scaffolding of the still unfinished church (E2/8; 7: 340). To forestall further objections, Tolstoy deliberately decided to end on the following phrase: "It is necessary to give up the nonexistent freedom and acknowledge the dependence imperceptible to us." By writing "Finis" (*konets*) he signaled that the discussion was closed (7: 355). Thus, for the first time Tolstoy attributes religious meaning to history, although he stops short—very short—of discussing the religious meaning of the individual human will, consciousness, or freedom. In this umpteenth rendition of Schlegel's enlightened historian who penetrates into the hidden decrees of divine wisdom in resplendent edifice of universal history, Tolstoy would not tolerate any mishandling of the law in the Lord's house.[48]

Tolstoy significantly concludes the book on questions about the moral meaning (*nravstvennyi smysl*) of historical evil. The last sentence in the drafts to the book asks how and why people bear responsibility for events and if they have the right to justify their decision. Tolstoy admits that in the moral sense there can be no permanent but only a temporary justification for war (15: 303). In the allegoric buffoonery of Christian comedy toward the end of the book, the Master of Ceremonies has already finished the drama and has come for the costumes, but Napoleon refuses to wash off his puppet's makeup, oblivious of the invisible hand that has been moving him. The Master of Ceremonies loses patience: "Don't you see now that it was not he but I who moved you? People, however, were stunned by the forced movement and took a long time before they could grasp this" (E1/4; 7: 256). In contrast to Napoleon, the pious Alexander emblazons a medal in honor of Russia's victory with the following motto: "Not unto us, not unto us, but unto Thy Name. I am a man just like you; leave me alone so I can live like a man and think about my soul and about God" (E1/4; 7: 257). In Tolstoy's explanation, Alexander remains obedient to the Lord's design, the war and the horrible costs it has reaped.

Theological nods notwithstanding, Tolstoy's gaps are yawning, especially when he gets down to matters of Christian metaphysics. In places, his discussion reminds one all too strongly of Leibniz's largely discredited determinism: "All is foreseen. . . . He knows in his infallible knowledge whether I will lift my arm [or] commit a murder. Thus I am not free."[49] Where Tolstoy comes close to arguing that through immediate union with God we align ourselves with His "infinite action," his source should be Spinoza, another butt of universal criticism in a century serious about history and skeptical about the possibility of the intellectual love of God.[50] Tolstoy's most poetic incursions into the vital force of freedom, the remainder that is inaccessible to historical law, leave unexplained where and how goodness and evil align themselves against this movement. For example, consider his weak rebuttal, in fragment number 319 of the drafts, of Schopenhauer's indictment of the Will of God for the imperfections in the will of individual creatures: "The question consists in that while we look at man as an object of observation, we find that man is subject to the same law of necessity as anything else that exists. But while we look at ourselves from the point of view of *the consciousness of life*, we feel in ourselves *the same force* that produces everything that lives. Man is God's creation. God made man what man is. And what is sin? This is the question of theology" (15: 244). Tolstoy is satisfied with assigning each problem to a specific science: responsibility to juridical sciences; good and evil to ethics; and the question of force to philosophy because only the process of history allows for a direct conversation between reason and consciousness (15: 244).[51]

For Joseph de Maistre, another staunch supporter of determinism whose ideas, especially those developed in "The Saint Petersburg Dialogues," have exerted influence on Tolstoy's choice of terms and his line of argumentation, the matter with historical justice and dispensation of morality looked more definite by far. Like Tolstoy, de Maistre thought God to be the "universal moving force" and considered other particles of creation to be moving in accordance with the nature given to them. Also like Tolstoy, he endowed history with the power to impose harmony between fortuitous human volitions and God's design. Unlike Tolstoy, de Maistre defended the necessity of evil, saying that he never understood "the eternal argument against Providence drawn from the misfortune of the just and the prosperity of the wicked."[52] The ultraconservative Catholicism of de Maistre accepted wars and other forms of violence on the ground that in order to become apparent a hidden divine force teaches the errant and thoroughly sinful humanity the principles of divine justice by choosing mostly violent means. In this war and political power alike, these two forces out of human control, are the preferred vehicles for demonstrating divine presence.

Given the lack of de Maistre's indoctrinated excuses, a catastrophic moral error of *War and Peace* to which Tolstoy acquiesces becomes apparent. His Copernican revolution prevents him from descending to the level of loathsome utilitarian and positivist explanations of life without forcing him to answer for metaphysics, while ironing out any wrinkles of the contradictory past by unfolding his novelistic carpet of unsurpassed genius: "And the more this canvas of the past unfurls itself before our eyes, the more apparently individual arbitrary wills are ironed out and the more apparent the correct and infinite ornaments that make up history become" (15: 269).[53] The metaphor of a flawlessly ornamented, complete carpet, woven out of the threads of fate and freedom represents a new polemical return to a dialogue with Herzen in 1860, when, in what was then to be his novel, Tolstoy was hoping to write about the conversion to faith, the reconciliation with God of the defeated Decembrists. Instead of Herzen's carpet of a stormy sea, Tolstoy's new canvas is a Hegelian idea of a peaceful ornament of fulfilled history without Hegel's certainty that history fulfils a definite meaning and goal and lifts itself up at the end of time to return back to heaven. To Tolstoy "freedom without time," is divine and not human (15: 293). And so the revelation of consciousness (*otkrovenie soznaniia*) (15: 254) remains to Tolstoy the only immediate moment of life and the only nexus to experiencing God.

NOTES

1. Friedrich Schlegel, *The Philosophy of History in a Course of Lectures*, by *Frederick von Schlegel*. With a memoir of the author, by James Burton Robertson, Esq. 2 vols. (New York: D. Apleton Co., 1841), 1: 77.

2. See chapter 4 of the present study.

3. Schlegel, 1: 81.

4. Schlegel, 1: 88–89.

5. Schlegel, 2: 41.

6. Stankevich, *Izbrannoe*, 130.

7. See Tolstoy's "Introductions, Forewords, and Variants to the Beginning of *War and Peace*" (Tolstoy 1928–58; 13: 53). Aside from these authorial comments, the remainder of the citations from the novel (including Tolstoy's explanatory note "A Few Words About the Book *War and Peace*") are to L. N. Tolstoy, *Sobranie sochinenii v dvadtsati dvukh tomakh*.

8. On the abusive "nonsense of detail," see Tolstoy, "Introductions, Forewords, and Variants to the Beginning of *War and Peace*," 13: 56. See Schlegel on the same, 1: 88.

9. The study of *War and Peace* through the lens of Schopenhauer's *Prize Essay on the Freedom of the Will* owes its beginning to Jeff Love's brilliant analysis in *The Overcoming of History in War and Peace*, 77, 93, 115; see also 133–46 on Schopenhauer's importance to Tolstoy. Although my interpretation does not differ from Love's points about the importance of unmediated experience that Tolstoy discovered in self-consciousness thanks to Schopenhauer, I broaden the discussion by examining the relationship between consciousness and personal quest in self- and character analysis and by approaching Tolstoy's narrative as a form of religion. The same broadening applies to Love's discussion of Schelling (Love, 121, 155, 183, 199–201).

10. Arthur Schopenhauer, *Prize Essay on the Freedom of the Will*, ed. Günter Zöller and trans. Eric F. Payne (Cambridge: Cambridge University Press, 1999), 10.

Schopenhauer wrote his essay in response to a set of questions put forward to contestants by the Royal Norwegian Society of Sciences.

11. Schopenhauer, *Prize Essay*, 44, 88.

12. The books most likely were Montesquieu's *L'Esprit des lois* (1748), Rousseau's *Contrat social* (1762), and Sismondi's *Tableau de l'agriculture toscane* (1801), *De la richesse commerciale* (1803), and *Nouveau principes de l'économie politique, ou de la Richesse dans ses rapports avec la population* (1819). Montesquieu would inform Count Nikolai regarding the optimum laws of the land to guarantee personal freedoms in relation to particular historical and natural conditions. Rousseau would reinforce his childhood belief that everything that derives from the Creator is virtuous and can only be improved away, and that man enjoys freedom thanks to an unspoken social contract that unites all wills into one. Jean Charles Lénard Sismonde de Sismondi's economic tracts would immerse Nikolai in the ideas that explain the contradictions and injustices of current economic laws, which, lest political disaster strikes, should be molded to protect the interests of those who toil.

13. Tolstoy, "Introductions, Forewords, and Variants. . . ," 13: 53.

14. Tolstoy, "A Few Words About the Book *War and Peace*," 7: 356.

15. Tolstoy, "Introductions, Forewords, and Variants . . . ," 13: 57.

16. Notebook no. 3, entry dated October 25, 1868 (48: 108).

17. Kant notably called freedom the highest good. See his *Critique of Judgment*, trans. James Creed Meredith (Oxford: Oxford University Press, 1952), 118.

18. See Hegel, *Lectures on the Philosophy of World History. Introduction: Reason in History*, trans. H. B. Nisbet (Cambridge: Cambridge University Press, 1975), 64–65.

19. G. W. F. Hegel, *The Philosophy of History*, trans J. Sibree (Amherst, N.Y.: Prometheus Books, 1991), 39–40, 41.

20. In this regard, Tolstoy names Schopenhauer's *World as Will and Representation (Die Welt als Wille und Vorstellung)*, *Prize Essay on the Freedom of the Will (Preisschrift über die Freiheit des Willen)*, and *On the Basis of Morality (Grundprobleme der Ethik)*, 15: 246. For Tolstoy "der intelligible Wille," the "ding an sich," Spinoza's *substantia*, and the "x" of divinity in theology are all equal: "What's remarkable in the history of this question is that for all those versatile thinkers who have been trying to solve this question, the higher the metaphysical number they were attributing to the unknown, the more fully they were denying freedom of will. Such is the 'x' for the theologians, *substantia* for Spinoza, das Ding an sich for Kant, der intelligible Wille for Schopenhauer" (15: 224–25).

21. In quoting Tolstoy, I am retaining his spelling in both German and Russian transcriptions.

22. Fragment no. 327 (15: 259).

23. See "Transcendental Dialectic," B362, in Kant, *Critique of Pure Reason*, 305.

24. See Immanuel Kant, *The Critique of Judgment*, 105 and Immanuel Kant, *Critique of Practical Reason*. Trans. T. K. Abbott (Amherst, New York: Prometheus Books, 1996), 191.

25. See A476/B504, in Kant, *Critique of Pure Reason*, 430.

26. Tolstoy must here be referring to the ideas of Henry Thomas Buckle, namely, that major historical actors and so-called civilizers of humanity who are not neces-

sarily only tsars define the historical activity of the masses. Tolstoy discusses this idea in the drafts of the epilogue (see fragment no. 305; 15: 187).

27. Tolstoy's "On Violence" contains the first mention of the "incomprehensible force" that moves nations. See chapter 3 of the present study.

28. Schlegel, 1: 92.

29. See Rousseau's defense of liberty, "the noblest faculty of man," in Jean-Jacques Rousseau, "A Discourse on the Origin of Inequality," in *The Social Contract and Discourses*, trans. G. D. H. Cole, rev. J. H. Brumfitt, John C. Hall, and P. D. Jimack (London: J. M. Dent, 1996), 104–5. Cf. Hegel's explanation of the limits of subjective freedom in G. W. F. Hegel, *The Encyclopedia Logic. Part I of the Encyclopaedia of Philosophical Sciences with the Zusätze*, trans. T. F. Geraets, W. A. Suchtig, and H. S. Harris (Indianapolis: Ind.: Hackett, 1991), 58.

30. See the fragment entitled "On the Goals of Philosophy" (*O tseli filosofii*) (1: 229–32).

31. Tolstoy, untitled fragment no. 9 (1: 233–36).

32. See Hegel, *Phenomenology of Spirit*, 159.

33. Arthur Schopenhauer, *On the Basis of Morality*, trans. Eric F. Payne (Providence, R.I: Bergham Books, 1995), 206–7. All subsequent references are to this edition.

34. Arthur Schopenhauer, *The World as Will and Representation*, trans. E. F. J. Payne, 2 vols. (New York: Dover, 1958), 2: 135.

35. See Schopenhauer's essay "On the Doctrine of Indestructibility of Our True Nature by Death," in *Parerga and Paralipomena*, trans. E. F. J. Payne, 2 vols. (1974; reprint, Oxford: Clarendon Press, 2000), 2: 270.

36. Arthur Schopenhauer, *The World as Will and Representation*, 2: 446–47.

37. Cf. Schelling's similar denial of moral freedom, which he calls absolute freedom of God's will in man. "Intimately connected with the concept of individual freedom are the concepts of evil, sin, guilt, punishment . . . To know that it is not we who act, but that a divine necessity acts in us, gives us peace and elevates us forever above all empty longing, fear and hope." Schelling, *Philosophical Inquiries into the Nature of Human Freedom*, xxxix.

38. Cf. Schopenhauer's dicta on unalterable actions. Inflexible human characters combined with predestined circumstances result in an unalterable action that could not have happened otherwise. Thus "everything that happens, from the greatest to the smallest, happens necessarily." Schopenhauer, *Prize Essay*, 53. See also Zöller's introduction, ibid., xxiv-xxv.

39. Immanuel Kant, *The Critique of Judgement*, 118–21.

40. Schopenhauer, *Prize Essay*, 81–88, esp. 86. For his criticism of Kant, ibid., 66.

41. Schopenhauer, *Prize Essay*, 83.

42. Schopenhauer, *On The Basis of Morality*, 144, 185, 209. Schopenhauer gladly borrowed the latter idea from the fourth book of Rousseau's *Émile*. Men are related by common desires and common fears and this is the only meaningful foundation for brotherhood, all things being an extension of *amour propre*.

43. Schopenhauer, *Prize Essay*, 66.

44. Schelling, *Philosophical Inquiries into the Nature of Human Freedom*, 59.

45. Schopenhauer, *On the Basis of Morality*, 141.

46. See Kant, *Critique of Judgment*, 43, 50, 232. Unlike Schopenhauer, both Kant and Schelling believe that "an account of human history will be of benefit to man" in teaching him not to blame providence for the evils which oppress him, and in assuming all responsibility for the misuse of his reason. Kant, *Critique of Judgment*, 233. Schelling, *Philosophical Inquiries*, 201–2.

47. Tolstoy must mean the following Old Testament miracles in Joshua: the waters of the River Jordan stood still to protect the ark of the covenant (3–4); the walls surrounding Jericho, under Israel's siege, collapsed (6); and the "sun stood still and the moon stopped" to protect the Israelites against the five kings (10). In making such optimistic declarations, Tolstoy must also be thinking of Leibniz's optimism and his treatment of freedom as a happy contingency standing in the wings of Newton's discovery.

48. In the drafts of the epilogue, Tolstoy initially likened the efforts of the representatives of the historical school of Christianity and positivists (Strauss, Renan, Vocht, Lewis, Mill, Littré) to the efforts of house painters imagining, while painting the roof, that the roof beams would hold because of their painting (fragment no. 319; 15: 243).

49. G. W. Leibniz, "Dialogue on Human Freedom and the Origin of Evil," in *Philosophical Essays*, trans. Roger Ariew and Daniel Garber (Indianapolis, Ind.: Hackett, 1989), 112.

50. Spinoza, *The Ethics of Spinoza: The Road to Inner Freedom*, ed. and trans. Dagobert D. Runes (New York: Citadel Press/Kensington, 1988), 62–63.

51. In the same fragment, Tolstoy merely enumerates the contradictions that belong to other spheres of knowledge: "For theologians, the question consists of a contradiction between omniscience and omnipotence of God the Maker and divine retribution for the deeds of Creation. [Tolstoy crosses out "and thus," which could promise a development of this view.] In ethics this contradiction is found between the law of necessity and responsibility; in juridical science between the law of necessity and human retribution; and in philosophy between the contradictory conclusions made by reason, in which one proves necessity while the other proves freedom" (15: 245). In all these cases, adds Tolstoy, the conversation continues between reasonable deductions, of which one is based on the data supplied by consciousness but not between consciousness and reason directly.

52. *The Works of Joseph de Maistre*. Selected, trans., and intro. Jack Lively. With a New Forword by Robert Nisbet (New York: Schocken Books, 1971), 187.

53. Tolstoy later adds: "The further the canvas of the past unfolds before us, the more distinct those correct lines become, in which one of the ends is hidden in the unknown and the other end is where our free will is located (15: 291–92).

Chapter Six

Tolstoy's Path toward Conversion: 1869–1875

THE EMERGENCE OF A MADMAN

In his own presentation of *War and Peace* Tolstoy claims that it was a revolution in artistic consciousness. Artistically the work did achieve a dynamic synthesis of the two opposites, namely, necessity and freedom, but it left too many doors open. The nature of the law as well as the true nature of freedom remained undisclosed. God was still an unknown factor, and the moral individuality of man at times looked too dubious. Moreover, Tolstoy failed to realize his original plan of a spiritual history of a generation of political fighters. The inscrutable answer supplied by Tolstoy viz. questions of evil and violence in the Epilogues and the novel itself exerted a heavy toll on his development as a writer and thinker and eventually brought him to an excruciating crisis only a few years later. In the final fragments of the drafts of *War and Peace* Tolstoy argued with himself and was protesting against his future faultfinding critics: "I am an artist! (*ia khudozhnik!*) and my whole life is spent searching for beauty, . . . but you are an artist, you can adorn."[1]

Despite his searches for beauty and God, Tolstoy abhorred the very idea of writing in the spirit of a religious rabble-rouser with a messianic cause, characteristic of Romantic nationalism and also of the decaying Slavophile ideology. In a facetious digression on the theme of religious patriotism, Tolstoy jokingly considers whether he could write something in the style of Zhukovsky's "Singer in the Camp of Russian Warriors" (1812), which asks the heavenly tsar for his sanctification in granting the Russians victory or immortality after death, and for protecting them with the "shield of Providence" (*shchit promysla*).[2] Tolstoy also defends his retreat into beauty from the new historical pragmatism initiated by Belinsky. For every of Belinsky's "types"

of superfluous men he can come up with a longer list of notoriously unhis-
torical, eternal characters that were born in response to pragmatism: Don
Quixote, Ajax, Clive Newcome, David Copperfield, Falstaff (15: 240). The
copious but cryptic notes on the relationship between historical writing and
religious art are well worth further deciphering. Tolstoy tells Nikolai Polevoy,
the conservative writer and historian, the enemy of Pushkin's historical drama
Boris Godunov, that he tried to learn from the patriots but failed: "I did try to
learn (from you) and I didn't" (15: 240). "Why do you need truths?" Tolstoy
asked Polevoy, who had intimated that Tolstoy's dichotomous ending
smacked of high-minded insanity.[3] The charge of obsolete and mad interpretations must be a reference to Tolstoy's clear lineage from Chaadaev's *Letters
Philosophiques*, incomprehensibly omitted from previous discussions of Tolstoy's historical postulates.

Chaadaev provided Tolstoy with a wealth of themes and terms to connect
individual "turnaround" with historical movement.[4] In the third letter, prefaced by an epigraph that resonates strongly with Tolstoy's program of "engulfing life," Chaadaev speaks of preparing for the turnaround before "our
decrepit nature dissolves," so that "our new man is born" (1: 122–26). By explaining that man is predisposed to acquiring freedom through submission,
Chaadaev employs Tolstoy's cherished division into the consciousness of
freedom and the reason of necessity. Arguing against the conceit of autonomous *moral law* (*l'ordre moral*), Chaadaev suggests that just like any
other law proven by the Copernican revolution and Newton's *celestial geom-
etry* (*la géométrie céleste*), it has its counterpart: "Every law of movement depends on the confrontation of two diametrically opposed forces. Before gravitation [*la gravité universelle*] there is the first push, or the projection
[*l'Impulsion initiale ou la Projection*]" (1: 130, 135–36). The same dynamic
parallelism is transferred by Chaadaev to the study of two forces acting in the
world of the spirit: "One force, of which we are conscious (*avons conscience*), our free will, our willing (*notre libre arbitre, notre vouloir*), and the
other force, by which we are unconsciously dominated, is the effect on our
essence [*notre être*] of *some force outside us* [*un pouvoir extérieur*] (1: 136).
In the state of "I am conscious," of "je connais," man realizes his obedience
to a higher force (1: 139). Chaadaev speaks of the submission of consciousness to necessity, when man notices that the force external to him dominates
his own *vital forces* (*les forces vitales*), and that he has to submit to it. "The
whole strength of our consciousness, of our mind," is its obedience and "the
more it realizes its obedience, the stronger it is for it" (1: 222–23, 130).

Consequently, only in the historical being of man and not in his individual consciousness, yielding vile "psychological history" (1: 181), is where
all the miracles of free consciousness based on God's law occur. It is the

good reason passing from generation to generation through the millennia from the first man until the arrival of Christ (1: 151).[5] Chaadaev's history ceases when in its final poetic move involving the completely engulfed Absolute it empties itself entirely into the formed void.[6] The last apocalyptic synthesis will lead to the birth of reasonable consciousness, or freedom in the womb of the word and God's law. Chaadaev destined Pushkin to fulfill these ideas in art. In effect, by writing his novel Tolstoy realized Chaadaev's dream, unfulfilled by Pushkin.[7] Thanks to Chaadaev, who corresponded with Schelling and simultaneously absorbed much of Hegel, Tolstoy found himself swept up in the maelstrom of "old-fashioned" Romantic ideas about history and the Christian meaning of art. According to Schelling's theory, by acknowledging the highest demands of the Christian poet, Tolstoy overcame the split by surrendering his artistic freedom to the law of necessity, thus achieving a blessed union of the conscious and the unconscious.[8] Tolstoy's treatment of history and freedom in the novel also echoes Hegel in the sense that "consciousness occasions the separation of the Ego, in its boundless freedom as arbitrary choice, from the . . . essence of the Will, that is, from the Good."[9]

However, Tolstoy attributes to creative force much more than Hegel, according to whose explanation the law is the stable image of unstable appearance unified by force into knowledge. In Hegel such externalization of force and the law is followed by the "inherent vital movement" of Christian reconciliation of God with man in history and is "manifested to man in the Christian religion."[10] The artist also has a role in this process. Acting as the unconscious tool of the spirit, often in an instinctive operation, as in Tolstoy's "involuntary" instincts of hive life, "like the building of a honeycomb by bees," the artist "blended the natural and the self-conscious [in] this ambiguous being which is a riddle to itself, the conscious wrestling with the nonconscious, the simple inner with the multiform outer."[11]

Thoroughly confident that "personal truth is art" and that Christianity "is totally artistic" and is entitled to uphold truths considered irrational according to the accepted point of view, Tolstoy was starting his work on the novel in a vigorous mood to produce religiously timed art.[12] In the same note where he first commented on the laws of zoology and his plans for the book, Tolstoy wrote in 1868: "Only art knows not the conditions of time, space, or movement. Only art provides essence" (48: 108). He thus equated art—or essence—with self-conscious freedom. As he confessed to Pogodin, and in his mental objection to Polevoy, he acknowledged belonging to the group of literary "madmen": "I understand the whole difference between the views I have expressed about history from the views of all historians. I am aware of this dilemma in all its terrible significance. Either I am a madman or I have discovered the new truth. (Tolstoy here deleted "I cannot accept the former.") I believe that I have discovered a new truth" (15: 242).

Tolstoy's self-diagnosis, namely, that of a madman who believes himself to be right, was confirmed by the authority of Herzen, a specialist on literary-historical dementia. In 1867, Herzen was asked to compose a sequel to "Doctor Krupov" and "The Damaged One." In the presence of such "vulgar materialists" as Carl Vogt, Herzen composed his last work, "Aphorismata a propos of the psychiatric theory of Doctor Krupov. Opus by the dissector and adjunct professor, Titus Leviathan-sky," his final caricature of history, and very possibly of Tolstoy's novel, which was already appearing in installments.[13] The comic name of the dissector hints at Titus Livius, the conservative historian of Augustan Rome, where gods disperse blessings to obedient masses and pious sovereigns, and certainly at Hobbes's *Leviathan* and its endorsement of determinism to subdue the unruly social swarm. From the point of Herzen's old polemic with Tolstoy, Herzen may hint at Tolstoy's conservative and antirevolutionary ideas supported by several positions in the novel. In the first name of the dissector, attentive readers of Tolstoy would also have recognized Titus, the book's famous but episodic peasant-soldier. His name in Russian rhymes with the verb "to mill," one of Tolstoy's synonyms for historical action; Tolstoy's Titus significantly refuses to go "run the mill" of history at the urging of his teasing comrades, snapping back lazily with the invariable "fool, I spit on you." Through such a thickly layered metaphor for his polemic, Herzen's comic materialist thanks Krupov for laying the medical foundation for the interpretation of universal history, yet he criticizes him for "religious-metaphysical phantasmagoria" that made concessions to Tolstoy-like "incremental movement without attainment."[14] While it is true that all is linked together in nature by the iron chain of necessity, nature is demure, and human creativity is real. Human creativity expresses itself in the frenzy of historical madness and its almost religious ecstasy of creation. In true history, all "calls for insanity (*bezumie*)," concludes Herzen; "everything has lived and lives by it."[15]

However, around 1869 Tolstoy already had a different program for short-cutting history and human freedom (or madness) into the Provinces of God. In his note "On Religion" (O religii) Tolstoy agreed with Herzen that religion itself is not the truth but rather a form of madness for the sake of salvation, because there were, are, and will be many religions.[16] But he then decided that humanity at large does not attempt to achieve any goals; only individuals may have tasks, which they do or do not fulfill: "Humanity and its life through the ages is not a *concept* (*poniatie*) but is *the word* (*slovo*), whose goal is to hint at *the boundless linkage of events and thoughts* that is quite incomprehensible (*neob'iatnoe stseplenie sobytii i myslei i sovershenno nepos-*

tizhimoe)" (7: 125). In a decisive change of tone since the conclusion of *War and Peace*, Tolstoy decides that the progress of humanity (*khod chelovechestva*) is unverifiable. Because for individual nonbelievers, "in the substitution of the calming answers there is a proud consciousness of the fact that man never deludes himself" (7: 126). Thus, only the discovery of a personal God can strike the needed balance between freedom and its distrust of laws, on the one hand, and the necessity to obey, on the other. Tolstoy reinterprets Schelling's metaphor of immortal linkages between the individual vectors of movement present in Christian history in the final drafts of *War and Peace*, where he is attributing to Christ a reconciliatory role in history—something Schopenhauer would never do, since such an ascription is purely Schellingian and Hegelian. Tolstoy's Christ is a tragic, revolutionary sufferer, who has lost life in order to redeem faith: "Christ says that not a hair of man's head will perish without the Father's will and he demonstrates by his sufferings the vanity of struggle against God's determined will" (15: 225).[17]

This version of Christ, who previously earned no more than five fleeting mentions in the whole corpus of Tolstoy's imaginative fiction and personal writings, is an altogether new development. Tolstoy is looking for a personal God, and the invisible God the Father frustrates and fascinates him. At the end of 1868 he wrote a note polemically aimed at Descartes that bore the title: "Not Cogito Ergo Sum" (Ne cogito ergo sum), where he rethinks his connection with the law of the father and necessity. He now thinks that human beings are individual dots caught in different moments of history. In order to become part of the infinite chain of linkages, people should think about correct "application of their abilities—movement in the direction given by Christ.—This movement provides the line, their combination and laws" (7: 132). Note that for Schopenhauer, by contrast, the worth of self-consciousness is not very great and correct thinking consists only "in the *endless combinations of concepts* which are carried out with the aid of words."[18]

In his new thrust to discover a personal God, Tolstoy found unexpected allies. The reaction to the philosophical sections of *War and Peace* that deny progress and historical freedom was mostly sour in the democratic and liberal camp.[19] More sympathetic and encouraging reactions praising the holistic, organic quality of Tolstoy's work were pouring in from such older Slavophiles as Mikhail Pogodin, Yury Samarin, Sergey Urusov, and such "men of the soil" as Dostoevsky and Strakhov.[20] To Pogodin Tolstoy bared his soul concerning his divided novelistic faith. With the devout Urusov he discussed the philosophical underpinnings of the Romantic calculus, deciphering vectors of the historical movement. To Samarin he wrote one of his most heartfelt and outlandish letters, urging this successful grassroots reformer to dissociate himself from the elemental hive life and become Tolstoy's religious partner.[21]

Tolstoy's instinctive move toward religious literature is evident in his acknowledgment of the anomaly of *War and Peace*, which he credits to the unexpected influence of Gogol's *Dead Souls* and Dostoevsky's *Notes from the House of the Dead*.[22] The choice is curious indeed. Russian literature knew greater generic oddities than a poem in prose with an unrepentant confidence man at its center and a fictional prison ethnography, plus an unrepentant, delicate, Bible-reading murderer as its narrative voice, but it did not know more successful combinations of moral vagueness and religious yearning. Strakhov's enthusiastic reviews of Tolstoy's novel hailed it as the long-overdue portrayal of healthy Russian life and lifted the stigma of nihilist—imposed by his late comrade Grigoriev—off Tolstoy's shoulders.[23] In his letters to Strakhov, Dostoevsky echoed his view of the "naked national idea of Russia" expressed in *War and Peace*.[24] In 1868–1869, Tolstoy's yearning for Christ coincided with Dostoevsky's firmed view that history is a struggle in transition toward the final state of humanity, its goal foretold in the "final nature" of Christ. While on earth, humanity should strive toward the goal of sacrifice, which is contrary to its egotistical nature, and suffer for it.[25]

Crime and Punishment (1866), which realized the idea of such a conversion in the second epilogue, was published in installments in Katkov's journal *The Russian Messenger* simultaneously with *War and Peace*. Dostoevsky chose to explore in his novel the possibility of a Copernican revolution of freed consciousness almost literally. In one of the decisive confrontations with Porphiry Petrovich, his prosecutor and devil's advocate, Raskolnikov elaborates on the special rights of the extraordinary people and the lawgivers and founders of mankind. He says: "I merely suggested that an 'extraordinary' man has . . . his own right, to allow his conscience to . . . step over certain obstacles. . . . [I]f . . . Kepler's or Newton's discoveries could become known to people in no other way than by sacrificing the lives of one, or ten, or a hundred or more people who were hindering the discovery . . . Newton would have the right, and it would even be his duty . . . to remove those ten or a hundred people. . . ."[26] This phrase in Dostoevsky most likely inspired Tolstoy to write his counterargument regarding the possibility of Copernican and Newtonian revolutions that do not contradict supreme laws of life. Tolstoy considered fitting his Pierre into Raskolnikov's shoes as Pierre nourished his dreams to assassinate Napoleon and liberate humanity. However, he did not allow his hero to commit this suicidal attempt or else make do for indiscriminate murder "of any Frenchman" since Napoleon failed to come Pierre's way (14: 300). Instead, Tolstoy sends Pierre through selection for execution by firing squad and then through captivity and its many horrible epiphanies, choosing to forego the hair-raising moral profits after the murder (Raskolnikov-style) en route to and in Siberia. Despite their differing approaches to the material, the attempt to achieve the synthesis of faith and reason in both works is undertaken in the second epilogue. Dostoevsky depicts the birth of a new word of salvation through the soul of a new man, "This could form a subject for a new story—but this one is finished."[27] Meanwhile, Dostoevsky's wavering ally Strakhov hailed the arrival of such word for Russian literature in the completed volumes of *War and Peace*. Dostoevsky refused to accept this view. The new word? Impossible! After Pushkin Russian literature will be incapable of achieving a greater breakthrough into the depths of religious truth.[28]

THE LIVING FORCE OF THE LAW

Leaving aside the suspicion that Dostoevsky was jealous, one might examine the nature of Tolstoy's horrific episode at Arzamas and ponder over a possibility that the new Tolstoy was then born. Yet neither Tolstoy's diaries nor his letters indicate that Arzamas was more than a fleeting episode, a figment of his rich imagination, suiting the lore of the fantastic, such as his previous abductions by the moon. Simply put, the Arzamas episode was too literary. Its description of symptoms strongly resembled Gérard de Nerval's nightmares in *Aurélia* (1855).[29] Moreover, it already resembled comparable descriptions in Tolstoy's earlier diaries and their refractions in his fiction:

> I saw in my dream that in my dark room the door opened suddenly and frighteningly and then closed again inaudibly. I was terrified, but I was trying to believe that it was the wind. Somebody told me: go and close it, and I went over and wanted to open it first, but somebody was unbendingly holding it from behind. I wanted to run away, but my legs failed me, and an indescribable terror possessed me. I woke up and I was happy with my awakening. What was I happy about? . . . Nothing dies, nothing is individual. . . . We call people higher beings. But what is higher or lower for God? Higher in terms of activity (from our point of view) and lower in terms of happiness—this is the essence of every existence.[30]

The habit of nocturnal dreaming was not given up after Arzamas. In her diary entry for April 19, 1872, Sophia Andreevna wrote: "The whole night, till dawn, Levochka was gazing at the stars."[31] The implication that another Russian writer just experienced a nightmare at the Arzamas inn would mean, by default, that his literary reversion and the birth of his new literary persona would be at hand. To Tolstoy, who only recently corresponded with Dmitry Bludov and exchanged views on his work with the survivors of the Pushkin circle, such implications should have been very clear. Although Tolstoy always found a way to insert his rich poetic experiences into his work, the Arzamas episode was withheld from literary representation until the conversion was almost over. Subsequent chapters will reexamine "The Memoirs of a Madman," for it is important to understand why Tolstoy revived the madness motif and the diary in accounting for the event.

In terms of personal experience, as the father of five children in 1872, Tolstoy adopted the tactic of sticking with the good and not asking for the best so as not to tempt fate: "the best is the enemy of the good" (le mieux est l'ennemi du bien).[32] He advocates the time-honored stoic virtues of patience and submission because the "farther distance one goes, the steeper the steps." Conserving the energy of maturing life, he is preparing to die when called.[33] The deaths of his brother Sergey's son, that of his own son Petya, and of his old Aunt Ergolskaya contributed to his humble acquiescence regarding the propriety of religious burial and its special meaning. Tolstoy sent an irritable letter to Fet to the effect that Schopenhauer's nirvana was nothing compared to humble religious resignation.[34] Leaving aside several months of relative idleness—which frightened Sophia Andreevna, who was still unaccustomed to transitions to new plots—more than ever Tolstoy was convinced that "forty centuries are watching" him "from the heights of these pyramids" and that "the world will perish" should he stop.[35] The latter jocular conviction, related in a letter to Alexandrine, pacified him for the moment with the toppled idol, Napoleon, to whom the words belonged.[36] The "whole fullness of this mess whose name is life" could not disgruntle him for long.[37] In the grips of his new "holy folly" (*eta dur'*), his creative demon, he was sketching a tale about the everyday lives of the cavalry regiment (the embryo of *Anna Karenina*), and confessing to Alexandrine about his only conversional experience of the time, his "terrible work with language" (*rabota nad iazykom uzhasnaia*).[38]

The realization that his language was to be reformed anew occurred simultaneously with the intense activity generated by his new intellectual involvements, the latter resulting from the unresolved competition between necessity and freedom. On the one hand, in *War and Peace* he advanced in the art of describing metaphysical and mental anguish. In this regard, Andrey and Pierre encapsulate the cumulative experience of Tolstoy's earlier doubting and seeking characters in their futile encounters with "what for?" On the other hand, Tolstoy continues to "restrain his Mephistopheles" and at critical moments distracts his heroes' attention from what is impossible to solve in human terms. When they look only to the stars, he directs them toward the low-hanging fruit of life, and vice versa. In the same scene where Pierre arrives at a comforting conclusion that is it horrible for him to die, Tolstoy distracts him by ruminations about the sufferings of Amélie de Mansfeld, Madame Suza's virtuous heroine: "Why did she fight against her despoiler—

he thought—when she loved him? God could not have implanted in her soul a striving that was contrary to his will. My ex-wife did not struggle and perhaps she was right" (II/II/1; 5: 70–71).[39]

Tolstoy's first step in distracting himself creatively was to study intensely the natural sciences in order to understand the processes that preserve and perpetuate life. His immersion in this field between 1870 and 1873 produced hundreds of sketches, calculations, and mysterious-looking schemes. At this time he wrote: "After death, life continues chemically as it here continues physically. Our Heavenly Father has many provinces in which to house life."[40] Eventually Tolstoy came up with his own conception of the vital force, which, to be sure, was unscientific or only partially scientific. In this he relied on his earlier conviction that "the Holy Ghost in the Gospels is *an unconscious force* residing in all people and acting in everyone contrary to his individual striving but in accordance with the universal good and truth."[41] Roughly two years earlier Tolstoy was convinced that man, too, is a force: physical, imaginative, and instinctively moral.[42] His interest lay in identifying points of contact between divine and human force. Dismissing most of the physical sciences (including "the new psychology," which studies "feelings about feelings"), his investigation of matter yielded an understanding of its infinite nature, divisibility, and perpetual motion.[43] Tolstoy's examination of the evolutionary theory of the species dissatisfied him. Darwin's evolutionary concepts did not bring him any further than the "staircase of the organisms," which conceals the secret wherein the primary cause of life is contained.[44] However, Tolstoy did not give up on organic life. On March 17, 1865, while observing and comparing a dog's and man's footprints in the snow, he guessed that there should be a special "instinct of deity" hidden in their dissimilar size, their mass in connection with God, and that their center of gravity should be involved: "This is God's wisdom, but this is no smarts, no intellect. This is an instinct of Divinity. This instinct is in us. Our mind simply enables us to veer away from the instinctive and to rationalize our deviations" (48: 59–60).

In general, Tolstoy's arguments about nature ally him most closely—in addition to Isaac Newton—with Michael Faraday, James Maxwell, and James Thomson, all thinkers who believe in the indestructibility of energy or in the immutable harmony between any temporal disequilibrium and the continuing force of life, proving that force or energy "could not be created or destroyed except by an act of divine power."[45] As new discoveries were made after the 1850s, Tolstoy became suspicious of the kinetic theory of gases and the increasingly microscopic divisions of matter within physics, chemistry, functional anatomy, cell theory, and cell pathology. He was not afraid of the increasing fragmentation of matter by means of which, in the view of the more recalcitrant, these scientific theories were doing away with matter. However, in these approaches to the study of life he observed the tendency not to explain life beyond the newly discovered divisions, which were literally particularizing life. One diary entry inquires impatiently: "Atoms of what? molecules of what?"[46] Aside from transmutations of matter and force, it was gravity, attraction, and repulsion that were still of greatest interest to Tolstoy: "it is not the bodies that are being attracted but the known centers of something. [W]hen the two points exert gravity on each other, which is inversely proportionate to the distances separating them, then the matter surrounding the center we take to be subject to the properties of the center and we say that all matter surrounding the center is subject to the law of inverse ratio to square distance. When will attraction stop? Obviously, only when the two centers coincide. This is the question" (1872; 48: 130–31).[47]

This dabbling with Newton's law of gravity is an attempt to see if the law is relative, that is, if it may be overcome so that the "stone" could fly back to heaven if the stone's and heaven's "centers of gravity" coincide. And what will become of the surrounding matter? For a while it *did* matter to Tolstoy. He felt that for happiness and for a moral life one needs flesh and blood.[48] In his doctrine of the indestructibility of our true nature, or universal will of which we are part, through death, which appeared in the new edition of *Word as Will and Representation*, Schopenhauer reinforced his idea that only phenomena die, and that the more developed self-consciousness becomes, the more painful and vain is its struggle with death.[49] Tolstoy first experimented with these ideas even before his serious reading of Schopenhauer began. Their first traces are visible in Olenin's daydreaming and envying the easy death of the mosquitoes (*The Cossacks*, 1862–1863), and the opposite reaction to the putrefaction of the flesh in Prince Vasily Ilarionovich's despair at the idea that the body will simply rot and then shrivel into dust.[50] In 1863–1864, Tolstoy responded to both reactions with the first drafts of the story "The Strider" (*Kholstomer*), where the scheme is more complex. In this story, the life and death of the man compares unfavorably to that of the horse. After a lifetime of hard work, the strider dies well, like the tree in "Three Deaths," his death serving a life-renewing purpose, since even his hide will be reused.[51]

Tolstoy's return in the late 1860s and the early 1870s to the ideas of good and bad deaths were stimulated by Schopenhauer as much as by his growing friendship with Nikolai Strakhov. Strakhov replaced Vasily Botkin, Tolstoy's closest philosophical and artistic supporter in his struggle for Goethe's *dahin*. Botkin died in 1869 and Tolstoy no longer shared his progressive, antireligious ideas. Strakhov was a perfect new friend for Tolstoy because he combined philosophical and scientific erudition with a distaste for the excessive rationalism of professional Western philosophy and the acumen of Russia's most active literary critic following the departure of Grigoriev.[52] Most of all, Tolstoy appreciated Strakhov's native predisposition for "pure philosophy"—imbibed with poetry and religious explanations—and his ability to express thoughts clearly, complementing delicacy with strength: "You do not tear apart with your fangs but with your gentle yet strong paws."[53] Gentle paws are well visible in how Strakhov mollifies Schopenhauer's indestructibility in his magnum opus entitled *The World as a Whole: Some Features of the Science of Nature* (1872), arguing for the organic hierarchy of the world, of which man is the "summit of nature and the nodal hub of being" (*vershina prirody, uzel bytiia*). Strakhov insisted that humans distinguish themselves from other constituent parts of nature's *panta rei* by understanding their limitations and their significance in the ongoing and self-enriching cycles of nature.[54] Strakhov's description of his consolation, namely, that the point of death is that it is fast and complete, although inspired by Schopenhauer, is filled with poetic awe at the sight of the grandiose destruction of man's superior organism, something to aspire to because "death is a great blessing. Our life is limited precisely because we can *live up* to something, that we can become *absolutely human*; death does not allow us to transcend ourselves."[55] In that sense, death is an added blessing because it fulfills the mysterious law of the universe, not allowing us to outlive our limit (*prezhit' sebia*) and transcend our humanity without depriving us of teleology: live, do, improve. The perfect body lives, acts, and falls, respecting the mysterious meaning of gravity.[56]

Strakhov argued that death occurs because nature needs to move forward as it defies stagnation and does not suffer the boredom of Ecclesiastes. Man also should act, exhibiting a "living striving for everything new" because "all exists only because it acts (*deistvuet*) and finds consolation in its practical solution, or in the possible fulfillment of *duty*."[57] Strakhov rejects the laments of Solomon concerning the futility of life because life is a project of constant practical self-renewal.[58] Tolstoy responded to Strakhov's *World as a Whole* with a lengthy letter in which he criticized Strakhov for labeling too many important questions impenetrable.[59] On the positive side, Strakhov was correct in distinguishing between organic and inorganic nature, and in explaining that materialists make matter divine and do not see any difference between organisms and man. He was also partially correct in arguing that cognition begins from the realm of the spirit and not from matter.[60] Rethinking his conclusions made in *War and Peace* Tolstoy argues that judgment of everything should be a judgment of *consciousness* (*soznanie*). Man does not live to perfect the spirit, but he lives to serve the cause of good, which is the whole and true content of man's life (61: 346–47). Strakhov's focus on the mystery of the spirit and the will did not explain to Tolstoy why the same will might act in a fly or fungi when it serves the goal of evolutionary perfection. (In one telling instance in Strakhov's book, fungi and mold are also shown to be breathing or driven by spirit.)[61] Tolstoy's rebuttal of Strakhov was a more serious rebuttal of his own duplicity after the epilogues. For the first time he gave consciousness a task to establish a clearer relationship with reason. Expressed according to Tolstoy's phrasings of the period, man's goal while he is alive is to establish coincident centers of gravity of reason and consciousness.[62] The two most eloquently expressed disagreements with Strakhov's book Tolstoy reserved for future discussions. He was shaken by Strakhov's Letter IX, "The Content of Human Life," which touched on the possibility of a midlife crisis, and compared man to a stone, a passive object for the mysterious future. Without going into any detail, Tolstoy suggested that Strakhov remove the chapter from his book (61: 347). Tolstoy also remained silent concerning the chapter on death.

Serious conversations on these matters would resume only in late 1875, when the first signs of Tolstoy's crisis appeared. In between Tolstoy wrote Strakhov about the necessity to reform the language of literature and to aim "low" (nizhe), to the hinterlands of culture to identify the popular (narodnoe) (61: 278). In letters to Strakhov, Tolstoy also complained about the repellent Anna Karenina, the false book he was burdened with and which distracted him from more vital tasks, the pedagogy and clarification of questions of life and death with his new friend, the youth of genius philosopher Vladimir Soloviev, author of a critique of abstract philosophy, who stayed with him in May 1875.

MAN AND SOCIAL HISTORY

Tolstoy's efforts to abandon his worries in the excitement of German Naturphilosophie or in the odd consolations of Schopenhauer's gloom did not fuel his optimism for long. Beginning with Goethe, the idea of organic morphology as applied to nature and culture, of organic evolution or "upbringing" (organische Bildung), strongly visible in Strakhov's book, prevailed and helped spread organic morphology in science, with its emphasis on the perfection of the "vital force" and education, on institutions that produce men who perfectly fit the respective cell in the beehive for which they trained or were born.[63] Thus, the atomistic picture of men, the billiard balls scattered randomly by the strike of the Master's cue was replaced in the Romantic and post-Romantic era by the idea of the swarm and then by the organically organized beehive, which was adopted in Russia by Westernizers who believed in the distribution of labor, Slavophiles who believed in the commune, and men of the soil who believed in serving society in one's social cell.[64] Tolstoy's study of the German method, derived from Goethe, during his trips abroad in 1857, and in 1860–1861 of the English method of education, derived from the moral idea of education based on the utilitarian foundation of happiness, involved him in the comparisons of the dogma (or the religious archetype) and the Protestant ethos of social usefulness.

His repeated search for freedom of action in social life was as inalienable a part of his quest after setting limits to freedom in *War and Peace*. Before 1875 Tolstoy tested the extent of this freedom in agricultural, legal, and pedagogical activity, which involved a combination of teaching and religious experimentation. By 1870 Tolstoy's nonacceptance of progress was almost complete. He was convinced that progress is a "belief in the miniscule God" (48: 121), a substitute for the law that moves nations, a shibboleth used by politicians and liberals to justify their materialist expansion for the sake of subjugating other forms of growth and exploiting the poor with an eye toward "general well-being" (48: 128).[65] Strakhov's idea of progress looked meaningless, for it is impossible to perfect infinitely the quality of human life on earth simply by being busy, but only by being busy in a special way. The logical upshot of these ideas was the retreat from history into the patriarchal— or, rather, matriarchal—way of life, which begins with the mother, or queen bee, the woman whose calling is to "lay eggs" and who ensures the life of the hive together with the male worker bee. The idea of the family as the holy nucleus of social life was born between 1868 and 1870.[66] By 1870 Tolstoy believed that he could make a difference in the life of his anthill and hive by assuming the role of a patriarchal master and provider. Yet a corrosive element in Tolstoy's thinking was also already present. While he was buying more land, his anarchic side was telling him in a dream about Proud'hon, that property is theft and that the whole nation should live like half-nomadic Cossacks, where the land is free.[67]

The effect of Tolstoy's incursions into law was equally incompatible with his religious mission. In 1866, while serving as a justice of the peace in the newly reformed administration, Tolstoy delivered a speech defending Vasily Shibunin of 65 Moskovsky Regiment, who was indicted for striking his commander in the face for his chief hounding to correct the spelling of company reports, which the torpid and tipsy Shibunin found humiliating. Shibunin had chosen Tolstoy to represent him in court. The latter built his case on the presumption of compassionate justice due to mitigating circumstances surrounding the life of a halfwitted, simple man who lacked the freedom to defend himself: "The state of the accused is, on the one hand, one of extreme stupidity, simplemindedness and inanity, foreseen by article 109 as a circumstance mitigating punishment. . . . At certain moments when he is under the

influence he is incited toward activity—the state of mental derangement stip-
ulated by article 116" (37: 474).

Tolstoy's attempt to tilt "the scales of justice . . . to the side of mercy"
failed. All but one member of the trial committee—who was not convinced
by the arguments that blackened Shibunin's humanity and obfuscated the
sense of moral choice of what is right for the sake of a man's release—
decided in favor of the death penalty. Tolstoy's appeal, which was written in
haste, omitted the number of the soldier's regiment and company. An inquiry
was sent to him, to which he responded immediately, but Shibunin had already been executed. Although Tolstoy's despair was boundless, he nevertheless repeated the same tactic of acquitting man of guilt in the remaining sections of *War and Peace* (1866–1869), whose ideas of justice closely resemble
Schopenhauer's view of law and morality in *On the Basis of Morality*.[68]

Tolstoy's next brush with the law took place in 1872, when he was under
investigation for the goring of a shepherd on his estate. The experience of
standing at attention at the signal phrase "The Court is in Session!" (*Sud
idet!*) and responding to the interrogating committee, many of whom he
knew socially and did not think highly of either intellectually or morally, was
more than Tolstoy could bear. He thought he could kiss the jailer's hand for
a promise to be left alone for a week so he could write. At the conclusion of
the hearings, which he feared could result in a six- to thirty-six-month im-
prisonment, he wrote an unfinished note entitled "The New Court in Its Application" (*Novyi sud v ego prilozhenii*, 1872).[69] Although the note opened
with self-pity—his system of entrenched safety was again broken into—
Tolstoy quickly switched to pointing out violations and the mishandling of
justice. Two adulterous murderers of their spouses—a merchant's wife and
an upperclass husband—were acquitted by the liberal judges and awarded
monetary rewards for the moral insult, while a petty thief, the moujik who
stole to feed his family, was locked away for years while his family was dying of hunger.

This note was a turning point in Tolstoy's early career as a public intellectual. There would be no social disaster after 1872 to which Tolstoy did not respond. In 1873 Tolstoy wrote an investigative report entitled "On Famine in
Samara" (*O Samarskom golode*), the first example of what was to become his
predominant style of social reportage. Defending the apparent laziness of
peasants who were forewarned of droughts, but did not prepare for the even-
tualities, he quoted his favorite verse from Matthew (Matt. 6.26), to prove
that the peasant alone behaves like the birds in the air who neither sow nor
reap and the heavenly father feeds them, "and should the disastrous year like
this arrive, he would bend his head humbly and say that he must have angered
God with his sins."[70]

Of all his social engagements, pedagogy proved the most fruitful, for it went hand in hand with both Tolstoy's ongoing spiritual investigations and his attempts to reorganize his writing. The school on his estate made headlines when Tolstoy serialized reports of the successes and failures of his anti-progressive educational experiments, including his experimental school, in the journal *Yasnaya Polyana*, which was published in 1861–62. Tolstoy's reports were greeted by Dostoevsky's *Vremya*; resulted in snide remarks from Boris Chicherin, with whom Tolstoy had ended his friendship; and were attacked by Chernyshevsky's journal *The Contemporary* (8: 612, 617). One facet of Tolstoy's pedagogical activity was his continued battle against the idea of Bildung, or education qua evolution, this good Goethean start-up which grew malignantly into the servant of progress, the new deity, "which by its very appearance destroys all questions, doubts, and proofs."[71] In his very first article addressed to the general public, "On Popular Education," Tolstoy shared his puzzlement with the amphibology of present-day education, its dubious position between dogmatism and contemporary science. On the one hand, students learn about the immortality of the soul. On the other hand, they are taught that frogs may be revived by a shot of electric current. Miracles of Jesus of the Nun are taught on the same day as the astronomy lesson advising them that the sun never rotated around the earth (8: 7). Nowhere in the practices of the German Bildung did Tolstoy witness the living appropriation of the eternal. Tolstoy published the results of his experiments with teaching students the Jewish Bible, the New Testament, the Lord's Law (*Zakon Bozhii*), religious history, world and Russian history, geography, math, the ABC's, creative literature, the natural sciences, music, and drawing.

The students' enthusiasm in creative reworking of the biblical and New Testament episodes delighted Tolstoy while modern representations of the biblical episodes in secular fine art left them cold. Tolstoy's attitude to these learning developments allows him to rediscover Kant's idea of a relationship between catechistic and didactic knowledge. For Kant the doctrine of virtue is a moral catechism that cannot be learned by rote and then scientifically applied. Superimposed ethics gives way to a synthetic revelation of the categorical imperative.[72] After *War and Peace*, Tolstoy returned to his idea that the didactic prevails over the secular and over the catechistic dead letter. He co-opted the best local teachers, Strakhov, and requested the assistance of Archimandrite Leonid of Tula, whom he asked to compile a list of "the best and, most of all, popular vitae" drawn from the Menology of Russian Saints and didactic stories to produce Popular Slavic Readers.[73] In drafts of a new essay on popular education—whose published version reiterated his belief that "what we call the soul" should not be analyzed but rather brought out in free interactive communication between teacher and student—he concluded

that in teaching and in learning man "should found his right on some indubitable truth, on the knowledge of what is necessary. This knowledge is unavailable from anywhere but what is given by faith."[74] Thus, the indubitable
truth of the didactic and sacred literature served Tolstoy as the best possible
link between the law of life and consciousness of this law in man's daily activity.

THE WORD INTO LOGOS: ABC'S AND MORAL ART

How was Tolstoy's literary activity related to his denial of the validity of the
existing literary Bildung? In 1867, he criticized Turgenev's novel *The Smoke*
(Dym; 1867) for its lack of the wit of the heart, and its artificially playful "wit
of the wit" (*um uma*) in condemning calculated infatuation of the mind with
politics and love. Concerning Turgenev Tolstoy added: "One more is done
for. I desire and hope that my turn will never come" (61: 172). Sensing his
friend's uncertainty about his own future after *War and Peace*, Fet wrote to
Tolstoy in August 1868 that he was unrivaled in combining freedom and the
law for the unity of representation.[75] Yet Tolstoy was no longer satisfied with
the abstruse competition between necessity and freedom in history: "If all
were known, there wouldn't be anything interesting about watching our comedy. And we would have stopped playing our roles so seriously."[76]

Since about 1868, Tolstoy was looking for new ways to create a complete
literary work: "Where are the laws? Either a mystic movement forward or an
artistic reproduction of the past" (48: 87). He was looking for his new labor
of love. In the summer of 1871 he read Herodotus while staying at his Samara
estate in Bashkiria. He was so enraptured by these myths devoid of forced
tension that he wrote to Fet in July 1871, vouching never again to write "ver-
bose drivel" (*mnogoslovnaia drebeden'*) of the type of *War and Peace*.[77] In a
letter dated May 31, 1873, to Strakhov, who praised the philosophical sections of the book, Tolstoy informed him about the excision of all "deliberations" from the new edition of the novel (62: 30–31). In the first chapters of
Anna Karenina written in 1873, Tolstoy was guided by Pushkin's humble la-
conism.[78] Although flexible about genre, he was increasingly less so about
language, of which verbosity was only a partial problem. To Sergey Urusov
Tolstoy confessed that a fable about the "law of the mortality of the tsars" that
he read in Herodotus—most likely the tale about the wise man Solon and the
king Croesus—introduced him to a different variation on the disclosure of the
law of life in literature.

Tolstoy's ingrained impatience with secular literature had been long in the
making. Some of the first criticisms leveled at him by advocates of gentle so-

cial art, such as Alexander Druzhinin and Turgenev, were against excessive psychological detail based upon physical reactions and his "hellish turns of phrase," a certain merchant-style vulgarity in his writing.[79] Now, through his pedagogical activity, he launched a revolution of poetic language. Numerous letters to Strakhov, Fet, and Alexandrine Tolstaya dating from 1871 speak about a "pause" necessary for reforming his language.[80] In his accounts of the experiments that he conducted in 1862 at his school for peasant children in Yasnaya Polyana, Tolstoy complained that in Russian there existed no "intermediary language" between the fairy tales or popular legends of Afanasiev and the literature of Karamzin and the Pushkin school. Belying its origin of precisely one such middle passage between religious literature of the Old Church Slavonic and the base vernacular tongues of the mob, the latter school was turning into a canon of aristocratic art. Tolstoy was looking for a transitional, provisional element, that certain elusive something (*chto-nibud'*), to bridge the gap between belles lettres and primitive art.[81] Such examples already existed on Russian soil. In the year of Herzen's death (1870), Tolstoy recalled Nikolai Ge's *succès de scandale* of 1863, his painting of the Last Supper, with Herzen serving as the model for Christ, and decided that such a sacred topic was *not* suitable for popular religious art (1870; 48: 118). The "middle style" of the 1850s and 1860s literature, with its mixed-estate (*raznochinnaia*) varieties, or popular stylizations in the works of the playwright Ostrovsky or the satirist Saltykov did not satisfy Tolstoy's effort to shield his natural man from democratic ethos. Tolstoy solicited further suggestions for the development of *transitional literature* (*perekhodnaia literatura*), his purgatorial project for the Russian spirit via Danteasque noble vulgar eloquence launched initially in his pilot journal *Yasnaya Polyana* (8: 61).[82] In this critical transitional period Tolstoy introduces a new era in the debates on languages and styles that reverses the route of progress and situates the literary paradise as the lost origin standing in need of recovery, and not as a cumulative result of enlightenment and modern evolution. Witness this typical rumination of the period: "A feeling for truth, beauty, and goodness is independent of the stage of development. When born, man represents a harmonious prototype for truth, beauty, and goodness; every hour of life, every minute in time . . . threaten to disrupt this harmony. Our ideal is behind us, not ahead of us" (1862; 8: 301–24).

This backward route to pure origins explains why, instead of returning to the Decembrist plot for another attempt at recovering the secret to their conversion, Tolstoy mined a much older historical period with abundant religious prototypes and decided to write a history of the persecution of the Old Believers at the dawn of the reign of Peter the Great. First drafts for this project were halted in 1873, when the plot of *Anna Karenina* speeded up. Let us recall Pierre's unending curiosity about the mass of peasants, "them" (*oni*), the impenetrable circles of Karataev's parables, and their indomitable yet unconscious connection to "that thing" (*ono*), the force of the law. Tolstoy's idea to open up the peasant, this thing-in-itself, and study him *alongside* the living force would seem logical from the point of view of Tolstoy's long search. The word "alongside" is key to understanding Tolstoy's new preoccupation with making the art of the parable again functional in the modern world. In this preoccupation, Tolstoy is again recuperating the archaic meanings; the word "parable" meaning "juxtaposition" and "comparison" in the Greek that he was teaching himself since 1869 originates from the verb implying the act of setting things alongside and comparing.

Tolstoy set off comparing the literary eras. In a letter to Strakhov, he devised a theory of literary ups and downs, which he called the "curve of Russian literature." On a horizontal line symbolizing eternity, Russian literature rises from nothingness at the time of Karamzin, reaches its peak with Pushkin, pauses at Lermontov and Gogol, begins its decline with "us, the sinful souls," and should descend and ultimately die. On March 3, 1872, Tolstoy concluded: "It seems to me that this is not a period of decay but death with a promise of resurrection in popular art" (61: 274). When Strakhov inquired about the nature of death and resurrection in the word, Tolstoy responded that death through literature was necessary, "to descend there, so we are free . . . What is lower is popular. I have changed the manner of my writing and my language . . . because this is necessary."[83] If ever a prototypical plot were to be found, and the popular character grasped, the archetype of literature—a circle of eternity, where nothing and everything are simultaneously present—would begin its life and crown Tolstoy's own literary Arzamas. In his effort to consolidate the forces of this new literature, which would bury the old world in order to give rise to the new, Tolstoy certainly saw himself as the primary sower of the logos. He could also count on participation of remarkable commentators and collectors of Old Russian literature and popular tales as Fedor Buslaev, Nikolai Tikhonravov, the followers of Aleksandr Afanasiev, the famous collector of popular and apocryphal legends, who died in 1871. Tolstoy was also eager to rely on the art of Nikolai Leskov, the author of tales recounting the criminal life of merchants, and master of the stylized folk idiom (*skaz*), who by 1873 had also published three novels based on the life of pilgrims and the clergy.[84]

At the time he wrote the letter to Strakhov, and before the project with Leonid of Tula could materialize, Tolstoy had already published two editions of ABC's for peasant children (1871, 1874) and four Russian readers (1874–1875). Among his tales published in the Russian readers, Tolstoy was especially proud of two: "God Sees the Truth But Waits" and "Prisoner of the Caucasus" (1872).[85] Bearing Tolstoy's warning in mind that the tales did not express the ideology of the soil, one notices that both stories rewrite the situations or subplots in *War and Peace* and Dostoevsky's *Notes from the House of the Dead*, Tolstoy's acknowledged inspiration for the latter. The longer but easier rewrite concerns "Prisoner of the Caucasus." Zhilin and Kostylin, two low-ranking Russian officers who are close to commoner status, find themselves swept up in the Tatar captivity and are at risk of losing their lives unless ransom, which neither can afford, is paid. Zhilin (from "tendon" or "vein") is the antithesis of Kostylin (the Crutch). The former is an enterprising and optimistic opportunist, the quintessence of freedom, who wastes no time in devising escape schemes and succeeds on his second try, albeit with the knowledge that if he is caught again he will be killed. The latter is the embodiment of passivity, resignation, and lack of zest for life. In a plot for the new literature, Karataev-Schopenhauer attitudes are clearly not favored: Zhilin, who survives and makes the rescue of his comrade possible, is the tale's unquestionable hero. Relative to Karataev's philosophy of nonresistance, Kostylin is released "barely alive," serving as the negative example. Echoing Dostoevsky, Tolstoy's tale celebrates strong types derived from Dostoevsky's book, criminals like Orlov or Kulikov, who never lose their dignity, fear punishment, or hesitate regarding whether to escape.

"God Sees the Truth But Waits" offers a more subtle rendering of the theme of resignation and guilt. The merry and carefree merchant Aksenov is slipped the knife with which his drinking buddy had committed murder. Aksenov is tried and sent to Siberia, spending twenty-six years at hard labor. His family all but renounces him. In the camp he reads the Bible and various holy books. With his white beard and humble but resolute demeanor, he resembles a wise old sage at fifty-one. Shortly thereafter Makar Semenovich, the man who had willfully framed him, is delivered to their prison. Not only does Aksenov guess Makar's identity, he witnesses his enemy digging a tunnel for escape. In defiance of Makar's threats and his offer to lead him out if he keeps quiet, Aksenov calls upon God as his witness for whatever he will do. He is pressed by the commandant, again in God's name, to tell the truth about the tunnel. Once again he overcomes the temptation, shaken as he is by the realization that Makar has ruined his life. At night Makar confesses his crime to Aksenov and begs to be pardoned in God's name. He petitions Aksenov to let him confess his crime publicly so that Aksenov can be released and his wrong undone. He does confess, but Aksenov refuses to leave prison, saying he has found the truth and can die. When his official pardon arrives, he has already died. For all its remarkable simplicity, the story's strong moral undercurrent is supported by very delicate markers: small details in the confrontation between divine and human law will be missed if parallelisms in the construction—with invocations to God, which coincide with the decisive challenges to conscience—are not considered in their concrete context. Aksenov waits, as does God, and their axes or centers of gravity coincide only when Aksenov feels no bitterness or wrong after forgiving his enemy. If he catered to the invocations to his holiness before, he would have taken the wand of justice out of God's hand and denounced Makar one way or another.[86] The story is remarkable in its own right, but doubly so, since it constitutes a complete rewrite of Karataev's bland parable told in *War and Peace* of a merchant who was wrongly accused and died passively. Passive as well was the reception of the tale as a plain anecdote by Karataev's audience, Pierre including. In addition, Tolstoy's psychological thriller on a moral theme harnesses two narrated stories overheard or witnessed by Gorianchikov, the unrepentant convicted wife-murderer and narrator of Dostoevsky's *Notes from the House of the Dead*. The dispassionately related injustices in a similar story about the Lomovs in Dostoevsky's book, the merchants who are wrongly accused and die in prison, are redeemed only by the impersonal and barely audible or noticeable prayers of the old holy man in the corner of the barracks.[87]

Tolstoy must have been bothered by the impassive demeanor of Dostoevsky's title character, the hungry collector of tales about suffering and repentance of other wife murderers, who has not shared a shred of his conscience while reaching epiphanies when his success in adjusting to life in the barracks is proven. Gorianchikov's unhappiness, loneliness, and speedy death while in exile in Siberia—after release his notes are "discovered" and collected by an anonymous editor to form the book—are only oblique indicators that he has paid for some unredeemable inner flaw. In an obvious gesture signaling his desire to leave no moral ambiguity unpunished, in 1875 Tolstoy drafted his own version of a similar crime and left the murderous husband thirsting for God's vengeance against himself alone with his thoughts: "As he was sitting on his cot he could hear commoners talk about his crime; one commoner felt satisfied that after the reforms masters would get the same for murder as 'them.' 'Trial,' he thought.—'Let it be. The knout. Siberia—let them be too. And let her see how the henchman will tear my flesh criss-cross while flogging me. She won't see. . . .' He tried to pray, but only fury against God was rising in his soul. At the same time he felt he was in His hands. He did not sleep two nights in a row and could not sleep."[88] The fragment breaks off enigmatically with the murderer undressing and entering the river for a mysterious conversion rite or suicide.

The contents of Tolstoy's ABC's, the Russian readers, and his other activities in 1869–75 suggest one of the most pious men in the empire. In the readers, David's Psalms, Genesis, the Ten Commandments, the verse about the birds of the air, the Symbol of the Creed, the Lord's Prayer, and ten other most important prayers of the Orthodox creed, the vita of Sergius of Radonezh— all are interlaced with fables of Aesop, moral parables from world folklore, and a few of Tolstoy's tales in the new language. This mixture also includes articles from the lore of the natural sciences about gases, heat, and atmospheric conditions. Those latter commissioned from and written by Strakhov offer no surprises. Those written by Tolstoy are transparent reflections of his hidden disquiet. The article "Bedbugs" (*Klopy*), about a traveler who is forced out of bed and leaves the inn in the middle of the night is a concealed retelling of the nightmare at the Arzamas inn (21: 213). There is one reminder of the unfinished business concerning the philosophy of nature and necessity: "Ballooned like a bubble rain water then broke into naught" (21: 59). William James commented as well on the role of the natural sciences in the lives of converts. He wrote to the effect that converts are something like the bubbles in which science recognizes the God of universal laws, "the bubbles on the foam which coats a stormy sea are floating episodes." To such a God of science, "our private selves are like those bubbles—epiphenomena" and their destinies "weigh nothing and determine nothing in the world's irremediable currents of events."[89] Only in our private and personal phenomena do we handle the actual, and egotistical, retail with God.

In his note "On Religion" Tolstoy asked precisely such a retail question of someone disillusioned with science, remembering, "with bitterness, *that he has no one to pray to*, that there is nothing up there? What am I? Why do I live? What will become after death? and if there is a connection between me and that higher power, can I plead to it—pray?" (7: 125). Anyone who studies conversion can't help remembering in this regard the anecdote with which A. A. Nock begins his exploration of the topic: "When [man] releases his hold on a stone which he has held in his hand and it falls to the ground, the result is always the same, and there is nothing to excite any feeling of dependence on unknown forces." What Tolstoy describes in his preoccupation with stones and gravitation is the dealings with the uncanny that inspire according to Nock a need of religion and consequently conversion arises.[90]

Busy at work on his purgatorial art project in the early 1870s, Tolstoy reflected on Plato's *Phaedo* and its themes of immortality and love to others. Plato's dialogue attracted him as he was bearing in mind that man thinks that his life is "a transient thing, the treble of Plato's lyre" (48: 68) only when he adopts the bird's-eye view on life, and he thinks the same of other lives. In a compassionate relationship with life built on love, Tolstoy reasoned, man will not be an indifferent tool of law for himself, others, and God. The artist in him was another unsolved enigma: "An artist of sound, lines, color, of the word and of the thought finds himself in a terrible situation when he does not believe in the meaningfulness of expressing his thought. What does it depend upon? It is not love of the thought. Love is anxious. And this faith is *quiet*. And there are times I do and don't have it. Why is that? A mystery" (48: 67).

Tolstoy had to decide whether in his art and personal fate he was ready to become a singer of Ecclesiastes.

NOTES

1. Fragment no. 318a (15: 241–42).
2. See Zhukovsky, *Izbrannoe*, 265–83. In his drafts, Tolstoy castigates Zhukovsky's lifelong infatuation with religious nationalism (15: 52).
3. Tolstoy is here responding to Polevoy's criticism of *War and Peace* in the *Russian Messenger (Russkii Vestnik)* (fragment no. 318a; 15: 240).
4. Chaadaev, *Polnoe sobranie sochinenii*, 1: 98–99, 204–5. Further references are cited parenthetically in the text.
5. This is a Hegelian scheme. See Hegel, *The Philosophy of History*, 319.
6. History is "spirit emptied out into time." Hegel, *Phenomenology of Spirit*, 492–93.
7. Tolstoy was aware of the awkward comparison. In the drafts he considered the merits of Pushkin's poem "The Hero" (Geroi, 1830), prefaced by "What Is Truth?" (Chto est'istina?), in which the poet chooses the lofty poetic lie over the "myriad of base truths" and sides with his chosen hero, despised by the mob. "What application is there for the base truth that all people are people and not heroes?" Tolstoy honors nameless doers of history: "Only this practical application of the base truth already proves that even a single base truth is dearer to us than the myriad of elevating lies" (15: 53). In 1869, Tolstoy disagreed with Chaadaev as he did with the whole German Romantic tradition where the role of prophets was concerned. By comparison, Chaadaev argues that acting through history and through the appointed prophets (Moses, David, Aristotle, Marcus Aurelius, Mahomet), the universal law governs the "moral movement of the centuries," and so history both mediates and meditates, observes and is observed, providing the scene for the collaborative effort of freedom and necessity, of consciousness and reason.
8. "Conscious and unconscious activities are to be absolutely one in the product. . . . The two are to be one for the self itself." Schelling, *System of Transcendental Idealism*, 222, 228.
9. Hegel, *The Philosophy of History*, 322.
10. Hegel, *The Philosophy of History*, 321–23. On Hegel's discussion of force, understanding and law, see Hegel, *Phenomenology of Spirit*, 90.
11. Hegel, *Phenomenology of Spirit*, 421, 424. For an alternative interpretation of the balancing act of *Verstand* (intuitive thinking) and *Vernunft* (analytical reason) in *War and Peace*, see Orwin, *Tolstoy's Art and Thought*, 132–40. For the same in relation to the dialectic of contradiction pertinent mainly to the Neoplatonic movement and Schelling's identity philosophy, see Love, *The Overcoming of History in War and Peace*, esp. 117–23, 150–54.
12. Cf. the following diary entry dated February 17, 1858: "There is personal and common truth. Common truth is 2 x 2 = 4 only. Christianity! It is totally artistic" (48: 73).

13. The work's Russian title is *Aphorismata po povodu psikhiatricheskoi teorii doktora Krupova. Sochineniie prozektora i ad'iunkt professora Tita Leviafanskogo.* See Herzen's explanation of the circumstances surrounding the writing, Herzen, 1: 468.

14. Herzen, 1: 471, 473.

15. Herzen, 1: 476.

16. The initial title of the fragment was "Could One Prove Religion?" The fragment was inspired by his reading, on October 16, 1865, of works by Henrietta Guizot-Witte, daughter of the famous historian and critic François Guizot. Tolstoy must have read one of the following: *Petites méditations chrétiennes à l'usage du culte domestique* (1862), *Nouvelles petites méditations chrétiennes* (1864), and *Histoire sainte racontée aux enfants* (1865). Tolstoy also used Montaigne's *Essais*, esp. the "Apologie de Raimond Sebond" (7: 366).

17. On this point I beg to differ with Sigrid McLaughlin, who sees Tolstoy's earlier attraction to Schopenhauer as based on humility, of which Christ is the emblem. See her article "Some Aspects of Tolstoy's Intellectual Development: Tolstoy and Schopenhauer," *California Slavic Studies* 5 (1970): 187–248. However, Tolstoy agrees with Schopenhauer on Jeremiah: "The Old Testament speaks about predestination (Jer. 10.23), and that man's deeds are not in his own power" (15: 225). Verses 23–25 from Jeremiah read: "O know, O Lord, that the way of human beings is not in their control, that mortals as they walk cannot direct their steps. Correct me, O Lord, but in just measure; not in your anger; or you will bring me to nothing. Pour out your wrath on the nations that do not know you." (*New Oxford Annotated Bible*, OT 979). A seemingly sudden inclusion of Christ where Israel is chastised for not following God's will could mean that Tolstoy's first interpretation of his historical role is that of submission and reconciliation (Jer. 4: 1–2 and 4: 14, 17–18). In Luke 21: 18 Christ predicts wars at the end of the world: "You will be hated by all because of my name. *But not a hair of your head will perish.*" (Luke 21: 9–22; *New Oxford Annotated Bible*, NT, 115). The corresponding Russian translation of "perish" is *spadet*/fall and of "lost" is *poterian*.

18. Schopenhauer, *Prize Essay*, 9–10.

19. See summary of these views in Knowles, *Tolstoy: The Critical Heritage*, 89–190.

20. For Tolstoy's collaboration with the older Slavophiles, see Boris Eikhenbaum, *Tolstoi in the Sixties*, trans. Duffiel White (Ann Arbor, Mich.: Ardis, 1982), 176.

21. See Tolstoy's letter to Samarin dated January 10, 1867 (61: 158–59).

22. In his essay "A Few Words About *War and Peace*," Tolstoy cites Gogol and Dostoevsky to prove that "in the new period of Russian literature there isn't a single work of fiction surpassing the mediocre that would completely fit into the form of a novel, narrative poem, or long short story" (16: 7).

23. For Strakhov's reviews of the first edition of Tolstoy's collected works, plus his four essays on *War and Peace*, see Nikolai Strakhov, *Kriticheskie stat'i ob I.S.Turgeneve i L.N.Tolstom (1862–1885),* ed. C. H. van Schooneveld. Slavistic Printings and Reprintings, 147. (The Hague: Mouton, 1968), 145–310. Strakhov's essays against "real" nihilism in literature originally appeared serially in 1861–1865.

24. See Dostoevsky's letter to Strakhov from Florence, dated February 26 (March 10), 1869, in Dostoevsky, vol. 29 (Part I), 17.

25. See Dostoevsky's note written at the foot of the casket of his first wife, Maria Isaeva in "Notebook, 1863–1864." Dostoevsky, 20: 174–75.

26. See Part III, chapter 5 of *Crime and Punishment* (Dostoevsky, 6: 199). Translated passage quoted from Fyodor Dostoevsky, *Crime and Punishment*, trans. Richard Pevear and Larissa Volokhonsky (New York: Vintage, 1993), 259–60.

27. For the scenes mentioned, see part 4, chap. 4, plus the second epilogue.

28. See Dostoevsky's letter to Strakhov dated March 24, 1870, in Dostoevsky, vol. 29 (Part I), 114.

29. Cf. the Arzamas jocular announcement of the new literary millennia through the adoption of the new secular word with Nerval's description in chapter 3 of *Aurélia*: "I went and slept at an inn where I was known. The innkeeper spoke to me of one of my old friends who lived in the town and who had blown his brains out after some unlucky speculation. . . . Sleep brought me dreadful dreams. I was in a room I did not know and talking to someone from the outside world." Gérard de Nerval. *Aurélia and Other Writings*, trans. Geoffrey Wagner, Tober Duncan, and Marc Lowenthal (Boston: Exact Change, 1996), 41.

30. Diary entry dated April 11, 1858 (48: 75).

31. Sophia Andreevna Tolstaya, *Dnevniki*. 2 vols. (Moscow: Khudozhestvennaia literatura, 1978), 1: 85.

32. Letter to Alexandrine Tolstaya dated July 5, 1865 (61: 93).

33. Ibid., January 18–23, 1872 (61: 71) and March 31, 1872 (61: 280–81).

34. Letter to Fet dated January 30, 1873 (62: 6–7). See also letters to Sergey Tolstoy (same date) (62: 7); to Tatiana Kuzminskaya, May 18, 1873 (62: 27–28); to Fet, November 18, 1873 (62: 55); and to Alexandrine Tolstaya, June 1–15, 1874 (62: 95).

35. Sophia Andreevna Tolstaya, *Dnevniki*, 1: 89.

36. Letter to Alexandrine Tolstaya dated December 15–30, 1874 (62: 130).

37. Ibid., September 23, 1872 (61: 320–21).

38. Ibid., April 6–8, 1872 (61: 281).

39. Note that at exactly the same time Dostoevsky pushes his characters toward the situation where they can flaunt their defiance against fate, "stick out their tongue at it," and fool contingency or the limits of human endurance (Dostoevsky, 5: 224).

40. Tolstoy, diary entry dated November 5, 1873 (48: 67).

41. Diary entry dated April 6, 1858 (48: 74).

42. Diary December, 7, 1868 (48: 88) and October 1868 (48: 106).

43. On March 18, 1858, Tolstoy wrote in his diary: "Magnetism, electricity, the most unexpected conclusions out of the simplest things and yet lack of concern how to apply them to life" (48: 74). The following note on matter was jotted down on March 16, 1868: "Matter is one. Matter is for itself. Matter is infinitely divisible. We don't know space without matter and can't imagine it" (48: 148). On moving matter, see the notes for January-February 1872 (48: 93).

44. Diary March 17, 1870 (48: 117). Cf. his caustic comment of November 26, 1871, against zoology and biology: "Let's search for eggs on a polyp and look for insemination in a fern" (48: 113).

45. P. M. Harman, *Energy, Force and Matter: The Conceptual Development of Nineteenth-Century Physics* (Cambridge: Cambridge University Press, 1982), 57.

46. Diary entry dated January 12, 1873 (48: 95).

47. Tolstoy is reformulating Newton's law of universal gravitational force: "That there is a power of gravity pertaining to all bodies, proportional to the several quantities of matter which they contain. The universe is composed of particles of matter all of which attract each other with a force proportional to the products of their masses and inversely proportional to the square of the distance between them." Richard S. Westfall, *The Construction of Modern Science* (Cambridge: Cambridge University Press, 1977), 155.

48. Letter to Alexandrine Tolstaya dated November 26–27, 1865 (61: 121).

49. Schopenhauer, *The World as Will and Representation*, 2: 267, 271.

50. See the discussion of the story "Distant Hunting Ground" in chapter 3 of the present study. Tolstoy returned to it in 1865.

51. Tolstoy finished the story in 1885.

52. Strakhov held degrees in physics, mathematics, and zoology and defended a thesis on the skeletal structure of mammals. Before attending university, he studied at a seminary. In short, he combined the perfect mixture of skills and personal characteristics. For the most comprehensive discussion of Strakhov's views and the fullest biography, see Linda Gerstein, *Nikolai Strakhov* (Cambridge, Mass.: Harvard University Press, 1971). For a history of Tolstoy's and Strakhov's intellectual and personal relationship, including their complete correspondence, see Leo Tolstoy and Nikolaj Strakhov, *Complete Correspondence in Two Volumes*, ed. Andrew A. Donskov and comp. Lydia Dmitrievna Gromova and Tatiana Georgievna Nikiforova (Ottawa and Moscow: Slavic Research Group at the University of Ottawa and State L. N. Tolstoy Museum, 2003). Andrew Donskov's essay plus bibliography, "Leo Tolstoy and Nikolaj Strakhov: A Personal and Literary Dialogue" (viii–lvi) is the best source of knowledge about Tolstoy and Strakhov's intellectual friendship.

53. See letter to Strakhov dated September 13, 1871 (62: 262).

54. Nikolai Strakhov, *Mir kak tseloe: Cherty iz nauki o prirode* (St. Petersburg: Tipografiia K. Zamyskovskogo, 1872), viii–ix.

55. Strakhov, Letter VII, "The Meaning of Death" (Pis'mo VII. Znachenie smerti), in *Mir kak tseloe*, 134.

56. Ibid., 173–76, 151.

57. Ibid., x, 115, 443.

58. Ibid., 201, 254.

59. Letter to Strakhov dated November 12, 1872 (61: 345–49).

60. Strakhov, *Mir kak tseloe*, 74. Tolstoy's refers to this page; see 61: 346.

61. Ibid., 61.

62. For other aspects of Tolstoy's interest in Strakhov's book and ideas, see Orwin's discussion of this letter and other correspondence in her *Tolstoy's Art and Thought*, 167–69 and 188–92.

63. On Goethe's idea of organic morphology, see Robert Richards, *The Romantic Conception of Life: Sciences and Philosophy in the Age of Goethe* (Chicago: University of Chicago Press, 2002), 477.

64. On organic versus atomistic society, of Enlightenment billiard balls changing into a Romantic swarm, see Peter Thorslev, *Romantic Contraries: Freedom Versus Destiny* (New Haven, Conn.: Yale University Press, 1984), 56–61.

65. On November 7, 1868, Tolstoy wrote Pogodin, sharing with him vague plans about starting a new journal, which he planned to name *Non-Contemporary* (*Ne-Sovremennik*), or the enemy of the democratic and single-mindedly progressive legacy of *Sovremennik*. See Tolstoy, "Progress" (Nov. 2 and 9, 1868; 7: 130–31).

66. Tolstoy, "On Marriage and the Woman's Calling" (O brake i prizvanii zhenshchiny) (1868; 7: 133–35).

67. "'La propriété c'est vol' . . . The Russian Revolution will not be against the tsar or despotism but against landed property.—I saw all of this in a dream. August 13." Notebook 2, August 13, 1865 (48: 85).

68. Tolstoy related his painful memories of this botched defense to his biographer Pavel (Posha) Biriukov. In 1908 Biriukov intended to publish the text of Tolstoy's defense in the second volume of his biography of the writer. In addition, he asked Tolstoy to write a memoir concerning the event. Tolstoy responded with his "Memoir About a Soldier on Trial" (Vospominaniia o sude nad soldatom, April 1908), representing one of the epiphanies of his teaching of nonviolent resistance to evil (37: 67–75).

69. Tolstoy, "The New Court in Its Application," 17: 319–23; 702–8.

70. Tolstoy, "On Famine in Samara," 17: 61–70.

71. Tolstoy, "Progress and the Definition of Education" (Progress i opredelenie obrazovaniia, 2nd vers., 1862; 8: 590). Subsequent references to this essay will appear parenthetically in the text. In general, subsequent references to essays published in *Yasnaya Polyana* omit the year, which the reader should assume is 1861–1862.

72. In *The Metaphysics of Morals*, as well as in his other works, Kant divides ethics into a doctrine of elements and a doctrine of method. See *The Metaphysics of Morals*, ed. Mary J. Gregor (Cambridge: Cambridge University Press, 1996), 221–26. See also "The Philosophy Faculty Versus the Theology Faculty," in *The Conflict of Faculties*, trans. Mary J. Gregor (Lincoln: University of Nebraska Press, 1979), 73.

73. Letter to Pavel Golokhvastov dated November 1–2, 1874 (62: 120).

74. Tolstoy, "O narodnom obrazovanii" (1874); 17: 79, 325.

75. See Fet's letters to Tolstoy in *Tolstoy: Perepiska s russkimi pisateliami*, 1: 398.

76. Letter to Urusov dated April–May 1871 (61: 253).

77. Letter to Afanasy Fet dated July 16–17, 1871 (61: 256).

78. Letter to Strakhov (unsent) dated March 25, 1873 (62: 16).

79. See Druzhinin's letter to Tolstoy dated October 6, 1856, quoted in *Tolstoy: Perepiska s russkimi pisateliami*, 1: 267.

80. See, for example, a letter to Strakhov dated March 22–25, 1872 (61: 277).

81. Tolstoy, "Yasnopolyanskaya School," first essay (8: 58).

82. Cf. the beginning of "Canto primo" of Dante's *Purgatorio* dreaming of a realm where human spirit can purge itself, "dove l'umano spirito si purga" in Dante Alighieri, *La divina commedia. Inferno. Purgatorio. Paradiso*. 3 vols. intro. Bianca Garavelli. Notes by Lodovico Magugliani (Milan: RCS libri, 1949. Reprinted by Milan: Superbur classici, 2001), 2: 51.

83. Letter to Strakhov dated March 22–25, 1872 (61: 278).

84. Leskov's novels drawn from the life of Old Believers and peasant pilgrims *Cathedral Folk* (Soboriane, 1872), *The Sealed Angel* (Zapechatlennyi angel, 1873), and *The Enchanted Wanderer* (Ocharovannyi strannik, 1873) solidified Leskov's reputation as the principal Russian chronicler of the life of the Russian religious mind.

85. The former, "Bog pravdu vidit da ne skoro skazhet," was included in the *Third Russian Book for Reading* (21: 246–53), while the latter, "Kavkazskii plennik," appeared in *The Fourth Russian Book for Reading* (21: 304–26).

86. For a detailed analysis of the artistic structure of the story, see the splendid essay by Gary Jahn, "A Structural Analysis of Leo Tolstoy's 'God See the Truth But Waits,'" *Studies in Short Fiction* 12 (1975): 261–69.

87. For the Lomovs' story, see part 2, chapter 5, of Dostoevsky's text.

88. "The Wife-Murderer" (Ubiitsa zheny) (1868–69; 7: 149–51).

89. James, *Varieties of Religious Experience*, 495.

90. Nock, Conversion: *The Old and the New*, xiii.

Part Two

Chapter Seven

The Course of Tolstoy's Conversion: From Philosophy to Christ (1875–1878)[1]

THE MAN AT THE SUMMIT AND HARMONY OF KNOWLEDGE

Tolstoy's exchanges with Strakhov in the early 1870s authenticated his deepening commitment to the question of life's meaning. The 1870s promised to confirm his suspicion, first expressed in the philosophical fragments of 1845–1852, that middle-aged people who refute the laws of religion watch in horror as their intellectual foundation (*opora*) collapses. In 1875, Tolstoy read Strakhov's fictional diary of the new brand of active idealism embodied in the person of "T-khov," a provincial doctor who endures the bitterness of life by serving his duty and even ends his letter unfinished, hurrying off to a house call.[2] Although Strakhov's idealist cuts the umbilical cord connecting him with nature, in his activity he respects and imitates its incessant drive toward change; he works in order not to think about the inevitable end. Tolstoy took the story to mean the defense of the old superfluous men whom nature feeds nothing but despair.[3] Conversations with Strakhov on activity and superfluity, the idealism of the crestfallen Hamlets of the Grigoriev type, and the place of autonomous consciousness in the organic universe were imbued with Schopenhauer's pessimism and Grigoriev's calls for the poetry of Ecclesiastes.[4]

In November 1875 Strakhov shared with Tolstoy his impressions of the written parts of *Anna Karenina*, expressing admiration for Tolstoy's outlook of a "benign Christian monk" who practices an active attitude (*deiatel'noe otnoshenie*) to life. Strakhov also brought in Tolstoy's old philosophical favorite, Kant's "three questions" (What can I know? What must I do? What should I hope for?), finding that the second question is the most important.[5]

On November 30, 1875, Tolstoy sent Strakhov a remarkable letter to address Kant's questions and "explain the meaning of life" (62: 219–30). Regarding the priority of putting Kant's questions forth, however, Tolstoy disagreed: "You will notice that of Kant's three questions (here our characters differ) I am only concerned (since my childhood have I been concerned) with the last question: What can we hope for?" (62: 219).[6] Through the disentangling of Tolstoy's questions, one can see that for him this is the first step in separating *true* philosophy of Spinoza, Descartes, Kant, Schelling, Fichte, Hegel, and Schopenhauer—that which answers the question about the meaning of life, from *speculative* philosophy—that which is dependent on a local analysis of facts based on the latest scientific experiments. In Tolstoy's explicit view of philosophy, the second of Kant's questions—"What can I do?"—is a bit premature. A person usually does not ask himself this question but simply lives; in both Hegel's and Rousseau's terms, he *is* just as what he *does*.[7] Being and doing are quite unselfconscious or unphilosophical until the need for hope arises. Considering Kant's question about hope Tolstoy arrived at Schopenhauer's old dictum that hope is the last treacherous tool of despairing self-deception. And he found himself in a position to inherit Schopenhauer's rich metaphorical arsenal to describe despair. Schopenhauer wrote that human puppets are dangling on the suspension rope strung by a mocking hand; they are supported by the flimsy ground beneath them (the objective value of life). Eventually "this rope becomes weak, the puppet sinks; if it breaks, the puppet must fall, for the ground under it supports it only in appearance."[8] The latter diagnosis thus matched Tolstoy's own premonition in 1852.

The following thought by Tolstoy in the same letter responds to both Schopenhauer and Rousseau's advice to fill life with useful activity between the "two useless extremities" of life and death.[9] To wish to live without hope means to love oneself; to wish to die is not to love oneself. Both outcomes are unsatisfactory. For the purpose of identifying a satisfactory solution, Tolstoy performs a purely ontological substitution. "Not to love oneself," Schopenhauer's solution to the evil of individuation, he equals with "to love not oneself," the overcoming of Rousseau's amour-propre, and Schopenhauer's cynicism denying the genuine love of another that is based neither on schadenfreude nor on the superstitious fear of suffering the identical pain. Not so much in terms of Russian grammar and syntax but rather in terms of Tolstoy's religion, the verb "love" requires an immediate object: "*not to love oneself, to love not oneself*—which is the same" (*ne liubit' sebia, ne sebia liubit'*—chto odno i to zhe) (62: 226). The two are not completely the same, however. The nonlovable "I" of Tolstoy tries to approximate the anthological Pascalian hated me (*moi, le haïssable*), whom self-hatred helps to believe in God and salvation.[10] This estrangement from the dreading self is necessary, however, in order to overcome the selfishness of personal survival. The non-I is now a subject, an author rather than an object of love. Since "I" is no longer an object of one's own personal love, it, along with other objects, becomes an object of impersonal or common (*obshchaia*) love. To the "I" that does not love itself but loves the commonly impersonal, death is no longer disagreeable.

However, in the second half of the letter Tolstoy forgets about the harmonizing project of the benign philosophizing monk and gives vent to his despair. The "I" suddenly materializes into the concrete character of the forty-seven-year-old Tolstoy at the apex of his achievement and dreading the inevitable descent: "I am forty-seven. . . . This age is the usual starting point of old age" in the ecclesiastical sense (62: 226). The ring of Solomon's lofty boredom is a polemic against several sources at once. Most obviously, Tolstoy responds to Letter Seven of Strakhov's *The World as a Whole*, which stated that nature does not tolerate the ecclesiastical world weariness and neither should man. Strakhov's letter also considered the situation of the man at the apex of his achievement, at the height of his capacity, his life fully concentrated in him: "But at last the fullness of life has been achieved. The man climbs to the extreme altitude accessible to him. . . . This period, *perhaps the brightest*, is often accompanied by grave suffering; the whole life is in man's hands, and he is asking: what to do with it? Oftentimes this is revealed in a crisis: people take the vows and take their monarchic crowns off."[11] The mild-mannered Strakhov did not elaborate on other choices—suicide, for example—the theme that Schopenhauer relished in similar descriptions. Strakhov's answer in Letter Seven mollified the despair by recommending the soul to aspire to the goal not yet achieved.

In "Counsels and Maxims" Schopenhauer ridicules the idea of "filling" the space of life with anything but genuine philosophical insight about the vanity of existence.[12] Either believe or philosophize! In old age, we do not nourish any hopes, we go into our capital; the trick is to spend it slowly and wisely. For men of great talent who have accumulated the most knowledge, the torture of a moment at the summit of achievement must be especially acute. But their consolation may also be greater because they replace passions with knowledge of Ecclesiastes and, having too little left of life, do not regret losing it.[13] Nevertheless, no matter what attitude we adopt, the progress of human life from birth to death is nothing but an insulting joke, with the classic five acts ending in tragedy.

Tolstoy, however, prefers to look more ridiculous than tragic and he philosophizes strictly in order to believe; he would rather be a walking advertisement of the paradigmatic bewildered traveler on the road of life. Tolstoy's man at the summit is reluctant to hide behind an ironic mask and adopt the nonchalant mien of a romantic who whistles while journeying down "life's steep path."[14] He is overcome by a sense of "bewilderment" (*nedoumenie*): a total awareness of life's emptiness and yet a perplexing lack of understanding regarding how this is possible (62: 227). There are subtle optimistic notes in this part of the letter, hinting at "I's" readiness to embrace both dread and hope. Tolstoy decides that the meaning he has been ascribing to life must be false: not many old people whom he knows await death in despair. He concludes: "My despair did not issue from the essence of life itself but from my view of it." He thus embarks on a search for a view that would "destroy the seeming meaninglessness of life" provided that the meaning of life is *not* destroyed by death (62: 228).

This instructive stasis in search of the right view is an undeniable staple of conversional classics about the perplexed, from Moses Maimonides' *Guide to the Perplexed* to Cardinal Newman's *An Essay in Aid of a Grammar of Assent*. The letter to Strakhov signals the beginning of a seminal change in both Tolstoy's thought and the form of his creative writing. He is posing as an allegorical philosophical agent, a paradigmatic philosophical searcher who deliberately aestheticizes his search. Even in this early conversion document Tolstoy purposefully presents himself in a proverbial, eternal light, for even a hopeless condition identified by true philosophy is itself timeless. Simultaneously Tolstoy willingly invites mockery of such a situation, for not only is it an honorable if hoary philosophical cliché of a glorious life examined well and given up as vain, but in his time it was also a pedestrian cliché, known from popular prints in every corner of the civilized world and in Russia. According to the worker Fedor Pavlov, cheap prints from the series "stages on life's way" covered the walls of artisans, merchants, and tradesmen.[15] In an age of scientific discovery dominated by theories of social and historical progress, it looked as if Tolstoy was engaging in another holy folly. Indeed, in its stylistic overtones Tolstoy's new idealistic manifesto looks little different when compared to the lament of the half-parodic Zhivnovsky and the whole tradition of Russian authors afraid of vertigo: "If one had the opportunity to avert one's gaze from this picture, wouldn't one? 'Where shall I go? What shall I do with myself?'" (Saltykov, 4: 181).

It is mostly the limits of time and space that bother Tolstoy. Just as life is a matter of time, so it is also a matter of space: "When we say 'lives,' 'life,' we think only of the space embraced by life" (62: 229). From within the bounds of this mortal life, our wishes and wills bounce back into the material world. Thus, during the first few years of his conversion project Tolstoy exacerbates and nurtures within himself this intense hatred of the material trappings of life. By harmonizing philosophy and faith in these first preliminary thoughts shared with Strakhov, the paradigmatic seeker pledges to carry out his new "daring plan" and establish "a religious harmony out of recent scientific thought" (62: 228) that would fill in Schopenhauer's and Strakhov's gaps: "I must do this. . . . I would also have done this had I not been writing now to you, a person close to me, but as if I were writing my *profession de foi* knowing that all of humanity is listening to me" (62: 220). In a subsequent criticism of Strakhov's organic theories, Tolstoy mentions that life as an organism is the province of physiology (or one of those "incomplete" sciences) and not of philosophy, which explains the meaning of life other than the life of cells. "Life as a subject of philosophy is life in its wholeness, that is, (. . .) it is *a translation into one harmonious whole* of all those foundations of human knowledge that cannot receive logical elucidations (62: 222, 223, 225). In the final section of this ontologically-informed letter Tolstoy relegates Schopenhauer's will (what was the consciousness of freedom in *War and Peace*) to temporal phenomena that are non-fundamental to life (62: 299). Love alone is not a solution either: "To love is a causal concept, for you can only desire what you love" (ibid.), and the solution is in the harmonization of timeless meaning and love. The abolition of the temporal will be Tolstoy's true goal in the next two or three years (1875–1878). Tolstoy spent 1875–77 writing philosophical and religious dialogues never intended for publication but mentally addressed to his doubts.[16]

His study of organic and inorganic matter continued. In January 1876 he reread Strakhov's *World as a Whole*, agreeing with him concerning the futility of finding the secret to immortality in inorganic nature but disagreeing more resolutely with Strakhov's division of people into "active" and "passive." Strakhov's division was based on Grigoriev's criticism (1862) of Tolstoy's alleged nihilism, his rejection of everything that is false and that does not result in the construction of new values. Stemming from his grouping of all characters into the predatory and the humble, Strakhov recommended that Tolstoy go the way of the humble rather than fight with the predatory. Grigoriev's recommendation was well received by Tolstoy between 1862 and 1876. But now Tolstoy begged to differ: the opposite of the humble are the riotous and the burning, fighting for hope (62: 237). The new idea of a burning and frenzied seeker was born, in part, thanks to the criticism of Nikolai Mikhailovsky. In 1875, following the disparaging remarks on sociology and progress made in *Anna Karenina*, this populist critic published the first lengthy evaluation of Tolstoy's creative contradictions, which he entitled "The Right and Left Hand of Lev Tolstoy" (Desnitsa i shuitsta L'va Tolstogo). Mikhailovsky appreciated Tolstoy's efforts to philosophize in his pedagogical undertakings, his desire to contribute to the cause of progress, reflected in the healthy and ardent side of his personality—his right hand. However, this right hand of the public intellectual was weak compared with the far more gifted left hand of a less socially resolute fiction writer who spawned nothing but useless tales drawn from the life of high society.[17] Mikhailovsky encouraged Tolstoy to acknowledge his duplicity and change his orientation and topics.[18] In response to intimations of his irresolution, however, Tolstoy had already assumed the dogged obstinacy of a seeker, taking refuge in Kant's "room for faith."

The fragment entitled "On Future Life Outside of Time and Space" (O budushchei zhizni vne vremeni i prostranstva; November 1875) considers three views, namely, that of materialists, idealists, and believers.[19] The materialist view is discarded because it is limited only to the physical perception of time and space, which is destroyed with the death of man (17: 338). For the idealists, time and space are not perishable products of perception but imperishable concepts, for example of Mikhailovsky's idea of social evolution. How, Tolstoy asks, can people—those perishable subjects of cognition and the carriers of temporal consciousness—step outside consciousness past the concepts that dominate their thoughts? Idealism, for Tolstoy, cannot explain future life without resorting to the concepts that limit life. In this Tolstoy sees a contradiction. He considers the religious view, which believes in the next world. However, there is still the question of "where" and "when" the future life begins: this question has no meaning, for by saying that the *future life lies beyond the grave* we are expressing temporally and spatially that which in its essence is neither temporal nor spatial (17: 388–89). Tolstoy is thus searching for the meaning of life, which not only transcends the form in which we can comprehend it, but also transcends limits as such. This is a major step forward from the simplistic presentation of consciousness in *War and Peace*.

In the next draft, "On the Soul and Its Life Outside of the Life Known and Comprehensible to Us" (1875), it is important to notice that the focus switches from perception, which is delimited by time and space, to the soul, which is interpreted Platonically. In keeping with Kant's criticism of rationalist theories of the soul, the fragment considers in earnest all that modern science has to say about the living (*zhivoe*), or organic, and the nonliving (*nezhivoe*), or inorganic.[20] Tolstoy concentrates on the moment when organic life becomes indestructible inorganic matter, but he cannot acquiesce to the fact that all living life is subordinate to the laws of inorganic matter constituting the unifying aspect of life (17: 340). The living man is his own laboratory in sorting out questions about "what we think, desire, suffer, and what awaits us there" (17: 344). It is true that all that we know we know, as Schelling and Chaadaev put it, "in two ways: as oneself and not as oneself" (17: 347). "Not oneself" (or the world) is available to me through experience, while I myself am available to myself only through immediate perception (17: 350). How can this immediate perception be inorganic or even immaterial? Now, in a clear departure from a similar division in the Epilogues to *War and Peace* adopted from Schelling, Chaadaev, and Schopenhauer, Tolstoy directs the experience of cognition and the goal of self-transformation at the immaterial "not I," the object of immaterial love and the source of immortality. The gravest mistake of materialism, as Tolstoy sees it, is that "materialism strives to learn about the soul experientially." By questioning this assumption of experiential inductive knowledge, "Man lives and dies; I live and I know from experience that I, too, will die" (17: 350), Tolstoy places himself at the forefront of the intellectual battle between logical positivists and idealists. However, at the end of 1875 Tolstoy's search for the essence of the soul was still not completed. He had no powerful counterargument against the certainty of mortality, whose proof is the objectively present remnant of life, namely, dead matter.

Although the fragment recognizes his stumbling in the face of spiritual survival, it grants memory a greater role than was the case in fragments on consciousness dating to the 1840s. Moreover, it illustrates Tolstoy's emerging belief in the paradoxical possibility of finding in consciousness and memory the key that will unify all the life that remains and what can continue. Tolstoy's theory of "the unification from the All" (*ob'edinenie ot vsego*) is his first attempt to set himself apart and not get trapped in the crossfire of philosophical disputes (17: 351).[21] Tolstoy rehearses the attempt hypothetically in the fragment entitled "Conversation About Science" (1875–76).[22] Its participants are the transparently encoded Nikolai Nikolaevich (Strakhov), the impudently confident Mikhailovsky ("the young supporter of progress with a beard"), and Pushkin's fictional collector of tales, I[van] P[etrovich] B[elkin], the kind yet dim-witted ideal of Grigoriev's "humble types" who hosts the dispute. When Nikolai Nikolaevich suggests that nations in Asia, Africa, and China succeed without progress, the young historian retorts that anything that is not progress lies outside the field of his interests.[23] Nikolai Nikolaevich and the narrator fail to counter this view effectively and mount their counteroffensive only as an afterthought. After Nikolai Nikolaevich departs, the naïve narrator continues his unanswerable questioning about progress and truth: Why should immortality be outside the scope of progress and science? Why should human questioning refuse to partake of the fruit from the tree of forbidden knowledge? In a simultaneously written letter, Tolstoy arrives at an anarchic rebellion of a bewildered naïf: "But if man can only comprehend life and can't comprehend the end of unifications, then he will necessarily have the idea of the living infinite, uniting all. But the unification of all is an obvious contradiction. This contradiction is the living god, and the god of love" (62: 244). For the first time in this secluded room for faith, Tolstoy reinstates the capacity of the individual self-consciousness of life (*soznanie svoei zhizni*) to approach God by harnessing himself to love, because it is both the tool and the goal of unifications.[24] The paradoxical relationship with God marked the beginning of a true relationship.

WISHFUL FAITH:
A GOD WHO DOES NOT EXILE THE MIND

In 1876 Tolstoy reread Pascal and Hume's essays and dialogues on religion back to back. In a famous scene of Hume's Dialogues, the naïf, Cleanthes, invites his Neoplatonic advocate and philosophical mystic, Philo, to imagine the unimaginable, namely, that an articulate voice could be heard from the clouds thanks to a "determination to believe what is most contrary to custom and experience."[25] Rather than seek manifestations of God or prove his complete absence, Pascal suggested his *Dieu caché*, the silent and invisible presence of divinity in the world.[26] Both possibilities—of the miracles of understanding of one's consciousness, Hume's trade-off with science and religion, in view of the impossible physical manifestation, on the one hand, and Pascal's mystical miracles of the heart and acceptance of the hidden God through Christ, the Gospels, and the church, who thus reveal his presence, on the other—motivated Tolstoy's search.

The paradigm of a stymied searcher from whom God is concealed was most likely suggested to Tolstoy by Pascal's example.[27] At forest clearings, in churches, within the family, at his writing desk, in intellectual disputes— everywhere he had been looking for the miracle of his consciousness, his *deus abscondis*. Chapter 5 of *A Confession* expressed this succinctly: "I've been looking everywhere" (23: 16). In a letter to Alexandrine dated March 20–23, 1876, Tolstoy expressed his admiration for the *Pensées* and Pascal's life, confessing as well that while he stopped believing in philosophy (like Pascal), he could not strike a wager and believe in prayer or plainly believe (unlike Pascal): "that I could believe, this seems impossible to me" (62: 262). After placing an undaunted exclamation point next to Pascal's dictum "Il faudra mourir seul," Tolstoy continues in a slightly later diary entry dated June 2, 1878: "One should not involve mediators and spectators in one's communication with God; genuine communication only begins eye to eye; when nobody knows and nobody hears, God hears thee [*Bog slyshit tebia*]" (48: 187). Exclusion of a third-party witness from Tolstoy's one-on-one communication was extended to Christ as well. Christ must have appeared to him an idle and silent witness (*sogliadatai*), whereas for this consistently reasonable seeker of faith, Christ the precursor who had found faith ought to be the riotous and burning word, as he argued to Strakhov. A faith in Him who watches invisibly in order to support the lone seeker reflects a faith in the Father, expressed in chapter 12 of *A Confession*: "He knows and He sees *my* search, *my* struggle, and *my* grief. He does exist, I told myself" (23: 44).[28]

This imperious epistemology had very little in common with Cartesian rationalism (much less clamorous in its doubts and certitudes), obviously punning on the syntactical choices and order of reasoning of the latter.[29] With Tolstoy, epistemology of faith amounts to no less than "I search, struggle, and grieve; therefore God exists." If it is not helpless rationalism, what is it? The few entries made in the diary at this time point at less than rational desperation: "How shall I save myself? I feel as if I perish—I live and I die, I love life and I fear death—How shall I save myself?" (48: 187). Tolstoy's responses to Alexandrine Tolstoya regarding Pascal certify that the painful "how" cannot be transformed into a simple "thus," that he cannot be converted by force, and that his conversion cannot strike him like a lightning bolt conveying miraculous salvation because he wished to undergo spiritual toil and suffering to earn his faith. He wrote to his friend: "I was also glad to hear your opinion (if I've understood it correctly) that sudden conversions rarely or never happen, but that one can pass through work and suffering. I'm glad to think so, because I've suffered and worked a lot, and in the depths of my soul I know that this work and suffering are better than anything else I've done in life. And this activity must have its reward—*if not the comfort of faith*, then *the consciousness of the work* which is its own reward. But the story of grace descending on man in the English Club or at a shareholders' meeting has always seemed to me not only stupid but immoral."[30]

The raptures about Pascal that Tolstoy expresses in his letters to Alexandrine Tolstaya concern only Pascal's happy combination of the faith of reason with the faith of the heart. Pascal's association with an organized faith (religion) meets with Tolstoy's approbation as a flight from certainty:

You say you don't know what I believe in. Strange and terrible to say: not in anything that religion teaches us; but at the same time I not only hate and despise unbelief, but *I can see no possibility of living, and still less dying, without faith*. And I'm building up for myself little by little my religious beliefs, but although they are all firm, they are very undefined and uncomforting. When questioned by the mind, they answer well; but when the heart aches and seeks an answer, they provide no support or comfort. With the demands of my mind and the answers given by the Christian religion, I find myself in the position, as it were, of *two hands endeavoring to cup while the fingers resist*. I long to do it, but the more I try, the worse it is; and at the same time I know that it's possible, that the one is made for the other.[31]

Tolstoy's metaphor of a rationally obstructed prayer (two hands—one of reason, the other of faith—unwilling to cup) is also an eloquent one because he insists that rational disbelief is immoral. The hands of a desperate seeker of God that fail to cup for prayer is a symptom typical of a thinker to whom "God comes to mind" instead of coming directly and intimately to his heart.[32] Although he knew that he could not be converted unless he earned his faith himself, in numerous letters to the people closest to him, for example to Sergey Urusov, Tolstoy revealed his obsessive "wish for faith" (*zhelanie very*) or for a "bedrock of faith" (*opora very*) in refutation of Schopenhauer's joke about its collapse (62: 248–49).

While he was repelled when people tried to convert him by explaining religion to him, he was impressed by a simple and unassuming faith of his social acquaintance, Aleksey Bobrinsky. "He's irrefutable because he doesn't try to prove anything, but says that he just believes, and you feel that he is happier than those who don't have his faith, and above all you feel that it is impossible to acquire the happiness of his faith by an effort of thought, but that you have to receive it by a miracle. And this is what I want and this is what I wrote about to Urusov" (62: 261).[33] To Urusov, Tolstoy sent his plea of "wishful faith" immediately following his visit on February 21, 1876: "I don't believe in prayer and cannot pray, but if it is true what you believe, then you can pray and your prayer can be heard; and so pray that God might give me the support of faith" (62: 249).[34]

Tolstoy's desire to apprehend the concealed God, came from agreeing with Kant ("Kant had shown me this") that God's existence cannot be proven and led him to disagreeing with Kant. "I nevertheless searched for God in the hope that I might find Him, and I would fall into an old habit and entreat *that which* I have been seeking and could not find."[35] One can ascertain that Tolstoy's first hours in Kant's room for faith were spent reverting to the old habit of entreaty and supplication common to prayer. The "inability to die" without believing that life has meaning causes Tolstoy the most suffering yet also saves him from suicide. The first four stances vis-à-vis death and faith that Tolstoy summarized, tested, and rejected as insufficient in *A Confession* (ignorance, Epicureanism, Stoicism, pessimism), helped him to elaborate the fifth stance, namely, of God seen on the strength of faith alone, and to recast his search in order to achieve the possibility of establishing a relationship with God. The way Tolstoy transcribed the earliest stages of his search illustrates that he gradually advanced from the third-person perceptual justification reliant on the equivocal demonstration of a stranger ("He," "that which") to the second, submissive, or provocative stage (you, "Thou"), and then to faith of a true relationship (I and you).[36]

Tolstoy would subsequently look for other ways to communicate with God, to learn how to "relate to that which I call God" (*A Confession*, 23: 44). As soon as Tolstoy placed his thoughts about God in the categories of phenomenal perception, or in terms of Kant's mediate consciousness practiced in *War and Peace*, God quickly turned into a skewed and volatile product of his own representation. The God whom he was able to envision in his understanding "melted like an ice block." But as soon as God is invoked as a possibility of belief and a spiritual relationship (*otnoshenie*), a possibility of communication, Tolstoy is revitalized. If God is invoked as an entity, a secure object of address and a form of address (which is the second meaning of the Russian word [*otnosit'sia, otnoshenie*]), an extended crisis follows. The former case is exemplified by "falling, by old habit, into an entreaty toward that which I have been seeking and could not find" (23: 44). Tolstoy uses the word *mol'ba* (entreaty), not *molitva* (prayer). He appeals to God that He *be* a possibility of communication. Not coincidentally, the draft of the same passage in chapter 12 has "turning toward *a something*," which here surely means an "undiscovered God," a God with potential.

Of special note are Tolstoy's pronouns. Had Tolstoy been praying conventionally, he would pray to "Him/him" not to "that." In place of Tolstoy's "entreaty toward that which I have been seeking" (23: 44) or "addressing myself to something" in the drafts (23: 504), it would have been "with a prayer to Him whom I was looking for" or "addressing myself to Somebody." Under the spell of temporary cowardice, the God of possible communication turns from an impersonal and inanimate pronoun "something" into the restrictive reference "that which," "whom," and then into the represented entity "The Creator, the guardian Lord" (*tvorets, promyslitel'*), who can be addressed and asked for things in a familiar way. Subsequently the entity He (one) will turn into a "nonentity" (nobody): "I fell into a state of panic and started to pray to the one whom I sought, in order that He might help me. And the more I prayed the more apparent it became that He did not hear me and that there was really no one to whom I could turn. And with my heart full of grief that there was no one, no God, I cried: 'Lord have mercy on me. Save me! O Lord show me the way!' But no one had mercy on me and I felt that my life had come to an end" (*A Confession*, 23: 44; Kentish trans., 64).

Tolstoy is alone in the forest, constantly thinking of God and trying to provoke His response. A form of address to God (*obrashchenie*) and a form of a relationship with God (*otnoshenie*) will determine the possibility of conversion, which in Russian is also rendered *obrashchenie* (both address and turn). However, a viable form of address and the possibility of conversion become possible only when it is based on understanding. How can such understanding operate and cooperate with God if God is nothing that is knowable and that can be something other than the god representable by fallible human means? Tolstoy goes into the conceptual arsenal of Kant's reason.

"But what about my concept of God, of He whom I seek?" I asked myself.
"Where does this concept come from? Where does this necessity come from?
This necessity is God." Once again, I felt joy. Everything around me came to life
and took on meaning. "But a concept of God is not God. It could be my personal
delusion," I told myself. Once again everything within me and around me began
to die. "Not a concept," I told myself, but a necessity—an exigency to know
God in order to live. Once I know God, I live, once I forget him, stop believing
in him, I die. This is not a concept but life. To know God and to live is one and
the same. God is life. (*A Confession*, 23: 44; Kentish trans., 64).

This remarkable picture of a tortuous "thinking for faith" illustrates the following crucial points: Tolstoy's God is meaning, but not merely a concept of
God, but something that is alive with meaning. Tolstoy's "resurrects" (*ozhilo*)
equates with the revelation of "having received meaning," an awareness of
God's presence.[37] Tolstoy's searches employ Kant's practical use of transcendental theology (nondogmatic explanations of God) "grounded on the ineluctable demands of practical reason."[38] Tolstoy embraces the necessity to
believe as his personal, human, and ethical command. In sum, Tolstoy needs
the substantiation that the reasonable knowledge (*razumnoe znanie*) of most
philosophies or sciences cannot provide.

At the beginning of 1877 Tolstoy sent Alexandrine Tolstoya a desperate rephrasing of Pascal's pari, explaining that he and Strakhov have nothing to
lose in holding onto the religious buoy without believing, for they know for
certain that their philosophical ship has sunk (62: 310).[39] The two were planning an expedition to Optina Pustyn in July 1877. Tolstoy carried with him
the assumption that all scientists and philosophers were "stupid," but that was
still not equal to faith, only a desperate substitution of one form of hope by
another. Yet he doubted as in this older diary note of 1873: "Admit incarnation and then transubstantiation of wine into blood and you get the whole
song and dance. Is there something in it?" (December 2, 1873; 48: 68). At
Optina, he planned to explain to the monks the reasons why he could not believe in sacraments (62: 310). During the visit, Tolstoy spoke with the Elder
Ambrose (Amvrosii) and with Father Pimen, who fell asleep during Tolstoy's
explanation. After the visit, Tolstoy decided that he lacked precisely "this
humble calm," this "love and calm."[40]

Nevertheless, from 1877 through 1878 Tolstoy toyed with Orthodoxy. The
origin of this attraction had its roots in his former hesitations between faith or
force. Doubts lingered ever since he wrote his first essay on religion in 1865,
which hazarded a daring plan to prove the existence of God, a plan stuck between the beads on the "rosary of human knowledge," one of Tolstoy's most
powerful metaphors of knowing:

The circle of human knowledge is a choker with many intervals between beads. The beads are our knowledge and they please us when we look on and we go through them with pride—it is the black thread, this chaos of thought, this un-knowable—that is frightful. In its primitive way religion will shake all beads to-gether; only it will keep in its hands the longer portion of the black thread at which we are not supposed to look, but as to the beads pressed together—what love, what symmetry, and no gaps or doubts. Nonbelievers divide the beads at equal intervals, with more or less art, in order to cover the thread, but it shows between every two beads If we narrow the interval when we eye it, more re-mains at the other side of the circle (7: 127).[41]

Tolstoy's first essay on religion after 1865, "The Meaning of Christian Re-ligion" (1875–1876) was not an attempt to hazard the look at the unknowable, but a social critique.[42] Briefly examining several religious attitudes of the nonbelieving society, he prefers honest atheists to sycophantic believers. Atheists will invariably be faced with the question of death and have a chance to reconsider. This point agrees with the 1852 essay "On Prayer," but conso-lation in honest atheism is impossible for Tolstoy in 1876. The fragment en-titled "The Definition of Religion-Faith" (Opredelenie religii-very; 1875–1877) divorces faith from the institution of religion and introduces a new term, *religiia-vera* (*religion-faith*), or a religion of faith, stringing the beads together and disregarding the distances still remaining between the beads on the rosary: "Religion is *a harmony of all* explanations and answers to those inevitable questions (or the only questions interesting in life) about life and death, to which reason gives me a particular answer and I don't know an answer more harmonious and therefore *I believe* in this answer and guide myself by it in every deed of my life. Religion in this definition cannot be contrary to reason or life. . . .Thus *beliefs* may seem false to me, while faith, as I define it, is always beyond doubt" (17: 357–58).

Christian religion for Tolstoy is not a faith but a *verovanie*, a term that has a clear heathen ring about it. It can variously be translated as "a conviction," "a customary thought," or even "prejudice." There can be many beliefs, but *the* belief is what would not be at loggerheads with reasonable explication or doubt, which gives one freedom of choice. In 1877 Tolstoy's definition is still philosophical in spirit and shares much in common with Hegel's and Kant's distinctions between true faith (*Glaube*) or moral freedom and its less reliable forms of variance and opinion (*Meinung*) in their discussion of the transition from individual morality to ethical life in society.[43]

The object of "Debates on Faith in the Kremlin" (1877) of the same year is a debate in the manner of a Hyde Park–type speaker that takes place within the walls of the Kremlin during Holy Week, in reality forbidden in Russia since the times of Catherine the Great.[44] The word "Resurrection," although never used, serves as the backdrop to the story, like the sketch of 1857, in which a nonbelieving author decides to join the parish during the celebration.[45] The narrator, a professor of philology, begins to feel that he has been duped by the materialism that has thus far guided him; he arranges to attend the debates and arrives in Moscow to stay with his old friend, an atheist and physiology professor. The author wanders from one group of the disputants to another, voicing no opinion of his own. He accords most of his sympathy to an officer, who announces that rituals such as the blasphemous sign of the cross cater to illiteracy. The narrator is also sympathetic to the schismatics, who are ready to overlook ritualistic differences for the sake of reestablishing a sincere faith. This sketch remains on the margins of belief and disbelief, reasonable and unreasoning faith, illustrating both advantages and disadvantages of ritual and prejudice.

In the same year of 1877, Tolstoy experimented with constructing his own catechism of faith based on his pedagogical findings of 1861–75. He used Luther's *Little Catechism*, which was published in 1875 by the Lutheran Press in Moscow, and the initially scandalous *Catechism* by Filaret Drozdov, in its day deemed a Protestant document but later revised and widely adopted for religious instruction.[46] Tolstoy's "Christian Catechism" (1877) is too raw and unfinished to be considered a "catechism" as such. It represents his exploration of the possibility of a compromise with the church. The writing of it was spurred on by his disgust at having overheard a catechism lesson given to children by a local priest.[47] Unlike its regular Orthodox counterpart—which begins with an explanation of the meaning of divine revelation, the holy books, and the structure of the catechism, and ends with the supplication prayer and the commandments—Tolstoy's version skips allegiance to Church altogether.[48] Tolstoy's Creed fails to mention the acceptance of the Holy Trinity, the divinity of Christ and the Incarnation, the Passion, the Resurrection and the Second Coming, the baptism, the raising of the dead, and life eternal. Tolstoy's holy Church lives "in the hearts of all people across the earth and expressed in the awareness of my goodness and the goodness of all in the life of men. I express this faith in the Christian teaching of the Orthodox Church, and therefore I believe in One God the Father Almighty, etc. Here is the Symbol of my Creed and therefore the adumbration of my catechism" (17: 363).

Tolstoy checks those thorny points of the Creed with which he can make no peace. His catechism is primarily a dialogue between "V" and "O." At first glance these initials might seem to stand for *vera* (belief based on reason) and *otkrovenie* (revelation based on miracles). Since the dialogue is precisely a deliberation on whether it is faith or revelation that leads to the discovery of the meaning of life, any literal application of an identity tag to a personified theological concept risks becoming a misnomer: we realize that "V" is a Q(uestion) (*vopros*) while "O" is an answer (*otvet*). This dialogue between a belief and revelation, which in form is common to all top-down catechistic responses, is not only a sly imitation of theological rhetoric, but also of Hume's dialogues on religion, and of the dialogue in which Pascal's wager is writen. Through question and answer Tolstoy elaborates the dyad of *razumnoe znanie* (reasonable knowledge) and *znanie very* (the knowledge of faith). Reasonable knowledge is scientific epistemic reason that Tolstoy thinks impossible without reasonable faith because it otherwise lacks the axiomatic base (the reason of reasons) (17: 364). The knowledge of reason suffers a split; the logical part of it serves to store and transmit revelatory knowledge and comes too close to the knowledge of faith, the lesser part depends on a progressive accumulation of scientific knowledge (17: 366). Once Tolstoy realizes that he is about to immerse himself in Kantian antinomies, he stops at the point where reason and faith dangerously and irrevocably risk parting ways. The catechism as a desired synthesis already arises as a contamination of healthy reasoning and reasonable faith. The two working concepts, "reasonable knowledge" and "the knowledge of faith," have fulfilled their cognitive function for Tolstoy. The knowledge of faith is essentially reasonable faith, "the indubitable knowledge of the meaning of the phenomena surrounding us by which we guide ourselves every minute of our lives," which does not contradict reason since the transmission of this knowledge of faith revealed by God in the soul of every man "was the cause of the knowledge of reason" (17: 364–66). For all its fragmentariness, the "Christian Catechism" may be regarded as the final overcoming of Cartesian solipsism, and the arrival at the conviction that faith is an immanent condition of creative reason, resulting from scrupulous, step-by-step progress across the circumference of "the beads." The beads that caused him obstruction were removed with the clear conscience of "reasonable and volitional faith."[49]

ANNA KARENINA:
A CONCATENATION IN THE SEARCH

Tolstoy's philosophical projects—coupled with the deaths of his newborn son Nikolen'ka and old aunt Pelageia Iushkova—surely absorbed him more than *Anna Karenina*, about which more and more complaints were voiced in letters to Strakhov, Fet, and other correspondents, where it is variously described as "stillborn," "dull and vulgar" (62: 199). He regretted that his artistic temperament did not permit him to finish the work in a slapdash manner. At times it seems that the novel is so divorced from Tolstoy's immediate and burning spiritual impulse that its initial plot—the illicit love affair, which strikes him as too literary and trivial from his new perspective—will cause the irrevocable collapse of his literary reputation, for which he seems to care little. When sections describing Anna's fall to Vronsky first appeared, he ridiculed the plot as one of those in which a "Russian prince murders his mistress and hollers: 'Oh, poor me!'" To Fet he announced that there has hardly ever been a writer less concerned for his success as himself.[50] In his bragging to Fet about successful horse purchases nothing but the occasional serious notes can give away the new intellectual turmoil.[51]

However, on October 26, 1875, Tolstoy announced to both Fet and Strakhov that he was establishing a new foundation (*podmostki*)—the artistic platform first mentioned in both versions of "A Dream," which Schopenhauer had since ruined (62: 209, 211). In these letters he confessed that literature without such a foundation was "horrifying" (*strashnaia*) (62: 211). The earliest, abbreviated version of the epigraph to *Anna Karenina*, "Vengeance belongs to me," fits well into this line of reasoning about rebuilding the foundation after vengeance for his wayward art has been wreaked.[52] Tolstoy is engaging in a polemic with Schopenhauer's use of the word "Herr," the dispenser of vengeance, which means "Lord" and "Master" and determines when and how God collects what is due. Tolstoy became satisfied with the novel only after the completion of part V, chapter 19, about which "he had been thinking much." This chapter described the death of Levin's brother Nikolai, following which the book's philosophical orientation started making more sense to Tolstoy and he could continue his battle against Schopenhauer's ethics and against his own wayward art. He related his satisfaction in a letter to Fet (April 28–29, 1876), the procrastinating translator of *World as Will and Representation*, in which Schopenhauer's truth about death built on pity, compassion, and a belief in nirvana supplants the cruel God of the Bible and the priests (62: 272).

Approaching the moment of his conversion, Tolstoy wrote remarkable lines to Strakhov explaining that art is an "endless labyrinth of concatenations" and that until the meandering author leads himself out, link by link, toward a satisfactory *end*, no isolated "idea" can serve as a thread: "Each thought, verbalized separately, forfeits its meaning, de-means itself terribly, when taken out of the concatenation in which it is a constituent part. The concatenation itself is not composed of thoughts (I think)."[53] Let's go back to Tolstoy's sketch "Not Cogito Ergo Sum" (1868)—which proposed that the goal of philosophy is to find general laws and that personality is not a series of dots forming a straight line but a movement "*in the direction given by Christ,* provid[ing] the line, their combination and laws" (7: 132). One may recall that Tolstoy thus corrected Schopenhauer's view of the meaning of philosophical thinking, which "consists in the *endless combinations of concepts*," eliminates the whims of hopeful self-consciousness.[54] Now Tolstoy is saying that art should also have the same laws ("those laws which serve as the foundation of these concatenations" [62: 269]), which are revealed at the end point of the work of art and form its very essence. What kind of link in this concatenated search was *Anna Karenina*?

Tolstoy's second novelistic masterpiece is not a gloss of Tolstoy's dialogues and philosophical fragments written in 1873–1877. It should be allowed to stand independently of its author's pressing spiritual concerns because Tolstoy preferred not to publicize his searches until he finished *A Confession* and other documents relating to his conversion. Yet the novel certainly reflects momentous themes and ideas that played a role in Tolstoy's spiritual reconstruction.[55] In offering my comments on the meaning of *Anna Karenina* for Tolstoy's conversion, I will limit myself to discussing only the most important links connecting Tolstoy's search with the text of his book.[56] The stages of Tolstoy's search certainly reflect *on* the stages of progress toward faith of Konstantin Levin, the second most important character in the novel, and yet the author's artistic discoveries are not confined to these few coincidences.[57] Levin is the only person in the book who lives haltingly, like an accidental tourist: thinking, watching, shifting from one state of mind to another, planning, or changing plans. He studies philosophies and listens to scholarly debates between his half-brother, Koznyshev, and a visiting professor, who pinpoint miniscule differences of opinion in distinguishing between the natural and psychic order of life yet shrug off as indecent Levin's question about the meaning of life (I/7; 18: 27–28).[58] Like his author, he reads theories of preservation of energy and matter, and theology, both Orthodox and Catholic, and rejects their mutually contradictory complexities, which still do not answer the main question (VIII/9; 19: 369–70).[59] On first encountering him, the reader sees Levin as a return to the superfluous type, "painfully out of harmony with himself" and frequently on the verge of suicide (VIII/8–10, 19: 369–73; 713–17). He thinks it is purposeless to do social work of any kind or serve instead of working on his estate alongside his peasants. He marries because he needs a love object and a source of understanding that can forgive him despite some shameful memories.[60] He watches his brother Nikolai die in order to understand what people think before they depart and where their spirit goes—while his wife, Kitty, and Nikolai's mistress take care of the dying man.

Yet in Levin we also see someone new, someone who "strained all his spiritual powers to escape from this condition" (VIII/8, 19: 369; 713). The novel ends with Levin's discovery of his inner conscience, his judge, imparted to him by his peasant, Theodore (meaning in Greek the gift of God), namely, that one lives for God and for enacting what is good, differently and uniquely in each man, neither with a cause (a motive of interest) nor with effect (a reward) (VIII/10; 19: 371). The same common knowledge, strikes Levin like a lightning bolt, felling trees during the almost simultaneous summer storm (VIII/12, 17; 19: 377–78, 394). His other instinctive discovery is that he must keep secret from everyone his pledge to abide by the willfully imposed commandment to do what is good and pray even if he does not understand the meaning. The discovery is not a conversion for which he hoped, but a mystery, an "imperceptive feeling—whether faith or not—needed for himself alone," which walks in "by way of suffering" and imposes indubitable meaning on everything (VIII/19; 19: 399).

Levin is the main reason why William James finishes his book with a vindication of Tolstoy's artistic mysticism, a proof for James that conversion consists of "faith-states" and a "will to believe," in which God is not known or understood but "used": "Tolstoy is absolutely accurate in classing faith among the forces by *which men live*. The total absence of it, *anhedonia*, means collapse."[61] Levin also brings back the sacramental question of the bubble raised by Tolstoy in *War and Peace* in Pierre's dream; he anticipates James' protests against examining faith through natural science wherein men are expendable bubbles and epiphenomena of natural evolution.[62] Levin wonders: "'In the infinity of time, in this infinite matter, and infinite space one little bubble, the organism is singled out; the bubble will float and then burst, and this bubble is me.' This was a tortuous untruth, but this was the last result of the labor of centuries of human thought in this direction" (VIII/9; 19: 370–71). What excites Pierre, Levin rejects as "tortuous untruth." The truce between "that force" and arbitrary will is the bad peace in *Anna Karenina* that Levin and Anna confront head on.

For Levin the injustice of life leads to the rejection of the indefinite "evil force" reducing him to the status of the bubble: "But this was not only untrue, this was some evil force, evil, adverse, the *force to which one ought not to submit*. One had to get rid of that force. And salvation was in the hands of everyone. One had to end this dependence on evil. And there was one means—death" (VIII/9; 19: 371). However, it is Anna who commits suicide. The novel presented clear individual reactions to "that force" and the choice of reactions led the novel's main characters to their destinations. Instead of committing suicide, Levin commits to the necessity of faith no matter what. Kitty rejects the religious bigotry of Varenka and accepts her husband's tortures as a truer form of faith. Vronsky admits to his secondary role of a tool and victim and refuses to be a free moral agent. Karenin consummates his vindictiveness in the role of self-righteous bigot. Dolly persists in her heroic drudgery in union with the fickle Stiva by punishments of children who fry raspberry on the candle and by harboring a secret envy of Anna's boldness. Stiva enjoys a lifelong career as destiny's forgiving favorite, hushing conscience as if it were gastric discomfort, and excusing his gut feelings for mental reflexes. Of all the characters, Anna and Levin possess the best instinctive ability to recognize the presence of the evil force in their mind and will.

Anna is transfixed by her evil deeds. Her inner judge never sleeps yet always votes for reasonable machinations and pretexts. In one of her moments of no escape, she remembers her son, Seryozha: "She *remembered that role of the mother*, partly sincere, although much overwrought," and invented her new goal in life, winning custody over Seryozha (III/15; 18: 305). When in similar trapped situations, Levin "felt the incessant presence of a flawless judge in his soul": "As soon as he was not acting as he should have, he felt it immediately" (VIII/10; 19: 373). Tolstoy's defense of Schopenhauer's theory of compassionate morality in the Epilogues of *War and Peace* reduced culpability for crimes based on the circumstance but inflicted punishment for the excesses of freedom. In 1868 Tolstoy wrote that we "*do not require retribution* for the crime" if we know anything about its circumstances and thus admit to a degree of this crime's "necessity." For the same reason, "we appreciate less the merits in a good deed" because if there are circumstances that lead us into committing what is good we are not completely free in committing to goodness (E2/10; 7: 345).

In the initial design of the adulterous plot, a possibility was hidden for the development of a murder with repentance and regeneration of the husband, assayed in "The Wife Murderer" (1868–1869). The reproach of the dying wife—who is imagined by the incarcerated murderer in the same posture as Anna in the scene of her post-partum fever, in which she assumes the right to forgive the lover and husband—resonated with the more scandalous early epigraph to the novel: "Vengeance belongs to me."[63] This prelude to the discussion of crime and punishment through the lens of preexisting polemics with Dostoevsky and Schopenhauer could now also include Herzen's "Who Is to Blame?" another story of adulterous crime, which echoes the same quotation from Rom. 12.19 and Heb. 10.30 and inquires as to who should bear the blame. Herzen chooses a bitter satiric tack by rewriting the New Testament into the report of a court bailiff about the devastation left after Beltov's intrusion into the life of the Cruciferskys (whose last name means "The Crucifieds"): "And this case, for lack of determined perpetrators, shall be entrusted to the vengeance of the Lord, while the court case shall be considered closed and archived."[64]

Although it was certainly possible, Tolstoy avoided the criminal unfolding and a dangerous conflation of moral situations with judicial rulings and random victimization. After Anna's suicide, moral crime continues. Vronsky feels that revenge has already been taken against him, that he is beyond the law. As he gets on the train to join the troops going to war against Turkey he behaves as a mere tool without moral will, going for the kill or agreeing to be killed (VIII/5; 19: 362). In a patent departure from the explanation of the responsibility for war provided in *War and Peace*, the irresponsibility of Christian governments and participating soldiers and officers for this war is named an unquestionable evil by the narrator (19: 387).[65] Life in the swarm and beehive of social history no longer exempts one from being held to personal account. The family unit, this smallest part of the honeycomb, is interesting to Tolstoy precisely when it is unhappy in its own way. For all the families joined in holy matrimony pass through the same mystery and take the same vows as do Kitty and Levin in the betrothal scene, described by Tolstoy in all its splendor and stern solemnity (V/3–4; 19: 13–21).

In *Anna Karenina* Tolstoy explores the extent of freedom in a tight network of individualized reactions to responsibility. The epigraph plays a central role in preventing justice from becoming entangled or vague. In its final formulation, it is the exact version from Heb. 10.30: "Vengeance is mine; I will repay." The context of this verse is the invective against the transgressors, who have "profaned the blood of the covenant by which they were sanctified, and outraged the spirit of grace. For we know the one who said, 'Vengeance is mine; I will repay.'" And again, "The Lord will judge the people." Certainly, the moral context of the book calls into question whether a more forgiving version of the same verse in Rom. 12.19 may be applied to the adjudication of everything that happens in the novel. The latter verse implores the beloved Christians not to repay evil with evil and to live peacefully with all: "Beloved, never avenge yourselves, but *leave room for the wrath of God*, for it is written, 'Vengeance is mine; I will repay, says the Lord.'"[66] Room left for the wrath of God has a deeper relation with Kant's room for faith than a mere textual resemblance.

The passage in Romans destroys the ambiguity of the abbreviated authorship of the utterance; yet it introduces another ambiguity in the process. If one repays the enemy with kindness, and in order that the evil done be avenged, the floodgates of God's wrath should be opened, for it is God's, not man's, work to punish. And if evil remains unpunished, then there is no room for faith. The passage in Hebrews, meanwhile, implies through Jesus' hidden authority that only the transgressors will face vengeance. In view of Tolstoy's ongoing dialogue with Schopenhauer regarding the meaning of responsibility and the place of faith, Schopenhauer's ardent rejection of Kant's allowance to man of tit for tat along with the practice of the autonomous moral will makes meaningful Schopenhauer's interdiction of moral violence. Only after Schopenhauer concludes that "no person has the authority or power to set himself up as a purely moral judge and avenger" he finally quotes from Romans: "Mein ist die Rache, spricht der Herr, und ich will vergelten" (Vengeance is mine, saith the Lord, and I will repay).[67] While Tolstoy supports Schopenhauer's view of compassion, he thinks that barring moral judgment is wrong in the context of the novel since Schopenhauer contradicts himself when insisting on the assumption of moral responsibility for one's acts, which forms character. Fet's translation of the same Schopenhauer section, about which Tolstoy must have consulted with his friend, is from Romans: "Mne otmshchenie, Az vozdam, glagolet Gospod.'"[68] Since Tolstoy selects the epigraph yet abstains from making an exact reference to the precise verse—or to Schopenhauer's book—his intention to pit the authorship of vengeance against the moral will of man in deliberations about the right to exact or visit retribution seems obvious.

In the scene describing her seduction by Vronsky, Anna decides to seek retribution and vengeance, while Vronsky pretends not to notice: "Dear Lord, forgive me! She felt so criminal that it only remained for her to humiliate herself and to beg forgiveness; and there was nobody else in life for her now but him, and so she directed this plea of forgiveness to him. He felt what a murderer should feel at the sight of the body just deprived of life" (II/11; 18: 157). He wants to conceal his guilt, "to hide the body," and he speaks of happiness. Anna interrupts: "What happiness!—she said in disgust and horror; and the horror involuntarily passed to him. For goodness' sake, no more, no more" (157). Anna understands her criminality and she attempts to wreak revenge for her transgression by proxy, not from God but from Vronsky, Karenin, or society: "Remember that I only needed forgiveness, and nothing more" (IV/17; 18: 434). This is a lie. Anna wants a divorce and seeks the status of a wife forgiven de facto. Nor does she intend to return to the weeping Karenin, whom she considers a saint. The scene in which the lover and husband are united at her post-partum bedside in the middle of a feverish delirium clouded by morphine is the most depressing vision of moral intoxication. Karenin is convinced of her criminality, calling her the bearer of a spirit of "evil and deception." Although unable to guide her conscience, he feels responsible for the propriety of the matter as long as her soul is subject to religion (II/8–10; 18: 152, 157).

The problem with Karenin is in attributing moral failures to everyone whom he treats with opprobrium. Karenin seizes the same moral authority and determines whom God wishes to destroy as Napoleon in the scene with the drowning troops in *War and Peace*. Moments before Anna's deathbed note begging forgiveness arrives, Karenin thinks the Latin dictum that Napoleon thinks on the bank of the Nieman, "Quos vult perdere, dementat" (18: 430–31). After the fiasco involving a sanctified ménage à trois, and newly unbeholden by the

bonds of forgiveness, Karenin abandons the role of abused kindness and en-
shrined sainthood in the same mood with which he approached it. He is too
firmly convinced that his wife is a criminal before whom he is and was a saint
(*tak mnogo byla vinovna pered nim i pred kotoroiu on byl tak sviat*) (V/25; 19:
91). Karenin is the despicable type who undergoes proverbial conversions at
the séances of the English club. We last see him when he mixes with the ranks
of born-again evangelicals who decide that it is wrong to grant Anna a divorce
despite Karenin's pronouncement with solemn gravitas that "sometimes grace
does not descend on those who toil for it and does descend on the unprepared,
like it did on Saul" (VII/21; 19: 313). Why Tolstoy is much kinder to the unprincipled Stiva and his atheistic protests when he arrives at the séance to in-
tercede on behalf of his sister the fallen Magdalene is the subject of frequent
debate. The above episodes unequivocally answer such questions.

   With its chief protagonist always on the brink of killing himself, with
Anna's suicide and Vronky's attempt at it, *Anna Karenina* is an unusual work
for Tolstoy who always disapproved of the act. Vronsky's impetus for self-
elimination—so that "shame is not felt"—is predictable as is his foiled suicide. Unlike Levin, who considered taking his own life to end the misery of
the centuries, or Anna, who wins her last selfish triumph over Vronsky and
literally "takes revenge," Vronsky is driven to the act by the mechanical repetition of what is socially implied (*razumeetsia*) and expected of all unhappy
lovers in officers' uniforms. He is surprised at himself when he finally shoots
and survives (18: 439). Anna's suicide—a means to "punish him and get rid
of them all and myself"—is quite another matter. She misses the first wagon
and is faced with a choice reminiscent of a baptismal moment, an invitation
to die to sin and be reborn in spirit: "The feeling akin to the one that she experienced when she was bathing and getting ready to sink into water possessed her and she crossed herself. A customary gesture of the sign of the
cross recalled in her soul a whole series of memories from her childhood and
girlhood; suddenly the darkness that had been enveloping everything for her
was lifted, and life appeared to her for a moment with all its bright joys of the
past" (VII/31; 19: 348–49). Instead she genuflects before the second wagon
and is horrified by what she has done: "'Lord, forgive me everything,' she uttered, feeling the impossibility of struggle."

   At this decisive moment, acknowledging the impossibility of exercising
her will against the overpowering force, we are not sure whether God accepted her retribution. The enigma of Anna's sacrifice is that she succumbed
to "the overpowering force." All we know about this novel is that the force in
question is evil, and it has to be resisted. And God's retribution assists only
those who resist. Before the candle that lights the book of her life goes out, in
place of the joyous memories of possible conversion Anna sees only a life

filled with "anxiety, lies, grief, and evil" (19: 349). Vronsky's crushing grief after her suicide is not alleviated by religious feeling. On all sides he hears that her death was "the death of a vile woman without religion" (VIII/4; 19: 360). In recalling her dead face, he could not remember her as "mysterious, loving, beautiful, looking for happiness and giving happiness," but only "cruelly vengeful," having triumphed in "fulfilling the threat of the ineffaceable repentance, not needed by anyone" (VIII/5; 19: 362).

The novel's conclusions about the meaning of death and man's encounter with the infinite complement the argument about misplaced sacrifice, in this case relaying a message of mixed results. Death in any form does not accomplish the same terrifying effect as it did in Tolstoy's works of the 1850s and especially in *War and Peace;* nor does it inspire the respect of the Lord's law fulfilled in "God Sees the Truth But Waits" derived from the new Christian humbleness and his reading of Herodotus. Nikolai's dying triggers a chain of unsolvable thoughts in Levin. Significantly, however, this death is not shown from within, the way Andrey's death was presented in *War and Peace*. Everybody is wrong about the timing or meaning of the final departure, including the priests, who administer extreme unction; Nikolai, who forgets about his atheism to bargain with God for his possible recovery; and Levin, who is exhausted after holding the hand of a virtual corpse. The distressing burden of dying recalls the descriptive details of the first death in "Three Deaths." The ugly expectation of the moment when Nikolai might finally be "finished" (*konchilsia*) is retarded by his possessive, almost malicious tenacity, which prompts his last words: "Not yet, but soon," reminiscent of Turgenev's lighter satire that inspired Tolstoy's "Three Deaths."[69] Although Nikolai's passing is no mystery of finished life (*konchilos'*) of Andrey, no ugly or degrading physical details can erase the brightened expression on his face, which persecutes Levin and forces him to contemplate those forces that perpetuate or destroy life.[70]

Levin concludes Tolstoy's gallery of sky watchers, who wonder about life's meaning. In the earlier, pre-metaphysical section of the novel Levin realizes that the sky's infinitely rewritten script of appearing and disappearing clouds and colors reveals *nothing* about life-changing decisions or the content of life itself (II/12; 18: 290–93). While for Andrey it could have been infinitely high, lofty, and quiet, promising nothing but quiescence; and for Pierre it could spell out anything, from his role in history, to his immortality; for Levin it signifies only "infinite silence" or God's impalpable presence.[71] After his conversation with Theodore at the end of the novel, Levin looks at the "high and cloudless sky" anew: "Don't I know that this is infinite space and not a round vault? But no matter how hard I squint my eyes, I cannot see it other than as a round and limited vault. And despite my knowledge of infinite spaces, I am certainly correct when I see a solid blue vault; I am more correct than when I try to see beyond it" (VIII/13; 19: 381–82). At this willful closing of infinity, of making his vault perceptual and solid blue, he stops watching and starts hearing heavenly voices (*golosa*), which ends for him the metaphysical terror of silent, infinite spaces and sends him into a wondering reverie if that what he experiences might be faith. Levin weeps and thanks God (ibid.).

With bolts of lightning traversing the sky and hinting at heavenly signs of conversion in the final scene of the novel, Levin looks at the sky again and wonders about what still confuses him if he already accepted that the manifest presence of God is the laws of goodness revealed to the world. Levin does not dispute the laws of nature in order to vindicate freedom; nor does he neglect his freedom to form the pact with necessity in imitation of the problematic conclusion of *War and Peace* (19: 398). Tolstoy observes an alternative law via his hero, who pledges to hold on to the mystery of his discovered will to believe and keep it undisclosed to others, while being empowered to invest life with the incontestable meaning of goodness in the service of those others.

INTERLOCUTORS AND LONELY SEEKERS: THE KNOWLEDGE OF FAITH

Given the variety of debates in *Anna Karenina* on burning social issues of the day, from feminism, to historical painting, to agricultural efficiency and political representation, and the war against Turkey, with the exception of public conversions at the proverbial English Club of the new Evangelicals, the absence of public debates on faith, the novel's final focus, is especially noticeable. Tolstoy more than recompensed the omission in his colloquy "Interlocutors" (1877–78). As in the first conversion document, his philosophical letter to Strakhov of 1875, the seeking philosopher in "Interlocutors" is again the same age as Tolstoy (forty-nine at the time). "I, Ivan Il'ich, 49 years old" is the last entry on the list of the dialogue's dramatis personae (17: 369–85). A congregation of jurors representing all flanks of rational knowledge (*razumnoe znanie*) and theology, who judge what he has to say in support of immortality, thrusts a very distraught protagonist into the epicenter of a fierce dispute. A young logical positivist, an idealist philosopher, a natural scientist, a dialectician-theologist, and a highly placed ecclesiastic assure a distraught Ivan Il'ich of his salvation from their admittedly limited perspectives. All participants deliberate on issues that torture Ivan Il'ich, such as immortality and the place of reason in faith. A Yunovich, who must be Soloviev's teacher of philosophy, Pamfil Yurkevich, described as a "keen sophist of faith," attacks

Ivan Il'ich, saying that his faith is subdued by ratiocination.[72] A monk, Father Pimen, whose prototype fell asleep during Tolstoy's visit to Optina Pustyn, shakes off his reverie to vouch for Ivan Il'ich's salvation because of his kindness ("he is kind, however; he will be saved"). The views of the dramatis personae in the colloquy overlap, in part because Tolstoy does not wish to sustain strict divisions between views. Ivan Il'ich leans toward the arguments of a "healthy idealist," encrypted "Strem," most likely the character Stremov in *Anna Karenina* (18: 310–15), a cynical and worldly peace-loving bureaucrat who combines the views of thinkers with whom Tolstoy is mostly sympathetic, namely, "Fet-Strakhov-Schopenhauer-Kant" (17: 369). "Strem" is trying to prove the impossibility of faith, which is contrary to pure reason, and argues that "in true reason," a small degree of faith is inevitable in essense and "in the enormity of its fruit" (17: 370).

When Ivan Il'ich demands a definition of faith, which Tolstoy fruitlessly demanded of Fet and Strakhov in letters written during these same years, every flank provides its own convincing reason for disbelief, belief against reason, or belief in spite of reason. Not giving up, Ivan Il'ich denies that new faith is consummated in a Mill-style social beehive, in Virchow's regeneration of cells, or in social communes.[73] Of special interest are the sketches of a thirty-seven-year-old Malikov, a social utopian and positivist who preaches Godmanhood and a thirty-five-year-old Bibikov who clamors for "the rejection of all foundations." A seventy-year-old monk named Father Pimen, who is there to preach humility and love and oppose with his kindness the smart sophists, Archbishop Stol'nikov, Yunovich, and the arch-Orthodox Urusov, rarely voices his opinions and remains asleep through most of the debate. Trying to provoke Pimen, Ivan Il'ich insists on the ethical foundation and social impracticability of belief. His rebellious and iconoclastic ethics surely reflect Tolstoy's "ardent" hopes, which belie Pimen's definition of a humble and meek old man: "Religion, by its very essence, is impractical—it did not come to bring peace but a Sword."[74] As soon as he comes under the attack from all directions of knowledge, Ivan Il'ich's courage recedes: "Ivan Il'ich is timorous and a sorry sight" (17: 371).

Tolstoy comes to the rescue, breaks off the polylogue, and continues with a dialogue on ethics between "K" and "I. I."[75] The exchanges seem to reflect Tolstoy's own spiritual fragmentation and his desire to refine his understanding of how immortality, understood here mostly to be an escape from death, can be justified from the points of view of reasonable knowledge, religion, and morality (17: 371–85). "Interlocutors," however, closes on too many points of view, whereas Tolstoy is in need of a single vision of the right end. "I. I." is most likely the same Ivan Il'ich, who still wishes to believe. "K" is merciless in sweeping away all those attributes of faith alien to reason. One may surmise that "K" may be Kant, who insists on the abyss between the perfect God and the imperfect man. The bridge between the two is the categorical imperative, the commandment to man's autonomous moral will. Tolstoy's apocryphal Kant claims that we destroy human freedom—and thus the possibility of a relationship with God for a thinking person—by praying to idols.[76] With this warning against idolatry, "K" departs. Ironically and significantly, "Interlocutors" reduces to one interlocutor whose inner voices of doubt and affirmation speak to each other on the ensuing pages of a diary, from December 20 through December 23, 1877. That diary has now become Tolstoy's own hidden diary of doubt (17: 373–82, 383–85).

"Interlocutors" begins as an exploration of knowledge and ends as a search for faith. Through Ivan Il'ich and "Kant," Tolstoy recommends answering the main question first: Who am I and how did everything surrounding me come into being? The question for Tolstoy is not that of Genesis (which he half-mockingly refers to as "how He managed to complete creation in 6 days," and what He created first, the solid ground or the storming sea). Both these environments are sinking and collapsing under him or swallowing him without faith in the creator. Tolstoy is interested solely in the genesis of the understanding of life's meaning. Though his dialogue is still not harmonious, the harmonizing agent has already been introduced. It is still not Christ, who is presented in the dialogue as a distrusted impostor who used contrivance (*izlovchilsia*) to substitute the New Testament for the old law. The agent in question is Moses, the same force that Pascal and Chaadaev both used in their transition to Christian faith (17: 379). Concerning Moses, in his *Letters Philosophiques* Chaadaev has recourse to Pascal's interpretation of divine miracles and traces this first miracle, Moses' miracle of recognizing the moment of his encounter with God and his understanding of the law.[77] Tolstoy also concentrates on the miracle of understanding God's pronouncement: "I am Who I am." The prophet is shown as the first successful seeker who expressed the inexpressible in the Word of *Genesis* after experiencing moments of an urgent quest and "*momentary clarity of thought (mgnovennoi iasnosti mysli)*," who for "one moment felt God, he felt where his own place was. He saw God (otherwise he would fail to express this feeling)" (17: 383–84). By paying tribute to the feeble organ of speech, Moses nevertheless said the main thing about his conversion experience: there is one God, the source of everything in time and in space, and man is his creation. Tolstoy joins in a conversation with Moses: "Now it is me, attempting to correct Moses. I am paying a much frailer tribute to the feeble word and am feeling that every word that I use is inadequate to the concept. One thing, however, is clear and indubitable—that the center of gravity, the gist, and purpose of the words uttered by Moses, is not and cannot be an exposition of the theory of genesis but an answer to the question: What am I? Whence do I come? What for?" (17: 383–84).

An instinctive turn to Moses aids the growth of Tolstoy's seeker. Tolstoy's alias, Ivan Il'ich, exercises personal hope, but he lacks the inner courage to let go of his diminutive *pros et cons* and accept faith in the vein of Moses, as supernatural revelation. Like Levin, he sees the fallen tree and the burning bush, but misses his chance at becoming a Moses. In Tolstoy's interpretation, in that imperceptible moment of clarity, Moses comes into possession of both the meaning and the Word (I am Who I am), a spiritual birth synonymous with his encounter with the one indivisible God who needs to be taken on trust alone. The insertion of Moses in Tolstoy's dialogue is an important remake of prophetic tradition in considering Christian revelation. A traditional converted prophet (Acts 9.1–19) and the prophet of Pushkin's poetry speaks neither in his own voice nor of his own free will. Dumb, blind, and bewildered, Saul is held hostage between life and death. When he regains the ability to speak, which the Russian idiom renders *dar rechi* (the gift of speech / the Word), he arises, is baptized, and *quotes* God's Word (Acts 9.18). In that sense he is a victim of intrusion through ventriloquism. Although Tolstoy's Moses fumbles for words to convey the Word, it resonates with his consciousness and he expresses the ineffable in his own way.

The miraculous element in acquiring the Word explains Tolstoy's simultaneous campaign against the historical school of Jesus, which sees in the Scriptures nothing but disconnected fragments of social evolution. As per his usual practice, Tolstoy carefully read such authors as Renan, Farrar, Müller, Bauer, Reiss, Burnouf, and Strauss, whose works were either supplied by Strakhov or acquired by other means in order to determine if he could side with them. "Is there in philosophy some definition of religion or faith aside from it being a superstition?" Tolstoy wrote Strakhov in November 1877, requesting the books on topics of theology (62: 353). Strakhov obliged, and although he expressed reservations about Strauss' Protestant pedantry in *Der alte und der neue Glaube* (1872), he was reckless enough to admire Renan's breadth and his immersion in religious emotions in *Les Apôtres* (1866) and his *Études d'histoire religieuse* (1857).[78] In a letter to Strakhov dated April 17, 1878, Tolstoy provides an extended and condensed critique of Renan's legacy and of the historical school as such, saying that he prefers the inconsistencies and questionable methods of the Synoptics to the corrections made by Renan (62: 413–14). If one follows Renan's precepts too faithfully, two equally pitiful consequences will result. Tolstoy lays bare the outcome of reasoning in the spirit of the historical school. First, Renan corrects Christ, who overlooked the sources of salvation, evolution, and progress, which were scientifically proven in the nineteenth century. As regards their relationship to evolution and progress, the Gospels and the Lord's Law may be treated as historical documents akin to Napoleon's Code. Christ can also be made part of social history and thus, inevitably, a member of a social party that politically did not win. Second, if he is regarded as a man, he will not be immune from the basest realities of human life (sweating, excreting, etc.), and is thus represented by the zealous historian with all the truthfulness of historical detail (62: 413–14). In a parallel diary entry Tolstoy focused on the historical school's opinion that Christ may not be an ideal model for humanity, and that ideas of social evolution and libertarianism are needed to supplement his teaching (48: 348–49).

Arguments against the historical school were already expressed (at greater length) in the drafts and final version of *Anna Karenina* of 1877 in relation to the artist Mikhailov's painting on the topic, which depicts the duel between Pilates and Jesus. Tolstoy has the art connoisseur, Golenishchev, a minor character, object to the historical school of Christology pursuing "that completely false direction. The same Ivanov-Strauss-Renan type of attitude to Christ and religious painting" (19: 34), in which Christ is represented not as a God but as a "Jew with all the realism of the new school." In the drafts of the scene, Golenishchev adds that Christ's face has already had his unique embodiment in the art of the old masters, who can neither be emulated nor surpassed: "So if they don't wish to represent a god but a revolutionary or a wise man, let them pick from history: Socrates, Franklin, but not Christ. We have grown accustomed to uniting in our understanding Christ with God, and so, when they show me a Christ who is head of a party, a man, I am confronted with an argument, with a doubt, with a comparison. Such a thing may not take place in art. They choose the same face, which cannot be chosen for art's sake" (20: 398).

Mikhailov's argument in defense of his method belaboring the sacred image "little by little" explains the meaning of the image for Tolstoy himself. He believes in the higher calling of his art only when, link by link and feature by feature, he comes closer to the miraculous source of his spiritual and religious discoveries and faith: "The face dearest to him, the face of Christ, the epicenter of the painting, which gave him such ecstasy at the time of its discovery" (19: 40). The cause of Mikhailov's torment is not that the choice of his topic is wrong but that his belief in it is not firm. He is prone to regarding his work through the eyes of skeptical beholders, such as Golenishchev and Vronsky. And when he does, it seems to him only a drab repeat of "the enumerable Christs of Titian, Raphael, and Rubens" (19: 40). He is also prone to reaffirming himself only in praise meted out to him. A validation of a more spontaneous Anna, who comments on the kindness and forgiveness of Christ's face, reaffirms for him not merely the sincerity of his art but the reality of kindness and forgiveness of Christ himself. In the internal monologue with which Mikhailov responds to Anna's comments, an expression of illumined ecstasy on his face, he now rapturously confirms to himself the presence in his Christ of the same kindness and forgiveness that prove to him the superiority of spiritual life over the life of the flesh that he wished to invest in his painting (19: 41). Hence, Christ is not a face or an image at all, but an attitude of kind forgiveness. Mikhailov's temporary illuminations and his gloomy assertions that he could not paint the Christ whom he would not have had in his soul reflects Tolstoy's simultaneous struggle between the visual-temporary appropriations of truth and its spiritual retention.

Tolstoy's criticism of the historical school hardly means that he subscribed to the inviolate purity of Christ's image but rather that he disbelieved this school's ability to render the timelessness it strove to uphold. Tolstoy therefore finds ludicrous Renan's effort to supplement Christ's teaching with the ideas of social evolution and social progress. Evolution is a logarithm of time, while Christ's purity, if one believes in it, stands above the forms of time and progress and above easy mimetic representation (62: 413–14). In 1877–1878 Tolstoy concludes that what we need to know about Christ is not necessarily true to his historical essence but rather true to the core of his teaching: "For us, all the degrading realistic human details have disappeared from Christianity for the same reason that everything disappears that is not everlasting; but the everlasting remains" (62: 413–14). Augustine's timeless Christian history in the last chapters of his *Confessions* is dearer to him than Max Müller's proofs (48: 348). The fact that none of the dialogues of religion of the historical school made it even tangentially into "The Interlocutors" authenticates the changed meaning of the Gospels for Tolstoy: not scenes drawn from the social life in the provinces of the Roman Empire but a new form of revelation, perhaps the last concatenation on the way to the law, with Jesus being the alpha and omega.

The historical school was not Tolstoy's only ideological target in defining the meaning of Christ. After the first accolades due Vladimir Soloviev for his criticism of abstract philosophical principles, Tolstoy familiarized himself with Soloviev's new publications. In 1878 he attended with Strakhov one of Soloviev's *Lectures on Godmanhood* (*Chteniia o bogochelovechestve*, 1877–1881), which changed Tolstoy's view of Soloviev. Soloviev opened his *Lectures* with an apologetic defense of positivism and materialism in the theories of progress, which had justifiably become so fashionable because science and not religion occupied the front posts of culture. Incarnation, Soloviev argued, was only "a more complete, more perfect theophany in a series of other, imperfect, preparatory, and transformative theophanies."[79] The new success of history could be ensured in the reaffirmed unity of the divine and human elements, in Godmanhood. "In the eternal, primordial world," Soloviev claimed, "ideal humankind is the body of the divine Logos. Similarly, in the world of natural becoming, the Church is the body of the Logos incarnate, that is, of the Logos historically individuated in the divine–human person of Jesus Christ."[80] While he could not but be sympathetic to Soloviev's creative vision of man overcoming his limits in the union with Christ and life eternal, Tolstoy had problems with Soloviev's general formalism, and the idea of Sophia symbolizing the role of the Orthodox Church.[81] His sharp criticism of Soloviev's version of divine humanity was expressed in a letter to Strakhov dated December 17–18, 1877 (62: 337–38). Tolstoy had just read Soloviev's "Critique of Abstract Foundations" (Kritika otvlechennykh nachal, 1877). He became suspicious of Soloviev's use of "the divine" (*bozhestvennoe*), sensing in it a new methodological ruse of Orthodox theocracy, Hegelian dialectics, and Soloviev's calls for material forms of historical altruism that revised divine law (62: 337–38). Tolstoy's criticism of Soloviev's theocratic dreams, which would determine their growing animosity toward each other in the years to come—also reveals his lack of any desire to improve Christianity or change its foundations, preferring to restore the primordial meaning of Christ's message. Letters to Strakhov in April 1878 forbid him to fall so low as to respond to Soloviev's "rubbish," which to Tolstoy was not far removed from Renan's "Darwinian Christianity," adding to it only the admixture of some "vile dogmas" and heresies (62: 413).

NOTES

1. This chapter expands and significantly revises the ideas initially examined in my earlier works, such my PhD dissertation, *Tolstoy's Projects of Transcendence (Reading the Conversion)*, 22–113 and shorter papers delivered in 2002, "Tolstoy's Conversion: Reexamination and Definitions" and "Tolstoy's Conversion: A Modified View."

2. N. Strakhov, *Vospominaniia i otryvki*, Russian reprint series, 44, ed. Alexandre V. Soloviev (1892; reprint, The Hague: Europe Printing, 1967), 293–94. "The Last of the Idealists: An Excerpt from the Unwritten Tale" (Poslednii iz idealistov. Otryvok iz nenapisannoi povesti) was first published in *Notes of the Fatherland* in 1866.

3. Reading Strakhov's "The Last of the Idealists" in August 1875, Tolstoy interpreted the tale his own way, seeing in it a defense of the umbilical cord of superfluity, whose juices still feed the likes of him, Hamlet, Turgenev's Hamlet, and Strakhov's Idealist (62: 196–97).

4. The often spiritual tone of Strakhov's correspondence with Tolstoy did indeed echo Grigoriev's last letters to Strakhov questioning "so-called 'activity'" of progressive people and opting for the vanity of vanities, "the most dreary book of Ecclesiastes." Quoted in Ianin, *Iz russkoi mysli o Rossii*, 78–79.

5. See *Leo Tolstoy and Nikolaj Strakhov: Complete Correspondence*, 1: 227–29. On Tolstoy's earlier interest in these questions, see chapter 2 in the present study.

6. This letter clearly and almost literally mentions themes, phrasings, and motifs in Tolstoy's later works that would be reworked in *A Confession, What I Believe? A Harmony and Translation of the Four Gospels, On Life*, and *What Is Art?*

7. Compare Heidegger's explanation of this unselfconsciousness, this inability to feel genuinely and creatively "perplexed": "are we nowadays even perplexed at our inability to understand the expression 'Being'? Not at all." See Heidegger, *Being and Time*, xix.

8. Schopenhauer, *The World as Will and Representation*, 1: 281, 299; 2: 356–59. See especially Schopenhauer's essay "On the Doctrine of Indestructibility," in *Parerga & Paralipomena*, 2: 269.

9. Rousseau, *Émile*, 211.

10. On Pascal's injunction of loving the Lord and hating the self, see his *Oeuvres complètes*, 373, 597.

11. Strakhov, *Mir kak tseloe*, 175.

12. See chapter 6, "On the Different Periods of Life," in *Parerga & Paralipomena*, 1: 477–97.

13. Schopenhauer, *Parerga & Paralipomena*, 1: 481, 489, 495.

14. For a comparison, see the paradigmatic Romantic treatment of the theme of descent in Xavier de Maistre's "Nocturnal Expedition Around My Room," in his *Voyage Around My Room*, 134.

15. Witness the memoir of the factory worker Fedor Pavlov: "On one side there is an infant ascending the stairs who then turns into a youth and then into a man with a stupid face wearing a top hat. This same man descends the stairs on the other side, finally reaching a coffin that is skillfully depicted in the lower right-hand corner. It is a rare room that does not have a print or two." *Russian Worker: Life and Labor Under the Tsarist Regime*, ed. Victoria E. Bonnet (Los Angeles: University of California Press, 1983), 115–16. Samples of these typical prints are available at the New York Public Library. Cf. the print "Stupeni chelovecheskogo veka" (Stages on Life's Way), image ID No. 479732 exemplifying the commonplace situation described by Tolstoy, of a "man at the apex of life" about to embark on his downhill journey toward old age and death. I thank Jeff Brooks for referring me to the image and NYPL permissions department for sending me the high-definition TIFF scan for research purposes.

16. In a letter dated April 15–17 (?), 1876, Tolstoy informed Alexandrine Tolstaya of his plans to dedicate the coming summer to the writing up of his philosophical and religious works, which he had already begun "not for publication but for himself" (62: 266).

17. Nikolai Mikhailovsky, *Biblioteka russkoi kritiki: Kritika 70-kh godov XIX veka* (Moscow: Olimp, 2002), 207–333.

18. For the connection between Mikhailovsky's criticism and those factions within progressive and liberal spheres that supported Tolstoy, see Eikhenbaum, *Tolstoy in the Seventies*, 52–55. See also Michael Denner, "Tolstoyan Nonaction: The Advantage of Doing Nothing," *Tolstoy Studies Journal*, 13 (2001): 8–22.

19. "O budushchei zhizni vne vremeni i prostranstva" (17: 338–39).

20. "O dushe i zhizni ee vne izvestnoi i poniatnoi nam zhizni" (17: 340–52).

21. Richard Gustafson renders the Tolstoyan phrase as "separation (*ot'edinenie*) from the All." See his *Leo Tolstoy: Resident and Stranger*, 94–95.

22. "Razgovor o nauke" (17: 139–41). I have based my deciphering of the encoded names on the conclusions of my analysis. The commentators of the Jubilee edition of Tolstoy's Complete Works point out parallels in the theme and directions of the argument between Levin and his half-brother, Professor Koznyshev (see part III, chapter 3, of *Anna Karenina*), without identifying participants in Tolstoy's philosophical dialogue (17: 619).

23. In a few lines Tolstoy captures the essence of the populist argument of Mikhailovsky's essay "What Is Progress?" (Chto takoe progress?; 1869), and his reviews of Herbert Spencer and Darwin. See N. K. Mikhailovsky, *Geroi I tolpa. Izbrannye trudy po sotsiologii v dvukh tomakh*, ed. V. V. Kozlovsky (St. Petersburg: Aleteia, 1998), 1: 307. For a general overview of Mikhailovsky and his intellectual circle, see James Billington, *Mikhailovsky and Russian Populism* (Oxford: Oxford University Press, 1958).

24. The ideas were reiterated in several letters to Strakhov in January and February 1876 (62: 243–45, 246–48).

25. At the end of Hume's "Second Scandalous Scene," miracles are considered as a possible alternative to science and reasonable proofs. See David Hume, *Writings on Religion*, ed. Antony Flew (Chicago; Open Court, 1998), 88.

26. See esp. fragments 229, 418, and 449. Pascal, *Oeuvres complètes*, 531, 550, 552.

27. The most authoritative explication of this paradigm is still Lucien Goldmann's *Le Dieu caché: Etude sur la vision tragique dans les Pensées de Pascal et dans le théâtre de Racine* (Paris: Librairie Gallimard, 1955); see Goldmann on "Que dois-je faire?" 294.

28. Leo Tolstoy, *A Confession and Other Religious Writings*, 64. Hereafter abbreviated *A Confession*. trans. Kentish.

29. See esp. Meditations Five and Six, in which Descartes reasons that God would be a deceiver if sense perception were not a more or less reliable form of belief. René Descartes, *Discourse on Method and Meditations on First Philosophy*, trans. Donald A. Cress (Indianapolis, Ind.: Hackett, 1993), 88–105.

30. Letter to Alexandrine Tolstoya dated April 15–17, 1876 (62: 266–67). Translation quoted from *Tolstoy's Letters*, 1: 295–96 (62: 266); my emphasis.

31. *Tolstoy's Letters*, 1: 296 (62: 266–67); my emphasis. I have amended the translation of the key phrase *slozhit'sia*, meaning "to cup for prayer," whose clearly religious connotation Christian's translation does not convey ("two hands endeavoring to clasp each other while fingers resist").

32. I am here using Emmanuel Levinas's phrase "Dieu qui vient à l'idée." See Emmanuel Levinas, "The Idea of God," in *Of God Who Comes to Mind*, trans. Bettina Bergo (Stanford, Calif.: Stanford University Press, 1998), 55–134.

33. This passage is quoted from Christian, *Tolstoy's Letters*, 1: 294.

34. Translation quoted from *Tolstoy's Letters*, 1: 291.

35. *A Confession*, trans. Kentish 63–64; I have modified the translation. Numerous variants to chapter 12 of *A Confession* show versions of the same hide-and-seek struggles; see esp. 23: 43–44, 504–5.

36. For the basic parameters of the believers' perception of God, see William P. Alston, *Perceiving God: The Epistemology of Religious Experience* (Ithaca, N.Y.: Cornell University Press, 1991), 119, 144.

37. The Russian word *poniatie* can be translated both as "concept" and "understanding" or "awareness." Tolstoy clearly intends the latter meaning. On such common equivocation by analogy of God with love, see Dan R. Stiver, *The Philosophy of Religious Language: Sign, Symbol, and Story* (Oxford: Basil Blackwell, 1996), 35.

38. Hans-Georg Gadamer, "Kant and the Question of God," in his *Hermeneutics, Religion, and Ethics*, trans. Joel Weinsheimer (New Haven, Conn.: Yale University Press, 1999), 9.

39. The last resort of the desperate, mysticism and spiritism, was jettisoned almost immediately. At the time, Strakhov was writing his *Essays about Spiritism*, in which he criticized spiritism and thus endorsed Tolstoy's views (62: 319).

40. Letter to Strakhov dated August 10–11, 1877 (62: 345). The best source documenting the role of Optina Pustyn in the creative lives of Russian writers can be found in the study by Leonard J. Stanton, *The Optina Pustyn Monastery in the Russian Literary Imagination* (New York: Peter Lang, 1995). On Tolstoy's four visits to Optina Pustyn in 1877, 1881, 1890, and 1910, see pp. 203–28.

41. Tolstoy, "O religii" (7: 125–27).

42. Tolstoy, "O znachenii khristianskoi religii" (17: 353–56).

43. See Kant, *Critique of Judgment*, esp. §30 (91), 140–49; and *Critique of Pure Reason* (A822/B850–A830/B 858), 646–51. See also Hegel, *The Philosophy of Right*, esp. §141–47, 189–91.

44. Tolstoy, "Preniia o vere v Kremle" (17: 145–50). On Russian government policies regarding public religious debates, see chapter 1 of the present study.

45. See chapter 3 in the present study. The impulse for Tolstoy's resorting to the rescuing power of revelation received by active self-consciousness must have been conveyed through Schelling's philosophy of revelation (*Philosophie der Offenbahrung*) that he studied in his youth and that came up frequently as a topic in his conversations with Strakhov in 1875–1877. Strakhov informed Tolstoy about his serious study of *Offenbahrung* in letters dated December 12, 1877, and January 20, 1878. See *Leo Tolstoy and Nikolaj Strakhov: Complete Correspondence*, 1: 382–83, 394.

46. See *Biblioteka Tolstogo*, vol. 3, part 1, 699. On the history of Filaret's *Catechism*, see chapter 1 of the present study. Tolstoy's desire to rework Filaret's *Catechism* could have also been dictated by his son Il'ya's difficulties in understanding its meaning and his consulting with the unquestioning Orthodox interpreters. Il'ya later recalled: "My understanding of God was always rather vague and confused. . . . The more I learned of the Scriptures, the more incomprehensible they seemed. In the beginning I tried to believe and understand, and asked all sorts of questions of maman and the priest who came to give me religious instruction, but their explanations did not satisfy me, and I became more and more confused. By the time I came to Filaret's

catechism and the church service, I was completely baffled." Il'ya Tolstoy. *Tolstoy, My Father: Reminiscences*, trans. Ann Dunnigan (Chicago: Cowles, 1971), 44–45.

47. See Tolstoy's letter to Strakhov dated November 6, 1877 (62: 347).

48. The Orthodox Symbol of Faith, The Creed, composed by Filaret states: "I believe in one Holy, Universal, and Apostolic Church." See Mitropolit Moskovskii Sviatitel' Filaret, *Pravoslavnyi katikhizis* (St. Petersburg: Pravoslavnaia Rus', 1995), 23. This reprint reflects the revised, canonical version of Filaret's text.

49. I have rephrased Robert Audi's "rational and volitional faith" to make the notion conform to Tolstoy's usage. See Audi, "The Dimensions of Faith and the Demands of Reason" in *Reasoned Faith*, ed. Eleanore Stump (Ithaca: Cornell University Press, 1993), 89.

50. Cf. Tolstoy's letter to Strakhov dated February 16, 1875 (62: 142). See also another letter dated February 23, 1875 (62: 152). See the letter to Fet dated February 22, 1875 (62: 149).

51. Unlike other critics, I am disinclined to consider the family episode of 1875 remembered by Tolstoy's teenage son Sergey to be indicative of his metaphysical distress. After the family's return to Yasnaya Polyana following a summer-long stay on the Samara estate in the steppes, Tolstoy, who must have gotten up without matches during the night, lost his way in the house, and desperately screamed after his wife. Older children were roused from their sleep and Sophia Andreevna suffered a fit of whooping cough with hysterics. We have seen that nocturnal nightmares or dreams have been part of Tolstoy's impressionable personality since his younger days. As Tolstoy's fabled and incessant changes, nightmares had a family tag attached and remembered by children as "The Arzamas misery." See Sergey Tolstoy. *Tolstoy Remembered by His Son* (New York: Atheneum, 1962), 25–26. It must be added that the Tolstoy household had family tags for a great many other occasions.

52. For the history of the epigraph to *Anna Karenina*, see the canonical explanation of Boris Eikhenbaum, who rejected the meaningfulness of the initial short version as a careless and hurried abbreviation and was the first to notice that the later more famous yet nonetheless enigmatic preface—"Vengeance is mine; I will repay"—was a direct translation of Schopenhauer's "Mein ist die Rache, spricht der Herr, und ich will vergelten" (see section 62 of *World as Will and Representation*) and not a biblical quotation. See Boris Eikhenbaum, *Tolstoi in the Seventies*, trans. Alfred Kaspin (Ann Arbor, Mich.: Ardis, 1982), 144–45.

53. Letter to Strakhov dated April 23 and 26, 1876 (62: 268–69).

54. See Schopenhauer, *Prize Essay*, 9–10. See chapter 6 of the present study for the discussion of "Not Cogito Ergo Sum."

55. Offering brief but eloquent comments in his guide for studying the crisis of the author and his characters, Gary Jahn summarized the differences: "In the novel Tolstoy goes beyond the specter of physical death and relates the despair of his main characters primarily to their unavailing attempts to realize themselves fully as individuals in the social and family context. . . . Anna, who capitulates, and Levin, who compromises, were forced to choose between the two responses that presented themselves to the author in the mid-1870s." Gary R. Jahn, "Crisis in Tolstoy and in *Anna Karenina*," in *Approaches to Teaching Tolstoy's Anna Karenina*, eds. Liza Knapp and

Amy Mandelker (New York: Modern Language Association of America, 2003), 67–73. In its chronological and occasional thematic evaluation of coincidences and differences between Tolstoy and his characters, Jahn's interpretation agrees with ideas raised in my "Tolstoy's Conversion: Reexamination and Definitions" (2002). I would like to thank Gary Jahn, the discussant, for his comments following my presentation. In the discussion that follows I am inclined to favor Jahn's approach only partially as regards the dynamic and the outcome of the struggle. For a more flexible interpretation of possible coincidences between Tolstoy's own searches and those of his characters see also Andrew Wachtel's "History and Autobiography in Tolstoy," in *The Cambridge Companion to Tolstoy*, 182–88, which also argues against conflating Levin's and Tolstoy's doubts and insists on their autonomous chronology.

56. For comprehensive analysis of the novel, see the following studies: Vladimir E. Alexandrov, *Limits to Interpretation: The Meanings of Anna Karenina* (Madison: University of Wisconsin Press, 2004); Barbara Lönnqvist, "Anna Karenina," in *The Cambridge Companion to Tolstoy*, 80–95; Amy Mandelker, *Framing Anna Karenina: Tolstoy, the Woman Question, and the Victorian Novel* (Columbus: Ohio State University Press, 1993); Donna Orwin, "The Morally Free Individual in *Anna Karenina*," in her *Tolstoy's Art and Thought*, 171–87, as well as other sections that discuss the novel (200–94); Richard Gustafson's "Anna's Battle for Love," "Levin's Search for Faith," and "The Theology of Sin and Suffering," in his *Leo Tolstoy: Resident and Stranger*, 118–55; and Gary Saul Morson's "Foreshadowing" (on Anna Karenina's "omens") in his *Narrative and Freedom: The Shadows of Time* (New Haven, Conn.: Yale University Press, 1994), 69–80.

57. If one compares the chronological content of Tolstoy's conversations, dialogues, and fragments about science, religion, and personal faith with the chronology of published installments of the novel, the coincidence and continuity of Tolstoy's and Levin's parallel searches becomes apparent. For an explanation of the impact that the serialization of *Anna Karenina* could have had on the integrity of the finished book, the significance of each individual link, and the dates of publication, see William Mills Todd III, "The Responsibility of Co-Authorship: Notes on Revising the Serialized Version of *Anna Karenina*," in *Freedom and Responsibility in Russian Literature: Essays in Honor of Robert Louis Jackson*, eds. Elizabeth Cheresh Allen and Gary Saul Morson (Evanston, Ill.: Northwestern University Press, 1995), 159–82.

58. Page and volume references are to the Jubilee edition of Tolstoy's works. The first roman numeral signifies the part, with the arabic numeral following it corresponding to the chapter within this part. Both numbers are followed by volume and page. Unless otherwise indicated, translated passages are quoted from Leo Tolstoy, *Anna Karenina*, ed. and trans. George Gibian (New York: Norton, 1995), with page numbers preceded by a semicolon.

59. Levin tried to substitute love for Schopenhauer's will, but this shred of consolation warmed him only for so long (19: 370).

60. In the famous debate with Stiva at the restaurant, Levin consciously contaminates a quotation from Pushkin's poem "A Memory" with a prayer of forgiveness (I/9; 18: 371).

61. Whatever the positive aspect of a faith-state, James writes, it gets "stamped in upon belief." He quotes his colleague, Leuba, as saying: "God is not known, he is not understood; he is used." See *Varieties of Religious Experience*, 506.

62. See chapter 6 of the present study.

63. See note 52 above.

64. Herzen, *Sobranie sochinenii*, 1: 124.

65. For this reason the conservative editor Mikhail Katkov refused to publish the eighth part of the novel in his journal.

66. Quoted in *The New Oxford Annotated Bible*, 223, 326.

67. See §62 of Schopenhauer's *World as Will and Representation*, 1: 348.

68. Although Fet's translation only appeared in 1881, there are reasons to suppose that Tolstoy and Fet discussed the passage, given their frequent exchanges on Schopenhauer, the progress of Fet's work, and Tolstoy's novel itself. See Artur Shopengauer, *Mir kak volia i predstavlenie*, trans. A. Fet (St. Petersburg: M. M. Stasiulevich, 1881), 426. I have consulted the passage from the copy in Tolstoy's library at Yasnaya Polyana. See *Biblioteka Tolstogo*, vol. 1 (part 2), 472.

69. See part V, chaps. 16–20 (19: 55–75) describing Nikolai's slow dying. See chapter 3 of the present study for the discussion of "Three Deaths" and Turgenev.

70. For the explanation of a difference between the physical finality of "konchilsia" and the mystery of finished life ("konchilos") see chapter 4 of the present study.

71. See Lydia Dmitrievna Gromova-Opulskaya, "Nedosiagaemaia tishina neba. O tekste romana *Anna Karenina*," in her *Izbrannye trudy* (Moscow: Nauka, 2005), 478–81. Through careful textological analysis, Opulskaya identified a copying mistake in the proofs of the novel held by Strakhov. Tolstoy's intended usage was "silent sky" rather than "tall sky."

72. Yunovich-Yurkevich is saying: "You are not a believer, you are a cogitator" (*vy ne veruiushchii, no razmyshliaiushchii*; 17: 371).

73. Aside from Rudolf Virchow, a cellular pathologist, other real-life representatives of natural and social knowledge are Emil Dubois Reymond, one of whose Berlin lectures in physics and physiology Tolstoy attended in 1860, and John Tyndall, an English physicist and author of popular books on heat as a mode of movement and sound. The Russian characters (Malikov, Maikov, Bibikov, Stol'nikov, Khomiakov, Urusov, Yunovich, Father Pimen) span all the flanks of social, philosophical, and religious utopia.

74. Ivan Il'ich is here surely quoting from Matt. 10: 34.

75. The colloquy breaks off at the phrase—which indicates Tolstoy's confusion of identity—"To my surprise I noticed that I. I." (17: 373).

76. Ibid. This imagined, overly rationalized Kant, who referred to faith as "science," was attacked by Tolstoy on the pages of his own first Critique. In the French version of 1835 used by Tolstoy (whose copy I was privileged to examine), one can witness numerous glosses such as "stupid" (*glupo*), "what nonsense" (*kakoi vzdor*) critiquing such phrases as "la foi et la science" (faith and science). Item no. 1720 in Tolstoy's library. Kant, *Critique de la raison pure*, 439, 448. See chapter 2 of the present study for a description of this item. See also *Biblioteka Tolstogo*, vol. 3, part 1, 555.

77. The presence of Moses is pervasive in Pascal's oeuvre. See esp. Fragments 224 and 236 in his *Oeuvres complètes*, 530–31. For further elucidation, see Chaadaev, *Lettres Philosophiques*, 1: 394–95, 421–26. In addition to Pascal, Chaadaev also uses the examples of Herodotus, Tolstoy's new infatuation since 1869, as well as Socrates, Plato, and Marcus Aurelius, Tolstoy's abiding intellectual companions. Chaadaev speaks of Moses at length in Letters Six and Seven of his *Lettres Philosophiques* in terms that strongly suggest that Tolstoy consulted him as a source in the middle of this rumination. "Let us begin with Moses," writes Chaadaev in explaining how he divined and then transcribed the law. Tolstoy repeats this phrase to a word. In a later edition of Chaadaev's work that survived in Tolstoy's library, the Moses sections— especially the phrase "Let us begin with Moses"—are heavily marked up, as are underlined mentions of Pascal. See *Biblioteka Tolstogo*, vol. 1, part 2, 430. Concerning Moses, Chaadaev has recourse to Pascal's interpretation of divine miracles and traces this first miracle of understanding.

78. See *Leo Tolstoy and Nikolaj Strakhov: Complete Correspondence*, 1: 382–83. In the 1890s Strakhov wrote a series of essays criticizing the historical school. Retail sale of Renan's books was forbidden in Russia. Strakhov sent Tolstoy duplicate copies withdrawn from the Saint Petersburg Public Library. Four books by Renan are catalogued at Tolstoy's Yasnaya Polyana library: #2718, *Saint Paul* (Paris: Calmann Lévy, 1869); #2719, *Vie de Jésus*, 2nd ed. (Paris: Michel Lévy frères, 1864); #2716, *L'Antechrist* (Paris: Michel Lévy frères, 1873); #2717, *L'Église chrétienne* (Paris: Calmann Lévy, 1879). This copy was carefully read and contains numerous jottings and notes in Tolstoy's own hand. See *Biblioteka Tolstogo*, vol. 3 (part 2), 232–35.

79. For these two citations, see Vladmir Soloviev, *Lectures on Divine Humanity*, trans. and ed. Boris Jakim (Hudson, N.Y.: Lindisfarne Press, 1955), 114 (Lecture Eight), 157 (Lectures Eleven and Twelve).

80. Soloviev, Lectures Eleven and Twelve, 164–65.

81. Neither Strakhov nor Tolstoy was sure about the correct identity of Soloviev's Sophia. Following the lecture, Tolstoy inquired after the matter and received information that in old Russian icons Sophia was a praying woman shown lifting her arms to heaven (March 16, 1878; 62: 400).

Chapter Eight

Turning with Christ (1878–1881)

THE BIRTH OF TOLSTOY'S CHRIST

The year 1878 signaled the peak of Tolstoy's Orthodox career. Reminiscences by his sons, Sergey and Il'ya, and the diary of Sophia Andreevna describe a typical pious pater familias who, when not at home, may be found in church attending mass.[1] As late as April 1878 Tolstoy's own diary is full of poetic recollections about moths attracted by the light of candles, in flight through the Holy Gates during services (48: 186).[2] The elder son Sergey remembered that Tolstoy's mood began to change in 1878, when he started to read the Gospels systematically.[3] Several baffling episodes in church put Tolstoy on the alert. On the eve of his visit to church in May 1878 he was reading the Gospels, finding more proofs that "everywhere Christ says that everything temporal is false and only the eternal is true," underlining his favorite lines about the birds in the sky, humility, and forgiveness. At the evening mass a prayer was recited for the conquest of Russia's enemies in the war against the Turks. "This is sacrilege," Tolstoy concluded (48: 70). He could still fast when needed and agree, without understanding the meaning of the act, "at least once a year . . . to drink wine, which is called the Lord's blood," but he could no longer find an easy way to accommodate the ritual and its symbols of faith with prayers "to kill more Turks" (62: 380).

In the simultaneous drafts of the novel about Old Believers, and the recurrent drafts of *The Decembrists*, historical characters pray profusely. The sketchiness of scenes and characters does not obfuscate their courageous and unbending submission to God's law. Prince Golitsyn begs the Lord: "Teach me and I'll do exactly this" (17: 165). At what surely proved to be the crucial moment, leading either to faith or suicide, Tolstoy entrusted his will to the

Lord in the hope that it would be in good hands and used properly and accepting the Lord's yoke: "What am I, abandoned in this world? Who shall I
address? Who shall I seek the answer from? From the people? They don't
know. . . . Lord, forgive me the delusion of my youth and help me to carry
Thy burden as joyously as I accept Thy yoke" (48: 351).

Tolstoy was still far from an open confrontation with "the people," but the
burden of the new yoke, his cross, finally turned him against the church, the
servant of this world in his new evaluation. "Let my freedom to be wrong be
mine," he declared in his diary in the spirit of Luther (48: 190). The three
brief notes that he composed for himself in 1879—"What a Christian May
and May Not Do," "The Kingdom of God," and "To Whom Do We Belong?"—show Tolstoy accepting in a clear declaration and for the first time
in his life "the law of Jesus Christ," which pitted him against the law of the
patriarchs.[4] In the first fragment Tolstoy repeated his earlier thought that the
world is no longer Christian. Under the guise of progressive history and historical Christianity, the servants of this world, from the incumbents to their
obedient slaves, serve the cause of destruction. In his effort to restore the possibility of the Kingdom, Tolstoy relies on John 19.12, Matt. 4.10 and 6.24,
and Luke 20.25 to assert that the whole life sphere should be divided into
what is properly God's and what is Caesar's and that spiritual life may not be
rendered unto Caesar. He thus declares his autonomy from the guardianship
of the state, Russia's spiritual police body since Peter the Great.

The fragments see the role of Christ in fulfilling the law of the Father manifestly, by forgiving his enemies at the cost of his life, and by exhibiting God's
spirit, which he proved to be alive in every man (90: 124). In this budding an-
archistic theology, which paraphrases Matthew 13.8; Christ is named God's
best son, who has elevated in himself the Son of Man (*syn chelovecheskii*):
"God is the spirit, the Father of that spirit, which is in man, and he is God the
Father only of those who recognize themselves to be His sons. And therefore
only those exist for God who retain what He has given them. Like Father, he
sows everywhere and collects what has remained his seed" (90: 125).

Tolstoy's Christ deviates from the interpretation of German Christian
metaphysics that so influenced his earlier religious development. To interpret Christ, Schelling introduced the momentous notion of *Versöhnung*, or
reconciliation, with the undeserved suffering, extending the notion onto
Christ as well. To believe in the Christian sense for Schelling is to reconcile
in one act freedom with necessity. For the arch-Romantic Schelling the idea
of unredeemable guilt possesses an artistic appeal, wherein freedom trans-
figures itself "into the highest identity with necessity."[5] Only through art can
one redeem that which otherwise cannot be explained, endured, or justified.
Hegel used Schellingian concepts very differently in *The Phenomenology of*

Spirit (1807), turning Christ, the logos of the Trinity, into the guiltless "self-offering Son," a reference point of reconciliation in history, and its epitome.[6] According to Hegel, Christ's reconciliation is more than a mere resignation to a fate endured in life. In Hegel's *Philosophy of History* the historical Christ is both the cause of historical *actualization* and its hero, who over-came his "anguished squirmings of the Unhappy Consciousness" by realiz-ing his bondage and finitude to something imperishable and endurable, the historical life of humanity.[7]

Tolstoy's Christ gave all people the ability to become his sons; he therefore does not interfere in the affairs of the world and material history, for example "God does not eradicate evil in the world because He does not destroy any-thing" that was created (90: 125). Tolstoy reserves all action for this world with man; thus, the will of the Father is only relevant in terms of how man in-terprets it. The vital force that decides man's life and where he belongs is fi-nally identified as *razumenie*, which is neither reasonable faith nor reasonable knowledge: "The Kingdom of God consists in relying on the son in order to retain one's *razumenie*" (90: 126) as the best answer to Kant's second ques-tion.

This Russian term that Tolstoy uses to define the meaning of divine logos defies adequate translation. It embraces a variety of meanings of the Trinity, including "understanding," "awareness," and "agreement." Tolstoy skillfully uses the term to imply that *razum-enie*, the seed, grew out of its root, *razum*, or divine reason, and included both the comprehension of it and its appropri-ation. The second element of the term, *-enie*, may signify the constituent part of the Russian words for consciousness (*so-zna-nie*), ability (*um-enie*), and will (*khot-enie*). In his liberal interpretation of Matthew, chapter 11, Tolstoy argues that Christ exercised his *razumenie* to put an end to the law of prophecy, that the Kingdom has come, that *razumenie* can now rule the world through man's action. Tolstoy rethinks the role of God the Father in the fol-lowing manner: "They say that He wrote the Law with his finger, that He walked into the burning bush, that He sent His son, and so on. Just as a liv-ing God—pitying, loving, and wrathful—is incomprehensible to people, so his own being, his own life, are incomprehensible to the mind of man. I am saying: the consciousness of my life, the consciousness of my freedom, is God" (90: 130).

In these formulations man's freedom (or consciousness) and God's reason discover each other in an intimate and mutually comprehensible relationship. The indecipherable Father appearing to Moses as "I am Who I am" was now re-transcribed in the deeds of his Son, in the teaching of Christ. "He is what He says" (*On to, chto on govorit*), Tolstoy wrote in a programmatic letter to Alexandrine Tolstaya dated February 2–3, 1880, announcing the change of his religion toward the definition of godliness through the free act agreeing with the law (63: 8). Thus by 1878–1879 Tolstoy finally overcame the long-standing contradiction of the philosophical epilogues of 1869: "it is obvious that if I proceed from reason to reason, I come to a fragment swirling in space. But this swirling fragment, like a reflex, requires an explanation." He adds that he will be stuck with Pascal's "infinity of indifferent spaces and time and the reason without reasons" if he does not radically change his own consciousness of life because man knows himself only through consciousness (48: 191). There will be no chance to make "the omniscient, eternal God, without cause" (ibid.) meaningful for consciousness unless consciousness itself undergoes transformation, which finds expression in Tolstoy's last discovery of 1879, *razumenie*. This discovery harmonizes the life of divine reason and human freedom. In 1879 Tolstoy finally accepts Jesus as reason and action expressed in the Word of his teaching; the fulfillment of divine will can be inherited by other Sons of God. Consciousness thus is either free or unfree, of the Kingdom of Heaven or of the devil. The notebooks of 1880 amass his discoveries into an excited pile of miraculous revelations: "The Kingdom of God is the sowing of the Word. Why didn't he eradicate evil? The weeds? Because the Kingdom of God is within you. . . . It is all clear and simple *what to do* and how. To be reborn in spirit. Change yourselves! *Metanoia*. So that the life of the spirit may be" (48: 324). His conversion was announced.

Tolstoy's iconoclastic position could not remain a secret from his inner circle, a privilege he granted Levin. As was his wont, he felt unable to keep his new discoveries to himself. The mutinous letter to Tolstaya in February 1880 heralded his faith in Christ's teaching, the foundation saved from the "melted ice" of doctrinal belief and phenomenological representations of divinity. Concurrently he heralded his break with the church: "What else should I believe in order to understand my soul and God's?" (63: 7–9). The belief could not be supported by Christ's place in the Trinity: "Who is Christ? God or man? He is what he says. He is the Son of God. He is the Son of Man. He says: I am what I am telling you: I am the truth and the way. . . . And as soon as they said: He is God, the second person of the Trinity, blasphemy, lies, and stupidity is the result. If he were around, he could tell them" (63: 8).

In 1878, after seventeen years of waging a silent war, Tolstoy made peace with Turgenev, as did Fet. In September 1878 Turgenev visited Yasnaya Polyana. All three had passed through the fire of Schopenhauer's pessimism. The conversations of the three neighboring landowner-writers revolved around aging and mental indisposition. Tolstoy and Turgenev exchanged several letters on the matter of intellectual crises, "the physiology of delusion," or "heavy bewilderment," as Tolstoy flirtingly put it in letters to Strakhov and Fet (62: 438, 441). Tolstoy did not take Turgenev or his gloom seriously: "His play is innocent and not repulsive if taken in small doses."[8] But Turgenev took it in earnest. Back in Paris, he wrote Tolstoy several letters urging him quickly to overcome his "mental indisposition" (*umstvennaia khvor'*). He warned Tolstoy against letting any of the anguished moods leak into his fiction: there are parts of the doubting soul that are not very proper to show.[9] In light of their discussions, Turgenev and Fet were suspicious about the direction of Tolstoy's next work, which he had already started (drafts of *A Confession*). Turgenev wrote from abroad: "You never tell me about your new work; rumor has it that you are working diligently."[10] Flaubert was sending his greetings to Tolstoy, and Europe gossiped that in the person of Tolstoy Russia finally had a writer "of Shakespearean quality." This was world fame.[11] However, Tolstoy's new rumored work had nothing to do with belles-lettres.

LOGOS INTO CHRIST

On September 26, 1880, Tolstoy inquired after the progress of Fet's translation of Schopenhauer's *World as Will and Representation* (63: 25). He had an ulterior motive in again thinking of the notorious demolisher of hope during his immersion in the critical reading of the Gospels. Schopenhauer supported the Platonic theory of logos, and was separating the experiences derived from live content, subject to instantaneous fading and vanishing, from the philosophical concept, which alone "is free from the power of time." Schopenhauer and Fet believed that concept alone preserves a pristine connection with the Word: "Therefore the Greeks called word, concept, relation, thought, idea, and reason (*Vernunft*) by the name of the first, *logos*."[12] A week after his inquiry, in his next letter to Fet Tolstoy announced his break with the idealistic philosophical doctrines of reason. In a lively re-creation of Christ's temptation in the desert and his response to Satan, Tolstoy illustrated the work of man's active and revealed logos, "only *razumenie* manifested God . . . I don't know others, I know myself. I know that I live by God, who in my life always stands by me; and I serve God alone. *Razumenie* is God, and about no other God do we have the right to speak" (63: 27). Fet wrote back with a careful defense of the philosophical reason, which, like Johannine logos, stand above the world and treat the latter as a medium of its creativity, in which man's understanding constitutes only a momentary "chain link" in the series of phenomenal manifestations, whose insights are only "ephemeral" (*kazhushshchi-iesia*) (62: 31). Such a presentation reflected Tolstoy's views of a decade ago. In his notebooks for November 1880 he chided Fet's obstinacy: "Whoever wills to create will know. My words are the spirit and the life. I am the Son of Man, the Son of God. You are children of the Heavenly Father. . . . Fet teaches and condemns me. What does he know?" (48: 324–25).

The rephrasing exhibits Tolstoy's growing frustration with the synoptic version and patristic interpretation dependent on miracles and other "distortions." The Gospels soon appear to him to be comprised of Christ's clear teaching plus unnecessary amendments and overlays added over the centuries to prove the truth of the teaching through illicit tricks: "Let us take the Holy Writ. It has been rewritten and translated over and over for 2,000 years, and written by whom? The grace of the Holy Ghost? This effaced and rotten manuscript?" (48: 326). He went on thinking about the content of the Nicene Creed, declaring Jesus' full deity: "I was not sure who was right or wrong . . . and then I remembered: What business should one have about the salvation of all? Salvation is only in fulfilling the commandments. And they disputed what? The commandments? No. The mode of carrying them out. So they were not even thinking of faith, but of something else. Live in the present. Enjoy the present in God, and there is no reward. So the Christianity as it exists is false?" (48: 326–27).

Tolstoy reaches in reality the point that he described as his moment at the summit in 1875: world fame, lack of faith, flimsy foundations of wrong views underfoot, and the realization of the necessity to revise wrong views in order to proceed. Therefore, he describes his turning toward Christ in the tradition of looking around everywhere for the appraisal of his wrong opinions. "I started looking for the foundation. People worse than me believed and I could not. . . . I have looked wider—in common folk there are deeds of faith and ignorance. . . . I must look in the teaching. . . .You can't say about Christ what you can say about Moses, that he is from God. He does not hand down the law, but he teaches how to fulfill; hence he is God only rhetorically speaking" (48: 327).

What canonical views of the church is Tolstoy ready to dispute? The Orthodox canon of Christology (consubstantiality) adamantly insists on Christ's Godmanhood, and stresses in equal measure the impenetrability of His two natures (the so-called *nesliiannost'*), the separate maintenance of his two hypostases.[13] In effect, the impenetrability of logos and human life was the philosophical point also raised by Fet. The destruction of the boundary was Tolstoy's first response to both philosophy and Orthodoxy. His second response had to do with the Orthodox doctrine of the incarnate Word, the "vision of the invisible," in which Christ, the second person of the Trinity, was hypostatically united by the Word as both fully God and fully man. The Orthodox Christ represents the hypostatical union rather than the fusion of his two natures, the asymmetry of such a union being overcome in the act of the incarnation of the logos. Christ is the Word that suffered in the flesh, and thus assumed a definite human nature, the "incarnate word of the unutterable father, the logos of the trinity."[14]

Tolstoy's approach was via a different route. In 1874 he read Justin the Martyr's writings in the hope that he could complete his *vita* for one of the four Russian readers. The fragment "Life and Suffering of Justin, the Philosopher" (Zhitie i stradanie Iustina Filosofa; 1874–75) remained a test of the force of logos to convert. The Platonic philosophy would conclude that from ideas one can ascend to the knowledge of God (*poznaniie Boga*) (17: 138). Tolstoy's Justin rejects the Stoic logos for its indifference to God, the peripatetics for their avarice, and the Pythagoreans for their substitution of astronomy for the study of God. Justin's final hope is his seashore encounter with a Neoplatonic philosopher who promises to explain incorporeal things through their likeness to corporeal things (*bestelesny veshchi s podobiia telesnykh*), heavenly things in the image of earthly things (*nebesnyi po obrazu zemnykh*), and to teach Justin how to derive the knowledge of God from the knowledge of ideas (*nauchit' ego znaniiu Boga po razumeniiu idei*) (17: 138). Not surprisingly, the earnest Justin refuses to fathom God in this manner: "But he could not attain the right Knowledge of God [*Bogopoznanie*] because Greek philosophy did not praise God as God but transformed the glory of imperishable God into the likeness of man, birds, quadrupeds, and reptiles. But Justin consoled himself in his spirit and trained himself in God-like Thoughts [*Bogomyslie*], learning God's Knowledge [*Bogovedenie*] as far as his unenlightened mind could take him" (17: 138).

Tolstoy substitutes God-thinking (*Bogomyslie*) and God-Knowledge (*Bogovedenie*) for a more traditional Theo-*logy* (*Bogoslovie*) as sources of God knowledge. Tolstoy's *razumenie* is already visible in his interpretation of Justin's "thinking for God," which corresponds to Justin's dictum that "to be Christian is to live with the logos."[15] Justin's refusal to convert to a celestial or "meteorological" interpretation of Neoplatonic logos and his association of striking effects with the work of the demons to imitate Christ certainly also served Tolstoy as inspiration.[16] Perhaps even more important for Tolstoy was Justin's linkage of Moses and Christ, the carriers of the Word of Genesis and God's spirit through the centuries.[17] Thus, the birth of Tolstoy's *razumenie* could very easily correlate with Justin's interpretation of conversion, "an illumination in the mind" in those who have chosen of their own free will to use their knowledge to "be born again."[18] Tolstoy's not so innocent distortion of the famous scene at the seashore seeks to minimize the impact of the advocate on the process of conversion and to make *razumenie* more proactive.

It took Tolstoy a year and a half of busy textological work with many sources in many languages (and even more hard thinking) to arrive at his rendering of logos (John I) precisely as *razumenie* rather than "God" or "Word":

"The understanding of life became the beginning of all. The understanding of life stood by, and for, God. The understanding of life *is* God" (24: 26). In view of all the considerations that Tolstoy set out, the best way to understand *razumenie* is "awareness." Christ himself achieves his awareness and converts to *razumenie* rather than being born into it. In the exegetic sections of his commentary on the Gospels, Tolstoy does not identify Christ's conversion with the moment of his encounter with John the Baptist and baptism in the River Jordan, but rather with his temptations in the wilderness and the recuperation of his will and God's word from Satan (24: 53–84). Only then does he return to John to relate the story of his illumination, of the logos he imbibed, and to tell him that he is ready for his ministry and passion for the fulfillment of life eternal.

The rendering of logos, including the interpretation of the birth of Christ as "embodied *razumenie*" (24: 36–37), Tolstoy considered to be fundamental to his entire project of rewriting the Gospels. This was the true nature of his work in 1880–1881. *Harmony and Translation of the Four Gospels* (Soedinenie i perevod chetyrekh Evangelii, 1880–1881) and its shorter version without extensive polyglot commentary, *The Gospel in Brief* (Kratkoe izlozhenie Evangeliia, 1881, 1883) will not stand up if criticized from the point of view of a devout Christian or a theologian. His most perspicacious Christian commentators have long done so. Andrzej Walicki classifies this expression of faith as a philosophy of God, "a specific version of theological immanentism."[19] Apart from the sacrilege of his undertaking, it is also true that Tolstoy's Greek was not strong enough for corrections, elimination, and reshuffling of verses and scenes. It is also true that he often had recourse to the expertise of the young classical philologist Ivan Mikhailovich Ivakin—hired in September 1880 to prepare the four Tolstoy boys for school entrance or degree exams—who was no theologian, to interpret difficult texts in Greek.[20] While easily pointing out his mistakes, several eminent Orthodox theologians appreciated Tolstoy's colossal spiritual effort. For example, Father Zenkovsky commented: "I do not judge Tolstoy for his unsuccessful attempts to delve into a sphere alien to him, of philology and exegesis; on the contrary, I am ready to kneel before the work that he has done. . . . Tolstoy's religious life is dear to me the way it was." Like James, he clearly understood the main thing about Tolstoy's revolts and revisions, namely, his desire to believe.[21] Tolstoy, however, did not see any problem in eliminating the church at the cost of establishing, through his understanding of logos, the familial relations of all humanity, for *razumenie* was the revelation open to everyone. Since His God could not utter a folly, Tolstoy called "a revelation that which provides an answer to the question, unsolvable by reason." Although not apprehensible (like the essence of God Himself), all conclusions that could be inferred from revelation should "satisfy *my* reasonable demands and the meaning thus accorded to my life would solve all the problems of my life" (24: 14).

This passage from Tolstoy's preface containing his rendition of the Gospels is written in the tone of a selfish child who has no use for God unless the meaning that God can give him (by providing him with "clear, reasonable, and true answers") would solve *all* the questions of his life. The solution might be easy, but the task that Tolstoy sets himself to procure the answer is not. In his prefatory comments to *The Gospel in Brief*, he accused the church, "this Christian Talmud" and his forerunner convert, St. Paul—along with dogmatic theology—of dimming Christ's light and hijacking the line "*of the concatenations in the chain of revelation*": "These false commentators call Jesus a God; . . . If God descended to earth to reveal the truth to the people, then the least that he could do was to open this truth so it might be understood by all; if he failed to do it, he was no God; if divine truths are such that even God fails to get his truths across, then people are even less capable of doing so. . . . The teaching of a great man is great only insofar as it expresses clearly and precisely what others have expressed unclearly and imprecisely" (24: 807–10).

Tolstoy's next important point of rethinking Jesus is his lack of foreknowledge about his purpose on earth. Tolstoy claims that "Christ earned his *razumenie*" (24: 37, 168). In other words, Christ became a son of God (*syn Bozhii*) by making himself a son of *razumenie* (*Khristos sdelalsia synom razumeniia*) (24: 36). In Tolstoy's interpretation of the scene, the waters of the Jordan were open to Christ, as they were for every other bather, and Christ had the courage to make his reasonable choice, making himself (*sdelalsia*) a son of God (24: 149). For this sole reason Tolstoy studies the Gospels as a case of successful conversion, from the greeting Jesus receives from John the Baptist (24: 149) to the last scene, in both the long and the shorter retelling, in which Jesus "entrusts his spirit" to the Father (24: 789, 934).[22] The act of "giving up the ghost" signifies reunion with the Father in the spirit: "Only the spirit truly exists—the Son of God" (24: 938). Tolstoy's interpretation of the coming of Christ as the first embodiment of logos (24: 131) makes impossible the arrival of the Day of Judgment, the Second Coming as the Last Coming. The spread of *razumenie* is a secure guarantee of the uninterruptible return of revitalized logos (24: 170). Now Tolstoy defines history as the spiritual task of the renewing logos sown in the world as a source of growing eternal life (24: 803).

The switch also responds to Tolstoy's concurrent reinterpretation of responsible consciousness. In his former views inherited from Cartesian tradition and German Idealism, especially Schopenhauer, reason and consciousness stand apart. *The Gospel in Brief* condemns this view on human life as suicidal, namely that "you are a casual concatenation of particles; there is no meaning in life and the very life is evil" (24: 806). According to the new view, man combines temporary and eternal life already in his conscious experience. Therefore, *razumenie* of life is the acceptance of law and its conscious implementation (24: 816–17). For the same reason Tolstoy concludes that it is wrong to deprive Jesus of his divine status by interpreting his role as if it were fulfillment of the last revelation. In doing so, the church deprives man, who follows Christ's teaching, of his duty to be responsible and free, for all "sons are free" (24: 812).

In one of his most poetic turns of phrase, Tolstoy rendered the parable of the sower (Matt. 13.3) and of Greek philosophical *logos spermatikos* or sowing logos as the eternal rejuvenation of logos (24: 177). The sower is the one who shows how to reveal logos when people forfeit it or persist, with the Pharisees, in the given doctrine of faith. Tolstoy's translation of the word "Pharisees" is *pravoslavnye*, meaning those who glorify correctly, or Orthodox believers (24: 104). The Pharisees are not unlike Russian Orthodox believers, who concentrate on the ritual of "correct glory" and use the word in vain. In a quite sophistic sleight of hand, Tolstoy treats Russian Orthodoxy (*pravoslavie*) as a righteous form of *slavie*, or vain praise, a willful collective deception, a commitment to the falsity of the sign. Pharisaic high priests become Orthodox bishops (*arkhierei*). This vain word of glory has no relation to the right meaning of logos. Tolstoy thus made his way to his old problem of prayer. According to the Orthodox doctrine, which relies on Matt. 6.9, 13 and Luke 11.2, 4, Christ condemned the diffuse wordiness of the Jewish prayer and instituted the Lord's Prayer, the Russian *Otche nash*. The habit of raising one's hands during prayer was only permitted for Orthodox priests during the liturgy. Tolstoy's idea of false oaths and vain praise in addressing God surely did not overlook this gesture, but it did not extend to the following requests in appellation to God (Matt. 6.11): Give us this day our daily bread; And forgive us our debts, as we forgive our debtors; And do not lead us into temptation, but deliver us from the evil one. But it discarded as Pharisaic the praise in the last verse, known in the Orthodox tradition precisely as "veneration" (*slAavoslOvie*) pronounced after the consecration of the holy gifts: "For Yours is the kingdom and the power and the glory forever. Amen."

Tolstoy's revision of the Sermon on the Mount (Matt. 4.35) and the Lord's Prayer eliminates oath in loyalty to Jesus and narrows down the sermon to five of the commandments that delineate the principles of active love (24: 197–284). The Christian principles that he accepts are as follows: "(1) Do not harm anyone and do not incite evil in anyone, for evil begets evil; (2) Do not pay court to women or leave the wife of your first intimacy, because leaving wives and their change creates all corruption in the world; (3) Do not take any oaths, because nothing can be promised, for man is in the power of his father, and oaths are made for evil purposes; (4) Do not resist evil but endure insult and do more than people demand: do not judge or go to court. Man is full of errors and can't teach others. By taking revenge man teaches revenge; (5) Do not discriminate between your fatherland and another, because all people are children of one father" (24: 839).

Following the conclusion of his expurgations, Tolstoy made an unexpected discovery. It seemed to him that the "so-called Lord's Prayer" provided a succinct expression of Christ's teaching in the same order as he had lined up his retelling of the Gospels. The excited Tolstoy juxtaposed the amended verses of the Lord's Prayer and his summary of Christ's teaching signifying chapter titles of his Gospels:

1. Our Father	(man is son of God);
2. Who is in Heaven	(God is the infinite spiritual foundation of life);
3. Hallowed be Your name	(let this foundation of life be holy);
4. Your Kingdom come	(let his power be realized in all men);
5. Your will be done in heaven	(and let the will of this infinite foundation be done in your own will);
6. and on earth	(and in your flesh);
7. Give us our daily bread	(temporal life is the bread of true life);
8. this day	(true life is in this moment);
9. and forgive us our debts, as we also have forgiven our debtors	(and let the mistakes and delusions of our past life not conceal from us this true life);
10. And do not bring us to the time of temptation	(and do not lead us into delusion);
11. But rescue us from the evil one	(and there will be no evil);
12. For this is Thy Kingdom and power and glory	(And let there be your power, and force and reason) (24: 803)

Subconsciously Tolstoy was reading the Bible as an artist would, creating a palimpsest of his faith-construction over a base proto-plot. Out of a multitude of changes and rephrasing, one can single out three essential elements that would infuse Tolstoy's post-conversion art, namely, his interpretation of three key Greek religious concepts that also signify essential aesthetic categories: *metanoia* (will to change), *kairos* (propitious moment or timing), and *khamartia* (sin or tragic flaw). Tolstoy interpreted these Greek words aesthetically and spiritually rather than as theological categories, which is how they initially had become known to him.

In Tolstoy's retelling of the Gospels, the call to "Change yourselves!" (*obnovites'!*, *metanoete*) is an invitation to convert to *razumenie*, the very words with which John the Baptist heralds the beginning of Jesus' conversion (24: 54–60). The term *metanoia* (will to change) was intended by Tolstoy to impart a stern spiritual dynamism to the search for meaning, without which neither an artistic nor a spiritual project is possible. It is explained by Tolstoy as a willingness to convert for good and therefore was dismissed either as merely a spatiotemporal change or a token conversion through the ritual of baptism. For example, it was not enough to join Jesus as his disciple, follow him, and call oneself a Christian; one must "give up one's life" for him. In Tolstoy's terms, such self-surrender amounted to giving up one's temporal life in the world in exchange for eternal life and salvation in *razumenie* (23: 340–41).

In this sense, the temporal and spatial phenomenal forms of life are not interpreted by Tolstoy as invitations of the decisive swap of priorities, but are regarded as secondary, false signs mimicking change. Thus, *kairos* (propitious timing), which for Augustine was the sacred timing of the descent of grace, is Tolstoy's synonym for *nonspiritual* time. It concerned itself with showing what was not essential to the understanding of meaning. It thus became a phenomenal portrait of delusion, of Pharisaic signs, convenient moments to do things in the interest of the socially proper side of life, or to conduct the politics of Judea and Rome (24: 433–35). In both *kairos* and *chronos*, or biological time, Tolstoy rejects the ephemera of the phenomenal nonspiritual being. In the seventh chapter of his retelling of the Gospels, the demand by the Pharisees of the phenomenal "sign" as proof of the existence of cosmic eternity is treated as a vivid example of *kairos*: "You are able to perceive the sight of the earth and the sight of the sky, whereas you fail to perceive this life. Why don't you judge yourselves correctly? (24: 433).[23] To this Tolstoy appended a rather cryptic commentary stating that "*kairos* is temporal life" (*kairos vremennaia zhizn'*) (24: 433). In the context of Tolstoy's renditions, this *kairos* most likely refers to the deification of emblems and "signs" or representations of temporal being: rain, clouds, etcetera, which, in other words, are not part of the eternal Genesis but rather form part of mutable "seasons." Like Levin in the final scene of *Anna Karenina*, Tolstoy rejects one of the three Sophistic applications of logos for the purposes of persuasion: the so-called *meterologoi*, or the meteorological proofs promoted by Gorgias, specifically, his claim that logos reveals itself to people in the form of heavenly bodies.[24] In Tolstoy's mind, the kairotic models that had been used by the Christian descendents of the Sophists for the sake of demonstrability of spiritual proofs of conversion likewise acted in the manner of Sophistic prophets of false wisdom.

Khamartiia remains the only true obstacle to the discovery of *razumenie*. The term *khamartiia* requires further exegesis. Tolstoy's interpretation of *khamartiia* was concerned with the origin and nature of inner conflict. He translated the term as "delusion" (*zabluzhdenie*), or the tragedy of being misled or tempted to live with the absent meaning of life (24: 52).[25] Such a reading correlates with Tolstoy's rendition of Jesus' torment in verses 10 and 11 of the Lord's Prayer. It also involves Tolstoy in the age-old aesthetic interpretation of evil and freedom of a literary action. The term was introduced into the aesthetic discourse on life and tragedy by Aristotle, for whom it signified the tragic entrapment of a protagonist. Aristotle ascribed *khamartiia* to the perverse refusal to pursue good while knowing what good is, the very defect, which makes people unjust. Ignorance of the choice between good and evil does not mean that an action is involuntary but only that it is bad. How does one become deluded? According to Aristotle, human plots imitate reality and what the imitator represents are "actions, with agents who are necessarily either good or bad." To form a whole action that could purge one's delusion through pity and fear, the plot should show a sequence of incidents with a beginning, a middle, and an end. This does not require that one man be its object, since "an infinity of things befall that one man." An action that purges through pity and fear should bring about reconciliation with an often undeserved change of fate. Aristotle is interested in the effect that action produces in the audience, how action affects the discovery of goodness, propriety, verisimilitude, and constancy of virtue. Although by all accounts virtuous men should exercise reason, which allows them to "prevent possible wickedness," "enjoy the benefits of the existing goodness," and the respect of the community, cosmic necessity does its own work. Wicked reason should give up its delusions, and virtuous reason needs to submit to its fate.[26] Schelling's resuscitation of the term of reconciliation with the undeserved suffering (*Versöhnung*) continued in his interpretation of Jesus, the new tragic hero of Christian art. Schopenhauer's interpretation of Christ's resignation as both the highest virtue and folly played off Hegel's use of the term. For Hegel *khamartiia* represents extreme subjectivity that perverts notions of good and evil and prevents them from becoming realized since it declares its own understanding of reality to be absolute. Christ's intercession, while on the cross, on behalf of his torturers would be "a superfluous request if the fact that they did not know what they were doing removed the quality of evil from their action so that it did not require forgiveness."[27] *Khamartiia* reinterpreted by Tolstoy exists only in the sense of willful or unwillful self-deception, the closing of conscious will that is unable or not eager to attain to *razumenie* (24: 433–35).

Since Tolstoy translated such a condition as "delusion" (*zabluzhdenie*) or the bewildered straying from *razumenie*, his sinners are consequently incapable of change. However, since sin is being equated with unreason, unreason always contains the potential for its own repair. Buoyed by this hopefulness, Tolstoy condemns the doctrine of damnation. Alongside that denial, he condemns the concept of "an eternal punishment for a temporary sin."[28] For this reason Tolstoy's new art is more open to conversion and salvation than the situation vis-à-vis divine justice described in *Anna Karenina*. The kind of justification that Tolstoy strives to attain in order to validate his heroes' striving toward *razumenie* as its own reward plays down the theme of sacrifice and consolation resounding in Schelling's, Hegel's, and Schopenhauer's *Versöhnung*. Tolstoy insists that salvation consists in the "deliverance from delusions" (*izbavlenie ot zabluzhdenii*) (24: 830).

Tolstoy's Christ the Redeemer requires no sacrifice other than trading one's delusion for the right understanding. This exchange also involves shifting one's allegiance to the new system of law. Tolstoy claims that Christ came to destroy the written law of the prophets, and he came as a criminal, an outcast, and a vagabond (24: 213). This idea is addressed directly in Tolstoy's reading of Luke 2.23: "Jesus says: one needs to be a vagabond to enter into God's kingdom, that is, one needs to suspend all forms of life. A vagabond has been, and would be, a despicable creature to whom everything is allegedly allowed, who is beyond the law. In verses 15 and 16 Jesus says: one ought to be a vagabond willfully, not against one's will. In those two verses, he again speaks about the necessity to be a vagabond, not the one to whom no law exists and all is allowed, but, on the contrary, to be a vagabond who is fulfilling the law, that is, certain right rules" (24: 215).

Tolstoy thus believes in self-accountability bordering on apostasy and anarchy that will be visited on the old-fashioned moral law, which will surely retaliate in its effort to resist change. This new divine legislature also involves God's silent observance of man's ability to account for his actions in making his decision concerning which law to serve. The only fear that remains is no longer the vengeance that God may sow but what man can destroy of his own in God's good works. One might say that Tolstoy deconstructs the mystical origin and authority of justice. In this sense, Tolstoy can hardly be called an anarchic destroyer or haphazard, lawless "vagabond." He is a skillful *moral reconstructor*, a denuder of the terms and senses of true justice, who is eager to preserve and rebuild as much goodness as possible.[29]

Although to Tolstoy Christ is not a supernatural miracle, his violent resistance to temptation and his nonviolent resistance to the ridicule of the Pharisees are Tolstoy's new miraculous tools for authentic, communicable art. In this sense, Tolstoy's "incorrect" retelling of the Gospels was a supremely artistic task, the quest of an author in search of a perfect hero. Tolstoy considered corrected Gospel moments to be strong and genuine artistic tropes that resist the striking effects and allure of miraculous, Pharisaic signs. His new frugal, severe, entertainment-free art, which bans both facetiousness and fancy, is part of the same anti-Pharisaic campaign, in which Jesus participates as the main hero. The New Testament served Tolstoy as a basic allegorical plot exemplifying a quest after the meaning of life. With partners and adversaries, true and false signs, his Christ the seeker successfully overcame all obstacles and avoided traps to fulfill his mission. Tolstoy was careful to translate "It is finished" (*koncheno*), Jesus' last word on the cross, rather than "It was finished" (*konchilos'*) in the report of Andrey's death as mystery in *War and Peace* or "he is finished" (*konchilsia*) in the report of Nikolai's death as physical cessation in *Anna Karenina* (24: 789, 934). "It is finished," by contrast, expresses fulfilled miracle of understanding.

There is a strict inner logic in Tolstoy's reasonably justifiable images of what is necessary or redundant for the understanding of the Gospels. He removed the episode at Cana of Galilee (John 2.1–11), where Jesus' identity at the beginning of his ministry is still hidden from the multitude but is revealed to his disciples during a wedding feast, where he transmutes water into wine. The same scene in the concurrently created novel *The Brothers Karamazov* plays a central role in the rebirth of Alyosha, who, as a result of its reading at the feast at Grushenka's, experiences the vision of the departed Elder Zosima and recovers his nearly shattered faith. Here are Tolstoy's reasons for excluding the scene: "This event at Cana of Galilee, described in so much detail, is one of the most instructive as regards the harmfulness of accepting the whole letter of the so-called canonical Gospels as something sacred. The event at Cana of Galilee does not present anything that is either remarkable, or instructive, or in any sense meaningful. If it is a miracle, it is senseless; if it is a trick, it is insulting; and if it is no more than a picture taken from life, it is simply not necessary" (24: 84).

Tolstoy's reason for his nonacceptance of the resurrection scene is more instructive than this suspicion of transubstantiation and the imaginary train of thought such symbolism may involve. He rejects the scene because resurrection in the body will mean the triumph of the temporal life and the restoration of the old law (24: 609–19). Yet Tolstoy is far from denying sacral meanings: Jesus' law establishes the new sacramental covenant over eternal meanings. Take, for example, Tolstoy's interpretation of the Eucharist based on the verse from John 13. His very choice is meaningful. Tolstoy chooses not to rely on Matthew 26, Mark 14, or Luke 22. The institution of the Eucharist, strictly speaking, is found only in Matthew, Mark, and Luke. John's version, preferred by Tolstoy, contains only an internalized declaration of the Eucharist (invisible, oblique, and practically silent). John's Jesus notably announces his departure for the House of His Father while washing the feet of his disciples, and then predicts the treachery among them. Although all four Gospels agree on Jesus' foreknowledge of his betrayal, they disagree on the manner of identification and the degree of exposure of this betrayal. David Friedrich Strauss, the interpreter Tolstoy criticized, notes that Luke's institution of the Eucharist *before* the banishment of Judas as the named traitor makes perfect sense: the Lord could not have allowed a declared fiend to partake of the divine sacrament. If Judas had consumed any of the wine or bread, it would have caused a profanation of the sacrament by cannibalism.[30] Tolstoy considers the possible options: either Jesus let an unnamed traitor partake of his flesh and blood and then forewarned him and others of the approaching sacrifice or Jesus first announced the betrayal and then instituted a covenant of love. Either way, he allowed his disciples to test their loyalty. Seeing that both of the above possibilities are present in John, while also recognizing Strauss' critical points, Tolstoy suggested that a lack of agreement among the synoptics is the most likely explanation for Christ's lack of foreknowledge of the exact identity of the traitor—or the manner of his betrayal. Rather than denying Jesus a foreknowledge of his mission, this suggestion implies that the dynamism of indecision arises from the unpredictability and desynchronized timing of the disciples' reactions to a covenant of love. In terms of how they are expressed, the mystery of unification by means of Jesus' logos will be revealed. Tolstoy insists that the bread and wine metaphor be judged as inseparable from the announcement of treachery and the washing of feet (24: 688–89). Contrary to the Orthodox liturgical interpretation, which excludes Judas from the circle of apostles receiving Christ's Eucharist, Tolstoy insists that "they all drank from the glass. If it did not refer to the traitor as well, it would not have been worth recording" (24: 688), because Jesus "ought to wash them all" (24: 695). After so many caustic comments about the Eucharist in Tolstoy's diaries, he finds the right tone for dealing with the scene. The Eucharist establishes the covenant of love, first igniting the intense drama of difficult choices regarding how to commit to acts of love (*delo liubvi*) in the face of hatred and treachery (24: 695). By immediately connecting the washing of feet with the metaphor of the eating of bread, and the drinking of wine, Tolstoy's interpretation signifies the moral bond that Jesus imposes upon the disciples not to violate the precept of forgiving the enemy: "The New Testament, that which in the synoptic has been expressed by resentment, is here expressed by love" (24: 700). Tolstoy felt ready to account for his Christ in rapture and joy, and for his faith—with feisty zest.

NATION UNSTABLE ISSUES THE RUMOR:
TOLSTOY IS MAD

The Russian literary scene during the few years of Tolstoy's absence was gloomy, dominated by Dostoevsky's adversaries, the writers of the new populism grouped around Nekrasov's and Saltykov-Shchedrin's *Notes of the Fatherland*. They included: prose writers Gleb Uspensky and Vsevolod Garshin; poets Dmitry Minaev, Semyon Nadson, and Leonid Trefolev; and the critic Mikhailovsky. The literary generation of Tolstoy's youth was slowly departing. In January 1878 Nekrasov died in Saint Petersburg after a long illness, composing on his deathbed a martyrology of civic poetry. Nekrasov's funeral turned into a display of civic tendentiousness, with the demonstrating radicals and students placing the poet-citizen above Pushkin. Tolstoy was struck by this death. Although he pitied Nekrasov the man and the spectacle of his funeral, he thought this sad end typified the "ruler of the minds," who was always hiding from the inner truths of existence.[31] Dostoevsky also diagnosed Nekrasov's disease as a form of spiritual illiteracy, displaying a thirst for darkness and demonic self-sufficiency.[32]

Saltykov also fit the diagnosis of moral lawlessness. In his grim masterpiece *The Golovlyov Family* (*Gospoda Golovlyovy*), which was completed in 1876 and published in a full edition in 1880, Saltykov describes the dying out of the bigot, Porphyry Golovlyov, nicknamed "dear little Judas" (*Iudushka*) and bloodsucker (*krovopivets*), and his decrepit kin, whom he helped to their graves. In a typical scene at the wake of his brother, Judas "crossed himself and drank the vodka, then he crossed himself again and swallowed a piece of caviar, crossed himself again and took a piece of smoked salmon."[33] At the end of the book, Judas leaves home during a blizzard, thirsting for God's justice and seeing the threatening ghost of his mother, Arina, whom he had robbed. Few scenes of repentance in world literature are more spiritually devastating than this character's final delirium.

At this time, Schopenhauer's philosophy was at the peak of popularity in Russian society and was considered by many critics, including Dostoevsky, to be a catalyst and jump start for the spoiled seed that had already been planted in their native soil.[34] Many so-called radical poets confused Schopenhauer's pessimism with political struggle. The most widely read younger poet, Semyon Nadson, who also published in the Nekrasov-Saltykov journal, sang of the "silt of earthly tremors" and sobs in a heart that was too empty to cry.[35] The titles of the superfluous protesters against existence from the 1840s through the 1860s, the damaged and the demented, had returned. The heartache in question had to do with the attempts of Uspensky and Garshin to revive the theme of conscience. "No, terrible is this word, conscience, it eats up a lot of folk," says the hero of Uspensky's story "The Incurable."[36] Turgenev's return to Russia in 1879 was greeted by the younger generation, who hoped that he might bolster the disillusioned spirits of the progressive literary fighters. However, Turgenev's *Poems in Prose* (*Poemy v proze*) from the cycles "Senilia" and "The New Poems" (1878–1882) only added to the pervasive theme of the slightly cynical yet attractive allegory of human melancholy, turning all hope and all earthly glory, including art, into dust. "I envy the stones!" declares one poem.[37] These sentiments were already palpable in Turgenev's earlier work, "Enough. An Excerpt from the Notes of a Deceased Artist" (1865).[38] In this manifesto of despair, the artist declares that before he is pulverized into ashes or drowns in the duckweed of self-denial and self-contempt he should maintain "the dignity of being conscious about his own nothingness. The sun goes down, the moths drop down like a weak drizzle and finis to their momentary life" (Turgenev, 7: 34–35). Giving up all fictions of self-deception, the narrator of the notes says that the artist can do two things: play with the mirror of life and deny that the reflection is horrible or fall forever silent. Turgenev's hero chooses the latter: "No . . . No . . . Enough . . . enough . . . enough. . . ." and finishes on the Hamletian: "The rest is silence . . ." (7: 38).

Mussorgsky's *Boris Godunov* (staged in 1874) and Tchaikovsky's *Eugene Onegin* (completed in 1878 and staged in 1881), both based on Pushkin, brought the theme of conscience and moral retribution to the fore. At the same time, both composers' lyrical efforts reflected the same premonitions of gloom. Mussorgsky's *Songs and Dances of Death* of the same years, although barely known, contributed to the spirit of hopelessness. Within the larger cultural scene, this gloom was counterbalanced by aggressive faith in the restoration of justice through violent means on the part of the democratic art. In Russian painting, individualization of faith was in order on the agenda of the Itinerants group of artists. The Itinerants had left the academy in protest over the uninspiring themes, many based on classical topics, which had a nationalist flavor and relied on monumental church art aesthetics. The Itinerants specialized in panoramic satires of the clergy and official Orthodoxy, and they sympathized with such popular scenes as the meeting of the icon by the common folk. In the 1860s the new Russian art glorified the oppressed, revolutionary, historical, or religious rebels—who variously opposed the regime. Calls for blood and new martyrdom introduced disequilibrium into secular art. The evasively allusive and provocative messianism of Alexander Ivanov's panoramic painting "Appearance of Christ to the People" finished in Italy in 1857–1858 and exhibited in Russia the following year inaugurated the new Christ. One figure preparing for baptism in the foreground was patterned on Gogol. In 1863, Nikolai Ge's controversial version of *The Last Supper*, which portrayed a grieving Christ patterned after Herzen who lets Judas depart to betray him, caused a scandal. In a few years the extremist left repaired the hesitant oversights of their aesthetic forerunners. In 1878, Vera Zasulich attempted to kill Fedor Trepov, and was acquitted thanks to the efforts of star lawyer Anatoly Koni and the writer-terrorist Sergey Stepniak-Kravchinsky assassinated the head of Russia's secret police, Nikolai Mezentsev. Russian terrorism was born. Trials against radical workers and students received much publicity. Famine in the countryside due to droughts aggravated the ravages of war with Turkey for peasants and fueled insurrection.

Responding to the wave of suicides that rocked the nation, Dostoevsky theorized about the problem in the December 1876 issue of *The Diary of a Writer*. In this sense, *Anna Karenina* bothered him considerably. After Mikhailovsky, the majority of critics condemned Tolstoy's near-indifference to social causes and, along with the alleged denial of freedom of action, also accused him of unburdening his religious insecurities on society through Levin, an issue not vital for the historical moment.[39] Dostoevsky's criticism was well founded. Before 1878, Tolstoy wrote next to nothing about burning political issues. He passed over in silence all the European revolutions from 1848 to 1870, and the vicious murder scandals in Russia associated with the Nechaev cell conspiracy, which became the subject of Dostoevsky's *The Devils* (1872). He wrote nothing about the first isolated and unsuccessful terror strikes of the 1860s, such as Dmitrii Karakozov's failed shooting of Tsar Alexander II in 1866. On all of these developments Dostoevsky commented extensively, condemning the radicals.

In a series of closely related "confessions of a Slavophile" devoted to the publication of part VIII of *Anna Karenina*, Dostoevsky expressed puzzlement at Levin's "gloomy separation" and, by means of an imaginary interlocutor, put forward the idea that Tolstoy is incapable of compromise when necessary to acquiesce to national calls of alarm. In order to see his truth, he needs "to make a full turn" (*povernut'sia vsem korpusom*). Dostoevsky insinuated that the author selfishly converted to the wrong cause while preventing his characters from digging deep into their souls and recovering their precious Russian instincts of "Mercy and Love"—thanks to such inherited Pushkinian traits as "universality" (*vsemirnost'*), "responsiveness" (*otzyvchivost'*), and the ability to transfigure in spirit (*perevoploshchat'sia*)—in order to consolidate the truce of lover, husband, and unfaithful wife at the foot of her bed into the anti-European manifestation of divine justice.[40] Tolstoy is right in claiming that there is a higher judge in heaven; however, Dostoevsky sees no sign of redemption at the end of Tolstoy's novel. Dostoevsky's God changes his mind: "No, not always is vengeance mine, not always do I repay." If Levin speaks for Tolstoy, he neglects what his character learned from the peasant to receive his Orthodox faith back. Dostoevsky concludes that the brilliant artist Tolstoy evidently failed to evince the three principles of religious art, universality, responsiveness, and transfiguration (25: 199).

Dostoevsky's dreams were answered by the great revival of Russian religious thought since the 1870s. The decades preceding and coinciding with Tolstoy's conversion and Dostoevsky's final years saw the flowering of religious mass media, which encouraged a dialogue with the lay reader and publications in the Russian vernacular of the bible and important texts in liturgy and homiletics.[41] A quick glance at the years 1878–79, when Tolstoy was starting *A Confession*, proves that his religious change did not occur in a spiritual vacuum but was a response to previous and current developments in Russian religious thought and culture. For the first time in Russian intellectual history, religious journals communicated with organs of secular learning. Soloviev advanced the issue of immortality from a purely academic topic to a veritable cause. Along with Dostoevsky, he closely followed the activities of Tolstoy's own favorite holy man, the librarian Nikolai Fedorov, who in these same years was developing his teaching on the resurrection of the dead, "the fathers" as the act of love of the sons and the ultimate goal of this common deed (*obshchee delo*) for humanity's presence on earth. Upon learning of Fedorov's ideas, Dostoevsky wrote: "Soloviev and I believe in the resurrection, which is real, literal, and personal, and which will be fulfilled on earth . . . maybe in the bodies like Christ's upon his resurrection before the ascension" (30[I]: 14).

Tolstoy's initial public ministry involved responses to terrorist activity. Compared with Ivan Turgenev's poetic glorification of Vera Zasulich as a "saint" in his poem in prose "Threshold" (Porog, 1878) or Iakov Polonskii's similar paean in "The Female Convict" (Uznitsa, 1878), Tolstoy's evaluation of the affair was uninspired in a profound way. In a letter to Alexandrine Tolstaya he condemned the government and the young terrorists: "All those who have justified the assassin and were sympathetic to her acquittal know very well that for the sake of their own safety one must not and should not justify murder, but for them the question is not who is right but who will win" (62: 409).

If to forgive Zasulich was wrong because that would justify murder, was it right to convict her in the name of the law? And which law would that be? Early in Russia's love affair with the revolution, Tolstoy was able to grasp that the result of the struggle depended on how well man could *simultaneously* act in the name of "what is right" and practice forgiveness toward the opponent of that right cause. In his letters to Strakhov, a determined critic of nihilism, Tolstoy called the Zasulich generation "the front-runners from the column we do not yet see; this looks to be boding the revolution" (62: 411).

Nevertheless, Tolstoy refused to regard terrorists as beasts and outlaws "acting in accordance with some psychological laws" (63: 68).

It will be profitable to compare Tolstoy's treatment of religious terror with Dostoevsky's exorcism of revolution in his novel *The Demons* (1872). Although the parable about "Legion, a man of the city who had [many] demons" and who begs Jesus to free him of the unclean spirit begins in Luke 8:26, and continues through 8:35, Dostoevsky prefaces his novel with an epigraph comprising only verses 32–35. There is a good reason for the choice. In verse 32, the focus is not on the individual man who has been undergoing torment and cure, but on the herd of swine that graze on the hillside, on the demons expelled from the man, and on the demons begging Jesus' permission to inhabit the swine. Permission granted, Dostoevsky celebrates the plunge of the herd in the abyss; he wills to see radicalism and reeling faithlessness shamefully self-destroyed. Dostoevsky's intent is to shift the absorption of terror to the spectator. It is those who hang about the scene who "became terrified" of the plunge (*uzhasnulis'*) and of the cost of the healing.[42] Dostoevsky's legion, strictly speaking, are not bomb throwers yet, only scandal rousers and spiders covering the country by their cocoon cells (*iacheiki*), nodes, and networks (*uzly i seti*). They excite and horrify the populace, their spectator, by their "fires and bonfires"(Dostoevsky 10: 418–19) and entertain hopes of inscribing their Russian "noble seminarian's" version of "new and terrible" freedom on the old Jacobin scroll of victimization and murder (10: 472–73).

Tolstoy's indwelling Kingdom that expels Legion has nothing to do with Dostoevsky's transmigration of evil. When he first thought about it, Jesus' kindness in the canonical Gospels to the demons' request not to be ordered to go back in the abyss perturbs Tolstoy: "If you admit that I expel evil, then it can't be that I expelled it with evil, because that way there would be no evil. If you expel evil, it is not with evil then . . . but by something else—by goodness" (24: 300-301). Tolstoy was tempted by this kindness and he even sought for a while to justify terror through government oppression and based on the necessity to explore new vistas for uninhibited action to achieve spiritual goals. In his fascinating and long letter to Mikhail Engelgardt, a radical who became interested in Tolstoy's new teaching, Tolstoy nonetheless begs the young man to accept Christian pacifism "instead of shootings, explosions and underground printing plants" (63: 112–14).

Tolstoy's inner circle had already disapproved of his new Christian enthusiasm. His elder son Sergey told him that the teaching of Christ is difficult. Tolstoy lost his patience: "One of us is insane: they or me" (49: 37–38). On May 29, 1881, he fell out with the Fets, who argued that Christian teaching is impracticable in modern society. The diary recorded his frustration: "Have they tried to practice it?" (49: 42). At another time Sergey confessed to his father that he liked the life of the flesh and believed in it (48: 47). On his next walking pilgrimage to Optina Pustyn' in peasant outfit in June 1881, Tolstoy went without Strakhov, accompanied by his servant, Sergey Arbuzov. Tolstoy was soon unmasked by his own dainty habits and imperious gentlemanly discretion and was promptly received by Father Ambrose.[43] Tolstoy was very satisfied by the lengthy debate with the elder, which could very well be considered a dispute, and wrote Strakhov and Turgenev to express his utter contentment (63: 69–72). In the diary he summed up the experience of deprivation: "I have not slept or eaten dry food in six days. I was trying to feel happy. Difficult, but possible, I have tasted my way toward it" (49: 46). Tolstoy started noticing with displeasure the champagne on the table in his home and deaths in the village from diseases caused by malnutrition, his uncouth peasants reading the Gospels, while the old uncle Turgenev "in luxury and idleness," fearing the talk or the name of God, dancing his cute, decrepit cancan with Tolstoy's work-shy progeny (49: 51, 57). Luxury and idleness caused the first destructive storms with Sophia Andreevna. After a happy summer stay in Samara, the family moved to Moscow in September 1881 to ensure proper schooling for the growing children, and for the elder son Sergey, who became a student of the natural sciences at Moscow University. The diary entry for October 5, 1881, reflects depression that has nothing to do with his religion, but has everything to do with its divorce from his immediate surrounding: "A month has passed—the most tortuous in my life, this move to Moscow. They all settle down. When will they start living? The wretches. And there is no life" (49: 58). In August 1882 he shouted at his wife angrily that his only sincere wish was to leave the family.[44]

With all that, Tolstoy's public ministry began in placid tones at the end of 1880. He made peace with Alexandrine in the first days of January 1881 on the strength of their belief in the same God (63: 42). Dostoevsky died at the end of January. In February 1881 Tolstoy wrote Strakhov, confessing his love for this "closest, dear, and sorely missed" man, as a result of whose departure a vital part of him broke loose, with whom it felt wrong to compete because the best products of his soul—for example, *The Wronged and the Injured*—brought Tolstoy joy and cured him of envy (63: 43). The assassination of Tsar the Liberator in March 1881 by the radicals of the terrorist group The People's Will allowed Tolstoy to continue this ministry of reconciliation and love. Between March 8 and 15, 1881, he drafted his letter to the new emperor, Alexander III, son of the victim of regicide. After the requisite tone of humility customary in the opening lines addressed to an imperial subject, Tolstoy abandoned obsequies and made an unprecedented plea to the young Christian brother, fearing that if no such effort were made, the tsar might overlook the obvious choice, namely, pardoning the criminals in the name of his human duties that take precedence over his duties as a tsar. The temptation was great to retaliate against the murderers of a fine and kind man who accomplished much good for Russia: "In this temptation consists the whole horror of your situation. Why not try to fulfill His Law [in performing] what is done in God's name" (63: 44–51). If the tsar were to hesitate regarding whether Christian law could be applicable to the release of the murderers, he would exhibit "cowardice" (63: 49, 51). The letter to the tsar was reinforced by a note to Constantine Pobedonostsev, the new Chief Procurator of the Holy Synod, Tolstoy's enemy after the publication of the last, anti–Pan Slavic part of *Anna Karenina* (63: 57). The tsar passed on a word to Tolstoy through Strakhov that if he were to be assassinated, he could well oblige, but he had no such right in relation to the current regicide (63: 55). The terrorists were executed in April. Two months later Pobedonostsev finally responded, opening communication lines with Tolstoy: "Our Christ is not yours. I know mine to be the Man of Virile Truth, who cures the infirm, and in your Christ I saw the infirm, who himself needs curing" (63: 59). This was a declaration of war.

Tolstoy was not discouraged. Memoirs of these conversations left by Tolstoy's interlocutors all agree on his ardor, strength, and sincerity. From the young Prince Alexis Obolensky he won sympathy despite the discomfiting disclosure, against the expectation of the young man, that in Levin's dispute with the priest Tolstoy meant the priest to be right. Vladimir Istomin, a young executive officer in education affairs at the Chancery of Moscow Mayoralty, who observed religious routines pro forma, was mesmerized by Tolstoy's discourse on immortality under the starry skies and in front of the stunned guests. The conservative critic Alexis Suvorin, the future patron of Anton Chekhov, met Tolstoy in 1880 after an eighteen-year hiatus and was struck by his youthful spirit and optimism. "Why don't you write?" Suvorin wondered. "Because we became teachers without knowing what to teach," Tolstoy replied. Vladimir Stasov, the veteran of art criticism from the liberal-democratic camp, paid Tolstoy a visit in the summer of 1880. At night Tolstoy subjected Stasov to a reading of his commentary on the Gospels, which the known atheist silently endured like a well-behaved guest. During a long walk the next day Tolstoy demanded a response. Stasov erupted with a diatribe against this utterly repulsive Asiatic book, the Bible. The scene continued with Stasov and Tolstoy "barking" at each other for thirty minutes and then silently walking home. Tension was relieved only when the good-natured Stasov told Tolstoy of the latest literary news. Rumors had already spread that Tolstoy was mad and couldn't write. In Stasov's and Turgenev's view of 1880, however, it was the new religious frenzy—unleashed by Dostoevsky's speech at the festivities commemorating the opening of the Pushkin monument in Moscow, which led to the coining of the new catchphrases about Russia's universality and messianism and sent the nation into convulsive raptures of insanity—that one had to be wary of.[45]

Given the bid for the dominant role in the spiritual leadership of the nation that was at stake, the speech affair and its possible influence on Tolstoy deserves closer analysis. Several at first apprehensive and then self-centered letters that Dostoevsky wrote to his wife in the last summer of his life before and after the Pushkin affair speak overtly about his ambition to be Russia's prophet.[46] The news about Tolstoy's nonattendance and Turgenev's indisposition pleased him: "Today Grigorovich told me that Turgenev, who had just visited with Lev Tolstoy, is ill, and Tolstoy is practically off his rocker and may now be quite insane" (30[1]: 166). The following day he confirmed the news: "About Tolstoy Katkov also is saying that he is quite demented" (30[1]: 168). On June 7, the eve of Dostoevsky's big day, fallouts began. According to Dostoevsky's reportage to his wife, in his speech Turgenev "demeaned" Pushkin by stripping him of his title of national poet. Turgenev expressed the opinion that Pushkin's worldview was narrow; his occasional praise of officialdom was disappointing, while his classical detachment was anachronistic. In scope, as a leader of the national tradition, he was no match for Shakespeare, Homer, or Goethe. Despite all that, he gave Russia its immortal sounds, and the return to Pushkin after the noise of the 1860s inspired Turgenev's expectations for the coming of a world-class genius.[47] For Dostoevsky the day was saved by the "colossal" impression of the *Brothers Karamazov*, which Dostoevsky could see reflected in the faces of those in attendance (30[1]: 182). On June 8 his triumph was complete: "No, Anya, never can you imagine or represent the effect of [my speech]! When I came out, the audience thundered with applause and for a long, long time they would not allow me to read. . . . It is all *The Karamazovs*! Finally I began. . . . When I announced the unification of all people of the world at the end, the room was nearly in hysterics; when I finished, I won't tell you of the roar, the howl of delight; people unknown to each other cried, sobbed, embraced, and vowed to each other to be better, and not hate but love each other. . . . Everyone streamed up to me onstage. All members of the Society . . . embraced and kissed me and everyone literally cried in ecstasy"(30[1]: 184).

If it was true indeed, Turgenev, in tears, ran up to kiss him, perhaps on account of a compliment Dostoevsky inserted in the speech. Ivan Aksakov ran onstage and proclaimed that Dostoevsky's speech was no mere speech but a historic event. Like the sun, Dostoevsky's word illumined the nation's cloudy horizon and prophesied that there would be brotherhood *without bewilderment (ne budet nedoumenii)*. For his next reading session of the day, Dostoevsky decided to pick Pushkin's "The Prophet" (30[1]: 184–85). The famous points of the speech, which the Turgenev circle thought stupid, speculative, and indecent, introduced the prophetic theme from the very first line. Dosto-evsky ascribed to Pushkin's prophetic spirit the discovery of several vision-ary phenomena. First, Pushkin discovered Russia's negative types, the Alekos and Onegins, the unhappy and proud wanderers in their native land. Second, he discovered that their disease could be cured by means of the humble sac-rifice and moral incorruptibility of its women, Tatiana in *Eugene Onegin* and Turgenev's resolute maidens, Tatiana's clones. Third, by his own "universal responsiveness" Pushkin impressed on the nation that Russia's destiny is in-contestably Pan-European and universal. If the proud wanderer humbles him-self and traverses his poor land with Christ in his heart, Russia will offer the world a solution erasing all contradictions and will head the all-humanitarian brotherly fellowship (26: 136–49). In short, Pushkin embodied those very three principles of true religious art "universality," "responsiveness," and the ability to transfigure in spirit that Tolstoy the artist lacked according to Dos-toevsky's earlier review.

Dostoevsky was soon challenged in the press by the right-wing thinker Constantine Leontiev's sober reminder that universal harmony cannot be achieved on earth. The young historian Aleksandr Gradovsky inquired about the origin and the reason for the existence of unhappy wanderers, wondering if their proud self-defense could have social explanations. Dostoevsky shot back with four essays—in what would be the last issue of his *Diary of a Writer*—explaining his Christian principles. In his firm view, the Russian peasant was thoroughly religious, whose mindset was crystallized by cen-turies of suffering and prayer in submission to God's will. With this precious humbleness and indifference to the false education of Rome, the nation could win if it assimilated the best of Western culture with the receptivity of Pushkin. At the moment, however, those who wished to deprive the nation of its chance to cleanse itself of its suffering and its accumulation of sin through blood and tears in the last war against the "oppressed Christian faith" were wrong (26: 151, 153). The last word in the debate was voiced by the legal scholar Constantine Kavelin in a letter to Dostoevsky. What should really en-joy pride of place, asked Kavelin, personal moral perfection or the improve-ment of those conditions that influence man's life in society? More than ever Russia was in need of positing for itself the question of moral truth, which was self-evident, necessary, and indubitable, and was not couched in self-appeasing rhetoric. Dostoevsky's speech provided such a model. Personal moral convictions were a fiction without a healthy social and religious order. Only the improvement of religious education and responsible social behavior, coupled with the assimilation of Christian teaching, could ensure victory over prejudice, drunkenness, and darkness.[48]

In support of his new religious cause, which was already in the planning stages, Tolstoy must inevitably have felt obligated to respond to these thinly veiled insinuations, even more so because themes of gloom led to the revival of debates over conciliatory faith and immortality. But now Dostoevsky was dead. His legacy was posthumously elevated by Soloviev—who used Tolstoy's letters to Strakhov for the task—to that of prophetic leader of the Russian nation under the aegis of Orthodoxy, its religious conscience. Ultimately the campaign played into the hands of Pobedonostsev, Ivan Aksakov, and the religious right. Under such circumstances, the meeting with Stasov and Turgenev's incessant pleas to write must have intensified Tolstoy's concern regarding his own future in literature.[49] His version of Christ and his new faith were the subject of vague but widely circulated rumor. Tolstoy had to decide whether he himself was planning to become a philosophizing prophet or a proselytizing philosopher, something of a Socratic-Christian sophist in the market square. Following a meeting with Nikolai Fedorov, the ascetic theorist of the revival of the dead, whom Tolstoy called "a saint," in a Moscow diary entry for October 5, 1881, Tolstoy compared the two options and contrasted his ideas with Soloviev's plans to "improve" Christianity on a world scale under the messianic banner of Dostoevsky, which Tolstoy had denounced as a sophism.[50]

As a result of his antipatriotic stance and advocacy of the terrorists, by 1881 Tolstoy, already an ingrate in the eyes of the authorities and the patriots, slowly let segments of his commentary on the Gospels become part of the common intellectual property. In addition to observing this slowly emerging opposition to the authorities, he was noticing a lack of understanding among his family and friends. He must also have discovered that less than a week before Dostoevsky's death Alexandrine Tolstaya had given him Tolstoy's correspondence and writings on matters of faith, which had been entrusted to her. One of Tolstoy's closest friends—whom he at times came close to offending but toward whom he invariably remained vulnerable and sincere in his religious soul-baring—inexplicably betrayed him. According to Tolstaya's memoir, Dostoevsky first asked her about Tolstoy's "new direction" in January 1881, during one of the social gatherings where Dostoevsky read from his *Brothers Karamazov*. To facilitate his understanding, she copied out Tolstoy's writings, which Dostoevsky arranged to pick up during a rendezvous at her place. Feeling ashamed to countenance "the great thinker" (*velikii myslitel'*) before her, she started reading. Dostoevsky clutched his head and ran around the room in despair: "Not right! Not right!" (*ne to, ne to*). Nonetheless, he grabbed "everything in writing that lay on the table: originals and copies of Lev's letters. From something that he said I inferred that a desire was born in him to dispute the false opinions of L. N. I do not regret the lost letters a bit, but I can't console myself that Dostoevsky's intention remained unfulfilled. Five days later, he was no more."[51]

Instead of implicating Tolstoy's iconoclastic religion in that final heartache that caused Dostoevsky's death or explaining away Dostoevsky's anxious re-action as a customary jealous spell, it might prove more profitable to sum up the extent of verifiable influences that Dostoevsky's extant religious work had, or could have had, on Tolstoy. Although Tolstoy's praise of *The Broth-ers Karamazov* did not appear until later, his admiration for the novel, which would remain his favorite, was total. Together with Dostoevsky's *Notes from the House of the Dead*, these novels, plus the short, futuristic dream of the late 1870s about love and kindness entitled "Dream of the Ridiculous Man," were Tolstoy's only two positive impressions.[52] Tolstoy disliked the corrosive and contradictory tone of *The Diary of a Writer*, thinking that it was injecting a spirit of dissent in society. In response to Strakhov's unsavory portrait of Dos-toevsky the man in the introductory essay to the first posthumous edition of the writer's works, Tolstoy abstained from comment, noting only in his letter of response dated November-December 1883 that it is wrong to place on a pedestal a man who is "all struggle" (*ves' bor'ba*) (63: 142).

In the midst of his conversion, Tolstoy never discussed or mentioned in his diary Dostoevsky's terrible doubts. Supposing that Ippolit Terentiev's confes-sion, with a laissez-faire to the world to destroy itself if he is destined to die or Kirillov and Stavrogin in *The Devils* (1872) interested him little, it is still curious not to have Tolstoy's reaction to other controversies. Neither the sanc-tified rebellion of the meek wife from Dostoevsky's eponymous story "The Meek One" (1876), who jumps to her death with an icon pressed to her chest. Nor Ivan's confrontation with the devil nor Christ's confrontation with the Grand Inquisitor, silently sealed with a kiss (*potselui*), the imperative of love, the verbal noun formed from the imperative "Kiss!," merited Tolstoy's com-mentary. If Tolstoy had had an opportunity to see Dostoevsky's second anno-tation in the Gospel of John—not the one confiscated by the police in 1849 that called for a death sentence but a present Dostoevsky received in Siberia from Natalia Fonvizina, wife of the convicted Decembrist—he would clearly have grasped the difference in their attitude toward Christ. Dostoevsky was mostly underlining and explaining verses that had to do with Christ's divin-ity and humanized beauty, his Oneness with the Father in the Trinity, the wine and the bread of the Eucharist, the Resurrection and resurrection of all in the body, mysteries, and the Apocalypses.[53] All of this loving underlining by Dos-toevsky related to the passages that Tolstoy expurgated or changed in John.

Nonetheless, records of one meeting late in 1881 seem to reflect Tolstoy's opinion of Dostoevsky's religion and the scope of the writer's accountability for his religious convictions. During his visit to the Moscow school where two of his sons, Il'ya and Lev, were students, Tolstoy shared his views about Gogol and Dostoevsky. He felt that the writer should not inflame others but rather burn with truth. Speaking of Gogol and, most assuredly, of Tolstoy's own changed religion, the Polivanovs thought they had to calm Tolstoy down on account of a possible artistic collapse. "You are a healthy person, unlike Gogol," they informed him. But Tolstoy disagreed with the Belinsky-spawned rumor that Gogol had experienced a defeat. He stressed that Gogol was undergoing a change that was only halted with his death. Evgeny Markov, a democratic critic who was also present during this conversation, wondered why Tolstoy didn't write of his change, given that society was in need of a new spiritual success story. Tolstoy replied that everyone in the literary guild seemed to feel the need to prove something. Dostoevsky was one: "His whole mistake was in his desire to teach everyone. Popping up is his feeling of everything good in the common folk, and he hastens to praise it; he feels something and so he lashes against one thing and extols another, but why?—he wouldn't know. He would feel, for example, that our Orthodox Church represents something good—and, his thought not yet formed, he goes preaching."[54]

Be that as it may, in February 1882, shortly after Dostoevsky's death, Tolstoy wrote Alexandrine several angry letters reminding her that Christ is not about treachery, but about "love and harmony" (63: 89). One especially abusive and bitter letter he chose not to send: "Your faith is a filthy fraud; your faith is the work of the devil" (63: 90–91). Having cooled off a bit, he all but put an end to the relationship and issued the following warning: "In my relationship to Orthodoxy, your faith, I do not find myself in the position of someone deluded or gone astray, but rather in the position of an accuser. I will not give in" (63: 93). This letter also remained unsent. It is under these conditions, egged on by expectations from the spiritually thirsty nation, that Tolstoy made up his mind about the structure and genre of *A Confession*, his most significant document accounting for his loss of faith and the beginning of its recovery. Drafts of *A Confession* were finished by 1879, the same year Tolstoy discovered *razumenie*. However, the final version, with the famous dream on the ropes at the end, was only completed in 1882. Between 1878 and 1881 Tolstoy had already experimented with forms of confession starting with the unrealized autobiography *My Life* (1878), a Rousseauean account of the life of a great sinner, which, in the space of only a few pages, covers the early years of Tolstoy's life (23: 561–63). Only years later would these first episodes of his conscious life be resurrected for Pavel Biriukov's biography. This work is nonetheless precious thanks to the confession that prefaces it: "My present condition, from the point of view of which I will be looking back and describing my life, I have chosen because it is only now, in little more than one year, that I find myself in a state of calm, lucidity, and firmness such as I have never heretofore enjoyed in my entire life" (23: 469). It was time for Tolstoy to account publicly for his religious change.

NOTES

1. S. A. Tolstaya, *Dnevniki*, 1: 93–104 (esp. the diary entries for 1878); Sergey Tolstoy, *Tolstoy Remembered*, 30–34; Il'ya Tolstoy, *My Father: Reminiscences*, 42–46.

2. The same experience is related in a letter to S. A. Rachinsky dated April 23, 1878 (62: 518).

3. Sergey Tolstoy, *Tolstoy Remembered*, 34–35.

4. See "Chto mozhno i chego nel'zia delat' khristianinu" (90: 123–24), "Tsartsvo bozhie" (90: 125–26), and "Ch'i my?" (90: 127–31).

5. F. W. J. Schelling, *The Philosophy of Art*, ed. and trans. Douglas W. Stott (Minneapolis: University of Minnesota Press, 1985), 255. Schelling's lectures were first published in 1856.

6. G. W. F. Hegel, *Phenomenology of Spirit*, 115, 525.

7. Hegel, *Phenomenology of Spirit*, 561. G. W. F. Hegel, *Lectures on the Philosophy of World History*, 38–39.

8. Letter to Strakhov dated October 27, 1878 (62: 445).

9. See Turgenev's letter to Tolstoy dated November 15/27, 1878, in Tolstoy, *Perepiska s russkimi pisateliami*, 1: 186.

10. Ibid., 1: 190.

11. Ibid., 1: 192.

12. Schopenhauer, *The World as Will and Representation*, 2: 63. For a comprehensive overview of interpretations of "logos" in classical Greek philosophy, see G. B. Kerferd, *The Sophistic Movement* (Cambridge: Cambridge University Press, 1981), 83ff.

13. On the doctrine of the consubstantiality of Christ see John Meyendorff, *Christ in Eastern Christian Thought* (Crestwood, N.Y.: St. Vladimir Seminary Press, 1987), 36–43, 65–89.

14. Ibid., 156, 183. The latter quotation is from Michael A. Meerson, *The Trinity of Love in Modern Russian Theology: The Love Paradigm and the Revival of Western Medieval Love Mysticism in Modern Russian Trinitarian Thought from Soloviev to Bulgakov* (Quincy, Ill: Franciscan Press, 1998), 22.

15. St. Justin Martyr, *Dialogues with Trypho*, 55.

16. St. Justin Martyr, *The First and Second Apologies*, 54–58; *Dialogues with Trypho*, 61.

17. St. Justin Martyr, *Dialogues with Trypho*, 44, 59–60.

18. Ibid., 67.

19. The authoritative view of Andrzej Walicki insisting on Tolstoy's rationalism overlooks Tolstoy's complete rethinking of reason in 1879–1880. See Andrzej Walicki,

A History of Russian Thought, 330–31, 338. In their studies concerned with issues of accuracy, David Redston and David Matual convincingly demonstrate that after Tolstoy's exclusion of all miracles, and his rejection of Grace and the Holy Ghost, or the Resurrection, "redundant" or "immoral" in Tolstoy's view—Tolstoy's religion corresponds to no known mainstream version of Christianity. See David Redston, "Tolstoy and the Greek Gospel," *Journal of Russian Studies*, no. 54 (1988), 21–33; and David Matual, *Tolstoy's Translation of the Gospels: A Critical Study* (Lewiston, USA: Edwin Mellen Press, 1992).

20. For Ivakin's reminiscences concerning his tenure at Yasnaya Polyana, see "Tolstoi v 1880-e gg" (Tolstoy in the 1880s), in *Literaturnoe nasledstvo*, vol. 69, part 2, ed. I. I. Anisimov et al. (Moscow: Akademiia Nauk USSR, 1961), 21–123.

21. V. V. Zenkovsky, "Problema bessmertiia u L. N. Tolstogo" (The Problem of Immortality in Tolstoy), in *O religii L'va Tolstogo* (Moscow: Put', 1912), 57–58.

22. The doctrine of *filioque* in Tolstoy's rendering is thus decreed not to have any relation to logos, because Christ earned his right at the possession of logos (24: 32).

23. The corresponding verse in Matt. 16.3 to which Tolstoy is referring reads as follows: "You know how to interpret the appearance of the sky, but you cannot interpret the signs of the times. An evil and adulterous generation asks for a sign, but no sign will be given to it except the sign of Jonah. Then he left them and went away." *The New Oxford Annotated Bible*, 24.

24. Gorgias argued that logos in the hypostasis of *meterologoi* makes things "unseen and lacking in credibility become apparent to the eyes of opinion." Critiquing Gorgias in his eponymous dialogue, Plato notes that Gorgias was inherently playing into the hands of deception (*apatē*). Plato insists on a radical gulf between logos and the things to which it refers. See Kerferd, *The Sophistic Movement*, 80.

25. Matual reads Tolstoy's translation merely as a "moral error," whereas my interpretation also encompasses aesthetic meaning. See Matual, *Tolstoy's Translation of the Gospels*, 75.

26. Aristotle, "Nichomachean Ethics, Book III.2," "Rhetoric to Alexander," and "Poetics," in *The Complete Works of Aristotle*, 2: 2317, 2323, 2326, 2327).

27. See paragraph 140 of *Hegel's Philosophy of Right*, 171. Hegel also quotes Pascal's discussion of Aristotle's Nichomachean Ethics III.2 and praises his distinction of those acting without perception from those acting from ignorance.

28. Tolstoy, *The Critique of Dogmatic Theology* (Kritika dogmaticheskogo bogosloviia, 1879), 23: 97.

29. See Jacques Derrida, "The Mystical Foundation of Authority," in *Deconstruction and the Possibility of Justice*, ed. Drucilla Cornell, Michel Rosenfeld, and David Gray Carlson (New York: Routledge, 1992), 3–67.

30. David Friedrich Strauss, *The Life of Jesus Critically Examined*, 2 vols., trans. Marian Evans (1860; reprint, St. Clair Shores, Mich.: Scholarly Press, 1970), 2: 715–19.

31. See Tolstoy's two letters to Strakhov dated January 3 and 27, 1878 (62: 369, 379).

32. See chapter 2 of the December 1877 issue of Dostoevsky's *Diary of a Writer* (26: 111–27).

33. Saltykov-Shchedrin, *The Golovlyov Family*, trans. Natalie Duddington and ed. James Wood (New York: New York Review of Books, 2001), 110–14.

34. See Irina Paperno, *Suicide as a Cultural Institution in Dostoevsky's Russia* (Ithaca: Cornell University Press, 1997), 82–83.

35. See "V tine zhiteiskikh volnenii" and "Rydat'? No v serdtse net rydanii," in S. Ia. Nadson, *Stikhotvoreniia* (Moscow: Sovetskaia Rossiia, 1987), 56–57.

36. Gleb Uspensky, "Neizlechimyi," in *Polnoe sobranie sochinenii* (Moscow: Academy of Sciences, 1940–54), 4: 191. The hero of Garshin's famous story "The Red Flower" (Krasnyi tsvetok) loses his mind in a failed attempt to restore justice, while the talented artist in "An Incident" (Proisshestvie) gives up art.

37. The narrator of "Higher Truth and Reality" (Istina i Pravda) would die for the higher truth of immortality but doubts: "but how can you 'possess it'? And, moreover, find bliss in it?" Ivan Sergeevich Turgenev, *Pesn' dushi. Stikhotvoreniia, poemy. Stikhotvoreniia v proze* (Moscow: Sovetskaia Rossiia, 1988), 304, 393.

38. "Enough. An Exceprt from the Notes of a Deceased Artist (Dovol'no. Otryvok iz zapisok umershego khudozhnika). Turgenev, *Sobranie sochinenii v desiati tomakh*, 7: 29–38.

39. For an exhaustive representation of differing views of the novel, see Knowles, ed., *Tolstoy: The Critical Heritage*, 233–370.

40. Quoted passages appear as follows: 25: 175, 194, 198–201, 218–23. See esp. subchapter 1 of chapter 1, chapter 2, and subchapter 4 of chapter 3 of *The Diary of a Writer*, July-August 1877, which came out in 1878. See also the subchapter entitled "*Anna Karenina* as a Fact of Special Significance" (*Anna Karenina* kak fakt osobogo naznacheniia) (25: 198–202).

41. The periodical *Christian Reading* (Khristianskoe chtenie) published on topics of science and belief and many reviews of Western and domestic theology. Other popular religious journals included *Dushepoleznoe chtenie, Pravoslavnyi sobesednik, Strannik*, and the weeklies *Voskresnyi den'* and *Troitskie listki*.

42. *Besy [Demons]*. Dostoevsky, 10: 5.

43. See Arbuzov's memoir about the trip in *L. N. Tolstoy v vospominaniiakh sovremennikov*, 2 vols. (Moscow: Khudozhestvennaia literatura, 1978), 1: 312–19.

44. Sophia Andreevna Tolstaya, *Dnevniki*, 1: 108–9.

45. For the memoirs and letters of Obolensky, Istomin, Suvorin, and Stasov, see *L. N. Tolstoy v vospominaniiakh sovremennikov*, 1: 239–47, 274–75, 276–81. Dostoevsky delivered his Pushkin speech at the Society of Lovers of Russian Literature on June 8, 1880. Its written version was published in the August issue for 1880 of his *Diary of a Writer* (26: 136–48).

46. See Dostoevsky's letters to Anna Grigorievna Dostoevskaya dated May 25–26, 27, 27–28, 28–29, 30–31, 31, and June 2–3, 5, 7, and 8, 1880 (30 [Part I]: 158–85).

47. See Turgenev, "Speech Delivered at the Dedication of the Monument to A. S. Pushkin in Moscow," in *The Essential Turgenev*, 839–49.

48. Konstantin Dmitrievich Kavelin, "Pis'mo F. M. Dostoevskomu," in his *Nash umstvennyi stroi: Stat'i po filosofii russkoi istorii i kul'tury* (Moscow: Pravda, 1989), 448–77.

49. Soloviev's three speeches in memory of Dostoevsky were delivered on January 30, 1881, February 1, 1882, and February 19, 1883, and published in a reworked form under the collective title "Three Speeches in Memory of Dostoevsky" (*Tri rechi v pamiat' Dostoevskogo*) in 1884.

50. "Nikolay Fyodorych is a saint. A tiny cell of a room. Must fulfill! That goes without saying. He refuses salary. No bedding and no bed. The poor Solovyov has condemned Christianity without understanding it and wants to invent something better. Chatter, endless chatter" (49: 58).

51. *Dostoevsky v zabytykh i neizvestnykh vospominaniiakh sovremennikov*, 257–58.

52. See Tolstoy's comments on the Christian standpoint in these works in his letter to Strakhov dated September 1880 (63: 24); Lev Nikiforov dated March 31, 1891 (65: 281); and to Sophia Andreevna Tolstaya dated November 1892 (84: 168). See also Tolstoy, *What Is Art* (30: 160, 177).

53. See Irina Kirillova's illuminating analysis in "Dostoevsky's Markings in the Gospel According to St. John," in *Dostoevsky and the Christian Tradition*, ed. George Pattison and Diane Oenning Thompson (Cambridge: Cambridge University Press, 2001), 41–50.

54. On Gogol and Dostoevsky, see the reminiscences of Lev Polivanov, headmaster of the all-male school in Moscow, and his wife. *L. N. Tolstoy v vospominaniiakh sovremennikov*, 1: 282–92.

Chapter Nine

Religious Experience and Forms of Accounting

IN SEARCH OF THE CONFESSIONAL VOICE

Modern commentators—most notably Lewis Rambo—agree that conversions have contexts and various stages of completion and that quest and its process would most certainly stand at the dynamic center of the conversion narrative. Such a narrative would normally include an encounter with the advocate or advocates and stages of acceptance or resistance to advocacy. This may involve entering into trial spiritual relationships or participation in rites and rituals and performing certain role-playing in the process of accounting for the transformations experienced. Often the "holistic" language of transformations and its anticipated metaphors would incorporate fretful movements, states of stalemate and disorientation, violent or appeasing dreams, and drowning and reviving.[1] Personal testimony at the end of transformation is "a common method for publicly displaying commitment" (Rambo, 137). Thanks to their presumed sincerity, autobiographies normally touch lives the way books of theology never do. The canonical phrases "And it dawned upon me," or "I started to realize" do not undermine but rather enhance the credibility of the "storytelling voice," whose presence is expected in advance in the confessional tale of the reviving soul.[2] Converts respond to the necessity to produce the expected story based on the assumption that they speak as *successful* converts. In this "motive-talk" and its clichés ("I knew that something in my life was going to happen—I could not continue as I am"), converts talk themselves into believing this to be the case, but no one wants to notice the sham.[3] These "artful narratives" constitute resources to countenance an "appropriate view of reality," bridging the gap between the dream of transformation and a return to reality.[4]

Tolstoy, however, is no ordinary convert or a "normal" writer-convert. *A Confession*, which in its final version bore the subtitle *An Introduction to an Unpublished Work*, was originally intended as an introduction to the long narrative of confessed wrongdoing and sin. In fact, at the beginning of the second chapter Tolstoy still promises to write the sad and instructive story of his life (23: 4). In his younger years Tolstoy depended on memory to secure the unstable impressions of consciousness. Yet he also distrusted memory, which could just as easily become an indiscriminate collection of moments. When exploring "reactions" to situations, no suitable narrative technique—in the absence of moral answerability of the self—had yet been found by him. Delightful storytelling fictions, Pierre's diaries in *War and Peace* represent an exercise in self-gratification and are presented as such in the novel. It could not have escaped Tolstoy in 1878–1879 that Schopenhauer was citing the example of two converts, Saint Augustine and Luther—both deniers of freedom of will and promoters of God's grace acting on man—to prove that such freedom exists. Now Tolstoy had to reconcile these old, partially solved problems of a responsible self with his new illuminations. Again, Tolstoy found a purely artistic solution. In all the forms in which he would practice the retelling of his spiritual experience in these first post-conversional years (a confession, notes, diaries, comparative records of death and near-death experiences), the act of narrating the event, or telling it back to the past, was dictated by the "knowing-forward," the new position of his awareness. The moment of decision, the life in the present, is dramatically positioned between the two narrative poles, one backward-telling, the other forward-looking.

"Notes of a Christian" (*Zapiski Khristianina*), begun in January 1881, was intended to replace Tolstoy's regular diary and signal a change in his spiritual calendar—two years following his acquisition of faith, which had followed thirty-five years of Godlessness. For this Tolstoy put a stop to his life journal, an account of a still-disoriented life, and started life afresh as a newborn Christian. Every daily experience, looked upon from the new perspective of *razumenie*, is extricated by him from its routine meanings and inserted into the "Notes" as an embedded test case of spiritual reckoning. Tolstoy explains the change of calendar: "how come (notes of a) Christian? Who may call himself a Christian? A true Christian is humble above all and does not dare call himself that, least of all make this a public announcement" (49: 7). Tolstoy's test failed. He could not bridge the gap between the projections of his new conscious desires, what was "pleasing and joyous," and the evil realities of life, what was "repellent, repulsive and sick" (49: 8). When he gave up on himself and switched to conducting an ethnographic tour of the grounds of his estate for the purpose of interviewing peasants from his village about their hand-to-mouth struggle to survive, the quality of the "Notes" improved. Peasants made the sincerity of their master look somewhat stupid and unworthy of their attention. In a brilliant decision to expose his own falsity, Tolstoy incorporated into his diary a vita (*zhizn'*) commissioned from a young peasant, Kostiushka (49: 13). The primary charm of this note, with its lapses of grammar and obvious spelling mistakes, is that it trades banter with its editor's desire to affirm the same true belief, only in a much more sterile form. When this occurred, the "Notes" were no longer Tolstoy's spiritual testimony of his own but a document of social exposure. The journal of a "two-year-old Christian" breaks off, then continues in the year 1881 as a regular journal of a fifty-two-year-old man, who argues about faith with the Fets, Turgenev, and his family (49: 8).

Tolstoy's need to verbalize his new awareness belongs in the long-standing tradition of religious and Christian lore. He expressed the gist of such a need with the characteristic clumsiness of a faith seeker, later calling it the task of a writer: "I think that the task of a person who writes is this: to communicate to other people those of *his* thoughts, beliefs that have made *my* life joyous."[5] The first paradoxical step in this determinedly selfish affair is to look back at the condition before vertigo.[6] The earlier drafts of *A Confession* contain the following phrase: "I have grown up, grown old, and looked back at my life" (23: 524). Donna Orwin suggested that Tolstoy's earlier conception of a human being as a mysterious atom is motivated by too many potential causes at any given moment; free will is known to him directly through consciousness that itself is in flux and where "a lifetime of moments" creates an individual.[7] Gary Saul Morson also assigns fluidity of process to Tolstoy's conception of personality, which is not a closed system with a riddle as it is in Dostoevsky. The mind rules over Tolstoy's characters through its "officers," as Morson describes them: attention, memory, and habit. Tolstoy's character psychologically agglutinates, or "accrues," and all of his changes are scrupulously conditioned, but not by himself. Just as history composed of infinitesimals and accidentals is beyond human judgment or control, so is his own very character. Often, Tolstoy's character does not notice important changes or thought processes within himself.[8] In other words, Tolstoy's character is irresponsible in the same way as history, which contains him.

With the ascendancy of Bakhtin's authority, it has become axiomatic to accept that the Tolstoyan hero never lives at the edge of the metaphysical abyss. These inherent and imposed difficulties make it easy to overlook an essential truth about Tolstoy's conception of personality. For Tolstoy time itself may be understood as a check point of accounting, a negotiated transit from death to life, that is, his anarchic competition with time, violating the naturally accepted human relationship with it. Tolstoy, who is all about living on the border, consciously creates his *aporias*, situations without a way out. He puts his life on hold so that he can understand how to go on breathing and eating with a clear conscience even as his talents, intellect, body, position in society and within his family reach their peak. There came a point for Tolstoy when he could not help breathing, eating, and sleeping, yet his life, the way he polemically described it in *A Confession* to argue with his youthful idol Rousseau, stalled (23: 11).[9] Tolstoy's narrative is always a dialogue of "auto-psychological states" and is thus built on memory and responsible accounting.[10] While fickle "officers" of perception or voluble self-unburdening of Rousseau style confession are not liable for moral blunders, it is important to admit that Tolstoy's mature accounting voice is no longer like that. After the experience at the apex, he experiences vertigo, then looks up and around, and looks back at himself in order to notice mistakes and change for the better. Yet Tolstoy's first public conversional statement did not become a retelling of his whole life experience with the happy ending, reflecting the twin ensembles of Christian obligations, self-understanding, and manifestation of faith, the display of wounds and the verbalized story in complete obedience to the will of the Father.[11] The active spiritual experience of the Tolstoyan post-conversion subject takes place between the poles of what I call "psychological transcendence" and "transcendental psychology." Psychological transcendence is the sum total of experiences that accompany growth in awareness. Transcendental psychology is the sum total of reflexes inherent *in* the right awareness. Psychological transcendence is the forward-moving experience of a conflicted soul. Transcendental psychology is an inward gaze, the impassioned contemplation of a self-sanctified soul. What is dramatized is the time of the soul—I am here borrowing an Augustinian term—at the midpoint of self-discovery.

A CONFESSION: IMMEDIACY AND
THE TRUTH OF FIGURAL ACCOUNTABILITY

Traditionally writers should have no problem with a literary reconstruction of their inner self. Their life experiences should provide the objective structure—verifiable biographical and historical events. Their artistic imagination, or the indestructible and immortal memory given them by Augustine, should add a subjective flourish.[12] Pushkin's poem "Memory," Tolstoy's favorite, could have served him as a model for unwinding the scroll of his past. In 1878–1879, however, Tolstoy's focus was not on the past but on the discovery of faith in the present, the moment of searching, and on sustaining faith in one's daily life. In the text of *A Confession*, his past is alluded to in an abbreviated paraphrase.

The first chapter explains his loss of faith in his teens by force of habit common in his circle. The second chapter initially promises to provide a full account of his life "someday" and again dwells, in general and anonymous terms, on the sins of the literary milieu. It speaks of his wrong priorities and reasons in choosing the career of a man of letters and a public educator. The third chapter continues in the same periphrastic mode: "I lived like that for another six years, giving vent to this madness until I got married" (23: 8). It speaks of Tolstoy's romance with progress, briefly interrupted by the witnessing of the guillotine and the death of brother Nikolai. Primarily employing the past continuous tense or imperfective verbal constructions ("I was swirling around the same insolvable problem"), Tolstoy achieves a sense of detachment from the past (23: 9). He lets us know that more important things will follow. Fifteen years of marriage and domestic bliss, which served as a substitute for his fascination with progress, merit no more than three sentences: "The new conditions of a happy family life distracted me completely from any searching of the general meaning of life. . . . Fifteen more years have passed" (23: 10). Finally, toward the end of the third chapter, Tolstoy arrives at the description of the incipient crisis: "So I lived, but five years ago something strange started happening to me: at first, minutes of bewilderment, and life's cessation, as if I did not know how to live or what to do, would come over me, and I would get lost and fall into dejection" (23: 10). These questions, at first intermittent but then more and more frequent, alerted him to the fact that this was no minor ailment but a chronic disease. The chapter ends with the famous expression of *aporia* borrowed from Mill's *Autobiography*: "Well, fine, so you will be more famous . . . than all the writers in the world—so what? And I had absolutely no answer." Tolstoy's thoughts sprawl over into the next chapter, his poetry of dejection finally given a chance to spread its wings at the point when life stopped: "My life came to a standstill" (23: 11).

The remaining thirteen chapters, or more than one-fifth of the work, will recount the agony of his struggle to find faith with a frequent recourse to traditional allegorical lore, of a seeker of faith in the person of a sailor caught amid the capricious river or sea, now benevolent, now hostile. In stark despair, the seeker clings to the concept of God as if it were his life jacket; then this sailor sees vigorous waves of life rising around him (23: 46). When he doubts, the waves rise to engulf and ruin him. However, he looks at other sailors and sees "countless barks that obstinately and uninterruptedly rowed against the current." He recalls the bank and the direction, and swims to the shore: "The shore was God, the direction was the parable, the oars were my freedom to row my way to the shore in order to join God. And the force of life was revived in me, and I again started to live" (23: 47).

Because the above apotheosis is only one among the intermittent stages of faith finding, in terms of genre, this work is not such an easy case. It is "*a con-fession*," one confession, of a faith lost and the much longer story involving the battle to regain it. The excising of the description of sins precludes the use of Rousseau's shame-flaunting ego in the plural of his *Confessions*. Ulti-mately the divulging of sins in this annoying manner, especially Rousseau's arrogant bargaining for love on account of his sincerity—however dubious—constituted a superfluous mixture of the clever, maudlin, and coy that Tolstoy could not respect, given his exposure to the confessions of the Russian su-perfluous types. As a precursor, Augustine might have fared better. After all, Augustine's *Confessions*, also in the plural, do provide enough life material to draw the requisite watershed between the temporal and the infinite. The scene in the Roman garden, signaling Augustine's emotional conversion, takes place at the very end of book 8. From the beginning of book 9—when Augustine thanks the Lord for breaking his chains and asks for his permission to sing His praises—through the end of book 13 we hear no more of Augus-tine, only his prayers and hymns to the splendor of the universe and his won-derment at the divinity of poetic speech. In the simultaneously written *Cri-tique of Dogmatic Theology* there is the following significant line: "Prayer is a reminder" of helplessness and sin (23: 281). Tolstoy could not write the whole confession as a form of prayer because prayers and entreaties ad-dressed to the God-entity turned God into an object, His world into a strato-sphere of meteorological materiality, and man into a "swirling" piece of mat-ter. This poetic replication of the universe could satisfy Augustine at the end of his book, but at precisely the same time Tolstoy gave up on such a world conception. Tolstoy could not freely adapt Augustine's pattern of conver-sional process for several additional reasons. Because he was already a bishop living among his clergy and could not have written his accounts other than with a political purpose, to some degree, in response to distortions of Chris-tianity by heretical ascetics and Manicheans, his *Confessions* are only par-tially a personal testimony of conversion. Secondly, Augustine's conversion was imitative. Until he heard of the conversion of two of the emperor's sol-diers, who followed the example of Saint Anthony, it was a very noncommit-tal relationship on Augustine's part. Thirdly, Augustine's conversion is de-scribed as a supernatural event. Book 8, chapter 12 of the *Confessions* describes the moment of conversion as a push from above that Augustine needed. When he was lying prostrate under the fig tree, a child's voice in-structed him to "take and read this" by pointing Augustine to the Gospels. Au-gustine understood this as the call of Saint Paul from Rom. 13.14.

Nonetheless, the long course of Augustine's searches involving conscious and unconscious transgressions, the reading of instructional literature, and meetings with good Christians whom he tries to imitate until the final moment of epiphany offer Tolstoy several important paradigms of conversion. The main one is, of course, the paradigm of a man divided: "My inner self was a house divided against itself."[13] Here as well, nevertheless, Tolstoy differed from Augustine, who held his belief that evil is a substantive force external to man to be obstructing his final turn, a view that Tolstoy gave up in 1879. Tolstoy also forgoes the descriptive detail of Augustine's formulaic descriptions of obstacles and promptings to converting: admonitions of his mother; the sermons by Saint Ambrose; the reading of the Gospels and epistles of Saint Paul; the examples of other "newly made" Christians; or a formerly outstanding Platonist (Victorinus).

Augustine's understanding of grace implies the benevolent willingness of God to turn toward a person and becoming one with Him, "converting me to yourself." Fully aware of his weakness, he confessed to being envious of Victorinus, a successful convert, who resolved "to be *made* a Christian" and was reborn through baptism.[14] Tolstoy's analogous envy of Buturlin in 1876–1877 did not translate into the appearance of this Augustinian episode in *A Confession*. Augustine was baptized following his conversion, which was a will to accept grace. Not unlike Paul, Augustine's turn from sin toward the ministry is the act of turning the world toward the Word through the Word. A significant and decisive difference between Paul and Augustine is the address of Jesus to Paul, the idea of grace offered as salvation through Christ's sacrifice. For Augustine conversion is not necessarily an act of empathy or imitation of Christ. Paul's radical sinfulness and guilt in the encounter with Him, whom he persecuted and who is still concealed, has a closer relation to the Old Testament law.[15] In *A Confession*, Tolstoy takes this latter path in dramatizing his resistance to convert, his back and forth moves against grace. Thus, Christ's presence in *A Confession* is limited to his concealment in the Eucharist, which Tolstoy's narrator demystifies as sham as he almost bolts from the service.

Whereas Augustine used the Gospels opened in the garden as a form of revelation and poetic departure, at the end of Tolstoy's *Confession* the narrator only promises to submit the Gospels and holy books to rigid scrutiny. There is a reason why Tolstoy did not finish *A Confession* in 1879, choosing to wait another three years in order to append the enigmatic parable of the dream on the ropes, which he felt was needed to consider the matter finished. By 1882 Tolstoy had completed his commentary on the Gospels and their harmony and all but finished his *Critique of Dogmatic Theology*. His suspense at the end of *A Confession* is only a matter of speaking. He had waited to achieve his desired state of clarity in order to undertake the writing of his *Biography of a Great Sinner*. For this reason, Augustinian memory seemed to Tolstoy too benevolent and too self-reverential in its recounting of a shameful experience as a penitential prayer. However, when he confronted the task of writing his long biography in 1903–4, in collaboration with Biriukov, Tolstoy again did not advance beyond the chapters of his childhood. To illustrate his disgust with standard biographies, Tolstoy included quotations from his real personal diary (such as the entry for January 6, 1903, which mentions those "infernal torments" that always accompany such an enterprise) (34: 345–46). In this later biography, Tolstoy begins with the declaration that reminiscences, as such, are a falsehood. He then summons Pushkin's "Memory" in the preface to the planned biography and at first uses Pushkin's metaphor of memory as a litany of bitterness, self-disgust, and lamentable wrong. Although the seventy-five-year-old Tolstoy remembers Pushkin's poem correctly, he finds it necessary to transform elegiac sadness into austere shame by substituting "shameful lines" (*strok postydnykh*) for "sad lines" (*strok pechal'nykh*): "But I do not efface those shameful lines" (34: 346).[16] The moments of spiritual clarity in which shameful lines could be kept intact only because they had already been inwardly corrected did not suit Tolstoy's pugilistic mood. Thus, to be considered a confessional trilogy, his accounting was to consist of *A Confession*, representing the pre-critical stage of search; *Harmony and Translation of the Four Gospels* (1880–1881) and *Critique of Dogmatic Theology* (1879–1880; completed 1884), representing the critical phase of search; and *What I Believe?* (*V chem moia vera?*; 1882–1884), representing the positive phase.

In choosing such a complex structure, Tolstoy had a rich array of brilliant confessional patterns to choose from, both Western and native. There were Pascal's divisive *Pensées* and his *Memorial*. There was Fonvizin's *vita*, divided into four periods of life: childhood; youth; young adulthood, when faith was lost; and middle age, when faith was supposed to be regained. The moving *vita* was interrupted by Fonvizin's death and ended on a meeting with the advocate. There was a possibility of Bunyan's allegorical flight and pilgrimage, also available as a scene of a flight from home in Pushkin's rendition. There was Rousseau's atheistic "discourse-history," the narrative built on the "passé composé," the approximate French equivalent of the present perfect, which was constantly bringing the past into the present and, in concert with picaresque details, maintaining tension and providing entertainment. There was Chateaubriand's autobiographer-diarist of the *Mémoires d'outre-tombe*, who "contaminated" the record of his long life with events that could only have been known to him from a distance and yet still discovered faith.[17] Although he would employ Rousseau's stylistic experiments with tenses, Tolstoy could not accept the crude mixture of the life of the flesh and the spirit found in Rousseau, nor could he accept the mixture of politics and social life—and man's dependence on them for changing his religious orientation—

found in both Rousseau and Chateaubriand. Herzen's historical confession *My Past and Thoughts* ("not so much historical notes as a confession") provided another intriguing alternative, but it, too, was not an option.[18] Herzen worked on his tale for decades, completing it a little more than two years before his death. Toward the end, he became so absorbed in the vicissitudes of political struggle that he finished his narrative on a rebuke to Otto von Bismarck. Soon, Herzen regretted his choice of reckoning to time (7: 488). After bidding a bitter farewell to "Messieurs Conservatives," Herzen returned to the letters of his youth, trying to recover the lyrical element of his confessions (7: 488).[19]

Or there was Viazemsky, who in 1875–1878 continued to think on the effectiveness of a writer's psychological memoir. In his own experiment with the genre extracted from the treasury of his famed lifelong personal Notebooks, veritable annals of his epoch (Staraia zapisnaia knizhka), the Memoir Viazemsky started in his last decade, he stuck to the more traditional structure of a European intellectual biography. He subscribed to the motto that "a public confession is subject to public judgment," finding no difference between deeds large or small (*malykh ili bol'shikh del ne byvaet*). Public character belongs to the public but the writer's tact in composing his account before death (*otchet*) determines how his property, his testament will be "touched," handled and to what effects it is used. Viazemsky also stressed that repentance is a misplaced notion in an autobiography. Sincerity is not the point: it is presumed as a *starting point*. Repentance happens not once, at the end of life, or at select points in the time of one life, but *many times* throughout life. The last written account, therefore, bears special weight and bears much on the writer's ability and sensibility to the word.[20] Viazemsky's *Autobiography* came out in 1878, the year he died, when Tolstoy started his work on *A Confession*.

How many narratives were needed and whom he was supposed to address occupied Tolstoy as well. Publishing a collection of letters—and he had something to offer—was another venerable and controversial home-grown tradition, from the posthumous letters of Stankevich to his friends and Chaadaev's philosophical letters to Gogol's *Selected Passages from Correspondence with Friends*. Tolstoy knew from experience that a publication of a collection of confessional addresses on religion to friends by a living Russian author would invariably cause a scandal and a call for subsequent confessions, with apologies, to the reader and the nation (Gogol) or high-society trickery, with condescending pretense, to wriggle out of the nasty predicament (Chaadaev).[21] This was unacceptable to Tolstoy, who favored an open emotional debate with the nation, as well as an open battle with the church. Similarly inappropriate was Rousseau's choice. After his irreligious *Confessions*, in the final two or three years of his life Rousseau added two more sets of pessimistic autobiographical narratives in dialogue form, in which the writer Rousseau judges Jean-Jacques the man and pities himself in ten walks/meditations of the *Reveries of a Solitary Walker*. In the *Confessions* Rousseau declared: "The real object of my Confessions is to contribute to an accurate knowledge of my inner being in all the different situations of my life. What I have promised to relate is the history of my soul; I need no other memoirs in order to write it faithfully."[22] But this memorable statement turned out to be untenable. Rousseau's unprecedented decision to send out as many copies of his afterthoughts to the *Confessions* "to all Frenchmen who still love justice and truth" met with indifference and coldness. Rousseau's decision to retreat from the world and detach himself from human affairs at the end of the dialogues filled him with a new hope that with the approaching death all desires would soon be extinguished, yet he could not do without writing.[23] In the *Solitary Walker* Rousseau's autobiographical character still takes stock, mentally apologizing for his past wrongs and counting on some unexpected charity for his upkeep in old age, but he addresses the nation no more.

Personal religious history could, of course, also be represented in a fictionalized form, as in Musset's *Confession of a Child of the Century* or Lermontov's *Hero of Our Time*. However, both of these were youthful works. Musset made it clear that his fictional choices were dictated by his youth: "Before the history of any life can be written, that life must be lived; so that it is not my life that I am now writing" (Musset, 1). The typicality of the loss of faith and the instructional element of a life lived and ended in disaster was once again a theme, influenced by Schopenhauer and Hartmann, that reverberated in the works of Russia's younger writers, such as Garshin and Nadson. The point of writing an account, which portrayed the loss of faith in his youth and its painful recovery in middle age, was that he could not resort to the old, discredited genre—which Tolstoy condemns, along with other literary ruses—involving the "playing with the mirror" of life in the second and third chapters of *A Confession*. The same should have applied to the other extreme, Turgenev's "Enough" or *Senilia*.

There is also the question of structure. In the two autobiographies most influential in Tolstoy's time, Mill's *Autobiography* (1873) and Newman's *Apologia Pro Vita Sua* (1864), the issue is resolved by combining the chronology of a life with the period of spiritual development. Mill streamlines his life story in the following manner. Moral influences of his father follow the period of his childhood. The stage of youthful propaganda follows the first stages of self-education. The period of crisis ensues. After his father's death, Mill's writings on social issues and his professional relationships around 1840 alter little in his life afterwards. The long period from 1840 inaugurates the general view of the remainder of Mill's life when he enjoyed the success-ful career of a liberal thinker. The crisis chapter does not divide Mill's life equally. Although Mill was young at the time of the crisis, the chapter is placed closer to the end of his life story. Newman's book consists of a pref-ace and five chapters charting history of his religious opinions in the periods from birth to the year 1833, 1833 to 1839, 1839 to 1841, 1841 to 1845. The final chapter, "Position of My Mind since 1845," describes the remainder of Newman's life after the conversion to Catholicism. Despite Newman's early focus on the development of religious opinion—and its even, incremental growth covering comparable periods between three to four years before the year 1845—it is evident that Newman's life resembles Mill's in that the apex of their spiritual development is followed by a tranquil and enjoyable period interrupted only by their deaths.

The convert's *vita* rewrites Schopenhauer's grim scheme of a decline after the apex, changing the allegory of ascent-descent and the hovering in limbo over the abyss. The vertigo leads to reorientation and faith. While drafting his life chronology for Biriukov's biography, Tolstoy similarly rewrote the Schopenhauer parable to which he had subscribed at the beginning of his cri-sis. The scheme of ascent-descent-ascent is found in a letter to Strakhov dated November 1875, representing his first blueprint for *A Confession*. In 1903 Tolstoy explained the chronology of his spiritual life, dividing it into four pe-riods: (1) 1828–1842: religious childhood; (2) 1842–1862: a period of brusque debauchery, vanity, and lust; (3) 1862–1880: a period reflecting "the morality of this world," from his marriage to his spiritual birth; (4) 1880 and after: a period "in which I now live and in which I hope to die, and from the point of which I see the whole meaning of my past life, which I would not want to change in any way, except for changing the evil habits acquired in my past periods" (34: 347). Disregarding the fact that Tolstoy failed to write the long version of his life, one needs to appreciate his acceptance of this struc-ture, initiated by Augustine—struggle for faith, acquisition of faith, tranquil life in faith—as the best and finest. One should also note that *A Confession* refuses to adhere to this structure.

Another significant question involves timing. Tolstoy was reluctant to wait a long time and started *A Confession* three years after the first signs of his crisis, paralleling the writing with his search and stopping the fictional search a few steps before the discovery of *razumenie*, which had happened in real time in 1879. In this sense Tolstoy's conversional account is one of the most authentic. By comparison, Augustine relates the experience of conversion in the Roman garden in A.D. 386–88 fourteen years later, *ex officio* of a Bishop of Hippo. Luther related his 1518 illumination in the Tower as late as 1545, a year before his death, offering a traditional description of a miraculous transformation by the grace of the Word.[24] Newman wrote about his 1845 conversion in 1864. Mill and Fonvizin both wrote at the "end of life," aged forty-seven, both same age, but while Mill described the life already accomplished and his crisis distant, Fonvizin did not have a chance to put a final stop to his autobiography. Tolstoy began at age forty-five or forty-seven, carefully timing his crisis in the letter to Strakhov and the third chapter of *A Confession.*

By examining the nature of the underlining in his copy of the French edition of Augustine's *Confessions,* most of which occur in books 10, 11, and 12, one may deduce that in constructing his tale Tolstoy evinced the most interest in the question of spiritual time and its passage, and timing things in the process of search.[25] In perhaps the most famous book of his *Confessions* (book 11) Augustine says that there is a present to the past in the form of memory, and a present to the future in the form of anticipation or apprehension. The form most appropriate for reliving an experience of remembrance for the moment of "now" is a recital of a psalm. This is Augustine's solution to the problem of temporality, which determines inner chronology and spiritual periods in the book, and which lasts for as long as twelve years. He describes a period of a prolonged delusion in nine books, and eternity in the space of four books. Need be, he could write one psalm only to address God in thanks after the conversion has taken place. Tolstoy's terms of periodization—"five years," "six more years," "and so I lived for another fifteen years"—fits this scheme. Eternity waits to be discovered in one of his moments of anguish, in the "now" of his searches.

Again following Augustine, Tolstoy adamantly refuses to merge the rhetoric of temporality and eternity. When the mixture seems proximate, an extended arrest of life follows, as if Tolstoy's spiritual organism were highly allergic to the mixture. One such example is Tolstoy's depiction of a forced return to life and reentry into his finite body after his lengthy dialogues with God, a return that causes a fit of characteristic disgust: "The life of the body is evil and a lie" (23: 22). In a symptomatic veiled quotation, Tolstoy refuses to accept Schopenhauer's response to the question concerning what we become following death. In Schopenhauer's dialogue between Thrasymachos and Philalethes, the following conclusion is reached:

Thrasymachos: To be brief, what am I after my death? Now, be clear and precise!

Philalethes: Everything and nothing.

T: There we have it! A contradiction as the solution to the problem. The trick is played out.

P: To answer transcendent questions in the language created for immanent knowledge can certainly lead to contradictions.[26]

Tolstoy does not accept Schopenhauer's compromise (all *and* nothing), opting instead for a response with one alternative (all *or* nothing) (23: 20). *A Confession* can thus be classified as a suspended type of temporality, a "frozen time" in which memory flashes back to represent moments of connection to the eternal in its *distended crisis*. Parables told—of Socrates, Solomon, Buddha, the traveler fallen into the well of death—are all identified with the narrator, and are important only for this reason; these and the dream at the end all contribute to the apotheosis of crisis in the absolute categories that seek personal finalization in the eternal. The twelfth chapter describes the resolution of a prolonged crisis experienced by Tolstoy's narrator. He restores the metaphorical sequence of losing life (dying) and then coming back to life (reanimation), connecting the stages to his varying stances toward God. Once he remembers that he lives only in those moments when he believes, the crisis ends with an ecstatic shriek: "So what else am I looking for? A voice was shrieking within me.—Here he is. He is that without which life is impossible. To know God and to live is the same. God is life. . . . And I was saved from suicide" (23: 45–46).

A Confession closes with the hope of finding faith and is therefore offered up as an introduction to the yet-to-be-written definitive version of *the found* truth. The suspense that we witness at the conclusion of *A Confession* illustrates how Tolstoy seeks a form in which he can accommodate his staple terms of reference in the rhetoric of accountability: the demands of a truth that transcends life and the demands of a life that takes stock of itself as it "moves on." Like Tolstoy's fragments and dialogues on religion, which were written in the 1870s, it offers patterns of belief and agnosticism. Unlike the dialogues, however, it exposes the experience of the search: the author tells us where and why he stumbles and what he plans to do to overcome the next "bewilderment." *A Confession* manages to captivate the reader without recourse to the imperative voice ordering him or her to follow him, the tactic abused by the young Tolstoy. In the calendar of its stasis, followed by escalating tensions and the new cataclysmic disruptions, cyclical time or seasonal changes and expectations of what might happen in the fullness of opportune time add nothing to the understanding of this seeker's spiritual discoveries. Tolstoy has successfully transplanted the reader onto the psychological-spiritual plane and the trip never loses a sense of suspense.[27]

How spiritual moments are determined by Tolstoy in this first narrative exercise following conversion remains to be determined in view of his insistence on the necessity to change yet also his rejection of *kairos* and *kronos*. Here one might cite Frank Kermode's provocative distinction between *kairos* ("narrative seasons") and *kronos* (time as such). Because books are "fictive models of the temporal world," says Kermode, we deserve the "regressive pleasure" of self-recognition in real temporal forms that we find in the *kairoi* models.[28] All illuminations and revivals of life that Tolstoy's character experiences in *A Confession* are his only forms of pleasure as such, and these are exclusively forms of spiritual pleasure. Similarly, all disgust is also caused by purely spiritual instincts. A significant difference between Tolstoy and *kairoi* poets, the players with the mirror of opportune timings, is that his account remains strangely unadorned and spare, considering his heavy use of allegorical descriptions. He rejects *kairoi* models as deceptive symbols of spiritual transformation and *kronos* models as a tempting way to substitute the historical contingency for personal responsibility.

How does one resonate with one's new being (the tick of spiritual birth) to a temporal event (the tock of physical death)? One can juxtapose, as did Augustine, "time of the soul" with Aristotle's *kronos*. As Paul Ricoeur suggests with reference to Augustine's *Confessions*, "eternal time" is immobile, it is "forever still" (*semper stans*) in contrast to things that are never still. In eternity nothing moves into the past: all is present (*totum esse prasens*). Time, conversely, is never all present at once.[29] There is a disjunction that is more sufficient, however. In Augustine's analysis it is not clear, how "time of the soul," the real time of confessional narrative, can become part of eternal time. It is distinguished from chronological time in that it is the internal perception of reality, the "now" of memory, which Tolstoy so prized at the end of the 1870s. Augustine shows that memory distends as a long expectation of the future, over the course of being, and is traversed by a "long remembrance of the past" until the past increases and is able to absorb the whole of the future, and the "whole becomes past," and the life is over.[30] This picture of life absorbed into the history of the world, subsumed in God-made time, was acceptable to the author of *War and Peace* but was rejected by the author of *Anna Karenina*. Augustine keeps himself separate from the "maker of All Time."[31] Herein lies the difference: Tolstoy is in no hurry to leave the distending crises because he is sure that as long as he looks, his life will not explode like a fictive bubble of *kairoi* and the soap bubbles of his old playful art, but will enable him to discover the meaning of life. Tolstoy is sure that the story of seeking faith, which is every believer's personal passion, is perhaps even more exciting than the tidy story of faith found.

In the first three chapters of *A Confession* Tolstoy explains the reasons for the loss of faith (*otpadenie ot very*) by the divorce of "the doctrine of faith" (*verouchenie*) from life (23: 2). Tolstoy deploys several techniques that make the narrative of losing faith and simulating faith in the interest of the government office so powerful. The impression that everything was happening naturally and inevitably is conveyed by simple tenses reflecting the fait accompli: "A person of our circle who does not study and is not employed in government service . . . could have spent dozens of years without remembering a single time that he lives among Christians and is himself considered a Christian professing Orthodoxy" (23: 2). The combination of scant personal information—like the stories of his brothers Dmitry and Nikolai—with social events—such as the guillotine episode or vain disputes in the writers' circles—coupled with broad generalizations create the impression that what was happening from the 1830s (the time of Tolstoy's childhood) to the 1880s was personal yet also quite common.

Already in these early sections one recognizes familiar themes that are often literally repeated from Tolstoy's writings and diaries of his youth and maturity, or taken from his correspondence and literary works. For example, the satire in the second chapter on writers as instruments of progress who brag of their "artistic rank" (*chin khudozhnika*) (23: 6) reproduces the jousting tones and expressions from the denunciation of progress and self-parody of his authorial conceit in the opening chapter of *The Decembrists* (17: 7–9). The acrimonious and self-pitying pattern of the artist's choice to abandon his play with the mirror and fall silent, as, for example, was practiced in Turgenev's "Enough," parodies its lachrymose tone. The mockery of fame at the end of the third chapter is used by Tolstoy to respond polemically to Strakhov's, Fet's, and Turgenev's goading that he keep on writing, as well as to rhetoric at Nekrasov's funeral and the Dostoevsky speech affair (23: 11). In this sense, Tolstoy's testimony is documentary and does comprise "selected passages" from his correspondence with friends and diary entries—a Gogolian work, with the important difference that he is describing the loss of Christian life rather than its hypothetical and artificial importation couched in the form of dank sermons mistakenly chosen by Gogol. Combining these two basic strands with artistic, biblical, and philosophical allegory, Tolstoy creates a complex testimony that is personal and impersonal, true and allegorical, documentary and—despite its polemical antireligious tenor—hagiographic.

Such is his pervasive deployment of forms of address and stylistic turns borrowed from Ecclesiastes in conveying the futility of achievement. Neither what "I have acquired" nor the new distractions (from pleasure to wisdom) could save him, "the Teacher and King of Literature," from the terrible truth, that everything under the sun is vanity. Whether wisdom, or madness or folly "the same fate befalls all of them."[32] Such is his allegorical summary of the four mutually exclusive choices available to an atheist: ignorance of the fact that life is evil; Epicureanism; suicide; and suicide not committed. In these last ranks of the weak, in the company of Schopenhauer and Solomon, Tolstoy places himself (23: 29). Even where Tolstoy does not paraphrase Ecclesiastes—and he does so often—he still adopts its tone. Consider the following: "And it seemed to me that I learned abroad to do it [teach], and, armed by all this utter wisdom,

I returned to Russia in the year of peasant liberation, and having taken the post of the intermediary, started to teach the uneducated folk in schools and educated folk in the journal that I began publishing. Business went well, it seemed, but I felt that I am not quite sane in my mind and that it can't go on for long. . . . Or I thought about that glory, which my works will earn me, and I told myself: 'All right, so you will be more glorious than Gogol, Pushkin, Shakespeare, Molière, and all the writers in the world, so what!' And I had no answer."[33] The insane and self-deceiving world of bigotry—in which "all that exists is reasonable" and where "there was no difference with the asylum"—presented to us by Tolstoy leads the reader directly to such underhandedly satiric works as Chaadaev's "Apology of a Madman" and Herzen's "Doctor Krupov," "Aphorismata," and chapters from *My Past and Thoughts* (23: 7).

In its every shape and shade, allegorical or satiric, the account presented by Tolstoy carefully reproduces stages and episodes of his lifelong search for the meaning of life—without skipping one link. The same strange and blind "force" that was pushing him away from life as it had been pushing him toward life (23: 12), made him imagine that up there somewhere there is "someone who is poking fun while looking down at me" and his need to discover the identity of the authority in charge—"I stay there, a fool of fools at the top, understanding clearly that there is nothing to life, never has been, and never will be. And He feels like laughing" (23: 13). The narrator's search for meaning becomes a search for faith at this stage of renunciation of knowledge and God. The search will continue—as it did in Tolstoy's real life—in lonely conversations with God, "when reason was working, but something else was working too" (23: 31). The accuracy of Tolstoy's description of his struggle for faith may be expressed in his handling of metaphors of search. In the sixth chapter, for example, he returns to his mainstay metaphor of frustration, the bubble-particle, and his mainstay metaphor of hope, the globe, first introduced in *War and Peace*. His companion is not a fellow immortal, like Virgil, but cynical knowledge of doubt, which responds with "because" to the question why life exists. "What is the meaning of my life?" Tolstoy's narrator demands. "You are what you call your life—you are that temporal, accidental concatenation of particles. . . . the interaction of these particles will cease and all that you call life will cease, and your questions will cease. You are an accidentally agglutinatcd ball of something. The ball rots. . . . The ball will break apart and the rotting and all the questions will stop" (23: 22). It is then that one also begins noticing Tolstoy's poetic hyperbole. Tolstoy does have companions. The "honest voices" above provide in a chorus a retelling of the ideas of Schopenhauer, Solomon, and Buddha (23: 22). The voice that ultimately overbears and assists him in his hope is the voice of Socrates' statement concerning the philosopher's duty toward death.[34] Tolstoy practiced the technique of voice-over for the sake of wishful faith earlier. Back in 1874, in his real diary, Tolstoy wrote: "Having lived almost to the age of fifty, I became convinced that earthly life gives you nothing, and that the clever man who looks at it intently, seriously— will go shoot himself immediately. . . . But Schopenhauer let it be known that something prevented him from shooting himself. This something is the goal of my book. What do we live by? Religion."[35] Schopenhauer's answer could not be religion; this is clearly Tolstoy's voice-over answer.

In the allegorical partner-seeking re-creation of his suicide fantasy in *A Confession*, Tolstoy abandons the company of Socrates and Buddha, who do not teach pessimism as a life attitude, aligning himself with the pessimists, Solomon and Schopenhauer (23: 37). Soon enough even the believer Solomon makes an inconvenient partner, and Tolstoy purposefully leaves himself in the frightening and life-negating company of Schopenhauer. In the seventh chapter, however, he asks himself: "Could it be that only Schopenhauer and I have been intelligent enough to understand the senselessness and evil of life?" (23: 30). In keeping with the veritable tradition of confessional narrative this last partner is also dropped and the allegorical Tolstoy confronts his doubts and his hopes alone. Reminding of Tolstoy's fragments in which his inner voices of reasonable knowledge and reasonable faith communicate in a recalcitrant interview, *A Confession* re-creates this mind-boggling equation (*uravnenie*) of "zero-identity" (*a zero tozhestvo*) wherein one element negates the other and a whole person of "mine, Schopenhauer's and Solomon's wisdom" neither progresses nor changes: $a = a$, $x = x$, $0 = 0$ (23: 34, 37).

The distraught consciousness of "zero identity" looking for self-reintegration is portrayed in a frantic, desperate repetition of first-person pronouns. In the tenth chapter the accumulation of "I" (*ia*), in its struggle for self-identification, will help the identity to be restored. This is visible through an elaborate distribution of pronouns separating "I" from Solomon's and Schopenhauer's collective "us" in an attempt to reunite with the rest of humanity, who live as "they": "I could see this, but it did not make things easier for me. I was now prepared to accept any faith as long as it did not demand a direct denial of reason, which would have been a deceit" (23: 37). By watching the peasants, Tolstoy realizes that the zero equation would be restored to a customary $2 \times 2 = 4$ once he identifies with evangelical truth taken on faith by the multitude, that "life is not evil and meaningless." "I came to love good people and to loathe myself, and I acknowledged the truth. And then it all became clear to me" (23: 41).[36] The choice of an easy $2 \times 2 = 4$ identity becomes the choice of an escape from oneself (23: 43, 45). Although his relation (*otnoshenie*) to truth is a tremendous discovery, Tolstoy reveals that he again knocked on the wrong door while attempting to find his God. After the discovery of the Gospels in the Roman Garden, Augustine asks God to accept his confessions and not to disparage them, and thanks God for breaking his spiritual chains (Augustine 175, 192, 202–3). Tolstoy defamiliarizes the discovery and postpones its realization at the cost of exposing himself as a satanic guest who runs from the entrance to the Gates of Heaven leading to the altar where he was attempting to receive the holy gift of the Eucharist from the priest, too impatient with Orthodox "gibberish" (*tarabarshchina*) (23: 48). In the fourteenth chapter we read about his near flight from the Eucharist: "when I approached the Royal Doors and the priest asked me to repeat what I believe, and that what I was about to receive was actually the body and blood, my heart contracted; it was a cruel demand made by someone who evidently had never known what faith is. I could not do it a second time" (23: 51).[37]

In his letters and diaries, Tolstoy sarcastically remarked that mundane matters occupy peasants more during the Communion than the transubstantiation of bread and wine. He proved this to be true for his circle in every work of fiction where this religious rite is described with understated irony. The culmination of his mockery of the Eucharist occurs in his late novel *Resurrection (Voskresenie)*, resulting in his excommunication from the church in 1901. However, in 1878–1882 only one comparable episode of a near-scandalous departure from Orthodoxy could have served as a prototype. This was Turgenev's 1877 tale entitled "The Story of Father Alexis" (*Rasskaz ottsa Alekseia*). It concerns Iakov, the only son of a priest, a seminary graduate and former university student, who is tortured by doubts "from the devil" during his Communion. Following confession Iakov pauses before imbibing the wine, crushes the wafer, drops the chalice, and suddenly rushes out of the church. Falling ill and on the verge of death, Iakov confesses to his father the reason for his behavior, namely the appearance of the devil behind the priest's back during the priest's solicitation of the oath: "because every crime may be forgiven except that against the Holy Ghost." Iakov died, unconscious and without repentance, "passing on like a senseless worm from this life unto life eternal." Following his death, Iakov's face regained its former earthly beauty and he appeared younger; his hair started curling again and his lips were smiling.[38] Turgenev's narrator failed to find a consoling word for Father Alexis. They soon parted. Tolstoy's flight from the Eucharist must have been inspired by Iakov's courage and postmortem transfiguration.

Tolstoy's last and perhaps most vivid example of a creative dialogue with other voices of *A Confession* is his reinterpretation at the very end of his work of Schopenhauer's pun about the life of the puppet on the ropes, losing its footing.[39] Tolstoy's unrelenting seeker wakes up from this pun as if from a nightmare, reminding us that as long as he maintains the hope of finding faith and persists in his effort, he will have his support. This consolation resonated with Kierkegaard's ironic escapade of a faithful rope jumper and acrobat performing somersaults of existential sublime, whose philosophy was gradually gaining headway in European literary markets.[40] In tandem with a confessed rejection of the Eucharist and the holy gifts, the dream with the ropes and the earlier retelling of a parable from *Prolog*, the Slavic book of lives, prominently posited the possibility of holy madness in the world of the self-deceived.[41] The *Prolog* allegory of human life is another tale of spiritual suspense. The traveler runs from the frenzied unicorn and jumps in the well, suddenly realizing that the open maw of a dragon awaits below. The only choice is to hang onto the branches of a wild bush that grows in the well. They drip honey, but one can see that a black and white mouse, representing night and day, nibbles at the branches and makes them ever weaker. The parable stops at this point, providing sufficient information to decipher the allegorical meanings of the finality of life. Although Tolstoy does not rewrite these explanations, he commits one of his fearful substitutions, suddenly inserting himself in the well in place of the impersonal everyman of the allegory: "And so I am holding onto the branches of life. . . . And I am trying to lick this honey, which used to console me before, and which doesn't anymore. . . . And this is not some tale but a real, indubitable truth, applicable to all" (23: 14). Tolstoy's hopeful rendition of the parable in the well represents a powerful and open polemic with Saltykov-Shchedrin's shocking treatment of moral reckoning in *The Golovlyov Family* that appeared in 1878. In the chapter aptly titled "The Reckoning" Saltykov has his hypocrite Iudushka Golovlyov, who is very fond of reading books like *Prolog* and *Lives of the Saints*, sink in the stone well of his moral agonies where he perishes without a hope of being forgiven and is not given a chance to come back to life:

Such awakenings of a neglected conscience are extremely painful. When a man's moral sense has not been trained it does not reconcile him to himself, does not reveal to him the possibility of a new life; his conscience merely tortures him endlessly and vainly, giving him no hope of seeing the light in the future. A man feels as though he *were in a stone well* [*chelovek vidit sebia v kamennom meshke*] pitilessly sacrificed to suffer the agonies [*bezzhalostno otdannym v zhertvu agonii*] without any chance of ever returning to life. And the only means of stifling the pain that wears *him away to no purpose* [*besplodnuiu raz'edaiushchuiu bol'*] is to take advantage of a moment of gloomy resolve and break his head against the walls of stone.[42]

The prediction of Sophia Andreevna Tolstaya in a letter to her sister that there will hardly be ten people in Russia who might be interested in *A Confession* was wrong (23: 517). Tolstoy has more than achieved his goal of inciting "revulsion" (*otvrashchenie*) in his life, an intention he had shared with Strakhov in November 1879 (62: 500), while also demonstrating his hopefulness of recovery. He drew the attention of the whole nation to the precedent he set for wrestling with the oppressive state and its ideology for freedom of conscience. One of the very first listeners to a few private readings of sections from Tolstoy's work that he gave in Moscow in April 1882, caught the interest of Sergey Iuriev, Tolstoy's good acquaintance, Chairman of the Society of Lovers of Russian Literature, and publisher of the intellectual periodical *Russian Thought* (*Russkaia mysl'*). Iuriev decided to publish *A Confession*, still without its final title and its sequels, Tolstoy's work-in-progress, *Critique of Dogmatic Theology*, and *What I Believe?*, in his journal. The third redaction of proofs for Tolstoy's introductory piece was approved by him. Iuriev prepared final proofs with a three-page editorial introduction, stressing the importance of Tolstoy's work in "our days of despondency, searchings of indefinite nature, and disillusionment leading to suicide" (23: 520). Iuriev touted Tolstoy as a teacher of faith (*uchitel' very*). Unable to decide what to do with the proofs, the Metropolitan Makarius, author of the monumental five-volume *On Dogmatic Theology*, who had spoken with Tolstoy in 1879, kept the proofs for quite a long time. Tolstoy was finally advised that the essay could be published on one condition. Without changing a word, he was to append to the enigmatic conclusion—with the dream on the ropes and a promise to critique Orthodox scripture—his explanatory statement that the opinions expressed in the essay represented his old and erroneous view and that in the year that elapsed since he wrote the essay he had reunited with the Church.

Tolstoy refused to recant (23: 521). Galleys with the essay were disassembled and all but several copies of the pilot offprint burned. In 1884, an independent Geneva-based publisher, Mikhail Elpidin, published Tolstoy's work in Switzerland. The so-far-anonymous work, called "a confession" in the family vernacular and Tolstoy's circle, was finally legitimized as *A Confession. Introduction to an Unpublished Work*. There is no doubt that Tolstoy supervised the new redaction and approved of it. He never disputed the title, as was his wont in case of the slightest displeasure with editorial decisions. Before the Elpidin publication, the surviving copies of *The Russian Thought* were immediately lithographed, copied in longhand, and debated nationwide in private conversations and correspondence. For the first time in his life, Tolstoy's non-fiction was read and in demand and inspired both love and hatred. Liberal writer Pyotr Boborykin sought a meeting with Tolstoy because the reading of one of the proofs gave him a glimpse into Tolstoy's inner life. "At the crossroads," Tolstoy's inner life irresistibly claimed Boborykin's attention.[43]

In September 1882, Tolstoy exchanged letters with the dying Turgenev, who still upheld his earlier point that the genre of confession is not literary work. However, he asked Tolstoy to send him a copy, promising to read the piece the way Tolstoy told him it should be read: without having to agree, with an attempt to understand, and to believe that it was written sincerely.[44]

The young critic Mikhail Gromeka managed to include lengthy quotations from *A Confession* in his review of *Anna Karenina*, which he imagined was the novel's direct sequel on faith. Gromeka's book-long essay, "The Last Works of L.N. Tolstoy" was bravely published by *The Russian Thought* at the end of 1884. Subsequent correspondence with Gromeka and other young critics opened a new page in Tolstoy's advocacy of religious conscience. In these conditions, Tolstoy honed the final two parts of his conversional accounting, *Critique of Dogmatic Theology* and *What I Believe?*

CRITIQUE OF DOGMATIC THEOLOGY

On September 27, 1879, on Strakhov's referral, Tolstoy went to speak with Metropolitan Makarius of Moscow. In the next couple of days, Tolstoy went to see other eminent prelates at the Monastery of the Trinity and St. Sergius in Moscow. There are no indications of an open confrontation between Tolstoy and any of these top hierarchs of the Russian Church. Reportedly, the elder archimandrite with whom Tolstoy spent a lengthy time together in a discussion behind the closed doors said after Tolstoy's departure, "He is infected with the pride, whose likeness I have rarely seen. Am afraid he will not end well."[45]

In a letter to Strakhov in October 1879, Tolstoy sounded positive when he wrote, "On your advice and after my conversation with Khomiakov-the son about the Church, I was in Moscow at the Trinity and spoke with Vicar Alexis (Lavrov-Platonov), Metropolitan Makarius, and Leonid Kavelin. All three are wonderful people, and smart too, but I am more confirmed in my conviction. I am anxious and restless and my spirit is embattled, and I suffer; but I thank God for this condition" (62: 499).

In the introductory comments of his *Critique*, which he began shortly after the visit, Tolstoy built a bridge between *A Confession* and *The Critique*. He explained that critiquing Orthodoxy was never on his mind: "I was firmly convinced that there is sole truth in this teaching, but many and more manifestations of this teaching, contrary to those conceptions, which I had on God and his law, forced me to the study of the doctrine itself. I did not suppose at the time that the doctrine could be false; I was afraid to suppose it, because one lie in this teaching could destroy it all. And then I would lose that main foothold. . . . And I began to study the books" (23: 60). Tolstoy immediately found textual contradictions and lapses of logic in all of his target texts, primarily *Confessions* of faith by Peter of Moghila, Kievan Metropolitan of the seventeenth century, and Makarius' Dogmatic Theology, which incorporated the teaching of John Damascene and his main text, *The Fount of Knowledge*. Tolstoy also considered catechisms by Platon Levshin and Filaret of Moscow and the third edition of *Orthodox Dogmatic Theology* in two parts by Filaret, Archbishop of Chernigov, which was published in 1882.

Because Tolstoy had just completed his own *Harmony and Translation of the Four Gospels*, the "indubitable disagreement" in John Damascene and Makarius and their comments, which intended to clarify the postulates of the doctrine, struck Tolstoy with its forced, "artificial" harmony (23: 60, 62). He accused the writers of clouding the crystal-clear teaching in order to enslave the reader into discipleship and impose themselves and the Church as shepherds and interpreters of something that did not need any mediation. For example, the doctrine claimed that divine truths were revealed to humanity. If they were revealed, Tolstoy asked, how could it be that these truths of the Old Testament waited for centuries to be rewritten into dogmas and then disputed at several councils in the early centuries of Christianity? "I am a man. God had me in mind too. But don't forget: all that you are saying you are addressing to reason. It could not be that God could have responded to people in this manner, those people whom he has created, to whom he gave reason so that they could understand Him. . . . A decent human being when he speaks with another would not use foreign incomprehensible words. How could God speak with me and use the vocabulary so as I would not be able to comprehend him?" (23: 65–67, 76). Tolstoy explains that his trust in reason and his own consciousness and their divine causes saved him from lapsing into complete atheism. Firstly, in his own way, Tolstoy discovered the inevitability of acknowledging the necessity of faith. Secondly, he saw that faith serves as the foundation of life for all people. Thirdly, the embattled need of faith was reinforced in him despite all of his doubts. Fourthly, credulity was not for him the only foundation of his faith. Finally, not all of the faith he had in God was inspired from the books on theology (23: 60).

Throughout his *Critique*, Tolstoy maintains one main argument against the doctrine of the Church. Namely, he insists on man's direct line with God through fulfilling the revealed commandments. In his view, the church maintains the opposite perspective, reserving for itself, the church, the role of a deciphering link that explains revelation and the right to administer mysteries and sacraments (23: 73). Tolstoy spends a long time disputing this point and starts with the doctrine of the Trinity. To him, preverbal human reason is primarily a mathematical concept. The first truth that God revealed to man could only be that He is He ("I Am Who I Am"), that he is One and indivisible. In considering the sums of the Trinity, I am=3, 3=1 and 1=3, Tolstoy recoils in disbelief from the consideration that God could have possibly revealed himself in such enigmatic formulas; speaking with men, he would have spoken in human terms in explaining Himself as "the beginning of all beginnings, the cause of all causes. God is God. God is One" (23: 76). God cannot be a Person (23: 104). Spirit can't have personal qualities (23: 124). Spiritual truths cannot be communicated in nonspiritual, essential qualities. God (the law and the way) can mean only what is opposite to essence of human life experienced in consciousness.

On this ground, Tolstoy collides again with the doctrine of vengeance and punishment and offers a new humanizing revision of his former views on the essence, or human freedom. Lest he be confused with a Protestant, opting for justification and election or election and predestination, he explains his resolute disagreement with various explanations of entitlement to grace by Luther and Calvin (23: 232–36). What is the real relationship between justice and grace, and how do they mutually define each other? In all Christian doctrines, Orthodox, Catholic, and Protestant alike, Tolstoy found that justice and grace work separately and are mutually exclusive of each other. If God is eternity and spirit, how could he wreak vengeance and impose eternal punishment for temporary sin? "If God should be believed to be kind and just, he would not resort to correction by punishing mankind eternally" (23: 97). The whole doctrine of The Fall appears to Tolstoy that "putrid bog" and pretext for baptism and sacraments in which the Church had been drowning the credulous. Tolstoy uses Luther's term "cooperation" to illustrate that he could have drowned in this baptismal font of falsehoods too if he had not used the best and surest source of salvation with which God graced men—reason and freedom of choice, his only "good offices" (*sodeistvie*) (23: 121, 136).

It is not in The Fall that Tolstoy identifies man's sinfulness and his troubles, "illness and death for the body for all humanity and expulsion from Paradise" (23: 138). The picture of the world in which there could be a happy God and an unhappy man looks too improbable to him. The Church postulates that God's good offices to the post-lapsarian humanity consisted in sending his son for sacrifice and expiation of human sin. Tolstoy sees a big problem with this redemption theory. To begin with, why humanity is still sinful after the Redemption and why do righteous men continue to suffer, he asks. Secondly, what are his role and the role of other men in the world? (23: 154). If a person accepts the doctrinal view of the Catholics and the Protestants, the righteous suffer in this world because they will receive their award in the afterlife, but the sinners, depending on how culpable they are, will suffer in their afterlife. The traditional Orthodox view mollifies this structured system of credit and debit by insisting that all will be forgiven during the

Second Coming and the Last Judgment of the world. These views do not answer satisfactorily Tolstoy's question about suffering and unhappiness, and they ignore his main question to Providence: "And I have my own business (on earth). I will especially appreciate the important treasuries of my business being explained" (23: 159).

To answer the two questions, Tolstoy returns to Jesus' conversation of "man among men" with Nicodemus. All questions will fall away if one believes what Jesus says: "The Kingdom of God has come, and it is in you." Man's salvation is not in the expectation of rewards or punishments in the afterlife but in giving unto God what is God's in this life. In Tolstoy's whole career, this reinterpretation is so far the strongest defense of conscience and human agency. If sons are free, they should stop believing in redemption and administration of Church rites, in Jesus the Pantocrator who sanctified the hierarchy to be his proxies on earth by making an injunction to the flock to be obedient. The modern concept that a person can truly be sanctified by faith on assumption that he is baptized, goes to Church, and takes all other sacraments is madness, Tolstoy cries out. In Tolstoy's most inspired revision of the sacraments so far, he defines baptism as *metanoia*, a will to change and enter the Kingdom. The Eucharist is the practice of forgiveness of the enemy and love. Repentance should only be done in private with someone who might have been wronged, and with God being a disinterested witness who neither accepts a bribe nor offers a reward except the condition of clear conscience (23: 251–61, 273).

Tolstoy's conception of faith is now complete. He has nothing to share with the Orthodoxy, a collection of "shorn people, very confident, deluded and poorly educated, in silk and velvet" who keep millions under the heel so that, under the pretext of the administration of the sacraments, they can rob people of their freedom (23: 296). Tolstoy would not concede to the idea that Orthodoxy could be a free congregation united by faith. "A collection of believers?" he asks. Yes, there are other associations of interest, such as lovers of Wagner's music who congregate in clubs or believers in social theories who gather to dialogue, but faith is a personal affair. As a teacher, the church is a concept alien to the spirit of Christianity. Tolstoy finishes his second confession on an inspired anthem of free conscience strongly resonating with Kierkegaard's injunction to choose oneself in order not to lose oneself. "I can select the color of my pantaloons, I can choose my wife, and I can build a house according to taste, but the rest, this in what I feel my humanity, in all of that I must seek consultation from them – from these idle, deceptive, and ignorant people. . . . This is terrible!" (23: 296–97). This passionate cry was uttered in spite of the fact that *Critique* had been inspired by his conversations with clever and pleasant clerics. Tolstoy ends his work with a blessing and words of encouragement for that "inner struggle" that divides the kingdoms of existence into the right and wrong ones (23: 302–3). The last corrections in *Critique of Dogmatic Theology* were entered in October 1884, but the work remained unpublished and circulated in this form until Elpidin found a way to publish it in Geneva (1891).

WHAT I BELIEVE?

It is in this work that we first have a firm feeling of the fruits of Tolstoy's conversion finally at work. Here he puts on Kant's "new man" without apology. He is the born-again man who has embraced his new understanding of life and no longer requires the hagiographic qualities of *A Confession* for a universal, edificatory, and allegorical appeal. In his new role, his experiences of a new convert are cast as the life of a great sinner from which everyone could learn. The last in the series of documents of Tolstoy's accounting and summary of his new creed, *What I Believe?* should not mislead by the question mark at the end of the title. The question is polemically posed. Foreseeing the destiny of the book that could possibly undergo censorship, at his own expense, Tolstoy published a limited edition of fifty copies, which sold like a fire, despite the considerable price of 25 rubles a copy. On February 14, 1884, the work was officially banned; however, Leonid Urusov's French translation of the work, *Ma religion*, appeared in Paris in 1885.

What I Believe? is a symbiosis of a journal and a public announcement. Dated January 22, 1884, it begins with an indication of Tolstoy's biological age (fifty-five years), thirty-five years of which are said to have been lost to atheism, of which only five were lived in the spirit of right faith, a fact that the former sinner and a false Christian and now a real Christian, Tolstoy is ready to make public (23: 304). In the new genre of a told rather than a retold Gospel, Tolstoy does not interpret, but *comments*: "I don't want to interpret (*tolkovat'*) the teaching of Christ, but only to explain how I understood it" (23: 304). To deliver a preventive blow to his foes, the Pharisees (or Orthodox believers), Tolstoy forgives them in advance: "I harbor no wrath against my detractors . . . Christ opened my eyes." Tolstoy relates the parable of the robber on the cross who believed Christ's teaching and was saved and presents himself as one such robber (23: 455). If Tolstoy ever described his conversion as dramatic event and a moment of dawning, it was this moment of becoming a believer when *suddenly* he started understanding the meaning of Jesus' teaching on nonresistance. "And *suddenly* I heard Christ's words, understood them, and life and death ceased seeming evil; and instead of the desperation, I experienced joy and happiness, which could not be destroyed by death" (23: 305). After this conventional prelude of a typical convert, the accounting for what has happened to him is less than regular from the Orthodox standpoint.

Without a hint of humility, Tolstoy refers to the writing of this catechism of faith as a God-given task of a successful convert: "My life and death will serve to the salvation of all—this was, after all, what Christ taught" (23: 402). In fact, he quoted God's instruction to Jonah with an implication that his own task is just the same: "Your knowledge of truth was only necessary to be transmitted to those who did not have it" (23: 413). The meaning of such return to faith is not overrated because Tolstoy speaks of a return to faith with a damning indictment issued to all modern versions of Christianity, which he argues to be devious violations of Christ's word. To Tolstoy, spiritual transcendence found in Christ's teaching was a perfect example of *metanoia* and the only "change in one's life" (*peremena zhizni*) or "new mode of life" (*nov[yi] obraz zhizni*) that he would advocate to replace the existing world order (23: 340–41). Because of exposing and relating his faith to anticipated detractors and hoped-for allies, Tolstoy had to find a way of keeping his arrogantly confessing presence yet hold himself subordinate to the content of a good life and new awareness that he was intent on describing. He approached the matter of his own authorial omnipresence with discriminating caution and explained the difference between "being there" to stand for what one preaches and hiding behind the authority of the Big Truth, which he had exposed in *Critique of Dogmatic Theology* (23: 93).

The surest way to avoid the trap of indoctrination is to offer an example of daily choices in whether to follow rules from Christ's teaching or to find them too cumbersome. There are rules in the teaching that look as if they are addressed to everybody in person, Tolstoy begins. Remembering his honest profligate, Stiva Oblonsky, who quoted the Gospels, reiterating that faith without deeds is dead (23: 311), Tolstoy pauses to recapitulate his position on the doctrine of Redemption and other safe conducts that allow men to do nothing with their choices of behavior (23: 313–14). He describes several of his numerous Moscow encounters. One was with Rabbi Solomon Minor, his Hebrew instructor, who wondered if all Christians really turn the other cheek. The question discomfited Tolstoy, because not all Christians certainly do. The second time he was embarrassed for the state of contemporary Christianity near the Borovitsky Gates in Kremlin, guarded by a sentry and occupied by beggars. The guard hushed off the beggars. Tolstoy asked him why he would do such an anti-Christian thing and if he had read the Gospels. The guard asked Tolstoy if he had read military instructions (23: 316–17). To Tolstoy, the answer epitomized the current state of affairs in all modern societies, "the lost and the insane," who, at the pretext of serving the rules of this world, claim that Christian rules are impracticable and have liberated themselves from moral responsibility (23: 361–68).

As in *Critique of Dogmatic Theology*, the culprit for moral nonaction is the convenient belief in the Fall and Redemption shared by both believers and nonbelievers. To nonbelievers it is convenient because it allows them to believe in material Paradise on earth. To believers it is convenient because the assumption that their immortal soul was breathed into them at birth, coupled with their outwardly correct behavior and obedience to rites, guarantee salvation (23: 377). Here, in returning to the exposition of the Two Kingdoms, Tolstoy finally reveals the crux of his faith: the task of life, which is a struggle between the animal and the reasonable nature, consists in subordinating the animal nature, the life of this world, to the reasonable nature, the demands of life eternal (23: 376). The source of evil in modern mentality, which violated man's links with his most direct line to life—eternal nature, labor, family, the world beyond national confines and an ability to die a healthy and painless death—was finally identified (23: 421). Tolstoy points out that eternal life proper is mentioned in the Bible but twice. The Jewish *khaie-oilom* refers to the infinite cosmos created by God, with man as its finite particle (23: 396). This life would be nothing but a wicked joke indeed and would come to a terrible end (23: 386). Regarding the view that life is expendable Tolstoy considers reports about two disasters and the terror they inspired, the collapse of the railway mound that caused a train crash and the burning of the circus in the Ukrainian provincial capital of Berdichev, both of which record great loss of life. The circus burned for one hour, and people pushed each other away from the door causing a stampede. In the same way, humanity had been burning for 1800 years since Christ had disclosed the source of salvation, which was rarely followed. Tolstoy calls us to "step back from the door, and remember that your life and your body does not belong to you," which is not the attitude of a particle waiting for its hour to be removed from the scene of life. Tolstoy refuses to accept ascetic solutions that man was given life to work the graveyard of his master and to serve other lives in order to save his own (23: 417). There is a delicate boundary between serving the evils of this world, "the chariot killer of consumption" (23: 421), toiling endlessly to no avail by catering to its wrong needs or by parasitically reaping its rewards, and making conscious choices that will agree with reasonable interests of the eternal kingdom. "Life can't be satisfied," sums up Tolstoy, but it can be spent up in Christian work (23: 426). The wicked *harnessing force* of progress (*sila stsepleniia*) makes people beholden to the wrong chain of historical necessity, of servants of this world (23: 448). At this point, Tolstoy makes an unexpected return to Strakhov's metaphor of true idealism, of true activity, the metaphor of the umbilical cord that he disputed in 1875. If Christ has conquered this world (*pobedil sei mir*) and his truth looks uncomfortable, it is because the umbilical cord keeping people enslaved to the life of this world has already been cut (23: 448). In explaining his own birth of a free moral agent, Tolstoy acknowledges that his life of profligacy and superfluity is over. He was feeling the push of *reasonable life* (*razumnaia zhizn'*) (23: 461), no longer a blind and hostile force, but that imperative that pushes him forward, a meaningful dot in the mutually dependent chain of eternity that believes that "the good awaiting me is possible only when all people will fulfill the teaching of Christ. I believe that the fulfillment of this teaching is possible, easy, and joyous" (23: 456). "Don't be afraid, little flock," he concluded, quoting from Luke 12.32, "for it is your Father's good pleasure to give you the Kingdom" (23: 465).

NOTES

1. See Lewis Rambo, *Understanding Religious Conversion*, 21, 87, 90–91, 137–59. For a splendid analysis of violent metaphors of change, see Ann Taves, *Fits, Trances, and Visions: Experiencing Religion and Explaining Experiences from Wesley to James* (Princeton, N.J.: Princeton University Press, 1999).

2. See Ralph Metzner, "Ten Classical Metaphors of Self-Transformation," *Journal of Transpersonal Psychology* 12, no. 1 (1980): 47–62.

3. See Brian Taylor, "Recollection and Membership: Converts Talk and the Ratiocination of Commonality," *Sociology* 12 (1978): 320.

4. See James A. Beckford, "Accounting for Conversion," *British Journal of Sociology* 29 (1978): 250–51. See Gerald Peter, *The Mutilating God: Authorship and Authority in the Narrative of Conversion* (Amherst: University of Massachussets Press, 1993), 159. See also Richard A. Hutch, *Biography, Autobiography, and the Spiritual Quest* (London: Continuum, 1997), 152–56.

5. Quoted from a letter to Fedor Zheltov dated April 1887 (64: 40). For similar pronouncements on the question of sincerity in memoir writing, see Tolstoy's later assessment of the *Journal Intime* of Henri Amiel. In 1893 Tolstoy was working on the translation of Amiel's journal in collaboration with his daughter, Maria L'vovna. The latter appeared in 1894, with a brief preface by Tolstoy, in his popular edition *Posrednik* (29: 360–61).

6. On a convert's need to look back, see William Earle, *The Autobiographical Consciousness* (Chicago: Quadrangle, 1972), 37–41. According to Earle, the consciousness that writes its autobiography from the point of view of ontology, or the meaning of life, necessarily includes intentionality and reflexivity (41).

7. Orwin, *Tolstoy's Art and Thought*, 191.

8. See Morson, *Hidden in Plain View*, 200–205. For Ginzburg's view of conditioned responsible choice see *On Psychological Prose*, 365.

9. For Rousseau's precepts on active life, see chapter 2 of the present study.

10. See Gustafson, 88, 110, 240; see also Wachtel's "History and Autobiography," 184–87.

11. See Michel Foucault's "Christianity and Confession," in his study *The Politics of Truth*, ed. Sylvère Lotringer and Lysa Hochroth (New York: New Press/Semiotext[e], 1977), 199–236.

12. See the canonical statements in Hans Meyerhoff's *Time in Literature* (Berkeley: University of California Press, 1955), 27, 57.

13. Saint Augustine, *Confessions*, 170.

14. Ibid., 160.

15. For in-depth treatment of Augustine, see Karl Frederick Morrison's *Understanding Conversion* and the companion volume *Conversion and Text: The Cases of Augustine of Hippo, Herman-Judah, and Constantine Tsatsos* (Charlottesville: University Press of Virginia, 1992).

16. Caryl Emerson notes that "Vospominanie" was the only poem by Pushkin that Tolstoy truly appreciated precisely because he considered it amendable. See Boris Eikhenbaum, "Pushkin i Tolstoi," *O Proze*, 169. See also Caryl Emerson, "What Is Art? and the Anxiety of Music," *Russian Literature* 40 (1996): 449.

17. In contrasting the techniques of Rousseau and Chateaubriand, I employ Jean Starobinski's classic approach to these autobiographies. See Jean Starobinski, "The Style of Autobiography," in *Literary Style: A Symposium*, ed. and trans. Seymour Chatman (London: Oxford University Press, 1971), 285–93. Like Rousseau's *Confessions*, Chateaubriand's multivolume work was lovingly preserved in Tolstoy's library, with dried flowers tucked between the pages. See *Biblioteka Tolstogo*, 3(1): 224.

18. See Herzen's preface (4: 7).

19. The last of the many "self-digging" confessions was the slightly earlier one written by Ogarev, completed in 1860–1861. This late-life confession, entitled "My Confession" *(Moia ispoved')*, focuses on the years of his childhood and the development of his revolutionary spirit. See Ogarev, *Izbrannye proizvedeniia*, 2: 392–425. In 1878–1882 it could only have been available to Tolstoy in lithographed or longhand copies.

20. A year before he died, Viazemsky also finished his farewell in verse, a poem harking back to Pushkin's thoughts on quilted gowns in the metaphorical life of a poet. "Our life in old age is like a well-worn gown. And like a warrior treasuring his cloak shot in the battle / I tend to my gown with love and respect." ("Zhizn' v starosti – iznoshennyi khalat") (1875–1877). Viazemsky, *Sochineniia* 1: 370. See also Viazemsky's "Iazykov i Gogol'" and "Iz avtobiografii" in *Sochineniia*, 2: 162–84, 239–81, esp. 170–73.

21. Buried in the margins of one of the books in his library Chaadaev wrote the following bitter inscription: "They find that I am pretending. How would you not, living with bandits and nitwits. This conceit in me, it is a grimace of grief." *Petr Ia. Chaadaev, Pro et contra. Lichnost' i tvorchestvo Petra Chaadaeva v otsenke russkikh myslitelei i issledovatelei. Antologiia* (St. Petersburg: Russkii khristianskii gumanitarnyi institute, 1998), 59.

22. Rousseau, *Confessions*, 266.

23. Jean-Jacques Rousseau, *Rousseau, Judge of Jean-Jacques: Dialogues*, ed. Roger D. Masters and Christopher Kelly (Hanover, N.H.: Dartmouth College and University Press of New England, 1990), 230, 251, 253.

24. See Harran, 182.

25. Aurelius Augustinus, *Les Confessions de Saint Augustin*, trans. d'Arnauld d'Andilly (Paris: Garnier, 1861), 374–75, 471, 473. For a meticulous analysis of Tolstoy's reading of this volume at different ages, see Alla Polosina, "L. N. Tolstoi i Avrelii Avgustin o pamiati, vremeni i prostranstve," in *Lev Tolstoi i mirovaia literatura. Leo Tolstoy and World Literature: Papers Delivered at Third International Tolstoy Conference, Yasnaya Poliana, 28–30 August 2003, in Memory of Lydia Dmitrievna Opulskaya*, ed. Galina Alexeeva (Moscow/Tula/Yasnaya Polyana: Yasnaya Polyana Publishing House, 2005), 65–76. My independent investigations agree with Polosina's findings.

26. Arthur Schopenhauer, "Short Concluding Diversion in the Form of a Dialogue: On the Doctrine of Indestructibility," in *Parerga & Paralipomena*, 2: 279.

27. Michael Holquist brilliantly explains a typical "confessional mode of autobiography" in the life of a self-acknowledged sinner caught between "two poles of knowing," namely, his former delusion and his new awareness. See Michael Holquist, *Dostoevsky and the Novel* (Princeton, N.J.: Princeton University Press, 1976), 95.

28. See Frank Kermode, *A Sense of an Ending: Studies in the Theory of Fiction* (Oxford: Oxford University Press, 2000), 196.

29. Paul Ricoeur, "The Aporias of the Experience of Time: Book 11 of Augustine's *Confessions*," in his *Time and Narrative*, 3 vols. (Chicago: University of Chicago Press, 1984–1885), 1: 25.

30. Ibid., 19.

31. Augustine divorces himself from the Maker of All Time (bk 11, chap. 13: 15).

32. Eccles. 1.12, 2.1, 12–14. Quoted in *The New Oxford Annotated Bible*, OT, 842–43.

33. This typical medley of "Ecclesiastical" style and syntax has been culled from chapters 2, 3, and 4 (23: 9, 11, 16, 23).

34. Plato, *The Collected Dialogues, Including the Letters*, ed. Edith Hamilton and Huntington Cairns (Princeton, N.J.: Princeton University Press, 1961), 49–50.

35. See Tolstoy's notations on unbound sheets dated February 27, 1874 (48: 347).

36. My translation closely follows Kentish's in Tolstoy, *A Confession*, 60.

37. Tolstoy, *A Confession*, trans. Kentish, 71.

38. Turgenev, *Sobranie sochinenii v desiati tomakh*, 8: 244, 250.

39. For Tolstoy's response to Schopenhauer's parable of the ropes, see chapter 7 of the present study.

40. Kierkegaard, *The Sickness Unto Death*, ed. and trans. H. V. Hong and E. H. Hong (Princeton, N.J.: Princeton University Press, 1980), 32.

41. See *Prolog*, 4 vols. (Moscow: Sviato-troitsko vvedenskaia tserkov', 1875), 3: 190–92.

42. See chapter "The Reckoning" (*Raschet*) in Saltykov-Shchedrin, *The Golovlyov Family*, 327. I have slightly amended the translation to give full justice to Saltykov's

terms such as "light," hopelessness, and the senseless pain. I have used M. E. Saltykov-Shchedrin, *Sochineniia v dvukh tomakh*, ed. M. Senchenkova (Moscow: Start. 1994), 2: 269 as the source of the Russian text.

43. *Tolstoy v vospominaniiakh sovremennikov*, 1: 261.
44. Tolstoy. *Perepiska s russkimi pisateliami*, 1: 198–99.
45. N. N. Gusev, *Lev Nikolaevich Tolstoy. Materialy k biografii s 1870 po 1881* (Moscow: USSR Academy of Sciences, 1963), 584–85.

Chapter Ten

Logos and its Life in the World (1880–1886)

LIFE IN THE CHRISTIAN CITY

During his visit to the Monastery of the Trinity and St. Sergius in Moscow in 1879, Tolstoy was asked by Professor Kudriavtsev of The Theological Academy if he would soon please the readership with a new work like *War and Peace* and *Anna Karenina*. Tolstoy responded by quoting St. Paul, stating that he would not want to be "like a dog that returns to its vomit" (2 Peter 2.22).[1] Apart from his short tale, "What Do Men Live By" (*Chem liudi zhivy*), published in the magazine, *Children's Repose* (*Detskii Otdykh*), and "Strider," finally finished in 1885, Tolstoy wrote little fiction from 1878 until 1885. His readers saw nothing from Russia's greatest living author in the manner of conventional writing. The sketches of his two novels from the times of Peter the Great and *The Decembrists* were never finished.

In the first post-conversion years, he searched for new forms that could accommodate his faith, and he rethought principles of his art. The first anxious reviews of his new art were a mixed blessing. Ivan Aksakov, whom Tolstoy despised, greeted the first popular tales with admiration and heaved a sigh of relief on behalf of Orthodoxy: "There has been much talk about the new, allegedly mystic trend in this author, and that he died for art. The story just published testifies to the contrary. The realist artist has not died in him but has become an artist spiritually enlightened, for whom art has become sanctified and the new world of creativity and moral service has opened to him."[2] Fedor Buslaev, a noted scholar of popular art, expressed a negative view of the new Tolstoy who, "being tempted by a fiendish suggestion to exhort and harangue, causes insult to his own spiritual nature by willfully abdicating his innate artistic talent. Count Tolstoy has been mercilessly dissipating his great poetic gift on the cheap ABCs of morals, scholastic interpretations, and various didactic experiments and endeavors." Buslaev called *A Confession* something like "lachrymose repentance" and "a fancy allegory about a fabulous Unicorn."[3] Tolstoy did not relent and added to the list about a dozen more tales and legends written in 1885, a note on the Moscow census, and a polemical social treatise entitled *What, Then, Should We Do?* (1882–1886). At last, he discarded the never-to-be-finished "The Memoirs of a Madman" in favor of his first post-conversion masterpiece, *The Death of Ivan Il'ich* (1886), the drafts of which were started in 1882 and for almost two years interloped with "The Memoirs."

In 1882–1884, Tolstoy made peace with Alexandrine Tolstaya on condition that they stop interfering into each other's convictions. In the face of his growing alienation from the establishment, he used Alexandrine's connections at court to plead the cause of arrested and persecuted sectarians and politicals, who were increasingly seeing in him a source of moral solace and practical support. On the one hand, his oldest friends were becoming distant. Even to Strakhov Tolstoy intimated that they would never be the same with each other unless Strakhov too made his own turnaround (63: 105). Sometimes, Tolstoy deliberately avoided intellectual exchange. In 1879 his old friend Boris Chicherin published *Science and Religion* (*Nauka i religiia*). Tolstoy saw no benefit in exchanging religious views on philosophical justification or refutation of theology and scientific explanation of faith with Chicherin, who fruitlessly expected Tolstoy's response after sending him two copies of the book.[4] In August 1883, Turgenev died abroad after sending Tolstoy a touching last letter with a request not to be despondent.

In addition to the growing interest in his religious personality in the nation and among the young, by the end of 1884 Tolstoy found himself surrounded by new intellectual associates—the radical teacher Vasily Alexeev, vice-mayor of Tula, Prince Leonid Obolensky, who was terminally ill with cancer, and another seriously ill new friend, Gavril Rusanov, the former legal servant. The two people whose friendship he would cherish the most were Nikolai Ge, the veteran religious painter, and Vladimir Chertkov, the young aristocrat who left a brilliant military career to assist Tolstoy in faith-building. In 1885, the ranks of Tolstoy's inner circle were filled by the young man of letters and publisher, Pavel Biriukov, his future biographer, and the antipositivist philosopher, Nikolai Grot.

The first post-conversion years were difficult, and sometimes Tolstoy felt lonely. He confessed to the young radical journalist, Mikhail Engelgardt, who sought Tolstoy's ethical counsel: "You can't possibly imagine how lonely I am, and to what extent the real "I" is being despised by everyone around me . . . and therefore my hope, almost my certitude in finding in you, who sincerely walks the same road with me towards the same goal, is very joyous to me" (63: 112). Not unlike Kant, Tolstoy soon started receiving letters with requests of counsel or advice by basketfuls and was turned to by atheists, agnostics, believers, and the wavering. In responses to such requests, Tolstoy normally repeated the major points of *What I Believe?* just as he did in his lengthy response to Engelgardt: "Do not suffer for the sake of suffering, but do not begrudge temporary suffering in fulfilling Christ's law in its direct application to life. Do not hide behind national causes to justify violence in the manner of Aksakov, Dostoevsky, and Soloviev" (63: 112).

In the letter to Engelgardt and in adjacent letters, Tolstoy opened his methodical war against property. This was the war with apology, for Tolstoy saw no immediate instrument for removing property relations from modern life or his own life: "You sermonize, and how do you live?" he asked himself. "I can only sermonize by my deeds, and my deeds are vile. . . . Incriminate me as I incriminate myself, but do not incriminate that path along which I proceed . . ." (63: 123). In two of his major tracts on practical Christian behavior in society Tolstoy addressed the question of pain and suffering accompanying labor and associated joyful labor with the parable in the Lord's vineyard. The shorter work, "On the Census in Moscow" (*O perepisi v Moskve*) (1882), and a long tract, *What, Then, Should We Do?* (*Tak chto zhe nam delat'*) (1882–1884) were both written on the spur of his endless and often uncomfortable excursions around the poorest corners of the old capital. In both, Tolstoy brought his theory of action to logical conclusion. The latter work, which Tolstoy was trying to publish under the title *Life in a Christian City* (*Zhizn' v khristianskom gorode*) clearly invoked Augustine's *Civitate Dei*.[5] In the selfless service to their community of a 2000-strong core of young volunteers who did not shun the poorest, disease-infested slums and dross houses of Moscow in order to take record of everyone in need—and not in the bail-off charity money of the rich, Tolstoy saw a ray of hope. "Why not hope that the real deed is being done not thanks to money but thanks to real work, and that the enfeebled drunks, the thieves yet uncaught, the prostitutes who still have a chance to return will be saved? The whole of evil might not be corrected, but there will be consciousness of it and struggle with it by inner means. . . . Why not think and hope that the cells of our society will revive and will revive the whole organism? We don't know in whose power the life of the cell, but we know that our life is in our power. By concert efforts, brothers, let's go!" (25: 180–81).

What, Then, Should We Do? is more sober. Those who imagine to be residing in the Christian city all but reneged on twin tasks bequeathed by the Bible to the humanity: man is accountable to the law of labor, and his wife should bear children. In Tolstoy's view, only women still partially perform their duty. The work inspired by visits to slums and inspection of prostitution quarters from the safe distance in the street also bears the indelible shame of a stampede in which his attempt to distribute alms in the dross-house almost resulted, prevented only by a violent intrusion of a police officer. On his return home to a dinner in five courses served by two lackeys in white gloves, Tolstoy felt the same unbearable nausea experienced thirty years earlier at the sight of the crowd cheering at the killing by the guillotine in Paris.

The daily genocide of the rich against the poor led Tolstoy to a relentless querying of the members of his circle about what indeed could be done. "Nothing, but a good idea" was the most common response to his obstinate reminder that all Christians should be equal. Tolstoy blames Hegelian philosophy that taught the nineteenth century to justify everything that exists for this evasive response, and social Darwinism, and positivist theories of happiness in its stead. The modern art "of Pushkin, Dostoevsky, Turgenev, L. Tolstoy, the pictures of the French salons and our painters portraying naked dames . . . the music of Wagner" did nothing to assist in building that morally independent personality and nothing to explain "how to acquiesce the demand of personal well-being with conscience and reason" (25: 350, 367). The answers supplied by modern artists, intellectuals become more and more sophistic, self-admiring; herein is the trick, warns Tolstoy. The task of the real thinker and the real artist is to suffer their way back to the origins, to the examples by Confucius, Buddha, Moses, and Christ: "And from the voice of their conscience and from the considerations imparted to them by people who formerly lived and people contemporary to them . . , these great teachers deduced their teachings—simple, clear, and comprehensible to all and that could be carried out" (25: 367). And so should the modern artist, "L.Tolstoy," the only surviving author from the group of other adulated sinners, Pushkin, Dostoevsky, and Turgenev, sacrifice his personal well-being for the sake of Christian revival of society (25: 373).

ART AS IT SHOULD BE

The use of *A Confession* as an example could suggest that Tolstoy was ready to play the role of a demented prophet. Such a path of a lunatic poet running away from town and falling into a well and refusing rescue ropes was prefigured in Horace's *Ars Poetica* and continued in the Christian lore of Bunyan and his Russian imitators from Fonvizin to Pushkin, Gogol, and Turgenev: "How do you know but that he threw himself in on purpose and does not wish to be rescued?"[6] Now that his metaphysical Arzamas was over, Tolstoy was expected to sing again, either "burn people's hearts" like Pushkin's prophet or be ridiculed and ousted like Lermontov's. The chatty broadsheets published caricatures of Tolstoy. One of those displayed Tolstoy, cried over by his muse, his marble bust of the author of *War and Peace* surrendered to the adulating mob, while the unnoticed author takes no heed, staff in hand, clad in a dervish garb, he steals out of town into the desert.[7]

The poet of sounds and colors, as he rapturously described himself in 1873, was now dead. Also dead, however, was the poet described in his parable "A Dream" rejected in 1863 by Aksakov, the vainglorious poet deserted by his contemptuous muse who felt schadenfreude at his own unhappiness.[8] Like Mill, Tolstoy could now reread other people's *Dejections* or compose his own, or he could repeat with Wordsworth, that the eye "cannot chuse but see," that he "cannot bid the ear be still," and that his heart still watched and received cultivating the new artistic-religious perception.[9] This path was more or less the one that Tolstoy chose to take. At the time of his "return" to literature only one other living compatriot, Soloviev, had a developed notion of literary-religious logos. Soloviev's logos was moving steadily in the direction of Hegelian concrete idealism of a concrete being. How can Christians transform abnormal reality abounding with moral evil, oppression, and plunder into the world that should be?[10] The general law of nature would not be perceived as evil, concluded Soloviev, if another, ethical law of Christianity did not exist, perhaps still in an embryonic blind form, unconscious of its inner power. Not unlike Tolstoy, Soloviev also explained that Christ was the first incarnation of this inner power of the soul over the material power on earth. The speech in which these ideas were aired caused the termination of Soloviev's academic career, but it must have caught Tolstoy's eye at the time when Tolstoy was rejecting Platonic hierarchies "as very artificial" and leaning more decisively toward ethical action (63: 62, 155). In February 1884 he wrote Buturlin: "Leave God alone as long as what our conscience demands of us (as a term, 'the categorical imperative' is too unclear and imprecise) were reasonable and therefore obligatory and common to all people. The whole task is in it and this task has been solved (to me) by Christ or by the teaching that is called Christian" (63: 155). His preoccupation as an artist, after all, was now to identify new transformative moments in art that would not mislead by their exterior semblance to the divine, but, instead, touch the core of inner being. Tolstoy set his eye on representing reason in practice. His new task was to create a form in which man is coerced by nothing but his impulse to do what is good and resist provocation from distracting challenges and temptations. On first reflection, Tolstoy found his new religious art better suited to the form of the parable, which underlay the realist, sometimes-naturalist representation in his elaboration of the Christian prototype. Is there a pure form that guarantees pure art? "A work of art is good or bad depending on what the artist says and how he speaks and whether he speaks *from the soul* [*ot dushi*]," Tolstoy begins his note "On Art" (*Ob iskusstve*) (30: 213) and with it resumes in the early 1880s his critique of polluted art. As he had announced earlier in the 1860s, natural man gained little from the invention of the printing press (8: 341). The printing press had to become itself re-consecrated in order to infect.[11]

With this goal in mind, in 1884 and 1885 Tolstoy oversaw the creation of two publishing ventures for the people—*Intermediary* (*Posrednik*) and *Flower Constellation* (*Tsvetnik*). The former was founded in 1884 with major assistance from Chertkov to ensure the spread of Christian literature in resistance to the dominance of banal popular art. Tolstoy served on its editorial board and until 1887 actively contributed his religious tales to its rich hopper.[12] The policies of *Tsvetnik*, founded in 1885–1886 on the initiative of a female education propagandist, Alexandra Kalmykova, were closely monitored by Tolstoy. In this, he fulfilled his aspiration to superintend the production of good art, from its conception to printing. In the 1880s, Tolstoy also wrote several shorter manifestoes in preparation for the magisterial *What Is Art?* (1897–1898): "A Letter to N. A. Aleksandrov" ("*Pis'mo N. A. Aleksandrovu*"), "A Preface to *Tsvetnik*" ("*Predislovie k sborniku Tsvetnik*") (both in 1886), and "On Art" (*Ob iskusstve*) (1889). All three establish new parameters for the transmission of harmonious joy through art.

The "Preface to *Tsevtnik*" is one good example of Tolstoy's war against false artistic signs. From the start, he quotes Jesus' admonition to the Pharisees' request for a sign (Matthew 12:34–37): "You brood of vipers . . . for by your words you will be justified, and by your words you will be condemned."[13] Tolstoy commented on this verse in his retelling of the Gospels, in which he changed "brood of vipers" (*porozhdeniia ekhidny*) into a much milder "reptile breed" (*zmeinaia poroda*) (NT 18). Tolstoy quotes verse 34 of Matthew 12:34–37, which takes on imperative tones, and the ethical choice is directly posed to the group (*govoriu zhe vam*), which is Tolstoy's exhortation against pharisaic art and artists (26: 307). In concert with the use of the future perfect (*kto napishet*), the second person imperative implies that following the command will result in a remunerative justice, while disobeying in retributive justice. The bad art of a bad artist will be punished. Certain orientations in art are "contrary to" (*protivno*) or "in accordance with" (*soglasno*) the new task. Tolstoy explains: The task to be truthful to the world *that is* (the artistic mimesis gliding over the appearances) is "contrary to." It is in accordance with the task *not to be truthful* to this world that is, but to be truthful to the world that *should be*. The license of the improbable, of the fantastic realm of the Kingdom of Heaven, of truer than the truth of what appears is accorded to those who possess Christ's wisdom: "Christ spoke in parables, and his parables endured as the eternal truth. He would just add, 'Only be observant as you listen to [parables]'" (26: 309). A genuine work of art is not a servant to the vile realistic mimesis, it is a work of miracles, a revelation of the "mysteries of life" (*otkrovenie tain zhizni*) (30: 215). "On Art" and Tolstoy's letter to Aleksandrov openly invoke the essence of true art as a harmonious revelation of Artistic Trinity: truth, goodness, and beauty (*istina, dobro, i krasota*). Only in this harmonization of the trinity in the soul of the artist can art function as a good work and can it reveal. The artist is warned in advance that by his word he will be saved or cursed. Suddenly Tolstoy returns to the Old Testament epithet, "brood of vipers" and overrides his milder translation of the same phrase in his retelling of the Gospels. Following Tolstoy's substitution, we may interpret the larger costs of artistic transgression against the word, a gift of grace to be preserved in the spirit of religious consciousness of art.

The "Preface to *Tsvetnik*" states how all creative literature should be judged if they attempt to show what there must be: "In order to show [life] in this way, one cannot describe only how it is in the world. . . . So as to have truth in what you write, you must write not what *is*, but what *should be*, describe not the truth of what is, but the truth of the Lord's Kingdom, which is close to us but is not here yet" (26: 308). Furthermore, any description of what is commonly known to be human happiness is *not* one, Tolstoy says. Tolstoy provides a catalog of conditions and plot sequences for a hero's "false" happiness: "[T]owards the end [he] is joined with his love interest and becomes notable, rich and happy." This false happiness is earned after a lifetime of picaresque adventure: "[H]e endures torture, tortures others, tolerates danger, misery, uses cunning, combats others. . . ." In this mockery, Tolstoy clearly parodies a typical plot of a typical European novel of education, *Bildungsroman*, which allows one to learn from life experiences by passing through life's customary stages (26: 308). Nevertheless, in his diatribe Tolstoy is not merely debunking traditionalist plots. If one attentively looks at what he proposes, he is also describing the regular, normal, and terrible plot of human life itself. The new art of his aspiration is the ideal world of the Kingdom, in which the unhappy is happy, the happy is unhappy, and the reversal of justice is achieved.

In 1884–1887 Tolstoy experimented with several parables, hagiographic tales in prose and dramatic forms and with vitas exemplifying moral education. The hero of Tolstoy's historical parable from the life of the early Christians, "Roam the World While There is Light" (*"Khodite v svete poka est' svet"*) (1886–1887), Julius (Iulii), receives advice from his childhood friend, Pamfilii, to give up his riches and join the Christians, a project that haunts Julius throughout his life. Taking Pamfilii up on his word that it is never late for a man to save himself and that he can roam this world as long as there is enough light in his soul that will guide him to where he ultimately belongs, the doubtful Julius keeps postponing. Major biographical episodes in Julius' life replicate the false engagements with life that Tolstoy ridicules as typical to a realist novel in his "Preface to *Tsvetnik*." Julius struggles for financial independence, gains it, and then suffers losses. He joins his love interest in holy matrimony. He has affairs but is won back by his wife. His children grow up in prosperity and turn into profligate, selfish spendthrifts. By the end of his life, Julius is a well-established, reasonable, honest *pater familias* and a statesman. However, Tolstoy does not let Julius die well in ripe old age. The pinnacles of Julius' worldly success are shown as dubious, deceptive, and catastrophic for his moral well-being. During one of Julius' despairing flights from home he meets an advocate against Christian conversion: "A deception of the Christians or their mistake . . . consists precisely in that they are reluctant to acknowledge man's nature. A perfect executor of their teaching can only be an old man who has outlived his passions" (26: 261). Allowing Julius to experience the gamut of reasonable doubts and passions, Tolstoy prepares him for joining the Christian world as an old man readied as a modest worker to a vineyard tended by other Christians who have left the corrupt confines of this world. The parable offers the first in a series of Tolstoy's rhetorical survivals within the body but without the body. Julius dies of old age, but he continues in his newly acquired eternal life; he dies and "did not notice the demise of his flesh" (26: 301). Tolstoy needs something that already does *not* belong in the norm and stands out, so as to bypass "what needs be" and make it into what "should be." Death is one such liminal situation and Tolstoy tests its narrative possibilities in one tale after another in 1885–1886. In his famous reworking of a Bashkir legend in the story "How Much Land Does a Man Need" (*Mnogo li cheloveku zemli nuzhno*) (1886), the good peasant Pakhom also does not notice how he dies, but this lack of attention signifies complete self-loss. Devilish promptings of greed inspire Pakhom and his wife to become involved in capitalist agriculture. His business is so good that he expands and then expands further. The whispers of the demons that are brought to life and are audible in the story thanks to Pakhom's avarice propel him to go to the Bashkirs and buy as much land as possible. The Bashkirs freely dispose of the land; bemused, they invite Pakhom to run around a vast field between dawn and sunset and claim as much space as he finds fit. Pakhom's daylong rush with a spade to the sound of the Bashkirs' titter ends on his missing the time of his life's sunset: he drops dead before he can close the circle and claim his property. He is buried the same day. Six feet from head to toe was all he needed (25: 78).[14] Tolstoy taunts and lulls us by the question he poses: "*mnogo li*" literally means "is it really that much?" The question invites an exit from the real (from what *is*).[15]

The next death on the roster has to do with admission of past crime. After the crime, the criminal's life turns into wakeful hell. Still, despite his sharp lookout for danger, he overlooks the moment of his death in a bad way. In his January–April 1886 revision of a Gothic crime story published by a lesser Ukrainian writer, Nikolai Kostomarov in 1881, Tolstoy forgoes the Romantic oracle-type curse that had been issued on the murderer who was to be punished in forty years.[16] Because no bolt from heaven arrives to strike him dead, the rich Trofim takes all measures of precaution against other people and arouses the fear of God in his potential robbers and murderers, something in which he did not believe himself. Trofim dies twelve years after the crime, peacefully, and in his sleep. He is buried as a respected citizen in the Alexander Nevsky cemetery. During the obsequies of hypocritical mourners who were reluctant to accept Trofim's confession shortly before he died the narrator adds: "Nobody but God knew of Trofim's crime, or of the punishment that had befallen him the minute he had lost God in himself" (26: 118).

Tolstoy's "Dramatization of the Legend of Aggei" ("*Dramaticheskaia obrabotka legendy of Aggee*") (1886) is a reworking of legend 24 from Afanasiev, "The Tale of the Czar Aggei and How He Was Afflicted by Pride" ("*Povest' o tsare Aggee i kako postrada gordostiiu*").[17] All the episodes of Aggei's punishment in Afanasiev are skimpy, succinct, and drawn in the spirit of mystic *kenosis*, symbolic rather than literal physical voiding of sin. Tolstoy's acquaintance with the picaresque Western version of the same plot based on the rowdy, adventurous, and action-packed Polish rendition of the Renaissance collection *Gesta Romanorum*, benefited his intention to stage a humorous and raucous conquest over evil. His proud Aggei is punched in a brawl with robbers, flogged for philandering with his master's wife where he is hired as a seasonal worker, and so on. Vsevolod Garshin's novella on the same plot, "The Lay of the Proud Aggei. A Reworking of an Old Legend" ("*Skazanie o gordom Aggee. Pereskaz starinnoi legendy*"), written as a florid neo-romantic stylization of Church Slavonic homilies was an unlikely explanation for why Tolstoy never tried to publish or stage his dramatization.[18] He was rather using the legend for his laboratory of the new art much in the same spirit as he used his philosophical fragments of the 1870s for the elaboration of his knowledge of faith. Both Garshin's story and Afanasiev's legend center on Aggei's profanation of a biblical verse that the rich will be punished. Aggei's punishment in Afanasiev finishes with an admonition never again to utter sacrilege on holy books (Afanasiev, 186). Garshin's version ends with Aggei walking the earth with blind paupers and holy people as a holy man named Alexis (Garshin, 311). Tolstoy's Aggei is forgiven when he merely pledges never to tear apart Evangelical verses that are not to his liking; he vanquishes his arrogance by serving dinner to his servants, a perfect return into the physical world and its material nourishments (26: 500). Tolstoy's Aggei is a merry bruiser and an irreverent atheist whose anticlerical antics Tolstoy seems almost to admire:

> Third Servant: He's beaten Pyotr to a pulp. Took away Semyon's wife, Fyodor's daughter. People are sufferin', they curse 'im, but he, he don't care, has a good time. Drinks from mornin' to night, goofs off, goes huntin' . . . Only why does God put up with his sins?
>
> Second Servant: Repent? Fat chance! . . . Just wait, he'll pull a stunt in church (Thunder and lightning).[19]

In this remarkable passage, we witness that Tolstoy's inveterate sinners are sincere and, therefore, liable to correction. Consider God's cooperation with Aggei, his ginger prompting by thunder and lightning, and lack thereof, save for devil's giggles and other eerie warnings, in the case of Pakhom and Trofim. While it is a breathtaking risk to sin so exceptionally as to tempt God's ire for dramatic effect in a backstage re-creation of thunder and lightning, Tolstoy looks for undramatic and tested remedies in order to repair the evils. Religious legends, evangelical verses, and popular tales with their veiled simplicity serve the purpose of returning the straying sinner back onto the road of truth by means of a symbolic deterrent from choosing errant ways. In his dramatizations and in accordance with Tolstoy's understanding of *khamartiia*, it is the delusion (*zabluzhdenie*), and not the character as such, that receives punishment. Pan Aggei is called "the deluded one" (*zabludiashchii*) by one of the robbers before being given a thorough beating (26: 492). This purposeful folksy slippage contaminates "lost" (*zabludshii*) and "erring" (*zabluzhdaiushchiisia*) and implies degrees of a lost direction: being deluded from life's purpose and straying from the path of searching on the main road. It is not unlike the healthy therapeutic effect described by Freud in which the actor and author allow the spectator to *identify* with the hero, but spare him by tacit implication that he *cannot* experience that very *same* grotesque suffering and is able to feel healthy emotions of resistance to moral pathology.[20]

EVIL AND THE WORLD AS IT SHOULD BE

Tolstoy understood justification before God as a radical change in status, but certified neither by the Church nor by manmade court. While his reinterpreting of the heavenly law invited sour reactions from the authorities, the sophistic justification underlying the coercive administration of law is attacked by Tol-

stoy at the peril of being accused by liberals of anarchist relativism "blunting
. . . moral discrimination."²¹ Tolstoy sees evil to be endemic in human lives; as
unavoidable is their urge to repent and correct. This is the topic of his famous
drama, *The Power of Darkness* (*Vlast' t'my*, 1886). The play has a subtitle built
off the Russian proverb: "the claw is stuck, the whole bird is gone." The cal-
lous Akulina, his ladylove, and Matrena, his mother, lead a weak-willed peasant lad Nikita into crime over the inheritance. He is the "bird" in question, both
criminal and victim, and first attempts to shrug off responsibility: "what have
you done to me?" he hollers in despair (26: 212). Although led to stand trial and
then face time in jail, he is the bird saved and free when he confesses his crime
"My design, my crime. Lead me anywhere you like" (26: 243).

In the parable "A Repentant Sinner" ("*Kaiushchiisia greshnik*") (1885), a
man lives until a ripe old age and dies at seventy, in total oblivion of his sins:
"this man would not repent" (25: 79). Only at his final hour, did he break into
tears and plead with the Lord to forgive him: "Oh Lord! As you did the robber on the Cross, forgive me too!" (25: 79). His imploring was enough to release his still sinful soul and let it *fall* in love with God's grace. In the ensuing exploits of Christian comedy, the sinner arrives at the closed gates of
Heaven. He bangs on the door, but Peter, David, and John refuse to let him
in. Unlike Kafka's man before the law, Tolstoy's sinner politely reminds each
of the demystified gatekeepers that none is blameless. The sinner reminds Peter how he slept after the Last Supper, how he thrice abdicated Christ, and
how he broke into tears when the rooster sang. He reprimands David for for-
getting about his taking another man's wife and life. He reminds John that it
is a sin to renege on his own word that "God is love," and not to forgive. Peter and David walk away from the gate in shame, but John, representing infinite love and forgiveness toward someone *so* willing to justify himself, allows
the sinner to enter the Heavenly Kingdom.

In the same unorthodox manner, Tolstoy approached the loud Mel'nitsky
case, the most conspicuous Moscow crime of the season that made national
headlines in 1882. In December 1883–January 1884, Tolstoy sketched a curious letter to an unidentified addressee, most likely Konstantin Odarchenko, a
barrister from Moscow, explaining his reaction to the case. The letter, never
sent, was in defense of Fedor Iliodarovich Mel'nitsky, treasurer of the Moscow
Orphanage, who had been indicted for embezzlement.²² On November 3,
1881, Mel'nitsky, fifty-one years of age, accompanied by an accountant Litvinov, set out for the Moscow Office of the State Bank in order to receive
339,000 rubles of state funds for the orphanage. Upon receipt of the sum in
cash, Mel'nitsky set aside 31,500 to cover current expenses and sent the
money on with Litvinov. He put the remainder (307,500) in a leather briefcase
and headed for the Merchants' Bank to make a deposit to the Orphanage's

checking account. According to his deposition, he felt lightheaded and sat down to recover. When he came to, the briefcase was gone. He immediately reported the incident to the attorney at the Chamber of Justice and then to the Chief of Police requesting his own apprehension. The investigation, however, took into account Mel'nitsky's overall performance on the job and concluded that the robbery was simulated and that the briefcase in reality had been handed over to Mel'nitsky's son, Boris F. Mel'nitsky, who was fined 5 rubles for no-show and contempt of court.[23] Facts of office abuse and malfeasance exposed during the investigation led to the elder Mel'nitsky's arrest. He was indicted, disfranchised, and sentenced to exile in the Tomsky Gubernia. Litvinov was acquitted. The trial ended on a contradictory note. It was a story, on the one hand, of embezzlement and heartless greed for the sake of the financial survival of his family. On the other hand, it was a story of reckless generosity, care for his daughters (whom he was marrying off) and sons (to whom he was trying to provide a good education), and service to the community in the provinces.

Tolstoy's intention in invoking the case, it seems, was to expose the societal reflex to condemn morally and then penalize legally someone who is but one of the many, a common man. For Tolstoy, one of the best proofs of the impossibility of establishing guilt was the report of a policeman who was given orders to search the road allegedly taken by Mel'nitsky when the crime occurred: "I was handed a lantern and told: Walk around and search; I walked around, but had no idea what I was searching for."[24] Making his plea for the Mel'nitsky family in his unusual reaction to the crime, Tolstoy speaks of Mel'nitsky's "Gospel-smart" crime: "Smart, precisely smart, as Christ presented to us the deed of [the] disloyal manager, saying that, in a sense, the sons of this world are smarter than the sons of light. The criminal nature of this deed to the sons of the world I stubbornly refuse to see. Mel'nitsky has once and for all done what we have allowed ourselves a lifetime to do, and has done so under great peril. So I cannot help saying that his deed was more moral. And everyone saw that his deed would be even smarter had it been pulled through, and everyone became envious" (63: 153). Tolstoy befriended Mel'nitsky's son, Petr Fedorovich, the younger brother of Boris, the unconfirmed accomplice of his condemned father. Petr Mel'nistky quit his promising military career to take up the case of his family. Long after the trial concluded, Tolstoy and Petr Mel'nitsky continued to stay in touch on matters of ethical justice and religion.[25]

In this outrageous outburst in defense of a criminal, Tolstoy is responsible enough not to deny the crime itself. However, as hard as it is to accept this logic, especially with its recruitment of the Gospels as support, it is very symptomatic of where Tolstoy locates moral responsibility and legal irresponsibility. The same equivalent of honest thievery has the right to be only in the picaresque fairy tale world, the imperfect and mocking parody of imperfect reality. We may recall here his tale, "The Tale of Ivan the Fool" (1885), in which the Fool outsmarts his wicked brothers and death itself, let alone the old demon with a retinue of three petty aids.[26] To accomplish this, Ivan plays havoc with justice and state institutions because evil relies on these forces to achieve its goals. When, in his customary foolish manner of turning up at the right moment and without much desire, Ivan becomes Tsar, he can practice unrestricted tomfoolery with the law of the land: "People came to Ivan's court. Says one: He stole my money. Says Ivan:—So, good! He needs it, then. It became known that Ivan was a fool" (25: 129).

Unlike Dostoevsky, Tolstoy had little interest in criminal intentions because he had little interest in the hyperbolized personality with a riddle to solve. Ingenious crimes, the intricacy of illegal ploys, were simply extensions of the most common vices, catalogued by him quite early in his diaries. Even the most vicious crimes held few surprises for him. Tolstoy's intricacy lies, rather, in a quite dispassionate, slightly humorous and condescending tricking of the vices. Slipping unobserved, undeterred, and unrecognized into the midst of human relations, vices personify *themselves* in human bodies rather than men personifying them. In a topsy-turvy reality of a picaresque tale, a religious parable, or a dramatization of a miracle play, Tolstoy's experimental parables and his response to the Mel'nitsky trial provide an antiworld of the Russian antiquity and the Baroque, a laughing mockery of corrupt reality that can be saved not by simple reversals, but by a complete turnaround.

Tolstoy's response to vice and moral error was a parable he related in *What I Believe?*: "Christ and his apostles roamed the world and dropped in on a rich man and the rich man would not let them in; they dropped in on a poor widow to eat her only heifer, and she let them in. So then He ordered that a barrel of gold roll to the rich man, and he sent a wolf to a widow in order to eat her only heifer, and the widow felt well, while the rich man felt ill." Tolstoy adds that in his version of legislature this story is true, it is what should be, even though "none of what it describes has been or could have been" (26: 308). His new moral character becomes a carrier of a moral bond that liberates and prepares for the reception of "what should be," the miraculous. Tolstoy himself does not interpret the demands of the new miraculous art as a form of restriction. His understanding of freedom may be illustrated in the interpretation of Jesus' words that "the sons are free" (*syny svobodny*). Tolstoy takes these words to imply that every son of God fulfilling his will is not to be bound by "anything human."[27]

Among the postreform jurists and theorists of moral responsibility, Tolstoy befriended a small minority who did not merely debunk or criticize the existing legal structure, but investigated the ethical foundations of law and insisted on moral privacy and the integrity of trial. This is how, in 1885, Tolstoy made friends with Nikolai Grot. Grot wrote one of his earliest, famous essays, "On Moral Responsibility and Juridical Imputation" (1885), inspired by the French translation of Tolstoy's *What I Believe?* and dedicated a published version of his lecture on moral and legal judgment "to the deeply respected author of *A Confession.*" He sent the essay to the writer by way of self-introduction, with precisely this inscription.[28] This work by Grot is one of the earliest exemplars of the moral tradition of legal thought in Russia. It is a remarkable attempt, highly appealing to Tolstoy, to edify professional jurists morally, a move that Grot, trained as a philosopher and psychologist, thought necessary at this crucial moment for the new courts.

The main message delivered by Grot's essay (first delivered as a talk in the Circle of Lawyers of Odessa) was the necessity, from the point of view of empathetic psychology, to discriminate between moral responsibility and legal liability. Grot asserts that the facts of moral life should be taken into consideration as sufficient evidence (Grot 1885: 5). Conscience and moral responsibility manifest themselves in the relativity of human life conditioned by competition between the motives of selfishness and altruism. Grot's definition of mature moral responsibility is a conscientious act of altruism stemming from Nietzsche's anarchic "love of the distant one" (Grot 1885: 7–13), with assumption of responsibility for his personal acts and absolution of any responsibility to the invisible absolute authority or the collective. It is here that we encounter the idea most precious for Tolstoy: Society must accept his justification from a wrongdoer and assist him in finding it by nonretributive means: "to understand is to pardon" [*comprendre c'est pardoner*]; "moral accusation, on the other hand, would be a form of compassion" (Grot 1885: 38). Tolstoy left many marks of approval in his copy of Grot's thin booklet. In his letter to Nikolai Strakhov on May 20, 1887, Tolstoy compared Grot and Soloviev, two of Russia's most promising young philosophers, according to their understanding of moral responsibility and decided that Grot won (64: 48–49). The young philosopher's endorsement of his ideas must have reminded Tolstoy of his failed defense of Shibunin and the reason why it failed: he insisted on understanding the criminal and pardoning him without allowing him to be a morally responsible party.

RHETORIC OF HOLINESS, MORAL ACTION, AND SYNTHESIS OF A RELIGIOUS ART-FORM

The following question arises immediately: how can one be morally in the realm of what should be, in what is estranged from the forms in which we are accustomed to comprehend and appreciate life? Tolstoy asks human experience to bypass its regular mimetic zone and to orient itself to the Christian principle of being, but without imitating Christ. Compared to the concealed God considered in the previous chapters, in art, Tolstoy associates the hidden (*abscons*) with the obscure (*temno*) rather than with the miraculous.[29] One learns from miraculous art, which transmits the revelation of Christ's *razumenie*, but not from miracles in art. Two tales, "Two Old Men" and "Three Elders," both written in 1885, praise unwitting or unpremeditated holiness rather than active planning. In the former, two peasants, Efim and Elisey, set on their pilgrimage to Jerusalem, but Elisey falls behind and never reaches the Holy Land. He is held back by a disaster that struck an unknown Ukrainian family from whom he stops to ask some water to drink and with whom he remains to help until they are healthy. During the Mass at the Lord's Sepulcher in Jerusalem Efim sees Elisey's face. Only upon his return home and after hearing Elisey's story the meaning of the miracle becomes transparent, but the moral gain is Efim's only: the idea of his sainthood frightens Elisey, and he quickly walks away (25: 98). In "Three Elders," prefaced with Matthew 6.7–8, Tolstoy continues his exploration of unpremeditated holiness, again concentrating on the proper manner of the Lord's worship.[30] During his visit at the remote island in the Far North, the Archbishop meets three elders who don't know how to pray correctly. Their jumbled prayer is a blasphemy of the Holy Trinity: "Three of You, three of us, forgive us!" (25: 103). Patiently, the Archbishop teaches them how to say Our Lord in Heaven. Then he departs, and the miracle happens. After his ship, a frail boat carrying the three elders rushes across the waves picking up speed: the elders forgot the correct prayer. Realizing his own impuissance in the face of such an overpowering faith, now clearly sponsored by God, the Archbishop crosses himself and asks the elders to say their version of the prayer on his account too.

In January 1885, Tolstoy was approached by Aleksandra Kalmykova, his colleague on the editorial board of *Tsvetnik*, to co-author a popular biography of Socrates for publication in *The Intermediary*, which was ultimately published, unsigned, as "Socrates, the Greek Teacher" (*"Grecheskii uchitel' Sokrat"*) by *Tsvetnik*. Tolstoy became enthusiastic about the prospect of creating a homiletic portrait of the ideal human being.[31] Thanks to Tolstoy's invasive editing and rewriting, there gradually emerged an image of Socrates- that-should-be, "the skinny righteous odd man" (*khudoi pravednik-chudak*) (26: 453). Tolstoy became so possessive of his idea of Socrates (not a political fighter for Athens independence or a historical revolutionary, as intended by Kalmykova), that he withdrew from the project quite late, probably because the factual rather than edificatory nature of the latter part of Kalmykova's book left less room for acting on his own intentions.[32]

Tolstoy's and Kalmykova's Socrates does nothing less or nothing more than preach Tolstoy's teaching in the public squares of Athens. Socratic *elenchus*, the celebrated philosophical dialectics of creative doubt, in Tolstoy's reproduction, is skillfully whittled down to two incompatible choices, to be picked by a queried party. The selected choice always happens to be a tenet of Tolstoy's belief. Most likely based on lessons given by Socrates in the original *Protagoras* and *Gorgias*, the chapter in Socrates' vita, "What Every Man Ought to Know?"(*Chto nuzhno znat' kazhdomu cheloveku?*), inquires about what makes a greater evil: fever (*likhoradka*) or lack of love from fellow humans (*to, chto tebia vse liudi ne liubiat*) (25: 449). The interrogated party votes for a temporary discomfort of fever in exchange for a comfort in brotherly love.[33] Tolstoy sees a connection between brotherly love, which in Greek means *Phila-Delphia*, and that is to be connected to the celebrated inscription on the portico at Delphi, "know thyself." When asked how to implement his creed in brotherly love in real life, Tolstoy's Socrates responds:

Take for instance this inscription on the temple. What does it say? . . . Does it not speak about what we are discussing—how man should live with other people?

—It says: "Know thyself" and tells you nothing about how people should live.
—Well, maybe it talks about "Knowing thyself." Maybe if we know ourselves, we shall find out the way to live.

—Explain this to us, Socrates,—says one.

—You are aware that I do not know how to explain things—said Socrates,—I can only question, and you *explain this all* to me. Here it is: oxen carry grapes. Do tell: who knows oxen and who knows the grapes? Is it the one who eats beef and the grapes or the one who knows how to run the oxen and the vineyard? (25: 449).

The tale concludes with this summary: "Socrates lived four hundred years before Jesus Christ's coming into the world" (25: 461). From Socrates to Christ and thereon lives the idea of personal sacrifice to truth. In several unfinished fragments of 1885—Christ's Temptation, Christ's Passion, two martyrs' vitae, and the life of Buddha similarly, Tolstoy invited the reader to enter as it were into the prototypical situation of the strife without its passive imitation.[34]

The story, "What Do Men Live By?" caused so much censure and admiration in its first readers because the question about the sufficiency of human life in the world was asked and answered in it by a superhuman authority. Tolstoy based the story on a sparse plot called "Angel" from the collection of legends by Aleksandr Afanasiev (1859), somewhat expanded by a traveling peasant storyteller, Vasily Petrovich Shchegolenok (1806–1880), who visited with Tolstoy in August 1879 and consented with pleasure to summer-long dictation sessions.[35] "What Do Men Live By?" is based on Shchegolenok's page-long parable "Angel On Earth" (*"Angel na zemle"*), itself a partial re-make of the famous "The Life of Saint Martin" circulating since the early centuries of Christianity. It is a story about Archangel Michael's demotion from paradise for his refusal to take the soul of a young woman, a new widow who had just given birth to twin girls.[36] The archangel falls to earth, feels hunger, and goes to work for a cobbler. During his three-year apprenticeship, the disguised Archangel speaks only when asked and smiles just twice. In the third year, the cobbler presses his worker to explain why he smiles so seldom. Michael explains that his first smile was for the two grown orphan girls whom he saw walk by the window alive and who would not have survived without God's mercy. The second smile was due to a rich man's demand for Michael to make him high boots that would stay unbroken after a year of wear. He died the following morning and funeral slippers were sown instead. Shchegolenok's tale ends with the cobbler's request for Michael to prove that he is the Angel he claims to be and to sing The Cherubim anthem from the roof of his home. The Angel obliges, the roof collapses, and the Angel flies up to heaven.

Tolstoy starts his tale in the plain and humble tones of gruff realism sparked by peasant humor and withholds the need to discuss the worker's identity until the very end of the story. In his version, the undercover mission of Michael was possible only thanks to the selfless compassion of the cobbler, Simon. Simon shared his shabby clothes with an anonymous stranger, the wingless and naked Michael, found by Simon near a dilapidated chapel. The slightly tipsy Simon had just failed to scrape enough money to buy a single fur coat for himself and his demanding wife, Matrena, and drank up twenty kopecks out of frustration. At first, Simon walks by the naked stranger. Then he stops and scolds himself, as if bewitched by an imperative to be kind to-ward the unknown man who said that God had punished him. Simon helps against his immediate profit: "And when he thought of his Matrena he felt sad, but when he looked at the stranger and remembered how he had looked up at him at the shrine, his heart was glad" (25: 10).[37] From this point on, mir-acles, coinciding with moments of kindness and love, begin to happen. The grumpy Matrena is similarly bewitched by goodness. She shares emergency reserves of food and clothing, causing Michael to give her his first angelic smile: "When she remembered that he had eaten their last piece of bread and that there was none for tomorrow and thought of the shirt and trousers she had given away, she felt grieved; but when she remembered how he had smiled, her heart was glad" (25: 14).[38]

After "God Sees The Truth But Waits," this story is the first in a series in which Tolstoy lets human time with its worries and constant fear of dispossession be tested by the demands of the higher order. The competition of the Godly and the human may seem unfair. The silent and rarely smiling cobbler Mihaila needs no rest, no clothes, no food, no fresh air, and no money. Year after year, he works twenty-four hours a day, watching the human world and trying to understand why he was mistaken in his kindness in trying to prevent the mother of two orphans from dying. In his re-creation of the moral universe, people amend their threshold of poverty and personal need in the same terms as Tolstoy explained them most fully in *What I Believe?* Pity from an angel to humans, a desire to protect them from grief is not love, as it turns out, but a crime that deprives man from his ability to do what is good, a crime for which, in this story, a heavenly body is cast into a human one. God's love continues only in human deeds. Only when it interrupts its work that evil creeps its way into human relations. In the end, Mihaila, now Michael and in the blinding armor of an Archangel, relates to his hospitable foster family the summary of his illumination into the nature of their human and superhuman task: "I understood that God does not reveal to (men) what each one needs for himself. In truth it is love alone by which they live. He who has love is in God, and God is in him, for God is love."[39] Upon uttering this truth, Michael rises, leaving an awe-stricken Simon in his hut that "stood as before, and there was no one in it but his own family."[40] The illuminated lodger ascends to heaven and accomplishes his mission on earth. Shchegolenok's apocryphal tale allowed no clashes of human and superhuman agency. In Tolstoy's story, the angel learns everything about kindness and love, and about what is Godly, from men.[41]

Tolstoy's parable, "The Godson" ("*Krestnik*") written in February-March 1886, is another vivid illustration of the miraculous dawning of spiritual wisdom in the life of man. The Godson, the allegorical Christian, transgresses his godfather's prohibition and enters the latched room in the palace. The room provides him with an omniscient vision of what can happen to people near and far. Like Michael in the previous story, the Godson is tempted with a possibility to shield humanity from their future mistakes and grief. Overloading his son with eloquent examples that such deterrent kindness brings on more evil than it strives to prevent, the infuriated godfather expels him from home. To return to his [G]odfather's home, the godson needs to become a God's Son literally. The symbolic cost of his return is by now clear. As in the Gospels, the spiritual successor of the Son of God is a robber who converts after he witnesses the act of expiation of sins through forgiveness of traitor and enemy (25: 147–61). "The Godson" establishes a pattern of contagious goodness after witnessing the works of love, but as a work of art this story is neither strong nor original. A more successful and controversial description of moral action in a synthesis of artistic form and religion Tolstoy achieves in the companion written to Nikolai Ge's *The Last Supper*. In 1870 Tolstoy refused to accept Ge's Christ. On March 13, 1870, he observed in his notebook that Ge painted *the civilian Christ* (*grazhdanskii Khristos*) most excellently, but that the divine topic was inappropriate for an event in civil history (48: 118). Like most of his contemporaries before his conversion, Tolstoy had considered Ge's Judas a conflicted messenger of political freedom, and his Christ a hostage in the battle for progress, while the whole group with the apostles nondescript conspirators in a failing cause. Tolstoy entered his disagreements with Ge in a short diary entry, but with his view on Christ and the Eucharist changed, he made the artist his closest ally in 1884.[42]

Even before he started writing stories for *The Intermediary*, Tolstoy engaged in compiling explanatory texts for the religious paintings that he himself picked or that Chertkov found for him as subjects.[43] Strictly speaking, verbal commentary on a painting was not Tolstoy's invention; instead, it was Belinsky's recommendation to adopt the practice of French periodicals for effective visual propaganda. In the 1840s, Belinsky advertised the usefulness of illustrations to a text reproduced from an engraving on a wooden plaque.[44] In the 1860s, when the Itinerant artists concentrated on finding true-to-life forms to transmit their socio-religious message, it became customary for writers to add commentary-review to ensure a correct social reception of an exhibited painting. Nevertheless, what Tolstoy endeavors is innovative. In 1885, Tolstoy writes five textual companions to paintings on religious or ethical subjects. In all five, Tolstoy chooses frozen frames of spiritual anguish when a character faces choices and chooses either Christ or death. Christ as a hero of art returns. In 1874, Ivan Kramskoy, the Itinerant and friend to both Dostoevsky and Tolstoy, rendered his version of "Christ in the Wilderness" ("*Khristos v pustyne*") presenting a seated and very realist Christ, a paradigm of all searching humanity, engrossed in an absorbing mental anguish.[45] In the 1870s, Kramskoy's Christ was better received than Ge's, yet Tolstoy offered his criticism of Kramskoy's trend of Christology through the conversations of Golenishchev and the artist Mikhailov in *Anna Karenina*. Ge's version engages also naturalistic descriptive means by combining them with historical accuracy of the setting and by developing the theme of mystique implanted in Leonardo's legendary mural on the same topic. When the scandal over Ge was at its peak, the atheist Vladimir Stasov, leader of democratic aesthetics, described Ge's painting as an "invented debate of Godforsaken origin" and refused to admit that the painting represented the Eucharist.[46] Saltykov-Shchedrin saw in the painting a "socially significant" event and Christ's self-sacrifice to Judas' fight for Judea's liberation.[47] In his *Diary of A Writer*, an

1873 review of the painting that Ge included in the Itinerants' tour en route to Vienna, Dostoevsky rebuked the compliments awarded to Ge's "regular genre painting" by his sworn ideological foe, Saltykov: "There sits Christ— but is that Christ? This is not the Christ we know. How is it possible that from such an ordinary quarrel of such ordinary people gathered to have supper, such as Mr. Ge depicts, there could arise something so colossal?"[48]

Ge focuses on the moment of tension between the announcement of betrayal and Judas' decision whether or not to leave the room (he is making his way to the exit). The tension is sustained: there is the possibility of a positive or negative outcome, depending on the response not simply of Judas himself but also of Jesus, the disciples, and the spectator. All of these responses and possible outcomes, whatever they are and from wherever they stem, will be both individual and interconnected. Judas' figure, in a dark hooded cloak that he is throwing over himself, ready to step out, is shown with his head bent down, invisible to us, his back to the brooding Christ. Christ is also looking down, but he is not majestically serene; he is tormented. The disciples, in different states of perplexity, do not engage in debates amongst themselves as in Leonardo's mural, but watch Judas leave. Tolstoy was among those few able to grasp the depth of Ge's understanding of the Gospel conflict and to accept its profound novelty in the revelation of the Eucharist through the visibly mundane. In 1884, Tolstoy expressed a tardy appreciation of Ge's Eucharist in his friendship with the painter and in the collaboration with him in the genre of textual commentary on paintings with a religious subject. Like Ge, Tolstoy does not take for granted that any preordained meanings may be embedded in Christ. Here, as in the rewriting of the Gospels, Christ's martyrdom, his Passion, was neither beautiful nor a miracle; it was the laborious struggle of a man tortured by senseless tormentors and by the conflict within himself, and it had to be represented as such. Consequently, according to Tolstoy, Christ's mission had to be reproduced with all the intensity and unpredictability, the open-endedness of a man's struggle for faith and salvation.[49] Countering Dostoevsky, the Christ whom we know for Tolstoy, is the Christ who reveals himself only through the deeds of his teaching. On March 2 or 3, 1884, Tolstoy wrote Ge a letter of affirmation in response to his new sketches of the Passion scene: "we are living through the period, not of Christ's preaching or his resurrection, but the period of the crucifixion. I won't believe for anything that He was resurrected in the body, but I shall never lose the belief that He will be resurrected in His teaching. Death is birth, and we have lived to see the death of his teaching, therefore birth is already close at hand" (63: 160).[50]

Tolstoy's "A Companion to Ge's 'The Last Supper'," ("*K kartine Ge 'Tainaia vecheria'*") (25: 139–43) was written in the course of a week, January 16–23, 1886, and aimed at no less than "resurrect[ing] Christ in His teaching" without defiling or beautifying his body and with achieving a living synthesis of art and religion. Only a synthesis of this kind would contain a unitary concept of "beauty-truth-goodness," wherein Christ is the embodied meaning of life, the Eucharist of brotherly love. To Tolstoy, Ge's painting illustrated the cavils of contemporary religious reception, namely that society considered Christ an incomplete answer to its demands. He was motivated by criticism of Ge's Christ as historically inauthentic, apolitically determined, not conventionally beautiful, and, therefore, unrecognizable, and "strange." Tolstoy's commentary harmonizes both his interpretation of the Last Supper in his actual revision of the Gospels in 1880–1881 and Ge's painting itself, which was tainted by its politicized reception.

According to Tolstoy, the center of conflict, of attraction and repulsion within the painting, is Jesus' Eucharist as love. This is dramatized by Judas' failure to return to Jesus and by the failure of John the Evangelist and Peter Simon to understand why Jesus lets Judas go. The next focus for Tolstoy is the struggle within Judas himself between pride and an impulse to seek Christ's forgiveness. In this description, Tolstoy diverts from Ge's original and voices the silent dialogue between Judas (who in Ge is only a blot of darkness) and Jesus: "Judas rose to his feet, picked up his clothes, threw them over his shoulders and made the first step, but his eyes are fixed on the face of his saddened Teacher. There is still time. . . . Jesus is reclined, leaning on his elbow, not looking up, but he sees and knows what is going on in Judas's heart and is waiting, suffering for him: He feels compassion for the Son of Destruction" (25: 142). Tolstoy exaggerates Ge's version of Judas' difficult move, his move against Christ's legacy of love, and Christ's forgiveness in the name of that legacy. In the same vein, he highlights the unwitting acts of treachery of the other eleven disciples, who yield to the temptation of blaming one another. In this manner, Tolstoy creates a sophisticated version of the Eucharist in which private timings of individual choice are entering "eternal time," a communion in love. His editing of the painting results in an insertion into the canvas of a dramatized moment of struggle between understanding of the main demand of life, which needs no specifically recognizable shape, defies it, even—and unreasonable conviction, the fatal mistake, the satanic delusion, which, clinging to the safety of one assumed truth, drives the soul to destruction. In the final variant of his commentary, Tolstoy places one part of his explanatory text above the painting, captioning it with a reference to John 13. It is a retelling of Tolstoy's translation of John ending on verse 35 (love of one another is what distinguishes them as his disciples) out of the canonical 38 verses. The lower part is the exegesis of Ge's painting proper. The religious censors found Ge and Tolstoy's co-authorship with John blasphemous.[51]

THE SACRIFICIAL MADMAN AND
TELEOLOGICAL KNIGHT

Even people who were the closest to Tolstoy voiced objections against putting his superb art in the employ of religious propaganda. The steadfast reasoning in *What Then Must We Do?* is compared by Chertkov unfavorably to
"What Men Live By." In a letter to Tolstoy in 1885 Chertkov calls "What
Men Live By" a success story because it gently elicits "penetrating thoughts
into the very core of the reader" while promoting his message. *What Then
Must We Do?*, meanwhile, produces different impressions because its judgments "are not convincing. As soon as there a slight imprecision, understatement, all this catches the eye unwittingly and arouses prejudice against the essay's major idea" (85: 154). Tolstoy insisted that the only understatement he
committed was in the presentation of the white-gloved lackeys at his home.
His overstatement concerned his inclusion into the group of dead and unim-
peachable classics. Tolstoy knew he had to give up the attractive realm of the
parable that served him well and again focus on man's internal space. The
conflicts of this internal sphere developing, to borrow Coleridge's phrase, out
of "anxious spirit of minute teleology" will become the primary interest of his
art after 1885.[52]

Tolstoy's daily tortures were many. Here is one characteristic day on June
19/July 1, 1884: "Cleaned my room in Seryozha's presence. A merchant came
to buy a strider. I went back on my word. 250 rubles. The falsity of my situation is evil" (49: 105). Already in accordance with his earlier design, when
one transcends the vile reality one need not ascribe seriousness to household
combat, nor ought one do battle against the oppression of the environment
with its base morality. "How Much Land Does a Man Need" was in part autobiographical in that it connected the question of property with mortality.
Tolstoy heard the legend from the Bashkirs near Samara where he went to buy
land back in 1869 and where on the way to the location he had experienced
his legendary Arzamas horror. He first rented the estate in the Bashkir steppes
and then purchased it. The family took practically annual trips to the steppes
ever since. Tolstoy's self-identification with Pakhom's avarice is surely a result of his owning too much and his keen sense about the value of landed
property. In the early years of his marriage, in December 1864, he wrote to
Ivan I. Orlov, manager of the Tolstoy's Nikol'skoe-Viazemskoe property, also
near Tula: "I am in great need of money. You have set a price too high for the
dung. See at a cheaper cost but make sure that it sells for sure. Don't miss the
time for the sale of rye. Take it to the mill and keep available. I intend to sell
it wholesale at the best price . . ." (90: 226). There were additional exciting
instructions about the cows and the calves and the art of husbandry. Tolstoy

was not a foe of property as late as in the 1870s when, much in the spirit of Adam Smith, he wrote that it helps to propagate activity because it sustains *energeia*. It is roughly in the period of 1883–1886 that things have changed, and everything associated with property owning came to define evil. On January 1, 1883, Tolstoy arrived at a new epiphany: free productive labor brings joy, but property protected by violence engenders slave labor and suffering (49: 60). Simultaneously with the writing of "How Much Land Does a Man Need," Tolstoy reviewed the work by peasant Timofei Bondarev titled "Love of Work or the Triumph of the Agrarian" (*Trudoliubie ili torzhestvo zemledel'tsa*) glorifying the labor of plowing and sowing. Tolstoy's logos spermatikos was thus literally becoming a religious law of labor like the Jewish Sabbath, the Christian fasting, or a quintuple praying in Islam. In the review, Tolstoy names the "breadly labor" (*khlebnyi trud*) a prophylactic means against idleness and a source of saving humankind (25: 463–75). The problem with his Pakhom was then that he confused working on land with buying land that he justified by special family interests.

In "Colloquy of Idlers" (*Beseda dosuzhikh liudei*) (1886), written as a preface to the parable "Roam the World While There is Light," people argue whether family interests should be sacrificed to the life with God (26: 246–49). Although most of them agree on the necessity of this sacrifice, they also agree that the plan is untenable in the real world. The chapter of Socrates' vita that Tolstoy wrote for Kalmykova's biography of Socrates portrayed a selfless man without a selfish family interest, who refuses to take pay for his lessons, to the utter dissatisfaction of the money-obsessed Xantippe who needed it to buy food for Socrates' children (25: 441). Ivan the fool, Tolstoy's beloved unselfish madman from the eponymous tale of the same year, is blessed with a wife who in oblivion of the sniggering environment chooses to be "a fool as well" and, like her husband the fool, live without money (25: 129).

In an 1888 letter to Nikolai Grot, which appears to be the result of an ongoing debate, Tolstoy delivers a tirade against spiritual traitors who adjust the demands of their moral activity to the material conditions of the daily grind.[53] In order to choose oneself correctly, insists Tolstoy, one will inevitably transgress most immediate loyalties. Christ left his immediate family and does not, according to Tolstoy, require any sacrifice other than abandoning delusion, for the life is the spirit of logos (24: 205). Tolstoy's anarchic individualism dictates that one should be prepared to sacrifice all temporal attachments if they represent lies and delusions and impede with the main priority. The call of the main purpose overrides the existing code of ethics, which is made null and void by what Kierkegaard, in 1885 Tolstoy's soon to be discovered inspiration, calls "teleological suspension of justice" or "teleological suspension of the ethical."[54]

Tolstoy's family did not share his excitement about this individual *telos*. He could not comprehend their selfish reasons and treacherous resistance. In May 1884, Tolstoy speaks with God at night and prays that He converts his wife (*chtoby Bog ee obratil*) and then scolds himself on the naiveté and revolting absurdity of such requests (49: 94–95). In June 1884, Tolstoy recommends to an unknown addressee to break free out of the family prison (63: 175–76). In a letter to Chertkov (July 24, 1884), Tolstoy describes the treachery of the moral monster who shares his bed: "On one occasion this year I was lying in bed beside my wife. She wasn't asleep, nor was I, and I suffered painfully from the awareness of my own loneliness in the family because of my beliefs, and the fact that they all in my eyes see the truth but turn away from it. I suffered both for them and for myself . . ." (85: 81).[55] During one of the most heated family scenes in December 1885, when Lev Nikolaevich announced his need to depart, Sophia Andreevna intimated that he was mad (85: 297). The newly insinuated madness translated into Tolstoy's vacillations among the titles of the future *The Death of Ivan Il'ich*, which included, almost interchangeably, *The Memoirs of a Madman*, *Death of the Judge*, and the *Diary of a Sane One*.[56] Tolstoy's subsequent gift of the story to Sophia Andreevna, who was publishing a new edition of his works, is a dubious symbolic gesture. The diaries of Tolstoy for the years 1884–1885 and his letters to Chertkov are rife with reports of self-torture, the imagery of trials, and the heavy cross. They recount desperation at the discovery that his family would not share his new spiritual strivings, that he is hated by the son Sergey and by his aunt Alexandrine Tolstaya for his faith: "as if my life were at their expense; the more I am alive, the deadlier they are . . ." (8/20 May 1884, 49: 91). The unsent letter to Chertkov (December 1885) arrested by Sofia Andreevna depicts the climax of Tolstoy's despair. He explains it by his failure to stay in a relationship with God, which he "searches for and misses" and affirms that his life is no better than the life of the people close to him from whom he attempts to alienate himself (85: 294–96).

The opposition of his family was likely to remind Tolstoy of the writings of Kierkegaard, with which he had just become acquainted and of which he became instantly enamored through the introduction of their mutual Danish admirer, Peter Hansen. Tolstoy read Kierkegaard in German translation most likely no earlier than 1885, but when he did, he immediately recognized in the Dane's leap of faith by means of self-choice toward affirmation a passionate revival of Luther's and Kant's project. In Kierkegaard's protest against this "greatest hazard of all, losing the self" Tolstoy found a powerful ally.[57] Tolstoy's understanding of individual *telos* is in agreement with the radically anti-Hegelian idea of Kierkegaard's *Fear and Trembling*, that the ethical component in the individual's life is established in a self-controlled and socially unmediated relation to God as a lonely feat of fright and courage.[58] Kierkegaard and Tolstoy see the meaning of individual moral action in stepping outside universal morality, of suspending its justice, and of last-minute catastrophic acquittal in the face of God. The pursuit of *telos* is an act of conscious resignation of faithfulness to the universal that does not require absolute faith, but that without such an infinite resignation, there can be no faith altogether.[59] Therefore, both make a rigid distinction between the religious order and the ethical order that govern the life of society. The latter they call a "sordid universal" of a multitude, which needs to be bypassed for the sake of establishing a direct relationship with the absolute, the *All*, and which, by definition, is in contrast to the universal.[60] In Kierkegaard's description, the religious *telos* of transgression is a lonely feat of fright and courage, as exemplified in Abraham's sacrifice: "Faith is namely this paradox that the individual is higher than the universal . . . the single individual isolates himself as higher than the universal . . . the single individual as the single individual stands in an absolute relation to the absolute."[61]

Tolstoy understood the mission of Abraham in the same fashion as Kierkegaard. In *What I Believe?* he placed Abraham's personal sacrifice (*zhertva lichnosti*) on the highest scale, comparable only to the sacrifice offered by Christ: "They can pray to God and they can take communion, yet they are appalled at Abraham's cruelty! . . . They feel incapable to sacrifice their own son, as did Abraham, while Abraham would not even think twice whether to sacrifice his son to God—who was providing for him the sole meaning and goodness of his life. Likewise, neither Christ nor his disciples could fail to sacrifice their lives to others because in that was the sole meaning and goodness of life" (23: 406).

It is apparent and indeed appalling that Tolstoy disregards the difference between his own son's life being sacrificed to the call of absolute faith and one's own life being sacrificed for the anonymous sons. This disregard looks offensive, but Tolstoy's hidden purpose *was* to cause offense. In this outburst, Tolstoy pursues the same amplified role of a loner driven by a higher religious purpose that is not yet shared by the world clinging to the convenience of their quasi-religious views: "How shall I stay alone in this human world which does not believe in Christ?" (23: 384). That Abraham would keep his *telos* in secret from his family commanded Tolstoy's respect after his own thwarted attempts at an explanation with Sophia Andreevna, daughter Tatiana, and son Sergey. It is not coincidental that in their stress on exceptionality of individual *telos* Kierkegaard and Tolstoy find an inspiring example in Socrates who sacrificed his life to his combat with the communal morality for the sake of his eternal consciousness. Working his way toward the end, a task so elegantly discharged by Socratic trial, now he had to be transformed into a creative decision. As such, the Socratic break with the past was inspiring, but, from the artistic standpoint, too radical and evasive to demonstrate its affective potential. As Kierkegaard explained by citing Aristotle's criticism of Socrates' evasive virtue and self-sufficiency of consciousness, "being-in-and-for-itself as the being-in-and-for-itself for thought . . . made the individual alien to the immediacy in which he had previously lived."[62]

The years 1885–1886 in which *The Death of Ivan Il'ich* was finished Tolstoy spent in struggles to define his primary duty and Kant again became relevant. Kant also spoke of philistine cowardice and of life according to legitimized morals. Kant saw liberation in standing trial before a tribunal of conscience rather than in a secretive flight from the family explored by Bunyan. "Every human being has a conscience and finds himself observed, threatened, and, in general, kept in awe (respect coupled with fear) by an internal judge."[63] What is the metaphysical component of everyday life? It is the ability to be one's own judge, impute, hold court, accuse, and condemn one's own inadequate behavior. Kant's chapter from which the above quotation is taken is fittingly titled "On a Human Being's Duty to Himself as His Own Innate Judge." It is at this stage that Tolstoy finally holds on to Kant's insistence of wearing one's "new man" and bearing an "ought" in a manner that is unconditional. These were the complex undercurrents of *The Death of Ivan Il'ich*, Tolstoy's unquestionable post-conversion masterpiece.

NOTES

1. N. N. Gusev, *Tolstoy. Materialy k biografii. 1870–1881*, 585.

2. Ivan Aksakov, "O rasskaze L. N. Tolstogo 'Chem liudi zhivy.' K. S. Aksakov, I. S. Aksakov," *Literaturnaia kritika* (Moscow: Sovremennik, 1981), 281.

3. Fedor Buslaev, "Znachenie romana v nashe vremia," *O literature. Issledovaniia. Stat'i* (Moscow: Khudozhestvennaia literatura, 1990), 461–72, quotation, 464–65.

4. Boris Nikolaevich Chicherin, *Nauka i religiia* (Moscow: Tipografiia Martynova, 1879). Tolstoy made a few negative remarks about the book only on January 24, 1894 (52: 109, 254, 352) and then in February 1901 (54: 88–89).

5. Chertkov and Obolensky, who acted as Tolstoy's publishing agents for *Russkoe bogatstvo*, suggested he take the word "Christian" out of the title. Tolstoy reluctantly agreed (85: 155–56).

6. Horace quoted from Hazard Adams, ed. *Critical Theory Since Plato* (San Diego/New York/Chicago: Harcourt, Brace, Jovanovich, 1971), 75.

7. For a more extensive background of this caricature placed on the front cover of the current study, see Michael A. Denner, "'Be not afraid of greatness . . .' Lev Tolstoy and Celebrity." Forthcoming in *Popular Culture*, 2009. The caricature is reproduced on page 3 of Denner's essay. Taking the occasion, I thank Professor Denner for referring me to the plate with this caricature in Vladimir C. Mikhnevich, *Nashi*

znakomye (St. Petersburg: Graficheskaia masterskaia Rudometova, 1884), plate no. 50. I also thank Professor Denner for providing me with a high definition scan of this image.

8. See chapter 3 of this book.

9. See "Expostulation and Reply" and "The Tables Turned" in William Wordsworth, *Complete Poetical Works* (Oxford: Oxford University Press, first publ. 1936), 377.

10. "Soderzhanie rechi, proiznesennoi na vysshikh zhenskikh kursakh professorom V. S. Solovievym 13 marta 1881 goda." Vladimir Soloviev. *Izbrannye proizvedeniia* (Rostov-on-Don: Feniks, 1998), 536–41, especially 537–38.

11. See Tolstoy's essay from the 1860s, "Progress and a Definition of Education" (*Progress i opredelenie obrazovaniia*) (8: 325–55).

12. For a detailed account of Tolstoy's involvement with *The Intermediary*, see Robert Otto, *Publishing for the People. The Firm Posrednik*. Unpublished PhD Dissertation. University of Wisconsin Press, 1983.

13. *The New Oxford Annotated Bible*. NT, 18.

14. For an incisive interpretation of this tale, see Gary R. Jahn, "Tolstoj's Vision of the Power of Death and 'How Much Land Does a Man Need?'" in *Slavic and East European Journal*, vol. 22, No. 4 (1978): 442–53.

15. The story, perhaps influenced by Herodotus, was among those for which Tolstoy later relinquished copyrights to his wife, S. A. Tolstaya (84: 81–82). Written in February-March 1886, it was published in the thick journal *Russkoe bogatstvo* (1886) and later in Tolstoy's *Intermediary* edition with his other tales. On April 6, 1886, Professor Storozhenko of Moscow University gave a public reading of the story to a packed and enthusiastic young auditorium which broke into big applause. See L. D. Gromova-Opulskaya, *Lev Nikolaevich Tolstoy. Materialy k biografii s 1886 po 1892 god* (Moscow: Nauka, 1979), 24.

16. "Okonchanie 'Malorossiiskoi legendy Sorok let iszdannoi Kostomarovym v 1881 g." (26: 114–18). Concluding Kostomarov's legend in April 1886, Tolstoy planned to publish it abroad, through *The Intermediary* press in Russian, English, French, and German. The plan was not realized (26: 697). The tale, heavily excised, was first published in a collection of popular fiction in Penza, 1899.

17. A. N. Afanasiev, *Narodnyia russkiia legendy*, ed. S. K. Shambinago (Moscow: Sovremennye problemy, 1914), 182–86. Tolstoy worked with one of the first editions of the Legends (1859). In 1877–1879, Tolstoy's acquaintance and scholar Nikolai Tikhonravov published the Russian version of *Gesta Romanorum* (Rimskiia Dieianiia), a collection of picaresque and didactic Christian legends popular in the late Renaissance and Baroque Europe from the Polish seventeenth-century original. A number of Tikhonravov's legends from *Gesta Romanorum* had been included by the famous collector Afanasiev in his collection of oral Russian versions of the same legends. *Rimskiia dieianiia (Gesta Romanorum)* (St.-Petersburg: Obshchestvo liubitelei drevnei slovesnosti, 1877–1878). Tikhonravov's edition is to this day the only complete extant Russian variant of *Gesta Romanorum*. Tolstoy's close association with Tikhonravov during these years revolved around the newly discovered legends that Tikhonravov was collecting and publishing. See Tolstoy's references to Tikhonravov

in his Notebooks (48: 252, 304). In addition to being the editor and publisher, Tikhonravov was also a serious textological scholar. Since 1884, Tolstoy was also friendly with Alexander Pypin, another prominent student of old Russian tales and folklore. See Tolstoy's letter to Pypin of January 10, 1884, on truth and truthfulness in Turgenev's art (63: 149–52). The Western title of the tale is "Of Too Much Pride; And How the Proud Are Frequently Compelled to Endure Some Notable Humiliation." *Gesta Romanorum*, trans. from the Latin by Charles Swan, revised, Wynnard Hooper (New York: AMS Press, 1970), 100–06. The vulgate title of the same legend is "De superbia nimiia et quomodo superbi ad humilitatem maximam seperveniunt; satis notabile" (ibid.). See Tale LVII in Tikhonravov edition of *Rimskiia dieianiia*, 69–89. The same legend, "Orgueil et présumption de l'empereur Jovinien" and its Russian variant, published by Tikhonravov, "On the Proud Caesar Evinian (*O gordom tsesare Eviniane*) must have been Tolstoy's source also.

18. Vsevolod M. Garshin, "Skazanie o gordom Aggee (Pereskaz starinnoi legendy)," Garshin, *Sochineniia* (Moscow/Leningrad: GIKhl, 1963), 303–11. See also the discussion of Tolstoy's hagiography and its dramatic reworking in the Aggei legend in Margaret Ziolkowski's classic work, *Hagiography and Modern Russian Literature* (Princeton: Princeton University Press, 1988), 114–16 and 221–24.

19. Translation quoted from "Dramatization of the Legend About Aggeus." Leo Tolstoy, *Plays in Three Volumes. Volume One 1856–1886*, trans. Marvin Kantor and Tanya Tulchinsky. Intro. Andrew B. Wachtel (Evanston, Ill.: Northwestern University Press, 1994), 1: 155.

20. "Psychopathic Characters on the Stage." Sigmund Freud, *Writings on Art and Literature*, eds. Werner Hamacher and David E. Wellbery. Foreword by Neil Hertz (Stanford: Stanford University Press, 1997), 87–94; quotation, 88–91.

21. Such is a critique of Tolstoy by Reinhold Niehbuhr: "It is . . . impossible to construct a socio-moral policy from this religio-moral policy of Jesus as, for instance, Tolstoy attempted in his rejection of jails and other forms of social punishment." See Reinhold Niebuhr, *An Interpretation of Christian Ethics* (San Francisco: Harper and Row, 1987), 28.

22. The court chronicle section of *Moskovskie vedomosti* published minutes of the trial. *Moskovskie vedomosti*, November 5–13, 1882 (nos. 307, 312, 313, 314). See also 63: 154.

23. *Moskovskie vedomosti*. November 5, 1882, no. 307, 4.

24. *Moskovskie vedomosti*. November 11, 1882, no. 313, 4–5.

25. See Tolstoy's Diary of 11/23 March 1884 about an intended casual visit with Mel'nitsky (49: 66–67). In October 1884 Tolstoy communicated with Mel'nitsky through Sophia Andreevna, then on a trip in Moscow. Mel'nitsky left her a letter for Tolstoy with a request of either securing a professional defense attorney for his father or (preferably) of Tolstoy's own defense of his father at his father's retrial in District Court on October 18, 1884 (83: 437, 439). Mel'nitsky's and Tolstoy's friendship, firmed wholly on religious grounds, lasted a long time. See Tolstoy's notebook of November-December 1896 (53: 296–97).

26. "The Tale of Ivan the Fool and his Two Brothers, Simon the Warrior, Taras the Fat-Belly, the Dumb Sister Malania, the Old Devil and the Three Demons" (*Skazka*

ob Ivane durake i ego dvukh brat'iakh, Semyone Voine, tarase Briukhane, nemoi de-vkemalan'e, i o starom d'iavole i trekh cherteniatakh . . .) (25: 115–38).

27. From a letter to Aleksandr Buturlin, (February 19, 1884; 63: 155).

28. Nikolai Iakovlevich Grot, *O nravstvennoi otvetstvennosti i iuridicheskoi vme-niaemosti* (Odessa: Tipografiia Odesskogo vestnika, 1885). See the description of this item in Tolstoy's library. *Biblioteka Tolstogo*, I (1), 225. Further references to this essay appear in text.

29. In the drafts to Chapter XXVII of *What is Art?*, *La messe noire* and *Là-bas* by Huysmans and the prose of Mallarmé are reproached for their meaning not only being hidden (*abscons*), but also obscure (*temno*) (30: 366). See also Richard Gustafson's discussion of the later Tolstoy's *abscons* in entries of his 1904 Diary (55: 51). Gustafson, 93.

30. For an in-depth explanation of this tale through Tolstoy's politics of "doing nothing" see Michael Denner, "Tolstoyan Nonaction: The Advantage of Doing Nothing." *Tolstoy Studies Journal*, vol. XIII (2001): 8–22.

31. See Tolstoy's positive comments about Kalmykova's work in his letters to her and Urusov (63: 215, 220, 225, 248) and to Chertkov (85: 174, 197, 207).

32. N. N. Gusev, *Tolstoy. Materialy k biografii. 1881–1885* (Moscow: Nauka, 1970), 425. The book was published with the numerous emendations that he had already entered. Tolstoy wrote part of Chapter IV on the life in the family and probably Chapter VII, on brotherhood (25: 429–61). See Gusev, *Materialy k biografii. 1881–1885*, 427.

33. Famous passages in *Gorgias* (493d–497a) compare good or bad lives to conditions of health and sickness. Plato, 275–79.

34. See "Iskusheniia Gospoda nashego Iisusa Khrista" (25: 26–27), "Stradaniia gospoda nashegoIisusa Khrista" (25: 114), "Stradaniia sviatogo muchenika Feodora, i Pergii Pamfiliiskoi" (25: 462), "May 18. Stradaniia sviatykh Petra, Dionisiia, Andreiia, Pavla i Khristiny" (25: 538–39), "Siddarta, prozvannyi Buddoi" (25: 540–43).

35. See Tolstoy's letter to Stasov, of August 2–3, 1879 (62: 494–95) and editorial commentary to "What Do Men Live By?" with drafts of the story (25: 665–70). In addition to "What Do Men Live by?" Shchegolenok inspired the writing of several remarkable tales in 1885: "The Two Old Men" (*Dva starika*), "The Three Elders" (*Tri startsa*), and others.

36. See the variants of Tolstoy's first draft of the story, "Angel On Earth" (25: 544–51) and a transcription of Shchegolenok's story (25: 666).

37. Translation, slightly amended, is from *The Portable Tolstoy*. ed. John Bayley (London/New York: Penguin Books, 1978), 488.

38. *The Portable Tolstoy*, 492.

39. *The Portable Tolstoy*, 504–5.

40. *The Portable Tolstoy*, 505.

41. In several articles, Gary Jahn demonstrated Tolstoy's avoidance of miracles in his thinking and in his later art. However, where his realism bounds on popular art or is cast in folk genres, as Jahn shows, Tolstoy admits direct comparisons of his heroes' conversions to Christ's Passion and spiritual resurrection. Gary Jahn, "A Note on Miracle Motifs in the Later Works of Lev Tolstoy." Reprinted in *Tolstoy's Short Fiction*, ed. Michael R. Katz (New York: Norton & Co, 1991), 481–86.

42. Their passionate friendship began in the course of Ge's work on his famous portrait of Tolstoy finished in the Moscow home of the writer in 1884.

43. See Tolstoy's correspondence with Chertkov on the issue in June 1885 (85: 235–37; 254).

44. Vissarion G. Belinsky, "O knizhnoi illiustratsii." *Literaturnoe Nasledstvo.* vol. 57 (Moscow: Nauka, 1951), 329–30.

45. On Kramskoy, see George Heard Hamilton, *The Art and Architecture of Russia* (New Haven and London: Yale University Press, 1983), 376–78. In the early 1880s, Kramskoy painted another controversial work, "Inconsolable Grief" (*Bezuteshnoe gore*), showing a woman in inconsolable mourning over a lost child or husband and thus putting immortality and religious consolation into doubt.

46. V. V. Stasov, "Akademicheskaia vystavka 1863 g" [1864]. V. V. Stasov, *Izbrannye sochineniia v trekh tomakh. Zhivopis', skul'ptura, muzyka* (Moscow: Gosudarstvennoe izdatel'stvo Iskusstvo, 1952), 113–22. Quoted passage, page 119.

47. Mikhail E. Saltykov-Shchedrin, "Nasha obshchestvennaia zhizn'. Kartina N. N. Ge Tainaia vecheria." (Our Social Life. The Last Supper, a Painting by N. N. Ge). M. Saltykov Shchedrin. *Polnoe sobranie sochinenii*, 6: 148–55.

48. See Dostoevsky, *A Writer's Diary* (Chapter IX for 1873) (21: 68–76). Quoted passage is from the translation by Kenneth Lantz. See Dostoevsky, *A Writer's Diary* in 2 vols, trans. Kenneth Lantz. Intro. Gary Saul Morson (Evanston, Ill.: Northwestern UP, 1994), 1: 215–16. See other criticism of Ge by Dostoevsky in the notebooks to *The Devils* in Complete Works (Dostoevsky, 11: 192; 12: 354). Dostoevsky's Underground Man ridiculed Saltykov-Shchedrin's praise of Ge's painting (5: 109, 383). On the details of this polemic, see Inessa Medzhibovskaya, "On Moral Movement and Moral Vision: The Last Supper in Russian Debates," *Comparative Literature* 56, no. 1 (winter 2004): 23–53.

49. Tolstoy confessed to Chertkov that "his own idea about Christ's last night with his disciples, matured by the time, fully coincided with what N. N. Ge had conveyed in his painting" (85: 320).

50. Translation quoted from R. F. Christian's *Tolstoy's Letters*, 2: 367.

51. See Tolstoy's 1886 correspondence with Chertkov, esp. 85: 319–20. For an expanded discussion of Tolstoy and Ge collaboration, see Medzhibovskaya, "On Moral Movement and Moral Vision." Tolstoy's text appeared for the first time in Chertkov's complete English edition of Tolstoy's forbidden works.

52. S. T. Coleridge, *The Collected Works. Logic*, ed. J. B. de J. Jackson. Bollingen Series LXXV (Princeton: Princeton University Press, 1981), 75.

53. Grot is attacked by Tolstoy because he confuses priorities. If spiritual survival is at stake, abandoning family and material effects should not be an obstacle. See Tolstoy's letter to Grot of July 15, 1888 (64: 179–80).

54. Kierkegaard, *Fear and Trembling* in Søren Kierkegaard, *Fear and Trembling. Repetition*, ed. and trans., Howard V. Hong and Edna H. Hong, with Intro and Notes (Princeton, N.J.: Princeton UP, 1983), 54.

55. Quoted from Christian's translation, *Tolstoy's Letters*, 2: 373.

56. Tolstoy's doubts about the title for *The Death of Ivan Il'ich* are recorded in the diary (March 30 to May 9, 1884; passim 49: 75–89).

57. Søren Kierkegaard, *The Sickness Unto Death*, ed. and trans. H. V. Hong and E. H. Hong (Princeton, N.J.: Princeton University Press, 1980), 32–33.

58. Kiekegaard, *Fear and Trembling*, 55–56.

59. Kierkegaard defines faith as a competing struggle between faithfulness to the universal and individual *telos*. See *Fear and Trembling*, 54. See also Kierkegaard, *Either/Or*. 2 vols., ed. and trans. Howard V. Hong and Edna H. Hong (Princeton, N.J.: Princeton UP, 1987), 1: 387–431.

60. On Tolstoy's idea of self-separation for the sake of reunification, see Gustafson, 94–95.

61. *Fear and Trembling*, 55–56. In *Sickness unto Death, Concluding Unscientific Postscript*, and "The Balance Between the Aesthetic and the Ethical in the Development of Personality" of *Either/Or*, Kierkegaard develops the idea of despair as the welcome and necessary stage before a leap to the ethical stage.

62. Søren Kierkegaard, *The Concept of Irony With Continual Reference to Socrates. Notes of Schelling's Berlin Lectures*, ed. and trans. Howard V. Hong and Edna H. Hong (Princeton, N.J.: Princeton UP, 1989), 228.

63. Immanuel Kant. *The Metaphysics of Morals*, 188–89.

Chapter Eleven

The Death of Ivan Il'ich

MIXED IDENTITIES, THE LOST DIARY, AND THE SOUL THAT ESCAPED

It is usually believed that the immediate impetus for the writing of Tolstoy's most famous novella was the death in 1881 of his neighbor in the Tula province, former member of the Kharkov and then of Tula District Court, Ivan Il'ich Mechnikov.[1] Ivan Il'ich had two other brothers, Il'ia Il'ich, the famous scientist working on projects of longevity and the less famous brother, a member of the radical intelligentsia, Lev Il'ich Mechnikov. The latter was infuriated at how Tolstoy portrayed what he believed was the career and death of his late brother Ivan, whose soul, in the words of Lev Il'ich, was turned into "a square of poorly polished parquet."[2] There is no reason to disbelieve that Mechnikov's death bore some relation to Tolstoy's story, and Tolstoy supposedly did admit in a conversation with the journalist Sergey Spiro in 1909 of "some relation" of his story to the death of that "nice and quiet man."[3] According to his sister-in-law Tatiana Kuz'minskaia's record of her stay at Yasnaya Poliana, Tolstoy "fell in love" around 1864–1868 with his neighbor Mechnikov, then still a rather young man in his late thirties (26: 680).

Anatoly Koni, who won the case for the terrorist Vera Zasulich in 1878, reports an interesting and unnoticed detail about the real-life Ivan Mechnikov, namely his reluctance to get involved, so that an unpopular or trying case could be shoved onto another colleague. Ivan Il'ich Mechnikov was one of those friends who turned his back on Koni after his fall from grace for his involvement in the defense of the radicals.[4] These character traits are true for the fictional Ivan Il'ich Golovin, the protagonist in Tolstoy's novella as we know him. Lest his story be confused with social commentary or direct-hit satire, Tolstoy changed the original title, "Death of The Judge" (*Smert' sud'i*), to delete any hint of a specific prototype. However, the legal connection does not stop with Mechnikov alone. One of the chief players in the enforcement of the legal reform was Aleksandr Vasilievich Golovnin (also spelled Golovin) who wrote memoirs about the reform that Tolstoy knew quite well (48: 467).[5] Golovachev was the name involved in the famous Mel'nitsky embezzlement trial, in which Tolstoy took great interest. The "Me'vinsky case" is mentioned at the beginning of the story. Furthermore, in 1884 Tolstoy's neighbors were the Golovins (Iakov Ivanovich and Olga Sergeevna), a jovial, merry, and still happy young couple who loved the good life and liked to laugh exactly like Tolstoy's characters.[6]

It is already obvious that the death of his neighbor-the-judge was an additional, but largely coincidental influence; the multiple confusing coincidences illustrate Tolstoy's desire to make Ivan Il'ich inconspicuous and ubiquitous, so that enough of Ivan Il'ich is seen in everyone. Tolstoy himself had a great deal of Ivan Il'ich in him. Tolstoy's fictional Ivan Il'ich was born in the series of unfinished dramatic satires Tolstoy commenced in 1856, "The Noble Family" ("*Dvorianskoe semeistvo*") (7: 152–63) and "Man of Affairs"("*Prakticheskii chelovek*") (7: 164–68). In both plays, Ivan Il'ich is an unhealthy and unsavory character, a scheming hanger-on in his forties. The fictional scoundrel Ivan Il'ich later acquired wider literary fame in the characters of the bureaucrats of the postreform Russia, who like distractions and a game of whist but dislike getting involved in cases with moral implications. These characters are Dostoevsky's Ivan Il'ich Pralinsky of the story "The Stupid Joke" (1862) and Chernyshevsky's Ivan Il'ich, the high official from his last novel, *Prolog* (1871). Tolstoy's vita of Ivan Il'ich is famous for its satiric, even vicious, assaults on the obtuse selfishness and parasitic life of members of Ivan Il'ich's environment. His colleagues, who start scheming the moment they realize that this death creates an appetizing job vacancy, and his family members, who go to the opera and plan his daughter's wedding as he withers in pain, are all targets of these assaults. Tolstoy mercilessly lets them vent their complaints of insomnia at Ivan's wake: In his last days the sick man cried so loudly that three rooms' distance could not save them a wink of sleep. The satiric tone that Tolstoy is unwilling to hide does legitimize the recent interpretation by James Rice, who saw in the story no seriousness at all, but a merry-go-round charade of comic devices.[7]

It is significant to remember, however, that the life of Ivan Il'ich was also an autobiography. In 1877, Ivan Il'ich, Tolstoy's alter ego and partner in faith-search in the tragicomic dialogue *Interlocutors* drives out everyone but Kant and stays in his room for faith with an attempt of a dialogue with his philosophy, which brings him to the question of revelation of faith, Lord's Law communicated to Moses, and the inner voice of conscience.[8] The unfinished "Memoirs of a Madman" that uses the encounter with death as an invitation to spiritual awakening but runs into the impasse of misunderstanding and the falsity of alms giving, both of which were just condemned in *What, Then, Should We Do?* made the prospect of finishing the tale as a tale of conversion to faith impossible.

There are several additional clues explaining Tolstoy's inspiration and final choices for the story that was finished in March 1886. In 1884, disputing the genres of spiritual confession in his letters to Alexandrine and bearing the dying Pascal in mind, Tolstoy explained to her that it is "terribly dangerous to look at oneself as a martyr" of faith (63: 167). Tolstoy opens chapter 2 of *DII* with the famous enigmatic account of Ivan Il'ich's life: "Ivan Il'ich's life was most simple and ordinary and most terrible" (26: 68). He similarly summarizes Pascal's life: "A life, most simple and ordinary [if judged] by its external events, and a life most terrible, tragic (if judged) by its inner content" (42: 488).[9] Pascal's *vita* inspires not only that hair-raising conjunction of "ordinary . . . and most terrible," but also a way to account to death. After his conversion, Pascal lived with a look directed toward death. When death did arrive, as a slow torture of some form of abdominal cancer, the cause of death also for Ivan Il'ich, Pascal did not greet it as a joyous conclusion to a painful journey, but with fear and regrets, lacking an assurance that he will be saved.[10] Tolstoy must have been struck by the fact that the Memorial of a Christian sown into his clothes did not inspire Pascal to die well. He will use this theme of oaths and transgressions in *DII*.

After his rewriting of the Gospels and involvement with artists in commentaries on Christ's passion the association of pain and faith acquires a greater role for Tolstoy. In the same period, he tried to experiment with intense pain, a process that was not difficult to induce because of his irregular and unsettled diet of those years with the sudden exclusions of succulent meats and other customary treats. On May 9/21, 1884 he wrote in the diary: "Terrible abdominal pain at night. Started figuring out how it is, to die. It did not look joyous, but neither was it terrifying" (49: 92). Silent dialogues with God accompanied by severe intestinal colic are a recurring motif in the diary and letters surrounding the writing of the story. Nightmarish silence and expectations of "something" accompanied the hours he spent gazing at the wallpaper that—detail after detail, scroll after scroll—concealed in the stencil work the logarithm of the unsolvable enigmas of life. Reading the handwriting of death on the wall is the only element that Tolstoy saved from "Memoirs of a Madman" to transpose into *DII*.

The same themes of physical immobility, solitude, and the necessity to die alone are discussed in letters with friends and strangers (1884–1886). To his terminally ill fellow-Christian and translator into French of *What I Believe?* Prince Urusov, Tolstoy sends consolations set in riotous tones of a rebuke for entrusting his ailing body to the care of an atheist doctor. "They will all die— now or twenty years later, but if they die with the energy of their belief, the movement of life will continue" (63: 203). Letters to Gavriil Rusanov, a bed-ridden, paralyzed, forty-year-old judge and another spiritual ally, constantly revolve around the meaninglessness of the death of the flesh and the impor-tance of continuing in the spirit (63: 217). To Rusanov's further queries about how the transfiguration takes place, Tolstoy responded that he has not under-stood the mechanism yet and was working on it (63: 224). To Biriukov, he wrote about the dangerous state of suspense that he envisioned, "One leaves the physical body and has not yet reentered one's spiritual body. If the force of inertia throws one back into the state before the crisis and 'normal life' re-sumes, this is death. This is what drove Judas to suicide: he was afraid to tear himself out of the old law and give himself over to Christ" (63: 254–55). At this crucial moment, Tolstoy arrives at the lifelong enigma of the stone's sta-sis, gravitation, and flight all along associated for him with freedom of will and immortality. In letters to Ge and Chertkov, written in the early months of 1885, Tolstoy compared man's mission in the world to that of a flying stone. In the early illumination of 1885 Tolstoy hastened to write Chertkov: "Every one of us is *a force that knows itself, a flying stone* that knows where and why it is flying and feels joy that it is flying and knows that in and of himself he is nothing, a stone, but that his whole meaning is in the flight, in that force that threw him, that his whole life is this force" (85: 136). In this new inter-pretation of man's teleological mission, Tolstoy repeats the same discovery about the good force and quotes Christ as saying in his letter to Ge that *each of us is a flying stone*, a force understanding itself: "Its universal goal and therefore striving toward that goal with joy" (63: 207). In the final chapter, Tolstoy will have Ivan Il'ich embark on such a flight, but not before we wit-ness his dead body from the start. In *DII*, Tolstoy reinterprets the horror ex-perienced at the sight of the corpse.

Terrible and wonderful, simple and miraculous, Life, opening its meaning on the fly, is the primary and sacred theme of *DII*, despite the fact that the fi-nal lines of the last chapter dispassionately describe the moment of Ivan's physical end: "and he died" (26: 113). This paradoxical story of salvation be-gins with the announcement of the hero's death and the enactment of its posthumous rituals and ends with death. In the first chapter, the cadaver is put on display, silently articulating its menacing reproach to the living. Carefully sniffing at the heavy air, the fake mourners convene to say a few required platitudes to the insincerely aggrieved wife. However, they look with pity at the sincerely grieving Vasia, the teenage son of the deceased, and retreat as soon as decorum permits. Ivan Il'ich's dead body does not reproach the audience in the manner of the society lady in "The Three Deaths" or the little Princess in *War and Peace*. The dead man's mien articulates that all that needed to be done was done and something of import was accomplished. However, the mystery of this accomplishment looks too horrifying to the onlooker. Adding a plethora of naturalistic details, Tolstoy gratifies this fear and abandons the body to the inevitability of its physical degradation. The body is left to indifferent spectators and grievers in much the same fashion as it is given up in Tolstoy's favorite Platonic dialogue, *The Phaedo*, whose theme of the escaped soul is thinly veiled in the story.

Tolstoy writes *DII* as a philosophical fantasy about the transition from the temporal to eternal time-consciousness as he described the idea in the letters just discussed. Artistically, the situation is fraught with the creative *aporia* that Tolstoy himself experienced and described in his searches of faith in *A Confession*. Ivan's *aporia* arises when, intrigued by the famous syllogism on immortality and mortality, he begins to seek answers to transcendent questions in the language created for immanent knowledge: "The syllogism he had learnt from Kiesewetter's Logic: 'Caius is a man, men are mortal, therefore Caius is mortal,' had always seemed to him correct as applied to Caius, but it certainly didn't apply to himself. That Caius—man in the abstract—was mortal, was perfectly correct, but he was not Caius, or an abstract man, but a creature quite separate from all others" (26: 93).[11]

The syllogism comes to Ivan Il'ich's mind at the beginning of chapter 6, when he begins to contemplate the possibility of his death and relates this possibility to the ontological experience of humans in the abstract. The syllogism connects his unrepeatable identity with the fate of other people and with the main question: does immortality exist? When this search leads Ivan to many curious contradictions, he, like the king of deconstruction, Jacques Derrida in *Aporias* (1993), unwittingly engages in a polemic with Epictetus: "When I am not, what will there be? There will be nothing. Then where will I be when I am no more?" (26: 91). To remind the reader, this famous quip of Epictetus, a Stoic expecting death, goes, "When *you* are, it is not. When *it* is, *you* are not." For Derrida, the wisdom of Epictetus triggers his deconstructive-reconstructive meditation on death and immortality. He reduces everything to what is also Tolstoy's favorite aporetic moment: how does one provide an account of one's own death when the space between being "I" and *not being at all* is but one step? How does one experience death and account for it becoming the force understanding itself during its transit from "here" to "there"? In Derrida's words, "'My death,' this syntagm that which relates the possible to the impossible, can be figured flashing like a sort of indicator-light (a light at a border) installed at a customs booth."[12]

The customs booth on Ivan Il'ich's route to eternal consciousness was installed by Constantine Leontiev the moment he read the story: "But we decidedly do not know what *man feels and thinks* when traversing that intangible border that is called death. To describe a succession of feelings or thoughts in a wounded or contused man is artistic courage; however, to describe the posthumous condition of the soul is not courage but helpless pretense—and nothing more."[13] Mikhail Bakhtin, who waved a red flag to Ivan's passage, signaling the foreignness of eternal consciousness to human experience, reinforced the roadblock more securely. Indeed, neither Tolstoy nor his hero will take the step of dying until death is understood. No matter how much he suffers, Ivan Il'ich resists a plain and simple transfer from here to there. The precipitation of finality or their postponements are intrinsically useless in Tolstoy's eternal time. The physiological cessation of being is always a de-synchrony of vital functions, as Tolstoy wrote: "(Ivan) stopped at half breath, stretched and died" (*ostanovilsia na polovine vzdokha, potianulsia i umer*) (26: 113). Another sort of synchrony involves Ivan's found purpose and his fictional end as a story.

Bakhtin complained that in Tolstoy consciousness marches in and out of the dying body as easily as if one walks from one room into another. Bakhtin's attention was fixated on the final flicker that dies into complete and non-negotiable darkness with the death of the flesh. The light of the eternal consciousness of one person continues in another's living consciousness. However, in Tolstoy's scheme of things, the dimming flicker is still the consciousness of perception, a form of temporal consciousness, to which eternal consciousness has no business relating. To him they are in two different rooms indeed. Only the eternal consciousness of one person, several persons, or the entire brotherhood knows how to be accountable to the experience of death without the fallacy of constantly looking back at oneself with the eyes of "I-for-myself," the narcissistic self-referentiality of the mirror consciousness (*samoogliadka*) that Bakhtin identified as the reason for Tolstoy's inability to create genuine dialogue.[14] Bakhtin is right in one thing: The paradox is that this accounting of living consciousness without the body is beyond all known norms of accounting and representation. He distrusts the fantastic flights of imagination and Kierkegaard's leaps of faith. If art is to be trusted, however, with all its *aporias*, antinomies, and paradoxes, Tolstoy's story of the burial of the old self, his fantastic escape, and resurrection invisible can, and perhaps should, be built only on accountable, questioning, and loving trust available only through artistic revelation or religious ecstasy.

In Tolstoy's opinion, this trust rests on secure foundations. The most persuasive form of trust to Tolstoy in this story is a thinking voice from which both the body and temporality with all of its lies have been removed. Such will be the dying and saving thoughts of Ivan Il'ich, for the plan of the story will ultimately crystallize into "the story of a commonplace death of a commonplace man, described from within."[15] Noncoincidentally, the rather elaborate diary of Ivan Il'ich in the drafts is lost in the final version. Tolstoy rewrote the story from the third person point of view, in which rhetoric is at its purest because it occurs within consciousness, in the immediacy of thinking itself. In the drafts, Praskovia Fedorovna, Ivan's widow, considers the discovered diary a very flawed account with a bizarre way of ordering and connecting events. As a result, she believes that "truth is on the side of the materialists" and that the mind is the first organ to succumb to physical decay: "He was no longer himself" (*on uzhe byl ne on*) (26: 508). Praskovia compares Ivan's diary unfavorably to his masterful accounts of court cases: "Missing are the sense of connection, clarity, strength of expression. His reports were sheer masterpieces. While here, she said, leafing through the notebook with her plump fingers studded with rings, it is so weak, so contradictory. No logic, that logic in which he used to be so very strong!!!" (26: 507). Praskovia gets rid of the diary and shoves it on Petr Ivanovich, whom Ivan Il'ich designated for the role of a more humane reader of this memoir of spiritual rather than physical suffering and who feels most scared and out of sorts at Ivan Il'ich's wake in the final version (26: 509–10). In the drafts, Petr Ivanovich is shattered by his late friend's account of his mistaken past and the horror of dying in lies written during "intervals of a half hour to an hour between terrible attacks of pain" (26: 508). It is the reading of the diary that makes Petr Ivanovich undertake a narration of Ivan's life and death and provide his own account of what Ivan's diary has changed in *him*. Petr Ivanovich in the drafts is the final authoritative editor who, unlike Ivan's widow or the incompetent readers of the posthumously discovered notes in Tolstoy's earlier stories, is competent to comprehend the painful memoir. His whole attention is focused on the little book that he carries home after paying his last respects to the late author of the journal. Petr Ivanovich comes to his senses immediately after reading the journal. After a sleepless night (one of the many to follow), he pays another visit to Praskovia Fedorovna first thing next morning. The rest of the early draft of the book takes on a rather modernist tact reminiscent of Nabokov's technique in *The Real Life of Sebastian Knight*. Petr Ivanovich plays the sleuth in search of his late friend's soul. He interviews witnesses, hires the servant Gerasim in his service, and consults records in order to create a vita. He bases his hagiographic reconstruction on what he finds in the notes and what he hears from those who witnessed Ivan Il'ich's illness (26: 510).

What follows is the famous beginning of the tale of Ivan Il'ich's most ordinary and most terrible life, in which Petr Ivanovich narrates the commemorative account of Ivan Il'ich's final year. Petr Ivanovich's narration deviates only slightly from chapters 2 through 5 in the final text. It narrates Ivan's life from its terrible start to his transfer to Moscow (St. Petersburg in the final version) and his fatal fall off the ladder doing home improvements. At this point, quotes from the diary dwindle to a bare minimum. Interpolated, they impart a sense of innocent ignorance to Ivan Il'ich's immersion in his rehabilitated career at the cost of his life: "He wrote: I feel as if fifteen years have been shaken off me" (26: 516). Gradually, Petr Ivanovich's narration becomes indistinguishable from the third-person narration that Tolstoy chooses for the final text.

Tolstoy does not preserve the memoir direction for several reasons. Petr Ivanovich's description, based on interviews and documents, cannot contain the final moments of Ivan Il'ich's life. Furthermore, the account of Ivan Il'ich's life, aside from the notes, is compromised by the lies of spiritually untrustworthy witnesses of the "sordid universal." Deliberately, Tolstoy gives up on a rich national tradition of impuissant deathbed confessions or letters, from Fonvizin and Stankevich through Saltykov and Ogarev in which the environment is blamed for failures in life and for the lack of trust in immortality. In the final version, Ivan Il'ich's death can only potentially help Petr Ivanovich, who does all he can to avoid imagining himself in the position of a mortal, someone who will also die: "an ordinary thought came to his aid that this thing happened to Ivan Il'ich, not him" (26: 67). In the final version, the private journal of dying turns into the collective memory of dying: Ivan's son Vasia and Petr Ivanovich show promise of arriving at it. They are connected with their future by the terrible memory and likeness of Ivan Il'ich (26: 68).[16]

By introducing death as an indecent joke in the eyes of timorous bureaucrats in the final version, Tolstoy puns on the meaning given to death in Strakhov's *World as a Whole*, specifically its Letter VII, which says: "We call something news when there was a fire or that Ivan Petrovich died while Anna Petrovna got married . . . [but] for the deeper minds, there is little new in our news."[17] In the final version, Strakhov's "Ivan Petrovich" became Tolstoy's "Petr Ivanovich," who was as equally unselfconscious. In the final version, at least at the beginning, Ivan Il'ich himself is exceedingly less self-conscious. He recalls his sins only fleetingly and parts with unpleasant memories lightheartedly: "At school he had done things which had formerly seemed to him very horrid and made him feel disgusted with himself when he did them; but later on when he saw that such actions were done by people of good position and that they did not regard them as wrong, he was not exactly able to regard them as right, but to forget about them entirely or not be troubled at all by remembering them" (26: 70).[18] In the final text, Ivan's real self-evaluations do not occur until chapters 9 through 12, in the silent dialogues with his conscience. While gazing at geometric stencils on the wall and brocades on the back of his sofa, Ivan remembers his childhood in unformed fragments of inner speech. Unlike the Madman from the aborted "Memoirs," or Anna Karenina in the final decisive moment, Ivan remembers only what is good for him to remember. Only in the last three hours of his life, in chapter 12, Ivan retrieves the negative memory of his past—a terrible life which was "not the right thing" and concentrates on finding "the right thing" so that his dying and the final illumination be drawn in terms of Christ's death on the Cross in Tolstoy's retelling of the Gospels.

CAIUS AND IVAN IL'ICH:
BETWEEN SYLLOGISM AND DEATH

The syllogism was included in the very first variant of the story.[19] At first, the syllogism affords only a very remote chance to provide Ivan with access to spiritual knowledge. As a lawyer trained to think in maximally general forms and then apply them to particular cases, Ivan needs to take them outside of the courthouse and out of the legal code, make them strange, and undo their abstractness. In order for that to happen, the syllogistic form must be spiritually domesticated and personalized. The syllogism becomes inextricably connected with Ivan's inner voice (*vnutrennii golos*): "'If I had to die like Caius I should have known it. *An inner voice* would have told me so, but there was nothing of that sort in me; I and all my friends felt that our case was quite different from that of Caius. And now there it is!' he said to himself. 'It can't be. It is impossible! But here it is. How's this? How's one to understand it?'" (26: 93).[20]

The structure of memory here is obviously different from the unhappy memory that we saw in Ivan's diaries and notes. Trying not simply to deduce or reject but to understand, Ivan weighs judgments as metaphysically healthy or morbid. He reaches an *aporia* because the morbid side of the problem transcends his understanding, but the healthy, formally infallible side does not aid his understanding. Ivan attempts to reverse the course of syllogistic reasoning, his *train of thought* (*khody mysli*): "To replace that thought he called up a succession of others, hoping to find some support in them. He tried to get back into the former current of thoughts that had once screened the thought of death from him. But strange to say, all that had formerly shut off, hidden and destroyed the consciousness of death, no longer had that effect. Ivan Il'ich now spent most of his time attempting to reestablish that old current" (26: 93).[21]

What Ivan needs to remember and resists for some time is his concrete (rather than abstract) relation to mortality. He must overcome the temporality of these memories unavailable to Caius and make peace with having to lose them all—Mitia and mama, cake riots at law school, memories of childhood smells and sounds (26: 93). When Tolstoy, in passing, referred to Epictetus' phrase in *A Confession*, he noticed the way it cowardly reduces the experience of death to a nonchalant joke. Tolstoy makes Ivan rephrase the same in such a way as to concur with the philosophies of the creative aesthetics of dying, of death as a process, and of the future. Emmanuel Levinas similarly attacked the Epictetus phrase in his essay "Death and the Future" for effacing our personal relationship with death, which is a unique relationship with the future, an "impossibility of possibility" of going beyond nothingness and the lack of ability to grasp this in human terms.[22] Tolstoy's inspirations of 1884, Epictetus and Plato's *Phaedo* allowed him to think of death in much the same terms. Ivan Il'ich's spiritual manipulations with logic that put death on hold is one of the major themes of *DII*.

Ivan Il'ich unfolds a masterful case through direct demonstration of the flaw in Aristotle's syllogistic theory, primarily, its inability to discriminate between universal and individual statements. In *Syllogistic*, Aristotle circulates the syllogism on the mortality of all Greeks, in which everything not abstract (everything with a body and numerically singular)—"Socrates' being an emblem of a primitive universal"—has to be subsumed under a universal quality (for example, mortality). One man ought to die because "all Greeks die."[23] Through singular propositions "not obviously of these forms" ("Socrates is a man"), Aristotle regarded mere variants of them, of which nothing could be predicated.[24] Having spent his entire career practicing the principles of judicial logic and rhetoric, Ivan Il'ich shifts his pursuits at the end of his life toward transcendental alternatives, rethinking logic in accordance with the demands of soul-searching.[25]

To treat Tolstoy's syllogism successfully, we will do well by subjecting it to closer scrutiny relying on time-honored critical views that considered logic an inalienable part of Tolstoy's writing method. Eikhenbaum thinks that logic for Tolstoy is a productive creative principle that resolves the contradiction between generalization and minuteness and expands experience.[26] Lydia Ginzburg sees a high point of the nineteenth-century's psychological discovery in the novella's ability to describe spiritual states. She adds, however, that the end is illogical and not conditioned, that we "all circumvent or discount the tale's ending, where harmony is restored in that joyous suffusion of light."[27] The fluidity of consciousness and spiritual growth that she elsewhere ascribes to Tolstoy stumbles here against faith and requires a brave supra-logical leap. Gary Saul Morson tends to see in *DII* an example of "timeless, anonymous, . . . categorical . . . and non-falsifiable" statements.[28] Morson also notices that Tolstoy is prone to omitting generalizing premises, committing so-called enthymemes, in order to reach the desired logical conclusion. This is hardly surprising, I should add. The creator of the syllogistic structure, Aristotle, while being content with discussing syllogisms only as universal judgments in logic, in rhetoric hopes to elicit a particular response, or pathos, through a missing link that has to be restored, as in an enthymeme.[29] Aristotle's discussion of particulars "with bodies" became more enlivened by rhetorical demands. Although he would admit in *Rhetoric* of the importance of individual cases and interests in judicial pleadings and medicinal investigations, he still insists on the preeminence of law over the discursive aptitude of the judge trying to plead for another individual and of illness (the universal) over the patient, whose case is a specific instance of a given disease. Tolstoy creates a bitter subtext for Ivan, who sees a double irony of his situation. A top-notch lawyer, he understands that only the universals are right. He should die because the disease in general is of most interest to his doctor who fails to see the originality and uniqueness of Ivan's malfunctioning kidney or perhaps caecum and why these two suspect organs are to Ivan a soulful matter (*zadushevnoe delo*) and a matter of life and death (26: 90–91). He should also die because all men die. Ivan will stage a revolt. In a curious understatement, Bakhtin's love of irony could not but notice vast creative potentials in *DII*, despite his general suspicion toward Tolstoy's descriptions of death: "Tolstoy's death consciously perceived from within does not exist at all."[30] In 1963, in the partially decodable stenography of his reworking of *The Problems of Dostoevsky's Poetics*, Bakhtin acknowledged the disruptive threshold in Tolstoy's story, therefore, implying the possibility of two conditions of consciousness or even two different types of consciousness, of a special relationship between Ivan Il'ich's "Caius"-consciousness and his "I"-consciousness.[31]

Tolstoy's favorite philosophers found a flaw in the syllogism, which reduced the question of mortality to formal deduction. Descartes suggested that we use syllogisms in order to intuit our thinking essences, including our eternal essences, to which Pascal adjoined his logic of the heart.[32] The Caius case came to define for Tolstoy the fate of consciousness itself. In *Phaedo*, reread by Tolstoy a few times in 1885 and 1886, Socrates heralds logic for preserving the "undying invisible," which cannot be realized if reason is defiled by "misology" (hatred of logic) and which eludes the objective evidence of death, the dead body.[33] In *Rhetoric*, written explicitly for the lawyers, Aristotle remains blind to these powerful exhortations of his philosophical teacher. Trying to enounce something meant for Aristotle to enounce either universally or not universally with nothing in between: "all men" was equated with "every man" and was antithetical to "every *not* man." Here is how Tolstoy was brought to his anti-Aristotelian choice.

In the 1880s, Tolstoy was undoubtedly exposed to the ongoing debates in logic on how to quantify and individualize personality in formal propositions, with Caius again in the epicenter. The notebook of 1880 mentions the reading of Svetilin's manual of formal logic (*Uchebnik formal'noi logiki*) (1871) in the midst of a rather heated cogitation about the reasonableness (*razumnost'*) of Christ's teaching (48: 329). Svetilin thought the essence of logical activity to be contained in operations of differentiation and identification. At Kazan, Tolstoy most likely studied only historical and social applications of Hegelian dialectics.[34] According to a historian of philosophical education in Russian institutions of higher learning and gymnasia, Ernest L. Radlov, Kant's logic and its simpler versions in the reworking of Baumeister and Kiesewetter were still taught as core sources of philosophical knowledge throughout the 1830s and 1840s, the time when many members of Tolstoy's circle were finishing their formal schooling.[35]

Radlov notices that changes in the teaching of logic in Russia came into effect when original Russian thinkers, such as Vladislavlev and Matvey Troitsky, the teachers of Nicholai Grot and Nicholai Lossky, began to reinterpret foundations of the Western systems of logic.[36] Taking into account Tolstoy's close friendship during those years with Grot, the author of *The Question of Reform in Logic* (1882) (*K voprosu o reforme logiki*), Tolstoy may be presumed to be in the epicenter of disputes about the future of logic. Grot proved inconsistency of strictly metaphysical or empirical formats of logical inquiry and insisted on the importance of the psychological factor as a means to transform exterior sensations into interior "movements of thought" (*dvizheniia mysli*).[37] Around 1885–1886, Grot's new metaphysical outlook in revolt against positivism influenced the policy of the Moscow Psychological Society, which had been created in 1885 and which Grot took over as chairman in 1887. The Society was deeply indebted to Kant's ideas about autonomy of the self and transcendental psychology.[38]

The Society's neo-idealism came as well in response to John Stuart Mill's inductive and anarchist proposition: "unless we are certain that all individual men—past, present and future—are dead" we cannot assert that one man is mortal. Mill attacked Aristotelian injustice upon noticing that in the generally accepted classification of the forms of syllogisms "no place is assigned to *singular* propositions (man); . . . they are ranked, for the purposes of the syllogism, with universal propositions (men)."[39] Mill insists that we can only assert that Socrates has the attribute of mortality, not that he is mortal (Mill, 135). Strictly speaking, nothing can be proved about death of an individual man until it has been experienced as fact. Like Mill's *Autobiography*, his logic too was used effectively by Tolstoy. He makes Ivan Il'ich notice the Aristotelian contradiction contained in the middle member. The singular man contained in the category of the species "men" immediately sees that he has to be promoted to the class of mortals by simple accretion, but he refuses to submit to such a promotion. Also thanks to two major inspirations, Kant and Schopenhauer, Tolstoy resorts to the Caius syllogism.

Kant attributed to syllogistic thinking its creative capacity: "The proposition 'Caius is mortal,' I can indeed derive from experience by means of the understanding alone. But I am in pursuit of a concept . . . (man) that contains the condition under which the predicate of this judgment is given; and after I have subsumed the predicate under this condition taken in its whole extension ('All men are mortal'), I proceed, in accordance therewith, to determine the knowledge of my object ('Caius is mortal')."[40] The unconditioned alone (Caius) makes possible the totality of conditions. The decision on a singular mortality (related to the universal *a priori* idea of it) can be made insofar as long as one's relation to the world has been defined. On Kant's and Tolstoy's terms, Caius and Ivan Il'ich *are* the condition of judgment, not its passive mechanical instancing. As Kant puts it, "There is only one Caius." In the singular sentence, "Caius is mortal" an exception can take place no more or no less than in the universal, "All men are mortal."[41] The exception (an extraordinary) equals the possibility of the ordinary.[42] Tolstoy was also fascinated by the appeal of infinite judgments discussed by Kant in § 22 of *Logik*, and took them for an invitation to rethink Schopenhauer's critique of Kant's logic assimilated in 1869. Those earlier convictions were on the point that reason cannot transcend the boundaries of experience and cannot be logically invoked for the purpose of demonstrating the existence of some absolute first principle, while consciousness does not deal with infinite judgments at all.[43] In his rethinking of logic in 1886, Tolstoy shuts the door forever on Schopenhauer's irrationalism and ridicule of logic.

Schopenhauer provocatively compared syllogism with a voltaic pile. According to him, syllogistic thinking processes judgments not unlike the voltaic pile processes currents whose force enlivens the living bodies or reduces them to the indestructible dust.[44] In his complex metaphor of indestructibility, Schopenhauer identifies thinking with substance to which actualizing electric force of will has been applied. He further claims that the voltaic pile can be regarded as a sensible image of the syllogism. The voltaic pile of will treats all forms of life equally and does not discriminate between individual or general instances of life. Therefore, it treats "man" and "men" or "animals" as if it were a point of indifference, the middle member traduced through the pile into the magic dust, out of which new forms of life will be created: "in the syllogism: All men are mortal; Caius is a man: I can exchange the middle term 'man' for 'animal being.' As an external characteristic, by which the figure of a syllogism is at once recognized, the middle term is certainly very useful. But for the fundamental characteristic of a thing to be explained, we must take what is essential to the thing."[45] Schopenhauer goes on to prove subordination of self-consciousness to will, this merciless incinerator of conscious life into the unconscious, in the eternal cycle of reversals and renewals of life forms.[46] Socrates, Kant (he adds Kant to be a character in one of the syllogistic premises), and Caius are amassed and sacrificed for the spark of will in the grand finale of syllogistic conclusion. Why in *DII* Tolstoy invokes Kiesewetter's book, *Grundriß einer allgemeinen Logik nach Kantischen Grundsaßen*, to counter Aristotle and Schopenhauer, becomes clear only once you realize that this book was a splendid fictional device, and as such it came in handy.

Twice a victim of potshots that Schopenhauer took at him and other overzealous Kantians, Johann G. C. Kiesewetter, once a popular promulgator of Kant's philosophy, might not have been an absolute authority in logic.[47] Kiesewetter's textbook was nonetheless an exciting, almost artistic phenomenon, one of its kind. It probed death and mortality syllogistically on all sides and from all angles, citing the syllogism that questioned Caius' mortality in all sorts of variations at least 150 times. Ten minutes with Kiesewetter's book will persuade any reader that Caius, even "my friend Caius," as Kiesewetter put it, is anything but an abstraction (I: 33). He is a lovable chap of flesh and blood with a believable narrative CV, who is now healthy and then sick, and who has a son, Titus, and a friend, Livius, whose soul is at first pure and immortal and then sinful, like everybody else's (I: 349, 354). He is a "sittliche Mensch" (man of habit), living by the force of convention, a magistrate or ruler (*Reg[l]er*), the pride and phoenix of logical community and he loves playing cards (I: 390). Involving Ivan Il'ich in labyrinths of questions and doubts about the immortality of the soul, the cruelty of God, the need to cope with fatal illness—all cast in syllogisms—Kiesewetter's textbook prompted to Ivan Il'ich and his author many of their riotous, deductive steps. Especially ambiguous are examples where Caius is ill and the diagnosis fails to be precise, so that one cannot help thinking, as in the case with Ivan Il'ich, that the physical cause is irrelevant (I: 217). When his Caius is ill, Kiesewetter, just like Ivan Il'ich, commits blasphemy deliberating in different figures whether God is merciful or cruel, whether he exists or not.

When Caius becomes morally upstanding (*tugendhaft*), although also more ill (*krank*), in the syllogistic conclusion he is in a halo of white and levitates in joy (I: 177). Kiesewetter asks to define everyone's private horizon (*Privathorizont*) by one's capacity to acquire knowledge (*Erkenntnisskraft*) while striving toward one's definite end (*seine bestimmten Zwecke*) (I: 111–12), the delimited space between mortality and immortality (I: 161). Toward the end of Kieseweter's book, Caius strives toward (*strebt nach*) spiritual righteousness (II: 279), absolves his sins, stops indulging in his voluptuous habits (I: 341), quenches malice (I: 417), loves, and is, therefore, active (II: 279). He enters into the spectrum of white and is beatified into the sanctum of logical sainthood. It comes as no surprise that Kiesewetter gained fame by his serialized versions of spiritualized logic.[48] It also comes as no surprise that his textbook of logic was used primarily in Russian schools of theology and religion.[49] It is now clear why at the right moment of awareness, coinciding with the escalation of his illness, Ivan Il'ich recalls Kiesewetter, whose syllogisms are quite high on the promise of salvation.

By contrast to this striving to the private horizon of immortality, the mentality of Ivan Il'ich's immediate environment is a facsimile of syllogistic reasoning that predicts all human movement. Chapter 1 of *DII* demonstrates the communal mentality at work: people deduce new placements and social transfers, occasioned by Ivan Il'ich's dropping out of the carousel and vacating his place. While Ivan Il'ich was terminally ill, but still formally employed and "kept his place" in the bureaucratic-syllogistic structure (*mesto ostavalos' za nim*) (26: 61), the poly-syllogism of promotion was already being constructed around him (26: 61–62). We involuntarily begin to transport Ivan Il'ich's colleagues syllogistically and metaphorically. If Alekseev takes the coveted place of Ivan Il'ich, then Vinnikov (or Shtabel') will take the place of Alekseev. Because it is Fedor Vasilievich who is identified as someone who can get the appointment of either Shtabel' or Vinnikov, then we know a few things for sure. 1) Ivan Egorovich Shebeck will be neither involved nor concerned by any transfer (he is, therefore, superior to everyone, including the late Ivan Il'ich). 2) Ivan Il'ich was superior to the rest of the gentlemen (*sotovarishchi*) concerned. 3) Alekseev was inferior to Ivan Il'ich, but superior to Vinnikov and Shtabel'. 4) Fedor Vasilievich held the lowest rank of all. This ladder of bureaucratic beings is surely an irony, but also a situation fraught with ordinariness and horror. By dying or moving from spot to spot, everyone is obliging everyone else. Somebody's loss is another's temporary gain. Tolstoy brings in the discussion of the terrible distance noncoincidentally: "they live so terribly far away . . . Far from you, you mean. Everything's far from your place" (26: 62).

The terror of the situation is that after all the interim members fall one by one or transfer one by one into a new category, the "empty spot" of Ivan Il'ich is not really empty, only vacant. After Ivan Il'ich moves into the place of Caius, somebody else in the story ought to move into his living space and then empty the space for a new "somebody else" and so on. Therefore the joy that "it is he who is dead and not I" is only premature (26: 62). Tolstoy deliberately clutters names and patronymics so that they indeed become analogically and, therefore, syllogistically connected. He even compares body parts of the sick and the healthy: thighs, limbs, hairlines, the envy of the sick toward the healthy and the squeamishness of the healthy toward the sick.

Most of the names in the story begin with a "major-premised name" (Ivan-Fedor-Vasilii-Petr), and extend into first name namesakes and patronymics: Ivan Egorovich, Fedor Vasilievich, little Vasia, Praskovia Fedorovna, and the noumenal relative of everybody else in the superlative degree, Fedor Petrovich Petrishchev. Petr Ivanovich, Ivan Il'ich's best friend, bears a special bond to the late hero because he also acknowledges his indebtedness to Ivan Il'ich (*schital sebia obiazannym Ivanom Il'ichem*) (26: 62). The sense of debt is reinforced by the following categories of inclusion, massively repeated in the text. The irony of mutual belonging in the ontological community fraught with eventual dying is reinforced by the constant repetition of designators of membership (members [*chleny*], comrades, and co-workers [*so-tovarishchi*]) and by reflexive iterative verbs with a common destination (convened, got together [*soshlis'*, *s'ekhalis'*]). All spheres of identity overlap on the person of Ivan Il'ich, who had been "a comrade of all convened" (*so-tovarishch sobravshikhsia*) (26: 61). In the description of how the still healthy Ivan Il'ich, the master of syllogistic behavior, danced (generally and in particular), Tolstoy employs a teasing logical riddle: "While he had been an official on special service he had been accustomed to dance in general, but as an examining magistrate it was exceptional for him to do so" (26: 72). The conclusion tells us that "If he [Ivan Il'ich] danced now, he did so as if to show that though he served under the reformed order of things and had reached the fifth official rank, still, when it came to dancing he could do it better than most people." So at the end of an evening, he sometimes danced with Praskovia Fedorovna (26: 72–73).[50] After showing the rewards of a thinking convenience in accordance with the major premise, Tolstoy shows us their stupefying horrors and investigates the ways of a productive fallacy. The ontological distance between "me" and "Caius" is all that matters.

LEGAL BIOGRAPHY AND
THE BIRTH OF THE INNER JUDGE

Walter Benjamin calls death "the sanction for everything that the storyteller can tell." In modernity, when "death has become less omnipresent and less vivid," the storyteller borrows his authority from death in an especially blatant gesture.[51] Tolstoy is, therefore, ambitious and sanctimonious enough to begin his story with Ivan's obituary, the dead body, and the funeral. Like Pascal and Benjamin, he knows that "no one dies so poor that he does not leave something behind."[52] In chapter 2, Tolstoy begins the retrospective recovery of his hero's lost life with what may be called an "*un*-exciting" force.[53] After the grim funeral description, we have a discouraging introduction into Ivan's past life, "most simple and most ordinary and most terrible." However, something here makes the story more than a mere retelling of an inconspicuous and routine life. This something resembles what Tomashevsky calls narrative excitement—"disturbing the tranquility of the initial situation and provoking action" (Tomashevsky, 72). This excitement and psychological suspense result from Tolstoy's combination of safe, crisis-free ordinariness and its supreme terror. The exposition of life in this life's wake delays the "excitement" until chapter 6 when the hero begins to approach his intuitive being, paradoxically, through a fixated form, through the "grounded motif" of mortality in the syllogism. From this position, the dynamic syllogistic symbol and other paradigmatic formulas—maxims, oracles, and parables—motivate the progression toward the final state of awareness.

Formally, *DII* is a biography of the judge. Richard Posner has suggested that biography as such is a legal genre, a matrix for the building of penitent vitae. The first biographies developed out of trial records in which the villain's life, often his confessions, was chronicled and publicly exhibited and therefore conciliatory measures were often unnecessary to protect the autonomy of judgment over the accused unless a thorough degree of secrecy is required for the procedure.[54] Another peculiarity of a judiciary biography is that biographies of prominent lawyers were textbooks for younger colleagues, and they highlighted professional feats: all biographical data are sifted into the funnel of cases won or lost.[55] From a literary view, these biographies are hagiographic in orientation, dull, and anticlimactic, and crises—if they occur—become turning points in a given career.

Many lawyers of Tolstoy's generation, mostly jurists (*pravovedy*), the graduates of the most prestigious School of Law (*uchilishche pravovedeniia*), the elite institution for lawyers in St. Petersburg that Tolstoy had his hero attend, were writing memoirs and reminiscences in the postreform years. The initial plan to write the tale in the form of the diary was prompted by the reading of the reminiscences of his good friend Stasov that appeared in *Russian Antiquity* (*Russkaia starina*) (1880–1881).[56] Stasov's memoirs provides a treasure trove of details that help to interpret Ivan's character rather than simply attribute to it his rather flippant and superficial wickedness. Stasov points out that music loving, dancing, rigorous gymnastics training, and card playing were all the signature traits of the graduates of the School of Law. The motif from Stasov's memoirs that Tolstoy put to profit in *DII* was of the disillusioned idealist who looks back on his life from the "green upholstered card-table later at night" and through the whirl of the balls at which he danced away "through more than one momentous civic agenda" sees himself, a pretty curly youth "so beloved by all."[57] This passage was surely noticed by Tolstoy, who seemed to have borrowed at least several of its themes and even borrowed entire phrases.

When we analyze the description of the judicial milieu in Tolstoy's work from the point of view of the sources that informed his knowledge of it and his interest in it, we indeed find nothing extraordinary or especially sinful in Ivan Il'ich's character. He is a typical legal servant, who shares all of these typical lawyerly traits: verbal manipulation, emotional aloofness, distrustfulness, ethical relativism, frugality, and social passivity.[58] The first graduates of the School of Law (Stasov's generation) were career wanderers in search of more fruitful assignments and virtuosos in separating their feelings from the task in which they were involved and the case from abstract principles.[59] From chapter 2 to chapter 5, Tolstoy patiently lets us follow his hero's peregrinations and career leaps around the juristic institutions of Russia, first on the eve, and then in the midst of her legal reform. In the conversional context of the story, Ivan's service in the category of a new man on special assignments introduces an unsettling but meaningful ambiguity. Ivan is a victim of another sort, of the delusion that when he applies his skills so masterfully and is so loyal to the institution, he should be properly remunerated with a fulfilled life. Ivan's first terrible night on his long road to conversion is spent on a summer veranda, when he realizes that only 5,000 ruble salary will save his life. In chapter 3, through a fortuitous meeting with the right bureaucrat, the enemy of his enemies, Ivan Il'ich procures the desirable slot, Miller's vacancy (*mesto Millera*), and transfers to St. Petersburg two ranks above his former comrades (*sotovarishchi*). In the new posh apartment that his new position allows him to move into, Ivan Il'ich climbs the ladder to fix the curtain rod and falls off this metaphorical ladder of success to suffer what turns out to be a lethal injury. In chapter 5, Ivan Il'ich's peregrinations are over, and our hero learns life's true destination: death. In chapter 6, he is confronted with his alter ego, Caius.

Shocked and demoralized at first, Ivan is repelled by his failing body and its inability to perform in the Supreme Court and repulsed by the pity, ranging from all undertones from solicitous indifference to indifferent interference, that others show him, indifference to the fact that he might be on trial for an unspecified crime. Most harshly he incriminates God, condemning *Him* in the second person singular for having thrown *him*, "little Vania," into life and then for abandoning him there, with no explanation and no guidelines, to die just at the point when life was beginning to yield its fruits. That same vision of the end about which his medallion, *Respice finem* (*beware of the end*) has been warning him since he put it on in his youth, now stands in front of his eyes as his materialized final purpose and as the final meaning of his life. From chapter 10 to chapter 12, all alone, one-on-one with his pain and the unanswerable question, "what for?" tossing and turning in the "black sack" into which he was shoved by an invisible hand (26: 105), Ivan continues to struggle for the final meaning. As soon he understands that physical pain and physical death have no meaning and are not "that thing" (*ne to*), but the real meaning, "that thing" (*to*) has yet to be found, Ivan embarks on a symbolic flight. Like a stone dropped by somebody else, he is disoriented, feeling only that he is flying away from death (chapter 10, 26: 109). Ivan Il'ich's flight acquires an orientation only after he acknowledges his former delusions about choosing the right goal. At this realization, he falls through the black sack and concludes his flight toward his final destination. At the end of the journey, there is no death: "Instead of death there was light. . . . So that's what it is! . . . What joy!" (26: 113). This breathtaking and self-steering flight toward the final goal is Tolstoy's artistic contribution to an understanding of human teleology, or justification of life.

The paragraph from chapter 2 describing Ivan's promotion to a position of court investigator clearly states the power of judgment over the destiny of someone whom the lawyer adjudicates: "All without exception are in his hands. Ivan Il'ich never abused his power, but his consciousness of it and the possibility to mollify it comprised for him the main interest and attraction of his new job" (26: 72). Judicial judgments are formed on the strength of precedents. An unprecedented case, then, must be brought against a precedent. Ivan passes judgment on Caius' mortality based on the observance of similar cases: "all men are mortal," meaning that "all lives are punishable by death."[60] In self-defense, he argues to himself that his case is unique: "Could Caius possibly have held court session in my manner?" (26: 93). By professional reflex, then, Ivan Il'ich conducts an extensive forensic recounting of his life, episode by episode, as soon as he begins to "suspect" himself as a possible criminal. In chapter 5, when Ivan Il'ich starts to judge himself, Tolstoy's voice recedes. Despite the fact that it conveys the story, it is Ivan Il'ich's deliberations on his past guilt and thoughts of what is to be done to repair the damage of his past wrongs that take center stage.

The inquisitor tries himself in the torture chamber of his conscience, the black sack. The sack represents a stage in Ivan Il'ich's detainment and should be read as a figurative representation of Ivan's self-inflicted punishment. The sack was among the most popular means of torturing criminals in the dark ages when customary law prevailed in Europe. Up to the thirteenth century, ordeals were resorted to in the absence of legal prosecution. In recovering the sack and temporarily entombing Ivan, Tolstoy returns justice to its crude, chaotic, natural application: "For three whole days, during which time did not exist to him, he struggled in that black sack into which he was being thrust by an invisible, irresistible force" (26: 112).[61] Tolstoy's hero swears under oath and in the face of imminent death, that he is not guilty. There is no apparent crime in *DII* because there is no burden of accusation. Ivan is being tortured "for nothing."[62] "The trial is on," thinks Ivan. "But I am not guilty!" (26: 107). Tolstoy is surely extracting a confession from his hero—but how? Exculpation by oath and exculpation by ordeal were the two principal varieties of medieval trial, in which "the absence of evidence, or witness, or even of accusers was a necessary precondition for the use of ordeal."[63] First, Tolstoy makes him physically suffer. Then he makes him suffer spiritually. Finally, by admitting to his guilt of mistaken direction, Ivan releases his spirit and dies in his body. Without doubt, Ivan's "successful" suffering resulting in his spiritual release from the sack represents as well Tolstoy's continued argument with Saltykov-Shchedrin's description of useless suffering in the stone well of conscience, which Tolstoy first disputed in *A Confession*.[64]

The doctor whom Ivan Il'ich sees in chapter 5 at the advice of Petr Ivanovich treats sick organs as if they were malfunctioning mechanisms, which can or can't be repaired. Ivan Il'ich, who, in the drafts of chapter 4, was presented as a direct follower of the so-called vulgar materialist Molleschott, at first also visualizes his body from the inside and, imagining the kidney that fails, decides that ailing nature needs to be helped or condemned (26: 90). For a while, the kidney remains Ivan Il'ich's *soulful case* (*zadushevnoe delo*), Ivan's intimate affair with his material constitution. By taking on the defense or prosecution of his kidney, for the first time in his career, Ivan Il'ich conflates personal matters with his work.

The doctor who visits Ivan Il'ich in chapter 11 (for the last time in the story) gives his final solution: opium. By then Ivan realizes that lulling the pain at the cost of clouding consciousness will be a mistake: "It was true, as the doctor said, Ivan Il'ich's physical sufferings were terrible, but worse than the physical sufferings were his mental sufferings which were his chief torture" (26: 110).[65] Similarly, when the priest, the spiritual doctor, visits Ivan Il'ich in the same chapter to offer the sacraments of communion, he only rekindles the false hope of physical revival: "'To live! I want to live!' he said to himself" (26: 111).[66] By taking on the case of pain, Tolstoy clashes moral absolutes and expediency. Tolstoy says that Ivan Il'ich's pain is absolute because his moral suffering has reached its absolute. This sort of physical pain is uncontrollable and is not meted out in reasonable proportion.[67] Tolstoy pushes to the limit the discreet, low-key moral sensibility of his reader. Up until chapter 9, Ivan's juristic mind demands that now that he is sick, he includes himself in the category of "us, the sick" (*my, bol'nye*), who oppose the category of "you, the healthy ones" (*vy zdorovye*), and at a higher degree of alienation from the sick are those who are extremely healthy, like animals (*skoty*) (26: 84, 91, 101).[68]

As in health, he expected retribution in the realized happiness, so in illness he expects retribution through pain. If he suffers in pain, it must be for *something*.[69] This conclusion, so discomforting from the point of view of moral philosophy, may pose an "evidential problem for theists," who believe simultaneously in an omniscient being with control over the world and in the biological and "moral value of pain and pleasure."[70] Following this argument, by inducing pain on his hero, Tolstoy is doing what God does in order to inform us of the value of our freedom. Amoral pain must exist in order to teach us how to avoid it; while in life, we are "good patients," actively suffering while waiting until the right pain killer is available (ibid., 171–72). Modern moral philosophy tends to treat pain as moral expediency, as the price paid for bridging the moral and espistemic gap between God and ourselves.[71] In short, it is not immoral to live one's life as a mortal, but it is amoral not to recognize the true sources of our pain. However, pain as such is *for nothing* in Tolstoy's novella. For quite a long time, Ivan judges the success of his self-trial by the degree and intensity of physical pain: if the pain recedes, he begins to think that he is forgiven, the pain will go away, and the old, pleasant life will make its long overdue return. If his pain intensifies, he accuses God of senseless and treacherous cruelty. In the medieval trial of ordeal, if the accused called on God as witness of his innocence, very specific instruments of torture were applied to determine guilt or innocence. If the accused was unharmed, this was proof of innocence. If he was harmed by the torture, this indicated guilt (Bartlett 14). Ivan is harmed most treacherously after enduring his fall from the ladder like a "fine gymnast" (26: 80).[72] Ivan calls on God as witness of his innocence and then attacks God as a corrupt silent witness, blind to his suffering, and permissive of it while knowing that Ivan has committed no crime.

God changes His legal face in the story. He is at times a forensic witness, at other times a defense attorney, and still at other times a cruel prosecutor. "Why did You do all this? Why did you bring me here? Why, and what for do you torture me so terribly?" (26: 105). This cruel, invisible God, to rephrase Benjamin Cardozo's dictum, performs the sacrificial rite on Ivan with averted gaze, convinced, as he plunges the knife, that he fulfills the duty of his office.[73] When finally Ivan condemns himself, in a split second of spiritual time, God ceases to be a remorseless killer and becomes a forgiving father. There is a recurrent image in Tolstoy's diaries of pushing one's sins out of oneself and pushing oneself through (as if through a narrowing cone) toward salvation. The further one goes, the greater a push is required. Ivan Il'ich falls through the sackcloth only after he realizes that what holds him is justification of his past life: "He was hindered from getting into it by his conviction that his life had been a good one. That very justification of his life held him fast and prevented his moving forward, and it caused him the most torment of all" (26: 112).[74] Tolstoy's reinterpretation of *tragic flaw* (*hamartia*) in the Gospels (24: 52) allows him to test and tease Aristotelian plot with its prediction of fate and complete action into which the protagonist is thrust. Aristotelian scheme implies an event that treacherously be*falls* the hero without his knowing it. By changing the meaning of contingency—falling off the ladder, career opportunities befalling Ivan, and his final free fall, flight away from death—Tolstoy implies that truly happy contingencies are created strictly out of moral and spiritual creativity. Instead of waiting for fortuitous meetings on the train, free individuals become their own moral trains.

RESPICE FINEM: THE STONE THAT KNEW ITS FLIGHT

The first concrete encounter with Ivan's possibility of the impossible is found in chapter 2, when Ivan Il'ich dons the medallion with the inscription *respice finem* (look forward to the end) and pays a visit to "the prince" (26: 70). We shall linger on both the phrase and the "prince" because they connect in the most fascinating fashion. Before making it onto Ivan Il'ich's medallion, the Latin phrase, *respice finem*, had long been a signature statement for the lawyers. In its Latin form, it was first used by Caesar in his *Gallic War* when he used the phrase to refer to the extent of power over territories and domains.[75] The phrase later became one of the maxims in the *Digestae*, collected quotes from outstanding Roman lawyers and statesmen that formed part of Justinian's *Corpus Iuris Civilis*, known as Roman Law. Tolstoy's study of Latin and Roman law at Kazan is recorded on the pages of his daily planner for 1847 (46: 249, 251, 255, 256). For those who were entering the legal profession in Russia simultaneously with Ivan Il'ich in the 1860s, it became unpopular to seek communion with the eternal law "through contemplation of death. Immortality was guaranteed in an ineluctable historical process and not through impossible individual exploits" (Wortman, 227).

Not surprisingly, in the early drafts, Tolstoy makes his hero impress upon one pessimistic colleague (initialed "I. P.") the idea of personal happiness: "But come on, are you really happy?—Me? I certainly am" (26: 523). Ivan Il'ich explains his happiness by a special talent to face only practical questions tied to tenable goals and not bothering himself with matters outside his scope of comprehension ("I never aspire to unfeasible goals") (26: 523–24). Good professional performance, aside from making him "absolutely happy" (26: 424) also makes him indifferent to death.[76] Absolute unhappiness, complete dissatisfaction, and horror of death would pour onto the pages of his diary, a tardy deathbed confession of a mistaken final goal.

The final version of *DII* is written as an allegory of the search for the final goal (from deception to revelation and redemption). Like in Holbein's famous Dance of Death, One Man, is shown in his archetypal rivalry with his inexorable fate, which the good dancer and logician Ivan Il'ich will be learning first generally and then in particular, as Death's beloved partner. The medieval morality drama of a quest on a road to salvation, such as *Everyman*, is also crucial for the understanding of *DII* and Ivan's resilience to encountering the untimely, always unwelcome, but always inexorable visitor. Like Ivan, Everyman in the play is to be called before God to account for his life. Everyman pleads unready and asks for some time to balance his accounts (improve the understanding of his life). Everyman turns to Fellowship, which refuses to accompany him and all of Ivan Il'ich's friends likewise treat death as Ivan's own adventure. Only Good Deeds, whose friendship Everyman has regained by penance, descends with him into the grave. It must have warmed Tolstoy's heart to read that Knowledge in the medieval play leads Everyman (who for that reason is crying for joy) to Confession, after which an Angel announces that Everyman's soul is pronounced virtuous. The Doctor (a non-lying one, a real healer of ailing souls) concludes the play by proclaiming that all Christians must live wisely and remember that only Good Deeds can accompany one to the Final Judgment (902–21).[77] Tolstoy's reinterpretation of the traditional devices of the morality play occurs primarily on the level of quest imagery. However, this imagery strikes deep to the very core of Ivan's pageant with death: "The story sayth: Man, in the begynnynge / Loke well, and take good heed to the endynge, / Be you never so gay!"[78]

It is on the tension of the transcendental psychology of the hero and on the presumption of the final purpose in the motto *respice finem* that the spiritual suspense of the story is built.[79] If we examine how the educated people of Tolstoy's circle understood the meaning of the Roman saying, it will become clear that stress was rarely eschatological or even serious, let alone tragicomic as in Tolstoy. The phrase was used to recriminate with humor those oblivious of their human frailty and remind them to make responsible judgments. Tikhonravov's translation of tale 103 in his Russian edition of *Gesta Romanorum*, where the phrase occurs is cheerful: "what you do, do it with wisdom and watch till you are done" and recommends never to forget about the arrival of the final hour: "look to the end . . . remember of your last day."[80] During the years of legal reform, portent wisdoms about final goals were routinely ridiculed in their broader social application.[81] Avoiding these crude satires, Tolstoy's use of the phrase embraces all three elements of the philosophical *telos*, and all three are recorded on Ivan Il'ich's medal: firstly, the necessity to see the end; secondly, the understanding of the purpose that leads to the end; and, thirdly, self-orientation toward the ultimate goal in accordance with the main purpose. One of the long-debated issues of the structure of *DII*—why it begins its narration "from the end"—can now be explained.[82]

According to Herodotus, who recorded the legend of Solon and Croesus, Solon advised man "to look always to the end of everything" and "never consider himself happy until he is dead."[83] Ivan does not heed the inscription on his watch chain, which in its original Greek form was one of the few written (absolute) laws of Athens and carved over the portico at Delphi. Herodotus relates how it became law (Book 1.29–92). Croesus was about to be sacrificed on a pyre erected by his victorious enemies. Earlier, Croesus had punished Solon for questioning the happy ending of his life by exiling him (I: 32; 47). Now Croesus realized that he was indeed mortal and repeated Solon's injunction to his captors, who then spared him. Croesus' fetters were taken to Delphi, with Solon's *gnome* carved on them (I: 90–91; 76). Thus, the law was born.

Herodotus' tale of King Croesus and Solon was the title tale for "Tsar Croesus and Teacher Solon" (*Tsar' Krez i uchitel' Solon*) that Tolstoy's *The Intermediary* published in 1886, the same year as *DII* was finished and published.[84] Herodotus' rendition (chapters 29 to 90 of Book I) lists one case of *peripeteia* after another in order to impress upon the stubborn Croesus that "man is entirely what befalls him" (I.32: 47). By contrast, the redaction of the legend in *The Intermediary* is very succinct. The Croesus in *The Intermediary* abides by the same easy and pleasant principle of disregarding the end as did Ivan Il'ich before his illness: "I will live well while I can afford to live well." Utterly humiliated by his inglorious defeat, Tolstoy's Croesus could only break into tears and say: "akh Solon, Solon!" As soon as he said that, he was let go, just as Ivan Il'ich was allowed to slip through the black sack upon acknowledgment of his wrong.[85] Directly referring himself and his reader to Solon's semi-apocryphal adage, Aristotle, in *The Nichomachean Ethics*, laid the foundations of the theory of *telos* as happiness in activity, with the sober advice not to tempt the end until the end arrives.[86] Consider Aristotle's reworking of Solon's phrase "let no man consider himself happy until he is dead." Whereas, for Solon, worldly effects are no proof of blessed life and only the moment of death can bear such proof; for Aristotle even the moment of death does not prove anything.

In *The Nichomachean Ethics*, Aristotle advises people to wait and look toward the end result of their accomplishments, and, paradoxically, beyond the end of their lives in order to verify their success (I, XI). Uncertain about the immortality of the soul (these uncertainties were expressed in *De Anima*),

Aristotle alters the meaning of Solon's saying as follows: "Should we consider no one happy, then, while he is living, but wait, as Solon said, to see the end of his life? . . . But is not this entirely absurd, especially since we have maintained that happiness is some sort of an activity?"[87] There was no way that a person could counter the unavoidable and perilous instabilities of fate and circumstance that befell his progeny after death: "(*[I]f we are to look to the end*: this is not accomplished by following a man's fortunes, past or future, since fortunes come and go, but by ascertaining his constancy in happiness, and happiness, once again, is activity."[88] Aristotle's ethical teleology taught that man achieves what is good for him to achieve. Rational activity determines what man is. Neither Aristotle's moral teaching nor its derivative—his aesthetic theory of plot and character development—was acceptable to Tolstoy because of their insistence on predestination, that no matter what one accomplishes, nothing beyond the fabula of one's predestined life can be accomplished or retold. A chance or unexpected circumstance of which Aristotle warns be*falls* a human being as part of the preordained design—reflected in personal destiny, in the life of the state, in historic fates, in artistic characters, in cosmogony.[89] Tolstoy used Aristotle to lay to rest the old nagging question of agency, of man serving a mere instrument to the fulfillment of universal laws.[90]

Thanks to Aquinas' contribution to natural law, which linked justice, moral law, and happiness, conscience became a power stronger than physical might, and reason became the supreme judge.[91] Kant's paradoxical *moral teleology* (or *deontology*, which refuses to witness the world from the angle of cause and effect) was the direct heir of natural law and made one point abundantly clear: a person was not supposed to confuse the final goal of moral effort with the material means of its achievement.[92] The source of highest human happiness lay in the ability to judge.[93] Kant's faith in this ability was so great that he found it necessary to cap his third *Critique* with a lengthy appendage called "Critique of Teleological Judgment." Moral judgment, on which human happiness is contingent, is invested there with extraordinary legislative agency, making "the furtherance of happiness in agreement with morality the final end."[94] The spiritual energy that a morally motivated human being possesses (*vis locomotiva*) propels him forcefully to the level of omniscience fitting for the "final end of creation." The imagery of a self-propelling noncorporeal moral force possessed by the soul intervenes when Kant discusses the differences between physico- and ethico-theology. Kant defines the highest level of human moral omniscience as "inner theology."[95]

Kant's teleology provides an unexpected gloss to the phrase on Ivan's medallion. Ivan Il'ich's visit to the prince in chapter 2 is usually understood as a sign of Ivan Il'ich's discreet servility, but Ivan Il'ich is not visiting any prince, but is paying a personal final round to Prince von Oldenburg, the founding father of the School of Law: an honorable, highly principled, charitable and merciful man. In a typical expression of reverence to this man, Stasov dedicated his memoir to Oldenburg. Oldenburg was also an avid Kantian, and his agenda for the select group of students whom he accepted was to prepare a team of dedicated followers who would combine a high level of professionalism with a high standard for moral justice. So that they would never forget their moral calling, Oldenburg chose for the school's motto the phrase, *respice finem*, which was engraved or otherwise displayed in the hall of assemblies.[96] At graduation, Oldenburg presented newly minted lawyers with the newly minted medallions bearing the motto and addressed them with an instructional parting word, calling the motto an "oath" (*kliatva*): "At the minute of temptation which inevitably awaits everyone, remember your oath and you will be returned on your right ways."[97] The students, under sway of ideas more progressive than Kant's, lovingly complained about Oldenburg's old-fashioned principles.[98] Ivan Il'ich graduates high in his class (with the tenth rank) and is obviously one of the favorites because of his personal final round to Oldenburg. Ivan Il'ich's farewell with his mentor is for him a gesture of empty formality to which Tolstoy gives a pejorative meaning, saying about Oldenburg's motto that Ivan "hung that little badge" (26: 70). Ivan Il'ich does not spend time thinking about the puzzle contained in the motto: he replaces a devotional ministering to the final goal (as Solon, Kant, or Oldenburg would have it), with service or activity in accord with Aristotelian and Hegelian prescriptions.

Only when the vision of death hovers before Ivan, and his petrified gaze is fixed upon it, the *telos* from his medal is realized in its most primitive, literal sense: "look to the end." No matter how much and how long Ivan holds his gaze upon it, he does not see the purpose of his living and dying: "could it be the only truth?" (26: 94). There was neither an answer in his formerly meaningful activity nor in this meaningless suffering. Ivan Il'ich is overwhelmed with bewildered *why* in chapters 9 and 10. "Why, and for what purpose, is there all this horror? But however much he pondered, he found no answer. 'Why these sufferings?' And the voice answered, 'For no reason—just so.' Beyond and besides this, there was nothing" (26: 107).[99] Ivan's bewilderment replicates the desperation of Tolstoy's two big *Why's*—"for what purpose?" (*zachem?*) and "for what?" (*za chto?*), both of which were countered in the philosophy of the Frankfurt sage with "for no purpose" and "for no reason." For the author of *A Confession*, Schopenhauer's temptation of this resignation to purposelessness ("Truth was that life is meaningless") (23: 12) is shaken off in subsequent chapters and fantastic suspension acts. It takes four weeks and three chapters of unspeakable physical pain and moral suffering for the hero to question the happiness of his past, pleasing, and successful, life. It takes him one hour *before* death to acknowledge the mistake, the horror of his past life, and find his purpose.

As Ivan gradually focuses on understanding his purpose, it is very clear that he isolates himself, even from the good and obliging peasant lad Gerasim, the only person in the household who is not squeamish emptying Ivan's commode. In *DII*, we find a compelling fictional corollary to the exceptional nature of individual *telos*, of self-isolation in search of this individual *telos*, that is also found in Kierkegaard. Before his illness and the ensuing change of orientation toward the absolute goal, Tolstoy's hero engages in frustrating and pointless quibbles with his wife over Vasia's schooling, over bakery bills and, at early stages of his illness, over which doctor to see and which medication to apply. However, after he begins to be his own judge, Ivan Il'ich discusses nothing, drives out Gerasim, is largely silent, and only listens, as does Abraham, who is anxious to discern his higher *telos*.[100] That Abraham would keep his *telos* a secret from his family would command Tolstoy's respect after his own thwarted attempts at an explanation with Sophia Andreevna, with his daughter Tatiana, and with son Sergey. The only remaining hope that he held out was for the spontaneous understanding of his youngest sons. We find the same picture in Ivan Il'ich's story: the complete misunderstanding of Praskovia, his daughter's selfish indifference, and the timid pity of the little Vasia.

From this point of view, we might analyze the case of teleological self-authorship exemplified by Ivan's flight toward the final goal in chapters 10 to 12 in Tolstoy's retelling of the stone parable. Ivan Il'ich does not immediately embark on a self-regulated flight, of the same fantastic discovery as related by Tolstoy in 1885 to Chertkov and Ge. At the beginning of his life, when he thought that he knew his purpose for sure, and the purpose to him was a career, he was drawn to the higher placed people as a fly would be drawn to light, toward its death (26: 69). When he was sick and imagined a flying stone that was falling downwards, he identified himself with Schopenhauer's stone thrown into life "for no reason," "without goal," and "for nothing" that falls downward because of the power of gravitation, driven by the force of blind will, toward its death.[101] Identifying himself with this stone at the moment of its fall, Ivan was "awaiting that dreadful fall and shock and destruction" (26: 109).[102] However, Ivan Il'ich does not fall to his death. He will be suspended in isolation. He will have to become the stone that begins to know the purpose and regulate the direction of its flight, to come into possession of its own agency. Speaking about the moral responsibility of a given thought-project, Kierkegaard recalls Aristotle's *telos* in *Nicomachean Ethics* (III, 5, 1114a) and deliberates whether a depraved person is still empowered to change himself and the quality of his flight "just as the person who throws a stone has power over it before he throws it but not when he has thrown it."[103] Aristotle does not think that if man is unjust and wishes to stop, he will stop and be just. "For neither does a sick person recover his health (simply by wishing); nonetheless, he is sick willingly, by living incontinently and disobeying the doctors." In Aristotle's terms, Ivan has forfeited the time when "he was free not to be sick, though no longer free once he has let himself go, just as he was up to throw a stone, since the origin was in us, though we can no longer take back once we have thrown it" (1114a).[104] Aristotle's stone, fatalistically, cannot be entirely "responsible for how (the end) appears to him," although virtuous actions are voluntary, just as is our responsibility to initiate them (1114b). Kierkegaard, meanwhile, invests immense energy in the power of conversion. The stone flying badly can still reverse its trajectory and reorient itself toward the right purpose.[105] Schopenhauer's stone, by contrast, flies in a manner that is already outside Tolstoy's moral universe. To cite Schopenhauer: "Spinoza says (Epist. 62) that if a stone projected through the air had consciousness, it would imagine it was flying of its own will. I add merely that the stone would be right. The impulse is for it what the motive is for me, and what is the case of the stone appears as cohesion, gravitation, rigidity in the assumed condition, is by its inner nature the same as I recognize in myself as will, and which the stone would also recognize as will, if knowledge were added in its case also." Schopenhauer added, "The will proclaims itself in the fall of a stone as in the action of a man."[106]

When Tolstoy invokes the image of the stone in chapter 10, Ivan experiences a Schopenhauerean degree of loneliness, purposelessness, and abandon-ness (*zabroshennost'*), which "that could not be more complete anywhere—either at the bottom of the sea or under the earth . . ." (26: 107).[107] A stream of remembrance carries him in a direction opposite to his progressing illness: one spot of light, there, behind, at the inception of life, and it grows darker and darker, and moves faster and faster. It rushes in regressive proportion to the square distance toward death (*obratno proportsional'no kvadratam rasstoianii ot smerti*) (26: 109), the image of the stone gaining speed after being dropped (a stone in free fall "downwards with increasing velocity," fell into his soul). I am flying (*ia lechu*), thinks Ivan Il'ich, while lying with his face to the back of the sofa, his life and its series of increasing suffering flying ever and ever faster (26: 109). At this point, Ivan Il'ich is still unable to justify or explain the magnitude of suffering that this flight is causing him. It is obvious, however, that he realizes the flight's outward velocity and direction (into more suffering, but life flies *from* death [*ot smerti*]). He is conscious of this flight, and tries to account for it. Ivan Il'ich thinks to himself: "Yes, it was all not the right thing," but that doesn't matter. The "right

thing" can still be done. "'However, what *is* the right thing?' he asked himself and suddenly grew quiet" (26: 112).[108] At that time, Ivan Il'ich "fell
through, saw the light and it was revealed to him that though his life had not
been what it should have been, it could still be rectified" (26: 112).

Lest it be forgotten, the image of a train (or a locomotive) that is used in
chapter 12 helps define the direction of the stone's movement and originates
in the locomotive energy of the soul discovering its final end that Kant introduced into moral teleology. In his drafts of the story, Tolstoy makes Ivan
Il'ich a believer in Büchner and Moleschott, who dismiss the possibility of
immortal soul (26: 524–25). In the final chapter, Ivan Il'ich realizes the
wildest idealist dream of his author: the flight of spiritual escape. Ivan's
much discussed and still enigmatic slip of the tongue, the intended
"farewell" is pronounced "stay out of my way" or "let me pass" (*propusti*).
In the final chapter, it can be read as the acquisition of full spiritual liberty
from the physical world. On a spur of this now unstoppable movement, Ivan
utters an interchangeable "let me pass." His final purpose is found in striving and embarking on a self-directed spiritual flight. At that moment, he
feels pity for those remaining. Those who keep vigil at Ivan's deathbed at
the end of the twelfth chapter and at his bier at the beginning of the first unwittingly participate in the act of his resurrection. In Orthodoxy, twelve
Gospel chapters or so-called "twelve Gospels" are read during the Easter
Vigils and they signify that "he knew that his hour had come to depart from
this world and to go to the Father. Having loved his own who were in the
world, he loved them to the end."[109] The death of Ivan Il'ich itself may be
thus the final chapter in Tolstoy's rewriting of the Gospels and of the Christian ritual.

So what is the teleology of human life, according to Tolstoy? It is absolute,
uninterrupted and uninterruptible striving toward goodness, for it is never late
to set things right: "Human life is a striving for goodness," Tolstoy wrote at
the conclusion of his great treatise *On Life*—"what man is striving for will be
redeemed to him: life that shall not be death and goodness that shall not be
evil" (26: 435). In *On Life*, started in 1886, Tolstoy tells us the parable of
"man as a dropped object." The madman, claims Tolstoy, is not the one who
persists in choosing his purpose and authoring his own flight but rather is the
one who, when told that he was dropped, said "clink" (*dzin'*)—and died (26:
409). Powerful art knows how to build a case of sublimity (most terrible) out
of a case, both most abstract and most ordinary. After the novella had been
published, Tolstoy related to a friend partly as a joke, partly in serious tone,
but very pleased: "My brother (Sergey) tells me tongue-in-cheek after scan-
ning critical reviews of *Ivan Il'ich*: 'you are being praised for having discovered how people die. Of course nobody has known it before you."[110] The

praise was not completely satisfactory. Tolstoy started writing *On Life* on the spur of *DII*. Its initial title was *On Life and Death* (*O zhizni i smerti*). After Ivan's mission accomplished, the work could only be called *On Life* (*O zhizni*).

NOTES

1. Editors of the Jubilee edition of Tolstoy's Complete Works list this death as one of the defining dates for Tolstoy's creative chronology in the 1880s (49: 162). Hereafter the title of Tolstoy's story is abbreviated in the text as *DII*.

2. L. D. Opulskaya, *Tolstoy. Materialy k biografii s 1886 po 1892 god*, 14.

3. N. N. Gusev, *Tolstoy Materialy k biografii s 1881 po 1885 god*, 88.

4. Anatoly Koni, "Vospominaniia o dele Very Zasulich." See A. F. Koni, *Sobranie sochinenii v vos'mi tomakh* (Moscow: Iuridicheskaia literatura, 1966), 2: 213.

5. Tolstoy's personal acquaintance. See mentions of Golovin in Tolstoy (8: 551, 557; 48: 467). Another eminent legal reformer, the author of the influential *Ten Years of Reform* (*Desiat' let reform*), Aleksei Andrianovich Golovachev, is mentioned by Tolstoy in his letters and diary (48: 178; 62: 339).

6. Tolstoy mentions them a great many times in his diary in August 1884 (49: 100, 111, 119, 238, 293, 243, 244). Tolstoy had at least ten acquaintances by that name.

7. James Rice, "Comic Devices in the Death of Ivan Il'ich," *Slavic and East European Journal*, Volume 47, No. 1 (2003): 77–95.

8. See chapters 7 and 8 of the present study.

9. See Tolstoy's unfinished life of Pascal, continued over the years from 1886 (when he compared Pascal and Gogol), to *The Circle of Reading* (*Krug chteniia*) (1904; 42: 488–91). For Tolstoy's passage about Pascal, see 42: 488.

10. Text of Memorial summarized here quoted from Coleman, 60.

11. Unless amended and so indicated, all translated passages from *DII* are from *Tolstoy's Short Fiction. A Norton Critical Edition*, ed. Michael Katz (New York & London: W. W. Norton, 1991). This passage, 149.

12. Jacques Derrida, *Aporias*, trans. Thomas Dutoit (Stanford: Stanford University Press, 1993), 23.

13. Constantine Leontiev, *Analiz, stil' i veianie. O romanakh gr. L. N. Tolstogo* (Providence: Brown University Press, 1968), 50.

14. See Bakhtin, *Sobranie sochinenii*, 5: 71, 72–79, especially 71–72.

15. Tolstoy shared this plan in his letter to L. D. Urusov, on August 20, 1885 (63: 282).

16. Tolstoy stresses the motif of terrible likeness by means of repetition of the crucial phrase "terribly alike" (*uzhasno pokhozhim*) that unites human experience of the living by the terror (*uzhas*) of dying.

17. Strakhov, *Mir kak Tseloe*, 114–15. Echoing Strakhov's *Ivan Petrovich* in chapter one of *DII* thinks that death is news that can happen to Ivan Il'ich, not to himself.

18. Translation quoted from *Tolstoy's Short Fiction*, 130.

19. Opulskaya, *Lev Nikolaevich Tolstoy. Materialy k biografii s 1886 po 1892 god*, 11.

20. *Tolstoy's Short Fiction*, 150.

21. *Tolstoy's Short Fiction*, 150.

22. "Time and the Other." *The Levinas Reader*, ed. Seán Hand (Oxford/Cambridge: Basil Blackwell, 1989), 37–58, quotation 41. On the question of amending logic artistically, see Jean-François Lyotard's essay "Levinas' Logic" in *The Lyotard Reader*, ed. Andrew Benjamin (Oxford and New York: Basil Blackwell, 1989), 275–313. In the same vein as Levinas' logic of alterity, Tolstoy's remake of logic in *DII* is also "an affront of the logic and grammar of the Western philosophical tradition." See Robert Bernasconi, "'Only the Persecuted . . .': Language of the Oppressor, Language of the Oppressed," *Ethics as First Philosophy. The Significance of Emmanuel Levinas for Philosophy, Literature and Religion*, ed. Adriaan T. Peperzhak (New York and London: Routledge, 1995), 77–86, quotation, 78. On Levinas' interpretation of Socrates' logic and his final moments, see Emmanuel Levinas, "The Philosopher and Death," *Alterity and Transcendence*, trans. Michael B. Smith (New York: Columbia University Press, 1999), 159.

23. "For so-and-so to be Wholly Within such-and-such, and for such-and-such to be Predicated of Every so-and-so, is just the same. We say 'Predicated of Every' so-and-so when you cannot pick any so-and-so of which the other thing will not be said. Similarly for 'Predicated of None'." See "Prior Analytics," Book One, Chapter One, *Aristotle, A New Reader*, ed. J. L. Ackrill (Princeton, N.J.: Princeton University Press, 1983), 25.

24. Aristotle, *A New Reader*, 35.

25. The clarity of light that Ivan Il'ich sees at the end makes most of the critics either wince or glower. Critics who are sympathetic to Ivan Il'ich's transformation tend to overlook or explain away his rationality; when he sacrifices thinking—part of his sinful bureaucratic nature—for feeling and compassion, he is rewarded. Those who stress his rational side insist on his cerebral stupor, his moral inertia. Ivan's task in dying is to undo the tight grip of formulations and sage maxims, but in the end Ivan becomes a type of an abstract average rather than a unique individual. The verdict on Ivan Il'ich that he "finds no understanding in the exemplary syllogism from Kiesewetter's textbook of logic" is still in force. Boris Sorokin observes that Ivan's "innate obtuseness stands in a puzzling conflict with his otherwise manifest wit, mental agility . . . and legal training." See Boris Sorokin, "Ivan Il'ich as Jonah: a Cruel Joke," *Canadian Slavic Studies* 5 (1971): 487–507, 491. For other views discussed above, see James Olney, "Experience, Metaphor and Meaning: The Death of Ivan Ilych," in *Journal of Aesthetics and Art Criticism*, vol. 31 (1972): 101–14, quotation, 108. Gary Jahn, *The Death of Ivan Ilych: an Interpretation* (New York: Twayne Publishers, 1993), 57–58.

26. Boris Eikhenbaum, *The Young Tolstoy*, trans. Gary Kern (Ann Arbor, Mich.: Ardis, 1972), 17, 43–44.

27. Ginzburg, *On Psychological Prose*, 330–31.

28. Morson, *Hidden in Plain View*, 9.

29. See M. F. Burnyeat's essay "Enthymeme: Aristotle on the Logic of Persuasion." *Aristotle's Rhetoric. Philosophical Essays*, ed. Dadid J. Furley and Alexander Nehamas (Princeton, N.J.: Princeton University Press, 1994), 2–56.

30. Bakhtin, *The Problems of Dostoevsky's Poetics*, trans. and ed. Caryl Emerson (Minneapolis: Minnesota University Press, 1984), 290.

31. Bakhtin, *The Problems of Dostoevsky's Poetics*, 295–96.

32. René Descartes, *Discourse on Method and Meditations on First Philosophy*, trans. Donald A. Cress (Indianapolis/Cambridge: Hackett Publishing Company, 1993), 70.

33. See "Phaedo" in Plato, 73.

34. Should Tolstoy know Hegel's *Lectures on Logic*, he would be undeniably revolted at Hegel's making utility of Christ who perishes from his singularity into the universality of the Hegelian spirit in the first out of the three syllogisms of Hegel's revealed religion (before nature, history, and philosophy). Hegel's famous syllogisms of revealed religion are found in §575, 576, 577 in *Encyclopedia of Philosophical Sciences*. See G. W. F. Hegel, *Theologian of the Spirit*, ed. Peter C. Hodgson (Minneapolis: Fortress Press, 1997), 153.

35. Ernest Leopol'dovich Radlov, "Ocherk istorii russkoi filosofii," in *Russkaia filosofiia na putiakh samopoznaniia. Stranitsy istorii* (Sverdlovsk: Izdatel'stvo ural'skogo universiteta, 1991), 96–216.

36. *Russkaia filosofiia na putiakh samopoznaniia. Stranitsy istorii*, 374.

37. The work was Grot's doctoral dissertation written in Tübingen, and published as a book under the same title in Leipzig, 1882. He views logic as the science of cognition which involves both mental and psychological activity of men. See Nikolai Grot, *K voprosu o reforme logiki, opyt novoi teorii umstvennykh protsessov* (Leipzig, 1882), especially 107, 211–60.

38. See P. P. Sokolov, "Filosofskie vzgliady i nauchnaia deiatel'nost' N.Ia. Grota," Nikolai Iakovlevich Grot, *Filosofiia i ee obshchie zadachi. Sbornik statei pod redaktsiei Moskovskogo Psikhologicheskogo obshchestva* (St. Petersburg, Tipografiia A.S.Suvorina, 1904), lxvii-civ; especially lxxii. In his influential study of the Society, Randall Poole writes that Russian neo-idealism was "distinctive in its return to the ontological reality of Kant's concept of the noumenal," in contrast to the phenomenological bent of German neo-Kantians. See Randall Poole, "The Neo-Idealist Reception of Kant in the Moscow Psychological Society," *Journal of the History of Ideas* vol. 60, no. 2 (April 1999): 319–43, especially 319, 324.

39. John Stuart Mill, *A System of Logic. Ratiocinative and Inductive: Being a Connected View of the Principles of Evidence and the Methods of Scientific Investigation* (New York: Harper and Brothers Publishers, 1874), 127, 141.

40. See A 322/B378. Kant, *Critique of Pure Reason*, 315.

41. Immanuel Kant, *Logic (1800)*, trans. and intro. Robert S. Hartman, Wolfgang Schwarz (Indianapolis & New York: Bobbs-Merril Company, 1974), 108.

42. On the possible humanistic content of Kant's syllogism, see Béatrice Longuenesses's, *Kant and the Capacity to Judge. Sensibility and Discursivity in the Transcendental Analytic of the Critique of Pure Reason* (Princeton, N.J.: Princeton University Press, 1998), 94–95.

43. On the assimilation of this idea by Tolstoy in 1869, see Harry Walsh in *Schopenhauer. New Essays in Honor of his 200th Birthday*, 300–311.

44. Schopenhauer, *The World as Will and Representation*, 2: 472.

45. Schopenhauer, *The World as Will and Representation*, 2: 117.

46. Ibid., 2: 213.

47. See ibid., 1: 443–44 and 2: 52–53. J. G. Kiesewetter, *Grundriß einer allgemeinen Logik nach Kantischen Grundsaßen. Zum Gebrauch für Vorlesungen. Erster Theil, welcher die reine allgemeine Logik enthält. Zweiter Theil welcher die angewandte allgemeine Logik enthält* (Berlin: Lagarde, 1802–6). In all references to Kiesewetter's textbook (1806) a Roman figure will designate the volume of his book, in which volume one contained the description of pure universal logic, and volume two contained the description of applied logic. Since the Russian adapted translation of this book is a rarity, I will therefore use the German original, providing my own translation or paraphrase in quotes as necessary.

48. Kiesewetter's *Fassliche Darstellung der Erfahrungsseelenlehre zur Selbstbelehrung für Nichtstudierende* (Wien: Franz Haerter, 1817) was his other bestseller, which has seen numerous editions.

49. According to the information supplied by Russia's most authoritative dictionary of the nineteenth century, "Kiesewetter's manual of logic in Russian translation was in heavy use with our schools, especially those of theology." See *Entsiklopedicheskii slovar',* eds. F. A. Brokgauz and I. A. Efron (St. Petersburg: Tipo-litografiia I.A.Efrona, 1895), volume 15, page 45.

50. *Tolstoy's Short Fiction*, 132–33.

51. See "The Storyteller. Observations on the Works of Nikolai Leskov" in Walter Benjamin, *Selected Writings*, eds. Howard Eiland and Michael W. Jennings. 4 vols. (Cambridge, Mass.: The Belknap Press of Harvard University Press, 1996–2003), 3: 150–51.

52. Benjamin recalls Pascal's phrase in "The Storyteller." Benjamin, 154.

53. Here I am rephrasing Boris Tomashevsky's formalist recipes for carrying off an effective narrative, which usually begin on an "exciting force." See Boris Tomashevsky, "Thematics" in *Russian Formalist Criticism. Four Essays*, trans. and introduction by Lee T. Lemon and Marion J. Reis (Lincoln and London: The University of Nebraska Press, 1965), 61–98, especially page 72 on imparts an exciting force to the plot.

54. Richard Posner, *Law and Literature. A Misunderstood Relation* (Cambridge, Mass. & London: Harvard University Press, 1998), 354–57.

55. Richard Posner, *Law and Literature. A Misunderstood Relation*, 359.

56. V. V. Stasov, "Uchilishche pravovedeniia sorok let tomu nazad, 1836–1842," *Russkaia starina*, vol. 29, no. XII (Dec. 1880): 1015–42; vol. 30, no. II (February 1881): 393–422; vol. 30, no. III (March 1881): 573–602; vol. 31 (1881): 247. Tolstoy thanked Stasov for sending him the journal and asked for other installments. See Tolstoy's letter to Stasov, May 1?, 1881, thanking him for the memoir, "your essay about the School of Law" that he enjoyed reading (63: 61–62). See also *Lev Tolstoy i V.V.Stasov. Perepiska 1876–1906*, ed. V. D. Komarovsky and B. L. Modzalevsky (Leningrad: Priboi, 1929), 59.

57. Stasov, *Russkaia starina*, vol. 29: 1034–35. Stasov's memoir may also help to solve the old enigma of the name of Ivan Il'ich's son. There is only one surviving boy in the family, but Tolstoy uses two names: Vasia and Volodia. These are first names and patronymic of Stasov's.

58. Ivan Il'ich comes from the hereditary bureaucracy, which relied solely on its salaries for income (the most populous category in the profession). Ivan Il'ich's father is a highly placed official and his elder brother accrued sinecures. The younger brother is a dropout from the School of Law and a professional failure serving for the railroad ministry. His sister attending the wake is said to be married to a Petersburg government official, Gref. Finally, Ivan Il'ich's daughter, Liza, is affianced to Petrishchev, a court investigator, the usual prestigious rank for a beginner legal professional at his age.

59. For the description of a typical Russian lawyer in the nineteenth century, see Wortman, 220.

60. See Posner's example to the effect that every opinion in the judge's practice tends to become a law. Posner, *Law and Literature. A Misunderstood Relation*, 268.

61. *Tolstoy's Short Fiction*, 166.

62. As Bartlett writes in his comprehensive study of the medieval trial, "only the suspect's confession counted as full proof. Moreover, in many systems, capital punishment could only be inflicted if the suspect confessed. The stringent application of the so-called 'legal proof' thus placed enormous emphasis on extracting a confession." See Robert Bartlett, *Trial by Fire and Water. The Medieval Judicial Ordeal* (Oxford: Claredon Press, 1986), 141.

63. See Bartlett, 30.

64. For the beginning of Tolstoy's polemic with Saltykov, see chapter 9 of the present study.

65. *Tolstoy's Short Fiction*, 164.

66. *Tolstoy's Short Fiction*, 165.

67. Daniel Rancour-Laferriere, who takes this route of interpretation, considers the possibility that Tolstoy wished Ivan Il'ich to be a follower of Christ, the absolute masochist who suffers for all. See Daniel Rancour-Laferriere, "Narcissism, Masochism, and Denial in *The Death of Ivan Il'ich.*" *Tolstoy's The Death of Ivan Il'ich. A Critical Companion*, ed. Gary R. Jahn (Evanston: Northwestern University Press, 1999), 117–33, especially 126.

68. The earliest stages of religious consciousness, according to Ronald Green, "characteristically affirm the reality of retribution in concrete, this-worldly terms: righteousness finds its reward in this world. The hope of upright persons is to end life surrounded by wealth and progeny, to 'come to [the] grave in ripe old age'" (Job 5.26). See Ronald Green, *Religion and Moral Reason. A New Method for Comparative Study* (New York/Oxford: Oxford University Press, 1988), 16–17 and 16–23.

69. David Danaher, in an essay dedicated exclusively to the presence of pain in *DII*, reads the pain figuratively and as a structural device. "Ivan's pain, like the image of the black bag, represents a logical extension of his life. . . . Ivan suffers because the effect of the pain—complete alienation—is an extreme form of how he lived his life.

His agony physically represents his life reduced to its unfortunate essence." According to Danaher, Ivan only learns when he listens to pain (24), which fills the story with a full variety of images and sounds. As the story ends, there is no pain. The conclusion? "The pain liberates Ivan from the deadening consequences of a formulaic life and is the focal point of his transformation from death to spiritual rebirth. Tolstoy suggests by this that meaningful spiritual growth cannot take place without discomfort." See David Danaher, "The Function of Pain in Tolstoy's *The Death of Ivan Il'ich*," *Tolstoy Studies Journal*, vol. X (1998): 20–28. Quoted passages, pp. 22–23, 25.

70. See Paul Draper, "Pain and Pleasure: an Evidential Problem for Theists," *Philosophy of Religion. The Big Questions*, eds. Eleonore Stump and Michael J. Murray (Makden, Mass./Oxford, UK: Basil Blackwell, 1999), 164–75.

71. On this, see Richard Swinburne, "Natural Evil and the Possibility of Knowledge," *Philosophy of Religion. The Big Questions*, 210–22, and John Hick, "Soul-Making and Suffering" in *The Problem of Evil*, eds., Marilyn McCord Adams and Robert Merrihew Adams (Oxford: Oxford University Press, 1990), 168–88.

72. In bringing up gymnastics, Tolstoy surely has recourse to Kant's discussion of the cultivation of "powers of spirit, mind, and body" in order to best fulfill one's social duties. These principles were applied in the curriculum of The School of Law. Kant, *The Metaphysics of Morals*, 95.

73. This phrase from Cardozo's "The Growth of the Law" (1924) was quoted from Posner, *Law and Literature. A Misunderstood Relation*, 280.

74. *Tolstoy's Short Fiction*, 166.

75. The phrase "respicite [respice] finitimam Galliam" is found in Book VII of the *The Gallic War*. Caesar, *The Gallic War*, trans. H. J. Edwards (Cambridge, Mass: Harvard University Press, 1994), 16.

76. Advancing the response of legal ethos against their complaints about the misery of life (in Russia and in humanity at large), Ivan Il'ich was trying to prove to one liberal in the drafts that he was absolutely happy. In the next draft, Ivan Il'ich was assuring his friend Ivan Petrovich that he was not afraid of dying and did not understand the fright of death, living by the joys of today, disregarding the evils of tomorrow (26: 524–25).

77. See "Everyman" in *Early English Drama. An Anthology*, ed. John C. Coldewey (New York & London: Garland Publishing, Inc., 1993), 43–67.

78. See "Everyman," verses 9–12 in *Early English Drama*, 43–44.

79. The term "transcendental psychology" is used here in the same sense as Kantian scholarship uses it: as a sum total of spiritual responses to antinomies of reason. See Patricia Kitcher, "Kant on Logic and Self-Consciousness" in *Logic and the Working of the Mind. The Logic of Ideas and Faculty Psychology in Early Modern Philosophy*, ed. Patricia A. Easton (Atascadero, California: Ridgeview Publishing Company, 1997), 175–190 and Patricia Kitcher, *Kant's Transcendental Psychology* (Oxford: Oxford University Press, 1990).

80. Tikhonravov, *Rimskie deianiia*, 117–25. The phrase in Russian (*smotri kontsa, pominai poslednia svoia*) is found in "Tale or Parable About Death So That Every Man Would Do Good Thinking" (*Priklad sirech' pritcha o smerti chto by vsiak che-*

lovek, vsem dobry rozmyshleniie tvorili). The original expression "Whatever you do, do wisely and think of the consequences" (Quicquid [sic] agas, prudenter agas, et respice finem) comes from tale 103 of Gesta Romanorum, "On Doing All Things with Concord and Forethought" (De omnibus rebus cum consensu et providencia semper agendas) in *Gesta Romanorum*, 177–80.

81. In Saltykov's dialogues on social issues "Year Round" (*Kruglyi god*) the phrase *respice finem* is used to make a case for the reforms (Saltykov 13: 234). In his satiric tales on bureaucracy and liberal reform, Saltykov repeatedly uses *respice finem* or its versions "Look out, look sharp" or even "avoid the end" the motto of the bureaucrats lying comfortably in the silt on the bottom of safe and still ponds. See Saltykov's tale "The Wisest Gudgeon" (*Premudryi piskar*) and "Kippered Fish" (*Vialenaia vobla*). Saltykov, 16: 62–3, 101. Saltykov's fleeting interest in *DII* was evidenced from the questions in a number of his letters to different addressees but his opinion of the story is unknown. Tolstoy referred to Saltykov's satires of those years as "Shchedrin's silly chatter," which consumed his former talent. See Tolstoy's letter of March 31, 1884 to Chertkov (85: 288–93). The attempts of Tolstoy and Chertkov to co-opt Saltykov's talent at its best for the purposes of the religious education via Tolstoy's firm *Intermediary* were thwarted by Saltykov's obstinate withdrawal from cooperation. See Tolstoy's letter to Saltykov-Shchedrin December 1–3?, 1885 (63: 307–8).

82. For alternative interpretations, see Gary Jahn's "The Death of Ivan Il'ich— Chapter One." *Studies in Honor of Xenia Gassiorowska* (Columbus, Ohio: Slavic Publishers, 1983), 37–43, and its reworked version in Jahn, *The Death of Ivan Il'ich: An Interpretation*, 31–40.

83. See Herodotus I: 32 in Herodotus, The History, trans. David Grene (Chicago & London: The University of Chicago Press, 1987), 48.

84. I am in agreement with C. J. G. Turner who also believes that Herodotus' tale served Tolstoy as a reminder of *respice finem* in *DII*. See C. J. G. Turner, "Tolstoy and Herodotus," *Tolstoy Studies Journal*, vol. XI (1999): 55–59, especially page 58.

85. In August 2000, I had the privilege to examine this booklet, sewn by Sophia Andreevna Tolstaya into a collected volume of two- to three-page long popular tales published by *The Intermediary* in the same year. See *"Tsar' Krez i uchitel' Solon i drugie rasskazy"* (Moscow: Posrednik, 1886), 1–4. See the description of this, and a later edition of the tale, in *Biblioteka Tolstogo*, volume 1, part 2, 420. In *What Then Should We Do?* Tolstoy mentions Solon among those rare prophetic minds (Confucius, Moses, Socrates, Solomon, Homer, Isaiah, David) who managed to inscribe imperishable wisdoms on the historical memory of humankind (25: 369).

86. Donna Orwin suggested that the theme of kings seeking "diversions rather than confronting the reality of their lives" that proves their unhappiness in the face of "inescapable death and disease" was first prompted to Tolstoy by Pascal. See Orwin, *Tolstoy's Art and Thought*, 146.

87. Although elsewhere I resort to Terence Irwin's translation of *Nicomachean Ethics*, I quote from Aristotle, *Selected Works*, trans. Hippocrates G. Apostle and Lloyd P. Gerson. Commentaries by H. G. Apostle (Grinell, Iowa: Peripatetic Press, 1982), 432, since this rendition of the passage appears to resemble Tolstoy's text most closely.

88. See *Nichomachean Ethics*, I: XI–XIII in Aristotle, *Selected Works*, 432–33, emphasis mine.

89. See Tolstoy's discussion of necessity and Aristotle in the drafts to *War and Peace* (15: 224 passim 243) and of Aristotle's idea of goodness in *What is Art*? and its drafts (30: 40, 67, 74–76, 292, 304, 318, 330, 338, 342, 347, 353) and in Diary (March 1, 1897; 53: 140–41, 304). In the mid 1880s, there were exchanges on Aristotle between Tolstoy and Nikolai Grot: precisely in connection with immortality, the fulfilled life and the practice of judgment (see Tolstoy's response to Grot, October 7, 1887 [64: 100–110]). In *On Life* Tolstoy names Aristotle's doctrine insufficient (26: 330). It is indicative that Aristotle's positive answer to personal fulfillment is associated for Tolstoy with the materialist systems of Bacon and Comte. Tolstoy, nevertheless, considered seriously the benefits of studying Aristotle in peasant schools (see 8: 6 passim; 386).

90. On the same, see Tolstoy's letter to Chertkov. Dec. 31, 1889 (86: 284–85).

91. See Aquinas's notations to Aristotle's theory of happiness in St. Thomas Aquinas, *Commentary on Aristotle's Nichomachean Ethics* trans. C. I. Litzinger. Foreword Ralph McInerny (Notre Dame: Dumb Ox Books, 2000), 61. See J. Owens, "Aristotle and Aquinas" in *The Cambridge Companion to Aquinas*, eds. Norman Kretzmann and Eleonore Stump (Cambridge: Cambridge UP, 1993), 38–59.

92. Best summarized in Kant's *The Metaphysics of Morals*, 147.

93. Ibid., 142.

94. Kant, *The Critique of Judgment*, 119.

95. Kant, *The Critique of Judgment*, 159. The Latin phrase *vis locomotiva* in the original text was not rendered in Meredith's translation. My reference here will be to the original German text. Kant, *Kritik der Urteilskraft* (Stuttgart: Philipp Reclam, 1991), 469.

96. See Georgy Siuzor. *Ko dniu LXXV iubileia imperatorskogo uchilishcha pravovedeniia, 1835–1910* (St.-Petersburg, 1910), 35. Siuzor is incorrect attributing the phrase to Horace (36), in whose entire oeuvre no such phrase has been found.

97. Siuzor 36; Wortman 208. Oldenburg, an immensely erudite, charitable and stoic man, treated his students like members of the family. Tolstoy was personally acquainted with one of the Oldenburgs, Petr Aleksandrovich (1868–1924), and appreciated this family's charity and its commiseration with political and religious dissenters. See Tolstoy, 73: 71–72; 90: 320–21. He requested the Prince's intercession with the Emperor for the persecuted Molokans (73: 71–72). In May 1901, he addressed the Prince personally to plead the cause of Maxim Gorky, who was then under arrest (90: 320–21). Gorky was released.

98. Wortman, 206–7.

99. *Tolstoy's Short Fiction*, 162.

100. Kierkegaard, *Fear and Trembling*, 82–120.

101. *The World as Will and Representation*. Book Two, 24 (vol. 2: 126).

102. *Tolstoy's Short Fiction*, 163.

103. Kierkegaard, *Philosophical Fragments*, 17.

104. Aristotle, *Selected Works*, 68–70.

105. For Kierkegaard, "the ethical demand is that one become *infinitely* interested in existing" (*Concluding Unscientific Postscript*, esp. 1: 207–26). The purpose of this

ethical subject, therefore, "is not simply to know the truth but to *become it*, not to produce objective truth but to transform one's subject's self." See James C. Livingston, *Modern Christian Thought. From the Enlightenment to Vatican II* (New York: Macmillan Publishing Co., Inc.; London: Collier Macmillan Publishers, 1971), 315.

106. *The World as Will and Representation*, volume 2, 299 and 24. Similar pronouncements on the stone are scattered throughout the book. See vol. 1: 131, 214, 404, 503 and vol. 2: 174, 303, 443.

107. *Tolstoy's Short Fiction*, 162.

108. Ibid., 166.

109. See John 3.1. Quoted from *The New Oxford Annotated Bible*. NT, 147.

110. See Tolstoy's letter to L. E. Obolensky in May 1886 (63: 357).

Chapter Twelve

On Life and Conclusion

SPIRITUAL FORCE

When Tolstoy was working on the final version of *DII*, he communicated with Nikolai Grot about the book that Grot had just finished, *On the Soul, in Relation to the Latest Doctrines of Power* (*O dushe v sviazi s sovremennymi ucheniiami o sile*).[1] Grot's book constructs a theory of spiritual force (*sila-dukh*) and separates itself passionately both from Schopenhauer's pessimism and from any connection with materialistic teachings of power (Büchner, Molleschott). This active spiritual force directly confronts Büchner's famous work, *Force and Matter* (*Kraft und Stoff*; 1860). Grot inscribed the book to Tolstoy as a personal gift and glossed its entire content, footnoting the topics that he and Tolstoy discussed "the other day." To these comments by Grot, Tolstoy added his responses, so the book's margins bear physical marks of Tolstoy's approval.[2]

Not only does Tolstoy support Grot's idea of the soul's liberation from matter and its striving toward goodness, he also inscribes what seems to be the Russian letter "O" against the paragraph in which Grot depicts the soul's flight towards liberation. This letter could be the first initial standing for "*Os-vobozhdenie*" (Liberation). Grot speaks of the liberation of the soul referring himself constantly to Plato's *Phaedo*, with which he begins the genealogy of his theory. The liberation of the soul is what specifically connects Plato's final Socratic dialogue, Grot's essay, and *DII*. This connection with his beloved dialogue helps explain Tolstoy's enthusiastic endorsements of Grot's fantastic picture of the soul's flight of escape: "Liberation? Only liberation" (*Os-vobozhdenie? Tol'ko osvobozhdenie*) and "Liberation? Only an active one" (*Osvobozhdenie? Tol'ko aktivno*) and, then, with regards to the improbability of such escape, "As an impossibility, still, a statistic" (*Kak nevozmozhnost', a statistika*).[3]

The statistic of the soul's liberation is ascertained immediately following Grot's proclamation of the saving force of his teleology: "Manifestly, our doctrine of spiritual force could serve as a foundation for the reworking of all moral, individual, and social ideals of humanity. It justifies, among other things, teleological view of nature and refutes the doctrine of pessimism" (Grot, 90). By March 25, 1886, the date inscribed at the end of his account of Ivan Il'ich's passion for the goal, Tolstoy had already found the name for his own discovery of liberation, and he called it "reasonable consciousness" (*razumnoe soznanie*).[4] Ivan Il'ich unites in his flight the force of the first push that cast him into life with his striving toward his first and final cause, the desired outcome of Tolstoy's search of nearly forty years.[5] Reasonable consciousness provides a crucial backdrop for the ideas that motivated Tolstoy's depiction of the awakening of purpose in the dying Ivan Il'ich and for sustaining Tolstoy's conversion. Reasonable consciousness neither vanishes with the physical cessation of being nor is dispelled by posthumous revelations or accidents already beyond all control (26: 400). Reasonable consciousness is a special orientation toward life, an imperative to attain what is good, and the identification of one's own unique supra-personal relationship with life.

As a union of reasonable necessity and conscious freedom, reasonable consciousness is immortal and is not limited to the time frame of the physical life cycle. In ecstatic possession of this newly discovered key to immortality, *On Life* was started in the summer of 1886. Tolstoy was helping a poor peasant widow collect straw for the winter and badly hurt his leg. The wound was seriously inflamed, and other complications followed, rendering Tolstoy bedridden for several months. Suddenly the illness was grave enough for Tolstoy to start thinking of death. His health soon started improving, but his cooperation with Grot facilitated his philosophical line of thinking on the topic of dying. When in March of 1887, Sophia Andreevna Tolstaya was preparing a fair copy from the finished part of the manuscript, she named it "On Life and Death" (*O zhizni i smerti*; 26: 753). Tolstoy also refers to his emerging work still "On Life and Death" (*O zhizni i smerti*) in his letter to Chertkov of April 2, 1887 (86: 42). Somewhere after May of 1887 and after he had read a synopsis of the second half of the work at the session of the Moscow Psychological Society on March 14, 1887, following Grot's talk "On the Freedom of Will" (*O svobode voli*), Tolstoy changed his mind about the twin title. He confessed in a letter to Vasily Alexeev in September-October 1887 that his work was really *On Life* alone and that death should be let go (64: 48–49). The work still involved several redactions in 1888. Grot was responsible to a degree for correcting spelling mistakes and for insisting on Tolstoy's sticking to his own terms of argumentation. Some of his corrections were not for the better. For example, Grot substituted "animal creatures" for Tolstoy's more poetic "living creatures" (26: 426, 790). The correction introduced a crude dichotomy of the animalistic versus the spiritual unintended by Tolstoy. Nonetheless, in the course of about five hundred pages in longhand, thirty-five chapters, and two addenda Tolstoy expostulates in his own voice on the meaning of reasonable consciousness and on secrets of its attainment.

In *DII*, and *On Life*, Tolstoy provides a summary of his earlier interpretations of the "connection between delusion and suffering" (*sviaz' zabluzhdeniia i stradaniia*) (26: 428). He continues to support the points of *What I Believe?* and *What, Then, Should We Do?* in that suffering or martyrdom by choice are not the real goals of earthly and spiritual toil. He confirms that suffering makes itself first known in human experience only within the confines of time and space and in illness, in accidents beyond control, and in various forms of social injustice. Rather than cultivate suffering in the Romantic, ascetic, or masochistic spirit, Tolstoy vehemently rejects its edificatory function unless it is first internalized, and then leads to overcoming the source of suffering. The change in orientation, turn or turnaround toward the right priorities, this new and latest understanding of conversion, can be done any time — even two or five minutes before death. Ivan Il'ich's escape was an example of narrative immortality. As Tolstoy half-jokingly stressed in his letter to Chertkov in November 1885, more realistic conversions and not those on the deathbed are much tougher to endure (85: 280). In its often-ironic portrayals of the reality whose true essence is not always what it appears to characters, *DII* already gave us a taste of the double reality of life, which if left undetected, creates all the torture, and all the dissatisfaction with existence. "Real life is joyous," says Tolstoy over and over, page after page in *On Life*. In the novella, we were witnesses of the two temporal zones of life, real and illusory, which are allowed to exist on their own terms. Liza, Ivan's daughter, pays Ivan a visit at his sickbed, looks at her watch, which Tolstoy describes in a suggestive parenthesis ("her father's present") and says: "Should we go, it is (now) the time" (26: 104). The family members are making ready to go to the theater. Eager to dissociate herself from the precarious zone of mortality, Liza makes an effort to make "should we go" conditional on "it is time." Her time is naturally the time of biological life that Ivan already considers a lie. When they leave, Ivan feels better (26: 105).

The relativity of time is similarly accentuated by the deceptive urgency with which the lawyers in the story try to get to the card table and enter the game "on time." Not only the moment but the number of entering the game may not be fortuitous for the player, who has a greater chance to become redundant or "dead" if his number is not good. Such is the least aspired number five at the end of the first rubber that Petr Ivanovich makes after paying his respects to the dead Ivan Il'ich (26: 68). The healthy and self-confident Ivan Il'ich made a point never to play the number five, fraught with a "very painful getting out of the game" (*uzh ochen' bol'no vykhodit'*; 26: 82). Already far along in his illness, Ivan Il'ich tries to stay in the game as long as his strength will afford him; he stops playing only when he notices that his partners feign defeat in his favor and when he requires a break for rest. This is unthinkable for a high-quality player who, while gambling and in choosing the highest stakes, approximates eternity (26: 88). After Ivan's enigmatic escape into eternity in chapter one, Petr Ivanovich and the dark, flippant Schwarz conspire to sneak out of Ivan Il'ich's funeral chamber as quickly as possible to get to the game. They forget that in the games of poker and whist the likely winner has a trump card that in the game's jargon is called "death" (*smert'*).[6] Ivan Il'ich, as Schwarz's sly look implies, "has cut a stupid deal" or, in the card jargon of the same phrase, "has dealt his pack stupidly" (*glupo rasporiadilsia*; 26: 63). Metaphysically speaking, however, Ivan also has the trump card and is a winner.[7] Having lost their own bearings in the relativity of time in *DII*, editors and translators of the story correct Tolstoy. For example, in the final chapter twelve, to make the time count adequate to the perception of the physical witnesses of Ivan's agony, translators substitute "this occurred at the end of the third day, *one* hour before his death" for Tolstoy's "*two* hours before his death" in the same phrase.[8] For those present, Tolstoy really implies that the agony would indeed drag out for another two hours, while after Ivan's most significant moment of understanding, its meaning would not change for another hour while his physical body is still in agony.

At earlier stages of his illness and tired of the meaninglessness of his biological hours, Ivan asks the servant for his watch. The Russian word "chasy" means "watch" and "hours." Ivan is destined to while away the hours that are of no use to him. He begins to count his schedule by his own special secondary symptoms—by the light of dawn, by the curtains drawn back, or by the doctor's visits (26: 100). Ivan's physical time is counted by his doctors, by his family, and by his brother-in-law who alerts Ivan's wife that her husband looks doomed to him, a dead man whose physical disintegration is a matter of weeks (26: 89). When Ivan was anxiously counting hours and years between promotions, time had a vile sign of the inertia of life. Gradually, his time in sickness becomes allegorically drawn out until it collapses into a decrepit slough of physical and then moral pain. Whether Ivan Il'ich chooses to go to his job and preside at trials at the court or to stay at home, time itself becomes his meaningless unavoidable trial. He is destined to while away the time with the same twenty-four hours a day, each of which was a torture (26: 89). Three days before death, he hushes the doctor away for good when the doctor arrives at his "usual hour" no longer to promise Ivan an extension on his life, but only to make the hours that he will live insensitive to pain (26: 110). Ivan Il'ich squeezes the morass of mortal time and space out of his spiritual schedule—the task that Tolstoy disbelieved to be possible in human terms in *War and Peace* and that cost him years of hardship and experimentation with causality and temporal-spatial limitations of life. What bothered him since 1869 were these problems: the conception of a human tool being only instantaneously free in the solipsistic games of denial of time and space, in self-loss in the swarm of animal life or the social hive. Long after writing his essay, "On Future Life Outside of Time and Space" (1875), reason and consciousness for Tolstoy still oppose each other. Only in the throes of his final struggles does Ivan Il'ich drop the semi-obnoxious questioning reminiscent of Pierre in captivity: "And who is me?" and divines in silence his flight away from death.

In his portrayals of fictional immortality in the manner of how it should be rather than how it really is, Tolstoy did not feel that he was committing a crime against truth. In his letter to a younger writer, Alexey Potekhin, Tolstoy repeated his belief of several years that mimetic truthfulness to visible life is a sham and that only that what should be in the ideal of human striving is the goal of writing. He who fails to see the boundary dividing true life from false has no right to write (64: 15). Writing itself may be redundant. Truth worth recording is the highest form of the expression of life's meaning; it will not die even if left unrecorded. Such is the undying element of Christ's teaching: "The reader must remember that Jesus never wrote any book, as did Plato, Philo or Marc Aurelius; he never transmitted his teaching, as did Socrates, to literate and educated people, but he spoke to those illiterate people whom he met in his life. It is much too late after his death that people noticed the absence of what he had been saying in written form and that it would not hurt to write it down" (24: 804–5). The same immortal force of the ideas of faith is explained in *What I Believe?* the nearest precursor of *On Life*: "A basis for faith is the meaning of life which judges what is important and good in life and what is unimportant and bad" (23: 406). Silent art of consummate inner beauty may be the final goal of art and spiritual activity. Like Heidegger much later, Tolstoy is convinced that the word speaks us and needs our assistance in speaking the language of life. Reasonable consciousness needs its writer so that its voice may be heard and so that it may assist the reader's conversion to the word of truth.[9]

On Life crowns the literature of Tolstoy's conversion. Despite its initial title "On Life and Death," the book was soon nicknamed by Strakhov a "book in philosophy on the predominance of consciousness" and on the "immortality of reason."[10] Aside from the oblique reference to Gogol's restrained and cautious "reasonable consciousness," Tolstoy's choice of the title and the topic may have been informed by Zhukovsky's "Letters to Gogol" (1847–1852) and another work titled *On Life*, a much earlier work by Shelley (1819), finally gaining in popularity after its first appearance in print in 1832. One of Zhukovsky's letter-mediations to Gogol in this period was called "On Death" ("*O smerti*") and was written on the occasion of the death of his daughter in-law. Like Tolstoy in his work, Zhukovsky calls death a transition to life outside space and time, the key that opens the door to immortality. In this consciousness plays the role of the key. If this consciousness is one of enduring love, the living and the dead are connected by uninterrupted succession of timeless communication of the two worlds. In fact, the very division of life into two worlds is an illusion of earthly consciousness oppressed and aggrieved by the seeming finality of death. Zhukovsky reappoints the binary: there is a true and enduring God's world and another, illusory, finite world of human delusion.[11]

Shelley's *On Life* adds more dimensions to the discussion of life, calling it the greatest mystery of unfolding eternity, "an astonishing thing," obscured by familiar perceptions. "What is life?" asks Shelley, stressing that life sifts through our impressions of it as we age and change. Is life confined only to our perceptions of who we might be, or does it answer the main question by considering "whence do we come, and wither do we go? Is birth the commencement, is death the conclusion of our being? What birth and death? The most refined abstractions of logic conduct to a view of life, which, though startling to the apprehension, is in fact that which the habitual sense of its repeated combinations has extinguished in us. It strips, as it were, the painted curtain from this sense of things." Shelley then addresses "the shocking absurdities of the popular philosophy of mind and matter" and pledges his allegiance to the alternative view that regards man to be a "wanderer through eternity" for whom life is "an education of error," and what remains of such education does not merely dissolve in the universe. This remarkable fragment remained unfinished.[12] Zhukovsky's, Shelley's, and perhaps also Viazemsky's term, "terrible consciousness," discussed in chapter 1 of the present study and as it was applied to Gogol's prophetic consciousness must have informed Tolstoy's choice of topics in *On Life*. So did Tolstoy's practically lifelong overcoming of Hegel's competition of the living force with unhappy consciousness and the enduring essence of life, Schelling's, Hegel's, and Schopenhauer's versions of reconciliation of freedom with necessity, and Belinsky's terrible affirmation to Botkin that addled the youths of his generation: "Nothing, Botkin! Nothing remains. . . . Only death is immortal." The earlier Tolstoyan notions of consciousness in its states of uninterruptible motion and memory's complete dependence on the body as well as the later notion of separation from the All of life (*ot'edinenie ot vsego*; 17: 351) were also brought into play.

THE CROWN OF CONVERSION

Grot tried one desperate exchange after another with religious authorities to publish *On Life*. The Archbishop of Kherson Nikanor spoke for spiritual authorities in general when he issued a negative review of *On Life*, saying that it was a powerful display of wit, sometimes running deep, but diffused with sophisms.[13] Nikanor was right in fearing the work.[14] Tolstoy's treatise was a personal and autobiographical statement that was geared toward a pluralistic audience of open-minded readers and listeners. He gave one of his numerous public readings in front of a conveniently commissioned grand jury, which he wished to consist of an attorney, a philosopher, and a "representative of religion."[15] The parallel with the triumvirate of professionals dispensing three sorts of judgment (lawyer, doctor, priest) in *DII* is striking. It was Tolstoy's clear intention to pass his two perfectly correct systems of logic by the jurors of his choice. The same two systems, one true, one false, are also present in Zhukovsky and Shelley. What were the two systems of logic that Tolstoy elaborated in his treatise on reason? He approaches the discussion of life from the standpoint of logic, in search of its main, all-embracing concept. He discards scientific descriptions because of his well-known suspicion of the possibility to grasp phenomena from and on all sides: "what matters in every reasoned thought is not reasoning itself, but what is in pride of place (position taken by it); in other words, in order to think fruitfully, one ought to know what to think on first and what next. . . . And the reasoning dissociated from the ultimate end of all reasoning is insane, no matter how logical it is" (26: 314).

Tolstoy explains life from the most "needed and important side" (26: 321), and he does so by making it clear why he chose three epigraphs to preface his work. *On Life* is prefaced firstly with Pascal's fragment that describes man as the thinking reed who knows that it is fruitless to attempt to engulf with his being as much space and time as his physical limit permits and yet over whom, endowed with reason, no physical calamity unleashed by the unthinking universe may have any advantage (26: 313).[16] The second epigraph is from Kant's *Critique of Practical Reason*, his most poetic piece, and describes the wonderment of *Verknüpfung* (harnessing or concatenation) in man's living and receptive being of the star-bedecked sky above and the moral law within, Tolstoy's long sought after harnessing and concatenating device of *sopriazhenie* and *stseplenie* adopted from Stankevich.

After a long history of rejecting the categorical imperative for fear of its abstraction and his warming up to the concept in the 1884 letter to Buturlin, Tolstoy finally embraced Kant's moral law and reinforced it with John's treatment of love.[17] The last epigraph is Tolstoy's favorite verse from John (12.34), the injunction to love each other that he also used for his commentary to Ge's *Last Supper*. Kant's inclusion in Tolstoy's trinity of saving graces marks his final rejection of Schopenhauer in the famous letter to Strakhov on October 16, 1887, in which Kant is extolled and Schopenhauer is called "a talented scribbler" (64: 105). Page 194 in Tolstoy's own edition of Kant where the paean to stars and moral law appears is encircled by Tolstoy's elaborate scroll beaming of enthusiasm and fondness.[18] But in his definition of reasonable consciousness Tolstoy went much further than Kant. For Kant, 'I think' is not a moral act, but a spontaneous act of representation culminating in "transcendental unity of self-consciousness," the one that accompanies all other representations of reality, but that "cannot itself be accompanied by any further representation."[19] Transcendental unity of self-consciousness is not relative to Tolstoy's reasonable consciousness. According to Kant, heteronymous apperception of the world is linked with rational principles only insofar as those latter are construed as the principles of happiness, linked, in their turn, with the physical and moral aspects of human life, or its empirical reality.[20] Kant claims that we obey moral law thanks to the dependence of our practical reason on external conditions of life.[21]

In constructing his reasonable consciousness, Tolstoy would disagree on the extent and hierarchy of such dependence; in particular he will object to Kant's insistence that reason is a special faculty opposed to understanding.[22] At the same time, Tolstoy pursues Kant's most radical and paradoxical ideas to the extreme. Thus, he takes literally Kant's repeated suggestion that practical employment of reason may enable us to transcend the limits of possible experience; especially Kant's celebrated phrase that "though I cannot *know*, I can yet *think* freedom" emboldens Tolstoy to equate man's hoping to be happy with his yearning to fulfill the laws of morality, so that the fulfillment of Kant's *ought to be* may point man to the "kingdom of grace."[23] Tolstoy makes lucid use of Kant's unclear definition of the degree of dependence of autonomous will on heteronymous, or sensible and physical, conditions of life. Tolstoy's interlude on logic after the epigraphs starts really on a philosophical parable about the miller and the river common in Buddhist explorations of higher wisdom. The miller lives by the river, and his mill performs perfectly without his knowing its structure and causes of its motion; his business is good. Suddenly, the miller decides to understand the mechanism. He now knows his mill perfectly, and he also soon realizes that it is the river and the dam that really cause his mill to work. The miller stops working for work's sake, and only launches the mill to tabulate the amounts of produced flour to the force that moves the winds that moves the arms that moves the grinding wheels and so forth. His business collapses, although his outwardly correct logic perfects itself.

Tolstoy told us similar parables in *War and Peace* in order to impress on us that we need to observe causes of power rather than its vestiges and neglect the immediate consciousness of will for the sake of the law that moves everything—the mill, the clock, the train, the troops, and the masses. He also stressed in *War and Peace* that divine will and its law may be observed only in historical movement rather than in the life of a single individual. Deity decides of its own volition whether man should move or how and when he should move. In *On Life*, as he did in *DII*, Tolstoy says the opposite. Man determines his own movement. The miller should not have wasted the time trying to understand the movement of the river. It is impossible. He should have tried to understand his relationship with the river and the mill that feeds him. In the diary entries adjacent to *On Life*, we find corroboration of this interpretation. In June 1886, Tolstoy writes that everything lives together and apart and that every effort to engulf more life only nears death. This contradiction would be insolvable if reason did not reside in man; reason living in man is a force that destroys his egoism and makes him a moral being who can understand death and life in a cardinally different way (49: 127). How does man employ his reason? In February 1887, Tolstoy clarifies: "Man uses his reason to ask why and for what reason? . . . and reason shows him that there are no answers. . . . Reason is not given to man to answer these questions. The very fact of asking these questions means that reason is deluded. Reason decides only the main question: *how*. And in order to know [this] *how*, he decides within the limits of (his) finitude the questions *why* and *what for*? How to live? Blessedly . . . Bliss is the making of one's bliss. There is no other" (49: 131). In essence, Tolstoy invites us to practice Kant's second question (what to do?) and decide not just what to do, but also *how to do it*. For this, we need to elaborate, through reason, our own unique relationship with the world and life.

On Life explains that all that man knows of the external world he knows thanks to his discovering three different relations to the world within himself: his reasonable consciousness, his physical being in the world, and the substance of life inclusive in his being.[24] In the external world, man discriminates between reasonable beings, animals and plants, and inanimate substances because he enjoys all three sources of perception (26: 357). All three modes of existence appear to man as if they constituted his own past, something he has lived through, the remembrance of his past lives (26: 359). This is Tolstoy's reinterpretation of the Orthodox conception of personality and man in the world that I have discussed in chapter 1. Using the word "life" as a concept, Tolstoy does not ascribe the quality of life to "little cells," something he never did even at the height of his passion for science or Schopenhauer. In doing so, Tolstoy distances himself not only from theological conceptions but also from traditionalist philosophy. Life is ascribed by Tolstoy to the definite *quality of consciousness* (26: 318).

A paradox is laid out: although life is not limited to a play of physical and mechanical forces, it takes place in the sphere of observable phenomena, where the struggle of evil and goodness cannot be seen. The fear of death arises from consciousness of the unsolvable contradiction of life, that my self-aware being, struggling to be and do good, will perish (26: 398). Tolstoy says that at this point only we arrive at the two strictly logical views on life: one false, and one true (26: 399). In the false one, life appears to us in the visible changes that occur in the body. In the true one, life is the invisible consciousness of that which endures and of the goodness and love that we bear in ourselves. In the false and very ancient view, life is but a chance (haphazard) game of forces made manifest in a substance existing within space and time, with swirling and falling objects and disintegrating matter. What we attribute to our consciousness of that form of life is not the consciousness of life eternal, but the consciousness of momentary and transient flickers, which burn out one by one until the darkness of death envelopes this perishable consciousness (26: 399).

This is precisely the consciousness of personal, egotistic striving that Tolstoy had difficulty embracing since 1847 and which he summarized in the epilogues to *War and Peace* and then reformulated in the final chapter of *Anna Karenina*. Observing the world, this consciousness of disparate moments sees itself as a particle in the limitless game of accidental forces or as a bubble that balloons and then bursts. Tolstoy even makes a rhyme to bury his once precious bubble for good. When the bubble of personal life is no more, it bursts with the sound of *bryzn'* (splash out). However, this "bryzn'" of a splash is not synonymous with *zhizn'* (life) (26: 318). Life is what I am conscious of *in myself*. I realize my life in the present, not in what I was or will be, but in that what I am, knowing that I have no beginning and no end.

The concept of space and time is nonconnectible with this consciousness of my life in the present. The life which I realize (*soznaiu*) is fully realized (*soznaietsia*) by me already outside of time and space. Tolstoy purposefully employs the terms from the Epilogues of *War and Peace* to highlight the fact that reasonable consciousness, this right attitude to the world, suffers no detachment from the reasonable laws of life. Only because of that, temporal and spatial termination cannot change anything or disrupt my genuine, eternal life (26: 400). It is not the death of their flesh that people are frightened of, but the prospect that the absence of true consciousness of life will render all suffering useless (26: 401). Reiterating the latter point already made in *What, Then, Must We Do?* Tolstoy reminds us that we die every day, we die when we fall asleep, and we die of old age as surely as we do of terrible accidents. What saves is the orientation in consciousness toward true life. The orientation toward eternity in reasonable consciousness does hold together moments of discrete consciousness (flickers) of temporal perception so as to turn them into the uninterrupted fluidity of continuing movement toward light without beginning or end. This explanation of reasonable consciousness of self by Tolstoy is very close to Kantian invisible individuality (*Persönlichkeit*), which, through the moral law orienting me toward worthwhile goals, represents me in the world as possessing true endlessness (*wahre Unendlichkeit*). The social life-habits of people (*privychka zhizni obshchestv liudei*) reflect the opposite, an acknowledgement of temporal consciousness only (26: 335).

When the realization of the split of consciousness (temporal and reasonable) inevitably arrives, it generates unspeakable pain (26: 340). In Tolstoy's terms, pangs of suffering accompany the birth of reasonable consciousness, unobservable temporally and invisible in its cyclical movement, but more real than objective reality. Tolstoy's description of the split of consciousness into reasonable and unreasonable is quite picturesque. The deluded consciousness clamors for the inalienable rights of personality and insists that life should be easy, pleasant, and merciful to all physical needs. It stages the rebellion against the demands of reasonable consciousness, and the two enter the fray. Reminding us of Ivan Il'ich's silent conversations with himself, his fondness for the old life and his realization that a return is impossible and has little to do with physical pain or the very question of physical survival, reasonable consciousness in *On Life* cuts the dispute short: "I don't want to hear any of this" (26: 368). Thus, Tolstoy brings us to the unfolding of a very special theology of *On Life*. He repeats his earlier illuminations achieved in 1881–1884 that true life is always stored in man, just as it is stored in a grain, and reasonable consciousness brings this truth out (26: 346). He mentions Christ for the first time only in chapter XVII, "The Birth in The Spirit" (*Rozhdenie dukhom*) about midway into the discussion to time Christ's appearance at the exact moment in the description when reasonable consciousness is taking seed. Tolstoy explains that reason (logos) is seeded in every man; whether it grows or not depends on the orientation of man's consciousness. Christ's response to the commandments of reasonable consciousness is a living example of immortality in action.

Tolstoy uses remarkable formulas to elaborate his finest statements on realized immortality, or man's conversion to the endurable in life. Man is brought to the necessity to be born the second time after his physical birth and maturation. When he attains reasonable consciousness, he is born again, and if he wins in his persistent inner struggle for merging with reason, the law of life, he will be saved. With death, we do lose our singular "I" (personality), which connects the body and a series of discrete consciousnesses revealed at separate moments over time (26: 406). Death of the flesh destroys what holds the body together—the consciousness of temporary life. However, will death destroy what connects all these subsequent consciousnesses into one, that is, into my understanding of the world (*moe otnoshenie k miru*)? One must prove that this consciousness was born together with the being of his flesh and will therefore die with it; therefore, Tolstoy would say that this is how it is *not* born (26: 407). Only a singular, unrepeatable attitude to the world independent of the influences of sensory perception and enslavement to selfish communal values constitutes the singular "I," which is not a result of an external cause, but *is* the main cause of all other events/phenomena (*iavlenii*) of life. One's singular attitude toward life and commitment to goodness from moment to moment of our life in the world guarantee perpetuation of life.

Against a common misconception, Tolstoy is not saying that we should deny our humanity and live our lives like incorporeal abstractions. Quite the contrary: "not the renunciation of personality, but its submission" to reasonable consciousness is what he insists on (26: 376). Tolstoy accepts the possibility that his position may be confused with Buddhism, but he makes it clear that he would rather be confused with a Buddhist than profess the life of selfishness or live in the loveless hell of Lermontov, whose crisis of love he brings into play alongside the question of love and suicide (26: 384). Suicide, such as Lermontov's duel or Schopenhauer's pessimistic renunciation of the will to live or ascetic self-emaciation, resolves the matter of crisis conscientiously, in its own twisted logic of "good faith." The line of reasoning of pessimists is this: since the insatiable striving for life cannot be satisfied, life should be forcefully curtailed or ended. What is required instead, in Tolstoy's creed, is subjugation of personal striving to reason. Human suffering results from man's commissioning his reason to satisfy the ever augmenting personal demands (26: 378). One should not disavow his person, because personality is one of the basic conditions of life; the life of personality, however, should not eclipse the *whole of life* (26: 378).

Tolstoy again returns to the task of establishing one's special relation (*otnoshenie*) to the world. In ourselves, we can always notice a movement toward this attitude in a greater subordination of our material nature to reason. Life is a constant reestablishing of new relations. The movement of life, or the reestablishing of relations, is what destroys Schopenhauer's representations, his phantoms (*predstavlenie, Vorstellung*) of death. A person who stays put in the relation with which he was born to the world and with the same experience of love or hatred anticipates death in fear (Schopenhauer's unchangeable "character" is under attack here), and feels the stopping of life and the nearing of death (*emu predstavliaetsia smert*; *Tod [im] vorgestellt*) (26: 409). But a person who understands life knows that he has contributed his unique attitude to the world. In the trains of his thoughts memorable to him, man can notice how his attitude to the world was changing and how the subordination to the law of reason was increasing, and so the sphere of his wellbeing was growing (as he was approaching greater light), even though the scope of his personal existence was decreasing (as he walked out of his dark shadow). The example below demonstrates Tolstoy's remarkable sense of spiritual perception in the play of shadow and light:

> For a person who comprehends life for what it really is, to speak about the diminishing of his life during illness and old age and to despair about it is the same as if the person who is approaching light would despair about his shadow getting thinner and thinner the closer he comes to light. To believe that his life expires when his body expires is the same as to believe that the expiration of the object's shadow after the object enters completely into the sphere of light amounts to the expiration of the object itself. Such a conclusion would be possible with somebody who has stared at the shadow for so long that he has imagined that the shadow is the object itself. For a person who knows himself not only as a reflection in his spatial and temporal being but as his grown loving relation to the world, the demise of the spatial and temporal conditions is rather a proof of the greater measure of light. For a person who understands his life as a certain known relation to the world with which he merged in his being and with which he was growing the more his love to it was growing, for this person to believe in his expiration is the same as for a person who knows the laws of the world in its external phenomena and believes that his mother found him on the field under cabbage leaves and that his body will evaporate somewhere so that no trace of his would remain (26: 411).

In the depiction of this metaphor of light as growing awareness, Tolstoy repeats the metaphor of light from its Evangelical rendition with which he agreed in his own retelling of the Gospels: "light shineth in darkness and darkness does not absorb it" (*svet vo t'me svetit i temnota ego ne pogloshchaet*) (24: 31). The incomprehensibility of suffering inflicted in the absence of any apparent wrongdoing proves to man most convincingly that his life is not merely the life of a person, begun with his birth and ending in his death (26: 423). Such is the metaphor in Ivan Il'ich's physical sensation of the blade of pain (*vintit*) that may have its origin in Tolstoy's synecdoche of physical malaise, first introduced in the opening chapters of Book II of *War and Peace*, in Pierre's impuissant ruminations about the blade (*vint*) as the source of pain in the world. For Pierre at this stage in his search, evil is a mechanism falling apart, where a certain part which begins to falter can undermine the function of the whole (such also as a loose bolt [*vint*] of a railway track for Tolstoy in the second epilogue). *On Life*, on the other hand, makes every part responsible for the functioning of life by subordinating the work of this part to the main relationship with the world (26: 423–24).

The trespass into an eternal form of consciousness described by Tolstoy finds its origin in Kantian moral transcendence, of the soul first as an object of inquiry and then as a subject having achieved its end. This is how Tolstoy resolves his longstanding creative contradiction of man's knowing himself individually and not individually.[25] *On Life* proposes all the parameters of spiritual and artistic behavior that we shall find merged in Tolstoy's works after 1886. Perhaps the most important of them is the question of love. Who is the neighbor, asks Tolstoy attributing this form of the question to Christ. Whom should one serve—people or society? Fatherland or friends? Friends or family? Wife or brotherhood? (26: 387). These are artificial questions, extensions of the selfish, temporal consciousness. There is no abstract love, and there is no real choice of priorities as soon as love is not projected into the future and judged by the results of its possible applications. There are no degrees of separation if love is real, active, and responsible. It never acts from the future nor is it based on the knowledge of things past because it is focused on the moment in the present, which is life. Therefore, suffering as a test of compassion professed by Schopenhauer is for unreasonable beings. Suffering, any suffering, can be mitigated only by the realization of the true meaning of life in the attitude we assume to the world (26: 435). If the attitude is right, we bring love into the world.

The Buddhist legend with which Tolstoy opened *On Life* is famously reworked in Hermann Hesse's *Siddhartha*. At the end, Siddhartha finds his peace by acknowledging that the river alone knows the secret of being, and man may work only as its ferryman. Siddhartha's lack of goals is a form of love: "when you throw a stone into the water, it finds the quickest way to the bottom of the water. It is the same when Siddhartha has an aim, a goal. Siddhartha does nothing; he waits, he thinks, he fasts, but he goes through the affairs of the world like the stone through the water. . . ." Accused of lack of real love to the beings in the world, Siddhartha continues his searches and realizes that being obsessed with the goal is wrong, that freedom of enhancing goodness opens one to practicing it at every moment.[26] Many years later, in his letter to Rusanov (November 28, 1903), Tolstoy sketched his understanding of himself as a continuous spiritual entity, the river of the law, by drawing parallel lines within which human destinies could position themselves either vertically (and therefore terminally) or horizontally (and therefore eternally), parallel with eternity. On the diagram, the line of life shown last is shown horizontally: "Parallel lines, disappearing on either side into eternity, and having neither a beginning nor an end is a true, spiritual, godly life. By joining ourselves with it, we grasp what we have a right to call life. . . . The best of lives is the one where it merges with eternal life, and death is ended" (74: 245).

On Life resolved Tolstoy's remaining contradictions about life in the world and immortality. Life no longer remains tragically caught between the law of reason (necessity) and the indefinite "x" of consciousness, or freedom, with its arbitrary and often morally indifferent cravings. In *War and Peace*, the law observes and rules, consciousness is observed, but it blocks out the possibility of accepting its complete dependence and bowing down to reason so that life could continue; it denies its serving a mere tool of reason. In *On Life*, finally, the two are operating and cooperating, as they should in the practice of complete turns in true conversion. Tolstoy's reasonable consciousness adopted from Gogol achieved a synthesis of thought, faith, and art unavailable to Gogol. In his "Letter on Gogol" (1886), written from the heights of his new faith, Tolstoy confirmed that Gogol, the inventor of reasonable consciousness the term, had only enough strength to reject the art steeped in charms (*soblazny*), lacking the strength to remain firm in his new conviction and nourish and reinforce his new word. Like Fonvizin in the earlier times of transition, he failed to communicate this conviction.[27] He also did not understand how to love three things: God; Belinsky, his censurer; and his own faith. Tolstoy clearly invokes Gogol's apologies to society in "Author's Confession," in which Gogol apologized to the public for his incorrectly chosen vocation, and for the opacity and inability of his failing word.[28] But what Belinsky could not overlook was more than redeemed for Tolstoy in the second, mailed version of Gogol's private response to Belinsky, where, in tones of passionate yet coolly exercised restraint, Gogol heralded the arrival of "*the age of reasonable consciousness*" (*vek razumnogo soznaniia*).[29] In an unfinished essay on the life of Pascal, which compared Pascal and Gogol, the two most famous fugitives from success into faith, Tolstoy also explains why Pascal's recommendations are tragic in their delusions and why he could not agree that God condescends to operate on the mind of man without the participation of man's will of reasonable consciousness.

THE TURNAROUND AND THE LOOK AHEAD

The examples above implying a Buddhist link are fitting. Tolstoy did sympathize with certain precepts of Buddhism, Daoism, and Confucianism, such as the teaching of visible and invisible reality, transience of physical life, following the stages of growth to increase wisdom and merge with the law of life. Yet he used principles of these various teachings reflexively and never let go of Socratic inner voice (*daimonion*) or of a secret belief in *concursus dei* (the intermediate communication of the soul with God) and, above all, of Kant's moral law. Becoming less aggressive about postulating individual *telos*, Tolstoy never tired of defending the logic of moral action. Therefore, the picture of the river of eternity above is nothing like a concealment of truth in the Lethe of passive oblivion. In dialogues of reasonable consciousness with the unreasonable part of temporal self, Tolstoy prescribes writing the endless personal catechism of the river of unconcealment, by posing only meaningful questions and finding concrete answers. From a diary entry on October 22, 1904, we learn that the final answer of the "personal catechism-in-progress" started in dialogues of faith and revelation in 1877 Tolstoy was hoping to utter at the moment of death, in a state of the ultimate lack of questions in the presence of the final answer, and in the form of the final verse of the Divine Liturgy: "Then would I say: 'Now lettest Thou Thy servant (depart in peace, O Lord, according to Thy word)'" (55: 92–93).

On Life threw yet another bridge over the river of eternity, for it showed how Tolstoy now approached the question of humanity. "Humanity" as such is not subject to question or ridicule in that earlier work than the more famous *The Kingdom of God is Within You* (1893–1894). *On Life* shows only sporadic instances of polemical humor or psychological wit that characterizes *The Kingdom of God* and debunks the myth of "humanity" and various charitable acts committed on its behalf, including patriotic and liberation wars. "Humanity" is represented in Tolstoy's later work as a concept inviting empty speculation and is replaced by a collective of interdependent human individuals, each endowed with a special responsible place within the moral universe. *On Life* concentrates on the eviction of personal love and not on the eviction of humanity at large, which would be Tolstoy's next controversial step. In *On Life*, notably, he contrasts forms of "narrow love" or selfish love to the nearest kin with Nietzschean "distant" love, embracing also "all people" and "patriotism" (for example, altruistic love of Fatherland).

Tolstoy would not be Tolstoy, of course, if he let his discoveries up to the year 1887 rest comfortably on the laurels of majestic assurance. For him, too much in human life was yet an obstacle to liberating flights like Ivan Il'ich's. The problem of humanity and escapism received a new, more terrifying solution already in his next story, *The Kreutzer Sonata* (started in the same 1887), in which hedonistic and craven passions, and not an illusory utopia of public activity, stand in the way of happiness: "But why should we live?" asks the desperate wife murderer Pozdnyshev, "If life has no reason, if it has been given us for its own sake, we have no reason for living. Observe that if the purpose of life is happiness, goodness, love or whatever, and if the goal of mankind is what it is stated to be by the prophets, that all men are to be united by love, that swords are to be beaten into ploughshares and all the rest of it, what prevents it from being attained? The passions do. Of all the passions, it is sexual, carnal love that is the strongest. It follows that if passions are eliminated, and together with them the ultimate, strongest passion, carnal love, the goal of mankind will be attained and there will be no longer reason for it to live any longer" (27: 29–30).[30]

Despite his avowed spirit of Christianity, *On Life*, *The Kreutzer Sonata*, and later works, such as *The Kingdom of God is Within You* and *What is Art?* have solidified Tolstoy's reputation of a Russian Nietzsche. In 1893, Grot published a significant essay, "Friedrich Nietzsche and Lev Tolstoy. Moral Ideals of Our Time" (*Friedrich Nietzsche i nravstvennye idealy nashego vremeni*) that praised Tolstoy, who commits acts of transgression against corrupt norms on behalf of Christian morality. Even the praise of his closest allies was not without misgivings. Grot regretted Tolstoy's tendency to weave his own fables out of metaphysics.[31] Meticulously and professionally, point by point, Grot catalogued the philosophical weaknesses of Tolstoy's views: 1) extreme and often unproductive radicalism; 2) absence of objectivity (Tolstoy's choice of philosophical facts is based on his own needs) because Tolstoy ignores facts that could compromise his inferences; 3) lack of a historical criterion. "Tolstoy," Grot continues, "generally tends to confuse the ideal and its execution, or the degree of approximation to the ideal that is practically plausible; hence all the strained interpretations and inconsistencies."[32]

Despite his criticisms, Grot does not underestimate Tolstoy's real philosophical worth, which lies in the correct reinterpretation of the Christian ideal that had been distorted or forfeited by modern society. According to Grot, Tolstoy sought to integrate the loftiness and clarity of exposition found in Christian teaching with the scientifically advanced reason of modern times. The masses whose spiritual vehicle is blind unquestioning faith would never understand him; for them and for the Church, Tolstoy would forever remain a heretic. However, as Grot explains, "a mind given to philosophic reasoning rejects the notion of heresy as dogmatic. Such a mind knows only truth and delusion, or better, only different stages in the approach to the truth." For Grot, the stigma of Tolstoy as heretic was the simple result of dogmatic indoctrination of humanity. In his view, Tolstoy is a thinker who has advanced much further than his age in his progress toward truth, by nipping in the bud the arguments of atheists and narrow materialists. Precisely, in this sense, should one seek to comprehend his importance: he was writing for *thinking individuals*, not for the masses and not for those who subsist on feeling. He is an aristocrat of a thinker; with the time, his teaching should be democratized, so that it will become accessible to the people.[33]

Grot wrote these words when the so-called journal crusade against Tolstoy was only beginning. Russian religious philosophy, an active warrior in the crusade, painted a comprehensive yet largely unflattering picture of Tolstoy's importance. Early in the past century, Lev Shestov, the advocate of Tolstoy's vertigo, stated that one believes Tolstoy when he is in doubt—a philosopher's prerogative—but disbelieves him when he preaches moral action (and lapses into doctrinaire impostorship):

> The "religious consciousness of our time" which Tolstoy wished to make obligatory for all, refused its service where it would have been welcomed as gospel. It seems that it does not depend on the will of man to believe or not to believe, and thereby Tolstoy's fundamental idea that man has only to wish it in order to find a moral support in life is changed from an axiom into a theory, or—to be frank—into a statement that cannot be in any way proved. At the same time, however, it becomes clear that the entire task Tolstoy undertook was not fulfilled by him, that he shunned the obligation to lead men to religion and, instead, took upon himself the right to lash them for their unbelief. . . . Tolstoy believes that it is possible not to tell his disciples of the emptiness of his heart above which he erected the—from the literary point of view—brilliant edifice of his preaching. . . . Must he not tell himself that the indignation he pours out on unbelievers, and the prescription of physical work that he recommends as a universal panacea, can seem to us nothing other than a skillful—perhaps also unskillful—means of evading his own doubts?[34]

A skillful or unskillful means of evading his own doubts is a harsh accusation of a life and art project, especially from Shestov who valued Tolstoy's doubt (the moment of vertigo), but not his overcoming of vertigo after the conversion. Symbolist writer and critic Dmitry Merezhkovsky, who most highly evaluated Tolstoy's ability to see into the mystery (*tainovidenie*) of a complete human being in the flesh and interpreted Christ's lesson as a secret (*tainyi*) test by way of temptation (*soblazn*), questioned Tolstoy's sincerity when he *was* trying to share his doubts in *A Confession*.[35] The poet and aesthetic thinker Viacheslav Ivanov held doubt as such to be half-creative. Tolstoy knew emancipation (*raskreposhchenie*) only in its negative form; this paradoxical kenotic striving was his half-hearted gesture toward the absolute "yes" of absolute being.[36] According to Ivanov, Tolstoy's doubt, unlike its Socratic counterpart, was but half-completed until his *act* of "completed personality"—a departure from home in 1910 and, soon thereafter, from life—had taken place. Tolstoy, added Ivanov, is *memento mori* to modern culture and a *memento vivere* to the Symbolism striving toward what is supra-real (ibid., 223).

On the question of turning Tolstoy's grandiose doubts into an epic, George Steiner, the eminent critic of the twentieth century, who wrote on Tolstoy from the wreckage of culture after WWII, cautions: "But in saying 'behind,' in suggesting that a novel may be facade or a mask for a philosophic doctrine, we involve ourselves in error. The relationship between thought and expression is at all times reciprocal and dynamic."[37] The relationship is also a subtle one. Critics since Mikhailovsky have perhaps toyed too literally with the possibility of an allegory of the two recalcitrant hands (left and right) or beasts (the hedgehog and the fox) lodged within Tolstoy's creative psyche. Like Mikhailovsky, Sir Isaiah Berlin, the creator of the allegory, believed that "the Muse cannot be cheated," but surely he could not have predicted that his philosophical allegory would become a staple device to interpret Tolstoy's conflicts.[38] Aileen Kelly sought to soften her mentor's censure of Tolstoy's efforts to maintain a bilateral truce. She made the point that art in doubt is more powerful, for each time it reconciles the two choices in a creative synthesis.[39]

If Tolstoy may be given the floor in this debate, he would add: "Incriminate me as I incriminate myself, but do not incriminate that path along which I proceed" (63: 123). The areas where and the reasons why Tolstoy's path to conversion is vulnerable are well known. He is vulnerable, as is any creator of any religious-philosophical system in that, according to Paul Ricoeur, he needs to be meaningful and true.[40] High art that realizes its immortal hopes needs no excuse for trying to be both, especially if we recall how Tolstoy excused himself in response to the Synod's Edict of excommunication (April 4, 1901, Moscow). In his response, Tolstoy borrowed the final lines of Dashkova's memoir to conclude his statement about honest dissidence and prefacing his letter with Coleridge's "Aids to Reflection" contra those who love Christianity as a sect rather than as Truth. Tolstoy wrote: "What I believe is this: I believe in God, whom I understand as spirit, and in Love as the beginning of everything. I believe that He is within me and I am within Him. I believe that the will of God is most clearly and understandably expressed in the teachings of the man called Christ, but I consider it the greatest of blasphemies to look on this man as God and to pray to Him. . . . Whether or not these beliefs of mine offend, grieve or tempt anyone, whether or not anyone dislikes them or finds them a hindrance, I am no more able to change them than I am able to change my own body . . . truth corresponds for me to Christianity as I understand it. And I hold to this Christianity; and in so far as I hold to it *I live calmly and joyfully, and calmly and joyfully* approach my death."[41]

So much for *anhedonia*. As is so often the case, it was the controversial turn of the century thinker Vasily Rozanov who found the most adequate words to express our perplexed admiration for Tolstoy's conversion when he said: "He covered the whole way from Hector to the Apostle Paul . . . covered this whole endless way alone in his thoughts, trials, looking for life, taking his measure of life. This is not a doctrine or a catechism . . . The study of Tolstoy's personality will yield more of interest than the study of all those great reformers of belief, all those catechists, from Calvin to the most recent."[42] In this sense, Rozanov added, "Tolstoy's search for faith, in his corrupt and indoctrinated age, is an act of heroism comparable to Dante's alternative version of Christianity for the Middle Ages" (ibid.). In order to develop Rozanov's intriguing cultural metaphor, Tolstoy's effort may be that of a historical Purgatory reminiscent of Hamlet's purgatorial sublime. Hamlet, the first incarnation of modern man, was haunted by spectral visions of his indecision and strove for the impossible replacement of hell and heaven with his own version of religion in a world that was out of joint. As Stephen Greenblatt argued, Hamlet is the first example of modernity in which literature and the course of history redefine each other.[43] Semifictional and semiautobiographical texts related to Tolstoy's conversion reveal that he was likewise not afraid to pose as a quintessential moral agent who freely partook of the history of conversion and its fictional accounts of his time and times past. In this he was Russia's first modern man, the first defender of the autonomous freedom of conscience, its first consistent and courageous point of contact, its open practice and forum.

It is far from accidental that the 1886 note on Gogol and the rethinking of his role of holy madman coincided temporally with Tolstoy's return to his "The Memoir of a Madman." Tolstoy was not only a reformed Russian Hamlet of the 1840s but its reformed Don Quixote, who had learned from his own "bitter experiences" and came to abominate them. Tolstoy's new teleological knight could repeat after the errant knight on his deathbed: "I was mad, but I am sane now."[44] The birth of his difficult religious epiphany synthesizing Turgenev's dream of Hamlet and Don Quixote (1860) occurred as the religious worldview of his time collapsed under the onslaught of pragmatism, Darwinism, and materialism. Tolstoy was driven toward his "sane madness" in much the same way as what prompted Don Quixote's pursuit of signs and resemblances of sameness of his spiritual origins in the new reality where they have "dissolved their former alliance," a pursuit "verging upon a special form of visionary madness."[45]

Tolstoy's longing for the sincere primitiveness and naïveté of early Christianity and its artistic expressions should not be confused with an instinctiveness of the impuissant simplifier. According to Wittgenstein, who was deeply impressed by Tolstoy's religious persona, Tolstoy's playing hide-and-seek with God based on the whim of his obstinate reason would mean that he "lives his life by a picture," by an allegorical picture (a variant of a language game) that needs justification. "The believer's attempt to justify his faith has an apparent similarity to scientific language—but that is only an illusion."

The point is that if there were evidence, this would destroy the whole business. So what remains of justification in religion? "Wittgenstein suggests that religion has to do with living one's life by a picture, and one either does or does not have such a picture."[46] This implication of a "game" should not suggest that a believer is insincere, only that his allegory is utilized as a means of spiritual cognition. Tolstoy certainly has his picture and his game. In his many renditions Tolstoy's retrieval of preverbal imagery of religious truths yielded an unforgettable polyphony of allegories and metaphors of search.

In *What I Believe?* Tolstoy added his name to the annals of successful seekers: "My life and death will serve the salvation of all—this is, after all, what Christ taught" (23: 402). If any given successful conversion benefits all humanity, this outrageous statement should hold true—even if Tolstoy's conversion and refashioning of his literary and public persona was primarily an expression of the "oldest fear" of humanity, the fear of death.[47] After all, this fear would signify the fulfillment of the eternal agony in the twentieth century primarily. As Kafka perceptively wrote, "The man in ecstasy and the man drowning—both throw up their arms. The first does it to signify harmony, the second to signify strife with the elements."[48]

I interpret this "fear"—which culminated in the rewriting of the Gospels and a rethinking of the death experience—as an expression of the struggle of the genius against the traditionalists and the deniers. In this sense, Tolstoy's religious career and his fashioning of new rules about what art and the world should be is a healthy reaction against persecution and oppression of the right of free expression.[49] The most significant, provocative, overt and covert dialogues with Tolstoy—with a range of his questions such as "Why I am Not a Christian?" "What I Believe?" "How I Believe?" which were raised by thinkers as diverse as Bertrand Russell and Pierre Teilhard de Chardin—continue to this day. For scholars of religious approaches to literature, philosophy, art, history, and ethics Tolstoy will and should remain forever relevant and challenging. Tolstoy's life in the art and intellectual thought of the twentieth and twenty-first centuries is the subject of my next book.

NOTES

1. Nikolai Grot, *O dushe v sviazi s sovremennymi ucheniiami o sile. Opyt filosofskogo postroeniia N.Ia. Grota.* Prof. Filosofii Novorossiskogo Universiteta (Odessa: tipografiia Odesskogo vestnika, 1886). I am grateful to the publishing and research sections of Tolstoy's personal library at Yasnaya Polyana (Galina Alexeeva, Liudmila Miliakova) for allowing me to examine this book from Tolstoy's personal collection, August 2000.

2. On page 77 of Grot's book Tolstoy has bent the upper corner where Grot speaks of the soul as a modification of other natural forces. ("The soul is a modification of other active forces of nature" / *[D]usha est' modifikatsiia drugikh aktivnykh sil prirody*.)

3. Tolstoy made this inscription on page 78, which he bent twofold. In the text of the chapter, I repeat the version suggested by the editors of *Biblioteka L'va Nik. Tosltogo v Iasnoi Poliane*, part 1 (vol. 1), 225. The editors tentatively suggest (a question mark is put next to their reading) that Tolstoy wrote "'*Osvobodit'sia? Tol'ko osvobozhdenie'* (?)." My opinion and that of Liudmila Pavlovna Velikanova, who assisted me in deciphering Tolstoy's hand, is that Tolstoy wrote "*Osvobozhdenie? Tol'ko aktivno*" (Liberation? Only an active one.) The second inscription runs vertically along the concluding part of Grot's picture of self-saving soul (98).

4. E. B. Greenwood and Andrzej Walicki have given excellent explanations as to why the narrowly rationalistic eighteenth century associations are unacceptable if applied to Tolstoy's reasonable consciousness and why *razumnoe soznanie* should translate "reasonable consciousness" rather than "enlightenment" or "rational consciousness." See E. B. Greenwood, "Tolstoy and Religion," *New Essays on Tolstoy*, ed. Malcolm Jones (Cambridge: Cambridge UP, 1978), 149–74. See also Walicki's Chapter "Two Prophetic Writers," especially section "The Phases of Moral Crisis. *A Confession*" in Walicki, *A History of Russian Thought*, 328–47. G. W. Spence was the first to discuss the term in its complexity. He also translates "*razumnoe soznanie*" as "reasonable consciousness": "The word 'reason' in *On Life* is used synonymously with 'reasonable consciousness', whereas the discursive 'reason' of the close of *War and Peace* is concerned only with phenomena and corresponds to the 'observation' (*nabliudenie*) of the later essay (*On Life*)." See G. W. Spence, *Tolstoy the Ascetic* (Edinburgh/London: Oliver & Boyd, 1967), 17. However, I cannot agree with Spence's treatment of reasonable consciousness as the assemblage of animal perceptual consciousness and endowed with a meaning (82–90).

5. Gary Jahn has written a succinct summary of major thematic connections between *DII* and *On Life*. See Jahn, *The Death of Ivan Il'ich. An Interpretation*, 93–102.

6. Nikolai Rozaliev. *Kartochnye igry* (Moscow: Grand, 1998), 316.

7. Schwarz's smug air exemplifies the tardy wit of *l'esprit d'escalier* when a departing guest, still searching for a witty repartee, might think, too late, of some mordant response. Schwarz of course had his witticism ready only *after* he left the room with the dead body. His tardiness may be Tolstoy's self-reference to his "Conversation About Science" (1875). See chapter 7 of the present study.

8. *Tolstoy's Short Fiction,* 166.

9. See Tolstoy's letter to Evgeny Ivanovich Popov (October 1–20, 1887; 64: 108).

10. See Opulskaya. *Lev Nikolaevich Tolstoy. Materialy k biografii s 1886 po 1892 god*, 88 and correspondence between Tolstoy and Grot (26: 752).

11. Zhukovsky, *Sochineniia v stikhakh i proze*, 945–53.

12. Percy Bysshe Shelley, *The Major Works*, ed. Zachary Leader & Michael O'Neill (Oxford: Oxford University Press, 2003), 633–36.

13. Opulskaya, *Lev Nikolaevich Tolstoy. Materialy k biografii s 1886 po 1892 god*, 110.

14. On the philosophical reception of *On Life*, see James P. Scanlan, "Tolstoy Among the Philosophers: His Book *On Life* and Its Critical Reception" in *Tolstoy Studies Journal*, vol. XVIII (2006): 52–69.

15. Before sending *On Life* into print, Tolstoy invited Grot to Yasnaya Polyana for its final reading. The timing was perfect, because the Kuzminskys (his in-laws) were also staying. A. M. Kuzminsky, the husband of Sophia Andreevna's younger sister Tanya, was an attorney. Grot represented philosophy and A. A. Tolstaya was a "representative of religion," all of whom Tolstoy wanted, in precisely this composition, to be present at the reading (Opulskaya, 106–7). This was, in effect, a revised composition of *Interlocutors* to whom Tolstoy, the matured Ivan Il'ich, could read his own opinion about immortality.

16. See fragment 200 in Lafuma numbering. Pascal, *Oeuvres complètes*, 528.

17. On Tolstoy's use of the categorical imperative in his letter to Buturlin of 1884, see chapter 10 of the present study.

18. I enjoyed the unforgettable privilege of seeing this copy of Kant in Tolstoy's library. Immanuel Kant, *Kritik der praktischen Vernunft*, ed. J. H. Kirchmann (Berlin: Gebrüder Grunert, 18—? last two digits illegible), 194.

19. Kant, *Critique of Pure Reason*, 135, 152–53.

20. Kant, *Critique of Pure Reason*, 83–86, 156–58.

21. Kant, *Critique of Pure Reason*, 465.

22. Ibid., 176–77, 300–301.

23. Ibid., 28, 136–44.

24. Knowing that Grot substituted "animal" (*zhivotnyi*) for Tolstoy's "living" (*zhivoi*) I think it is wrong to attribute to Tolstoy the meaning not intended and translate the epithet as that pertaining to "animal" life. This is especially legitimate because in the nineteenth century the slightly obsolete meaning of the Russian word "*zhivotnyi*" (living, related to life) was still current.

25. The first record of this recurrent idea connected with subsequent conversion is found in diary entry of July 21, 1870 (48: 127).

26. Herman Hesse, *Siddhartha*, trans. Hilda Rosner (New York: Bantam Books, 1971), 60, 140–41.

27. Tolstoy, "O Gogolie" (26: 648–51).

28. "I thought, upon reading my book, I would be told: 'Thank you, brother' and not: 'Thank you, teacher!' Am I not myself only human? I can't be thankful enough to those who, upon sensing that it was all too much for a feeble human nature, have hoisted me with a hand of a brother mourning over me and commanded me to cheer up. God reward them: I don't know a higher feat than extending a hand to the one enfeebled of spirit." Gogol, *Sobranie sochinenii*, 7: 298, 332.

29. See chapter 1 of the present study.

30. Translation quoted from Leo Tolstoy. *The Kreutzer Sonata and Other Stories* (Oxford: Penguin Classics, 1985), 54.

31. See Tolstoy's responses to Grot in 1887, and especially on October 7, 1887, in defense of his views (64: 100). Tolstoy's reminiscences of Grot (*Vospominaniia o N.Ia. Grote*; 38: 421–25) explain their intellectual affinities and disagreements, but stress that what aligned them was more important.

32. Nikolai Iak Grot, *Filosofiia i ee obshchie zadachi. Sbornik statei pod redakt-siei Moskovskogo Psikhologicheskogo obshchestva* (St. Petersburg: Tipografiia A.S. Suvorina, 1904), lii. Tolstoy was aware of these criticisms. They are found in the same posthumous collection of Grot's essays that was sent as a gift to Tolstoy by the family of the late philosopher, who died in 1899. See *Biblioteka L.N.Tolstogo*. Part I, vol. 1, 225.

33. *Filosofiia i ee obshchie zadachi*, lii.

34. Lev Shestov, "The Good in the Teaching of Tolstoy and Nietzsche: Philosophy and Preaching," in *Dostoevsky, Tolstoy and Nietzsche*, trans. Bernard Martin (Ohio: Ohio University Press, 1978), 86–88. The Russian original was first published as *Dobro v uchenii gr. Tolstogo i F. Nitshe (Filosofiia i propoved')* (Berlin: Skify, 1923), 78.

35. Dmitry S. Merezhkovsky, *L.Tolstoy i Dostoevsky* (Moscow: Nauka, 2000), 82, 140–42. It has become customary to forget that Merezhkovsky's legendary character-ization of Tolstoy as '*tainovidets ploti*' (the seer of the flesh) brings nothing to bear on the flesh as such but on the eucharistic interpretation of the human being as having partaken in his body of what is intrinsically divine.

36. Viacheslav Ivanov, "Lev Tolstoi i kul'tura," in *Rodnoe i vselenskoe* (Moscow: Respublika, 1994), 273–75.

37. George Steiner, *Tolstoy or Dostoevsky: An Essay in Old Criticism* (New Haven, Conn.: Yale University Press, 1996), 232.

38. Isaiah Berlin, "The Hedgehog and the Fox," in *Russian Thinkers*, ed. Aileen Kelly (London: Penguin, 1979), 81. The enduring authority of Berlin's celebrated essay, first published in 1953, has not been shattered in almost fifty-five years of making the rounds on the academic circuit. However, the appellation stuck as too trivial as it was based on a trivial dictum (the hedgehog knows one big thing at a time, and for all time, whereas the fox knows many small things at once and at all times).

39. See Aileen M. Kelly, "Tolstoy in Doubt," in her *Toward Another Shore: Russian Thinkers Between Necessity and Chance* (New Haven, Conn.: Yale University Press, 1998), 80–90.

40. Paul Ricoeur, *Figuring the Sacred. Religion, Narrative, and Imagination* (Minneapolis: Fortress Press, 1995), 35. Confer Ricoeur's statement with Tolstoy's preface to his version of the Gospels. Tolstoy wrote that the answer God should give him must be "not only reasonable, clear, but also true" (24: 14).

41. "Otvet na opredelenie Sinoda ot 20–22 fevralia i na poluchenie mnoi po etomu sluchaiu pis'ma" (A Reply to the Synod's Edict of February 20–22 and On Letters Received By Me On the Same Occasion), 34: 245–53, esp. 251–52, 253, trans. Robert Chandler, from *The Lion and the Honeycomb. The Religious Writings of Tolstoy* ed. A. N. Wilson (London: Collins, 1987), 129–30. Translation amended by me. Tolstoy prefaces his letter with quoting from Coleridge's "Aids to Reflection in the Formation of a Manly Character on the Several Grounds of Prudence, Morality and Religion" (1825): "He who begins by loving Christianity better than truth will proceed by loving his own sect or church better than Christianity, and then end in loving himself better than all" (34: 245).

42. V. V. Rozanov, "Tolstoy mezhdu velikimi mira" (Tolstoy Among the World's Greats), in Rozanov, *O pisatel'stve i pisateliakh* ed. A. N. Nikoliukin (Moscow: Respublika, 1995), 307–12, esp. 312.

43. See Stephen Greenblatt, *Hamlet in Purgatory* (Princeton, N.J.: Princeton University Press, 2002), especially 10–46 and 258–62.

44. Cervantes, *Don Quixote*, trans. J. M. Cohen (London: Penguin, 1950), 936, 938.

45. See Michel Foucault's illuminating description of Don Quixote's "poetry of sameness" and his "indispensable cultural function" not of someone who is certifiably sick, but "as an established and maintained deviant" in Michel Foucault, *The Order of Things. An Archaeology of the Human Sciences* (New York: Vintage Books, 1994). Quoted passages in the text occur on p. 47. Quoted passage in the notes occurs on p. 49.

46. Stiver, *The Philosophy of the Religious Language*, 68.

47. Emil Cioran, "The Oldest Fear: Apropos of Tolstoy." E. M. Cioran, *The Fall Into Time*, trans. from the French by Richard Howard, intro. by Charles Newman (Chicago: Quadrangle Books, 1970), 141–54. Cioran makes a comparison of Tolstoy and Dostoevsky, which is unfavorable to Tolstoy. Cioran's right-wing brand of existentialism justifies Dostoevsky's archconservative views, anti-Semitism, and support of autocracy as the more humane and sincere expressions of the primordial fear of death than Tolstoy's conversion, his defense of the poor, and his teaching of nonviolence. Cioran's evaluation finds an ally in Prince Dmitry Mirsky's discussion of Tolstoy's "extraverted narcissism." See Mirsky's essay of 1929, "Some Remarks on Tolstoy." Dmitry Mirsky, *Uncollected Writings on Russian Literature*, ed. G. S. Smith (Berkeley, Calif.: Berkeley Slavic Specialties, 1989), 311.

48. See Kafka's November 24, 1917, entry in the "Third Notebook." Franz Kafka, *The Blue Octavo Notebooks.*, ed. Max Brod, trans. Ernst Kaiser and Eithne Wilkins (Cambridge, Mass: Exact Change, 1991), 26.

49. In this sense, Tolstoy's career is little different from the ostracized writing of Maimonides or Spinoza. On the topic of ostracized thought and the art of self-expression, see Leo Strauss, *Persecution and the Art of Writing* (Chicago and London: The University of Chicago Press, 1988). See especially Strauss' essay on Maimonides' *Guide to the Perplexed* as an example of persecuted writing, which elaborated its tropes and methods of self-defense (pp. 38–94).

Appendix I

Tolstoy, "On Prayer" (1852)

Only those people who are middle-aged and have a family and who have no permanent connection with the secular youth of this century might not know that the majority of this youth does not believe in anything. . . . Disbelief has cast deep root in the contemporary generation of the highest circles and has become so widespread that it is frightful even to consider the fate awaiting our fatherland. . . . There are three foundations of disbelief: intellection, vanity, and weakness; according to this division, there are three classes of disbelievers: intellectuals, the vainglorious, and the weak. —To the first class there belong people endowed with a strong intellect and big energy. They feel such an insurmountable need to subjugate everything to the implacable laws of reason that they can't help but refute the laws of religion, which are based on faith and revelation. —Why are they given to this capability to refute these laws intellectually? Why should they pass through a tortuous condition of doubt and uncertainty? —These are the questions that man is not able to answer. —All that he can say is that they are less guilty than they are unhappy —they see that against their will, more than that, unconsciously —they watch in horror as that which what used to be their firm foundation (*opora*) collapses; and *an unknowable, insurmountable force* draws them towards destruction. —This class of disbelievers has existed always and everywhere, mostly toward their old age; when the energy diminishes and the need to reflect decreases, they return to religion in repentance. To the third class there belong all who—out of intellectual weakness and will and out of imitation— submit to the opinion of the majority and stop fulfilling the dogmas of Christian religion and finally stop believing in it. The number of disbelievers of all classes is so great that they comprise the majority in the young circles. How can a young lad withstand public opinion—in his heart of hearts he is afraid since he feels that he is not behaving well—he would be glad to sign himself with a cross, but he is being watched, and he is threatened with . . . ridicule. . . . —The whole trouble of these people is their youth, their weakness and vanity. —Should they be thrust into the circle of virtuous people, they would become virtuous—but they found themselves in the circle of disbelievers, and they turned into ones too. —To the second class there belong those who having found themselves enticed by intellectualism and philosophical theories (which the novels have made accessible to everyone), have swapped Christian beliefs, instilled in them from childhood, for pantheist ideas, intricate suppositions of witty writers, or their own inventions. —Each of them puts together his own special religion, which has neither consequence nor foundation, but which is congruent with its passions and weaknesses. They believe in what pleases them, refute what is difficult for them, sacrifice their former beliefs in order to pamper their petty self-love—to impress others or themselves with a poetic fancy or witticism and on the wreckage of religion to erect the temple to their vanity and weaknesses.[1]

NOTE

1. See "On Prayer" (*O molitve*) (1: 247–48). Textual commentators note that the manuscript is executed with calligraphic precision characteristic of Tolstoy's meticulous juvenile handwriting. In his diary entry for April 1, 1852, Tolstoy described his state of mind when the note on prayer was being composed: "Have been writing a chapter on Prayer. Was moving droopily. . . . I kept writing and writing and then I started noticing that my reflection on prayer lays claims to logical consistency and intellectual depth, but it is inconsequential. Have made up my mind to finish it somehow, on the spot, and now burned half of it —I won't place it into my novella but will preserve it as a memorial" (46: 105).

Appendix II

PRAYER FOR GRANDDAUGHTER SONECHKA (1909)

Lord has told all people to do one thing: to love each other. One must learn to do this. And in order to learn to do this, the first thing is needed: never let yourself think badly of anyone no matter what; secondly, never speak ill of anyone; thirdly, never do to another what you would not will to be done to you.

Whoever learns this, will love all people, whoever they are, and will know the greatest joy in the world—the joy of love. So I will study this with all my might (90: 85).

PRAYER (1909)

I do not know whether I will live until tomorrow, whether they will live, those whom I love and who love me, or whether they will pass this noon or tomorrow, before me. I do not know whether I will be healthy or sick, sated or famished, respected or censured by people. I know only that everything that will happen to me and with everyone I love will happen in accordance with the will of the one who lives in the whole world and in my soul. And all that happens in accordance with his will is good. Therefore, I will not think about what might happen to me and to all those whom I love. Only one thing shall I endeavor: to be always with him, the one whom I know within myself thanks to love. I need one thing for this: love everybody in deed, in word, and in thought, that is, do as much of the good thing as I can to everyone I encounter, tell nothing ill either to anybody or about anybody and above all not allow myself, even in my thoughts, to think ill about people. I shall remember this and apply all my powers to this (90: 145).

Bibliography

Aertsen, Jan A. "Aquinas Philosophy in Its Historical Setting." 12–37 in *The Cambridge Companion to Aquinas*, Norman Kretzmann and Eleanore Stump, eds. Cambridge: Cambridge University Press, 1993.

Afanasiev, A. N. *Narodnyia russkiia legendy*. ed. and Foreword, S. K. Shambinago. Moscow: Sovremennyia problemy, 1914.

Aksakov, K. S., and I. S. Aksakov. *Literaturnaia kritika*. Moscow: Sovremennik, 1981.

Alexandrov, Vladimir E. *Limits to Interpretation: The Meanings of Anna Karenina*. Madison, Wis.: The University of Wisconsin Press, 2004.

Alighieri, Dante. *La divina commedia. Inferno. Purgatorio. Paradiso*. 3 vols. intro. Bianca Garavelli. Notes by Lodovico Magugliani. Milan: RCS libri, 1949. Reprinted by Milan: Superbur classici, 2001.

Allert, Craig D. *Revelation, Truth, Canon and Interpretation: Studies in Justin the Martyr's Dialogue With Trypho*. Leiden: Brill, 2002.

Almazov, Aleksandr Ivanovich. *Istoriia chinoposledovaniia, kreshcheniia i miropomazaniia*. Kazan': Tipografiia Imperatorskogo universiteta, 1884.

———. *Soobshcheniia zapadnykh inostrantsev XVI–XVII vv o sovershenii tainstv v russkoi tserkvi*. Kazan': Tipografiia Imperatorskogo universiteta, 1900.

Alston, William P. *Perceiving God: The Epistemology of Religious Experience*. Ithaca, N. Y.: Cornell University Press, 1991.

Andrews, E. A., LLD, Lewis, Charles, Rev. Short, Charles, eds. *A New Latin Dictionary*. New York/Cincinatti: American Book Co., 1907.

Aristotle's Rhetoric. Philosophical Essays. eds. David J. Furley and Alexander Nehamas. Princeton, N. J.: Princeton University Press, 1994.

Aristotle. *The Complete Works of Aristotle*. 2 vols. The revised Oxford translation. ed. Jonathan Barnes. Princeton, N. J.: Princeton University Press, 1984.

———. *(A) New Reader*. ed. J. L. Ackrill. Princeton, N. J.: Princeton University Press, 1983.

———. *Nicomachean Ethics*. trans. Terence Irwin, Indianapolis/Cambridge: Hackett Publishing Company, 1985.

———. *Selected Works*. trans. Hippocrates G. Apostle and Lloyd P. Gerson. Commentaries by H. G. Apostle. Grinell, Iowa: Peripatetic Press, 1982.

———. *Treatise on Rhetoric*. trans. Theodore Buckley. Amherst, New York: Prometheus Books, 1995.

(The) Art of Prayer: An Orthodox Anthology, compiled by Igumen Chariton of Valamo; trans. E. Kadloubovsky and Elizabeth Palmer. London: Faber and Faber, 1997.

Arzamas: sbornik v dvukh knigakh, eds. Vadim E. Vatsuro and Aleksandr L. Ospovat Moscow: Khudozhestvennaia literatura, 1994.

Arzumanova, N. A, ed. *I dum vysokoe stremlen'e*. Moscow: Sovetskaia Rossiia, 1980.

Aquinas, Saint Thomas. *On Law, Morality and Politics*. eds. William P. Baumgarth and Richard J. Regan. Indianapolis/Cambridge: Hackett Publishing Company, 1988.

———. *The Pocket Aquinas*, ed. Vernon J. Bourke. New York: Washington Square Press, 1960.

———. *The Cambridge Companion to Aquinas*, eds. Norman Kretzmann and Eleanore Stump. Cambridge: Cambridge University Press, 1993.

Augustine. *Confessions*. trans. R. S. Pine-Coffin. Penguin Classics, 1961.

———. Aurelius Augustinus, *Les Confessions de Saint Augustin*. trans. d'Arnauld d'Andilly. Paris: Garnier, 1861.

Aurelius, Marcus. *Marcus Aurelius and His Times. The Transition from Paganism to Christianity*. Roslyn, N. Y.: Walter J. Black, 1945.

Baillie, John. *Baptism and Conversion*. London: Oxford University Press, 1964.

Bakhtin, Mikhail M. *Art and Answerability*. trans. Vadim Liapunov. eds. Michael Holquist and Vadim Liapunov. Austin: The University of Texas Press, 1990.

———. *Dialogic Imagination*. trans. Caryl Emerson. ed. Michael Holquist. Austin: The University of Texas Press, 1981.

———. *Problems of Dostoevsky's Poetics*. trans. Caryl Emerson. Minneapolis: Minnesota University Press, 1984.

———. *Sobranie sochinenii*. 5 vols. Moscow: Russkie slovari, 1996-.

Bakunin, Michael. *God and the State*. New York: Dover, 1970.

Barnard, L. W. *Justin Martyr: His Life and Thought*. Cambridge: Cambridge University Press, 1967.

Bartlett, Robert. *Trial by Fire and Water. The Medieval Judicial Ordeal*. Oxford: Claredon Press, 1986.

Bayley, John. *Tolstoy and the Novel*. Chicago: The University of Chicago Press, 1966.

Beckford, James A. "Accounting for Conversion." *British Journal of Sociology* 29 (1978), 249–62.

Beiser, Frederick C. "Hegel's Historicism." 270–300 in *The Cambridge Companion to Hegel*. ed. Frederick C. Beiser. Cambridge: Cambridge University Press, 1993.

Belinsky, Vissarion G. "O knizhnoi illiustratsii." 329–30 in *Literaturnoe Nasledstvo*. vol. 57. Moscow: Nauka, 1951.

———. *Sobranie sochinenii v deviati tomakh*, 9 vols. Moscow: Khudozhestvennaia literatura, 1982.

Bell, John. "The Judge as Bureaucrat." 33–56 in *Oxford Essays in Jurisprudence. Third Series.* eds. John Eekelaar and John Bell. Oxford: Claredon Press, 1987.

Benediktov, Vladimir G. *Stikhotvoreniia.* ed. V. I. Sakharov. Moscow: Sovetskaia Rossiia, 1991.

Benjamin, Walter. *Selected Writings.* 4 vols. Cambridge, Mass.: The Belknap Press of Harvard University Press, 1996–2003.

Berdiaev, Nikolai. *Filosofiia svobody. Smysl tvorchestva.* Moscow: Pravda, 1989.

——. *Izbrannye proizvedeniia.* Rostov-on-Don: Feniks, 1997.

Berlin, Isaiah. *Russian Thinkers.* ed. Aileen Kelly. Penguin Books, 1979.

Bernasconi, Robert. "Literary Attestation in Philosophy: Heidegger's Footnote on *The Death of Ivan Ilyich.*" 7–36 in *Philosophers' Poets.* ed. David Wood. London/ New York: Routledge, 1990.

——. "'Only the Persecuted. . . ': Language of the Oppressor, Language of the Oppressed." 77–86 in *Ethics as First Philosophy. The Significance of Emmanuel Levinas for Philosophy, Literature and Religion.* ed. Adriaan T. Peperzhak. New York and London: Routledge, 1995.

Bernshtam, T. A. *Prikhodskaia zhizn' russkoi derevni.* St. Petersburg: Russian Academy of Sciences. Peter the Great's Museum of Anthropology and Ethnography (Kunstkamera))/Peterburgskoe vostokovedenie, 2005.

Biblioteka L. N. Tolstogo v Iasnoi Poliane. Bibliograficheskoe opisanie. Parts I, II, III. Moscow: Kniga, 1972–2000.

Biblioteka russkoi kritiki: Kritika 60-kh gg. XIX veka. Moscow: Astrel', 2003.

Biblioteka russkoi kritiki: Kritika 70-kh godov XIX veka. Moscow: Olimp, 2002.

Billington, James. *The Icon and the Axe: An Interpretive History of Russian Culture.* New York: Vintage, 1970.

——. *Mikhailovsky and Russian Populism.* Oxford: Oxford University Press, 1958.

Blake, William. *The Complete Poetry and Prose of William Blake.* New Revised Edition. ed. David V. Erdman. Commentary, Harold Bloom. New York: Anchor Books, 1988.

Bocharov, Sergey. *Roman Tolstogo Voina i Mir.* Moscow: Khudozhestvennaia literatura, 1978.

Bonnet, Victoria E., ed. *Russian Worker: Life and Labor Under the Tsarist Regime.* Los Angeles: The University of California Press, 1983.

Bulgakov, Sergius. *A Bulgakov Anthology.* eds. James Pain and Nicholas Zernov. Philadelphia: Westminster Press, 1976.

——. *Pravoslavie.* Moscow: Folio, 2001.

Burbridge, John W. *Hegel on Logic and Religion. The Reasonableness of Christianity.* Albany, N. Y.: SUNY Press, 1992.

Burnyeat, M. F. "Enthymeme: Aristotle on the Logic of Persuasion." 2–56 in *Aristotle's Rhetoric. Philosophical Essays.* eds. David J. Furley and Alexander Nehamas. Princeton, N. J.: Princeton University Press, 1994.

Buslaev, Fedor. *O literature. Issledovaniia. Stat'i.* Moscow: Khudozhestvennaia literatura, 1990.

Caesar. *The Gallic War.* trans. H. J. Edwards. Cambridge, Mass./London: Harvard University Press, 1994.

Carden, Patricia. "The Expressive Self in War and Peace." *Canadian-American Slavic Studies*, vol. 12 (1978): 519–34.

Cervantes, Miguel de. *Don Quixote*. trans. J. M. Cohen. London: Penguin, 1950.

Chaadaev, Petr Iakovlevich. *Polnoe sobranie sochinenii i izbrannye pis'ma*, 2 vols. ed. Z. A. Kamenskii. Moscow: Nauka, 1991.

Chances, Ellen B. *Conformity's Children: An Approach to the Superfluous Man in Russian Literature*. Columbus, Ohio: Slavica Publishers, 1978.

Chateaubriand, François-Auguste-René de. *Atala/René*. trans. with an introduction by Irving Putter. Berkeley, Calif.: The University of California Press, 1980.

Chernyshevsky, Nikolai G. *Polnoe sobranie sochinenii v piatnadtsati tomakh*. Moscow: Gikhl, 1949.

——. *Sochineniia v dvukh tomakh, Filosofskoe nasledie, 101*. Moscow: Akademiia Nauk, USSR. Institut filosofii. Izdatel'stvo Mysl', 1987.

Chicherin, Boris Nikolaevich. *Nauka i religiia*. Moscow: Tipografiia Martynova, 1879.

——. *Nauka i religiia*. Moscow: Respublika, 1999.

Chistiakova, M. "L. N. Tolstoy i Saltykov." 508–18 in *Literaturnoe nasledstvo. 13–14 (II Shchedrin)*. Moscow: Zhurnal'no-gazetnoe ob'edinenie, 1934.

Christian, R. F. *Tolstoy's War and Peace*. Oxford: Oxford University Press, 1962.

Cioran, Emil M. *The Fall Into Time*. trans. from the French by Richard Howard. Intro. Charles Newman. Chicago: Quadrangle Books, 1970.

Clay, George R. *Tolstoy's Phoenix. From Method to Meaning in War and Peace*. Evanston, Ill.: Northwestern University Press, 1998.

Coleman, Francis X. J. *Neither Angel Nor Beast. The Life and Work of Blaise Pascal*. New York/London: Routledge and Kegan Paul, 1986.

Coleridge, S. T. *The Collected Works of Samuel Taylor Coleridge. Biographia Literaria. Volumes 1 and 2 Complete in One Volume*. eds. James Engell and W. Jackson Bate. Bollingen Series LXXV. Routledge & Kegan Paul. Princeton, N. J.: Princeton University Press, 1983.

——. *The Collected Works of Samuel Taylor Coleridge. Logic*. ed. J. B. de J. Jackson. Bollingen Series LXXV. Routledge & Kegan Paul. Princeton, N. J.: Princeton University Press, 1981.

Critical Theory Since Plato. ed. Hazard Adams. San Diego/New York/Chicago: Harcourt, Brace, Jovanovich, 1971.

Danaher, David S. "The Function of Pain in Tolstoy's *The Death of Ivan Il'ich*. *Tolstoy Studies Journal*, vol. X: (1998): 20–28.

Dashkova, Ekaterina. *Zapiski 1743–1810*. ed. G. N. Moiseeva, Yu. V. Stepniak. Leningrad: Nauka, 1985.

de Man, Paul. *Aesthetic Ideology*. ed. and intro. Andrzej Warminski. Minneapolis: University of Minnesota Press, 1996.

——. *Blindness and Insight. Essays in the Rhetoric of Contemporary Criticism*. intro. Wlad Godzich. Minneapolis: The University of Minnesota Press, 1983.

Delaney Grossman, Joan. "'Philosophers, Decadents, and Mystics': James's Russian Readers in the 1890s," 93–112 in *William James in Russian Culture*. ed. Joan Delaney Grossman and Ruth Rischin. Lanham, Md.: Lexington Books, 2003.

Del'vig, Anton. *Stikhotvoreniia*. Moscow: Sovetskaia Rossiia, 1983.

Denner, Michael A. "'Be not afraid of greatness . . .' Lev Tolstoy and Celebrity." Forthcoming in *Popular Culture* (2009).

——. "Tolstoyan Nonaction: The Advantage of Doing Nothing." *Tolstoy Studies Journal*, volume XIII (2001): 8–22.

Derrida, Jacques. *Aporias*. trans. Thomas Dutoit. Stanford, Calif.: Stanford University Press, 1993.

—— "The Mystical Foundation of Authority." 3–67 in *Deconstruction and the Possibility of Justice*. ed. Drucilla Cornell, Michel Rosenfeld, and David Gray Carlson. New York & London: Routledge, 1992.

Derzhavin, Gavrila. *Sochineniia*. Moscow: Pravda, 1985.

Descartes, René. *Discourse on Method and Meditations on First Philosophy*. trans. Donald A. Cress. Indianapolis/Cambridge: Hackett Publishing Company, 1993.

(A) Dictionary of Christian Theology. ed. Alan Richardson. Philadelphia: The Westminster Press, 1969.

Dobroliubov, Nikolai Aleksandrovich. *Izbrannoe*. Moscow: Sovremennik, 1984.

Dostoevsky, Fedor Mikhailovich. *Polnoe sobranie sochinenii v tridtsati tomakh*. Leningrad: Nauka, 1972–1988.

Dostoevsky, Fyodor. *Great Short Works of Fyodor Dostoevsky*. ed. and intro. Ronald Hingley. New York: Harper and Rowe, 1968.

——. *Crime and Punishment*. trans. Richard Pevear and Larissa Volokhonsky. New York: Vintage, 1993.

——. *Notes From Underground*. trans. and ed. Michael R. Katz. A Norton Critical Edition, 2nd edition. New York/London: Norton & Company, 2001.

——. *A Writer's Diary in 2 vols*. trans. Kenneth Lantz. intro. Gary Saul Morson. Evanston, Ill.: Northwestern UP, 1994.

——. *F. M. Dostoevsky v zabytykh i neizvestnykh vospominaniiakh sovremennikov*. ed. S. V. Belov. St. Petersburg: Andreev i synov'ia, 1993.

Dostoevsky and the Christian Tradition. eds. George Pattison and Diane Oenning Thompson. Cambridge: Cambridge University Press, 2001.

Drozdov, Vasilii. *Sochinenie Filareta, mitropolita Moskovskogo i Kolomenskogo. Slova i rechi 1803–1867* in 5 vols. Moscow: Tipografiia Mamontova, 1873–1885.

——. Mitropolit Moskovskii Sviatitel' Filaret, *Pravoslavnyi katikhizis*. St. Petersburg: Pravoslavnaia Rus', 1995.

Earle, William. *The Autobiographical Consciousness*. Chicago: Quadrangle, 1972.

Early English Drama. An Anthology. ed. John C. Coldewey. New York & London: Garland Publishing, Inc., 1993.

Easton, Patricia A., ed. *Logic and the Working of the Mind. The Logic of Ideas and Faculty Psychology in Early Modern Philosophy*. vol. 5. North American Kant Society. Studies in Philosophy. Atascadero, Calif.: Ridgeview Publishing Company, 1997.

Eikhenbaum, Boris M. *Lev Tolstoy. Shestidesiatye gody*. Leningrad: Khudozhestvennaia literatura, 1974.

——. *Lev Tolstoy. Semidesiatye gody*. Leningrad: Sovetskii pisatel', 1960.

——. *Molodoi Tolstoi*. Peterburg-Berlin: Izdatel'stvo Grzhebina, 1922.

————. *O Proze*. Leningrad: Khudozhestvennaia literatura, 1969.

————. *Tolstoi in the Sixties*. trans. Duffield White. Ann Arbor, Mich.: Ardis, 1982.

————. *Tolstoi in the Seventies*. trans. Alfred Kaspin. Ann Arbor, Mich.: Ardis, 1982.

————. *The Young Tolstoy*. trans. Gary Kern. Ann Arbor, Mich.: Ardis, 1972.

Emerson, Caryl. "The Tolstoy Connection in Bakhtin." *PMLA*, volume 100, No. 1 (January 1985): 68–80. revised 149–170 in *Rethinking Bakhtin. Extensions and Challenges*. ed. Gary Saul Morson and Caryl Emerson. Evanston, Ill: Northwestern University Press, 1989.

————. "What is Infection and What is Expression in *What is Art?*" 102–27 in *Lev Tolstoy and the Concept of Brotherhood*. Papers and presentations from a conference held at the University of Ottawa, 22–24 February 1996. Ottawa: Legas, 1996.

Encyclopedie ou dictionnare raisonné des sciences, des arts et des métiers. 2 vols. ed. Alain Pons. Paris: Flammarion, 1986.

Feuer, Kathryn B. *Tolstoy and the Genesis of War and Peace*. eds. Robin Feuer Miller and Donna Tussing Orwin. Ithaca, N. Y. and London: Cornell University Press, 1996.

Fichte, Johann Gottlieb. *Early Philosophical Writings*. trans. and ed. Daniel Breazeale. Ithaca, N. Y.: Cornell University Press, 1988.

————. *Science of Knowledge: With the First and Second Introductions*, trans. and ed. Peter Heath and John Lachs. Cambridge: Cambridge University Press, 1982.

Filaret Moskovskii. See Drozdov, Vasilii.

Florovsky, George. *Puti russkogo bogosloviia*. Paris: YMCA-Press, 1983.

Fonvizin, Denis Ivanovich. *Sobranie sochinenii v dvukh tomakh*. Moscow/Leningrad: Gosudarstvennoe izdatel'stvo khudozhestvennoi literatury, 1959.

Foucault, Michel. *Discipline and Punish. The Birth of Modern Prison*. trans. Alan Sherdian. New York: Vintage Books, 1979.

————. *The Politics of Truth*. eds. Sylvère Lotringer and Lysa Hochroth. New York: New Press/Semiotext[e], 1977.

————. *The Order of Things. An Archeology of the Human Sciences*. New York: Vintage, 1994.

Frank, Semion L. *Russkoe mirovozzrenie*. St. Petersburg: Nauka, 1996.

Freeze, Gregory L. *From Supplication to Revolution: A Documentary Social History of Imperial Russia*. New York: Oxford University Press, 1988.

Freud, Sigmund. *Writings on Art and Literature*. eds. Werner Hamacher and David E. Wellbery. Foreword by Neil Hertz. Stanford, Calif.: Stanford University Press, 1997.

Gadamer, Hans-Georg. *Hermeneutics, Religion, and Ethics*. trans. Joel Weinsheimer. New Haven and London: Yale University Press, 1999.

Garshin, Vsevolod M. *Garshin. Sochineniia*. Moscow/Leningrad: GIKhl, 1963.

Gellrich, Jesse M. *The Idea of the Book in the Middle Ages: Language Theory, Mythology, and Fiction*. Ithaca, N. Y.: Cornell University Press, 1985.

Geraci, Robert P., and Michael Khodarkovsky. eds. *On Religion and Empire. Missions, Conversion, and Tolerance in Tsarist Russia*. Ithaca, N.Y. and London: Cornell University Press, 2000.

Gerstein, Linda. *Nikolai Strakhov*. Cambridge, Mass.: Harvard University Press, 1971.

Gesta Romanorum. trans. from the Latin by Charles Swan, rev. Wynnard Hooper. New York: AMS Press, 1970.

——. ed. Hermann Oesterley. Berlin: Weidmannsche Buchhhandlung, 1872.

Gifford, Henry. *Tolstoy.* Oxford: Oxford University Press, 1982.

Ginzburg, Lydia. *O psikhologicheskoi proze.* Moscow: Intrada, 1999.

——. *On Psychological Prose.* trans. Judson Rosengrandt. Princeton, N. J.: Princeton University Press, 1981.

Goethe, Johann Wolfgang von. *Faust.* ed. and trans. Stuart Atkins. Princeton, N. J.: Princeton University Press, 1984.

——. *Selected Poetry.* Bilingual edition. trans. with intro and notes by David Luke. London: Penguin Books, 2005.

Gogol, N. V. *Sobranie sochinenii v vos'mi tomakh.* Collected Works in 8 vols. Moscow: Terra, 2001.

——. *Selected Passages from Correspondence with Friends.* trans. Jesse Zeldin. Nashville, Tenn.: Vanderbilt University Press, 1969.

Goldmann, Lucien. *Le dieu caché. Etude sur la vision tragique dans les Pensées de Pascal et dans le théâtre de Racine.* Paris: Librairie Gallimard, 1955.

Goncharov, Ivan Aleksandrovich. *Sobranie sochinenii v shesti tomakh.* Moskva: Gosudarstvennoe izdatel'stvo khudozhestvennoi literatury, 1959–1960.

Grant, Robert. *The Politics of Sex and Other Essays.* Foreword by Raymond Tallis. Hampshire and London: Macmillan Press Ltd, 2000.

Green, Ronald. *Religion and Moral Reason. A New Method for Comparative Study.* New York/Oxford: Oxford University Press, 1988.

Greenblatt, Stephen J. *Hamlet in Purgatory.* Princeton, N. J.: Princeton University Press, 2002.

Greenwood, E. B. "Tolstoy and Religion." 149–74 in *New Essays on Tolstoy.* ed. Malcolm Jones. Cambridge: Cambridge University Press, 1978.

——. *Tolstoy: The Comprehensive Vision.* New York: St. Martin's Press, 1975.

Grigoriev, Apollon. *Vospominaniia,* ed. B. F. Fedorov. Moscow: Nauka, 1988.

Gritsch, Eric W. *Born Againism: Perspectives On a Movement.* Philadelphia: Fortress Press, 1982.

Grot, Nikolai Iakovlevich. *Filosofiia i ee obshchie zadachi. Sbornik statei pod redaktsiei Moskovskogo Psikhologicheskogo obshchestva.* St. Petersburg, Tipografiia A. S. Suvorina, 1904.

——. *Nietzsche und Tolstoi.* trans. Alexis Markow. Berlin: Hugo Stenitz Verlag, 1898.

——. *O dushe v sviazi s sovremennymi ucheniiami o sile. Opyt filosofskogo postroeniia N. Ia. Grota.* Prof. Filosofii Novorossiskogo Universiteta. Odessa: Tipografiia Odesskogo vestnika, 1886.

——. *O nravstvennoi otvetstvennosti i iuridicheskoi vmeniaemosti.* Odessa: Tipografiia Odesskogo vestnika, 1885.

Gusev, N. N. *Lev Nikolaevich Tolstoy. Materialy k biografii s 1870 po 1881.* Moscow: USSR Academy of Sciences, 1963.

——. *Tolstoy. Materialy k biografii. 1881–1885.* Moscow: Nauka, 1970.

Gustafson, Richard. *Leo Tolstoy: Resident and Stranger. A Study in Fiction and Theology.* Princeton, N. J.: Princeton University Press, 1986.

Hamilton, Heard. *The Art and Architecture of Russia*. New Haven and London: Yale University Press, 1983.

Handbook of Religious Conversion. H. Newton Malony and Samuel Southhard, eds. Birmingham, Alabama: Religious Education Press, 1992.

Hardon, John A. *The Catholic Catechism: A Contemporary Catechism of the Teachings of the Catholic Church*. New York: Doubleday, Image Books, 1981.

Harman, P. M. *Energy, Force and Matter: The Conceptual Development of Nineteenth-Century Physics*. Cambridge: Cambridge University Press, 1982.

Harran, Marilyn. *Luther on Conversion. The Early Years*. Ithaca and London: Cornell University Press, 1983.

Hasker, William. *God, Time, and Knowledge*. Ithaca, N. Y.: Cornell University Press, 1989.

Hegel, G. W. F. *Elements of the Philsophy of Right*. trans. H. B. Nisbet, ed. Allen W. Wood. Cambridge: Cambridge University Press, 1991.

———. *The Encyclopedia Logic. Part I of the Encyclopaedia of Philosophical Sciences with the Zusätze*. trans. T. F. Geraets, W. A. Suchtig, H. S. Harris. Indianapolis/Cambridge: Hackett Publishing Company, 1991.

———. *Lectures on the History of Philosophy*. intro. Tom Rockmore, trans. A. S. Haldane and Frances H. Simon. Abridged edition. Amherst, N. Y.: Prometheus Books, 1996.

———. *Lectures on the Philosophy of World History. Introduction: Reason in History*. trans. H. B. Nisbet, intro. Duncan Forbes. Cambridge: Cambridge University Press, 1975.

———. *Phenomenology of Spirit*. trans. A. V. Miller, intro. J. N. Findlay. Oxford: Oxford University Press, 1977.

———. *The Philosophy of History*. trans. J. Sibree. Amherst, N.Y.: Prometheus Books, 1991.

———. *Theologian of the Spirit*. ed. Peter C. Hodgson. Minneapolis: Fortress Press, 1997.

———. *Vorlesungen über die Ästhetik I/II*. Stuttgart: Philip Reclam Jun., 1995.

———. *Vorlesungen über die Ästhetik III*. Stuttgart: Philip Reclam Jun., 1984.

Heidegger, Martin. *Being and Time*. trans. Joan Stambaugh. Albany, N. Y.: SUNY Press, 1996.

———. *Poetry, Language, Thought*. trans. Albert Hofstadter. New York: Perennial Classics, 2001.

Herodotus. *The History*. trans. David Grene. Chicago & London: The University of Chicago Press, 1987.

Herzen, Alexander. *Sobranie sochinenii v vos'mi tomakh*. Moscow: Pravda, 1975.

Hesse, Hermann. *Siddhartha*. trans. Hilda Rosner. New York: Bantam Books, 1971

Holquist, Michael. *Dostoevsky and the Novel*. Princeton, N. J.: Princeton University Press, 1976.

Hugo, Victor. *La préface de Cromwell. Texte* (par Victor Hugo). intro. and notes by Maurice Souriau. Geneve: Slatkine Reprints, 1973.

———. *Dramas. Oliver Cromwell*. trans. I. G. Burnham. Philadelphia: George Barrie & Son, 1896.

Hume, David. *Treatise of Human Nature*. Buffalo, N. Y.: Prometheus Books, 1992.

——. *Writings on Religion*, ed. Antony Flew. Chicago: Open Court, 1998.

Iazykov, Nikolai M. *Sochineniia*. Leningrad: Khudozhestvennaia literatura, 1982.

I dum vysokoe stremlen'e, ed. N. A. Arzumanova. Moscow: Sovetskaia Rossiia, 1980.

Irwin, Terence, ed. *Classical Philosophy*. Oxford: Oxford University Press, 1999.

Istoriia pravoslaviia i russkogo ateizma. Moscow: USSR Academy of Sciences, 1960.

Ivanov, Viacheslav. *Rodnoe i vselenskoe*. Moscow: Respublika, 1994.

Iz russkoi mysli o Rossii, ed. Igor Trofimivich Ianin. Kaliningrad: Iantarnyi skaz, 1998.

Izenberg, Gerald N. *Impossible Individuality: Romanticism, Revolution, and the Origins of Modern Selfhood, 1787–1802*. Princeton, N. J.: Princeton University Press, 1992.

Jahn, Gary. *The Death of Ivan Ilich. An Interpretation*. New York: Twayne Publishers, 1993.

——, ed. *Tolstoy's The Death of Ivan Il'ich. A Critical Companion*. Evanston, Ill: Northwestern University Press, 1999.

——. "The Death of Ivan Il'ich —— Chapter One." 37–43 in *Studies in Honor of Xenia Gasiorowska*. Columbus, Ohio: Slavic Publishers, 1983.

——. "A Note on Miracle Motifs in the Later Works of Lev Tolstoy." 481–86 in *Tolstoy's Short Fiction*. ed. Michael R. Katz. New York: Norton & Co, 1991.

——. "A Structural Analysis of Leo Tolstoy's 'God See the Truth But Waits,'" *Studies in Short Fiction*. volume 12 (1975): 261–69.

——. "Crisis in Tolstoy and in *Anna Karenina*." 67–73 in *Approaches to Teaching Tolstoy's Anna Karenina*, ed. Liza Knapp and Amy Mandelker. New York: Modern Language Association of America, 2003.

——. "The Role of the Ending in Lev Tolstoi's *The Death of Ivan Ilich*." *Canadian Slavonic Papers* 24, no. 3 (1982): 229–38.

——. "Tolstoy and Kant." 60–70 in *New Perspectives on Nineteenth-Century Russian Prose*. ed. George J. Gutsche and Lauren Leighton. Columbus, Ohio: Slavica Publishers, 1981.

——. "Tolstoj's Vision of the Power of Death and 'How Much Land Does a Man Need?'" *Slavic and East European Journal*, vol. 22, no. 4 (1978): 442–53.

James, William. *The Varieties of Religious Experience*. London: Penguin Classics, 1982.

Justin Martyr, Saint. *Dialogues With Trypho*. trans. Thomas B. Fallsand, ed. Michael Shlusser. Washington, D. C.: Catholic University of America Press, 2003.

——. *Saint Justin Martyr: The First Apology, The Second Apology, Dialogue with Trypho, Exhortation to the Greeks, Discourse to the Greeks, The Monarchy; or the Rule of God*. ed. Thomas B. Falls. New York: Christian Heritage, 1949.

——. *Saint Justin Martyr, The First and Second Apologies*. trans. Leslie William Barnard. New York: Paulist Press, 1966.

Kafka, Franz. *The Blue Octavo Notebooks*. ed. Max Brod, trans. Ernst Kaiser and Eithne Wilkins. Cambridge, Mass: Exact Change, 1991.

Kaizer, Daniel H. "Quotidian Orthodoxy: Domestic Life in Early Modern Russia." 179–92 in *Orthodox Russia. Belief and Practice Under the Tsars*. ed. Valerie Kivelson and Robert H. Green. University Park, Pa.: Penn State University Press, 2003.

Kant, Immanuel. *The Critique of Judgement*. trans. James Creed Meredith. Oxford: Oxford University Press, 1952.

———. *Critique de la raison pure*. Traduite de l'allemand par C. -J. Tissot, 2 vols. Paris: Ladrange, 1835–36.

———. *Critique of Pure Reason*. trans. Norman Kemp Smith. New York: St. Martin's Press, 1965.

———. *Kritik der Urteilskraft*. Stuttgart: Philipp Reclam, 1991.

———. *Logic (1800)*. trans. and intro. Robert S. Hartman and Wolfgang Schwarz. Indianapolis & New York: Bobbs-Merril Company, 1974.

———. *The Metaphysics of Morals*. trans. Mary Gregor. Cambridge: Cambridge University Press, 1996.

———. *Perpetual Peace and Other Essays on Politics, History, and Morals*. trans. Ted Humphrey. Indianapolis/Cambridge: Hackett Publishing Company, 1983.

———. *Philosophical Correspondence, 1759–99*. ed. Arnulf Zweig. Midway Reprint, Chicago: The University of Chicago Press, 1967.

———. *Political Writings*. trans. H. B. Nisbett. Cambridge: Cambridge University Place, 1991.

———. *Prolegomena to Any Future Metaphysics*, newly revised by James W. Ellington. Indianapolis/Cambridge: Hackett Publishing Company, 1977.

———. *Religion Within the Limits of Reason Alone*. trans. with intro. and notes, Theodore M. Greene and Hoyt H. Hudson. With a new essay by John. R. Silber. New York: Harper Torchbooks, 1960.

Karamzin, Nikolai. *Sochineniia v dvukh tomakh*. Leningrad: Khudozhestvennaia literatura, 1984.

Kaufmann, Walter. *Religion From Tolstoy to Camus*. Garden City, N. Y.: Doubleday & Co., 1961.

———. *Tragedy and Philosophy*. Princeton, N. J.: Princeton University Press, 1968.

Kavelin, Konstantin Dmitrievich. *Nash umstvennyi stroi: Stat'i po filosofii russkoi istorii i kul'tury*. Moscow: Pravda, 1989.

Kelly, Aileen M. *Toward Another Shore. Russian Thinkers Between Necessity and Chance*. New Haven and London: Yale University Press, 1998.

Kerferd, G. B. *The Sophistic Movement*. Cambridge: Cambridge University Press, 1981.

Kermode, Frank. *The Sense of an Ending*. New York: Oxford University Press, 2000.

Kierkegaard, Søren. *The Concept of Irony With Continual Reference to Socrates. Notes of Schelling's Berlin Lectures*. eds. and trans. Howard V. Hong and Edna H. Hong. Princeton, N. J.: Princeton University Press, 1989.

———. *Concluding Unscientific Postscript to Philosophical Fragments*. 2 vols. eds. and trans. Howard V. Hong and Edna H. Hong. Princeton, N. J.: Princeton University Press, 1992.

———. *Either/Or*. 2 vols. eds. and trans. Howard V. Hong and Edna H. Hong. Princeton, N. J.: Princeton University Press, 1987.

———. *Fear and Trembling. Repetition.* eds. and trans. Howard V. Hong and Edna H. Hong, with Introduction and Notes. Princeton, N. J.: Princeton University Press, 1983.

———. *Parables of Kierkegaard.* ed. Thomas C. Oden. Princeton, N. J.: Princeton University Press, 1978.

———. *Philosophical Fragments.* eds. and trans. Howard V. Hong and Edna H. Hong. Princeton, N. J.: Princeton University Press, 1985.

———. *(The) Sickness Unto Death.* eds. and trans. H. V. Hong and E. H. Hong. Princeton, N. J.: Princeton University Press, 1980.

Kiesewetter, J. G. C. *Fassliche darstellung der erfahrungsseelenlehre zur selbstbelehrung für nichtstudierende.* Wien: Franz Haerter, 1817.

———. *Grundriß einer allgemeinen Logik nach Kantischen Grundsaßen.* Zum Gebrauch für Vorlesungen. Dritte Auflage, Erster und zweiter Theil, Berlin, Lagarde, 1802–1806.

Kirillova, Irina. "Dostoevsky's Markings in the Gospel According to St. John." 41–50 in *Dostoevsky and the Christian Tradition.* ed. George Pattison and Diane Oenning Thompson. Cambridge: Cambridge University Press, 2001.

Kitcher, Patricia. *Kant's Transcendental Psychology.* New York/Oxford: Oxford University Press, 1990.

Kiukhelbecker, Vil'gelm Karlovich. *Izbrannye proizvedeniia v dvukh tomakh.* 2 vols. Moscow and Leningrad: Sovetskii pisatel', 1967.

Kivelson, Valerie, and Robert H. Green. eds. *Orthodox Russia. Belief and Practice Under the Tsars.* University Park, Pa.: Penn State University Press, 2003.

Kondakov, Yury E. *Gosudarstvo i pravoslavnaia tserkov' v Rossii: evoliutsiia otnoshenii v pervoi polovine XiX veka.* St. Petersburg: Izdatel'stvo Rossiiskaia natsiolanl'snaia biblioteka, 2003.

Koni, A. F. *Sobranie sochinenii.* 8 vols. Moscow: Iuridicheskaia literatura, 1966.

Kontsevich, I. M. *Optina pustyn' i ee vremia.* New York: Jordanville, 1970.

Language in Religion. eds. Humphrey Tonkin & Allison A. Keef. Lanham, Md. and NY/London: University Press of America, 1989.

Leibniz, G. W. *Philosophical Essays.* trans. Roger Ariew and Daniel Garber. Indianapolis and Cambridge: Hackett Publishing Company, 1989.

Leo Tolstoy and Nikolaj Strakhov. Complete Correspondence in Two Volumes, ed. Andrew A. Donskov and comp. Lydia Dmitrievna Gromova and Tatiana Georgievna Nikiforova. Ottawa and Moscow: Slavic Research Group at the University of Ottawa and State L. N. Tolstoy Museum, 2003.

Leone, Massimo. *Religious Conversion and Identity. A Semiotic Analysis of Texts.* London and New York: Routledge, 2004.

Leontiev, Konstantin. *Analiz, stil' i veianie. O romanakh gr. L. N. Tolstogo.* Providence: Brown University Press, 1968.

Lermontov, Mikhail Iur'evich. *Izbrannye proizvedeniia v dvukh tomakh,* ed. Irakly Andronikov. Moscow: Khudozhestvennaia literatura, 1973.

Lermontov, Mikhail. *A Hero of Our Time.* trans. Paul Foote. London: Penguin, 1966.

Lev Nikolaevich Tolstoy. Materialy k biografii s 1881 po 1885 god. ed. N. N. Gusev. Moscow: Nauka, 1970.

Lev Nikolaevich Tolstoy. Materialy k biografii s 1886 po 1892 god. ed. L. D. Opulskaya. Moscow: Nauka, 1979.

Lev Nikolaevich Tolstoi. Sbornik statei i materialov. Moscow: Akademiia nauk, 1951.

Lev Tolstoy i V. V. Stasov. Perepiska 1876–1906. ed. V. D. Komarovsky, B. L. Modzalevsky. Leningrad: Priboi, 1929.

Levinas, Emmanuel. *Alterity and Transcendence.* trans. Michael B. Smith. New York: Columbia University Press, 1999.

———. *Of God Who Comes to Mind.* trans. Bettina Bergo. Stanford, Calif.: Stanford University Press, 1998.

———. *Totality and Infinity.* trans. Alphonso Lingis. Pittsburgh: Dusquesne University Press, 1992.

(The) Levinas Reader. Emmanuel Levinas. ed. Seán Hand. Oxford/Cambridge: Basil Blackwell, 1989.

Livingston, James C. *Modern Christian Thought. From the Enlightenment to Vatican II.* New York: Macmillan Publishing Co., Inc.; London: Collier Macmillan Publishers, 1971.

L. N. Tolstoy, Dokumenty, fotografii, rukopisi. comp. M. Loginova and N. Podsvirova, ed. L. Opulskaya. Moscow: Planeta, 1995.

L. N. Tolstoy v vospominaniiakh sovremennikov, 2 vols. intro. K. N. Lomunov, ed. G. N. Krasnova. Moscow: Khudozhestvennaia literatura, 1978.

Locke, John. *Essay Concerning Human Understanding.* Amherst, N. Y.: Prometheus Books, 1995.

Logic and the Working of the Mind. The Logic of Ideas and Faculty Psychology in Early Modern Philosophy. ed. Patricia A. Easton. Atascadero, Calif.: Ridgeview Publishing Company, 1997.

Love, Jeff. *The Overcoming of History in War and Peace.* Amsterdam/New York: Rodopi, 2004.

Luther, Martin. *Christian Liberty.* ed. Harold J. Grimm. Philadelphia, Pa.: Fortress Press, 1957.

Lyotard, Jean-François. "Levinas's Logic." 275–313 in *The Lyotard Reader.* ed. Andrew Benjamin. Oxford: Basil Blackwell, 1989.

Maistre, Joseph de. *The Works of Joseph de Maistre.* Selected, translated and introduced by Jack Lively. With a New Forword by Robert Nisbet. New York: Schocken Books, 1971.

Maistre, Xavier de. *Voyage Around My Room. Selected Works of Xavier de Maistre.* intro. Richard Howard, preface Joseph de Maistre, trans. Stephen Sartarelli. New York: New Directions Books, 1994.

Maloney, George A. *Russian Hesychasm: The Spirituality of Nil Sorskij.* The Hague: Mouton, 1973.

Mandelker, Amy. "Tolstoy's Eucharistic Aesthetics." 116–27 in *Lev Tolstoy and the Concept of Brotherhood.* Papers and presentations from a conference held at the University of Ottawa, February 22–24, 1996. Ottawa: Legas, 1996.

Matual, David. *Tolstoy's Translation of the Gospels. A Critical Study.* Lewiston: The Edwin Mellen Press, 1992.

Maturin, Charles. *Melmoth the Wanderer.* London: Oxford University Press, 1989.

McLaughlin, Sigrid. "Some aspects of Tolstoy's Intellectual Development: Tolstoy and Schopenhauer." *California Slavic Studies*, vol. 5 (1970): 187–248.

Medzhibovskaya, Inessa. "Aporias Of Immortality: Tolstoy Against Time" in *Word, Music, History. A Festschrift for Caryl Emerson*. ed. Lazar Fleishman, Gabriella Safran, Michael Wachtel. *Stanford Slavic Studies*, volumes 29–30 (2005): 29: 370–84.

———. "On Moral Movement and Moral Vision: *The Last Supper* in Russian Debates." *Comparative Literature*, volume 56, No. 1 (winter 2004): 23–53.

———. "Tolstoy and Religious Maturity" forthcoming in *American Contributions for the XIV International Congress of Slavists*. Bloomington, Indiana: Slavica Publishers, 2008.

———. "Tolstoy's Conversion: A Modified View" in *The Over-Examined Life: New Perspectives on Tolstoy*. ed. Justin Weir and Julie Buckler. Essay accepted by the editors December 31, 2002. Forthcoming.

———. "Tolstoy's Conversion: Reexamination and Definitions." (Paper presented at the conference "Tolstoy: The Over-Examined Life" at Barker Center, Harvard University on April 19–20, 2002.)

———. "Tolstoy, evkharisitiia i Tainaia vecheria." 155–70 in *Leo Tolstoy and World Literature. Papers Delivered at IIIrd International Tolstoy Conference. Yasnaya Poliana August 28–30, 2003. In Memory of Lydia Dmitrievna Opulskaya*. Ed. Galina Alexeeva. Moscow/Tula/Yasnaya Polyana: Yasnaya Polyana Publishing House 2005.

———. *Tolstoy's Projects of Transcendence (Reading the Conversion)*. PhD Dissertation. Princeton University, 2001.

———. "Teleological Striving and Redemption in *The Death of Ivan Il'ich*." *Tolstoy Studies Journal*, volume XII (2000): 35–49.

———. "Vital Force or Deity? The Philosophical Quandary in the Epilogues to *War and Peace*." (Paper presented for panel "Lev Tolstoy: Revising and Revisiting the Critical Tradition" at the annual meeting of American Association of Teachers of Slavic and East European Languages, Philadelphia, Pa., December 28, 2006).

Meerson, Michael A. *The Trinity of Love in Modern Russian Theology: The Love Paradigm and the Revival of Western Medieval Love Mysticism in Modern Russian Trinitarian Thought from Soloviev to Bulgakov*. Quincy, Ill: Franciscan Press, 1998.

Merezhkovsky, Dmitry S. *L. Tolstoy i Dostoevsky*. Moscow: Nauka, 2000.

Meusel, Heinrich. *Lexicon Caesarianum* (confecit H. Meusel). Berlin: W. Weber, 1887–1893.

Metzner, Ralph. "Ten Classical Metaphors of Self-Transformation." *The Journal of Transpersonal Psychology* 12, no. 1 (1980): 47–62.

Meyendorff, John. *Christ in Eastern Christian Thought*. Crestwood, N. Y.: St. Vladimir Seminary Press, 1987.

Meyerhoff, Hans. *Time in Literature*. Berkeley, Calif., and Los Angeles: University of California Press, 1955.

Mikhailovsky, Nikolai K. *Geroi i tolpa. Izbrannye trudy po sotsiologii v dvukh tomakh*, ed. V. V. Kozlobsky. St. Petersburg: Aleteia, 1998.

Mikhnevich, Vladimir C. *Nashi znakomye*. St. Petersburg: Graficheskaia masterskaia Rudometova, 1884.

Mill, John Stuart. *Autobiography*. ed. Jack Stillinger. Boston: Houghton Mifflin Company, 1969.

——. *The Logic of the Moral Sciences*. La Salle, Ill.: Open Court Classics, 1994.

Mirsky, Dmitry. *Uncollected Writings on Russian Literature*. ed. G. S. Smith. Berkeley, Calif.: Berkeley Slavic Specialties, 1989.

Morrison, Karl Frederick. *Conversion and Text: the Cases of Augustine of Hippo, Herman-Judah, and Constantine Tsatsos*. Charlottesville, Va: University Press of Virginia, 1992.

——. *Understanding Conversion*. Charlottesville, Va.: University Press of Virginia, 1992.

Morson, Gary Saul. *Hidden in Plain View*. *Narrative and Creative Potentials in War and Peace*. Stanford, Calif.: Stanford University Press, 1987.

——. "The Reader as Voyeur: Tolstoi and the Poetics of Didactic Fiction." *Canadian-American Slavic Studies*, 12. no. 4 (Winter 1978), 465–80. Reprinted 379–94 in *Tolstoy's Short Fiction. A Norton Critical Edition*. ed. Michael Katz. New York & London: W. W. Norton, 1991.

——. "War and Peace." 65–79 in *The Cambridge Companion to Tolstoy*, ed. Donna Tussing Orwin. Cambridge: Cambridge University Press, 2002.

Morson, Gary Saul, and Caryl Emerson. *Mikhail Bakhtin. Creation of a Prosaics*. Stanford, Calif.: Stanford University Press, 1990.

Moskovskie vedomosti. Issues 307, 312–14. November 5–13, 1882.

Musset, Alfred de. *Confession of a Child of the Century*. trans. Robert Arnot. New York: Current Literature, 1910.

Nadson, Sergey Iakovlevich. *Stikhotvoreniia*. Moscow: Sovetskaia Rossiia, 1987.

Nerval, Gérard de. *Aurélia and Other Writings*, trans. Geoffreey Wagner, Tober Duncan, and Marc Lowenthal. Boston: Exact Change, 1996.

[The] New Oxford Annotated Bible. eds. Bruce Metzger and Ronald Murphy. New York and Oxford: Oxford University Press, 1994.

Niebuhr, Reinhold. *An Interpretation of Christian Ethics*. San Francisco: Harper and Row, 1987.

Nock, Arthur Darby. *Conversion. The Old and the New in Religion from Alexander the Great to Augustine of Hippo*. London, New York: Oxford University Press, 1933.

Ogarev, Nikolai Platonovich. *Izbrannye proizvedeniia v dvukh tomakh*. Moscow: Gosudarstvennoe izdatel'stvo khudozhestvennoi literatury, 1956.

——. *Stikhotvoreniia i poemy*. intro. S. A. Reyser and B. P. Koz'min, eds. S. A. Reyser and N. P. Surina. Moscow: Sovetskii pisatel', 1937.

Olney, James. "Experience, Metaphor and Meaning: The Death of Ivan Ilych." *Journal of Aesthetics and Art Criticism*. Volume 31 (1972): 101–14.

On Spiritual Unity: A Slavophile Reader. Aleksei Khomiakov. Ivan Kireevsky. With Essays by Yury Samarin, Nikolai Berdiaev, and Pavel Florensky. trans. and eds. Boris Jakim and Robert Bird. Hudson, N. Y.: Lindisfarne Books, 1998.

Opisanie rukopisei khudozhestvennykh proizvedenii L. N. Tolstogo. eds. V. A. Zhdanov and E. E. Zaidenshnur. Moscow: USSR Academy of Sciences, 1935.

Opulskaya[-Gromova], Lydia Dmitrievna. *Lev Nikolaevich Tolstoy. Materialy k biografii s 1886 po 1892 god*. Moscow: Nauka, 1979.

——. *Izbrannye trudy*. Moscow: Nauka, 2005.

Orwin, Donna Tussing. "The Return to Nature: Tolstoyan Echoes in *The Idiot*." *The Russian Review*, volume 58 (January 1999): 87–102.

——. *The Cambridge Companion to Tolstoy*, ed. Donna Tussing Orwin. Cambridge: Cambridge University Press, 2002.

——. *Tolstoy's Art and Thought. 1847–1880*. Princeton, N. J.: Princeton University Press, 1993.

Otto, Robert C. *Publishing for the People: The Firm Posrednik, 1885–1905*. PhD Dissertation. The University of Wisconsin-Madison, 1983.

(The) Oxford Dictionary of Quotations, 4th edition. ed. Angela Partington. Oxford/New York: Oxford University Press, 1992.

Paperno, Irina. *Suicide as a Cultural Institution in Dostoevsky's Russia*. Ithaca, N. Y.: Cornell University Press, 1997.

Parker, T. H. L. "Conversion," 73–75 in *A Dictionary of Christian Theology*, ed. Alan Richardson. Philadelphia: Westminster Press, 1969.

Pascal, Blaise. *Oeuvres complètes*. Paris: L'Integrale/Seuil, 1963.

——. *Penseés*. trans. A. J. Krailsheimer. London: Penguin, 1966.

——. *Pensées sur la religion et sur quelques autres sujets*. ed. Louis Lafuma. Paris: Edition du Luxembourg, 1951.

Pervukhina-Kamyshnikova, Natalia M. *V. S. Pecherin. Emigrant na vse vremena*. Moscow: Iazyki slavianskoi kul'tury, 2006.

Petr Chaadaev, Pro et contra. Lichnost' i tvorchestvo Petra Chaadaeva v otsenke russkikh myslitelei i issledovatelei. Antologiia. eds. A. A. Ermichev and A. A. Zlatopolskaya. St. Petersburg: Russkii khristianskii gumanitarnyi institut, 1998.

Philosophy of Religion. The Big Questions. eds. Eleonore Stump and Michael J. Murray. Makden, Mass. /Oxford, UK: Basil Blackwell, 1999.

Plato. *The Collected Dialogues*. ed. Edith Hamilton. Princeton, N. J.: Princeton University Press, 1961.

Polosina, Alla. "L. N. Tolstoi i Avrelii Avgustin o pamiati, vremeni i prostranstve." 65–76 in *Lev Tolstoi i mirovaia literatura. Leo Tolstoy and World Literature: Papers Delivered at Third International Tolstoy Conference, Yasnaya Poliana, August 28–30, 2003, in Memory of Lydia Dmitrievna Opulskaya*, ed. Galina Alexeeva. Moscow/Tula/Yasnaya Polyana: Yasnaya Polyana Publishing House, 2005.

Poole, Randall. "The Neo-Idealist Reception of Kant in the Moscow Psychological Society." *Journal of the History of Ideas*. Volume 60, no. 2 (April 1999): 319–43.

Posner, Richard A. *Law and Literature. Revised and Enlarged Edition*. Cambridge, Mass. and London: Harvard University Press, 1999.

——. *Law and Literature. A Misunderstood Relation*. Cambridge, Mass. and London: Harvard University Press, 1998.

Pravoslavnaia vera i traditsii blagochestiia u russkikh v XVIII-XX vekakh. Etnograicheskie issledivaniia i materially. eds. O. V. Kirichenko, Kh. V Poplavskaya. Moscow: Nauka, 2002.

[The] Problem of Evil. ed. Marilyn McCord Adams and Robert Merrihew Adams. Oxford: Oxford University Press, 1990.

Prolog, 4 vols. Moscow: Sviato-troitsko vvedenskaia tserkov', 1875.

Prutkov, Koz'ma. *Koz'ma Prutkov*. Rostov-on-Don: Feniks, 1996.

Pushkin, Aleksandr S. *Polnoe sobranie sochinenii*, 19 vols. Moscow: Vozrozhdenie, 1994–1997. Expanded reprint of *Polnoe sobranie sochinenii*, 17 vols. Moscow: Izdatel'stvo Akademii Nauk, 1937–1959.

——. *Sobranie sochinenii v desiati tomakh*. Moscow: Khudozhestvennaia literatura, 1974–1978.

——. *Eugene Onegin*. trans. James F. Falen. Oxford: Oxford University Press, 1995.

——. *Pushkin on Literature*, rev. ed. ed. and trans. Tatiana Wolff. Evanston, Ill.: Northwestern University Press, 1998.

Pushkin, Vasily L'vovich. *Stikhi, proza, pis'ma*. Moscow: Sovetskii pisatel', 1989.

Pustarnikov, Vladimir. *Filosofskaia mysl' v Drevnei Rusi*. Moscow: Krug, 2005.

Radlov, Ernest Leopol'dovich, "Ocherk istorii russkoi filosofii." 96–216 in *Russkaia filosofiia na putiakh samopoznaniia. Stranitsy istorii*. Sverdlovsk: Izdatel'stvo ural'skogo universiteta, 1991.

Rambo, Lewis. *Understanding Religious Conversion*. New Haven and London: Yale University Press, 1993.

——. "The Psychology of Conversion," in H. Newton Malony and Samuel Southhard, eds. *Handbook of Religious Conversion*. Birmingham, Ala.: Religious Education Press, 1992, 159–77.

Rancour-Laferriere, Daniel. "Does God Exist? A Clinical Study of the Religious Attitudes Expressed in Tolstoy's *Confession*." *Slavic and East European Journal*, volume 49, number 3 (Fall 2005), 445–73.

——. "Narcissism, Masochism, and Denial in *The Death of Ivan Il'ich*." 117–33 in *Tolstoy's The Death of Ivan Il'ich. A Critical Companion*. ed. Gary R. Jahn. Evanston, Ill.: Northwestern University Press, 1999.

Reardon, Bernard. *Religion in the Age of Romanticism*. Cambridge: Cambridge University Press, 1985.

Reasoned Faith. Essays in Philosophical Theology on Honor of Norman Kretzmann. ed. Eleonore Stump. Ithaca and London: Cornell University Press, 1993.

Redston, David. "Tolstoy and the Greek Gospel," *Journal of Russian Studies*, no. 54 (1988): 21–33.

Reyfman, Irina. "Turgenev's 'Death' and Tolstoy's 'Three Deaths'. *Word, Music, History. A Festschrift for Caryl Emerson*. ed. Lazar Fleishman, Gabriella Safran, Michael Wachtel. *Stanford Slavic Studies*, volumes 29–30 (2005): 29: 312–26.

Riasanovsky, Nicholas. *Russia and the West in the Teaching of the Slavophiles*. Cambridge, Mass.: Harvard University Press, 1952.

Rice, James. "Comic Devices in the Death of Ivan Il'ich." *Slavic and East European Journal*. Volume 47, No. 1 (2003): 77–95.

Richards, Robert. *The Romantic Conception of Life: Sciences and Philosophy in the Age of Goethe*. Chicago: The University of Chicago Press, 2002.

Ricoeur, Paul. *Time and Narrative*. 3 vols. Chicago: The University of Chicago Press, 1984–1985.

——. *Figuring the Sacred. Religion, Narrative, and Imagination*. Minneapolis: Fortress Press, 1995.

Rimskiia dieaniia [Gesta Romanorum]. St. Petersburg: Obshchestvo liubitelei drevnei slovesnosti, 1877–1878.

Rollinson, Philip. *Classical Theories of Allegory and Christian Culture*. Pittsburgh, Pa./Brighton, Sussex: Duquesne University Press, Harvester Press, 1981.

Rousseau, Jean-Jacques. *The Confessions*. Herfordshire, England: Wordsworth Editions Limited, 1996.

——. *Émile, or On Education*. trans. and intro. Allan Bloom. New York: Basic Books, 1979.

——. *The Reveries of the Solitary Walker, Botanical Writings, and Letter to Franquières*. trans. and annotated, Charles E. Butterworth, Alexandra Cook, Terence E. Marshall. ed. Christopher Kelly. *Collected Writings of Rousseau*. Series Editors Christopher Kelly and Roger D. Masters, vol. 8. Dartmouth: University Press of New England, 2000.

——. *Rousseau. The Judge of Jean-Jacques: Dialogues*. ed. Roger D. Masters and Christopher Kelly. trans. Judith R. Bush, Christopher Kelly, and Roger D. Masters. *Collected Writings of Rousseau*. Series Editors Christopher Kelly and Roger D. Masters, vol. 1. Dartmouth: University Press of New England, 1990.

——. *The Social Contract and Discourses*. trans. and intro. G. D. H. Cole. Revised and augmented, J. H. Brumfitt and John C. Hall. ed P. D. Jimack. London: J. M. Dent and Vermont: Charles E. Tuttle. The Everyman Library, 1996 reprint.

Rossiia pered vtorym prishestviem v dvukh tomakh. 2 vols. Moscow: Rodnik, edition of Sviato-Troitskii Monastery, Moscow, 1994.

Rozaliev, N. Iu. *Kartochnye igry*. Moscow: Grand, 1998.

Rozanov, Vasilii V. *Sobranie sochinenii*. 2 vols. Moscow: Pravda, 1990.

——. *O pisatel'stve i pisateliakh*. ed. A. N. Nikoliukin. Moscow: Respublika, 1995.

Russell, Bertrand. *A History of Western Philosophy*. New York: Simon & Schuster, 1945.

Russkaia poeziia XVIII veka, ed. G. P. Makogonenko. Moscow: Khudozhestvennaia literatura, 1972.

Russkie prosvetiteli (ot Radishcheva do dekabristov). Sobranie proizvedenii v dvukh tomakh. Moscow: Izdatel'stvo sotsial'no-ekonomicheskoi literatury Mysl', 1966.

Russkoe pravoslavie: vekhi istorii, ed. A. I. Klibanov. Moscow: Izdatel'stvo politicheskoi literatury, 1989.

Sankovitch, Natasha. *Creating and Recovering Experience: Repetition in Tolstoy*. Stanford, Calif.: Stanford University Press, 1998.

Saraskina, Liudmila. *Nikolai Speshnev: Nesbyvshaiasia sud'ba*. Moscow: Nash dom/L'Age d'Homme, 2000.

Scanlan, James P. "Tolstoy Among the Philosophers: His Book On Life and Its Critical Reception." *Tolstoy Studies Journal*, vol. XVIII (2006): 52–69.

Scharlemann, Robert P., and Gilbert Ogutu, ed. *God in Language*. New York: Paragon House Publishers, 1987.

Schelling, F. W. J. *The Philosophy of Art*. ed., trans., and intro., Douglas W. Stott. Foreword by David Simpson. Minneapolis: University of Minnesota Press, 1985.

——. *System of Transcendental Idealism* (1800). trans. Peter Heath, intro. Michael Vater. Charlottesville: University Press of Virginia, 1997.

——. *Philosophical Inquiries into the Nature of Human Freedom.* trans. James Gutmann. La Salle, Ill.: Open Court, 1992.

——. *Ages of the World.* trans. Judith Norman. *The Abyss of Freedom,* essay by Slavoj Žižek. Ann Arbor: The University of Michigan Press, 1997.

Schlegel, Friedrich. *The Philosophy of History in a Course of Lectures, by Frederick von Schlegel. With a memoir of the author,* by James Burton Robertson, Esq. 2 vols. New York: D. Apleton Co., 1841.

Schleiermacher, Friedrich. *On Religion: Speeches to Its Cultured Despisers.* trans. John Oman, ed. E. Graham Waring. New York: Ungar, 1955.

Schopenhauer, Arthur. *On the Basis of Morality.* trans. Eric F. Payne (Providence, R. I. and Oxford: Bergham Books, 1995.

——. *Parerga & Paralipomena.* in 2 vols. trans. E. F. J. Payne. Oxford: Claredon Press, 1974/reissue 2000.

——. *Prize Essay on the Freedom of the Will.* ed. Günter Zöller, trans. Eric F. Payne. Cambridge: Cambridge University Press, 1999.

——. *The World as Will and Representation.* trans. E. F. Payne, in 2 vols. New York: Dover Publications, 1958.

——. Artur Shopengauer, *Mir kak volia i predstavlenie.* trans. A. Fet. St. Petersburg: M. M. Stasiulevich, 1881.

Schopenhauer. New Essays in Honor of his 200th Birthday. ed. Eric von der Luft. Studies in German Thought and History. vol. 10, Lewiston/Queenston/Lampeter: The Edwin Mellen Press, 1988.

Shchedrin, N. *(M. E. Saltykov). Polnoe sobranie sochinenii.* 20 vols. ed. Kirpotin et al. Moscow: GiKhl, 1933–1957.

——. *Sochineniia v dvukh tomakh.* ed. M. Senchenkova. Moscow: Start, 1994.

——. Saltykov-Shchedrin, *The Golovlyov Family,* trans. Natalie Duddington and ed. James Wood. New York: New York Review of Books, 2001.

Shelley, Percy B. *The Major Works, Including Poetry, Prose, and Drama.* ed. Zachary Leader and Michael O'Neill. Oxford: Oxford University Press, 2003.

Shestov, Lev. *Apofeoz bespochvennosti. Opyt adogmaticheskogo myshleniia.* Leningrad: Izdatel'stvo Leningradskogo universiteta, 1991.

——. *Dobro v uchenii gr. Tolstogo i F. Nitsshe (filosofiia i propoved').* Berlin: Skify, 1923.

——. "The Good in the Teaching of Tolstoy and Nietzsche: Philosophy and Preaching." trans. Bernard Martin. *Lev Shestov. Dostoevsky, Tolstoy and Nietzsche.* Ohio University Press, 1978 (1–140).

——. *Sochineniia v dvukh tomakh.* Moscow: Nauka, 1993.

Shevzov, Vera. *Russian Orthodoxy on the Eve of Revolution.* New York: Oxford University Press, 2004.

——. "Letting the People into Church: Reflection on Orthodoxy and Community in Late Imperial Russia." 59–77 in *Orthodox Russia. Belief and Practice Under the Tsars.* ed. Valerie Kivelson and Robert H. Green. University Park, Pa.: Penn State University Press, 2003.

Shklovsky, Victor. *Lev Tolstoy.* trans. Olga Shartse. Moscow: Progress Publishers, 1978.

Silbajoris, Rimvydas. *War and Peace: Tolstoy's Mirror of the World*. London: Prentice-Hall International, 1995.

Sirotkina, Irina. *Diagnosing Literary Genius. A Cultural History of Psychiatry in Russia. 1880–1930*. Baltimore: Johns Hopkins University Press, 2002.

Siuzor, Georgy. *Ko dniu LXXV iubileia imperatorskogo uchilishcha pravovedeniia, 1835–1910*. St. Petersburg, 1910.

Soloviev, Vladimir. *Sobranie sochinenii Vladimira Serg[eevicha] Solovieva*. Bruxelles: Zhizn's Bogom, 1969.

———. *Izbrannye proizvedeniia*. Rostov-on-Don: Feniks, 1998.

———. *Lectures on Divine Humanity*, trans. and ed. Boris Jakim. Hudson, N. Y.: Lindisfarne Press, 1995.

Søren Kierkegaard. Modern Critical Views. ed. with an intro. Harold Bloom. New York/Philadelphia: Chelsea House Publishers, 1989.

Sorokin, Boris. "Ivan Il'ich as Jonah: a Cruel Joke." *Canadian Slavic Studies*, volume 5 (1971): 487–507.

Spence, G. W. *Tolstoy the Ascetic*. Edinburgh/London: Oliver & Boyd, 1967.

Spinoza, Baruch. *A Spinoza Reader. The Ethics and Other Works*. trans. and ed. Edwin Curley. Princeton, N. J.: Princeton University Press, 1994.

———. *The Ethics of Spinoza: The Road to Inner Freedom*. ed. and trans. Dagobert D. Runes. New York: Citadel Press/Kensington, 1988.

[M. M.] *Stasiulevich i ego sovremenniki v ikh perepiske*. 5 volumes. ed. M. L. Lemke, St. Petersburg, 1911.

Stankevich, Nikolai Vladimirovich. *Izbrannoe*. ed. G. G. Elizavetina. Moscow: Sovetskaia Rossiia, 1982.

———. *Nikolai Vladimirovich Stankevich. Perepiska ego I biografiia*. ed. P. V. Annenkov. Moscow: Tipgrafiia Katkova, 1857.

Stanton, Leonard J. *The Optina Pustyn Monastery in the Russian Literary Imagination*. New York: Peter Lang, 1995.

Starobinski, Jean. "The Style of Autobiography." 285–93 in *Literary Style: A Symposium*. ed. and trans. Seymour Chatman. London: Oxford University Press, 1971.

Stasov, Vladimir Vasilievich. *Izbrannye sochineniia v trekh tomakh. Zhivopis', skul'ptura, muzyka*. Moscow: Gosudarstvennoe izdatel'stvo Iskusstvo, 1952.

———. "Uchilishche pravovedeniia sorok let tomu nazad, 1836–1842." *Russkaia starina*, vol. 29 XII (Dec.) 1880; vol. 30 II (February) 1881; vol. 30 III (March) 1881; vol. 31 (1881).

Steiner, George. *Tolstoy or Dostoevsky: An Essay in Old Criticism*. New Haven and London: Yale University Press, 1996.

Stern, Fritz, ed. *The Varieties of History. From Voltaire to the Present*, selected and introduced, Fritz Stern. New York: Meridian Books, 1960.

Stiver, Dan R. *The Philosophy of Religious Language. Sign, Symbol, and Story*. Cambridge, Mass.: Blackwell Publishers, 1996.

Strakhov, Nikolai N. *Kriticheskiestat'i ob I. S. Turgeneve i L. N. Tolstom (1862–1885)*. ed. C. H. van Schooneveld, Slavistic Printings and Reprintings, 147. The Hague: Mouton, 1968.

——. *Mir kak tseloe. Cherty iz nauki o prirode.* St. Petersburg: Tipografiia K. Zamyslovskogo, 1872.

——. *Vospominaniia i otryvki.* St. Petersburg: Tipografiia br. Panteleevykh, 1892. Reprint: Russian reprint series. ed. Alexandre V. Soloviev, with the assistance of Alan Kimball. Volume XLIV. The Hague: Europe Printing, 1967.

Strauss, David Friedrich. *The Life of Jesus Critically Examined.* 2 vols., trans. Marian Evans. 1860; reprint, St. Clair Shores, Mich.: Scholarly Press, 1970.

Strauss, Leo. *Persecution and the Art of Writing.* Chicago and London: The University of Chicago Press, 1988.

Stromberg, Peter G. *Language and Self-Transformation. A Study of the Christian Conversion Narrative.* Cambridge: Cambridge University Press, 1993.

Taves, Ann. *Fits, Trances, and Visions: Experiencing Religion and Explaining Experiences from Wesley to James.* Princeton, N. J.: Princeton University Press, 1999.

Taylor, Brian. "Recollection and Membership: Converts Talk and the Ratiocination of Commonality." *Sociology.* volume 12 (1978): 316–24.

Taylor, Charles. *Hegel.* Cambridge: Cambridge University Press, 1996.

Thaden, Edward C. *Conservative Nationalism in Nineteenth-Century Russia.* Seattle: University of Washington Press, 1964.

Thorslev, Peter L. *The Byronic Hero.* Minneapolis: University of Minnesota Press, 1962.

Thulstrup, Niels. *Kierkegaard's Relation to Hegel.* trans. George L. Stengren. Princeton, N. J.: Princeton University Press, 1980.

Thunberg, Lars. *Man and the Cosmos: The Vision of St. Maximus the Confessor* Crestwood, N. Y.: St. Vladimir's Seminary Press, 1985.

Todd, William Mills III, "The Responsibility of Co-Authorship: Notes on Revising the Serialized Version of *Anna Karenina.*" 159–82 in *Freedom and Responsibility in Russian Literature: Essays in Honor of Robert Louis Jackson.* ed. Elizabeth Cheresh Allen and Gary Saul Morson. Evanston, Ill.: Northwestern University Press, 1995.

Tolstaya, Sophia A. *Dnevniki.* 2 vols. Moscow: Khudozhestvennaia literatura, 1978.

Tolstoy, Il'ya. *Tolstoy, My Father: Reminiscences.* trans. Ann Dunnigan. Chicago: Cowles, 1971.

Tolstoy, L. N. *Sobranie sochinenii v dvadtsati dvukh tomakh.* ed. M. B. Khrapchenko et al. Moscow: Khudozhestvennaia literatura, 1978–1985.

——. *Polnoe sobranie sochinenii.* ed. V. G. Chertkov. 90 vols. Moscow: Khudozhestvennaia literatura, 1928–1958.

Tolstoy, Leo. *Anna Karenina.* trans. George Gibian. New York/London: Norton and Co., 1995.

——. *Childhood. Boyhood. Youth.* trans. Rosemary Edmonds. London: Penguin Books, 1964.

——. *A Confession and Other Religious Writings.* trans. Jane Kentish. London: Penguin Books, 1987.

——. *The Gospel According to Tolstoy.* ed. and trans. David Pattersen. Tuscaloosa and London: The University of Alabama Press, 1987.

——. *The Gospel in Brief.* trans. Isabel Hapgood. ed. and preface by F. A. Flowers III. Lincoln and London: The University of Nebraska Press, 1997.

———. *Great Short Works of Leo Tolstoy.* intro. John Bayley, trans. Louis and Aylmer Maude. New York: Perennial Library, 1967.

———. *The Kreutzer Sonata and Other Stories.* trans. David McDuff. London: Penguin, 1983.

———. *The Lion and the Honeycomb. The Religious Writings of Tolstoy.* ed. A. N. Wilson. London: Collins, 1987.

———. *Plays.* 3 vols. trans. Marvin Kantor and Tanya Tulchinsky. ed. Andrew Baruch Wachtel. Evanston, Ill.: Northwestern University Press, 1994–1998.

———. *The Portable Tolstoy.* ed. John Bayley. London/New York: Penguin Books, 1978.

———. *Tolstoy's Diaries.* 2 vols. ed. and trans. R. F. Christian. London: The Athlone Press, 1985.

———. *Tolstoy's Letters.* 2 vols. trans. and ed. R. F. Christian. New York: Charles Scribner's Sons, 1978.

———. *Tolstoy's Short Fiction. A Norton Critical Edition.* ed. Michael Katz. New York and London: W. W. Norton, 1991.

———. *Perepiska s russkimi pisateliami.* 2 vols. Moscow: Khudozhestvennaia literatura, 1978.

Tolstoi i o Tolstom. Materialy i issledovaniia. ed. K. Lomunov and L. Opulskaya. Moscow: Nasledie, 1998.

Tolstoy. The Critical Heritage. ed. A. V. Knowles. London/Henley/Boston: Routledge & Kegan, 1978.

Tolstoy, Sergey. *Tolstoy Remembered by His Son.* New York: Atheneum, 1962.

Tomashevsky, Boris. "Thematics." *Russian Formalist Criticism. Four Essays.* trans. and introduction by Lee T. Lemon and Marion J. Reis. Lincoln and London: University of Nebraska Press, 1965 (61–98).

Tsar' Krez i uchitel' Solon. Moscow: Posrednik, 1886.

Turgenev, Ivan Sergeevich. *Sobranie sochinenii v piati tomakh.* Moscow: Russkaia Pravda, 1994.

———. *Sobranie sochinenii v desiati tomakh.* Moscow: Gosudarstvennoe izdatel'stvo khudozhestvennoi literatury, 1962.

———. *Pesn' dushi. Stikhotvoreniia, poemy. Stikhotvoreniia v proze.* Moscow: Sovetskaia Rossiia, 1988.

Turgenev, Ivan. *The Essential Turgenev.* ed. and with an intro. Elizabeth Cheresh Allen. Evanston, Ill.: Northwestern University Press, 1994.

———. *Rudin.* trans. Richard Freeborn. London: Penguin, 1975.

———. *Smoke.* trans. Constance Garnett. New York: Turtle Point Press, 1991.

Turner, C. J. G. "Tolstoy and Herodotus." *Tolstoy Studies Journal.* Volume 11 (1999): 55–59.

Uspensky, Gleb. *Polnoe sobranie sochinenii.* Moscow: Academy of Sciences, 1940–1954.

Velkley, Richard. *Being After Rousseau. Philosophy and Culture in Question.* Chicago and London: The University of Chicago Press, 2002.

Venevitinov, Dmitry Vladimirovich. *Stikhotvoreniia. Proza.* ed. E. A. Maimin and M. A. Chernyshev. Moscow: Nauka, 1980.

Viazemsky, Petr Andreevich. *Sochineniia v dvukh tomakh*. 2 vols. Moscow: Khudozhestvennaia literatura, 1982.

Wackenroder, Wilhelm Heinrich, and Ludwig Tieck, *Herzensergießungen eines kunstliebenden Klosterbruders*. Stuttgart: Reclam, 1994.

Wachtel, Andrew Baruch. *The Battle for Childhood: Creation of a Russian Myth*. Stanford, Calif.: Stanford University Press, 1990.

———. "History and Autobiography in Tolstoy," in *The Cambridge Companion to Tolstoy*, ed. Donna Tussing Orwin. Cambridge: Cambridge University Press, 2002.

———. *An Obsession with History: Russian Writers Confront the Past*. Stanford, Calif.: Stanford University Press, 1994.

Walicki, Andrzej. *A History of Russian Thought. From the Enlightenment to Marxism*. trans. from the Polish by Hilda Andrews-Rusiecka. Stanford, Calif.: Stanford University Press, 1979.

———. *The Slavophile Controversy: History of a Conservative Utopia in Nineteenth-Century Russian Thought*. trans. Hilda Andrews-Rusiecka. Notre Dame, Ind.: Notre Dame University Press, 1989.

Walsh, Harry. "The Place of Schopenhauer in the Philosophical Education of Leo Tolstoi." 300–311 in *Schopenhauer. New Essays in Honor of his 200th Birthday*. ed. Eric von der Luft. Studies in German Thought and History. vol. 10. Lewiston/Queenston/Lampeter: The Edwin Mellen Press, 1988

Westfall, Richard S. *The Construction of Modern Science*. Cambridge: Cambridge University Press, 1977.

William James in Russian Culture, ed. Joan Delaney Grossman and Ruth Rischin. Lanham, Md.: Lexington Books, 2003.

Wilson, A. N. *Tolstoy*. New York: Fawcett Columbine, 1988.

Wordsworth, William. *Complete Poetical Works*. Oxford: Oxford University Press, first publ. 1936.

Wortman, Richard S. *The Development of Russian Legal Consciousness*. Chicago and London: The University of Chicago Press, 1976.

Vishlenkova, Elena. *Zabotias' o dushakh poddannykh: religioznaia politika v Rossii pervoi chetverti XIX veka*. Saratov: Izdatel'stvo Saratovskogo universiteta, 2002.

Viswanathan, Gauri. *Outside the Fold. Conversion, Modernity, and Belief*. Princeton, N. J.: Princeton University Press, 1998

Zenkovsky, V. V. *A History of Russian Philosophy*. trans. George L. Kline. London: Routledge and Kegan Paul Ltd., 1953.

———. *Osnovy khristianskoi filosofii*. Moscow: Kanon, 1996.

———. "Problema bessmertiia u L. N. Tolstogo." *O religii L'va Tolstogo. Sbornik statei*. Moscow: Put', 1912 (27–58).

Zhdanov, V. A. and E. E. Zaidenshnur. eds. *Opisanie rukopisei khudozhestvennykh proizvedenii L. N. Tolstogo*. Moscow: USSR Academy of Sciences, 1935.

Zhukovsky, V. A. *Sochineniia v stikhakh i proze*. 10th edition. ed. P. A. Efremov. St. Petersburg: Izdanie knigoprodavtsa I. Glazunova, 1901.

———. *Izbrannoe*. ed. I. M. Semenko. Moscow: Pravda, 1986.

Ziolkowski, Margaret. *Hagiography and Modern Russian Literature*. Princeton, N. J.: Princeton University Press, 1988.

Index

accounting. *See* confessional literature; conversion narratives; self-accounting

abyss, xxviii–ix, 19, 37, 64, 77, 89, 186, 219, 233, 241

activity, 61, 64–71, 117–18, 123, 161, 162, 211, 265–73, 277–88, 318–20, 348, 350; Tolstoy on, 45–46, 64–71, 74, 84, 161, 257–58. *See also* work

Afanasiev, Aleksandr, 271–72, 279

Aksakov, Ivan, 222, 224, 263, 265

Alexeev, Vasily, 264, 334

All, 39, 85, 167, 287, 339. *See also* All-Unity; deity

allegory, 351, 353. *See also* imagery

All-Unity, 12. *See also* All

anguish, 138, 169, 211, 281–82. *See also* despair

anhedonia and anhedonic calculus, xxvii

Anna Karenina (Tolstoy): crime and punishment in, 179–84, 212, 217; death in, 180–84, 213; logos, 210–11; prayers, 178, 182–84; reactions to, 161, 165–66, 178, 217–18, 251; religious concepts, 175, 184–90, 251; writing of, 20, 138, 142, 146, 147–48, 175–84, 342

Annenkov, Pavel, 59

Aquinas, Thomas, 319

Aristotle, 211, 304–7, 316, 318, 321

Arsenieva, Valeria, 75

art: despair and, 215–17; laws of, 176–77; moral art, 71–77, 146–52; politics and, 215–17; religion and, 67–71, 131–37, 188, 267–73, 277–84; Tolstoy on, 133, 176–77, 188–89, 268–73. *See also* artist; artistic perception; music; paintings; writing

artistic perceptions, 24, 26, 45, 178, 267–73; Tolstoy on, 109–10, 131, 267–73. *See also* art; objective perspective; perception; subjective perspective; writing

artistic platform, 176

artistic rank, 245. *See also* fame

artists: artistic rank, 245; freedom, 133; God as, 45; as madmen, xxiv, 133–37, 215; task of, 113, 131–37, 151–52, 266–73, 277–84, 351; Tolstoy on, 113, 131–32, 151, 225, 266–73; Tolstoy's standing, 203, 215–27. *See also* artistic perception; artistic platform

Arzamas, xxiv, xxix, 17, 137–38, 285

Arzamas society, 17–18, 65, 90

atheism, 12, 16, 17, 22, 27, 49, 142; Tolstoy, 37–38, 41; Tolstoy's writing

About the Author

Inessa Medzhibovskaya is assistant professor of literature at Eugene Lang College, The New School for Liberal Arts in New York City, where she teaches a variety of courses in Russian and Central East European literature, theory of the novel, and movements such as romanticism and modernism. She holds a PhD from Princeton University in Slavic languages and literatures and degrees in Germanic philology (English literature) and international education. She is the author of many essays on Tolstoy, Pushkin, and topics of Russian intellectual history and culture, which have appeared in *Slavic and East European Journal*, *Comparative Literature*, *Tolstoy Studies Journal*, *Stanford Slavic Studies,* and other venues.